FOUNDATIONS IN MEDIA
General editor: Oliver Boyd-Barrett

Approaches to Media
A Reader

Edited by

Oliver Boyd-Barrett and Chris Newbold

A member of the Hodder Headline Group
LONDON

First published in Great Britain 1995 by
Arnold, a member of the Hodder Headline Group.
338 Euston Road, London NW1 3BH

Co-published in the United States of America by
Oxford University Press Inc.,
198 Madison Avenue, New York, NY10016

The advice and information in this book are believed to be true and
accurate at the date of going to press, but neither the authors nor the
publisher can accept any legal responsibility or liability for any errors
or omissions.

British Library Cataloguing in Publication Data
A catalogue record for this book is available from the British Library

Library of Congress Cataloging-in-Publication Data
A catalog record for this book is available from the Library of Congress

ISBN 0 340 65229 2

8 9 10 11 12

Produced by Gray Publishing, Tunbridge Wells
Printed and bound in Great Britain by MPG Books Ltd, Bodmin, Cornwall

Contents

Section 4. Political economy

Section 5. The public sphere

Section 6. Media occupations and professionals

Section 7. Cultural hegemony

Section 8. Feminism

Section 9. Moving image

Section 10. New audience research

General editor's preface

This volume is one of a series of five readers which aim to provide a comprehensive set of resources for media studies courses. Other volumes of the series address the following themes: media in global context; media industries and professions; audiences and reception; and media texts. Each volume of the series is intended to stand alone for the benefit of individual students or course organizers of courses at both undergraduate and postgraduate levels in media, journalism and broadcasting, communications, cultural and literary studies and, more generally, of courses in sociology, politics, and literature and education. Taken together, the volumes provide a broad introduction to the study of media, and they cover each of the major issues, topics, themes, approaches and methodologies encountered in the study of media. They are also intended to provide an international inflection both in source and in topic, which is in line with the processes of globalization of the media industries and with world-wide interest in the study of the media.

Oliver Boyd-Barrett

Editors' introduction: approaching the media

Oliver Boyd-Barrett and Chris Newbold

Our intention in this volume is to identify and illustrate what are arguably the major traditions of scholarly enquiry in the field of communications media since the 1940s.

Our principal purpose has been to provide convenient access for students of both undergraduate and postgraduate courses in mass communications to original articles that may be said either to have had a seminal influence or which have encapsulated in some way the major features of a tradition or part of one, and which students might otherwise have difficulty in locating. We think it is important to stress that our aim is to provide readers and students with a flavour of the concerns of each of the traditions we have identified, rather than try to include for each tradition an exhaustive or even a modestly complete range of all the key texts which it might reasonably be argued have been seminal. There is a strong historical inflection, given that it is often the older texts that are most difficult for students to track down, even though such texts often retain considerable influence on thinking within a field. We were inspired to set about this task in the context of preparation of the MA in Mass Communications (by Distance Learning) at the Centre for Mass Communications Research, University of Leicester, whose students are recruited from a number of different countries around the world, and whose access to good libraries is highly variable.*

A secondary purpose of the volume is to introduce and provide a companion resource for the series of five volumes of which this is the first, and which together aim to provide key source and illustrative material, as well as original contributions to the major dimensions of media research, here identified as media globalization, industries and professions, audiences and media reception, texts and language.

Needless to say, there is no one way of narrating the history of media research nor of illustrating that history. There are different accounts of the history of media study, and the tensions and contradictions between these accounts constitute an illuminating study in itself. Furthermore, we are talking of a relatively young field of enquiry, and there is still considerable scope for review and reconceptualization of the significance of what has occurred over the past 50 years. Although it is not possible nor is it desirable to try to establish water-tight boundaries between any of the traditions that are

*The volumes are course readers for the MA in Mass Communications (by Distance Learning) which has been developed by the University of Leicester for students on a world-wide basis. As such they offer what their editors believe to represent a range of rich resource materials for any course in the area of media. Readers of these volumes who would like more information about the CMCR distance learning degree should write to the Course Secretary, Centre for Mass Communication Research, University of Leicester, 104 Regent Road, Leicester LE1 7LT, United Kingdom.

variously identified here, it is useful to identify outstanding differences between different traditions of enquiry. This is because:

- many authors have been consciously influenced in their work by a sense of belonging, not necessarily exclusively, to one or more particular lines of enquiry;
- some authors are commonly identified – though not necessarily with their participation or consent – as belonging to one or another tradition;
- identifying differences between approaches, in the manner of a semiotic paradigm, can be an aid to the process of understanding any single approach;
- some of these traditions reveal a process of conscious self-reflection, development and progress which can best be understood through an awareness of the particular journeys which they have charted.

It is important to acknowledge that taxonomies (systems of classification) imposed upon a field of study can exaggerate differences and obscure interconnections, which is why it is best, where possible, to recognize the labels that researchers have tended to ascribe to themselves – although that in itself may not overcome the temptations of over-rigid compartmentalization. While media research is generally cautious if not critical of post-modernism, post-modernism's disregard for historical polarities and its relish for inter-textuality offers a reminder of the dangers of taking too seriously the outcome of divisions hermeneutically constructed.

The 'traditions' identified are not all of a kind, given that the sites and the motives behind any convergence among a group of scholars are different. We can speak of traditions which are represented in terms of the broad lines of their ideological trajectory: for example, pluralist studies are recognized by their premise that the media operate in a multi-interest society and are part of the process of competition for influence in such a society (whether or not particular authors who have been 'assigned' a place in this tradition were conscious at the time that they were likely to be thus assigned). Alternative points of convergence may be methodological, as in the new wave of ethnographic audience or reception studies, the significance of which can be understood only with reference to the strength of the proceeding popularity of hegemony theory, and the cruder or more reductionist assumptions which it sometimes made about the influence on the thinking and behaviour of individuals of systemic or élitist forces, operating through media.

Yet other points of convergence may be neither theoretical nor method-ological, but simply taxonomic labels which signify a general area of content, as might be the case with the 'public sphere'. In practice, convergences around theory, methodology and content tend to be inter-related. The 'public sphere' signifies a broad interest in the way in which communications media relate to opportunities or the lack of them for the formulation by individuals and social groups of ideas, policies and policy options, with a view to the exercise of influence on the political process. But the term itself has been coined by Habermas (1962), and carries with it the traces of his particular historical account of the development of democracy and the welfare state, and which has developed along a particular trajectory of concern tending to focus on the role of public media, and the influence of the contrary processes in recent decades of commercialization, privatization, consolidation and deregulation.

As well as recognizing differences, the volume draws attention to similarities, for example between the early 'functionalist' studies which asked how mass media functioned to integrate the lives and cultures of individuals with the broader, organic features of societies, and 'hegemony' studies which radically rephrased and humanized the question of the relationship between media and society – 'how do mass media participate in the construction of consensus among heterogeneous cultural groupings in the interests of ruling classes or élites?' It is not surprising, therefore, to find articles that could easily belong to two or more traditions. The classic study of Adorno and Horkheimer, for example, might have been identified as belonging to 'hegemony' theory or even to 'the public sphere'. It could as easily have been included as an introduction to cultural studies or located in a 'Marxist' category. Here, the editors have chosen a brief extract that serves as a robust statement of 'mass society' theory, a concern which inspired a great deal of sociological and literary writing at the time.

We are painfully aware not only that we cannot possibly do justice to any one of the traditions which we wish to exemplify, but that some traditions are barely acknowledged at all. In some cases this is simply for lack of space. In others it is because the tradition lies too far outside the scope of mainstream social science to be relevant to the editors' main purpose. In other cases omissions signal the intention to include further source materials in later volumes of this series. The field of 'cultural' or 'media imperialism' for example, is represented here only by Schiller's 1969 classic formulation and has been located under 'political economy'. It has not been possible to represent each of the major stages of 'media effects' research; nor is there explicit recognition of the particular contributions of psychology and social psychology, although these tend to be concentrated in the fields of early effects studies on voting, attitudes and questions of media violence. The new social historiography is here represented in the section on media occupations and professionals by an extract from Scannell and Cardiff's social history of the BBC.

The multiplicity of different taxonomies and different narratives about the study of media over the years serves in itself as a caution against any temptation to attribute to any one taxonomy a particular 'truth' value. A classification is informed in part by the ideas that researchers have had about their own projects and about their significance in relation to preceding projects, and in part by the particular inter-relationships and contrasts which the editors, from the vantage point of a particular moment in time, can identify and justify as meaningful. Inevitably, these judgements, while informed and influenced by our membership of a relatively small intellectual community whose common culture is sustained by a substantial degree of shared access to a range of discourses and literatures, are to an extent idiosyncratic, and they are certainly temporal. Alternative classifications would have been quite possible, so there is no claim to exclusivity. In choosing this particular taxonomy, we have taken account of the (conflicting) meta-narratives that others in the field have offered. The volume has ten sections, each with a section introduction which contains references for further reading. In each section we attempt to offer a good chronological range, with representation of different foci within each range.

In order to secure a reasonably broad range we have generally chosen extracts in preference to complete chapters or articles. The volume as a whole is organized in terms of a loose chronology, Sections 2 and 3 tending to reflect predominantly contributions from the earlier years of the discipline, moving through 'media effects', 'public sphere', media occupations, to cultural hegemony and feminist studies, moving image, and finally, to the post-Foucauldian period marked among other things by a vigorous ethnographic approach to audience or reception studies. The volume as a whole does not include as much work as we would have liked from 1990s sources, but later volumes in the series will compensate for this; the historical inflection of this, the first volume, underlines its status as a 'companion' to later volumes as well as providing an account, in its own right, of the different traditions of research in the field.

For us, this has been an enlightening experience, sometimes a faintly nostalgic one where we have revisited contributions that have lain neglected for decades. We have been encouraged by the evidence of progress and development in the field even as we are also impressed by the cyclical character of intellectual fashion. But cycles, spirals for example, need not necessarily be circles. There are still very great differences of position, focus, ideology in the field. The success of the wave of 'new audience studies' for example does not seem to us to have reduced the necessity to maintain an interest in media industries, production and media texts, which have a great deal of bearing on the range of cultural products that are made available. We suspect that the gulf between academics and professionals is almost as great as ever, although among the academics there are some who are more clearly working on behalf of professional training than of theoretical development. There is a gulf, too, between those who are still consciously directed by theory and the ambition of theoretical development and others who, distrustful of and disappointed by such ambition, manage to work with little or no reference to formal academic theories at all. In this volume, however, we have tended to privilege contributions to theory because we believe it is through theoretical development that some of the most significant advances in the field have been achieved. But we suspect that the passion which fuelled earlier clashes in the field, between Marxists and pluralists, for example, is not present in as much force in the field today. The extraordinary political changes that were introduced through the Reaganite and Thatcherite eras, the collapse of the Soviet Union and of the communist republics of Eastern Europe, the economic prosperity of many countries of Asia and Southeast Asia are among a number of the forces which have contributed to a loss of certainty, but leading, perhaps, towards a greater appreciation of the values of eclecticism, open mindedness and dialogue in theory, research design and methodology.

Acknowledgements

The work of compiling a course reader of this kind, while very different from authoring an entirely original text, is often a fairly considerable challenge of intellectual consolidation and organization. So we have found in this case, and we are also very conscious of the fact that without the support and back-up of the distance-learning team, and of our colleagues in the Centre for Mass Communication Research, this volume would have been even longer in the making than in fact proved to be the case. We are especially indebted to Jane Walker, the Course Secretary, for her work in tracing copyright holders and in organizing the permissions, and to Jim McKenna, Research Assistant, whose work in keeping track of the contributions, maintaining them in order, and marking up and marshalling the final manuscript, was vital to the whole enterprise. We are thankful to all our colleagues, students, and not least our families who had to put up with not a little disruption on our account.

The publisher wishes to thank the following for permission to use their copyright material:

ABLEX Publishing Corporation, U.S.A. for the extract from *Dependency Road: Communications, Capitalism, Consciousness*, pp. 40–7 © 1981 by D. W. Smythe.

Association for Education in Journalism and Mass Communication, U.S.A for the extract from *Journalism Quarterly*, Vol. 44, No. 3, pp. 419–21 © 1967 by P. Snider.

Blackwell Publishers, Oxford for the extract from *A Social History of British Broadcasting: The National Culture* (selection from Chapter 13), pp. 277–80, 286–9 © 1991 by P. Scannell and D. Cardiff.

Blackwell Publishers, Oxford for the extract from *The Structural Transformation of the Public Sphere*, pp. 37–8, 41–3 © 1992 by J. Habermas.

British Sociological Association, Solihull for the extract from *The Journal of Sociology*, pp. 359–80: Mass communication and modern culture: contribution to a critical theory of ideology © 1988 by J. B. Thompson.

J. Carey, U.S.A. for the extract from *Communication as Culture: Essays on Media and Society*, pp. 37–68 © 1989.

Chatto & Windus, London for the extract from *The Long Revolution*, pp. 57–70: The analysis of culture © 1981 by R. Williams.

Comedia Publishing Group, Gloucester for the extract from *Family Television, Cultural Power and Domestic Leisure*, pp. 146–50 and 153–8 © 1986.

Constable Publishers, London for the extract from *Journalists at Work*, pp. 106–14 © 1971 by J. Tunstall.

Cornell University Press, NY for the extract from *Story and Discourse: Narrative Structure in Fiction and Film*, pp. 15–42: Introduction, Chapter 1 © 1978 by S. Chatman.

J. Curran, London for the extract from *Culture, Society and the Media*, pp. 11–29 © 1982.

Elsevier Science, The Netherlands for the extract from *Theory and Society*, Vol. 6, pp. 205–53: Media sociology: the dominant paradigm © 1978 by T. Gitlin.

G. Gerbner, U.S.A. for the extract from *AV Communication Review*, Vol. 17, No. 2, pp. 137–48 © 1969.

J. D. Halloran, Leicester for the extract from *Communication and Social Structure: Critical Studies in Mass Media Research*, pp. 21–57 © 1981.

Longman Group, Essex for the extract from *Making the News*, pp. 72–6, 78–81 © 1979 by P. Golding and P. Elliott.

Manchester University Press, Manchester for the extract from *High Theory/Low Culture*, pp. 101–14: Narrative form in American network television © 1986 by J. Feuer.

The Merlin Press Ltd, London for the extract from *The Socialist Register*, pp. 207–23 © by G. Murdock and P. Golding.

Methuen, London for the extract from *Narration in the Fiction Film*, pp. 49–53.

The Open University, Milton Keynes for the extract from *Culture, Society and the Media*, pp. 56–90: The rediscovery of ideology © 1982 by S. Hall.

Open University Press, Buckingham for the extract from *Popular Culture and Social Relations*, pp. xi–xix: Popular culture and the turn to Gramsci © 1986 by T. Bennett.

Oxford University Press, Oxford for the extract from *Screen*, Vol. 31, No. 1, pp. 45–66: Questions of genre © 1990 by S. Neale.

Oxford University Press, New York for the extract from *Hearth and Home: Images of Women in the Mass Media*, pp. 3–17.

Pinter Publishers, London for the extract from *Communicating Politics*, pp. 45–53 © by N. Garnham.

Routledge, London for the extract from *Critical Communication Studies: Communication, History and Theory in America:* On ignoring history: mass communication research and the critique of society © 1992 by H. Hardt.

Routledge, London for the extract from *Cultural Populism: Populism and Ordinary Culture* ©1992 by J. McGuigan.

Routledge, London for the extract from *Narration in the Fiction Film*, pp. 48–62: Principles of narration © 1985 by D. Bordwell.

Routledge, London for the extract from *Watching Dallas*, pp. 102–11 © 1984 by I. Ang

SAGE for the extract from *Media, Culture and Society*, Vol. 1, No. 2, pp. 130–4.

SAGE, London, for the extract from *Journalists as War*, pp. viii–xiv © 1988 by D. E. Morrison and H. Tumber.

SAGE, London for the extract from *European Journal of Communication*, Vol. 1, No. 2: Patterns of involvement in television fiction: a comparative analysis pp. 152–4, 166–70 © 1986 by T. Liebes and E. Katz.

SAGE, London for the extract from *European Journal of Communication*, pp. 207–38: Five traditions in search of the audience © 1990 by K. B. Jensen and K. E. Rosengren.

SAGE, London for the extract from *Media, Culture and Society*, Vol. 4, No. 2: Women and the cultural industries, pp. 133–51 © 1982 by M. Mattelart.

SAGE, London for the extract from *Media Culture and Society*, Vol. 11, No. 2: Class and gender in the hegemonic process class differences in women's perceptions of television realism and identification with television characters © 1989 by A. Press.

SAGE, London for the extract *The Uses of Mass Communications: Utilization of Mass Communication by the Individual*, pp. 19–32 © 1974 by E. Katz, J. G. Blumler and M. Gurevitch.

SAGE, London for the extract *European Journal of Communication*, Vol. 5: The new revisionism in mass communication research – a reappraisal, pp. 145–51 © 1990 by J. Curran.

SAGE, London for the extract from *The Theory of the Public Sphere*, Vol. 10, No. 3, pp. 179–97 © 1993 by J. B. Thompson.

SAGE, U.S.A. for the extract from *The Functional Analysis and Mass Communication Revisited*, pp. 197–205 © 1974 by C. R. Wright.

SAGE, U.S.A. for the extract from *Prime-Time Television – Content and Control*, pp. 84–91 © 1980 by G. Cantor.

SAGE, U.S.A. for the extract from *Handbook of Political Communication*, pp. 476–85 © 1981 by J. Blumler and M. Gurevitch.

SAGE, London for the extract from *Television and Women's Culture*, pp. 11–21: Feminist cultural television criticism – culture, theory and practice © 1990 by M. E. Brown.

SAGE, London for the extract from *Mass Communication Review Yearbook*, Vol. 2, pp. 37–49: Mass communication research in Europe © 1981 by J. Blumler.

H. I. Schiller, U.S.A. for the extract from *Mass Communications and American Empire*, pp. 94–103 © 1992.

Simon & Schuster, Inc., New York for the extract from *Public Opinion and Communication:* The effects of mass communication © 1966 by J. T. Klapper.

Social Research, NY for the extract from *Social Research*, Vol. 45, No. 2, pp. 256–64, 266 © 1978 by G. Tuchman.

Speech Communication Association, U.S.A. for the extract from *Critical Studies in Mass Communication*, Vol. 4, No. 2, pp. 100–6: Feminist theories and media studies 1987 by H. L. Steeves.

Speech Communication Association U.S.A. for the extract from *Critical Studies in Mass Communication*, Vol. 5, No. 3, pp. 219–28 © 1988 by M. Allor.

Tuchman, G. for the extract from *Hearth and Home: Images of Women in the Mass Media*, pp. 3–17.

The University of Chicago Press, U.S.A. for the extract from *Public Opinion Quarterly* Vol. 36, No. 2, pp. 176–87 © 1972 by M. E. McCombs and D. L. Shaw.

The University of North Carolina Press, U.S.A. for the extract from *Social Forces*, Vol. 33, pp. 329–35 © 1955 by W. Breed.

University of California Press, U.S.A. for the extract from *Six Guns and Society: A Structural Study of the Western*, Chapter 8, pp. 185–94: Myth and meaning © 1975 by W. Wright.

University of Texas Press, Texas for the extract from *Morphology of the Folktale*, Chapter 2, pp. 19–24 © 1968 by V. Propp.

VERSO, London for the extract from *Women's Pictures: Feminism and Cinema*, pp. 21–42: The pleasure machine © 1982 by A. Kuhn

VERSO, London and Tanja Howarth Literary Agency for the extract *The Culture Industry: Enlightenment as Mass deception: Dialectic of Enlightenment*, pp. 120–4 © 1979 by T. W. Adorno and M. Horkheimer.

VERSO, London and The University of North Carolina Press, U.S.A. for the extract from *Reading the Romance*, pp. 10–15, © 1984 by J. Radway.

Every effort has been made to trace copyright holders of material produced in this book. Any rights not acknowledged here will be acknowledged in subsequent printings if notice is given to the publishers.

Section 1

The field

1

Defining the field

Oliver Boyd-Barrett and Chris Newbold

If the study of media represents a 'field', it is a field with indistinct boundaries; a playing field, marked out for a variety of different games, subject to distinctive titles and rules, each game with its own painted lines, but the lines of each game overlapping those of others. Each game also has its own spectators, and among these there are some who have come just for the game in which they have most interest, and there are others whose attention spans the field for sight of any match that looks interesting or exciting.

The work in this first section represents attempts by some leading players of these different games at defining both the relationships between different approaches or traditions of enquiry within the field, and those between academe and the society which it studies and attempts to address. It also gives us a sense of what were the 'dominant paradigms' – the most fashionable games – at given moments of the history of the development of the field.

Within the bounds of the extracts presented in this section, the notion of the field as a whole, although often flagged, is rarely discussed, and perhaps even more rarely established. A few collective endeavours have attempted to make connections between differently-inflected attempts to identify field boundaries, such as those signified by the terms 'mass communication', 'communication', and 'media studies'. Not the least of these endeavours was 'Ferment in the field' (*Journal of Communication*, 1983), and, again, in the more recent volumes of that same journal, articles entitled 'The future of the field I' and 'The future of the field II' (*Journal of Communication*, 1993a, b). This latter volume is subtitled 'between fragmentation and cohesion', an indication, perhaps, of the unsettled and unsettling debate that periodically comes to the fore. The nature of this debate need not detain or restrain us too long here, suffice to say that the field is a term which enables us to discuss under one umbrella the eclectic nature of mass communications research. It is also important to remember that while such field-boundaries have long histories, and are often jealously guarded, they may have little actual substance or meaning to those outside academic discourse, and their significations may seem very fluid and elusive even to those inside it.

Much of the debate represented in these extracts came from contributions to the study of 'mass communication', which is indeed one of the earliest labels used to identify the field. This term has particular strengths, as it invites our attention to the industries and industrial practices which lie behind communications media such as television, radio, newspapers, film, and music, and it underlines the extraordinary size of many of these operations in terms of their audience reach. There is, however, an ambivalence about the term 'mass' which increasingly requires qualification by those who are content to identify with this label and which has driven other scholars towards alternative signifiers that stress 'culture', 'media' or, simply, 'communication'. The term 'mass' has its roots in the original theories of 'mass' society from the nineteenth century. These theories resulted from interest, among other things, in the newly formed large urban populations of industrial society, and with crowd behaviour. There are implications behind the concept of great size, homogeneity, lack of distinctiveness or individuality, and of mindless, even irresponsible response.

Although the focus of media study does often involve cultural products that involve substantial numbers of people in their production and huge swathes of national and international populations in their reception, there is no longer any confidence in assumptions that the processes of meaning generated in the interaction between such products and individual members of the audience can be described in global terms. On the contrary, the meanings, experiences and pleasures which media products may help to generate are also uniquely particular to individuals, whose 'readings' of media 'texts' will also be an expression of their location within overlapping nexuses of cultural, social, ethnic, gender, linguistic, occupational and other sources of identity, while also a product of the immediate social and physical contexts of 'reading' (in the home or in the community, singly or collectively, with peers or with elders, etc.).

These sources of differentiation which are a universal feature of the 'meaning' of media communications, are accentuated by the advent of new technologies which enhance the potential of media for relatively small-scale communication, not just of 'mass' products for relatively discrete, single-interest audiences, as in the case, for example, of specialist magazines or video-on-demand services through cable networks, but also for one-to-one communication through such means as the telephone or electronic computer mail. The convergence of communication and computer technologies greatly extends the range of possible signification of the term 'media'. There is little to be gained by trying to confine the field to 'traditional' media, for these can be revitalized through entirely new delivery systems; 'new' media are defined in part by their echoes of the 'old'; and, besides, very much the same kinds of questions (but also some very different questions) can be asked of the 'new' as were asked of the 'old'. For example, the range of literacy practices encountered through use of computer technology both derives from features of traditional literacy, as in formulating sentences in word processing, while at the same time extending and transforming these, for example through the physical and social contexts in which computer composition occurs, and the possibilities which such technology allows for the instant combination of different texts and kinds of text, and the facilities for accessing and reading texts (and data-bases) that are peculiar to computers. These differences are relevant for our understanding both of one-to-one communication and for large-scale media communication in our contemporary world.

Contemporary use of the term 'mass communication', therefore, demands that we attend to 'recipients', 'audiences', 'readers', 'viewers', 'users', and to the detailed 'texts' which they create and consume, in all their diversity and richness, constructed and circulated as they are within the broader contexts of groups, cultures, societies. Another way of saying this is that the meaning of communication lies in its context, and there is no proper understanding of any feature of communication if context is left out of account. Mass communication research, as argued implicitly or explicitly in many of these extracts, has to start with society and social relations, moving only then to the analysis of media products and communication processes.

The focus of discussion in this section, therefore, relates to a very wide conception of mass communication, wider, certainly, than is sometimes indicated by alternative nomenclatures for the field. The signification of 'communication studies', for instance, sometimes tends towards a focus on messages and their construction, the relationship between senders and receivers, and with the nature of all forms of language, whether oral, written, or visual. Lurking behind the concept is sometimes a 'transmission' or linear view of the processes by which meaning is created, which is applied equally to interpersonal and organization as to mass or media communication. The terms 'media studies' and 'cultural studies' are infused much more by a model of meaning which stresses its generation out of the collaborative interaction of authors or producers, texts and readers within specific contexts. The former focuses particularly on 'mainstream' media texts; the latter is interested more globally in the symbolic codes available for social expression, and the ways in which the structure and exploitation of these codes both reflects social relationships and contributes to their formation.

But these are labels that were scarcely present in the early days of mass communication research; they are, rather, the product of its institutionalization, either on its own terms or in collaboration or partnership with other disciplines within academe. The early days were more clearly marked by a series of disciplinary claims to mass communication of which psychology was for a long time the strongest but not the only contestant, with literature, sociology, politics, economics, or professional studies in journalism, public relations, etc., lagging some way behind. But where these disciplines once struggled to absorb the study of mass communication within their own disciplinary boundaries, it is now truer to say that their struggle is for predominance within newer, over-arching disciplines that have secured departmental or faculty status.

Lest such discussion may tend to highlight differences between histories, approaches, institutional contexts, this is an appropriate point to refer to more recent attempts to identify what it is that all these tend to have in common. Bazalgette (1992), drawing on a framework designed by the British Film Institute, argues that across the different divisions of the field it is possible to identify a range of common questions or issues into which it is possible to place almost any media discussion. These points of commonality have to do with media technologies, categories, institutions, languages representations and audiences.

This section is ordered with a view to illuminating the main debates both *about* the field and *within* the field throughout its development (and it is not always easy to distinguish between these levels of debate). Later sections of the reader provide much more detail of the progression within each of the key approaches to media study. In this section, as in those that follow, there is an historical dimension – the organization of extracts draws our attention to the sequential logic within which specific questions were raised at specific 'moments' in the development of the field, and to the paradigms that were dominant at these times.

The extract from Hardt serves to introduce and discuss the influential period of mass communication research that emerged in the United States in the 1940s and 1950s. It also refers back to earlier periods to examine the roots of much of this thought. Hardt's approach is characterized by a whiggish 'great man' theory of mass communication history, and invites our attention to the approaches and controversies between 'father figures' such as Schramm and Lasswell, while illustrating the relevance of personal academic and social backgrounds in assessing the contentions that divided and united the field. He explores notions of 'critical' research and wrestles with the differences between 'field' and 'discipline'.

The relationship between various elements in the field is one of the central concerns of this section and Hardt helps to illuminate how, at least in the eyes of American academics, communication and media studies were transformed by their very institutionalization within academe. Some researchers harboured a desire for a scientific discipline, others wanted a multi-disciplinary environment, and many were tied to administrative and industrial interests and funding. All were committed to understanding the processes of communication and their role in the structuring of a democratic society, from within the frameworks and tools of traditional social science.

The extract from Todd Gitlin also invites us to examine how the specific circumstances of the generation of a theory can tell us a great deal about its strengths and weaknesses. In effect, Gitlin's paradoxical target is precisely the attempt to substitute for grand theorizing of media 'effects' along 'mass society' lines with the concept of *mediated* effects, the mediation in this instance represented by the inter-personal channels which were proposed by Lazarsfeld as crucial to the effectiveness of media as agents of attitude change. The concept of 'two-step' flow and personal influence became central tenets in a new orthodoxy in which the potential of media for individual change was seen to be modest, limited by a wide range of such mediating factors. Where Hardt concentrates on the early drive to explain media effects, Gitlin shows how the appearance of methodological rigour is no substitute for asking the right questions and no guarantee of valid answers: effects cannot be reduced to before-and-after methodology, and 'no change' is not at all the same thing as 'no effects'. Yet the model of the two-step flow (see also Section 3 on the media effects tradition) is largely responsible for discrediting the still-discredited stimulus–response Pavlovian, 'magic bullet' models of media effect, and it greatly advanced the search for intervening variables in the communication process. The model of 'intervening variables' dominated the field for at least three decades, especially in the United States, as Gitlin shows, where it was central to the identity of mass communication research in its transformation into institutional respectability within American academe, in ways which had repercussions for the nature of future research. It was an orthodoxy not only of subject matter and of methodology, but related to a positive world view of corporate capitalism and representative democracy. It reduced politics to opinions, and opinions to consumer choice, and marginalized the significance of media as institutions interacting with other powerful institutions in society. This for Gitlin is the essence of American mainstream sociology and its particular version within this dominant paradigm of media sociology.

The extract from Halloran further underlines the contribution, in theorizing the media, of the sociology of knowledge. Perhaps it is because researchers must by necessity ask questions about how the media represent the social world, that they quickly turn to questions about how, and why, research represents the media, examining the relationship, as does Halloran, between research, its context, and those elements that impinge on the research process. While he distinguishes between conventional 'administrative' research (subjugated to the immediate requirements of sponsors and funding) and critical approaches (more independent, perhaps, of industrial interests, but scarcely existing in a social vacuum), he also recognizes that these are both rooted in the intellectual traditions of western industrialized nations and must also be interrogated from positions beyond that framework. Thus, in this piece asking the right questions is only part of the equation; questioning the questioner is the place to start.

Hardt in an earlier examination of the field of study as it 'came of age' (Hardt, 1979, p. 17) emphasized that the 'study of mass communication can make sense only in the context of a theory of society' (Hardt, 1979, p. 35). Halloran here agrees, but leaves us with the pertinent question, which theory? The extracts discussed thus far provide some insight into the relationship between American and European research traditions. Blumler in his article even calls for more collaboration across the Atlantic. Not only does he distinguish between the more holistic European approach, and the focus on audience/effects in the American approach, he also relates this difference to differences in the media industries on the separate continents. Having created these straw men he proceeds to cut away at them, indicating areas of détente, and the need for a stronger audience-based research in the European tradition. The tradition of British empirical media sociology, with its emphasis on social survey and participant observation, had already revitalized the study of media industries and institutions with such work as that of Tunstall (1971), Schlesinger (1978), and Boyd-Barrett (1980). Even as Blumler was writing, the area of audience study was about to undergo a similar transformation (see Section 10) represented, in particular, by the work of Morley (1980).

The Thompson extract which concludes this section draws the study of mass communications and culture back towards their roots in sociology. 'Drawn back', not in the sense of a scolded puppy, but rather as final proof that it is possible to teach an old dog (sociology) new tricks.

The 'tricks' that sociology and social theory can learn from mass communication, according to Thompson, relate to its centrality in modern culture. The developments and debates reviewed in this section take us from narrowly defined 'effects'-based research, to much wider debates about the subject, its scope and rationale, and its methodologies. Thompson draws many of these together into a hermeneutic methodological framework; for him, the symbolic nature of interpretation is the crux of mass communication, even if a tripartite division of his object of study still remains at the core of this work. Although he does not talk of production, content, and audience, these divisions are still evident in his concepts of production/diffusion, construction and reception/appropriation.

There has been much criticism over time of the 'transmission belt' model of communication (see examples in Sections 2 and 3), and of the 'ideological apparatus' model (see examples in Section 8). Underlying both of them is a model of the receiver as implicitly naive and vulnerable. Thompson does not want to relinquish the relationship between culture, communication and ideology, but he does want to develop a more dynamic understanding, not one based on reproduction but one which considers how messages are mobilized by the media and taken up by the individuals who receive them.

References and further reading

Bazalgette, C. (1992) Key aspects of media education. In Alvarado, M. and Boyd-Barrett, O. (eds) *Media Education*, British Film Institute, London, pp. 199–219.

Blumler, J. G. (1977) The emergence of communication studies. *Journal of Educational Television*, Spring.

Boyd-Barrett, O. (1980) *The International News Agencies*, Constable, London.

Golding, P. and Murdock, G. (1978) Theories of communication and theories of society. *Communication Research*, Vol. 5, No. 3.

Hardt, H. (1979) *Social Theories of the Press*, Sage, London.

Hamelink, C. J. and Linne, O. (1994) *Mass Communication Research: On Problems and Policies*, Ablex Publishing, Norwood, NJ.

Halloran, J. D. (1974) *Mass Media and Society: The Challenge of Research*, Leicester University Press.

Journal of Communication (1983) Ferment in the field. *Journal of Communication*, Vol. 33, No. 3.

Journal of Communication (1993a) The future of the field I. *Journal of Communication*, Vol. 43, No. 3.

Journal of Communication (1993b) The future of the field II. *Journal of Communication*, Vol. 43, No. 4.

Lazarsfeld, P. F., Berelson, B. and Gaudet, H. (1948) *The People's Choice*, Columbia University Press, New York.

Morley, D. (1980) *The Nationwide Audience*, British Film Institute, London.

Schlesinger, P. (1978) *Putting Reality Together*, Methuen, London.

Tunstall, J. (1971) *Journalists at Work*, Constable, London.

UNESCO (1970) The mass media and society the need for research. UNESCO reports and papers on mass communication, No. 59.

2

On ignoring history: mass communication research and the critique of society

Hanno Hardt

From Hardt, H. (1992) *Critical Communication Studies: Communication, History and Theory in America*, Routledge, London, pp. 77–122.

> Most of the critics in this country want to see their criticisms within the present framework of the industry.
>
> Paul Lazarsfeld

By the 1940s the United States had made the transition into an age of mass societies, when dreams of the Great Community were reconstituted as opportunities for participation in a collective life, with promises of protection from mass manipulation and loss of liberty. Social theorists had become preoccupied with notions of depersonalization and the atomization of society, reflecting upon a hostile world that was increasingly dominated by totalitarian regimes. Their claims of authority championed the need for individuals to share a sense of community under the guise of their respective ideologies. Some of the circulating theories of American social scientists rested on analyses of modernization and its effects upon social organizations, taking into account the shift from notions of 'community' to considerations of 'society'. Other theories addressed the study of collective behaviour, that is, the effects of mass manipulation, including propaganda and advertising, on the nature of the social environment.

Under these circumstances, issues of communication and society figured prominently in the work of Chicago sociologists, who questioned the direction of urban growth and social commitment. In their writings public opinion was recognized as a powerful and essential source of strength for the maintenance of a democratic society and remained a major focus of theorizing about the nature of pluralism. Indeed, the character and conduct of large numbers of people coping with technological change and searching for meaningful conditions of existence, in an environment that had become more difficult to understand and almost impossible to conquer, had presented new opportunities for the study of social behaviour and control.

For instance, Herbert Blumer, whose work in the tradition of Mead and symbolic interactionism represented a pragmatist approach to the pathology of mass society, provided a now classic discussion of collective behaviour as a study of 'ways by which the social order comes into existence, in the sense of the emergence and solidification of new forms of collective behaviour' (Blumer, 1939, p. 223). For Blumer, communication played a significant role in his discussion of the processes of social movements. He differentiated among collectivities, such as publics, crowds and masses, and suggested that social movements centring on the mechanisms of the public or crowd give rise to the political and moral phases of the social order, while those which 'stress the mechanisms of the mass, yield subjective orientations in the form of common tastes and inclinations' (Blumer, 1939, p. 280). Accordingly, his presentation of public opinion and propaganda appears related to public activities, while issues of advertising ('mass advertising') are addressed as appeals to members of the mass.

In contrast to European discussions of mass society and the dangers of totalitarianism, Blumer and others provided an explanation of mass phenomena which rested on American middle-class experiences of massification, describing the conditions of social change under the pressures of technology and industrialization.

[. . .]

The frequent observations of media involvement in the process of organizing and manipulating people served as an obvious agenda for the study of communication. At about this time, in the early 1940s, Harold D. Lasswell had introduced the term 'mass communication' in his work about political power and propaganda. The term was meant to signify the modern conditions under which society is organized and to emphasize the role of bureaucracies and their communication technologies in political decision-making processes. It was also an acknowledgement of the importance of communication for the analysis of social phenomena.

[. . .]

Throughout the ensuing debates about mass society theories and their impact on the American experience, warnings about the dangers of powerful media and their effects on the welfare of society and the expression of democratic practices resurfaced in the literature. For instance, Louis Wirth wrote that in 'mass communications we have unlocked a new social force of as yet uncalculable magnitude' which 'has the power to build loyalties, to undermine them, and thus by furthering or hindering consensus to affect all other sources of power'. And he urged that it is important 'that we understand its nature, its possibilities, its limits, and the means of harnessing it to human purposes' (Wirth, 1948, p. 12).

Thus, when American communication and media studies emerged in the 1940s, their initial concerns reflected the needs of an expanding society, including the positioning of political and economic interests, while their intellectual foundations rested on the influence of the critical tradition of pragmatism and the sociology of the Chicago School. That is, the basic commitment to enlightenment and the improvement of society *qua* society was replaced by a definition of allegiance to special interests that equated the rising demands of the political and economic systems with serving the welfare of society. Along the way, the process of (mass) communication became identified with the creation and maintenance of the necessary conditions of the social environment and the quality of the democratic experience, while issues of communication and media rose to become commercially and politically relevant topics of social-scientific inquiry.

Although significant contributions to the field of communication and media research were made initially by individuals working in the traditions of sociology, social psychology or political science, there were also expectations for the creation of a separate discipline. With these promising beginnings of modern (mass) communication research grew an implicit assumption that its praxis could not only produce a theoretical understanding of the role of media and communication in a liberal-pluralist society, but also help legitimate social-scientific concerns about the nature of communication and establish mass communication as a scientific discipline. These hopes seemed particularly strong among those whose scholarship was organized exclusively around problems of media and communication, often under the auspices of journalism or mass communication departments within American colleges and universities, where contemporary references to mass communication research as a discipline continue to reside.

Shearon A. Lowery has provided a typical description suggesting that the 'move towards becoming a discipline' began with the institutionalization of mass communication research in university programmes, and is reflected in the presence of 'scholarly journals, scientific associations, textbooks, and the other trappings of a discipline' (Lowery and DeFleur, 1988, p. ix). Others, with strong academic groundings in sociology or social psychology, for instance, seemed less inclined to contemplate the status of the field. Although considerations of communication in the context of social theories, in particular, remained a considerable but never exclusive concern of most major contributors to the field, including Lasswell, Lazarsfeld, Deutsch, Lewin and Hovland, they never precluded other, related investigations of human relations or social structures. In fact, the ability to contextualize questions of communication in the specific problematic of established disciplines contributed significantly to insights into human nature and conduct.

On the other hand, individuals like Wilbur Schramm, who emerged (from journalism education) during this period as a leader in the field, yearned for a systematic and unified theory of communication.

[. . .]

When the field of (mass) communication theory and research turned from a cultural/historical interpretation of communication, reminiscent of pragmatism and the work of the Chicago School, to a social-scientific explanation, ideas of communication and media were processed in the context of quantitative analyses and investigations.

[. . .]

The fast rise of communication and media research paralleled social and political needs for knowledge about the power of information and its role in the control of society. It also reflected the presence of a social-scientific *instrumentarium*, like survey research or content analysis, to capture and describe the process of communication.

Wilbur Schramm identified Lazarsfeld, Lewin, Lasswell and Hovland as 'the 'founding fathers' of communication research in the United States' (Schramm, 1963, p. 2), following Berelson's designation of these individuals as leading social scientists (Berelson, 1959, p. 1), but completely ignoring the history of concerns about communication and culture that had characterized the Chicago School and continued to surface in literary and anthropological writings at the time. Instead, Schramm insisted on characterizing communication research as an exclusive exercise of a behavioural science orientation by suggesting that it 'is quantitative, rather than speculative. Its practitioners are deeply interested in theory, but in the theory they can test.' He insisted that 'they are behavioural researchers: they are trying to find out something about why humans behave as they do, and how communication can make it possible for them to live together more happily and productively' (Schramm, 1963, pp. 5–6).

According to Schramm, the 'science of human communication' had arrived only with the development of 'audience measurement, public opinion sampling, content study, and the measurement of social effect' (Schramm, 1948, p. 5). Such definitions would coincide with rising interests in methodological issues rather than with specific social or political problems of a post-war society that attempted a gradual adjustment to normality. [. . .]

The decisive shift to a scientific/empirical definition of the field emerged with a series of scientific models of communication and mass communication, particularly from the late 1940s and throughout the 1950s, which were preoccupied with functional aspects of various (mass) communication models and reinforced by specific positivistic methods. These activities served a number of immediate goals, specifically, the definition of the field, or, as some would argue, the discipline, the demonstration of its scientific nature, and finally its legitimation as a social-scientific enterprise.

Thus, when Lasswell offered a 'convenient way to describe an act of communication' (Lasswell, 1948, p. 37), he proposed what became an influential and considerably powerful formula for understanding human communication. He proceeded to identify not only the elements of the communication process – communicator, message, medium, receiver, and effects – but he also labelled the corresponding fields of communication research: media analysis, audience analysis and effect analysis (Lasswell, 1948, p. 37). The description revealed Lasswell's primary interest in the power of persuasive (political) communication, but also referred to organismic equivalencies within an approach dominated by the intent of the communicator and the effect of messages (Lasswell, 1948, p. 41). As such, his definition of communication harks back to the stimulus–response model, rooted in learning theory, which became a significant force in mass communication theory. Focused upon effects, this approach implied a concept of society as an aggregate of anonymous, isolated individuals exposed to powerful media institutions engaged in reinforcing or changing social behaviour.

Equally important and quite persuasive in its scientific, mathematical intent was the work of Claude Shannon and Warren Weaver (1949), whose model described communication as a linear, one-way process. [. . .]

In the following years, mass communication research was informed by a variety of communication and mass communication models. Stimulated by earlier efforts and by the rise of psychological models, which included aspects of balance theory and co-orientation (Heider, 1946; Newcomb, 1953; Festinger, 1957), they provided an attempt to order and systematize the study of mass communication phenomena (Schramm, 1954; Gerbner, 1956; Westley and MacLean, 1957). Their authors shared an understanding of the complexity of mass communication and its integration in society. At the same time, the impact of these models directed mass communication research toward an investigation of specific components and encouraged or reinforced a preoccupation with questions of communication effects. Furthermore, it accommodated the development and critique of research methodologies based upon a functional theory of society that had been firmly established with the creation of mass communication models.

Consequently, the field offered social-scientific explanations for the stability of the social, political and commercial system without critically evaluating its own communication-and-society paradigm. Indeed, it was not until a widespread paradigm crisis reached the social science establishment, particularly in the 1970s and 1980s, that communication and media research turned to acknowledge the importance of culture.

Nevertheless, even throughout these years, the field of (mass) communication research continued to be identified overwhelmingly with the mainstream perspective of social science research. Both shared the implications of a pragmatic model of society. Their investigations related to the values of individualism and operated on the strength of efficiency and instrumental values in their pursuit of democracy as the goal of individual members of a large-scale, consensual society.

The commercialization of everyday life, particularly prior to the Second World War, provoked an atmosphere of experimentation and innovation that raised questions about the expanding role of communication and media in society. The requirements of propaganda analysis, including the production, dissemination and reception of persuasive messages during the war, and the demands of a post-war economy, helped accelerate the study of communication in society without the need to reflect on the nature and intent of communication research.

[. . .]

By the middle of the 1950s, Schramm had a strong sense of the interdisciplinary nature of communication research, the potential of social science methodology, and its capability to answer practical questions, but no apparent theoretical framework for a critical assessment of the role of the media in American society. This was the beginning of a period when the search for improved research tools obfuscated the rationale for communication research, except to respond to a rather vague idea of the relationship between communication, media and democracy.

[. . .]

Schramm's initial contribution was journalistic rather than scientific; he reported about the state of communication research, but he did not engage in an informed critique of theories and methodologies of the field and their appropriateness for the study of society. However, he adopted a strong interest in the growth and development of the academic field, coupled with questions of freedom and responsibility, in which the support of communication research becomes a public responsibility in an effort to create and sustain a level of media performance that contributes to the development of a democratic society (Schramm, 1957).

Lazarsfeld was among those European (and particularly German-speaking) philosophers and social scientists who had arrived with the beginning of the Second World War. He called himself a 'European positivist' who had been influenced by Ernst Mach, Henri Poincaré and Albert Einstein, and who felt intellectually close to members of the Vienna Circle (Lazarsfeld, 1969, p. 273). When he encountered members of the Frankfurt School, particularly Theodor Adorno and Max Horkheimer, who were in their first years of exile, Lazarsfeld was not particularly familiar with critical theory. But he discovered a mutual interest in the problems of mass culture, which he had begun to analyse in his studies of audiences and media contents. On the other hand, in his association with Columbia University, Lazarsfeld was introduced to the theoretical work of Robert Merton, and the evolving collaborative efforts in the area of mass communication and community studies 'became an integral part of the "Columbia" version of structural functionalism', testifying to Merton's involvement in the rise of communication research (Robinson, 1988).

[. . .]

Elsewhere, Gerbner would offer a definition of 'masses' that emphasized the movement of messages rather than the organization of people. He argued that the 'key to the historic significance of mass media is . . . the association of 'mass' with a process of production and distribution'; consequently, 'Mass communication is the technologically and institutionally based mass production and distribution of the most broadly shared continuous flow of public messages in industrial societies' (Gerbner, 1967, pp. 53–4).

While Schramm defined the parameters of the field through the continuous publication of textbooks throughout the 1950s, Lazarsfeld delivered the social-scientific expertise and new insights into the role of communication in American society. His initial interest in methodological problems, applied to the study of media effects, resulted in a number of studies which helped mold the communication and mass communication establishment. Although communication research in the guise of propaganda and advertising analyses had existed for some time, Lazarsfeld helped establish the credibility of the field as a social-scientific endeavour in the university environment.

Lazarsfeld considered the study of radio a major undertaking which could provide insights into American culture and society, assuming that 'the operation of radio certainly bears the imprint of the present social system and is, in turn, bound to have certain effects upon social institutions' (Lazarsfeld, 1939, p. 5). He asserted that the investigation of radio could also lead to understanding social and cultural values in society, since 'what is or is not going on the air is greatly influenced by the respect for existing moral codes, the acceptance of today's distribution of property, and other features of American culture' (Lazarsfeld, 1939, p. 5). However, there is no indication here that Lazarsfeld entertained ideas about the social or political problematic of the power of ownership, or the control of content and its impact on other groups or classes in society, except to speculate about the social and economic consequences for established institutions, like the press and education. He identified the problems of joint ownership which arose a few years later with the profitability of radio and raised ethical questions about its effects upon news coverage. Concerned about the relationship between radio and newspapers, Lazarsfeld asked, 'What is the advertising policy resulting from joint ownership? How is news of social importance such as that of labour disputes and racial problems, handled under varying ownership structures of newspapers and radio stations?' (Lazarsfeld, 1941b, p. 13). Lazarsfeld's questions revealed a major problematic of commercialism and a specific weakness of contemporary media coverage. Discriminatory news gathering and dissemination practices involving the organization of labour and the participation of the black community were rarely addressed, and Lazarsfeld contributed a concrete and insightful comment on the need for socially relevant investigations of media behaviour. [. . .]

From his own political assessment of American society, and perhaps after his professional analysis of the economic power of the broadcasting industry, Lazarsfeld had come to the conclusion that 'freedom of speech is now a three-cornered proposition between the government, the communications industry and the individual citizen' (Lazarsfeld and Field, 1946, p. 74). His model assumed a separation of power and conveyed the impression that individuals were actually in control of their political or economic destiny, and, thus, viable partners in any alliance of power, while any notions of collective representation of various social, cultural or political interests remained unexplored.

Specifically, Lazarsfeld's research strategy was built upon the idea that such alliances shift depending upon the issues and their varying implications. Indeed, the demands of individuals for freedom of speech and the role of the broadcasting industry to 'maintain a vigilance to see that the government does not interfere with the freedom of radio as an institution' and to defend 'its commercial interests under the formula of free speech' (Lazarsfeld and Field, 1946, p. 74) constituted a major political problematic. It also contained practical consequences for Lazarsfeld's work. His strategy was to 'keep the Bureau [of Applied Social Research] maneuvring between the intellectual and political purist and an industry from which I wanted cooperation without having to "sell out" ' (Lazarsfeld, 1969, p. 321).

This period of communication research was also shaped by the political atmosphere leading up and through the experiences of the Second World War. Most obvious were the demands for information about propaganda effects; less visible, but equally important, were the encounters with *émigré* scholars whose presence in the traditions of logical positivism and Marxism began to enrich the intellectual climate of American universities. Both the search for specific answers to the power of communication and the availability of European expertise helped determine the development of the field into the 1980s.

For instance, Lazarsfeld continued to seek theoretical breakthroughs, and the subsequent presence of Theodor Adorno in the Princeton Office of Radio Research was based upon his hope to 'develop a convergence of European theory and American empiricism' (Lazarsfeld, 1969, p. 323). [. . .]

Lazarsfeld's encounter with Adorno and Horkheimer was fruitful only in that it led to a joint publishing effort and to his own definition of critical research.

[. . .]

The Institute of Social Research and the Office of Radio Research at Columbia University collaborated in 1941 on a special issue of *Studies in Philosophy and Social Science*, which was devoted to problems of mass communication. Lazarsfeld, used this occasion to offer his own under standing of the mass communication research establishment in the United States by drawing on his encounter with critical theory in the American context of social research. According to Lazarsfeld, '*administrative research* . . . is carried through in the service of some kind of administrative agency of public or private character', while '*critical research* is posed against the practice of administrative research, requiring that, prior and in addition to whatever special purpose is to be served, the general role of our media of communication in the present social system should be studied' (Lazarsfeld, 1941a, pp. 8–9).

[. . .]

Lazarsfeld's definition of critical research ignored the historical nature of critical research in the tradition of the Frankfurt School and failed to consider the role of culture in the positioning of the media, opting instead for his own ideological position. He has commented on his attitude toward critical theory, acknowledging his 'tendency towards cannibalism. In order to understand another system of thought I have to translate it into my own terms. It never occurred to me that I might thereby try to exercise dominance over the other fellow' (1975, cited in McLuskie, 1988, p. 34). Although sympathetic toward critical theory, Lazarsfeld insisted upon a deductive form of critical research, misunderstanding Adorno's theory of society, in which data are not phenomena which express a general theory, but 'mere epiphenomena upon the theory' (Rose, 1978, p. 98).

Indeed, Lazarsfeld, and many of his contemporaries, saw the problems of media and society in technological terms, dealing with the inevitability of industrialization, the massification of audiences, and the effects of these 'mass' media on people. They adopted a technological rationale, which Horkheimer and Adorno once defined as 'the rationale of domination itself' (Horkheimer and Adorno, 1972, p. 121), and which could only provide solutions consistent with the prevailing theory of society.

Furthermore, over time American (mass) communication research has remained insensitive to changing historical conditions which effectively define problems of communication. Instead, communication research typically aligned itself with the social and economic power structure and maintained an ideological position that would be exposed and attacked by Horkheimer and Adorno.

Mass communication research of this period, with its intensive effort to produce a variety of mass communication models since the 1950s, had also sought the theoretical unity and, therefore, political strength of the field. It had moved from a sociological perspective to a multi-disciplinary area of communication and mass communication studies, which offered new opportunities for critical research. Lazarsfeld had recognized this trend, but he was unable to forge his critical research perspective into a major, theoretical statement. Indeed, when he began to formulate his position *vis-à-vis* the reality of economic and political authority in mass communication research,

he offered a reading of critical theory (and the Frankfurt School) which ignored the theoretical premises and their practical consequences, particularly as suggested in the works of Horkheimer and Adorno.
[. . .]

The notion of a critical position ultimately meant a recognition of authority and a reconciliation with power; it also meant working with the necessity for change within the dominant paradigm and arguing for the convergence of existing theoretical or practical perspectives.

The critical research of Lazarsfeld was neither based upon a Marxist critique of society nor founded on traditional social criticism in the United States, with its questioning of authority in the populist, reformist sense. Nevertheless, Lazarsfeld's work helped define the American domain of communication research for decades to come. His remarks about critical research represented the repositioning of traditional social science research within the practice of what C. Wright Mills has called abstracted empiricism (Mills, 1970, p. 60). The notion of critical research, as opposed to administrative research, became a point of legitimation in the development of (mass) communication research. Its presence asserted the neutral and independent position of communication research as an established and recognized field of study and helped justify its claims as an administrative unit within the organization of American universities.

The field also represented a relevant and important *methodological* specialization as a branch of sociology. As a result, scholarly interests in methodological issues frequently became priorities and, ultimately, determinants of social research and research agendas. A reason for the failure to advance a unified theoretical proposition has been the legitimation of communication research through its methodological expertise combined with its service function for government and commerce, including media enterprises.
[. . .]

Mass communication research in this era of economic recovery and existential dilemmas typically isolated specific conditions of the environment. It delved into relationships among people, investigated questions of social identity, and, generally speaking, raised some doubts about the stability of individuals in their social relations. At the same time, there was a marked absence, however, of questions about the role of the media in the process of culture and ideological struggle, including the location of authority and the distribution of power. Thus, Gerbner's 'challenge for mass communications research' reflected his own commitment to a liberal-pluralist vision of society, based upon the participation of individuals in a 'genuine' public. He asked communication scholars

> to combine the empirical methods with the critical aims of social science, to join rigorous practice with value-conscious theory, and thus to gather the insight the knowledgeable individual in a genuine public must have if he is to come to grips (and not unconsciously to terms) with the sweeping undercurrents of his culture.
>
> (Gerbner, 1958, pp. 106–7.)

His challenge was a confirmation of Lazarsfeld's call for critical research, but it was also a reflection of a democratic ideal which characterized earlier reformist notions in American social science research. Although reform-minded in the sense of understanding itself as contributing to the betterment of society, (mass) communication research remained committed to a traditionally conservative approach to the study of social and cultural phenomena, in which instrumental values merged and identified with moral values.

[. . .]

During this period communication research had also come under the scrutiny of its own practitioners, but with rather limited and disappointing results, since social scientists practised a form of self-critique that was, for the most part, aimed at the methodological issues of the field. For instance, when Joseph Klapper published his research survey in 'The effects of mass media' (in mimeographed form in 1949 and as a book, *The Effects of Mass Communication*, in 1960), Lazarsfeld speculated in his introduction to the 1949 edition about the lack of knowledge concerning media effects, suggesting that the

> main difficulty probably lies in formulating the problem correctly. For the trouble started exactly when empirical research stepped in where once the social philosopher had reigned supreme. To the latter there was never any doubt that first the orator and then the newspaper and now television are social forces of great power.

And he concluded that a lack of sophisticated measurement techniques combined with the complexity of media effects were responsible for the current state of information about what media do to people (Klapper, 1949, pp. 1–2).

Lazarsfeld implied that empirical communication research must break with the line of argument and the logic of historical and theoretical analyses, and replace rather than supplement the previously held views on the power of communication in the hands of those who control it with the newly established truths of empirical research. However, a few years later Smythe began to raise a number of substantial issues pertaining to the conduct of communication research. He, not unlike Lasswell, exposed the dangers of scientism, observing that the 'bulk of the research in the interdisciplinary field coming to be known as "communication research" has been in the hands of persons who more or less consciously adopt the stance of "scientism". Consequently, the 'evidence from the fields of history, sociology, political science and economics are ignored as being unfit for acceptance as "science" ' (Smythe, 1954, pp. 24–7).

Smythe argued for a combination of empirical methodologies and rigorous logic to create 'non-scientistic' conditions for the pursuit of communication research and the development of a general theory of communication with premises and preconceptions that are rooted in historical consciousness. His sense of history demanded a recognition of the importance of culture and cultural institutions for an assessment of contemporary media effects, and he produced a 'substantive' thesis which held that over time and 'as our culture has developed it has built into itself increasing concentrations of authority' which are nowhere 'more evident than in our communications activities' (Smythe, 1954, pp. 24–7). He developed a historical scenario and reached the 'hypothetical conclusion' that 'as our social organization has become more tightly integrated on the basis of modern technology, authority has increasingly been built into it'; and he advocated that a further hypothesis be tested

> that our mass media, through cutting off feedback, through dealing in stereo-types, through specializing in a manipulative view of humanity (both directly through advertising and indirectly through the plot structures and motivations portrayed in entertainment and other program material), are capable of molding us more and more into authoritarianism.
>
> (Smythe, 1954, pp. 21–4.)

But while Smythe had raised critical issues from a theoretical perspective, Berelson now pronounced the end of communication research from within the establishment a few years later. His review of the field in terms of its 'distinguished past' (Berelson, 1959, p. 5) included a series of minor or less influential positions (besides those represented by Lasswell, Lazarsfeld, Lewin and Hovland) that consisted of a reformist approach (Hutchins Commission), a historical approach (Riesman, Innis), both of questionable scientific value, according to critics, as well as a series of perspectives represented by journalism (Schramm, Casey, Nixon), mathematics (Shannon, Weaver), psycholinguistics (Osgood, Miller) and psychiatry (Ruesch, Bateson). Interestingly enough, Berelson omitted significant contributions in other disciplines, revealing a blind-spot for considerations of communication and language in such areas as anthropology, linguistics and literature. On the other hand, he characterized Lazarsfeld as the only one 'who centered on communication *per se*' (Berelson, 1959, p. 5). But his solutions were rather disappointing; they followed established lines of communication research, observing new developments in popular culture and mass communication, and urging the adoption of an economic perspective on communication. Berelson failed to address specifically the poverty of the theoretical discourse, but seemed content with defining the 'vitality' and 'breakthroughs' of the field in terms of research activities and methodological advancements (Berelson, 1959, p. 6). In addition, there was no attempt on his part to connect (old and new) pursuits of communication research with questions of society, let alone issues of enlightenment and culture. Unlike other fields, mass communication studies had not specifically attracted the work of social theorists, but provided opportunities for specific research interests which were widely accepted, imitated and published. The theoretical debates in other disciplines, however, were not as readily reflected in the (mass) communication literature. Berelson's failure to respond to the interdisciplinary nature of the theoretical discourse serves as an additional indication that (mass) communication research had been project-oriented and dedicated to the practical application of research methodologies.
[. . .]

This period of communication studies, however, was defined in terms of specific research objectives. It was characterized by a decided emphasis on the idea of society, which had become the focus of social-scientific analysis. The notion of critical research remained within the administrative considerations of communication research, while criticism often involved methodological issues and was bound to threaten creative or innovative modes of inquiry.

At the same time, the need for theoretical advancement was scarcely considered in the relevant literature of communication and media studies. Such activity occurred – outside of communication research – in an interdisciplinary context, typically combining philosophical, literary and anthropological insights into the nature of language and culture. The results were alternative explanations of communication and media, based on the use of symbols in private and public discourse, the power of myths, and the symbolic functions of democratic institutions, which replaced the idea of society with the notion of culture.

At the end of the period, mainstream communication and media research had failed to address critical developments from within and without its boundaries. It had remained within specified categories of interests, reflected in an academic specialization in the study of communication that was interdisciplinary by its commitment to a behavioural science orientation, but without any significant or successful attempt to break out of its monadic circle. With the acknowledgement of a cultural approach to the study of society during the following decades, the field would demonstrate a willingness to co-opt specific theoretical or methodological aspects of a critical Marxist tradition, including Critical Theory, rather than to rethink its position in terms of the weaknesses or failures to produce a theory of communication that is also a theory of society.

References

Berelson, Bernard (1959) The state of communication research. *Public Opinion Quarterly*, Vol. 23, No. 1 (Spring), pp. 1–5.

Blumer, Herbert (1939) Collective behavior. In Park, Robert E. (ed.) *An Outline of the Principles of Sociology*, Barnes & Noble, New York, pp. 221–80.

Festinger, Leon A. (1957) *A Theory of Cognitive Dissonance*, Row & Peterson, Evanston, IL.

Gerbner, George (1967) Mass media and human communication theory. In Dance, Frank E. X. (ed.) *Human Communication Theory: Original Essays*. Holt, Rinehart & Winston, New York, pp. 40–60.

Gerbner, George (1958) On content analysis and critical research in mass communication. *Audio Visual Communication Review*, Vol. 6, No. 2, pp. 85–108.

Gerbner, George (1956) Toward a general model of communication. *Audio Visual Communication Review*, Vol. 4, No. 3, pp. 171–99.

Heider, Fritz (1946) Attitudes and cognitive information. *Journal of Psychology*, Vol. 21, No. 1, 107–12.

Horkheimer, Max and Adorno, Theodor W. (1972) *Dialectics of Enlightenment*, Herder & Herder, New York.

Klapper, Joseph T. (1960) *The Effects of Mass Communication*, Free Press, New York.

Klapper, Joseph T. (1949) The effects of mass media: a report to the director of the public library inquiry, Bureau of Applied Social Research, Columbia University, New York (mimeographed).

Lasswell, Harold D. (1948) The structure and function of communication in society. In Bryson, Lyman (ed.) *The Communication of Ideas*, Harper & Row, New York, pp. 37–51.

Lazarsfeld, Paul F. (1969) An episode in the history of social research: a memoir. In Fleming, Donald and Bailyn, Bernard (eds) *The Intellectual Migration: Europe and America, 1930–1960*, Harvard University Press, Cambridge, MA, pp. 270–337.

Lazarsfeld, Paul F. (1941a) Remarks on administrative and critical communications research. *Studies in Philosophy and Social Science*, Vol. 9, No. 1, pp. 2–16.

Lazarsfeld, Paul F. (1941b) Some notes on the relationship between radio and the press. *Journalism Quarterly*, Vol. 18, No. 1, pp. 10–13.

Lazarsfeld, Paul F. (1939) Radio research and applied psychology. *Journal of Applied Psychology*, Vol. 23, No. 1, pp. 1–7.

Lazerfeld, Paul F. and Field, Henry (1946) *The People Look at Radio.* University of North Carolina Press, Chapel Hill.

Lowery, Shearon A. and DeFleur, Melvin L. (1988) *Milestones in Mass Communication Research*, 2nd edn, Longman, New York.

McLuskie, Ed (1988) Silence from the start: Paul Lazarsfeld's appropriation and suppression of critical theory for communication and social research. Unpublished paper, Boise State University, Boise, ID.

Mills, C. Wright (1970) *The Sociological Imagination*, Penguin Books, Harmondsworth.

Newcomb, Theodore M. (1953) An approach to the study of communicative acts. *Psychological Review*, Vol. 60, No. 6, pp. 393–404.

Robinson, Gertrude J. (1988) Paul F. Lazarsfeld & Robert K. Merton: The Columbia School's contributions to US communication studies. Unpublished paper, McGill University, Montreal.

Rose, Gillian (1978) *The Melancholy Science: An Introduction to the Thought of Theodor W. Adorno*, Columbia University Press, New York.

Schramm, Wilbur (1963) *The Science of Human Communication: New Directions and New Findings in Communication Research*, Basic Books, New York.

Schramm, Wilbur (1957) *Responsibility in Mass Communication*, Harper & Brothers, New York.

Schramm, Wilbur (1954) How communication works. In Schramm, Wilbur (ed.) *The Process and Effects of Mass Communication*, University of Illinois Press, Urbana, pp. 3–26.

Schramm, Wilbur (ed.) (1948). *Communications in Modern Society*, University of Illinios Press, Urbana.

Shannon, Claude and Weaver, Warren (1949) *The Mathematical Theory of Communication*, University of Illinois Press, Urbana.

Smythe, Dallas W. (1954) Some observations on communication theory. *Audio Visual Communication Review*, Vol. 2, No. 1, pp. 24–37.

Westly, Bruce and MacLean, Malcolm S. (1957) A conceptual model for mass communication research. *Journalism Quarterly*, Vol. 34 No. 1, pp. 31–8.

Wirth, Louis (1948) Consensus and mass communication. *American Sociological Review*, Vol. 13, No. 1, pp. 1–15.

3

Media sociology: the dominant paradigm

Todd Gitlin

From Gouldner, A. W. *et al.* (eds) (1978) *Theory and Society*, Elsevier
Scientific Publishing Company, Amsterdam, Vol. 6, pp. 205–253.

Since the Second World War, as mass media in the United States have become
more concentrated in ownership, more centralized in operations, more
national in reach, more pervasive in presence, sociological study of the media
has been dominated by the theme of the relative powerlessness of the
broadcasters. Just as the national television networks – the first in history
– were going to work, American sociology was turning away from the study
of propaganda. In this essay I argue that such a strange conjunction of events
is not without its logic. I argue that because of intellectual, ideological and
institutional commitments, sociologists have not put the critical questions;
that behind the idea of the relative unimportance of mass media lies a
skewed, faulty concept of 'importance', similar to the faulty concept of
'power' also maintained by political sociologists, specifically those of the
pluralist persuasion, during the same period; and that, like pluralism, the
dominant sociology of mass communication has been unable to grasp certain
fundamental features of its subject. More than that, it has obscured them,
scanted them, at times defined them out of existence, and therefore it has
had the effect of justifying the existing system of mass media ownership,
control, and purpose.

The dominant paradigm in media sociology, what Daniel Bell has called
the 'received knowledge' of 'personal influence',[1] has drained attention from
the power of the media to define normal and abnormal social and political
activity, to say what is politically real and legitimate and what is not: to justify
the two-party political structure; to establish certain political agendas for
social attention and to contain, channel and exclude others; and to shape
the images of opposition movements. By its methodology, media sociology
has highlighted the recalcitrance of audiences, their resistance to media-
generated messages, and not their dependence, their acquiescence, their
gullibility. It has looked to 'effects' of broadcast programming in a specifically
behaviourist fashion, defining 'effects' so narrowly, microscopically, and
directly as to make it very likely that survey studies could show only slight
effects at most. It has enshrined short-run 'effects' as 'measures' of
'importance' largely because these 'effects' are measurable in a strict,
replicable behavioural sense, thereby deflecting attention from larger social
meanings of mass media production. It has tended to seek 'hard data', often
enough with results so mixed as to satisfy anyone and no one, when it might
have more fruitfully sought hard questions. By studying only the 'effects'

that could be 'measured' experimentally or in surveys, it has put the methodological cart ahead of the theoretical horse. Or rather: it has procured a horse that could pull its particular cart. Is it any wonder, then, that thirty years of methodical research on 'effects' of mass media have produced little theory and few coherent findings? The main result, in marvellous paradox, is the beginning of the decomposition of the going paradigm itself.[2]

In the process of amassing its impressive bulk of empirical findings, the field of mass media research has also perforce been certifying as normal precisely what it might have been investigating as problematic, namely the vast reach and scope of the instruments of mass broadcasting, especially television. By emphasizing precise effects on 'attitudes' and microscopically defined 'behaviour', the field has conspicuously failed to attend to the significance of the fact that mass broadcasting exists in the first place, in a corporate housing and under a certain degree of state regulation. For during most of civilized history there has been no such thing. Who wanted broadcasting, and toward what ends? Which institutional configurations have been generated because of mass broadcasting, and which going institutions – politics, family, schooling, sports – have been altered in structure, goals, social meaning, and how have they reached back into broadcasting to shape its products? How has the prevalence of broadcasting changed the conduct of politics, the texture of political life, hopes, expectations? How does it bear on social structure? Which popular epistemologies have made their way across the broadcasting societies? How does the routine reach of certain hierarchies into millions of living rooms on any given day affect the common language and concepts and symbols? By skirting these questions, by taking for granted the existing institutional order, the field has also been able to skirt the substantive questions of valuation: Does the television apparatus as it exists fulfil or frustrate human needs and the social interest? But of course by failing to ask such questions, it has made itself useful to the networks, to the market research firms, to the political candidates.

The dominant paradigm and its defects

The dominant paradigm in the field since the Second World War has been, clearly, the cluster of ideas, methods, and findings associated with Paul F. Lazarsfeld and his school: the search for specific measurable, short-term, individual, attitudinal and behavioural 'effects' of media content, and the conclusion that media are not very important in the formation of public opinion. Within this whole configuration, the most influential single theory has been, most likely, 'the two-step flow of communications': the idea that media messages reach people not so much directly as through the selective, partisan, complicating interpolation of 'opinion leaders'. In the subtitle of *Personal Influence*, their famous and influential study of the diffusion of opinion in Decatur, Illinois in the mid-1940s, Elihu Katz and Lazarsfeld were concerned with 'the part played by people in the flow of mass communications'.[3] One technical commentator notes with due and transparent qualification: 'It may be that few formulations in the behavioral sciences have had more impact than the two-step flow model'.[4] Daniel Bell, with his characteristic sweep, calls *Personal Influence* 'the standard work'.[5]

As in all sociology, the questions asked and the field of attention define the paradigm even before the results are recorded. In the tradition staked out by Lazarsfeld and his associates, researchers pay most attention to those 'variables' that intervene between message-producers and message-receivers, especially to the 'variable' of interpersonal relations. They conceptualize the audience as a tissue of inter-related individuals rather than as isolated point targets in a mass society. They see mass media as only one of several 'variables' that influence 'attitudes' or voting choices, and they are interested in the measurable 'effects' of media especially in comparison with other 'variables' like 'personal contact'. They measure 'effects' as *changes* over time in respondents' attitudes or discrete behaviours, as these are reported in surveys. In a sequence of studies beginning with *The People's Choice,*[6] Lazarsfeld and his associates developed a methodology (emphasizing panel studies and sociometry) commensurate with their concern for mediating 'variables' like social status, age, and gregariousness. But in what sense does their total apparatus constitute a 'paradigm', and in what sense has it been 'dominant'?

I want to use the word 'paradigm' loosely only, without history-of-science baggage, to indicate a tendency of thought that (a) identifies as important certain *areas* of investigation in a field, (b) exploits a certain *methodology*, more or less distinctive, and (c) produces a set of *results* which are distinctive and, more important, come to be recognized as such. In this sense, a paradigm is established as such not only by its producers but by its consumers, the profession that accords it standing as a primary outlook.

Within the paradigm, Katz's and Lazarsfeld's specific theory of 'the two-step flow of communication', the idea that 'opinion leaders' mediate decisively between mass communicators and audiences, has occupied the centre of scholarly attention. In any discussion of mass media effects, citations of *Personal Influence* remain virtually obligatory. As the first extended exploration of the idea – 'the two-step flow' appears only as an afterthought, and without much elaboration, at the end of the earlier *The People's Choice* – *Personal Influence* can be read as the founding document of an entire field of inquiry. If the theory has recently been contested with great force on empirical grounds,[7] the paradigm as a whole continues to be the central idea configuration that cannot be overlooked by critics. Joseph T. Klapper's *The Effects of Mass Communication* (1960) is the definitive compilation of the field's early stages; but the Decatur study, spread out as it is in detail, seems to me a better testing-ground for a re-examination of the whole paradigm. By having the power to call forth citations and critiques at its own level of generality, it remains central to the field. For twenty years replicating studies have proliferated, complicating and multiplying the categories of the Decatur study, looking at different types of behaviour, different types of 'news function' ('relay', 'information', and so on), some of them confirming the two-step flow on a small scale,[8] but most of them disconfirming or severely qualifying it.[9] All these studies proceed from the introduction into an isolated social system of a single artefact – a product, an 'attitude', an image. The 'effect' is always that of a controlled experiment (such, at least, is the aspiration), but the tendency is to extrapolate, without warrant, from the study of a single artefact's 'effect' to the vastly more general and significant 'effect' of broadcasting under corporate and state auspices. Whatever the particular findings, the general issues of structural impact and institutional change are lost in the aura, the reputation of the 'two-step flow'.

As Melvin L. DeFleur[10] and Roger L. Brown[11] have stressed, the course of mass media theory has to be understood as a historical process, in which theorists confront not only social reality but also the theories extant. Theorists, of course, respond to the going theories in the languages of social research then current, that is, within a social-scientific world view now 'normal', or becoming 'normal', or contesting for 'normalcy'. They respond, explicitly or not, in the light or darkness of history – of new, salient forces in the world, social, political, and technological. There are thus three meta-theoretical conditions shaping any given theoretical perspective: the nature of the theory or theories preceding (in this case, the 'hypodermic' theory); the 'normal' sociological world view now current, or contesting the ideological field (in this case, behaviourism); and actual social, political, technological conditions in the world. The theory of the two-step flow, and the specific approach to 'effects' in which the theory is embedded, are generated by a behaviourist world view which makes itself decisive – and invisible – in the form of methodological microassumptions. The dominant paradigm has to be understood as an intersection of all these factors.

The 'personal influence' paradigm is itself located within a critique of the earlier 'hypodermic' theory, which is in turn both a theory of society and a theory of the workings of mass media within it.[12] In the 'hypodermic' model, society is mass society, and mass communications 'inject' ideas, attitudes, and dispositions towards behaviour into passive, atomized, extremely vulnerable individuals. Katz and Lazarsfeld, who first named the 'personal influence' paradigm, codified it, and brought it to the centre of the field, were explicitly aiming to dethrone the 'hypodermic' theory.[13]
[. . .]

Behaviourist assumptions and damaged findings

But the 'personal influence' theory was founded on limiting assumptions, so that its solid claims would be misleading even if substantial. Indeed, as it happens, the theory does not even hold up in its own terms; the Decatur study, taken on its face, fails in important ways to confirm the theory it claims to be confirming. Moreover, the anomalies themselves help us grasp the theory's social context; the anomalies mean something. For now I want to isolate the theoretical assumptions of the entire paradigm, and to see how they were applied in *Personal Influence*.

It is worth stressing again that the theory was rooted in a strict behaviourism. 'Effects' of mass media lay on the surface; they were to be sought as short-term 'effects' on precisely measurable changes in 'attitude' or in discrete behaviour. Whether in Lazarsfeld's surveys or the laboratory experiments of Carl Hovland and associates, the purpose was to generate predictive theories of audience response, which are necessarily – intentionally or not – consonant with an administrative point of view, with which centrally located administrators who possess adequate information can make decisions that affect their entire domain with a good idea of the consequences of their choices.

Assumption 1. Commensurability of the modes of influence: the exercise of power through mass media is presumed to be comparable to the exercise of power in face-to-face situations. 'People' 'play a part' in the 'flow of mass communications'. The links in 'the general influence chain' are all of the same order; the relations between their influences can be characterized as 'greater' or 'lesser'. This was assumed rather than explicitly stated in *Personal Influence*, although there are points in the text (for example, p. 96) where the assumption lay relatively close to the surface. Discussing the two 'forms of influence' in the same breath, as functional equivalents or commensurables, is what made for the general effect.

This reduction of structurally distinct social processes to commensurables can be recognized as a cardinal operation in the behaviourist canon. But what is distinct about the two processes, of course, is that everyone has the opportunity to exercise 'personal influence' directly on someone else, albeit informally, and generally the relation is reciprocal, whereas the direct influence of mass media belongs routinely and professionally to the hierarchically organized handful who have access to it.

Assumption 2. Power as distinct occasions: power is to be assessed in case studies of discrete incidents. Katz and Lazarsfeld discussed and rejected two other possible criteria of influence: The reputational method, for one, (a) fails to reveal the frequency of influences, and (b) may elicit the names of prestigious individuals who have not actually directly influenced the respondent. Second, the counting of face-to-face contacts might let the decisive encounters through the sieve. Instead of these alternatives, they decided to ask respondents to recall 'incidents of influence exchange,' and the specific influentials involved therein.[14] In particular, they would ask respondents how they had changed their minds in each of four issue areas; then they would interview the next link in the chain. The occasion of influence was the face-to-face encounter in which individual A commended attitude 'a' or behaviour 'b' to individual B. Those who exercised influence on such occasions were defined as 'opinion leaders'.

Notice that this behaviouralization of power is identical to that achieved and insisted upon by the pluralist school of community political analysts who also came to prominence and began to dominate their field in the 1950s.[15] Here too the revolt against an earlier paradigm which emphasized the power of élites (the hypodermic model on the one hand, vulgar Marxism or élite theory on the other). Here too the tacit denial of patterns of structurally maintained power, or what will later be called 'non-decisions'.[16] Here too the insistence on studying discrete episodes of the exercise of influence, as if power were a kind of freely flowing marketplace commodity in a situation of equality, more or less; whence, as we shall see below, the discovery that opinion leadership, like the pluralist concept of influence, is issue-specific and 'non-pyramiding'.[17] 'Opinion leaders' in one sphere did not have influence over other spheres, just as Dahl's New Haven influentials did not 'pyramid' their influence. The structural homology of the two paradigms, personal influence and pluralism reveals something more significant than a coincidental similarity in the shape of their results; it reveals the similarity of problematics and methodologies, the common thrusts of the two fields.

Assumption 3. The commensurability of buying and politics: the unit of influence is a short-term 'attitude change' or a discrete behaviour; or, more exactly, the report of such 'change' or behaviour by a respondent, and one which the respondent can attribute to some specific intervention from outside. Katz and Lazarsfeld were concerned with 'four arenas of every-day decisions: marketing, fashions, public affairs and movie-going'.[18] These areas were assumed to be assimilable within a single theory.

The domain of their interest is most accurately conveyed with a look at the relevant questionnaire items.[19]

With regard to marketing:

> During the last month or so, have you bought any new product or brand that you don't usually buy? (I don't mean something you had to buy because it was the only one available.) Yes . . . No . . . . (If no) On which of these have you tried a new brand most recently? a. breakfast cereals . . . b. soap flakes or chips . . . c. coffee . . . d. None of these.

With regard to fashions:

> Have you recently changed anything about your hairdo, type of clothing, cosmetics, make-up, or made any other change to something more fashionable? Yes . . . No . . . (If so) What sort of change did you make?

With regard to movies, 'our starting point was to ask the respondent to tell us the name of the last movie that she saw.' (The respondents were women. For the reason, see *Personal Influence*, p. 236.)

And on public affairs, the interviewers asked a number of recent poll questions, then asked if the respondent had recently changed her mind about any 'like' them.

So in two of the four issue-areas, the concern was explicitly with changes in consumer behaviour; in the third, with another discrete behaviour in the realm of consumer choice; and in the fourth, with change in the opinion expressed. These issue-areas were taken to be comparable, and the presumed comparability of political ideas and product preferences distorted some of the actual findings. But more: the blithe assumption of the commensurability of buying and politics, never explicitly justified, never opened up to question, hung over the entire argument of *Personal Influence* like an ideological smog.

Assumption 4. 'Attitude change' as the dependent variable: more deeply, more tellingly, the microscopic attention to 'attitude change' was built on a confining approach to the nature of power. In *Personal Influence*, power was the power to compel a certain behaviour, namely buying; or, in the case of 'public affairs,' it was the power to compel a change in 'attitude' on some current issue. Respondents were asked if they had recently changed their attitudes on a current issue; if they had, they were asked who had influenced them.[20] If they had not changed their attitudes they were assumed not to have been influenced.

Now there are two ways in which this sense of influence is inadequate. First, it is possible that a respondent had begun to 'change her mind' on a given issue, only to be persuaded back to the original position by personal influences or, directly, by mass media. More important still are the ways in which attitudes failed to change at all. If one does not take invariance for granted, but as something to be explained, how are we to understand the resulting 'non-decisions'? For there is no compelling reason why constancy of attitude, in the capitalist age, must be taken for granted. Indeed, what in the modern age is called a constancy of attitude would have been inconstancy itself in previous times. Fickleness of loyalties is a prerequisite of a capitalist society, where private property routinely yields to the claims of wealth and accumulation.[21] In the phase of high-consumption capitalism especially, when 'new' is the symbolic affirmation of positive value and 'old-fashioned' an emblem of backwardness, 'changing one's mind' about products is a routine event. And in the realm of public life generally, one is frequently confronted with new political agendas (ecology, say), not to mention technological inventions, social 'trends', celebrities and cultural artefacts, on which one is provoked into having opinions in the first place. Shifting policies of state routinely call for the mobilization and shift of public opinion.

In this historical situation, to take a constancy of attitude for granted amounts to a choice, and a fundamental one, to ignore the question of the sources of the very opinions which remain constant throughout shifting circumstances. Limiting their investigation thus, Katz and Lazarsfeld could not possibly explore the institutional power of mass media: the degree of their power to shape public agendas, to mobilize networks of support for the policies of state and party, to condition public support for these institutional arrangements themselves. Nor could they even crack open the questions of the sources of these powers.

And this absence is not rectified by the presence of another major term in the Lazarsfeld canon: *reinforcement.* For Lazarsfeld and his school, especially Joseph T. Klapper, reinforcement is the way in which media influence makes itself felt. The media are taken only to 'reinforce existing opinions' rather than to change minds. Klapper's summary book, *The Effects of Mass Communication,*[22] remains the *locus classicus* of this argument, which comes forward to void criticism of the more general argument about the ineffectuality of media. Klapper and others who write in this vein think of reinforcement as a lower order affair compared to persuasion or mobilization. Yet reinforcement of opinion is an indispensable link between attitudes and actions. If media 'only' reinforce 'existing opinions,' they may well be readying action, or anchoring opinion in newly routine behaviour. Moreover, 'reinforcement' can be understood as the crucial solidifying of attitude into *ideology*, a relatively enduring configuration of consciousness which importantly determines how people may perceive and respond to new situations. But 'ideology' and 'consciousness' are concepts that fall through the sieves of both behaviourism and stimulus–response psychology. They have no ontological standing in the constraining conceptual world of mainstream media research.[23]

[. . .]

Assumption 5. Followers as 'opinion leaders'. Katz and Lazarsfeld took as given, definitive, and fundamental the structure and content of the media. The close attention they paid to 'opinion leaders' not only automatically distracted from 'the central importance of the broadcast networks and wire services, it defined 'opinion leading' as an act of following without the awareness – indeed, the amusement – that such confusion should have occasioned. They were looking at the process of ideas moving through society through the wrong end of the telescope.

Specifically, the Decatur women were asked to nominate 'opinion leaders' in relation to the externally defined news. To tell who was an 'opinion leader', Katz and Lazarsfeld asked them 'for their opinions on a variety of domestic and international problems then current in the news, e.g. on Truman's foreign policy, on demobilization policy for the army, etc.' Then the women were asked if they had 'recently changed their opinions' and whether they had been asked for advice.[24] 'Experts', meanwhile – those whose general public affairs influence overflowed the boundaries between issues – were defined as those nominated in response to this question: 'Do you know anyone around here who keeps up with the news and whom you can trust to let you know what is really going on?'.[25] In what sense, then, did an 'opinion leader' actually lead? What was an 'expert' expert in, and who decided the content of certified expertise?

The problem, to use the official language of sociology, is that the administrative mentality exaggerates the importance of 'independent variables' that are located closest in time and space to the 'dependent variables' under investigation.[26] Only their administrative point of view prevented Katz and Lazarsfeld from taking seriously the obvious: that their 'experts' were dependent for their expertise on a 'variable' explicitly ruled out of the scope of analysis. Respondents were being asked to name as influentials those individuals who they thought were most tuned in to the mass media. Katz and Lazarsfeld were taking for granted the power of mass media to define news; and they were therefore discovering not 'the part played by people in the flow of mass communications', but the nature of the channels of that flow.[27] Vague language (indeed, a vague concept of power, as we shall see) masked a crucial distinction. It is as if one were studying the influence of streets on mortality rates – during an enormous flood. A street is a conduit, not a cause of drowning. But the distinction is lost in bland language. When they came to address the issue, Katz and Lazarsfeld skirted the issue of institutionalized news this way:[28]

> Compared with the realm of fashions at any rate, one is led to suspect that the chain of interpersonal influence is longer in the realm of public affairs and that 'inside dope' as well as influencing in specific influence episodes is much more a person-to-person affair.

The suspicion of a 'longer chain of influence' is an evasion of institutionalized relations between broadcasters and audiences.

But an administrative point of view is likely, from the outset, to confuse a report of a certain sort of influence with originating power, since the institutional origin, by being more distant both conceptually and in time and space, will inevitably 'leak' in transmission. In the process of asking *how* decisions are made at the bottom of the influence structure, it cannot ask *why* the occasion for deciding exists in the first place. It asks, in other words, the questions an administrator asks, or, in this case, the questions a marketer asks.

Why did the *Personal Influence* study start by assuming that mass media influence is comparable to face-to-face influence, and that power exists as discrete occasions of short-term 'attitude change' or behavioural choice? How may we account for the theory's thin sampling of reality, for its discrepancies and their absence from the summary theory? And why did the field that grew from these beginnings preserve that thinness and those discrepancies in both theory and methodology? If we step back from the Decatur study and its successors to the general style of thought they embody, to their sociological tenor, we find a whole and interwoven fabric of ideological predispositions and orientations. We find, in particular, *an administrative point of view* rooted in academic sociology's ideological assimilation into modern capitalism and its institutional *rapprochement* with major foundations and corporations in an oligopolistic high-consumption society; we find a concordant marketing orientation, in which the emphasis on commercially-useful audience research flourishes; and we find, curiously, a justifying social democratic ideology.

When I say that the Lazarsfeld point of view is administrative, I mean that in general it poses questions from the vantage of the command-posts of institutions that seek to improve or rationalize their control over social sectors in social functions. The sociologist, from this point of view, is an expert who addresses problems that are formulated, directly or indirectly, by those command-posts, who are concerned, in essence, with managing the expansion, stability, and legitimacy of their enterprises, and with controlling potential challenges to them. In the development of media research in particular, as in the whole of the post-war positivist surge in social science, the search is for models of mass media effects that are *predictive*, which in the context can mean only that results can be predicted from, or for, the commanding heights of the media. The 'variables' are to be varied by those in charge of mass media production, and only by them; therefore they tend to be short-run in time span and behavioural rather than structural in focus. From the administrator's point of view, the mass media system in its structural organization is of course not at issue; it is the very premise of the inquiry. Thus, the administrative theorist (the term is Lazarsfeld's own self-characterization)[29] is not concerned, for example, with the corporate decision to produce radio and television receivers as household commodities rather than, say, public ones, although this fundamental choice had serious consequences for the social uses, power, and meaning of mass media.[30] The administrative theorist is not concerned with the corporate structure of ownership and control at all, or with the corporate criteria for media content that follow from it: he or she begins with the existing order and considers the effects of a certain use of it. What C. Wright Mills called abstracted empiricism is not at all abstracted from a concrete social order, a concrete system of power.

Over the course of the twentieth century, capitalism would work to present consumer sovereignty as the equivalent of freedom, in the common view and the common parlance. ('If you don't like TV, turn it off.' 'If you don't like cars, don't drive them.' 'If you don't like it here, go back to Russia.' 'If you don't like Crest, buy Gleem.' 'If you don't like Republicans, vote Democratic.') The assumption that choice among the givens amounts to freedom then becomes the root of the worldwide rationale of the global corporations, what Richard Barnet and Ronald Muller have called the vision of 'the global shopping center'.[31] Thus it is that a society develops in which voting and soap-buying, movie choice and political opinion, become more than methodological equivalents as objects of study; they become similarly manipulable and marginal acts that promise much while they deliver mostly preservative-stuffed 'goods' that flatten the ability to taste. By ignoring the systemic and institutionalized nature of these processes, and by fusing its administrative, commercial, and social-democratic impulses, the mainstream of American media sociology has done its share to consolidate and legitimize the cornucopian regime of mid-century capitalism. That the dominant paradigm is now proving vulnerable to critique at many levels is a measure of the decline of capitalist legitimacy, commercial values, and the political self-confidence of the rulers. But that is another story.

Notes

1. Bell, Daniel (1975) The end of American exceptionalism. *The Public Interest*, Fall, p. 218.
2. Some recent American departures from the dominant paradigm are the papers in Chaffee, Steven H. (ed.) (1975) *Political Communication*, Sage, Beverly Hills; and, more basically, Gandy, Oscar H. (1976) The economics and structure of bias in mass media research, a paper delivered to the Leipzig meeting of the International Association for Mass Communications Research. Against the Lazarsfeldian emphasis on the limited and mediated influence of the mass media, the widespread interest in agenda-setting functions of the media (following McCombs, Maxwell E. and Shaw, Donald L. (1972) The agenda-setting function of the mass media. *Public Opinion Quarterly*, Vol. XXXVI, Summer, pp. 176–87) is promising, but still too narrow and ahistorical: analytically it abstracts both media and audiences from their social and historical matrix. In England, the alternative approach of cultural studies, influenced by Marxist cultural theory and semiological 'readings' of content, seems to me the most promising angle of analysis. For a fine example, see Cohen, Stanley (1972) *Folk Devils and Moral Panics*, MacGibbon & Kee, London; the papers gathered in Cohen, Stanley and Young, Jock (eds) (1973) *The Manufacture of News*, Constable, London and Sage, Beverly Hills; and Stuart Hall's essays, gathered in a forthcoming collection from Macmillan in London. See also the discussion of the field in Gitlin, Todd (1977) 'The whole world is watching': mass media and the new left, 1965–70, unpublished PhD dissertation, Sociology Department, University of California, Berkeley, pp. 15–23 and Chapter 10. The Lazarsfeld paradigm retains considerable force and prestige despite all this: for a recent study in that tradition, see Patterson, Thomas E. and McClure, Robert D. (1976) *The Unseeing Eye: The Myth of Television Power in National Elections*, Putnam, New York.
3. Katz, Elihu and Lazarsfeld, Paul F. (1955) *Personal Influence: The Part Played by People in the Flow of Mass Communications*, Free Press, New York.
4. Arndt, J. (1968) A test of the two-step flow in diffusion of a new product. *Journalism Quarterly*, Vol. 47, Autumn, pp. 457–65.
5. Bell, loc. cit. (see Note 1).
6. Lazarsfeld, Paul F., Berelson, Bernard and Gaudet, Hazel (1948) *The People's Choice*, Columbia University Press, New York
7. See the following studies: Deutschman, Paul J. and Danielson, Wayne A. (1960) Diffusion of knowledge of the major news story. *Journalism Quarterly*, Vol. 37, Summer, pp. 345–55; Troldahl, V. C. and Van Dam, R. (1965) Face to face communication about major topics in the news. *Public Opinion Quarterly*, Vol.

29, p. 634; Troldahl, V. C. (1966–7) A field test of a modified 'two-step flow of communication' model. *Public Opinion Quarterly*, Vol. 30, Winter, pp. 609–23; Arndt, op. cit. (see Note 4); Allen, I. L. (1969) Social relations and the two-step flow: a defense of the tradition. *Journalism Quarterly*, Vol. 46, Autumn, pp. 492–8; Bostian, L. R. (1970) The two step flow theory: cross-cultural implications. *Journalism Quarterly*, Vol. 47, Spring, pp. 109–17; and Lin, Nan (1971) Information flow, influence flow and the decision-making process. *Journalism Quarterly*, Vol. 48, Spring, pp. 33–40. In the Chaffee volume cited in Note 2 above, Becker, Lee B., McCombs, Maxwell E. and McLeod, Jack M. (Development of political cognitions, pp. 29–31) reinterpret data from Lazarsfeld's own *The People's Choice* and its successor, *Voting*, to show that the media are more influential than Lazarsfeld concluded. For a collation of empirical criticisms of the two-step flow, citing later studies that tend to show direct media impact especially on the poor, the isolated, and the highly anomic, see Janowitz, Morris (1968) Mass communication: study. In *International Encyclopedia of the Social Sciences*, Macmillan and The Free Press, New York, Vol. 10, p. 51.

8. Rosario, F. Z. (1971) The leader in family planning and the two-step flow model. *Journalism Quarterly*, Vol. 48 Summer, pp. 288–97, in particular.

9. See all the other studies cited in Note 7.

10. DeFleur, Melvin L. (1970) *Theories of Mass Communication*, 2nd edn, McKay, New York, pp. 112–54.

11. Brown, Roger L. (1970) Approaches to the historical development of mass media studies. In Tunstall, Jeremy (ed.) (1970) *Media Sociology: A Reader*, University of Illinois Press, Urbana, pp. 41–57.

12. For more on 'personal influence' theory as a critique of the earlier 'hypodermic' theory, see Katz, Elihu (1960) Communication research and the image of society: convergence of two traditions. *American Journal of Sociology*, Vol. 65, March, p. 113, and DeFleur, op. cit. (see Note 10), pp. 112–17.

13. Katz and Lazarsfeld, op. cit. (see Note 3), pp. 16–17.

14. Katz and Lazarsfeld, op. cit. (see Note 3), p. 146.

15. See especially Dahl, Robert (1961) *Who Governs?* Yale University Press, New Haven; and Polsby, Nelson (1963) *Community Power and Political Theory*, Yale University Press, New Haven. Of course the literature on pluralism and élite theory is vast. For an earlier critique of pluralist theory along the present lines, see Gitlin, Todd (1965) Local pluralism as theory and ideology. *Studies on the Left*, Vol. 5, Summer, pp. 21–45. For an interesting critique of both pluralism and its 'non-decision' critique, culminating in a proposal for a 'three-dimensional' approach which integrates the strengths of each, see Lukes, Steven (1974) *Power: A Radical View*, Macmillan, London. There arises the question of whether the structural homology between pluralism and the two-step flow reflects an actual homology in their subject matters as well as, or rather than, in the respective theoretical problematics. In other words: Is there, or was there in the 1950s, an actual plurality of communication influence-sources parallel to an actual plurality of power sources? I cannot defend my answer to this question at length within the confines of the present essay, but I do want to put it forth: the answer is a qualified 'no'. The actual plurality of sources in both communities and media chains was drying up as both were becoming centralized and homogenized in the 1950s. The networks and the huge national security state were major national features of that decade: prima-facie evidence of the growing weight of nationalizing forces and therefore of the ideological nature of the two paradigms. Bachrach, Peter and Baratz, Morton S. (1962) The two faces of power. *American Political Science Review*, Vol. 56, pp. 947–52; and their (1970) *Power and Poverty: Theory and Practice*, Oxford University Press, New York.

17. Katz and Lazarsfeld, op. cit. (see Note 3), pp. 107–8, 332–4.

18. Katz and Lazarsfeld, op. cit. (see Note 3), p. 138.
19. Katz and Lazarsfeld, op. cit. (see Note 3), p. 341
20. Katz and Lazarsfeld, op. cit. (see Note 3), p. 271, n. 2.
21. See Arendt, Hannah (1958) *The Human Condition*, Anchor, Garden City.
22. Klapper, Joseph T. (1960) *The Effects of Mass Communication*, The Free Press, New York.
23. Thanks to William Kornhauser for pointing this out to me in conversation.
24. Katz and Lazarsleld, op. cit. (see Note 3), p. 271n. Emphasis added.
25. Katz and Lazarsfeld, op. cit. (see Note 3), p. 276n.
26. Thanks to David Matza for putting this point to me in conversation.
27. Even at that, the Katz–Lazarsfeld findings on 'public affairs influence' are the weakest in the book on their face, and do not warrant the exorbitant claims later made in their name. Nor did Katz and Lazarsfeld seem interested in the distinction between marketing and public affairs 'flows'. The differences might have spoken to the difference between consuming and politics.
28. Katz and Lazarsfeld, op. cit. (see Note 3), p. 319.
29. In Lazarsfeld, Paul F. (1941) Remarks on administrative and critical communications research. *Studies in Philosophy and Social Science*, Vol. IX, pp. 2–16.
30. This was an actual historical decision, first proposed for RCA, the first mass broadcasting apparatus, by the young David Sarnoff in 1915. See Lyons, Eugene (1966) *David Sarnoff*, Harper and Row, New York, pp. 71–3; and Barnouw, Eric (1966) *A Tower in Babel* (*A History of Broadcasting in the United States*), Oxford University Press, New York, Vol. 1, pp. 78–9.
31. Barnet and Muller (1974) *Global Reach*, Simon & Schuster, New York.

4

The context of mass communications research

James D. Halloran

From McAnany, E. G. *et al.* (eds) (1981) *Communication and Social Structure: Critical Studies in Mass Media Research*, Praeger, New York, pp. 21–50.

Imbalances and inadequacies

Several years ago it was stated quite unequivocally in a United Nations Educational, Scientific and Cultural Organization (UNESCO) publication that intelligent communication policies depended on the availability of information that only research could provide (Halloran, 1970). This statement was part of a plea for more research and for the development of communication policies and related research policies, and it seems reasonable to suggest that, together with many other forces and pressures, it played a part in the growth of mass communication research in recent years.

Because of the way research has been defined, initiated, supported, and organized, and because of the tasks it has been called on to perform (over perhaps the last 50 years), we find that it is not just a question of not having enough information. In addition, the information we have is partial and unbalanced. We know far more about some parts of the world than about others; we know far more about some aspects of the communication process than about others; and we have more analyses and interpretations from certain value positions than from others. An additional complication is that the implications of these imbalances are not properly understood, and as a result we not infrequently encounter universal generalizations and cross-cultural applications that simply are not valid.

In this chapter, then, I regard it as essential to emphasize at the outset that research is not initiated, organized, executed, or applied in a social and political vacuum. A true understanding of the nature of research and its application calls for an understanding of the historical, economic, political, organizational, professional, and personal factors that impinge on the research process in so many ways.

Briefly, these are the factors that govern what research is carried out and, perhaps more importantly, what research is not carried out. In some way or other the questions we ask in research are indications of what we consider important or problematic. They reflect our priorities, our values, and our concerns, as well as our compromises with regard to what is allowed or is otherwise possible.

Unfortunately, it would appear that many researchers, irrespective of their country of origin, do not recognize this situation. They accept as given, or take for granted as an unquestioned assumption, what ideally they should regard as problematic. This, not surprisingly, is reflected in their work: what work they do, how they interpret it, and how they seek to apply it.

The situation outlined above is an important consideration for those of us who regard research as essentially a conditioned or circumscribed attempt to construct reality. It does this by the areas or topics that are selected and by the use of concepts, techniques, categories, systems of classification and categorization, and the positing of relationships within these areas. Again, these concepts, categories, and relationships do not develop in a vacuum; they are not neutral, and therefore we should know about the framework within which they have developed and are being applied. This is particularly important when comparisons of different research approaches are being made.

I referred earlier to the unbalanced or uneven distribution of research internationally, and this is clearly a reflection of other areas of economic and informational imbalance that characterize the international scene. Certainly, as far as quantity is concerned, there is no doubt that the mass communication research field is dominated by research from western, industrialized nations.

[. . .]

Conventional research

Our point of departure must be the main stream of mass communication research (stemming mostly from the United States, although with widely scattered followers and advocates in other countries). For want of a better term, I shall refer to this as 'conventional research'. In broad, general terms, by 'conventional research' I mean that research having a mainly value-free, positivistic, empiricist, behaviouristic, psychological emphasis. However, in criticizing this approach in mass communication research, I do not want to be seen as throwing the baby out with the bath water. It is essentially a matter of emphasis and balance. Of course, there is much useful work that falls under the above-mentioned headings. I must also emphasize that my comments on this type of work should not be seen as an opposition to rigorous methods, experimental work, quantification, and so on. One may, however, criticize the primacy of this position, in which 'scientific' is defined solely or mainly in terms of method, and in which little or no attention is given to theory, concepts, or the nature of the relevant, substantive issues and their relationship to wider societal concerns.

In the United States, the main thrust of mass communication research[1] had developed, like other branches of social science, essentially as a response to the requirements of modern, industrial, urban society for empirical, quantitative, policy-related information about its operations. On the whole, research was carried out with a view to improving the effectiveness of the media, often regarded simply as objects of study or as 'neutral tools' in achieving stated aims and objectives, often of a commercial nature. This was at the heart of administrative or service research, where the emphasis was on improving methods to facilitate the achievement of specific goals rather than on refining concepts, developing theories, or achieving social change. Even when, in more recent times, the emphasis at one level shifted to a social-problem orientation (such as violence or pornography), audience use or effects models still predominated.

In this way the research, although often referred to as abstracted empiricism, was certainly not abstracted from the society within which it operated and that it was geared to serve. If we accept this, we should be more inclined to enquire about the questions that have not been asked in research, as well as those questions that have. In an approach centred on the media rather than the society, theory was neglected and the media were not seen in relation to other institutions. There were few, if any, questions about power, organization, and control, little reference to structural consid-erations, and only attempts to study the social meaning of the media in historical or contemporary contexts.

The emphasis on answers seen to be useful in the short term; the concentration on methods (particularly on what could be measured, with its false notion of precision); the focus on the individual as the unit of study, with the related restriction of media influence to attitude change; and the accompanying tendencies to ignore the possible influence of the media on institutions in defining social reality, setting the social–political agenda, and legitimating certain forms of behaviour and institutional arrangements, as well as on cultural change generally, have led to a completely inadequate understanding of the communication process and the notion of media influence. It must be remembered that these ideas were widely held, that they were exported, and that they are still with us, although, as we shall see, they are increasingly challenged, particularly outside the United States.

It has also been argued that contained in these value-free, positivistic, behaviouristic approaches is a view of people that exists mainly for the instrumental purpose of studying them. Whether or not this is true, it is certainly important to consider the images of persons and the models of society implicit in research; yet, regrettably, many researchers do not even think in these terms.

Of course, sociology is based on ideas as well as on tasks and operations, and there is no doubt that the ideas of the earliest workers in sociology, as well as the social concerns of the time, played an important part in the development of social science in the United States. But mass communication research in the United States was more closely linked to social psychology and to professional and commercial interests than to sociology. Admittedly, scholars like Lazarsfeld grappled with the problems posed by the conflict between critical and theoretical interests on the one hand, and empirical demands on the other, but the critical challenge and the theoretical concerns never really surfaced in sustained research programmes.

[. . .]

As already indicated, it would, of course, be quite unfair (and indeed inaccurate) to suggest that over the years all mass communication and related research in the United States had been slavishly administrative. It is not as simple as that. There have been many strands to the work, and critical messages, social concerns, and certainly professional accomplishments have not been entirely lacking. Still, even today, it is difficult to detect, in what is a vast body of work, any conscious underlying philosophy or purpose, or still less an overriding social or political concern.[2] Thousands of projects have been carried out, but there is little evidence of the systematic accumulation and development of a corpus of knowledge, and there have been few attempts to relate the work to an appropriate social theory. It is still mainly a matter of doing rather than thinking, of serving rather than questioning or challenging.

Critical and sociological research

What then of the 'critical research' that has been mentioned in passing as being opposed to the aforementioned conventional research? If it is dangerous to generalize about conventional mass communication research, then it is even more dangerous to do so about the so-called critical approach, which, although it owes much more to European thought and scholarship than does the conventional approach, nevertheless reflects the influence of American sociology.

It could be argued that the unity of the critical approach – if, in fact, a unity can be identified – lies in its opposition to conventional work rather than in any shared, more positive approach. For, as we shall see, the critical umbrella covers a variety of positions. In fact, there are those who would suggest that some of the more extreme ideological positions should not really be classified as social scientific research. There is also another problem with the use of the word 'critical', which has to do with the fact that researchers who share the same theoretical position or research approach are frequently selective in choosing their targets. Researchers from two different countries, or political systems, may confine their 'criticisms' to only one of those countries or systems, almost as though there was nothing to criticize in the other.

However, despite these difficulties, let me proceed (with a plea for tolerance) to write about critical, problem, and policy-oriented research, primarily with a sociological perspective. In view of current research development, it should be noted here that I make a distinction between policy-oriented research and policy research. The latter is frequently of the variety that seeks to bring about the efficient execution of policy and thereby make the existing system more efficient. On the whole, it is not concerned with asking questions about the validity of the system, challenging predominant values, or suggesting alternative policies or modes of action. Policy-oriented research, on the other hand, ideally addresses itself to the major issues of our time. It is concerned with (among other things) questioning the values and claims of the system, applying independent criteria, suggesting alternatives with regard to both means and ends, exploring the possibility of new forms and structures, and so on. It is not necessary to make an either/or issue out of these different approaches. We are not talking about incompatible concerns, but about the different implications for policy and society of, on the one hand, approaches that prevailed in the past and are still with us, and, on the other, those approaches of a more critical nature that are now emerging. To repeat, the conventional approaches of the past that characterized so much commu-nication research, explicitly or implicitly, served and supported rather than criticized or challenged.

On the whole, critical research, although stemming from a wide range of positions and reflecting different values, is less likely than conventional research to be encumbered by historical and institutional relationships with journalism and broadcasting. Moreover, it is not as closely linked with markets, audiences, and publics, and is less inclined to have a service, administrative, or commercial character. Needless to say, it is not without its value implications, but it is definitely more independent of the institutions that it studies.

As far as media institutions are concerned, the approach is more likely to be from the outside, with a critical policy or problem orientation. Critical research does not ignore problems central to the media, but ideally it never takes these problems as defined by media practitioners or politicians. Its starting points are the major social issues of our time, not necessarily the major media issues as narrowly defined by the professionals, owners, or controllers. It is worth noting that even today, in the United States, there are prominent names in the field (such as Weaver and Gray) who, from what they regard as 'a discipline all their own' strongly advocate a research approach that is 'more readily applicable and meaningful to the profession', rather than one that may 'slip back into the comfort of sociology and psychology' (1979). It is indeed interesting to see what is regarded as comfort.

At the risk of oversimplification, let me attempt to summarize the main characteristics of this emerging critical approach. First and foremost, it deals with communication as a social process; second, it studies media institutions not in isolation but with and in terms of other institutions, and within the wider social context (nationally and internationally); and third, it conceptualizes research in terms of structure, organization, profession-alization, socialization, participation, and so on.

One of the clear implications of this approach is that all aspects of the communication process should be studied. The factors (including historical, economic, political, organizational, technological, professional, and personal factors) that impinge on the production process and influence what is produced demand close scrutiny, as do the factors that influence how what is produced is used. In the past the emphasis in research was on use, reaction, effects, influence, and so on, not on relationships involving ownership, control, structure, organization, and production.

The same basic principles and questions are relevant, with the necessary changes, wherever the research is carried out. Moreover, this approach also shows the futility of studying communication in isolation, or of studying communication policies without reference to other related policies (educational, cultural, economic, social, and other policies).
[. . .]

Some illustrations of critical research

[. . .]

As indicated earlier, we now know that to restrict our understanding of media influence to what can be assessed by way of attitude change, imitation, or identification presents a very misleading picture of the part played by the media in society. There is no need here to dwell at length on the question of influence or effects, but over the past few years we have moved to a position where we now think of media influence in terms of association, amplification, legitimation, agenda setting, and so on. We also take into account units other than the individual as we attempt to assess the influence of the media on other institutions, on definitions of social reality, and on culture and society more generally. Of course, these phenomena are not so easily susceptible to what passes for scientific measurement as are attitude change and imitation, and in one way this is what caused a problem. The issues deemed worthy of investigation have tended to be those that could be measured by the *approved* available techniques. It is encouraging to see the newer approaches to mass communication research favouring a more flexible, imaginative, less hidebound approach to the study of media influence than we have had in the past. It is important to remember, however, that to support this change is not to offer support for some of the unsystematic, impressionistic, soft options that have appeared in recent years. Ideally, these newer approaches call for more ability, more discipline, more dedication, and more effort – not less.

We may also find evidence of past practices when we examine the general question of communication and information. There are many examples across a wide range of communication issues (including development, health education, family planning, agricultural innovation and adoption, social action, and social policy) where one still has the impression that those responsible for information campaigns and educational programs work on the assumption that their main – perhaps even their sole – task is to provide information, and the rest will follow.

Yet research shows this is not the case. The adoption of a sociological perspective, where the information process and the relevant individuals and groups are studied in the appropriate historical and social contexts, illustrates the importance of many other non-media factors. People may possess the necessary information on any given issue, but may not possess the social skills to translate the information into the appropriate social action. Others may possess the information too, but also have conflicting information or opposing attitudes or past experiences, any of which may act as obstacles and get in the way of the translation. The effective conversion and utilization of information may also depend on other institutional arrangements and support factors in the social structure generally. All these intervening factors are extremely important in any analysis of communication/information problems. An analysis may indicate, for example, that in any given campaign it would be more fruitful to concentrate on such areas as the transfer of information, the obstacles to its use, the intervening factors, and the conversion and utilization of information, rather than on its provision. Generally, we may say that information is a necessary, but never a sufficient, cause of social action, although there are even some instances where information becomes a substitute for action.

[. . .]

Perhaps the level where the various brands of critical research appear to have most in common is at the level of research operation and practice. It is beyond dispute that the aforementioned rejections of positivism, behaviouristic psychology with its simple causal hypotheses, and the extremes of functionalism, together with a preference for models of the communication process that, if nothing else, include sociological concepts, have led to research program and projects that were not much in evidence a decade or so ago.

Of course, there is much more to be done: other questions need to be asked, and there is a need for more evidence of the recognition of the implications of the assumptions that underlie the research, and for more precise and clear articulations of theoretical principles. But only the blind, the ignorant, or the profoundly prejudiced could fail to recognize that the questions that are being asked now represent an approach to mass communication research fundamentally different from the approaches that prevailed in the not so distant past and that persist in places today. Admittedly, the questions, the research approaches, and the social and policy concerns do not represent a single, clearly articulated 'theoretical' position. But, for me, with a clear preference for a plurality of models, this is all to the good, and a situation to be welcomed and encouraged. There are, however, those from widely differing standpoints who think the 'critical' label is misleading, concealing more than it reveals, perhaps even concealing quite dangerous and disruptive tendencies not appropriate to any scientific endeavour.

To recapitulate briefly, the last 20 years or so have seen changes in mass communication research reflecting changes in social science generally. One of the outcomes, more apparent in Europe and Britain than in the United States, has been the development of a critical, sociological approach that has challenged not only the supremacy of earlier, mainly positivistic research approaches, but also the service and administrative functions of these approaches and the claims and presumptions of the media systems that they serve. In more recent years, similar challenges, perhaps representing an interesting fusion between regional initiatives in the Third World, particularly in Latin America, and the aforementioned critical approach, have also developed.

Problems in sociology and mass communication research

The outlook so far seems encouraging. But there are those who now see a crisis in sociology that is bound to be reflected in some way or other in mass communication research. A prominent British sociologist, John Rex, has argued (1978) that we have gone astray. He welcomed the dethroning of the old approaches, but is not very happy with the new claimants and usurpers. Instead of the considered and thoughtful development of plural paradigms that enjoy complementary relationships (and that he and I would favour), he fears that a situation has developed, not of complementarity, but of conflict between warring schools. As he sees it, this situation is not marked by speculative and reflective approaches, or by careful examination, respect for evidence, consideration of alternatives, or the caution and tolerance that one might expect from social science, but by dogma, doctrinaire statements, selective use of evidence, unsubstantiated assertions, and, at times, arrogance and hostile intolerance. He likens the situation to the religious wars of the past. The positions, firmly held by the new high priests, brook no contradictions, and evidence must not be allowed to get in the way of faith. Like others who claim to be social scientists, he is more than a little worried about a situation where, if 100 hypotheses derived from a theory or set of beliefs were invalidated in research, the theory might still remain inviolate. This has certainly little in common with the 'rational, moderate, and democratic' approach advocated by many of those who would consider themselves to be critical researchers.

[. . .]

It has been argued that institutionalized sociology (it has, of course, been institutionalized in different ways in different places) would not necessarily be the source of inspiration for critical enquiry. According to Murdock and Golding (1977), this inspiration is more likely to be found in a commitment to the basic questions that they would regard as providing sociology with its original impetus.

To them, and to others holding similar views, what matters is that society is defined by the system of class relationships that prevail, and thus the prime focus for study should be 'the mass media , . . and the class system'. The second focus should be the way in which the media constitute one of the means by which that system is legitimated, and the third focus should be the sources of social dissent and political struggle. The task of 'research' is to show how the prevailing distributions of poverty and power and the dominant principles of control shape the structure of symbolic arrangements, how they enter into experience as interpretative procedures, and what are the conditions of their repetition and change. To accomplish this, it is suggested, research must be grounded more solidly and consistently than hitherto in general social theory, apparently in one specific social theory.

Some of the researchers and students of the media who adopt this or some similar stance are genuinely committed to research that attempts to demonstrate the validity of the above-mentioned relationships. But there are others who are concerned with assertion more than with validation or with the provision of concrete evidence from the systematic observations of social reality that might enable social theory to be put to the test. Some of them pay lip service to data collection and analysis, but others dismiss such laborious and irrelevant procedures (which also happen to be difficult to master and have the unfortunate tendency to prove one wrong) and readily accept that their main task – the main function of research – is to attempt to make reality appear to conform to ideology.

[. . .]

What kind of theory?

It was suggested earlier that in the world of mass communication research there was reasonably wide agreement on the need to develop appropriate theories. In fact, mass communication research, for much of its history, has been obsessed with the quest for theory. However, judging from recent international conferences, there is no clear agreement on the most appropriate level of theorizing. Two suggestions have recently been made: that a 'grand theory' is called for (an approach that is usually related to the desire to link mass communication research with the main issues of society); and that mass communication researchers should pursue theorizing of the middle range, since the time is not yet ripe for the formulation of a 'grand theory. '

Even allowing for the difficulties raised in this comment, it seems to be fairly generally acknowledged that we must pay due attention to the relationship between theory and empirical research (and the results of empirical research). It is, of course, relatively easy to point to the pitfalls of arid empiricism, but the issue of the best ways to develop fruitful connections between empirical research and the development of theory remains. Most of us accept that the importance of empirical research lies not in the data themselves. But we also recognize that in the interpretations made of the data, if we do embrace some form of grand theory, we must not fall into the trap of remaining at a level of theorizing that cannot generate hypotheses designed to test critically such theoretical issues.

The weaknesses and inadequacies of research that is not consciously tied to an articulated theory have been well illustrated, and they reflect what Carey (1978) has referred to as 'the absence of any informing relation between communications and social theory'.

Perhaps it might also be stated again that this does not mean that the conventional work has no theoretical implications. It represents a standpoint, a value position, even if this is not made explicit. In fact, one of the problems is that because the position is never articulated it can never be adequately criticized. Without an underlying theory of society, any research program will fragment into bits and pieces that can never possibly tell us anything about the relationship of media to society, and this is one of the reasons that the conventional approach is likely to be welcomed by the media establishment.

A theory of society is necessary – on this, perhaps, many of us can agree. But what theory? Carey suggests that there can be a theory of communication (and research) that has developed from a theory of society, or a theory of communication that is explicitly a theory of society. We need not pursue this question here, but we may quote Carey (1978) again and emphasize 'that powerful and fundamental work in this field, as in the other social sciences, will only proceed under the reflexive guidance and criticism of such theory. '

There is a task for us here, then, and the clearer articulation and exposition of our theories would bring a clearer understanding of various developments. Another way of bridging gaps, finding common denominators, coming together, and possibly carrying out research exercises might be to focus more on individuals and their communication needs.

Notes

1. There is a danger here of oversimplification, because there were scholars in the United States, even in the early days (Mead and Park, for example), who adopted a different, more critical approach to media/communication problems. Even so, these were not normally seen as dealing with mass communication research.
2. A possible exception is the attempts in recent years to counter critical and UNESCO-related research.

References

Carey, J. (1978) A plea for the university tradition. AEJ presidential address. *Journalism Quarterly*, pp. 846–55.

Halloran, J. D. (1970) Mass media in society: the need of research. UNESCO, Reports and papers on mass communication, No. 59.

Murdock, G. and Golding, P. (1977) Capitalism, communications, and class relations. In Curran, J. *et al.* (eds) *Mass Communication and Society*, Edward Arnold, London, pp. 142–73.

Rex, J. (1978) British sociology's wars of religion. *New Society*, May 11, 1978.

Weaver, D. H. and Gray, R. (1979) Journalism and mass communication research in the United States: past, present and future. Paper presented at the 1979 Annual Convention of the Association for Education in Journalism, Houston, Texas.

5

Mass communication research in Europe: some origins and prospects

Jay G. Blumler

From Cleveland Wilhoit, G. and de Bock, H. (eds) (1981) *Mass Communication Review Yearbook*, Vol. 2, Sage, Beverly Hills and London, pp. 37–47.

In recent years mass communication research has gradually come of age in many countries of Western Europe. Signs of this development are not only quantitative – such as increases in the number of university centres and appointments devoted to the field, expanded research activity, and the growing publication of books, articles, and specialist journals – but also qualitative – including gains in European scholars' sense of distinctive identity, self-confidence, and even sheer enjoyment of a path-breaking spirit as new research directions are explored. Here I shall pose and offer provisional answers to two questions that naturally arise in the minds of many observers of these striking trends.

One question has to do with origins and sources: How exactly did European mass communication research 'get that way'? Or rather, what features of historical time and societal space help to explain the emergence of certain outstanding tendencies of communication research in Western Europe – in contrast, say, to certain equivalent characteristics of American work?

The second question is related to the complex sense that many of us have of operating in a philosophically polarized field – although it is almost impossible succinctly to distinguish the rival camps without indulging in stereotypes, and it is increasingly difficult to equate our philosophic differences with geographic ones. It is still true that 'Europe is providing a congenial proving ground for . . . much critically grounded mass communications enquiry'.[1] Yet some major European figures do not regard themselves as critical researchers; and inside the critical school, some quite exciting disputes of analytical standpoint and approach to evidence are coming ever more insistently to the fore. Moreover, the mass communication literature also includes a conciliatory strand, one that seeks to throw bridges across the divisive gulfs. Recent expressions of that outlook include the Katz report for the BBC[2] and Kurt Lang's claim 'There is no inherent incompatibility between the "positivism" of administrative communication research and the critical approach associated with the Frankfurt school'.[3] In lineage, however, this conciliatory note is traceable to Robert Merton's early post-war plea for a consolidation of European sociology of knowledge with American studies of public opinion and mass communication, 'aiming towards that happy combination of the two, which possesses the scientific virtues of both and the superfluous vices of neither.'[4] Arising from all this, my second question is: what constructive steps can be taken by divergent research traditions in our field to bring them to easier speaking terms with one another?

Origins of European and American mass communication research

As I have implied, answers to the first question can be pursued along dimensions of time and space. Taking that of time first, the fact that Europe began to find its own mass communication research feet in approximately the mid-1960s is doubly significant. The European research surge originated shortly after the publication of Joseph Klapper's then seemingly authoritative account of the American state of the art as outlined in *The Effects of Mass Communication*.[5] Dominant impressions formed by many Europeans were that Americans had mainly concentrated on audience-level enquiries, effects research, and questions open to quantitative treatment by survey or experimental designs; and that as a result they had marched up a blind alley. Some Europeans attracted to communication study for the first time found little appeal in continuing to plough that furrow and began to suspect that they might have to define the field afresh.[6] For another thing, as Karl Erik Rosengren has pointed out, the middle of the 1960s was a time when European social science, after much pre-war speculation over issues of theory of knowledge and an early post-war period of immersion in American quantitative techniques, was hit by a wave of revived interest in Marxism, as well as hosting certain other specialized schools of thought, such as semiotics, structuralism, interactionism, sociolinguistics, contemporary cultural studies, and others.[7]

The conjunction of these temporal influences helps to explain three prominent features of European work. One is the characteristically 'holistic approach of European communication science',[8] or the conviction that mass communication institutions and processes must be studied especially in their linkages to surrounding social orders. Of course, such a broadly societal perspective is grist to a Marxist's mill. As Golding and Murdock have urged in this vein, 'we do not need a theory of mass communications but a theory of society to generate guiding propositions and research....'[9] But in Europe Marxists hold no monopoly over holism. A similarly comprehensive thrust can be found, for example, in Elisabeth Noelle-Neumann's spiral of silence theory (which postulates that media journalists, when emphasizing certain societal trends, manage to convey impressions of standpoints that are winning and losing ground to audience members, to create climates in which people feeling in the ascendant are more prepared to voice their views and so to enlist the powerful engine of interpersonal communication in the molding of public opinion).[10] It also can be seen in the efforts of Rosengren and his colleagues to inter-relate media content data and extra-media trend data so as to chart sources of change over the post-war period in the symbolic environment of Swedish society.[11] And it can be found in Gurevitch and Blumler's identification of diverse entry points into the analysis of political communication systems, the chief components of which they define as:

1. political institutions in their communication aspects;

2. media institutions in their political aspects;
3. audience orientations to political communication; and
4. communication-relevant aspects of political culture.[12]

This holistic impulse leads to a second European trait. Put negatively, methodological boundary lines are not always strictly respected. Put positively, research questions are often tackled by mixed methods. Noelle-Neumann's work, for example, relies on a combination of content analysis, panel research, and synchronized investigation of the opinions and perceptions held on certain matters by strategically placed communicators, such as journalists and ordinary members of the public.[13] Another example, from which publications are now emerging, is a project of cross-national research into the role of broadcasting in the 1979 elections to the European Parliament that was designed by a consortium of political communication scholars based in each of the nine member states of the European Community. This combined interviews with political party publicists; interviews with broadcasting executives and journalists; a content analysis of the themes of campaign programmes; post-election surveys; and, in some countries, before-and-after electoral panels as well – organized on comparative lines.[14]

Third, except perhaps for a few specialized subfields, such as research on election campaigns, the uses and gratifications approach, studies of children's responses to television, and research into the structure of adult viewing patterns,[15] there are relatively few coherently cumulative traditions of audience-level inquiry in Europe. It is as if, among critical researchers especially, the systematic attempt, empirically and quantitatively, to measure the impact on audience members' ideas of the flow of mass communicated messages has been given a 'bad name'. Effects research in particular is treated in some quarters as the brothel of media studies: the 'madam' rather than the 'queen' of our science.

The spatial origins of European mass communication research are particularly interesting, only two examples of which I will consider. First, in contrast to the United States, where mass communication research grew up alongside a commercially dominated media system, in Europe the predominant medium at the time when researchers were cutting their teeth was television, organized along public service lines. This meant that its programmes would be provided by public service corporations, which were enjoined to serve social interests impartially and were to some extent divorced from direct political control, although they were ultimately accountable to organs of the state. Now, such a system inevitably propels broadcasting right into the heart of the political arena, even in a country like Britain, where many safeguards of media autonomy have been carefully devised. For one thing, just because broadcasters are supposed to be impartial and serve the public interest, they are correspondingly and readily open to accusations of impropriety, bias, and neglect of duty, some sincerely voiced, others mounted to cloak the more naked pursuit of partisan advantage. For another, broadcasters are necessarily dependent on governments of the day for decisions vital to their continuing survival and welfare – to raise the level of its licence fee, as in the case of the BBC in Britain, or for authorization to open an additional television channel, as in the case of ITV. For yet another, public service broadcasting organizations are singularly lacking in self-sufficiency. They badly need outside support, much of it political, to keep afloat in turbulent societal seas. It is true that in the crises and rows that periodically erupt over TV's social role, broadcasters sometimes can exploit a lack of unity among surrounding political forces. In such circumstances, however, broadcasters can also be undermined by arguments, even from their political friends, that if they do not toe the line, it may be impossible to curb the wilder politicians who are clamouring for more control over television. It is for such reasons that the late Sir Charles Curran, former Director-General of the BBC, proclaimed a need for senior broadcasters continually to engage in 'the politics of broadcasting'. As he put it, 'The broadcaster's life has to be one of continuous political ingenuity'.[16]

Three further features of the work of many European mass communication researchers are traceable to the centrality of public service television in the communication systems of their societies. One is their preoccupation with the role of the mass media (and especially broadcasting) in politics and, more specifically, with the tensions that arise between the supposed neutrality and independence of television on one hand and its many ties to prevailing political structures, values, and interests on the other. Another is a frequent tendency to analyse mass media functioning through the concept of 'constraints'. Although I have not encountered an explicit definition of that important term in its application to our field, I suppose that 'constraints' might be conceived as institutionalized practices and patterned relationships, internal or external to media organizations, which serve to narrow, limit, or closely circumscribe their ability to realize their own professed social purposes. Yet another European characteristic which springs in part from this source is a keenness to address issues of media policy.[17] Compared with some Americans, many Europeans are less anxious about the purity and self-sufficiency of their professional research roles and are more ready, even eager, to mix in some way their professional with their civic roles. It is true that Europeans are internally split over how best to relate policy positions to empirical findings. Marxists ignore the positivistic gap between 'the is' and 'the ought', implying that it can be bridged by sensitivity to the class struggle and to history, while non-Marxists typically aim to draw a clearer boundary line between what they are saying on normative and empirical wavelengths, respectively. Nevertheless, Europeans often strive to express the policy relevance of their work – for example, in concluding chapters to the books they write, in giving evidence to public bodies with media responsibilities, and in contributions to conferences often convened on policy issues with joint broadcaster/academic participation.

A second major contrast of societal space may help to explain why Europeans and Americans tend to focus on different relationships between mass communication systems and social structures. It was historically true that in many European societies, fundamentally opposed ideological and political options were not only conceivable in principle but were translated into organized partisan cleavages, including radical challenges to prevailing distributions of wealth and power, as in the case of socialist and communist movements. Yet, over the post-war period, the reality of sociopolitical advance toward greater equality has seemed negligible, leaving as if unmodified the traditionally unyielding patterns of social stratification. In contrast, the United States is a country where historically the clash of fundamentally opposed ideological and political options has seemed muted if not inconceivable, while in the post-war period one societal subsector after another has been disturbed by unpredictable currents of social change. I was recently struck in this connection by the readiness of Samuel Becker and Elmer Lower, when comparing social conditions at the time of the Kennedy–Nixon debates in 1960 with those that prevailed when the Carter–Ford exchanges were staged in 1976, to refer to the intervening period as a time of 'America in political and social transition'.[18] In illustrating that theme, they noted a number of changes that had taken place during those 16 years: the decline of the cities; the nation's involvement in and later extrication from the Vietnam war; the emergence of unconventional lifestyles and sexual mores; and an ever-deepening loss of confidence in government. Had they wished, they could have additionally mentioned higher rates of geographical mobility; the dramatic erosion of voters' partisan identifications; the increasing incidence of marital instability; and a greater recognition of the formerly neglected civil rights of women, blacks, and other minorities.

Different formulations of the social role of mass communications do seem to arise from this contrast. In Europe, academics of a Marxist and critical bent especially regard the mass media chiefly as agencies of social control, blocking pathways of radical social change and propping up the status quo. Golding and Murdock manifest such a standpoint quite clearly when specifying their 'basic departure point' as a 'recognition that social relations within and between modern societies are radically, though variably, inegalitarian'. This causes them to focus in turn, they say, on 'the relations between the unequal distribution of control over systems of communications and wider patterns of inequality in the distribution of wealth and power' as well as on 'relations between the mass media and the central axis of stratification – the class structure'.[19]

In the United States, however, such formulations permeate the literature less pervasively, and the mass media are more often seen either as partial cause agents in social change, or as tools that would-be political actors can use to gain publicity and impetus for their pet projects of change, or as authoritative information sources on which people have become more dependent as the complexities of social differentiation and the pressures of a rapidly changing world threaten to become too much for them (as in DeFleur and Ball-Rokeach's hypothesis that 'audience dependency on media information increases as the level of structural instability [societal conflict and change] increases').[20]

Prospectus for conciliation and future research

Although the second question I posed at the outset referred to prospects of research camp reconciliation, it would be naive to expect certain deep-seated differences of outlook between rival approaches ever to be completely overcome. Take, for example, these ways of writing about mass media effects on audiences. On one side we have Gaye Tuchman's reference to media constructed news 'as a "frame" organizing "strips" of everyday reality and imposing order on it';[21] as well as George Gerbner's view of television as a 'medium of the socialization of most people into standardized roles and behaviors', the chief function of which 'is to spread and stabilize social patterns'.[22] On the other side we have Jack McLeod and Byron Reeves' opinion that 'it is from the unravelling of conditional and interactive relationships that the most interesting communication theory will come and not from simple assertions that the media set public agendas or that children learn from television';[23] as well as the view, recently expressed by Robert Hawkins and Suzanne Pingree, that the influence of television on viewers' construction of social reality should vary according to a whole host of intervening variables, including their information-processing abilities, critical awareness of television, direct experience of other sources providing confirmation or disconfirmation of TV messages, their place in the social structure, and their patronage of different forms of program content.[24] In one case, the mass media are regarded as imposing categories through which reality is perceived, by-passing potential neutralizing factors and engulfing the audience in a new symbolic environment.[25] In the other, mass media influence is conceived as essentially differentiated, filtered through and reflected by the diverse backgrounds, cultures, affiliations, and lifestyles of individual audience members. Ultimately, this division reflects a conflict of political philosophy between those who see society as governed by a more or less unified economic or power élite and those who still adhere to a pluralist vision of society.[26]

Even so, it is curious how the holders of certain positions in our field tend to restrict their appeal to already convinced devotees by arbitrarily narrowing the range of phenomena they study or by turning a blind eye to their own philosophic soft spots. Cross-camp debate could become more mutually enlightening, at least, if attempts were made to break down some of these unnecessary barriers. Let me conclude, therefore, by considering how such a prescription might be followed on both sides of the Atlantic, as it were.

A brisk diagnosis of the American field offered in this spirit might start by noting how it compares with the European scene – where, despite a wide scatter of work, much of it seems to get pulled toward a few focal points of theoretical and policy gravity by the presence of scholars who in their different ways are each trying 'to get it together'. In contrast, the American scene appears nowadays (as distinct from its pioneering era) to lack such a synthetic and binding quality, resembling more a boxing gym in which each individual is doing his own thing, so that some people are skipping rope, some are punching bags, some lifting weights, some sparring, some taking showers, and some are just having a rest!

Perhaps two ways forward from this state of affairs could be proposed. First, there should be more attempts to push already vigorous traditions of audience-level enquiry back not only to analyses of recurring patterns of media content, but also to those features of media organization that help to generate such systematically structured forms of output. Agenda-setting research is a striking case in point. As Steven Chaffee once remarked, 'Agenda-setting is [truly] one of the two or three best research ideas this field has seen in recent years'.[27] So far it has been pursued only in a truncated version, however, dealing over and over again with just the media content/ audience reception interface. Yet you cannot properly talk about agenda *setting* without also considering who or what managed to lay out the agenda in a certain way, so that the issue agendas which audiences may take over are then seen to have derived from weights and meanings, given to news events, that arise in turn from certain abiding features of news-media gatekeeping and story construction. This is not just a matter of looking at media organizations as processors of issue material; it is also one of expanding the range of actors whom we are prepared regularly to take into account when conducting research into mass communication as a social process. That is, we should increasingly be treating mass communication as a 'three-legged stool', involving not only audiences and journalists but also all those political and other interest groups that strive to reach audiences by developing strategies for influencing journalists.[28] So a more full and rounded version of agenda-setting still waits in the wings to be called onto the research stage, though its terms were already well stated in 1976 by Becker, McCombs, and McLeod when they pointed out that an agenda-setting framework

> specifies a set of relationships, beginning with the impact of the social system on media institutions, and, then, on their members, particularly reporters and editors. These media operatives make decisions which, the evidence shows, have impact on the cognitions of the media audience members. Those cognitions, for example, have been shown to affect voter turnout and election choice. Both behaviors can be seen as central to the political and social system. So the model takes us full circle.[29]

Follow up *that* prospectus and you really will have plenty to talk to the Europeans about!

Second, Americans should look again – and hard – at those four theories of the press, and particularly at the social responsibility variant among them, that were so influentially propounded by Wilbur Schramm and his colleagues nearly a quarter-century ago.[30] Searchingly realistic attention should be directed especially at the faith that was then pinned on the development of a sense of responsibility among mass media executives and staff communicators to ensure that standards of public service are adequately met. Unfortunately, that expectation seems at odds with the findings of many recent sociological studies of mass media organization, from which one more often receives an impression of institutions that are too hemmed in by externally and internally operative constraints for self-initiated reforms to yield significant results. Of course, I cannot recommend some particular way out of this impasse here; I am only urging scholars who consider that the mass media can and should serve worthier ends than the aggrandizement, through publicity, of dominant power interests to address themselves more closely to it. (Perhaps I may add, however, that in recent years my own response to this impasse in the news and political broadcasting field has taken the form of proposing policies that might act on the fabric of constraints themselves, hoping by pushing them back to give the media more elbow room for promoting more mature understandings of civic affairs in the electorate at large.)[31]

But should not Europeans also be asked to mend some of their ways in this spirit of research *détente*? Two thoughts occur to me here. One is that those Europeans who are hostile to or suspicious of audience effects research should give up their prejudices. It is a shocking indictment of the state of the field in Europe that it has so few cumulative traditions of effects research that can stand comparison with American work on, for example, agenda-setting, trust in government, and the social construction of reality. Such neglect should no longer be tolerated, for the study of mass communication as a process without systematic investigation of audience response is like a sexology that ignores the orgasm!

Second, it is high time those European radicals and critical thinkers who so repeatedly proclaim that mass communication only bolsters the status quo attended to some vital distinctions which so far they have tended to smudge. One is the distinction between *norm upholding* and *institutional support*. In itself, the critical school's assertion that much mass media content reflects a society's widely shared cultural norms and values is incontestable, first because that is one way in which large and heterogeneous audiences can be simultaneously addressed, and, second because in the field of news the operationalization of 'objectivity' cannot be wholly culture-free. It is therefore not at all difficult to accept the statement in *Bad News* (by the Glasgow Media Group) that 'the notion of cultural neutrality can never be achieved',[32] as well as the claim of Stuart Hall *et al.* in *Policing the Crisis* that much journalism presupposes that 'as members of one society . . . we share a common stock of cultural knowledge with our fellow men: we have access to the same "maps of meaning" '.[33] But the projection of such meanings does not automatically entail the legitimation of a particular institutional order. That equation is sustainable only in press systems where the prevailing institutions are regarded as near-perfect embodiments of the authoritative and shared norms. And that is certainly not the case in any straightforward sense in the media systems of liberal-democratic societies. It is fascinating to recall in this connection Lazarsfeld and Merton's classic definition of 'the enforcement of social norms' as one of three main functions of mass communication. 'The mass media,' they said, 'may initiate social action by "exposing" conditions which are at variance with public morality'.[34] In short, norm enforcement can undercut as well as prop up particular institutions and the leaders who run them, a possibility that members of the critical school have so far ignored in their analyses.

Of course, in order to counter such criticisms they might reply in effect: yes, but look at the heavy and regular coverage élite political actors can count on receiving in the news media of all societies. And it is again indisputable that such coverage tends to enhance the perceived status of such actors in the eyes of audience members. Even so, another crucial distinction needs to be made. Perceived status is one thing, but the inculcation of positive affect, respect, and a disposition to trust the actors concerned is quite another and does not automatically accompany the former. Recent experience in Britain of the regular sound broadcasting of Prime Minister's Question Time in Parliament provides an intriguing case in point. Many MPs were so horrified by the unfavourable impressions of politicians' behaviour in the House of Commons, which they feared this implanted in listeners' minds, that they exerted pressure on the BBC to take it off the air.[35]

Nevertheless, critical theorists might counterargue that media coverage tends to treat unorthodox approaches to the conduct of politics as if out of court and beyond the pale of the cultural consensus.[36] And once again it cannot be denied that radical minority opinions often do get short shrift from the mass media in this sense. Even so, yet another distinction has to be taken into account when assessing this tendency: it is one thing to shut off an option; it is quite another to legitimate the remaining ones. It is equally possible, after all, for the one to be blocked out while the others are *run down*. Such, at least, is the claim of those American scholars who regard the news media as implicated in some way in the generation of political malaise.[37]

Finally, it might be claimed that news is really the same the whole world over – that newsmen engage in essentially the same organizational routines and are locked in essentially the same way into the predominant values and power structures of their societies, wherever they may be operating. This is the essence of a position taken in a gem of a recent book by Golding and Elliott, entitled *Making the News*, which compares broadcast news bulletin content and newsroom procedures in the three societies of Ireland, Sweden, and Nigeria. In their words, the study shows that 'even in highly varied cultural and organizational settings broadcast news emerges with surprisingly similar forms and contents'. It is intriguing to realize when reading the book in detail, however, how such a provocative position can be sustained only by taking a very high analytical line. For it turns out that the position is valid only in the abstract sense that 'news is largely an artefact of the supply of information made available to the newsroom', constraints on which then arise outside the broadcasting sphere 'in the state, culture and economy of each country'. True enough very likely, but in concrete forms (still another neglected distinction) the constraints operative in individual countries may bear down quite differently on the newsmaking process. In fact, Golding and Elliott give the game away in a comment tucked into a short paragraph that is devoted to the topic of 'drama as news value'. Dramatic structure, they say, can often be achieved by the presentation of conflict, as in the matching of opposed viewpoints drawn from spokesmen of both sides of the question. Because of limited resources for film interviews, this technique is less available to poor newsrooms, and 'in Nigeria it is almost entirely absent because of the severe authority of government departments'.[38] To many of us, of course, there is no sense in which news systems which do give access to opposition voices can be equated with those that provide outlets for government sources only.

Notes

1. Blumler, Jay G. (1977/8) Purposes of mass communications research: a transatlantic perspective. First Founders' Lecture, delivered at the Annual Conference of the Association for Education in Journalism, Madison, Wisconsin, August, 1977 and published in *Journalism Quarterly*, Vol. 55, No. 2, pp. 219–230.
2. Katz, Elihu (1977) *Social Research on Broadcasting: Proposals for Further Development*, BBC, London.
3. Lang, Kurt (1979) The critical functions of empirical communication research: observations on German–American influences'. *Media Culture and Society*, Vol. 1, No. 1, January, pp. 83–96.
4. Merton, Robert (1951) *Social Theory and Social Structure: Toward the Codification of Theory and Research*, Free Press, New York.

5. Klapper, Joseph T. (1960) *The Effects of Mass Communication*, Free Press, New York.
6. The sense of being involved in a crisis of mass communication research, the means of resolving which must be discovered by Europeans drawing on their own intellectual resources, is well conveyed in a paper by Roberto Grandi, 'Some aspects of the studies and research conducted in Italy concerning mass communication', which was prepared for presentation to a seminar at The Annenberg School of Communication, University of Pennsylvania.
7. Rosengren, Karl-Erik (ed.) (1981) *Advances in Content Analysis*, Sage, Beverly Hills.
8. Nordenstreng, Kaarle (1976) Recent developments in European communication theory. In Fischer, Heinz-Dietrich and Merrill, John C. (eds) *International and Intercultural Communication*, Hastings House, New York.
9. Golding, Peter and Murdock, Graham (1978) Theories of communication and theories of society. *Communication Research*, Vol. 5, No. 3, July, pp. 339–56.
10. Noelle-Neumann, Elisabeth (1980) *Die Schweige-spirale: Offentliche Meinung unsere soziale Haut*, Piper, Munich.
11. Rosengren, Karl-Erik (1980) Cultural indicators: Sweden, 1945–1975. Paper presented to the 30th Annual Convention of the International Communication Association, Acapulco, Mexico, May.
12. Gurevitch, Michael and Blumler, Jay G. (1977) Mass media and political institutions: the systems approach. In Gerbner, George (ed.) *Mass Media Policies in Changing Cultures*, John Wiley and Sons, New York.
13. Noelle-Neumann, Elisabeth (1980) Mass media and social change in developed societies. In Wilhoit, G. Cleveland and de Bock, Harold (eds) *Mass Communication Review Yearbook*, Sage, Beverly Hills, Vol. 1, pp. 657–78.
14. See Blumler, Jay G. (1979) Communication in the European elections: the case of British broadcasting. *Government and Opposition*, Vol. 14, No. 4, pp. 508–30; and Blumler, Jay G. and Fox, Tony, The involvement of voters in the European elections of 1979. *European Journal of Political Research* (forthcoming).
15. Examples of recent work in these subfields may be found, respectively, in Blumler, Jay G., Cayrol, Roland, and Thoveron, Gabriel (1978) *La Television fait-elle L'election?* Presses de la Fondation Nationale des Sciences Politiques, Paris; Blumler, Jay G. and Katz, Elihu (1974) *The Uses of Mass Communications*, Sage, Beverly Hills; von Feilitzen, Cecilia, Filipson, Leni and Schyller, Ingela (1979) *Open Your Eyes to Children's Viewing*, Sveriges Radio, Stockholm; and Goodhardt, G. J., Ehrenberg, A. S. C. and Collins, M. A. (1975) *The Television Audience: Patterns of Viewing*, Saxon House, Westmead.
16. Curran, Charles (1979) *A Seamless Robe*, Collins, London.
17. Nordenstreng, Kaarle, op. cit. (see Note 8).
18. Becker, Samuel L. and Lower, Elmer W. (1979) Broadcasting in presidential campaigns, 1960–1976. In Kraus, Sidney (Ed.) *The Great Debates: Carter vs. Ford, 1976*, Indiana University Press, Bloomington.
19. Golding and Murdock, op. cit. (see Note 9).
20. DeFleur, Melvin L. and Ball-Rokeach, Sandra (1975) *Theories of Mass Communication*, Longman, London, 1975.
21. Tuchman, Gaye, (1978) Myth and the consciousness industry. Paper presented to the Congress of the International Sociological Association, August, 1978.
22. Gerbner, George and Gross, Larry (1976) Living with television: the violence profile. *Journal of Communication*, Vol. 26, No. 2, pp. 173–99.
23 McLeod, J. M. and Reeves, Byron (1980) On the nature of mass media effects. In Withey, S. B. and Abeles, R. (eds) *Television and Social Behavior: Beyond Violence and Children*, Lawrence Erlbaum and Associates, New Jersey.
24. Hawkins, Robert P. and Pingree, Suzanne, Television influence on constructions of social reality. A review prepared for *Television and Behavior: Ten Years of Scientific Progress and Implications for the 80's*, National Institute of Mental Health, to be published.

25. Katz, Elihu (1979) On conceptualising media effects. In *25 Jaar Televisie in Vlaanderen*, Centrum voor Communicatiewetenschappen, Catholic University of Leuven.
26. Blumler, Jay G. (1979) Models of mass media effects. In *25 Jaar Televisie in Vlaanderen*, Centrum voor Communicatiewetenschappen, Catholic University of Leuven.
27. Chaffee, Steven H. (1978) Book review of *The Emergence of American Political Issues: The Agenda-setting Function of the Press* (by Shaw, Donald L. and McCombs, Maxwell E., West, St. Paul, 1977). *Political Communication Review*, Vol. 3, No. 1, pp. 25–8.
28. Blumler, Jay G. and Gurevitch, Michael (1979) The reform of election broadcasting: a reply to Nicholas Garnham. *Media, Culture and Society*, Vol. 1, No. 2, pp. 211–19.
29. Becker, Lee B., McCombs, Maxwell E. and McLeod, Jack M. (1975) The development of political cognitions. In Chaffee, Steven H. (ed.) *Political Communication: Issues and Strategies for Research*, Sage, Beverly Hills, pp. 21–64.
30. Siebert, F. S., Peterson, T., and Schramm, W. (1956) *Four Theories of the Press*, University of Illinois Press, Urbana.
31. Blumler, Jay G. (1977) The intervention of television in British politics. Research paper commissioned by the Annan Committee, *Report of the Committee on the Future of Broadcasting*, Cmnd. 6753-I, Her Majesty's Stationery Office, London.
32. Glasgow Media Group (1976) *Bad News*, Routledge and Kegan Paul, London.
33. Hall, Stuart, Critcher, Chas., Jefferson, Tony, Clarke, John and Roberts, Brian (1978) *Policing the Crisis: Mugging, the State, and Law and Order*, Macmillan Press, London.
34. Lazarsfeld, Paul and Merton, Robert (1957) Mass communication, popular taste and organized social action. In Rosenberg, Bernard and White, David Manning (eds) *Mass Culture*, Free Press, New York, pp. 457–73.
35. Unpublished research into 'Innovation in political communication: the sound broadcasting of parliamentary proceedings', currently being jointly undertaken by the Centre for Television Research, University of Leeds, and The Hansard Society for Parliamentary Government.
36. Hall, Stuart, Media power: the double bind. *Journal of Communication*, Vol. 24, No. 4, pp. 19–26.
37. Robinson, Michael J. (1976) American political legitimacy in an era of electronic journalism. In Cater, D. and Adler, R. (eds) *Television as a Social Force: New Approaches to TV Criticism*, Martin Robertson.
38. Golding, Peter and Elliott, Philip (1979) *Making the News*, Longman, London.

6

Mass communication and modern culture: contribution to a critical theory of ideology

John B. Thompson

From *Sociology* (1988) British Sociological Publications, London, Vol. 22, No. 3, pp. 360–79.

My aim in this essay is to outline an approach to the study of mass communication as a central component of modern culture. It is an approach which is animated by the belief that the study of mass communication belongs among the core concerns of sociology; it is an approach which is informed by social theory, and by the writings of critical social theorists, but which seeks to move beyond the restricted view of many theoretical approaches.

[. . .]

The study of mass communication may be approached within the general context of the analysis of modern culture. The concept of culture is notoriously complex; endowed with a long history in different languages, the notion has been used in a variety of ways.[1] For the purposes of my argument here, I shall distinguish between four basic usages, which I shall refer to as the 'classical', 'descriptive', 'symbolic' and 'structural' conceptions. According to the classical conception, culture is a general process of intellectual or spiritual development. This usage reflects the origins of the term in the idea of husbandry, or the cultivation of growth. It is a usage which was prevalent in European historical and philosophical writing in the eighteenth century, when 'culture' and 'cultivated' were sometimes equated with 'civilized' and 'civilization', sometimes contrasted with them. It is a usage which remains with us today and which is exemplified by the description of someone as a 'cultivated individual', as a person with 'cultivated taste'. In the nineteenth century, however, a second basic usage began to emerge, in connection with the development of the discipline of anthropology. Writers such as E. B. Tylor sought to develop a 'science of culture' which would investigate the interrelated forms of knowledge, belief, art, morals, customs and habits characteristic of particular societies (Tylor, 1871). This anthropological approach has given rise to a broad, descriptive conception of culture, embracing the values, practices and beliefs of a people; culture, as Tylor remarked, is a 'complex whole', a vast and varied array which define the way of life of a society or an historical period.

[. . .]

We can discern a third usage of the term 'culture' and its cognates in the anthropological literature, a usage which can be described as the symbolic conception. Anthropologists such as White and Geertz have linked the study of culture to the analysis of symbols and symbolic action (White, 1949; Geertz, 1973). 'Culture', comments Geertz, is an 'acted document', an interwoven system of construable signs (Geertz, 1973, pp. 10, 14). The performance of a ritual dance, the writing of an article or a book, the creation of a painting or a musical score are cultural activities in this sense: they are meaningful actions producing meaningful objects and expressions which call for interpretation. However it is important to stress – and this is a consideration which is not always emphasized sufficiently in the anthropological literature – that cultural activities are always situated in specific social–historical contexts which are structured in certain ways. Cultural analysis is the analysis not only of meaningful actions, objects and expressions, but also of the relations of power within which these are located. This critical point provides a basis for what may be described as a structural conception of culture. I shall offer a preliminary characterization of this conception by defining 'cultural analysis' as the study of symbolic forms – that is, meaningful actions, objects and expressions of various kinds – in relation to the historically specific and socially structured contexts and processes within which, and by means of which, these symbolic forms are produced, transmitted and received. Hence cultural phenomena may be seen as symbolic forms embedded in structured contexts; and cultural analysis may be regarded as the study of the meaningful constitution and social structuration of symbolic forms.

[. . .]

Cultural phenomena do not subsist in a vacuum. They generally exist as substantial objects circulating in institutionalized channels of transmission or diffusion – for example, as commodities produced by private corporations, promoted by advertising agencies, distributed by commercial networks, sold by shops or chains of shops, consumed by certain categories of individuals. These channels constitute part of what we may describe as the modalities of cultural transmission by which symbolic forms are relayed beyond the contexts of their production and endowed with extended availability in time and space.

This approach to the analysis of culture provides a framework for considering the nature of mass communication and its impact on modern culture. The modalities of cultural transmission in modern societies have been profoundly affected by the development of institutions of mass communication. The development of these institutions – of newspapers, book publishers, broadcasting organizations, etc. – marked the emergence of new forms of information diffusion and cultural transmission. The production and circulation of meaningful objects and expressions became increasingly mediated by industrial organizations concerned with the commodification of symbolic goods.

[. . .]

In speaking of 'mass communication', we are presupposing a very special sense of the term 'communication'. In general the term communication refers to the transmission of meaningful messages. These messages are often expressed in language, but they may also be conveyed by images, gestures or other symbols used in accordance with shared rules or codes. A great deal of communication in everyday life takes place in the context of face-to-face social interaction: messages are conveyed to an individual or individuals who are physically present, and whose responses provide the person conveying the message with an immediate and continuous source of feedback. In the case of mass communication, however, the nature of the communicative process is quite different. Let me highlight four important differences. In the first place, while messages in mass communication are produced for an audience, the individuals who comprise the audience are not physically present at the place of production and transmission or diffusion of the message; mass communication involves what we may describe as *an instituted break between production and reception.* Hence the personnel involved in the production and transmission or diffusion of the message are deprived of the immediate and continuous sources of feedback characteristic of face-to-face interaction. The communicative process in mass communication is marked by a distinctive form of *indeterminacy,* since the message must be produced and transmitted or diffused in the absence of direct and continuous monitoring of audience response. The personnel involved in mass communication employ a variety of strategies to cope with this (see McQuail, 1969; Burns, 1969). They draw upon past experience and use it as a guide to likely future outcomes; they employ well-tried formulae which have a predictable audience appeal; they make occasional but highly selective use of audience monitoring devices, such as the information provided by market research or by the routine monitoring of audience size and response. These and other strategies are institutional mechanisms which enable them to reduce indeterminacy in a way that concurs with the aims of the institutions of mass communication.

A second difference between mass communication and the exchange of messages in everyday life concerns the nature of the technical means of mass communication. In contrast to everyday interaction, where the exchange of messages typically occurs as a transient verbal utterance or visual display, the messages are inscribed in texts or encoded in some other material medium such as film, tape, records or discs. These and other *information storage mechanisms* affect the nature of the message itself and endow it with a permanence which the utterances exchanged in everyday interaction do not have. They affect the nature of the message in the sense that they determine what can and cannot be recorded and transmitted in the medium concerned. In this respect there are significant differences between the various media which demand systematic and detailed analysis. The kinds of messages that are recorded in written texts such as books or newspapers, for example, are quite different from the messages recorded on film and transmitted on television, in so far as the latter consist of complex audio-visual constructs in which language is spoken in accordance with the grammar and conventions of everyday speech, and in which the temporal flow of the message is intrinsic to it. The recording of messages in the various media of mass communication also endows them with a permanence which extends beyond the moment of recording. The messages are stored in a medium which persists; they thereby acquire a temporality quite different from that characteristic of utterances in face-to-face interaction: they are extended in time, temporalized, historicized. Indeed, they become *part of* history, in the double sense of belonging to the past as well as the present and of constituting some of the resources through which the past is reconstructed and understood. The messages conveyed by the mass media form part of the tissue of tradition in modern societies and the legacy through which our historical memories are formed.

A third characteristic of mass communication which distinguishes it from the communicative process in everyday social interaction is that the messages in mass communication are generally commodified, that is, constituted as objects which are exchanged in a market. Mass communication may be regarded as *the institutionalized production and diffusion of symbolic goods via the transmission and storage of information/communication*. Media messages are incorporated into products which are sold, or which are used to facilitate the sale of other goods; hence calculations concerning the marketability of the product shape the character and content of the message produced. The commodification of messages is facilitated by the fact that they are *reproducible*, that is, fixed in a medium which enables them to be produced in multiple copies for sale and distribution. The mode of reproduction varies significantly from one medium to another. In each case, however, media institutions commonly seek to control the mode of reproduction, since it is a major source of the revenue derived from their products. The capacity to control the mode of reproduction has been threatened in recent years by the development of new technologies, such as tape recording, video recording and photocopying, which enable messages to be accurately and cheaply reproduced. Thus the property which facilitates the commodification of media messages is also the property which enables that process to be undercut. In this respect, the mechanisms and institutions of mass communication are embedded in a broader social field characterized by asymmetrical relations of power and ongoing struggles for access to, or for the preservation of, scarce resources.

A fourth distinctive characteristic of mass communication concerns the availability of the messages, that is, the fact that the messages are potentially available to an extended audience which is altogether different from the interlocutors of a face-to-face interaction. The fixation and transmission or diffusion of media messages extends their availability in time and space, enabling them to endure and to reach a large number of spatially dispersed recipients. But the fact that they are potentially available to an extended audience does not mean that they are actually available in an unrestricted fashion; on the contrary, their circulation is restricted and regulated in a variety of ways. It is restricted by commercial considerations, for example, in the sense that the institutions which produce them may also seek to control their diffusion in order to secure their financial return. The circulation of media messages may also be restricted by state institutions.

[. . .]

The capacity of media messages to circulate among an extended audience is one of the characteristics in virtue of which we commonly speak of *mass* communication: it is communication for a mass audience, for the masses. But the term 'mass' may be misleading on this context. For this term connotes not only a large quantity but also an indefinite shape, an inert, undifferentiated heap. However the messages transmitted by the mass media are received by specific individuals situated in definite social–historical contexts. These individuals attend to media messages with varying degrees of concentration, actively interpret and make sense of these messages and relate them to other aspects of their lives. This ongoing appropriation of media messages is an inherently critical and socially differentiated process. It is inherently critical in so far as the appropriation of media messages is a process of creative interpretation in which individuals actively construct sense and plot, actively approve or disapprove of what is said and done, and thereby assimilate media messages into their own social–historical context, transforming these messages in the very process of assimilation. The appropriation of media messages is also a socially differentiated process in the sense that the individuals who make up the audience are differentiated in terms of specific social attributes such as class, gender and age. Media messages are received by individuals who are situated in socially structured contexts. It cannot be assumed that these messages will be appropriated in the same way by different individuals in different contexts. On the contrary, it may be the case that there are systematic variations in their appropriation of media messages, variations which are linked to socially structured differences within the audience. I shall return to this hypothesis later, after considering some of the relevant methodological issues.

Analysing culture

So far I have been concerned primarily with the conceptualization of culture and mass communication; I now wish to address in more detail some issues of a properly methodological kind.
[. . .]
The methodological framework may be described as a form of 'depth hermeneutics'. There are several reasons why a 'depth-hermeneutics' methodology provides an appropriate framework for cultural analysis. It provides an appropriate framework, in the first place, because the object of analysis is a meaningful symbolic construction which calls for interpretation. Hence we must give a central role to the process of interpretation, for only in this way can we do justice to the distinctive character of the object domain. But in so far as we must also consider the social–historical context and institutional mediation of symbolic constructions, and in so far as these constructions are structured in certain ways, we must also employ other methods of analysis. These methods may illuminate various aspects of the object domain and may thereby facilitate the process of interpretation.
[. . .]
Let me begin by returning to the characterization of 'cultural analysis' as the study of symbolic forms in relation to the historically specific and socially structured contexts and processes through which, and by means of which, these symbolic forms are produced, transmitted and received. Cultural analysis thus involves the study of the social–historical context within which cultural phenomena are situated. I shall describe this phase of cultural analysis as *social–historical analysis*. The production and circulation of meaningful objects and expressions are processes that take place within historically specific and socially structured contexts or fields. These fields are characterized by social relations and institutions which involve asymmetries of power and resources. Individuals are located at certain positions within these fields and

draw upon the available resources in order to produce, transmit and interpret meaningful objects and expressions. The production of meaningful objects and expressions – from everyday utterances to works of art – is production made possible by the resources available to the producer, and it is a production oriented towards the anticipated circulation and reception of the objects or expressions within the social field. This orientation may be part of an explicit strategy pursued by the producer, as when television personnel seek to produce a programme for a particular market and modify the contents accordingly. However the orientation may also be an implicit aspect of a productive process, in so far as the aims and orientations of the producer may already be adapted to the conditions of circulation and reception of the objects produced, in such a way that the orientation does not have to be formulated as part of an explicit strategy. If the production of meaningful objects and expressions involves the utilization of resources available to the producer, so too their reception is a situated process in which resources are employed by the individuals who appropriate the object or expression. The reception of meaningful objects and expressions, like the production and transmission of them, is a process situated in a definite social–historical context. The task of the first phase of cultural analysis is to reconstruct this context and to examine the social relations and institutions, the distribution of power and resources, by virtue of which this context forms a differentiated social field.

The meaningful objects and expressions which circulate in social fields are also complex symbolic constructions which display an articulated structure. It is this characteristic which calls for a second phase of analysis, a phase that we may describe as *formal or discursive analysis*. The aim of formal or discursive analysis is to explicate the structural features and relations of the meaningful objects and expressions. As complex symbolic constructions, these objects and expressions are structured in various ways, in accordance with schemata such as grammatical rules, narrative logic or the systematic juxtaposition of images. The formal analysis of these structural features and relations can bring out such schemata, as well as highlight certain relations and patterns which are characteristic of the object or expression concerned.

The third phase of the depth-hermeneutical methodology is a phase that may properly be called *interpretation*. The process of interpretation builds upon social historical and discursive analyses; it draws upon the insights yielded by these analyses employing them as elements in a creative, constructive interpretation. While drawing upon these insights, it is not exhausted by them. However rigorous and systematic the methods of formal or discursive analysis may be, they can never abolish the need for a creative construction of meaning, that is, for an interpretative explication of what is represented or said. In explicating what is represented or said, the process of interpretation transcends the closure of the symbolic construction; it projects a possible meaning, puts forward an account which is risky and open to dispute. Symbolic constructions are representations of something, discourse says something about something, and it is this transcending character which must be grasped.

[. . .]

The tradition of hermeneutics also remind us that the symbolic constructions are the constructions of a subject. To analyse these constructions is to investigate an object which is produced by a subject and received – read, viewed, listened to, understood – by other subjects. The understanding of symbolic constructions by the subjects who produce and receive them is a vital aspect of the analysis. But the 'subject's understanding' is a complex phenomenon which must itself be analysed in a contextual and interpretative way. In producing a symbolic construction a subject expresses himself or herself; *how* this subject understands this construction is attested to by *what* he or she expresses, both in this construction and in other constructions, that is, in other utterances, actions, texts. In receiving a symbolic construction a subject interprets it, makes sense of it and incorporates it into other aspects of his or her life; *how* this subject interprets this construction is attested to by *what* he or she says about it (or does not say about it), or by *what* he or she does with it (or does not do with it). The subject's understanding of symbolic constructions is not a simple datum to which we can have recourse, but a complex phenomenon which must be analysed interpretively.
[. . .]

Analysing mass communication

The distinctiveness of this approach stems from the concern to analyse mass communication *as a cultural phenomenon,* that is, to study mass communication in terms of the historically specific and socially structured forms and processes within which, and by means of which, symbolic forms are produced, transmitted and received. Hence we shall not lose sight of the fact that we are dealing with meaningful objects and expressions which call for interpretation, while at the same time recognizing that the production and transmission of these objects and expressions are socially situated and institutionally mediated processes. The distinctiveness of this approach also stems from the concern to specify the ways in which the objects and expressions of mass communication may be studied as *ideological.*

Let me begin by distinguishing between three aspects of mass communication. These aspects are closely interconnected in the process of producing and transmitting media messages, but by distinguishing between them we can delineate three object domains of analysis. The first aspect is the process of production and diffusion, that is, the process of producing the material of mass communication and transmitting or distributing it via channels of selective diffusion. This process is situated within specific social–historical circumstances and generally involves particular institutional arrangements. The second aspect is the construction of the media message. The material transmitted by mass communication is a product which is structured in various ways: it is a complex symbolic construction which displays an articulated structure. The third aspect of mass communication is the reception and appropriation of media messages. These messages are received by individuals, and groups of individuals, who are situated within specific social–historical circumstances, and who employ the resources available to them in order to make sense of the messages received and to incorporate them into their everyday lives. These three distinct aspects enable us to define three object domains of analysis. We can focus our attention on each of these object domains in turn, analysing their characteristic forms and processes. But the fact that these object domains are constituted by abstracting from other aspects of mass communication implies that an analysis focused on a single object domain will be limited in certain respects. A comprehensive approach to the study of mass communication requires the capacity to relate the results of these different analyses to one another, showing how the various aspects feed into and shed light on one another.

By distinguishing between these three aspects of mass communication, we can see that the depth-hermeneutical approach is applicable in differing ways to the analysis of the respective object domains. I shall examine the applicability of this approach by focusing on the medium of television and by considering the analysis of its different aspects. Consider first the analysis of the production and diffusion of television programmes. Such analysis is concerned above all with what I described earlier as social–historical analysis, that is, with the study of the social–historical and institutional context within which, and by means of which, programmes are produced and transmitted. This context consists of, among other things, these characteristics: the institutional organization of producers and of transmission networks; patterns of ownership and control within broadcasting institutions; the relations between broadcasting institutions and state organizations responsible for monitoring output; the techniques and technologies employed in production and transmission; the routine and practical procedures followed by television personnel; the aims of producers and programmers and their expectations of audience response; and so on. Some of these characteristics can be examined by means of empirical, including documentary, research. Others, such as the routine and practical procedures followed by television personnel or their aims and expectations, can be elucidated only by employing a more contextual, interpretative approach.

[. . .]

The second aspect of mass communication is the construction of the media message. When we focus on its construction and analyse its characteristics, we give priority to what I described earlier as formal or discursive analysis; that is, we analyse it primarily as a complex symbolic construction which displays an articulated structure. Among the structural features that we may highlight in the analysis of television are the syntax, style and tone of the language employed; the juxtaposition of word and image; the angles, colours and sequences of the imagery used; the structure of the narrative or argument; the extent to which the narrative or argumentative structure allows for sub-plots, digression or dissent; the use of specific devices such as flashbacks and voice-overs; the ways in which tension is combined with features such as humour, sexuality and violence; the interconnections between particular programmes which form part of a finite or open-ended sequence; and so on. These and other structural features of television messages can be analysed by a variety of techniques, from different forms of content analysis to various kinds of semiotic, narrative and discourse analysis.[2] It is important to emphasize, however, that the analysis of the internal structural features of media products is limited in certain respects. It is limited, in the first place, in so far as it abstracts from the process of production and diffusion. Hence it does not take account of the social and institutional conditions within which, and by means of which, media messages are produced and transmitted. The analysis of the internal structural features of media products is also limited in so far as it abstracts from the reception and appropriation of media messages. Hence it does not take account of the sense which these messages have for the individuals who watch them, hear them, read them, nor of the ways in which these individuals interpret media messages, accept them, reject them and incorporate them into their lives.

The reception and appropriation of media messages is the third aspect of mass communication which defines a domain of analysis. A great deal of research has been done, and continues to be done, on the reception of media messages and on the size and nature of audience response. Researchers have sought to study, for example, the short-term and long-term effects of media messages, the ways in which audiences use the media and the gratifications which they derive from them.[3] But these approaches, however interesting they may be, pay insufficient attention to the ways in which different individuals and groups actively make sense of media messages and integrate them into other aspects of their lives. The different phases of the depth-hermeneutical procedure can be used to explore what we may describe as the *modes of reception* of media messages. Thus in the study of television we must examine, by means of social–historical analysis, the specific circumstances and the socially–differentiated conditions within which individuals receive television messages. The specific circumstances: in what contexts, with what company, with what degree of attention, consistency and commentary, do individuals watch programmes, or series of programmes, of differing kinds? The socially–differentiated conditions: in what ways does the reception of media messages vary according to considerations such as class, gender, age, ethnic background and the country of the recipient? The latter question can be pursued by carefully designed research which uses structured interviews to explore how different individuals, and different groups of individuals, make sense of particular programmes.[4] These interviews yield recipient texts which can in turn be analysed in various ways, for example by methods of formal or discursive analysis. The features of one recipient text can be compared and contrasted with those of others and together they can be considered in relation to the construction of the media message itself. The formal or discursive analysis of these texts does not displace the need for the creative interpretation of media messages and recipient responses. Drawing upon the formal analysis of structural features and the social–historical analysis of the conditions of production/diffusion and reception/appropriation, the process of interpretation seeks to explicate what is said and not said, asserted and implied, represented and obscured, in media messages and recipient texts. It seeks to unfold the possible meanings of media messages, and it seeks to show how recipients make sense of these and incorporate them into their lives. As an interpretation, this process necessarily builds upon, and potentially intervenes in, the everyday activities of the subjects who make up the social world.

Against the background of this general approach to the study of mass communication, we can reconsider what is involved in the analysis of ideology.

[. . .]

This approach enables us to see that the three distinct aspects – production/diffusion, construction and reception/appropriation – are all essential ingredients in the analysis of its ideological character. The study of production and diffusion is an essential ingredient because it elucidates the institutions and social relations which enable media messages to be produced and transmitted. Since these are the outcome of specific production processes and are circulated via channels of selective diffusion, the study of these processes and channels may shed light on the construction and availability of media messages. The study of the construction of media messages is an essential ingredient because it examines the structural features by virtue of which they are complex symbolic phenomena, capable of mobilizing meaning. By examining structural features such as the syntax and style of the language employed, or the structure of the narrative or argument, this kind of analysis brings out the constitutive characteristics of the message, that is, the characteristics with which the message is constructed as meaningful. The study of the reception/appropriation of media messages is an essential ingredient because it considers both the social–historical conditions within which messages are received by individuals, and the ways in which these individuals make sense of the messages and incorporate them into their lives. It considers how the meaning mobilized by media messages is taken up by the individuals who receive them; hence it examines the ways in which these messages are effective within the social relations in which the individual recipients are enmeshed.

If we adopt this general approach to the analysis of the ideological character of the mass media, then we can see that many of the crucial questions concern the relations between the production/diffusion and construction of media messages, on the one hand, and their reception/appropriation by individuals situated within specific social–historical conditions, on the other. It is within this semantic space that the meaning mobilized by media messages becomes (or does not become) effective in the social world, serves (or does not serve) to sustain relations of domination. The interpretation of ideology in the mass media cannot be based solely on the analysis of the production and construction of messages: it must also be based on an analysis of the conditions and characteristics of reception. Thus one of the tasks confronting the interpretation of ideology in the mass media is that of relating the production/diffusion and construction of media messages, on the one hand, to the production and construction of recipient texts, on the other. In this way the process of interpretation can begin to explicate the connections between the mobilization of meaning in media messages and the relations of domination which this meaning serves to sustain. What these relations of domination are, and whether this meaning serves to sustain or to subvert them, to reinforce or to undermine them, are questions which can be answered only by linking the production/diffusion and construction of media messages to the ways in which they are received and interpreted by individuals situated within specific social–historical contexts.

[. . .]

By attending to the complex ways in which media messages are received and interpreted, we can begin to examine how the meaning mobilized by them is transformed in the process of reception, is appropriated by individuals situated in the structured contexts of everyday life and serves therein to sustain or disrupt relations of domination. We can thus open the way for a dynamic, critical approach to the analysis of ideology in the mass media. While taking account of the production/diffusion and construction of media messages, this approach does not remain at the level of analysing their structural features but seeks to relate these features to the ways in which messages are understood by, and the sense which the reception of these messages has for, individuals situated in specific social contexts. The analysis of ideology in the mass media thus bears a potentially critical relation, not only to the construction of meaning in media messages, but also to the interpretation of messages by recipients and to the relations of domination which characterize the contexts within which these messages are received. To analyse ideology in the mass media is to offer an interpretation which may intervene, which may serve as a resource for critical reflection among the very individuals who receive and interpret media messages as a routine part of their everyday lives. It may enable the subjects who make up the social world to reflect critically on their understanding of media messages and on the structured social relations of which they are part.

Conclusion

In this essay I have been concerned to outline an approach to the study of mass communication as a central component of modern culture. It is an approach which enables us to do justice to the different aspects of mass communication – the production/diffusion, construction and reception/appropriation of media messages – and which enables us to analyse these different aspects in relation to one another. It treats media messages as situated in specific social–historical and institutional contexts, while recognizing their distinctive character as meaningful symbolic constructions. It combines different methods of analysis in a systematic way, enabling us to shed light, in a flexible but rigorous manner, on the different aspects and features of mass communication

Notes

1. For general discussions of the concept of culture see Williams (1976, 1981), Kroeber and Kluckhohm (1952).
2. The relevant literature is extensive. For a small selection see Rosengren (1981), Schlesinger, Murdoch and Elliott (1983), Davis and Walton (1983), Rowland and Watkins (1985).
3. For a selection of relevant literature see Halloran (1970), Seymour-Ure (1973), Gerbner and Gross (1976), Blumler and Katz (1974).
4. Interesting attempts to pursue this line of reflection may be found in Piepe, Emerson and Lannon (1975), Morely (1980, 1986), Hodge and Tripp (1986), Liebes and Katz (1986).

References

Burns, Tom (1969) Public service and private world. In Halmos, Paul (ed.) *The Sociology of Mass-media Communicators, The Sociological Review Monograph* Vol. 13, pp. 53–73.

Geertz, Clifford (1973) *The Interpretation of Cultures*, Basic Books, New York.

Mcquail, Denis (1969) Uncertainty about the audience and the organization of mass communication. In Halmos, Paul (ed.) *The Sociology of Mass-media Communicators, The Sociological Review Monograph*, Vol. 13, pp. 75–84.

Tylor, Edward B. (1871) *Primitive Culture: Researches into the Development of Mythology, Philosophy, Religion, Language, Art and Custom*. John Murray, London.

White, Leslie A. (1949) *The Science of Culture: A Study of Man and Civilization*. Farrar, Strauss and Cudahy, New York.

Section 2

Mass society, functionalism, pluralism

7

Early theories in media research

Oliver Boyd-Barrett

This section illustrates three early approaches to the study of media (mass society, functionalist, pluralist), and covers a period of transition from totalistic denigration of media, illustrated in Adorno and Horkheimer's despairing condemnation of mass culture, through to the more optimistic and varied range of functionalist and pluralist perspectives.

These traditions differ in the extent of their systematization and self-awareness. As a tradition of media theory, pluralism is the least systematized of the three. Researchers who worked within the premises of orthodox conceptions of the modern democratic society experienced least need to unpack the ideology within which they framed their questions. The 'pluralist' label was more often attributed to them by opponents than one they used of themselves. They shared a belief that society comprised many different interests wrestling on a (reasonably) level playing field for key resources of status, money and power, and whose struggle was policed and regulated by the state for the public good. The thesis is articulated by Galbraith's notion of 'countervailing forces', and accords with a Weberian view of society as ordered, heterogeneous and competitive, but, crucially, one in which ideas and beliefs are at least as important as economics.

As an analysis of social structure, mass society theory attracted intellectuals of both the Left (Adorno and Horkheimer, in this section) and the Right (Elliott, 1963 and Leavis, 1933), finding common cause in defence of an élite 'high culture' which had formed so significant a part of their own intellectual development, and against what they saw as the products, at once inconsequential and invidious, of a mass culture informed solely by the lust for profit. Mass society, as represented in the work of C. Wright Mills (1956), is characterized by a nexus of interlocking power élites (military, industrial, political) which manipulates the masses in spite of, or even by means of, the formal machinery of democratic procedure. Such a society is inherently conflictual, and undermines the functionalist models (especially the structural functionalism of Talcott Parsons, 1948), which talk of system 'needs' and 'goals', and which tend to see conflict as functionally directed to system survival. Mass society theory is not far distant from Marxist theory where culture is seen as part of the 'superstructure' of ideas determined by society's economic 'base'. But the cultural products themselves barely merit the effort of detailed analysis in either approach.

Early mass society debate focused on culture, and on the conditions which prepared the way for the production and mass distribution of cultural commodities. Primary among these conditions (articulated by Kornhauser, 1959, among others) were the processes of industrialization and consequent urbanization, and the disruption to traditional extended family structure and community ways of life, together with their authentic and historically-rooted cultures. In their place were now rootless, mobile and lonely city-dwellers tied to wage-labour, deprived of their traditional community associations, subject to the direct manipulation of capitalists and of state regulation, and consoled by the products of an industry of mass culture which worked at one and the same time to reap profit from consumption of cultural commodities and sale of advertising, and to further entrap audiences within what could be called the pluralist ideology of the autonomous individual in free competition for social goods. There were some, however, who, like Edward Shils in this section, took the concept of mass society as a useful description of an important historical shift in social structure while insisting on what he regarded as its positive benefits, even for the diffusion of high culture.

These three traditions were particularly influential in a period covering approximately the 40 years before the Second World War through to the mid-1970s. They each informed the study of media effects (cf. next section). The traditions do not die, but are transformed or, lying dormant for periods of time, are rediscovered and adapted. The Frankfurt wing of the mass society tradition, represented by Adorno and Horkheimer, grew out of the attempt of a group of scholars who fled Nazi Germany for the U.S.A. in the 1930s to make good the absence in the works of Marx of an extended treatment of the cultural industries. From their work is established a bridge, through Marcuse 1964, to the cultural wing of neo-Marxism of the 1960s and 1970s; the Frankfurt School was itself the 'critical' combatant in conflict with what Lazarsfeld had called 'administrative' research. The tension between 'critical' and 'administrative' traditions was stoked to flame and transformed at the end of this period, in the 1970s confrontation (as described by Curran *et al.* in this section) between pluralists and neo-Marxists.

The Frankfurt view of the audience is monolithic, giving little or no attention to the potential for audience diversity of readings or resistance to media texts. Not disposed to empirical investigation, there was little incentive for the Frankfurt school, which regarded positivistic science (and even accessible language) as a further symptom of capitalist techno-rationality, to investigate real-life audiences. The Frankfurt school bent towards the 'magic bullet' theory of media effects, which assume the direct impact of a media message. This was soon to be discredited, although more recently, (see Gitlin in Section 1), significant alternative models of media effect such as Lazarsfeld's 'two-step flow' have also attracted considerable criticism, leaving open the issue as to how far and in what circumstances the media can or do exert influence without interpersonal mediation. But other scholars (of whom Wilensky in this section is an example) developed mass society theory through empirical research, and both functionalist and pluralist models were easily subject to the methodological positivism which pervades almost the entire field in this whole period.

Gitlin's critique of Lazarsfeld notwithstanding, the 'mass society' period of media research has typically been regarded as something of a dinosaur, one that attributed too much power to media and underrated the importance of social contexts of media consumption and of the survival of social structures which mediated the relationship between state and the individual. The revival, restoration and internationalization of the capitalist ethic and capitalist ideology, marked by the accession to power of Republicans (1980) and Conservatives (1979) in the U.S.A. and the U.K., respectively, should at least invite a reassessment of mass society theory. In many countries of the so-called 'advanced' world since the 1960s long-term and community loyalties to political parties have been undermined; there have been successful assaults on support for trades unions, a progressive weakening and shattering of the nuclear family, deliberate destabilization and 'temporalization' both of blue-collar and white-collar employment, acceleration in rates of violent and non-violent crime; evidence of collusion between national power élites and international business.

Arguably, these tendencies have more effectively than ever before increased the manipulability of the individual by the state and by the economic interests which drive the policies of the state. Alternatively, those who advance the theory of the 'media as public sphere', as well as those who stress the role of media in the transformation of time and space, may argue that the media themselves, in the development of electronic communities and through their authority to interrogate the powerful, become ever more important sources of mediation and protection. Political economists on the other hand, examining the concentration, diversification, commercialization and internationalization of the ownership, control and content of the media may doubt whether the broad drift of the policies and actions of power élites are likely to be much affected one way or the other by whatever survives of oppositional or contested discourse in the media. Scepticism as to the possibility of a generalized relevance of media content to political change is also supported by scholars of 'new audience research' who focus on and possibly find reassurance in the multiplicity of (culturally-embedded) 'readings' and uses of media texts by different individuals at different times and in different contexts.

Each extract in this section has been chosen to represent an approach to media research but this does not mean that each extract belongs solely to one particular tradition. Some extracts might as easily have been assigned to other sections. The piece by Blumler and Gurevitch, for example, belongs equally to Section 6. Equally, there are articles in other sections which could have been assigned to this one (e.g. Tunstall's work on journalists as an example of the analysis of institutional goals within the functionalist tradition). Both Blumler and Gurevitch, and Tunstall, could be quoted as examples of the application of yet another approach, one which is not singled out for special attention in this volume namely, exchange theory (cf. Blau 1964), which was popular within sociology at the time they wrote.

Mass society

The Adorno and Horkheimer selection might have been located in any of a number of traditions – political economy or cultural hegemony, for example. But *The Culture Industry* is, among other things, a passionate statement of mass society theory, born of direct experience of fascism and economic depression, and anticipates modern political economy (in particular in its analysis of the consequences for cultural products of industrial monopoly) and studies of cultural imperialism. Its analysis is remorselessly depressing; everything, including the superficial appearance of diversity in the range of products, is interpreted reductionistically in terms of its role for invested capital, and it is in that totalistic, systemic sense that the mass society theory of the Frankfurt variety can even be represented as a sort of black funct-ionalism, one which works as much by suppressing inconvenient needs as by meeting them. The continuing relevance of the Frankfurt analysis, despite its naive assumptions of direct individual media effects and disregard for the importance of empirical investigation, lies in its identification of the relevance for media research of monopoly control, cross-ownership, com-mercialization, the subjugation of technological rationale to the interests of the economic élite, and control over access to mass audiences.

For Shils, in sharply contrasting valorization, mass society is an achieve-ment. He considers much the same things as Adorno and Horkheimer and sees them through quite different spectacles. Like them, his discussion is not over-burdened by the substantiation of assertion with empirical evidence; unlike them his underlying theoretical framework is implicit more than it is explicit. Perhaps drawing on the imagery of the American 'melting pot', Shils sees mass society as the development of a sense of national identity: the replacement of diverse individual attachments by a symbiotic relation-ship between individual and nation. The strengthening of ties between individuals and the nation – the outcome of industrialization, transport and communication technology – privileges national identity above other (and more divisive) sources of identity. In as much as this process loosens tradition (which, by implication, stands for things divisive, authoritarian and hierarchical), individuals are more equal, freer to form attachments and more receptive to new ideas. Industrialization, for Shils, is essentially liberating – above all, liberating from the 'burden of physically exhausting labor' . When he comes to the culture of mass society, Shils offers a tripartite division whose names are sufficient evidence of a 'high low' continuum. In a telling footnote he puzzles over evidence of a high level of consumption of 'mediocre culture' by large numbers of the social élite, and the 'mediocre' quality of much work within the genres of 'superior' culture, doubts which, had he pursued them, might have counselled a more critical look at the variety of indices which he offers for distinguishing between the three levels of culture (i.e. production quality, level of 'seriousness', 'penetration' of insights, and 'complexity' of symbolic content) but which he does not attempt to operationalize. This tripartite division is reminiscent of similar divisions of the period, not least in the U.K., where the BBC divided its radio channels between the stations of classical music (Third Programme), talks and current affairs (Home Service) and the Light Programme (popular music, comedy). His understanding of 'culture' is a long way removed from that of social anthropologists, where the term 'culture' is used to refer to ways of life or, somewhat more specifically, to the range of symbolic forms which communities use for the purposes of social expression.

The application of social anthropology to urban populations in the U.S.

and in the U.K. during the 1950s and 1960s provided evidence that despite the forebodings of Kornhauser and other mass society theorists, strong communities continued to flourish in modern society, managing to sustain participation in representative associations as a bulwark against central state power (although, as I have argued above, these reassurances may now be seriously out of date). The work of Wilensky offered a more complex view of mass society by focusing on the apparent contradiction in the more affluent countries between the considerable heterogeneity of social structure and the growing standardization of 'culture' in the narrower sense of media consumption. This is a particularly good example (although unfortunately there is insufficient space here to give a flavour of its methodology) of the application of positivism and empiricism to what hitherto had been issues discussed at a very broad level of abstraction and assertion. Wilensky is well aware of the rich diversity of social life that lies behind standard sociological variables. He addresses this diversity through refinement of the variables (e.g. differentiation between different occupations, and between different responses to media), and accesses these through detailed interview. By the standards of some 1990s' versions of 'ethnographic method' for whom it is enough to interview an informant in their 'natural' surroundings, Wilensky's approach might even qualify as ethnographic; the analytical categories, however, are not 'grounded' in the evidence, but rather are applied to it, and the results are then handled with considerable statistical sophistication. In contrast with the ambition of Wilensky's study, indeed, many ethnographic studies might even appear mean and impoverished, were it not for the fact that Wilensky's concentration on the continuous refinement of variables perhaps obscured the initial valorization which gave rise to those variables: as represented in the confidence, for example, with which he defines mass culture in opposition to high culture, or in his exclusion of women. His conclusion, not dissimilar to that of Shils but qualified by reference to the need for continuing research and refinement, is that the average cultural 'level' may ascend rather than descend in line with increased affluence and cultural standardization.

Functionalism

Functionalism has many sources and many forms but which share in common a focus on system-wide properties and on issues of system survival, adaptation and change – although in early manifestations functionalism was principally concerned with the maintenance of social stability. Different analogies are used to help conceptualize these processes; among these, the biological analogy, which Lasswell in this section uses in his analysis of the role of communication for society, has been particularly popular since the nineteenth century, but recently supplanted, first by mechanical and then by cybernetic metaphors.

The short extract from Lasswell contains his classic formulation of the 'act of communication' which long helped to define the principal questions of communication studies. To its credit, it included a robust emphasis on production, as well as on content, delivery and audience; the formulation tends to exclude or at least to hide the contexts of communication (immediate, historical, social, institutional contexts, among others), and it is expressed in a way which would now be recognized as lying closer to the linear 'transmission' model of communication than to the 'semiotic' model of negotiated meaning. In talking of the functions of communication, media are seen as acting on society much more than they are seen as acted upon; and their role is appraised positively, normatively, without reference to conceptions of ownership, motivation, profit, nor indeed to what we might loosely describe – if only to guard against our falling in step with the complacent attribution of goodwill which this kind of analysis exudes – the 'sleaze' dimension of the entertainment industries.

A more explicit functionalism was developed by Charles R. Wright across a period of 15 years (1959, 1960, 1974), of which an extract is presented in this section. For Wright, functions refer to the 'consequences of certain routine, regular and standardized components of communications'. He identifies a variety of different approaches to functional analysis, ranging from the general functions/dysfunctions of media for total social systems and for individuals, to the functions/dysfunctions of particular media (or of particular institutional or professional practices). Functional analysis looks at the inter-relationships between system components. It thus escapes the worst dangers of linear causality: as well as enquiring about the functions of media for society and for individuals it also looks at the functions of other social institutions and of individuals for media (including, in this example, the functions of the acquisition of media competencies such as literacy for media-related behaviours).

Wright (along with DeFleur, 1970, and others) regarded functionalism as a useful source of hypotheses about the inter-relationships between media and other elements of the social system, hypotheses which could be explored through empirical enquiry, and he gives many examples which demonstrate this potential very well. He extends this to consideration of functional alternatives: what are the consequences, for example, of the needs of individuals being fulfilled in one way (e.g. through mass media) rather than in others (e.g. interpersonal communication). But the system-focus of functionalism tends towards a rather mechanical way of asking and addressing questions. It lends itself well, at the theoretical more than at the practical or empirical levels, to the complexity of inter-relationships between the features of given systems; it is not well suited to the subtleties and ambivalences of social, cultural and economic processes, nor to analysis of the ways in which social meaning is developed within a given culture. Functionalism requires categories, and in the choice of determining what is functional for what lies a good deal of potential for selective partitioning of the world.

Pluralism

The conflict between Lazarsfeld and Adorno (referred to in Gitlin, in this volume) was described by Lazarsfeld himself as the conflict between administrative and critical theory. Administrative research (within western industrialized societies) tended to pose questions appearing to take for granted the innate rationality and social justice of the existing social order, whereas critical theory problematizes and relativizes social order as one which, to varying degrees of stability or instability, has been constructed in favour of certain interests over others.

Administrative research was research funded by the communications industries themselves, and the name has narrower signification, therefore, than the broader term 'pluralist' (sometimes called 'liberal-pluralist' or simply 'liberal') which came to replace it; its oppositional term, 'critical' theory, has proved broader than the 'Marxist' or 'hegemony' labels which competed with it for popularity in the 1970s. In the account of Curran, Gurevitch and Woollacott, in this section, the two approaches are seen to diverge radically in their view of media effects: pluralists holding that media power to change people is very limited, while neo-Marxists, heirs to the 'mass society' tradition, believed that effects were strong, serving not to change society but to reproduce it. Curran *et al.* argue that while this is essentially the same finding, namely that the media work principally to reinforce social order, the two traditions are separated by differences in the kind of questions they ask. Pluralists are interested in whether violence in media encourages individuals to be more aggressive. Neo-Marxists are interested in whether media portrayals of violence are designed to consolidate compliance with the forces of law and order. Curran *et al.* question whether pluralism is necessarily more wedded to empirical methodology than Marxism, and they detect growing interest among Marxists in empirical research.

The article was written in support of an Open University course first presented in 1977, *Mass Communication and Society*, whose production provided a battlefield between Marxists and 'pluralists'. (It also exhibited evidence of tension within the 'Left', namely between political economy and cultural studies approaches.) Less than 15 years later, in 1990, Curran would be reviewing the demise of Marxism, defending its strengths against the 'new revisionism' of the 'new audience' studies of the 1980s (see Section 10). The 'new revisionism', represented in Morley's 1980 study of *Nationwide* audiences, applied the insights of radical text-based studies (themselves divided between those which considered texts were 'polysemic', i.e. open to a plurality of different readings, and those which believed that they carried 'preferred readings', or that they 'positioned' or 'inscribed' audiences) and discovered a richer diversity of actual audience 'readings' than many had expected. Although this sounded a lot like the old pluralism (indeed, Curran argued that 'new revisionism' had simply re-discovered what was already well known from 1940s audience research), it had little to say about the narrow range of programming or about the restricted opportunities which prohibit the vast majority of citizens from any kind of access to mass audiences (least of all without the mediation of media professionals).

The extract from Blumler and Gurevitch is an astute and subtle analysis of a form of political communication. It should also be regarded as a potential entry to Section 6, since it focuses on such issues as the relationships between journalists and news sources, journalistic cultures, and conventions of news-gathering. A key feature of the analysis is its focus on roles and role-relationships as bounded by institutional goal-directed cultures. In this respect one might say this is also a functional analysis (functionalism is explicitly invoked in order to look at the consequences of role-anchored guidelines). But the extract mainly exemplifies the application of a pluralistic model of communication: its premise is that politicians and journalists essentially represent different institutional interests and different cultures, but that these interests and cultures converge, and their convergence requires a bounded common culture; the continuity of this common culture is maintained through institutionally developed roles, role relationships, negotiation and patterns of exchange. Very many of the quoted examples of this common culture at work are from election studies. Thus we have: elements of institutional and cultural difference (magnified when one includes a variety of different national cultures in the framework); possession by different institutions of scarce resources which they exchange for mutual advantage; and a focus on the achievement of system stability or controlled adjustment. The focus on system adjustment, even if it allows for incremental evolution, may not in itself explain the greater tensions that exist between press and politicians in the mid-1990s by contrast with late-1970s Britain, nor is it clear how and whether this system is sustained as successfully outside the confines of ritualized political events or contexts as within them.

A Marxist or critical perspective, as represented in parts of Sections 3 and 7 on political economy and cultural hegemony, respectively, might have framed evidence of collaboration here with reference to the ways in which journalists and politicians collaborated as members of the same social class formation, and on the ways in which such collaboration worked essentially to exclude certain topics, issues and interests. It might have provided evidence of mobility between journalistic and political roles, with many politicians entering politics from journalism, and returning to journalism following the demise of their political careers. It might also have looked at patterns of interaction between more senior members of both institutions. It would have focused more specifically on differences between different political parties, and different news issues, and would not have limited the focus of its attention to 'élite' media and 'élite' news. In other words, it would have been less concerned with how it is that members of marginally different camps of a privileged social élite manage to get on with one another, and much more exercised by the continuity of this system of privilege in a context of massive social inequality and the denial of access for non-élites, mediated or unmediated, to mass audiences. To have achieved this it would have focused less on the mechanics of election coverage, if it had focused on elections at all, and much more on the social construction of discourses which surround electioneering in relation to concepts of democracy, citizenship, individual freedom. It would more likely have looked at issues invoking direct conflict between advantaged and disadvantaged social groups.

References and further reading

Blau, P. (1964) *Exchange and Power in Social Life*, John Wiley, New York.
DeFleur, M. L. (1970) *Theories of Mass Communication*, David McKay, New York.
Elliott, T. S. (1963) *Selected Letters*, London.
Galbraith, K. (1969), *The Affluent Society*, Harmondsworth, Penguin.

Kornhauser, W. (1959), *The Politics of Mass Society*, Free Press, New York.

Lazarsfeld, P. F. (1941) Remarks on critical and administrative communication. *Research, Studies in Philosophy and Social Science*, Vol. IX, pp. 2–16.

Leavis, F. and Thomson, D. (1948), *Culture and Environment*, Chatto and Windus, London.

Marcuse, H. (1964) *One-dimensional Man*, Routledge and Kegan Paul, London.

Mills, C. W. (1956), *The Power Elite*, Oxford University Press, New York.

Parsons, Talcott (1960) *Structure and Process in Modern Societies*, Free Press, Glencoe.

Wright, C. R. (1960) Functional analysis and mass communication. *Public Opinion Quarterly*, Vol. 24, pp. 606–20.

Wright, C. R. (1974) Functional analysis and mass communication revisited. In Blumler, J. G. and Katz, E. (eds) *The Uses of Mass Communication*, Sage Publications, Beverly Hills, pp. 197–212.

8

The culture industry: enlightenment as mass deception

Theodor W. Adorno and Max Horkheimer

From Adorno, T. W. and Horkheimer, M. (1979) *Dialectic of Enlightenment* (translated by Cumming, J.), Verso, London, pp. 120–4.

The sociological theory that the loss of the support of objectively established religion, the dissolution of the last remnants of precapitalism, together with technological and social differentiation or specialization, have led to cultural chaos is disproved every day; for culture now impresses the same stamp on every thing. Films, radio and magazines make up a system which is uniform as a whole and in every part. Even the aesthetic activities of political opposites are one in their enthusiastic obedience to the rhythm of the iron system. The decorative industrial management buildings and exhibition centres in authoritarian countries are much the same as anywhere else. The huge gleaming towers that shoot up everywhere are outward signs of the ingenious planning of international concerns, toward which the unleashed entrepreneurial system (whose monuments are a mass of gloomy houses and business premises in grimy, spiritless cities) was already hastening. Even now the older houses just outside the concrete city centres look like slums, and the new bungalows on the outskirts are at one with the flimsy structures of world fairs in their praise of technical progress and their built-in demand to be discarded after a short while like empty food cans. Yet the city housing projects designed to perpetuate the individual as a supposedly independent unit in a small hygienic dwelling make him all the more subservient to his adversary – the absolute power of capitalism. Because the inhabitants, as producers and as consumers, are drawn into the centre in search of work and pleasure, all the living units crystallize into well-organized complexes. The striking unity of microcosm and macrocosm presents men with a model of their culture: the false identity of the general and the particular. Under monopoly all mass culture is identical, and the lines of its artificial framework begin to show through. The people at the top are no longer so interested in concealing monopoly: as its violence becomes more open, so its power grows. Movies and radio need no longer pretend to be art. The truth that they are just business is made into an ideology in order to justify the rubbish they deliberately produce. They call themselves industries; and when their directors' incomes are published, any doubt about the social utility of the finished products is removed.

Interested parties explain the culture industry in technological terms. It is alleged that because millions participate in it, certain reproduction processes are necessary that inevitably require identical needs in innumerable places to be satisfied with identical goods. The technical contrast between the few production centres and the large number of widely dispersed consumption points is said to demand organization and planning by management. Furthermore, it is claimed that standards were based in the first place on consumers' needs, and for that reason were accepted with so little resistance. The result is the circle of manipulation and retroactive need in which the unity of the system grows ever stronger. No mention is made of the fact that the basis on which technology acquires power over society is the power of those whose economic hold over society is greatest. A technological rationale is the rationale of domination itself. It is the coercive nature of society alienated from itself. Automobiles, bombs, and movies keep the whole thing together until their levelling element shows its strength in the very wrong which it furthered. It has made the technology of the culture industry no more than the achievement of standardization and mass production, sacrificing whatever involved a distinction between the logic of the work and that of the social system. This is the result not of a law of movement in technology as such but of its function in today's economy. The need which might resist central control has already been suppressed by the control of the individual consciousness. The step from the telephone to the radio has clearly distinguished the roles. The former still allowed the subscriber to play the role of subject, and was liberal. The latter is democratic: it turns all participants into listeners and authoritatively subjects them to broadcast programmes which are all exactly the same. No machinery of rejoinder has been devised, and private broadcasters are denied any freedom. They are confined to the apocryphal field of the 'amateur', and also have to accept organization from above. But any trace of spontaneity from the public in official broadcasting is controlled and absorbed by talent scouts, studio competitions and official programmes of every kind selected by professionals. Talented performers belong to the industry long before it displays them; otherwise they would not be so eager to fit in. The attitude of the public, which ostensibly and actually favours the system of the culture industry, is a part of the system and not an excuse for it. If one branch of art follows the same formula as one with a very different medium and content; if the dramatic intrigue of broadcast soap operas becomes no more than useful material for showing how to master technical problems at both ends of the scale of musical experience – real jazz or a cheap imitation; or if a movement from a Beethoven symphony is crudely 'adapted' for a film sound-track in the same way as a Tolstoy novel is garbled in a film script: then the claim that this is done to satisfy the spontaneous wishes of the public is no more than hot air. We are closer to the facts if we explain these phenomena as inherent in the technical and personnel apparatus which, down to its last cog, itself forms part of the economic mechanism of selection. In addition there is the agreement – or at least the determination – of all executive authorities not to produce or sanction anything that in any way differs from their own rules, their own ideas about consumers, or above all themselves.

In our age the objective social tendency is incarnate in the hidden subjective purposes of company directors, the foremost among whom are in the most powerful sectors of industry – steel, petroleum, electricity, and chemicals. Culture monopolies are weak and dependent in comparison. They cannot afford to neglect their appeasement of the real holders of power if their sphere of activity in mass society (a sphere producing a specific type of commodity which anyhow is still too closely bound up with easygoing liberalism and Jewish intellectuals) is not to undergo a series of purges. The dependence of the most powerful broadcasting company on the electrical industry, or of the motion picture industry on the banks, is characteristic of the whole sphere, whose individual branches are themselves economically interwoven. All are in such close contact that the extreme concentration of mental forces allows demarcation lines between different firms and technical branches to be ignored. The ruthless unity in the culture industry is evidence of what will happen in politics. Marked differentiations such as those of A and B films, or of stories in magazines in different price ranges, depend not so much on subject matter as on classifying, organizing, and labelling consumers. Something is provided for all so that none may escape; the distinctions are emphasized and extended. The public is catered for with a hierarchical range of mass-produced products of varying quality, thus advancing the rule of complete quantification. Everybody must behave (as if spontaneously) in accordance with his previously determined and indexed level, and choose the category of mass product turned out for his type. Consumers appear as statistics on research organization charts, and are divided by income groups into red, green, and blue areas; the technique is that used for any type of propaganda.

How formalized the procedure is can be seen when the mechanically differentiated products prove to be all alike in the end. That the difference between the Chrysler range and General Motors products is basically illusory strikes every child with a keen interest in varieties. What connoisseurs discuss as good or bad points serve only to perpetuate the semblance of competition and range of choice. The same applies to the Warner Brothers and Metro Goldwyn Mayer productions. But even the differences between the more expensive and cheaper models put out by the same firm steadily diminish: for automobiles, there are such differences as the number of cylinders, cubic capacity, details of patented gadgets; and for films there are the number of stars, the extravagant use of technology, labour, and equipment, and the introduction of the latest psychological formulas. The universal criterion of merit is the amount of 'conspicuous production', of blatant cash investment. The varying budgets in the culture industry do not bear the slightest relation to factual values, to the meaning of the products themselves. Even the technical media are relentlessly forced into uniformity. Television aims at a synthesis of radio and film, and is held up only because the interested parties have not yet reached agreement, but its consequences will be quite enormous and promise to intensify the impoverishment of aesthetic matter so drastically, that by tomorrow the thinly veiled identity of all industrial culture products can come triumphantly out into the open, derisively fulfilling the Wagnerian dream of the Gesamtkunst-werk – the fusion of all the arts in one work. The alliance of word, image, and music is all the more perfect than in Tristan because the sensuous elements which all approvingly reflect the surface of social reality are in principle embodied in the same technical process, the unity of which be comes its distinctive content. This process integrates all the elements of the production, from the novel (shaped with an eye to the film) to the last sound effect. It is the triumph of invested capital, whose title as absolute master is etched deep into the hearts of the dispossessed in the employment line; it is the meaningful content of every film, whatever plot the production team may have selected.

9

Mass society and its culture

Edward Shils

From Jacobs, N. (ed.) (1961) *Culture for the Millions*, D. Van Nostrand, Princeton, NJ, pp. 1–7.

Mass society: consensus, civility, individuality

A new order of society has taken form since the end of World War I in the United States, above all, but also in Great Britain, France, Northern Italy, the Low and Northern European countries, and Japan. Some of its features have begun to appear in Eastern and Central Europe, though in a less even manner; more incipiently and prospectively so, in Asian and African countries. It is the style to refer to this new order as the 'mass society'.

This new order of society, despite all its internal conflicts, discloses in the individual a greater sense of attachment to the society as a whole, and of affinity with his fellows. As a result, perhaps for the first time in history, large aggregations of human beings living over an extensive territory have been able to enter into relatively free and uncoerced association.

The new society is a mass society precisely in the sense that the mass of the population has become incorporated into society. The centre of society – the central institutions, and the central value systems which guide and legitimate these institutions – has extended its boundaries. Most of the population (the 'mass') now stands in a closer relationship to the centre than has been the case in either pre-modern societies or in the earlier phases of modern society. In previous societies, a substantial portion of the population, often the majority, were born and forever remained 'outsiders'.

The mass society is a new phenomenon, but it has been long in gestation. The idea of the *polis* is its seed, nurtured and developed in the Roman idea of a common citizenship extending over a wide territory. The growth of nationality in the modern era has heightened the sense of affinity among the members of different classes and regions of the same country. When the proponents of the modern idea of the nation put forward the view that life on a contiguous, continuous, and common territory – beyond all divisions of kinship, caste, and religious belief – united the human beings living within that territory into a single collectivity, and when they made a common language the evidence of that membership, they committed themselves, not often wittingly, to the mass society.

An important feature of that society is the diminished sacredness of authority, the reduction in the awe it evokes and in the charisma attributed to it. This diminution in the status of authority runs parallel to a loosening of the power of tradition. Naturally, tradition continues to exert influence, but it becomes more open to divergent interpretations, and these frequently lead to divergent courses of action.

The dispersion of charisma from centre outward has manifested itself in a greater stress on individual dignity and individual rights. This extension does not always reach into the sphere of the political, but it is apparent in the attitudes toward women, youth, and ethnic groups which have been in a disadvantageous position.

Following from this, one of the features of mass society I should like to emphasize is its wide dispersion of 'civility'. The concept of civility is not a modern creation, but it is in the mass society that it has found its most complete (though still very incomplete) realization. The very idea of a *citizenry* coterminous with the adult population is one of its signs. So is the moral equalitarianism which is a trait unique to the West, with its insistence that by virtue of their sharing membership in the community and a common tongue men possess a certain irreducible dignity.

None of these characteristic tendencies of mass society has attained anything like full realization. The moral consensus of mass society is certainly far from complete; the mutual assimilation of centre (i.e. the élite) and periphery (i.e. the mass) is still much less than total. Class conflict, ethnic prejudice, and disordered personal relations remain significant factors in our modern mass societies, but without preventing the tendencies I have described from finding an historically unprecedented degree of realization.

Mass society is an industrial society. Without industry, i.e. without the replacement of simple tools by complicated machines, mass society would be inconceivable. Modern industrial techniques, through the creation of an elaborate network of transportation and communication, bring the various parts of mass society into frequent contact. Modern technology has liberated man from the burden of physically exhausting labour, and has given him resources through which new experiences of sensation, conviviality, and introspection have become possible. True, modern industrial organization has also been attended by a measure of hierarchical and bureaucratic organization which often runs contrary to the vital but loose consensus of mass society. Nonetheless, the fact remains that modern mass society has reached out toward a moral consensus and a civil order congruous with the adult population. The sacredness that every man possesses by virtue of his membership in society finds a more far-reaching affirmation than ever before.

Mass society has aroused and enhanced individuality. Individuality is characterized by an openness to experience, an efflorescence of sensation and sensibility, a sensitivity to other minds and personalities. It gives rise to, and lives in, personal attachments; it grows from the expansion of the empathic capacities of the human being. Mass society has liberated the cognitive, appreciative, and moral capacities of individuals. Larger elements of the population have consciously learned to value the pleasures of eye, ear, taste, touch, and conviviality. People make choices more freely in many spheres of life, and these choices are not necessarily made for them by tradition, authority, or scarcity. The value of the experience of personal relationships is more widely appreciated.

These observations are not meant to imply that individuality as developed in mass society exists universally. A part of the population in mass society lives in a nearly vegetative torpor, reacting dully or aggressively to its environment. Nonetheless, the search for individuality and its manifestations in personal relations are distinctly present in mass society and constitute one of its essential features.

The culture of mass society

The fundamental categories of cultural life are the same in all societies. In all the different strata of any given society, the effort to explore and explain the universe, to understand the meaning of events, to enter into contact with the sacred or to commit sacrilege, to affirm the principles of morality and justice and to deny them, to encounter the unknown, to exalt or denigrate authority, to stir the senses by the control of and response to words, sounds, shapes, and colours – these are the basic elements of cultural existence. There are, however, profound variations in the elaboration of these elements, for human beings show marked differences in capacity for expression and reception.

No society can ever achieve a complete cultural consensus: there are natural limitations to the spread of the standards and products of superior culture throughout society. The tradition of refinement is itself replete with antinomies, and the nature of creativity adds to them. Creativity is a modification of tradition. Furthermore, the traditional transmission of superior culture inevitably stirs some to reject and deny significant parts of it, just because it is traditional. More fundamental than the degrees of creativity and alienation is the disparity in human cognitive, appreciative, and moral capacities This disparity produces marked differences in the apprehension of tradition, in the complexity of the response to it, and in the substance of the judgements aroused by it.

Thus a widely differentiated 'dissensus' has become stabilized in the course of history. The pattern of this 'dissensus' is not inevitably unchanging. The classes consuming culture may diminish in number, their taste may deteriorate, their standards become less discriminating or more debased. On the other hand, as the mass of the population comes awake when its curiosity and sensibility and its moral responsiveness are aroused, it begins to become capable of a more subtle perception, more appreciative of the more general elements in a concrete representation, and more complex in its aesthetic reception and expression.

The levels of culture

For present purposes, we shall employ a very rough distinction among three levels of culture, which are levels of quality measured by aesthetic, intellectual, and moral standards. These are 'superior' or 'refined' culture, 'mediocre' culture, and 'brutal' culture.[1]

Superior or refined culture is distinguished by the seriousness of its subject matter, i.e. the centrality of the problems with which it deals, the acute penetration and coherence of its perceptions, the subtlety and wealth of its expressed feeling. The stock of superior culture includes the great works of poetry, novels,

philosophy, scientific theory and research, statues, paintings, musical compo-
sitions and their performance, the texts and performance of plays, history,
economic, social, and political analyses, architecture and works of
craftsmanship. It goes without saying that the category of superior culture does
not refer to the social status, i.e. the quality of their attainment, of the author
or of the consumers of the works in question, but only to their truth and beauty.

The category of mediocre culture includes works which, whatever the
aspiration of their creators, do not measure up to the standards employed
in judging works of superior culture. Mediocre culture is less original than
superior culture; it is more reproductive; it operates largely in the same genres
as superior culture, but also in certain relatively novel genres not yet fully
incorporated into superior culture, such as the musical comedy. This may
be a function of the nature of the genre or of the fact that the genre has
not yet attracted great talent to its practice.

At the third level is brutal culture, where symbolic elaboration is of a more
elementary order. Some of the genres on this level are identical with those
of mediocre and refined culture (pictorial and plastic representation, music,
poems, novels, and stories) but they also include games, spectacles (such as
boxing and horse racing) and more directly expressive actions with a minimal
symbolic content. The depth of penetration is almost always negligible,
subtlety is almost entirely lacking, and a general grossness of sensitivity and
perception is a common feature.

The greatest difference among the three levels of culture, apart from intrinsic
quality, is the tremendous disparity in the richness of the stock available in
any society at any given time. What any given society possesses is not only
what it creates in its own generation but also what it has received from
antecedent generations and from earlier and contemporaneous generations
of other societies. Superior culture is immeasurably richer in content because
it contains not only superior contemporary production but also much of the
refined production of earlier epochs. Mediocre culture tends to be poorer,
not only because of the poorer quality of what it produces in its own generation,
but because these cultural products have a relatively shorter life span.
Nevertheless, mediocre culture contains much that has been created in the
past. The boundaries between mediocre and superior culture are not so sharp,
and the custodians of superior culture are not so discriminating as always
to reject the mediocre. Furthermore, a considerable amount of mediocre culture
retains value over long periods; and even though mediocre taste varies, as
does superior taste, there are stable elements in it, too, so that some of the
mediocre culture of the past continues to find an appreciative audience.

At the lowest cultural level, where the symbolic content is most impoverished and where there is very little original creation in each generation,
we come again to a greater, if much less self-conscious, dependence on the
past. Games, jokes, spectacles, and the like continue traditional patterns with
little consciousness of their traditionality. If the traditional element in brutal
culture has been large, this is due to the relatively low creative capacities of
those who produce and consume it. Here, until recently, there has been little
professional production, machinery for preservation and transmission is
lacking, and oral transmission plays a greater part in maintaining traditions
of expression and performance than with superior and mediocre cultures.

The magnitudes: consumption

The quantity of culture consumed in mass society is certainly greater than in any other epoch, even if we make proper allowance for the larger populations of the mass societies at present. It is especially at the levels of mediocre and brutal culture that an immense expansion has occurred, but the consumption of superior culture has also increased.

The grounds for this great increase, and for the larger increase in the two lower categories, are not far to seek. The most obvious are greater availability, increased leisure time, the decreased physical demands of work, the greater affluence of the classes which once worked very hard for long hours for small income, increased literacy, enhanced individuality, and more unabashed hedonism. In all these, the middle and the lower classes have gained more than have the élites (including the intellectuals, whatever their occupational distribution).

The consumption of superior culture has increased, too, but not as much as the other two categories, because the intellectual classes were more nearly saturated before the age of mass society. Moreover, the institutions of superior culture – the collections of connoisseurs, academies, universities, libraries, publishing houses, periodicals – were more elaborately and more continuously established in the pre-mass society than were the institutions which made mediocre and brutal culture available to their consumers.

Thus in mass society the proportion of the total stock of cultural objects held by superior culture has shrunk, and correspondingly the share of mediocre and brutal culture has grown.[2]

Note on the value of mediocre and brutal culture

Mediocre culture has many merits. It often has elements of genuine conviviality, not subtle or profound perhaps, but genuine in the sense of being spontaneous and honest. It is often very good fun. Moreover, it is often earnestly, even if simply, moral. Mediocre culture, too, has its traditions; many of the dramas and stories which regale the vulgar have a long history hidden from those who tell and enjoy them. Like anything traditional, they express something essential in human life, and expunging them would expunge the accumulated wisdom of ordinary men and women, their painfully developed art of coping with the miseries of existence, their routine pieties and their decent pleasures.

There is much ridicule of kitsch, and it is ridiculous. Yet it represents aesthetic sensibility and aesthetic aspiration, untutored, rude, and deformed. The very growth of kitsch, and of the demand which has generated the industry for the production of kitsch, is an indication of a crude aesthetic awakening in classes which previously accepted what was handed down to them or who had practically no aesthetic expression and reception.

Notes

1. I have reservations about the use of the term 'mass culture', because it refers simultaneously to the substantive and qualitative properties of the culture, to the

social status of its consumers, and to the media by which it is transmitted. Because of this at least three-fold reference, it tends to beg some important questions regarding the relations among the three variables. For example, the current conception of 'mass culture' does not allow for the fact that in most countries, and not just at present, very large sections of the élite consume primarily mediocre and brutal culture. It also begs the important questions as to whether the mass media can transmit works of superior culture, or whether the genres developed by the new mass media can become the occasions of creativity and therewith a part of superior culture. Also, it does not consider the obvious fact that much of what is produced in the genres of superior culture is extremely mediocre in quality. At present, I have no satisfactory set of terms to distinguish the three levels of cultural objects. I have toyed with 'high', 'refined', 'elaborate', 'genuine', or 'serious', 'vulgar', 'mediocre', or 'middle', and 'low', 'brutal', 'base' or 'coarse'. None of these words succeeds either in felicity or aptness.

2. This change in the relative shares of the three levels of culture has been distorted by contrast with the preceding epochs. The cultural life of the consumers of mediocre and brutal culture was relatively silent, unseen by the intellectuals. The immense advances in audibility and visibility of the two lower levels of culture is one of the most noticeable traits of mass society. This is in turn intensified by another trait of mass society, i.e. the enhanced mutual awareness of different sectors of the society.

10

Mass society and mass culture: interdependence or independence?

Harold L. Wilensky

From Smelser, N. (ed.) (1964) *American Sociological Review*, American Sociological Association, New York, Vol. 29, No. 2. pp. 174–6, 194–6.

Theories of mass society and the functions of the mass media

Traditional theorists of 'urbanism' or of the 'mass society' tend to be pessimistic in ideology and macroscopic in sociology; their empirical critics tend to be optimistic – some would say fatuous – in ideology and microscopic in sociology. Both seek to interpret the impact of industrialism and urbanism on social structure and culture. Together they have given us most of the imagery with which we construct our picture of the affluent society.

From Tocqueville to Mannheim[1] the traditional theorists have been concerned with one or both of two problems: (1) the debilitation of culture-bearing élites (and of the core values they sustain) brought on by their diminishing insulation from popular pressures; (2) the rise of the masses, who, for various reasons, are increasingly susceptible to demagogues and extremist movements.[2] These scholars are said to believe that the mobility, heterogeneity, and centralization of modern society destroy or weaken the ties that bind men to the common life, rendering the mass manipulatable, leaving mass organizations and the mass media in control. Although they vary in their depiction of the generating forces, they tend to accent either the atrophy of primary and informal relations or the atrophy of self-governing secondary groups and associations.[3]

Now the empirically-minded critics – a later generation studying a more industrialized society – have countered with these propositions: primary groups survive, even flourish. Urban-industrial populations have not stopped participating in voluntary associations, which in America and perhaps in other pluralist systems, continue to multiply. Moreover, in every industrial society, whether pluralist or totalitarian, there are potent limits to the powers of the mass media, the big organizations, and the centralized state.

I count myself as one of the critics,[4] but I am restive about the way the debate has progressed.[5] The parties talk past one another and ideological blinders obstruct the vision far more than in other areas of sociological investigation. Nowhere is this more true than in the sketchy treatment of mass culture in theories of the mass society and in the almost ritualistic recital of the 'two-step flow' slogan by the students of media ineffectiveness.

The main theme of the theorists is this: the mass society develops a mass culture, in which cultural and political values and beliefs tend to be homogeneous and fluid. In the middle and at the bottom – in the atomized mass – people think and feel alike; but thoughts and feelings, not being firmly anchored anywhere, are susceptible to fads and fashions. At the top, poorly-organized élites, themselves mass-oriented, become political and managerial manipulators, responding to short-run pressures; they fail to maintain standards and thereby encourage the spread of populism in politics, mass tastes in culture – in short, a 'sovereignty of the unqualified'.[6]

The empirically-minded critics of such theories are impressed by the diversity of modern life. Concerning the levelling and fluidity of culture, they point to an extraordinary variety of cultural products, assert that it is easier to prove that mass tastes have been upgraded than that such tastes have been vulgarized, and protest that high culture has not declined but merely become more widely available. Concerning the role of the mass media in politics and culture, the critics cite considerable diversity of media content as well as persistence in habits of exposure. And where diversity of content falls short, they argue, there is everywhere enormous diversity in response. While the optimists are well aware of the limits of their studies, they seem always to come to the same punch line: the burden of evidence indicates that the media are not omnipotent; they are absorbed into local cultures via the two-step flow from media to local group to person; and this absorption involves a self-selection of exposure corresponding to previous attitude.[7]

It is a pity that these students of the media who know mass communications best are not more ideologically sensitive and not more concerned with general characterizations of society; equally unfortunate is it that the theorists, at home in the world of ideologies and utopias, are not more sophisticated in the handling of data. For systematic observation and theoretical problems must be brought together if we are to understand the interplay of social structure, high culture, and mass culture.

Mass culture and high culture

For my purposes here the most useful definition that distinguishes high culture from mass culture is one that emphasizes the social context of production. 'High culture' will refer to two characteristics of the product: (1) it is created by or under the supervision of a cultural élite operating within some aesthetic, literary, or scientific tradition (these élite are the top men in the sphere of education, aesthetics, and entertainment who carry the core values and standards of that sphere and serve as models for those working in it); (2) critical standards independent of the consumer of the product are systematically applied to it. The quality of thought or expression of the cultural object and the social milieu in which it is produced define high culture. This definition has the advantage of leaving open questions about the organization and recruitment of cultural élites, the social controls to which they are subject (e.g. pressures from patron, market, or mass), the conditions under which a high quality product – a Shakespearian play, a Mozart symphony – can become popular, the ways in which the product is or is not absorbed into the culture of the consumer.

'Mass culture' will refer to cultural *products manufactured solely for a mass market*. Associated characteristics, not intrinsic to the definition, are *standardization* of product and *mass behaviour* in its use. Mass culture tends to be standardized because it aims to please the average taste of an undifferentiated audience. Common tastes shape mass culture; critical standards sustained by autonomous producing groups shape high culture. Another frequent but not inevitable correlate of mass culture is a high rate of mass behaviour – a uniform and direct response to remote symbols.[8] It is expressed in strong attachment to and dependence on distant public objects and concerns, e.g. acts, thoughts, and feelings regarding the nation (hyperpatriotism and xenophobia), class (Marxian class consciousness), race (racism). The definition leaves open questions about the relation of mass culture to high culture; the conditions under which a product of mass culture can meet the standards of high culture; the degree to which mass culture is fluid or, like folk culture, stable (characterized by little original creation in each generation); whether traditions of expression and performance develop in it; the extent to which the impact of the mass media is mediated by audience standards and the extent to which those very standards are themselves anchored in the media.

In short, these concepts permit sociological analysis of cultural products in the social contexts in which they are created and used. They have the disadvantage of being difficult (but not impossible) to apply in empirical research.

[. . .]

Implications for sociological theory

In applying the larger debate about the shape of modern society to the mass media and mass entertainment in America, I have brought systematic survey data to bear on the problem of the interplay of social structure, mass culture, and high culture. I have tried to resolve the paradox of a simultaneous growth of structural differentiation and cultural uniformity by re-examining the structural roots of media exposure and response. These data point up the need for a merger of the main characterizations of modern society – 'mass', 'industrial' and 'urban.' Specifically, three lessons can be learned.

1. The sketchy treatment of mass culture in theories of the mass society and the very limited idea of the two-step flow of mass communications, which accents the healthy absorption of the media into local cultures, demand more sophisticated treatment of the social structures in which the media are received. My data suggest that we need to slice up social structure in ways that capture both the persistence of older divisions (age, religion, occupation) and the emergence of newer ones (the quality and content of education) and to do it more precisely than usual. To say 'white collar' or 'working class' is to obscure most of what is central to the experience of the person and the structure of society. To say 'professional, technical, and kindred' captures more of social life but not much more. 'Lawyer' and 'engineer' move us closer to social reality, for these men develop quite different styles of life, rooted in diverse professional schools, tasks, work schedules, and organizational contexts. To say 'independent practitioner'

is to say even more, and finally, to particularize the matter with 'solo lawyer' vs 'firm lawyer' is to take account of the sharp contrasts in recruitment base (social origins, religion, quality of professional training), career pattern and rewards which divide the two.

In general, data both here and in other studies suggest that as predictors of life style variables especially cultural tastes and ideology – sex, age, and social-economic stratum are far weaker than religion, type of education, work and career – variables that represent positions in established groups. The implication is clear: return to the study of group life.

2. Television, the most 'massified' of the mass media, the one with the largest and most heterogeneous audience, has become central to the leisure routine of majorities at every level. The usual differences in media exposure and response among age, sex, and class categories – easy to exaggerate in any case – have virtually disappeared in the case of television. Even here, however, where we pinpoint social groups – an occupation supported by an occupational community, a religion buttressed by a religious community – some differences do remain. And among the printed media, where most competition prevails, the chances of such groups to stylize their uses of mass communications remains strong.

3. The paradox of the simultaneous growth of structural differentiation and cultural uniformity is thus partly a matter of our weak concepts and measures of social structure and our consequent failure to spot group-linked variations in life style. But it may also reflect the state of an affluent society in transition. In order to pin down the cultural impact of continued economic growth, we require data not now in hand. For countries at similar levels of economic development, having diverse cultural traditions and systems of education and communications, we need data on levels of mass taste, organization and self-conceptions of cultural élites, distance between educated and less educated in exposure to mass culture and high culture. Until we have such systematic comparisons, I will assume that structure and culture are congruent and massified in rapidly developing new nations and that they become increasingly incongruent at levels of development thus far achieved. Finally, as rich countries grow richer, homogenizing structures in politics, education, and mass communications combine with an already high level of cultural uniformity to reduce the hold of differentiating structures of age, religion, work, and locality, and bring about greater consistency of structure and culture – a new combination of 'mass' society and 'industrial' society, mass culture and high culture.

4. Many leads in my data point to the need for synthesis not only of ideas about industrial society and mass society but also of ideas about pluralism and totalitarianism. I can here merely indicate the direction of these findings. Briefly, what takes place in the economy and the locality – work, consumption, and participation in formal associations – forms coherent styles of life, one of which I have come to label 'Happy Good Citizen-Consumer'. The style includes these pluralist-industrial traits: strong attachment to the community (supporting increased school taxes, contributing generously to churches and charity, thinking of the neighbourhood as one's 'real home', voting in elections); consumer enthusiasm (planning to buy or to replace many luxury possessions); optimism about national crises; a strong belief

that distributive justice prevails (feeling that jobs are distributed fairly). It also involves long hours at gratifying work, little or no leisure malaise; wide-ranging, stable secondary ties and, to some extent, wide ranging, stable primary ties – the very model of a modern pluralist citizen. But this benign pattern of work, consumption, and participation is independent of participation in and feelings about mass culture. And both happy good citizenry and the uses of the mass media are more or less independent of approaches to national politics – or at least go together in ways not anticipated in received theory. Thus, the good citizen-consumers tend to be unusually prone to personality voting (party-switching, ticket splitting), dependent on the media for opinions on issues, susceptible to advertising and to mass behaviour generally (e.g. they score high on a measure of susceptibility to manipulation by the media in politics and consumption). Men who have confidence in the major institutions of American society distrust 'TV and radio networks'; men who trust the media distrust other institutions. Finally, men whose social relations are stable tend to have fluid party loyalties. To be socially integrated in America is to accept propaganda, advertising, and speedy obsolescence in consumption. The fact is that those who fit the image of pluralist man in the pluralist society also fit the image of mass man in the mass society. Any accurate picture of the shape of modern society must accommodate these ambiguities.

Notes

1. De Tocqueville, Alexis (1948) *Democracy in America*, Alfred A. Knopf, New York, 2 vols; Mannheim, Karl (1940) *Man and Society in an Age of Reconstruction*, Routledge & Kegan Paul, London.
2. Cf. William Kornhauser's treatment of 'accessible elites' and 'available masses' in (1959) *The Politics of Mass Society*, The Free Press, Glencoe, Ill.
3. Cooley, Mayo, and their students emphasize the functions of primary groups in the maintenance of social order, and cite reasons for their declining functions and authority. Since the primary group is the training ground for good citizenship, its decline, they felt, would produce mass men who would produce a 'mass society', 'anomie', or 'social disorganization'. Cooley, Charles H. (1927) *Social Organization*, Charles Scribner's Sons, New York; Mayo, Elton (1933) *The Human Problems of an Industrial Civilization*, Harvard University Press, Cambridge, esp. pp. 122 and (1945) *The Social Problems of an Industrial Civilization*, Harvard University Press, Cambridge, Chapters 2 and 5.
4. See Wilensky, Harold L. and Lebeaux, Charles N. (1958) *Industrial Society and Social Welfare*, Russell Sage Foundation, New York, Chapter 5.
5. For an assessment of the evidence on the vitality of social participation see Wilensky, Harold L. (1961) Life cycle, work situation, and participation in formal associations, in Kleemeier, R. W. (ed.) *Aging and Leisure*, Oxford University Press, New York; and Social Structure . . . , op. cit.; for an empirical study of the integrative potential of various types of social relations see Wilensky, Harold L. (1961) Orderly careers and social participation. *American Sociological Review*, Vol. 26, August, pp. 521–39.
6. Cf. Selznick, Philip (1951) Institutional vulnerability in mass society. *American Journal of Sociology*, Vol. 56, January, pp. 320–31; Rosenberg, Bernard and White, David Manning (eds) (1957) *Mass Culture*, The Free Press, Glencoe, Ill; and Kornhauser, op. cit.
7. See for example, Klapper, op. cit.; and Bauer, Raymond, A. and Bauer, Alice H. (1960) America, 'mass society' and mass media. *Journal of Social Issues*, Vol. 16, pp. 3–56.

8. Following Blumer and Wirth, the 'mass' is a collectivity which is big, heterogeneous (dispersed geographically and cross-cutting many groups and sub-cultures), and socially-unstructured (comprised of individuals who do not share norms and values relevant to the situation – individuals who are unattached for a time, not in role, and can therefore behave in a uniform, undifferentiated way). Blumer, Herbert (1946) Elementary collective behavior, in McClung Lee, Alfred (ed.) *New Outline of the Principles of Sociology*, Barnes & Noble, New York, pp. 185; and Wirth, Louis (1938) Urbanism as a way of life. *American Journal of Sociology*, Vol. 44, July, pp. 1–24. On the public, see also Park, Robert E. (1904) Masse und Publikum: Eine Methodologische und Soziologische Untersuchung, Inaugural-dissertation der Hohenphilosophischen Fakultaet der Ruprecht-Karls-Universitaet zu Heidelberg, Lack & Grunau, Bern.

11

The structure and function of communication in society

Harold D. Lasswell

From Bryson, L. (ed.) (1964) *The Communication of Ideas*, Cooper Square Publishers, New York, pp. 37–8.

The act of communication

A convenient way to describe an act of communication is to answer the following questions:

Who
Says What
In Which Channel
To Whom
With What Effect?

The scientific study of the process of communication tends to concentrate upon one or another of these questions. Scholars who study the 'who', the communicator, look into the factors that initiate and guide the act of communication. We call this subdivision of the field of research *control analysis*. Specialists who focus upon the 'says what' engage in *content analysis*. Those who look primarily at the radio, press, film and other channels of communication are doing *media analysis*. When the principal concern is with the persons reached by the media, we speak of *audience analysis*. If the question is the impact upon audiences, the problem is *effect analysis*.[1]

Whether such distinctions are useful depends entirely upon the degree of refinement which is regarded as appropriate to a given scientific and managerial objective. Often it is simpler to combine audience and effect analysis, for instance, than to keep them apart. On the other hand, we may want to concentrate on the analysis of content, and for this purpose subdivide the field into the study of purport and style, the first referring to the message, and the second to the arrangement of the elements of which the message is composed.

Structure and function

Enticing as it is to work out these categories in more detail, the present discussion has a different scope. We are less interested in dividing up the act of communication than in viewing the act as a whole in relation to the entire social process. Any process can be examined in two frames of reference, namely, structure and function; and our analysis of communication will deal with the specializations that carry on certain functions, of which the following may be clearly distinguished: (1) the surveillance of the environment; (2) the correlation of the parts of society in responding to the environment; (3) the transmission of the social heritage from one generation to the next.

Note

1. For more detail, consult the introductory matter in Smith, Bruce L., Lasswell, Harold D. and Casey, Ralph D. (1946) *Propaganda, Communication, and Public Opinion: A Comprehensive Reference Guide*, Princeton University Press, Princeton.

12

Functional analysis and mass communication revisited

Charles R. Wright

From Blumler, J. and Katz, E. (eds) (1974) *The Uses of Mass Communications*. Sage, Beverly Hills, pp. 199–205.

Functions of the total mass communication system

Mass communication *in toto*, or the very existence of mass media, is one kind of standardized social phenomenon whose consequences need to be examined. What difference does it make, especially for a society, to have a mass communication system? Can one design research to answer such a macro-sociological question? I (Wright, 1960, p. 607) concluded pessimistically that one cannot and that functional analysis at this level 'appears currently to be dependent primarily on speculation, and holds little immediate promise for the development of an empirically verifiable theory of mass communication'. I think now that this view was unduly pessimistic because it couched the question unrealistically (for purposes of contemporary research) in terms of all or nothing, that is, the presence or absence of mass media in a society. Recent research and theory have been both more realistic and more promising of obtaining a purchase on this macrosociological issue.

Imagine a society in which all communication was interpersonal. There were no media for mass communication. Everything that its members sought to find out about events in their environment (social and physical), everything they needed in order to discover the socially shared interpretations about these matters and prescriptions for reacting to them, everything about the values, rules and expectations of members of their society, everything that might serve as social lubricant – jokes, stories, songs, etc. - all these things were available only through direct communication between individuals. All communication needs had to be met in this way. One could conduct research to determine the extent to which individuals, or categories of individuals, made use of interpersonal communications to gratify their needs for information, guidance, and entertainment, but there would be no question about the mode of communication employed; everything had to be interpersonal.

Consider now the opposite type of imaginary society, one in which no one could communicate directly with anyone else, but all had access to mass communicated materials. One could conduct research to determine the extent to which individuals, or categories of individuals, made use of mass communication (in general, or various media in particular) to gratify their needs for information, guidance, and entertainment, but there would be no question about the mode of communication employed; everything had to be mass communication.

Societies of the first type (limited to interpersonal communication) are increasingly difficult to imagine, let alone find, except on a small scale of remote villages and exotic places. As national types they hardly exist. Societies of the second type (limited to mass communication) are entirely imaginary. In today's world, most societies have a total communications system that includes both capabilities – interpersonal and mass communication. Three questions of significance emerge: (1) what is the communication mix that characterizes a society? (2) what difference does this make? and (3) what are the conditions (both external and within the media systems) which affect the kinds of social consequences that the media have? Among the significant external conditions are other social institutions in the society (for example, forms of government); internal conditions include the pattern of media ownership and control, degree of centralization, and standardization of media content, among others.[1]

One can argue that the intrusion of any amount of mass communication into a social system creates a qualitative change that results in a society different from one solely dependent upon interpersonal communications. Beyond this, most macrosociological treatments consider variations in the facilities for mass communication. Students of modernization and development, for example, classify societies according to the quantity of various media for mass communication; for example, number of newspapers published, television transmitters in operation, cinema seats, radio transmitters, or in terms of some ratio of such facilities to total population (e.g. radio receivers per 100 persons). The assumption is usually made that increased facilities for mass communication are accompanied by an increase in their usage by more members of the population. This seems reasonable, although it is seldom documented by research.

Attempts to document the social consequences of a heavier or lighter mix of mass communications/personal communications are all too rare. Theorists of modernization argue that the intrusion and expansion of the mass media lead to changes in the members of the society and in social institutions which make both the population and the society more receptive to social change, more 'modern', more 'developed'. The intervening mechanisms and processes by which such changes come about vary from theorist to theorist and include such psychological factors as the development of empathy and such sociological factors as the ability to move ideas, goods, records, and other commercial items about with dispatch. Examples of theoretical and empirical efforts to come to grips with the study of the role of mass communication in social change and especially in social development can be found in the works of Hyman, Levine and Wright (1967), Lerner (1958, 1963), Lerner and Schramm (1967), Pye (1963), Rogers and Svenning (1969), and Schramm (1964). Since an excellent recent summary and analysis of various theories and research on the role of mass communication in social development is presented by Frey (1973), these will not be reviewed here.

One theorist, George Gerbner (1967, 1972), takes the view that mass communication (which he defines as the mass production and distribution of messages) provides the *main* thing that members of the 'audience' share and that, in this sense, mass communication creates its own *public*. Societies lacking in such facilities are also lacking in massive publics. This viewpoint suggests one macrosociological function of mass communication, namely, the creation of new publics.

Not only does mass communication provide a common stream of messages (message system) for its public, but also, in Gerbner's theory, these messages *cultivate* the images of society shared by its public. These message systems provide their audience with an interpretation of the world in terms of what *is*, what is *important*, what is *right*, and what is *related* to what else. In this manner they cultivate the audience's images of reality. This is difficult to prove, but research is now under way at the Annenberg School of Communications under a programme of studies on 'cultural indicators' directed by George Gerbner and Larry Cross. The programme at present consists of two prongs. The first is a continuing monitoring and analysis of the content of various mass media. In particular the project has included a systematic analysis of prime time network television drama. The second prong involves research on the public, aiming at discovering the extent to which their views about social facts correspond more to the televised presentation or more to reality. For example, are heavy viewers of television more likely than light viewers to believe that violent crimes are a common occurrence (an image of the world presented in many television dramas), and are the latter viewers more likely to have an image that corresponds more with the actual incidence of violent crimes as reflected in official statistics? To the extent that heavy viewers of television give answers more characteristic of the world as portrayed by biased television content than by life, the inference is made that their world view has been cultivated by the media. Cultivation, then, is a function of mass communication. One social consequence of these mass communicated latent messages could be the creation of widespread 'cultural false consciousness' (Gross, 1974).

An ingenious and illuminating series of studies of the sometimes subtle consequences of mass communication, especially television, on the political process has been conducted during the past two decades by Kurt Lang and Gladys Engel Lang. In their view (Lang and Lang, 1969, p. 19), 'the mass media structure issues and personalities. They do this gradually and over a period of time, and thus this impact seems less spectacular than the shift or crystallization of a particular vote decision'. They consider, among other social effects, the ways that public events, especially political, are structured and influenced by the presence of mass media, and the ways in which mass communication helps to shape the image of public events for individuals, with related social consequences for the political process. Although the focus is on television and politics, their research has broader implications for the functional analysis of mass communication in general; it demonstrates that such studies can be made through imaginative research designs exploiting contemporary social events covered by the mass media.[2]

Modes of mass communication

A second type of functional analysis considered in the earlier essay dealt with each particular method of mass communication (e.g. newspapers, television) as a subject for analysis. The basic research question posed was what functions (and dysfunctions) can be attributed to each medium and how can these be isolated through research. One research strategy suggested was to conduct studies in societies in which a particular medium is absent or when the normal operation of a medium is disturbed, for example, by a strike, providing one can account for the influence of other factors in the situation.

This research strategy still seems promising to me, although in practice it appears to have been more beneficial in illuminating the functions of particular media for individuals than for the social system. Kimball (1963), for example, conducted an instructive longitudinal study of the impact of a prolonged newspaper shutdown on the residents of New York City. This study was especially informative about the alternative modes of communication which people turned to for substitutes for the missing newspapers as the shutdown continued over time. It became clear that for many individuals these alternative modes were not functional equivalents for newspaper reading. The study also demonstrates the value of a research design that allows one to trace a changing awareness of functions over time. (But it was not designed to provide data on the impact of the press on the society and its social institutions.) Research opportunities need not await the total disappearance of a particular medium. Lyle (1962), for example, studied the impact of a double newspaper merger, which greatly reduced the number of daily newspapers available to residents of the Los Angeles metropolitan area. And Steiner (1963) provides some interesting qualitative data on what people did when their television set was broken, reactions which gave indirect clues as to the possible functions that television was having when in operation. Other research opportunities come to mind: the closing of a neighbourhood movie house; the termination of a major mass magazine such as *Life*; a near breakdown in a total communications system such as during a natural crisis.[3] These are, admittedly, atypical situations, but that is precisely why they are potentially useful as research sites. The purpose of such research is not to study the impact of the crisis *per se* (or other change in the communication facilities), but rather to use this moment of increased sensitivity to the missing (or changed) medium in order to cull clues as to the functions that it normally performs.

An alternative strategy is to search for occasions in which a new medium of communication is being introduced into a society, or in which an older medium is being augmented in scope or is reaching new segments of the society. Examples of studies of what happens when television is introduced into a community are found in the work of Campbell (1962), Himmelweit, Oppenheim and Vince (1958), and Schramm, Lyle and Parker (1961). The major emphasis in these studies is on the consequences of television for the individual, but some consideration is given to the larger social implications. The introduction of cable television, especially insofar as it provides for new local channel programme origination, should provide research opportunities for the study of its functions for both the individual and the community. An example of a new mode (if not medium) of communication for some people is brought about through the development of literacy. An example is a recent study by Heli de Sagasti (1972).

De Sagasti explored the social implications of newly acquired adult literacy in the context of an 'underdeveloped' society. Intensive interviews were conducted with adult women, migrants working as domestic servants in Lima, Peru, who had recently learned to read. Prior expectation, based upon prevailing theories about the impact of literacy upon members of developing societies, was that literacy would open the world horizons for these individuals, enhance their interest in and exposure to national and international issues, and expand their uses of the mass media. Change their lives it did; but not exactly in the ways anticipated.

De Sagasti (1972, p. 2) found that the major impact of newly acquired literacy was upon the private and social skills of the individual. 'Newly developed adult literacy facilitates interpersonal communication, both spoken and written; this constitutes a dominant advantage of literacy for the respondents'. As literate persons, the respondents now could enjoy the privacy of reading and writing letters; the advantage of greater ease in physical mobility through their ability to read signs and directions; less vulnerability in commercial transactions through their ability to read shopping lists, bills and other documents; and a new ease and facility in conversation with others. Their use of the mass media was changed only slightly, except for reading photonovellas for relaxation, occasional newspapers, and religious materials.

> The newly literate adults' print reading is limited in range and amount. The reading that is done is used in terms of particular needs, and especially the respondents' position as migrants in a very different new environment. . . . There is little evidence of literacy increasing broadcast media use [p. 3].

Other consequences of literacy for the individual are explored as revealed in case accounts by the women themselves.

Furthermore, de Sagasti proceeds to examine the possible implications of new adult literacy for the society. She notes that new adult literacy has a 'multiplying effect' as skills of reading and writing are shared with illiterates and as new literates attempt to influence illiterates to learn to read. Literacy appears to have a clear, if modest, impact on occupational role performance and on new occupational goals. It has a greater impact on the new literate's educational and occupational aspirations for her children. And it has implications for the development of personal characteristics that may allow the migrant to better adapt to and function within her new urban environment. New literacy is associated with a desire to remain in the city rather than to return to the rural homeland, thereby potentially affecting patterns of residential mobility and stability in the society. And new literacy leads to the desire and determination to have one's children more fully participate in the opportunities of the new urban society. Thus, this study touches upon both the individual and social consequences of acquiring a new mode of communication, one customarily associated with exposure to the mass media. It illustrates the feasibility and benefits of future functional research conducted on such strategic populations undergoing changes in major modes of communication.

Institutional analysis

A third application of the functional approach suggested in 1960 was in the institutional analysis of mass media and communication organizations, 'examining the function of some repeated and patterned operation within that organization' (Wright, 1960, p. 608). Case studies, comparative analyses of differently organized media, and experiments were suggested as promising research strategies. During the past 15 years there has been a rise in the attention given to sociological analyses of mass communication organizations and institutions. Examples can be found in Halmos (1969), Tunstall (1970), and Wright (forthcoming). Several of these studies adopt a functional perspective. Space constrains us to one illustration here, and we chose one that addresses the topic at a broad level – television as a social institution.

An implicitly functional approach to the analysis of certain features of television as a social institution is provided by Katz (1973) in his article 'Television as a horseless carriage'. Katz sets as his task an analysis of the problems faced in the introduction of television (especially in small and developing nations) and sees them, in part at least, as consequences of the uncritical transplantation of certain professional norms or conventions from radio broadcasting. Specifically, he considers three such professional norms (1973, p. 382): '(1) the goal of non-stop broadcasting; (2) the orientation toward an everybody audience; and (3) the striving for up-to-the-minute news'. The norm of non-stop broadcasting is seen as having the dysfunction of making television trivial, through the exhaustion of talent and through resorting to repetitive formula dramatic series, with the further effect of leading viewers to use television more as a background for other activities than as a significant cultural experience deserving the viewer's full attention. The norm of striving for large heterogeneous audiences – of all ages and social classes – has the dysfunction of failing to meet the needs of minority audiences. And the norm for up-to-the-minute news prevents the development of in-depth 'newsmagazine' treatments by television. Katz then proceeds to speculate on the consequences of these norms, inherited from radio, for television broadcasting in new nations. His central thesis is, to summarize, that (1973, p. 391)

> certain professional views – certain conventions – about the nature of television seem to me dysfunctional from the point of view of the inherent nature of the medium, and its essential, or at least potential, difference from radio. They are certainly dysfunctional from the point of view of the potential role of television in nation-building and in the stimulation of indigenous cultural expression and creativity.

Admittedly theoretical rather than empirical, Katz's presentation nonetheless illustrates the kinds of questions raised by a functional analysis of institutionalized practices in the mass media.

Examples of the consequences of other institutionalized practices in mass communication can be found in the work of Cantor (1971) on Hollywood television producers, Elliot (1972) on a television series production, Faulkner (1971) on hiring practices among Hollywood musicians, and Tuchman (1972, 1973a) on conventions of objectivity in news making and reporting through newspapers and television.

Functional analysis of basic communication activities

The fourth level of functional analysis advocated in the earlier essay is rather abstract but crucial for the development of a functional theory of mass communication. The central arguments in its formulation are, in briefest summary, as follows: mass communication, as institutionalized in modern societies, constitutes a social phenomenon qualitatively and quantitatively different from personalized communication. The several kinds of communication activities in which people engage (and four were identified at that time – surveillance of the environment or news activity, interpretation of the events surveyed and prescriptions for reactions to them, the transmission of social values and other elements of culture to new members of the society, young or old, and human amusement or entertainment) could be, and are, carried out both by means of mass communications and by other more personalized forms. The critical questions for research centre on what are the consequences (manifest and latent) of carrying out these communications activities by means of mass communication; consequences for individuals, groups of individuals, societies, and culture.

An important distinction, sometimes blurred in subsequent reviews, is between functions and communication activities. Our working quartet of communications – surveillance, correlation, cultural transmission, and entertainment – was intended to refer to common kinds of activities which might or might not be carried out as mass communications or as private, personal communications. These activities were not synonyms for functions, which, as noted, refer to the consequences of routinely carrying out such communication activities through the institutionalized process of mass communications.

Notes

1. A functional perspective also reminds us of the need for research on the consequences which other social institutions have for mass communication. What, for example, are the functional requirements for the existence and operation of mass communication in a society? We need to consider not only the material resources and technology necessary for mass communication but also the social, economic, political, and other organizational arrangements required. And we need studies of the effects of changes in social, governmental, economic, and other institutional areas upon the nature and operations of the communication system. These problems, however, cannot be explored in the current essay.
2. For a recent study of television and politics that combines a concern about the political consequences of mass communication with a consideration for the gratifications of the audience see Blumler and McQuail (1969).
3. Clues to the functions normally performed by mass communication also may come through research during moments of social crisis in which the media are fully operative but the public is sensitized to their importance because of the crisis. Examples of such social crises are political assassinations, urban riots, commodity shortages, and episodes of a suspected 'killer at large' in a community.

References

Campbell, W. J. (1962) *Television and the Australian Adolescent*, Angus & Robertson, Sydney.

Cantor, M. G. (1971) *The Hollywood TV Producer*, Basic Books, New York.
De Sagasti, H. (1972) Social implications of adult literacy: a study among migrant women in Peru. Ph.D. dissertation, University of Pennsylvania (unpublished).
Elliot, P. (1972) *The Making of a Television Series*, Constable, London.
Faulkner, R. (1971) *Hollywood Studio Musicians*, Aldine-Atberton, Chicago.
Frey, F. (1973) Communication and development. In Pool, I. *et al.* (eds) *Handbook of Communication*, Rand-McNally, Chicago.
Gerbner, G. (1972) Communication and social environment. *Scientific American*, Vol. 227, pp. 153–60.
Gerbner, G. (1967) An institutional approach to mass communications research. In Thayer, L. (ed.) *Communication Theory and Research*, Charles C. Thomas, Springfield, Ill.
Gross, L. (1974) The 'real' world of television. *Today's Education*, January, pp. 86–92.
Halmos, P. (ed.) (1969) The sociology of mass-media communicators. *Sociological Review Monograph*, Vol. 13.
Himmelweit, H., Oppenheim, A. M. and Vince, P. (1958) *Television and the Child*, Oxford University Press, London.
Hyman, H., Levine, G. and Wright, C. R. (1967) *Inducing Social Change in Developing Communities*, United Nations, Paris.
Katz, E. (1973) Television as a horseless carriage. In Gerbner, C. *et al.* (eds) *Communications Technology and Social Policy*, John Wiley, New York.
Kimball, P. (1963) New York readers in a newspaper shutdown. *Columbia Journalism Review*, Fall, pp. 47–56.
Lang, K. and Lang, G. E (1969) *Television and Politics*, Quadrangle Books, Chicago.
Lerner, D. (1963) Toward a communication theory of modernization. In Pye, L. (ed.) *Communications and Political Development*, Princeton University Press, Princeton.
Lerner, D. (1958) *The Passing of Traditional Society*, Free Press, Glencoe.
Lerner, D. and Schramm, W. (eds) (1967) Communication and change in the developing countries, East-West Center Press, Honolulu.
Lyle, J. (1962) *Audience impact of a double newspaper merger. Journalism Quarterly*, Spring, pp. 145–57.
Pye, L. (ed.) (1963) *Communications and Political Development*, Princeton University Press, Princeton.
Rogers, E. and Svenning, L. (1969) *Modernization Among Peasants*, Holt Rinehart & Winston, New York.
Schramm, W. (1964) *Mass Media and National Development*, Stanford University Press, Stanford.
Schramm, W., Lyle, J. and Parker, E. (1961) *Television in the Lives of our Children*, Stanford University Press, Stanford.
Steiner, C. (1963) *The People Look at Television*, Knopf, New York.
Tuchman, G. (1973a) Making news by doing work. *American Journal of Sociology*, Vol. 79, pp. 110–31.
Tuchman, G. (1973b) The technology of objectivity: doing objective TV news films. *Urban Life and Culture*, Vol. 2, April, pp. 3–26.
Tuchman, G. (1972) Objectivity as strategic ritual: an examination of newsmen's notions of objectivity. *American Journal of Sociology*, Vol. 77, pp. 660–79.
Tunstall, J (ed.) (1970) *Media Sociology*, University of Illinois Press, Urbana.
Wright, C. R. (forthcoming) *Mass Communication: A Sociological Perspective*, revised and enlarged edition, Random House, New York.
Wright, C. R. (1960) Functional analysis and mass communications. *Public Opinion Quarterly*, Vol. 24, pp. 605–20.

13

The study of the media: theoretical approaches

James Curran, Michael Gurevitch and Janet Woollacott

From Gurevitch, M. *et al.* (eds) (1982) *Culture, Society and the Media*, Methuen, London, pp. 12–16.

A reassessment of the impact of the mass media during the late 1940s, 1950s and 1960s gave rise to a new academic orthodoxy – that the mass media have only a very limited influence. This view was succinctly stated by Klapper (1960) in a classic summary of more than a decade's empirical research. 'Mass communications', he concludes, 'ordinarily do not serve as a necessary and sufficient cause of audience effects' (p. 8). Underlying this new orthodoxy, was a reassessment of man's susceptibility to influence. A succession of empirical enquiries, using experimental laboratory and social survey techniques, demonstrated that people tended to expose themselves to, understand and remember communications selectively, according to prior dispositions. People, it was argued, manipulated – rather than were manipulated by – the mass media. The empirical demonstration of selective audience behaviour was further reinforced by a number of uses and gratifications studies which argued that audience members are active rather than passive and bring to the media a variety of different needs and uses that influence their response to the media.

Underpinning this reassuring conclusion about the lack of media influence was a repudiation of the mass society thesis on which the presumption of media power had been based. The view of society as being composed of isolated and anomic individuals gave way to a view of society as a honeycomb of small groups bound by a rich web of personal ties and dependences. Stable group pressures, it was concluded, helped to shield the individual from media influence. This stress on the salience of small groups as a buffer against media influence was often linked to a diffusionist model of power. In particular it was stressed by a number of leading empirical researchers that the social mediation of media messages was not a hierarchical process. 'Some individuals of high social status apparently wield little independent influence', wrote Katz and Lazarsfeld (1955), 'and some of low status have considerable personal influence'. Wealth and power, it seemed, did not shape public opinion in the leading Western democracy.

Even the image of man as a natural prey to suggestion and influence was challenged by a number of persuasive theories of personality formation that apparently explained selective audience behaviour. In particular cognitive dissonance theory, which postulated that people seek to minimize the psychological discomfort of having incompatible values and beliefs, seemed to explain people's deliberate avoidance and unconscious decoding of uncongenial media messages.

In short, the conventional belief in the power of the media seemed to be demolished. A popular view based on flimsy anecdotal evidence had been confounded by systematic empirical enquiry. Even the assumptions about the nature of man and the structure of society on which the belief in media power had rested, had been 'revealed' as bankrupt and misguided.

During the late 1960s and the 1970s, the new orthodoxy was challenged from two quite different, indeed opposed, directions. Those working within the empirical effects tradition initiated what Jay Blumler has called the 'new look' in mass communications research. This has consisted partly of looking again at the small print of the pioneering studies into media effects obscured by the often polemically worded dismissals of media influence that are regularly cited in summary overviews of the literature. For although leading researchers like Katz, Lazarsfeld and Klapper reacted strongly against the conventional view of the omnipotent media in sometimes extravagantly worded generalizations, they were careful to qualify what they said by allowing a number of cases when the media may be or has been persuasive: when audience attention is casual, when information rather than attitude or opinion is involved, when the media source is prestigious, trusted or liked, when monopoly conditions are more complete, when the issue at stake is remote from the receiver's experience or concern, when personal contacts are not opposed to the direction of the message or when the recipient of the message is cross-pressured. More recently a number of scholars have also re-examined the empirical data presented in the early classic 'effects' studies and argued that they do not fully support the negative conclusions about media influence that were derived from them (Becker, McCombs and McLeod, 1975; Gitlin, 1978). Furthermore, it has been argued, social changes such as the decline of stable political allegiances and the development of a new mass medium in television require the conclusions derived from older empirical studies to be reassessed.

The limited model of media influence was also attacked by scholars in the Marxist and neo-Marxist critical tradition that became a growing influence on mass communication research during the 1970s. The initial response of many Marxist and critical writers was to dismiss out-of-hand empirical communications research as being uniformly uninteresting. The media, they argued, were ideological agencies that played a central role in maintaining class domination: research studies that denied media influence were so disabled in their theoretical approach as to be scarcely worth confronting (or indeed, even reading).

Some empirical researchers responded with evident exasperation to this sweeping dismissal by arguing that disciplined, rigorous empirical research had revealed the inadequacy of unsubstantiated theorizing about the mass media (e.g. Blumler, 1977). Indeed, a casual reader of exchanges between these two traditions might be forgiven for thinking that a new engagement had developed in which a view of the mass media as having only limited influence, grounded in empirical research within a liberal tradition, was pitted against an alternative conception of the mass media as powerful agencies, informed by an exclusively theoretical Marxist/critical perspective.

But while the two research traditions are, in some ways, fundamentally and irreconcilably opposed, they are not divided primarily by the differences highlighted in this debate. In fact, the classical empirical studies did not demonstrate that the mass media had very little influence: on the contrary, they revealed the central role of the media in consolidating and fortifying the values and attitudes of audience members. This tended to be presented in a negative way only because the preceding orthodoxy they were attacking had defined the influence of omnipotent media in terms of changing attitudes and beliefs. The absence of media conversion consequently tended to be equated with the absence of influence.

Ironically, Marxist and critical commentators have also argued that the mass media play a strategic role in reinforcing dominant social norms and values that legitimize the social system. There is thus no inconsistency, at an empirical level, in the two approaches. Indeed, as Marcuse has suggested, 'the objection that we overrate greatly the indoctrinating power of the "media" . . . misses the point. The preconditioning does not start with the mass production of radio and television and the centralization of their control. The people entered this stage as preconditioned receptacles of long standing . . .' (Marcuse, 1972). He could have added with justification, that a generation of empirical research from a different tradition had provided corroboration of the reinforcement 'effect' he was attributing to the media.

Differences between the pluralist and critical schools about the power of the mass media, at the level of effectiveness, are to a certain extent based on mutual misunderstanding (notably, an over-literal acceptance by some Marxist commentators of polemical generalizations about the lack of media influence advanced by some empirical researchers). This misunderstanding has been perpetuated by the tendency for researchers in the two different traditions to examine the impact of the mass media in different contexts as a consequence of their divergent ideological and theoretical preoccupations.

Consider, for instance, the vexed issue of media portrayals of violence. Most researchers in the Marxist tradition in Britain have approached this question in terms of whether media portrayals of violence have served to legitimize the forces of law and order, build consent for the extension of coercive state regulation and de-legitimize outsiders and dissidents (Hall, 1974; Cohen, 1973; Murdock, 1973; Chibnall, 1977; Whannel, 1979). They have thus examined the impact of the mass media in situations where mediated communications are powerfully supported by other institutions such as the police, judiciary and schools, and sustained by already widely diffused attitudes favourable towards law enforcement agencies and generally unfavourable towards groups like youth gangs, student radicals, trade union militants and football hooligans. The power of the media is thus portrayed as that of renewing, amplifying and extending the existing predispositions that constitute the dominant culture, not in creating them. In contrast, empirical researchers in the liberal tradition have tended to examine media portrayals of violence in terms of whether they promote and encourage violence in everyday life. They have consequently defined the potential influence of these portrayals of violence in a form that is opposed to deeply engrained moral norms supported and maintained by a network of social relationships and powerful institutions actively opposed to 'anti social behaviour'. That a 'limited effects' model of media influence emerged from such studies should come as no surprise: it was inherent in the way in which media influence was defined in the first place.

The same pattern of difference can be illustrated in relation to the question of voting. Some Marxist commentators have contended that media portrayals of elections constitute dramatized rituals that legitimize the power structure in liberal democracies; voting is seen as an ideological practice that helps to sustain the myth of representative democracy, political equality and collective self-determination. The impact of election coverage is thus conceived in terms of reinforcing political values that are widely shared in Western democracies and are actively endorsed by the education system, the principal political organizations and the apparatus of the state. In contrast, pioneering studies into the effects of the media on voting behaviour by Lazarsfeld *et al.* (1948), Berelson *et al.* (1954) and Trenaman and McQuail (1961) concluded that the media had only marginal influence in changing the way in which people voted. Their negative conclusions were based on an analysis of media influence in a form that was strongly opposed by powerful group norms, at a time when partisan allegiances were stable. Significantly, their conclusions have been modified as these contingent influences have weakened.

The alleged dichotomy between the 'grand-theoretical' and 'atheoretical' approaches to media study represented by the two opposed traditions of Marxism and liberalism is also a little misleading. The liberal tradition in mass communications research has been characterized by a greater attention to empirical investigation. But it does not constitute an 'atheoretical' approach: on the contrary, empirical communications research is based upon theoretical models of society even if these are often unexamined and unstated.

Indeed, the conventional characterization of liberal and Marxist traditions in mass communications research as constituting two opposed schools tends to obscure both the internal differences within each of these traditions and the reciprocal influence which each has exerted upon the other. The shift from a perception of the media as a stupefying, totally subduing force expressed, for example, by Marcuse (1972), to a more cautious assessment in which dominant meaning systems are moulded and relayed by the media, are adapted by audiences and integrated into class-based or 'situated' meaning systems articulated by McCron (1976), is characteristic of a significant shift within Marxist research that has been influenced, in part at least, by empirical communications studies. This has been accompanied by increasing interest within the Marxist tradition in empirical survey-based research into audience adaptation of media-relayed ideologies, exemplified recently for instance by Hartman (1979) and Morley (1980). At the same time, Marxist critiques have contributed to a growing recognition within empirical communications research that more attention needs to be paid to the influence of the media on the ideological categories and frames of reference through which people understand the world. Evolving from the relatively limited conception of media 'agenda-setting' (the ranking of issues, in terms of their perceived importance) in election studies, a new interest has developed in the wider 'cognitive effects' of the media that reflects a nearly universal dissatisfaction amongst researchers with the narrow conceptualization of media influence afforded by the classic effects studies.

References

Becker, L., McCombs, M. and McLeod, J. (1975) The development of political cognitions. In Chaffee, S. (ed.) *Political Communication: Issues and Strategies for Research*, Sage, Beverley Hills.

Berelson, B., Lazarsfeld, P. and McPhee, W. (1954) *Voting: A Study of Opinion Formation in a Presidential Campaign*, University of Chicago Press, Chicago.

Blumler, J. (1977) The political effects of mass communication. In DE 353, *Mass Communication and Society*, Open University Press, Milton Keynes.

Chibnall, S. (1977) *Law-and-Order News*, Tavistock, London.

Cohen, S. (1973) *Folk Devils and Moral Panics*, Paladin, St Albans.

Gitlin, T. (1978) Media sociology: the dominant paradigm. *Theory and Society*, Vol. 6.

Hall, S. (1974) Deviance, politics and the media. In McIntosh, M. and Rock, P. (eds) *Deviance and Social Control*, Tavistock, London.

Hartman, P. (1979) News and public perceptions of industrial relations. *Media Culture and Society*, Vol. 1, No. 3.

Katz, E. and Lazarsfeld, P. (1955) *Personal Influence*, Free Press, Glencoe.

Klapper, J. (1960) *The Effects of Mass Communication*, Free Press, Glencoe.

Lazarsfeld, P., Berelson, B. and Gaudet, H. (1948) *The People's Choice*, Columbia University Press, New York.

McCron, R. (1976) Changing perspectives in the study of mass media and socialisation. In Halloran, J. (ed.) *Mass Media and Socialisation*, International Association for Mass Communication Research.

Marcuse, H. (1972) *One-dimensional Man*, Abacus, London.

Morley, D. (1980) *The 'Nationwide' Audience: Structure and Decoding*, British Film Institute, London.

Murdock, G. (1973) Political deviance: the press presentation of a militant mass demonstration. In Cohen, S. and Young, J. (eds) *The Manufacture of News*, Constable, London.

Trenaman, J. and McQuail, D. (1961) *Television and the Political Image*, Methuen, London.

Whannel, G. (1979) Football, crowd behaviour and the press. *Media, Culture and Society*, Vol. 1, No. 4.

14

Politicians and the press: an essay on role relationships

Jay G. Blumler and Michael Gurevitch

From Nimmo, D. and Sanders, K. (eds) (1981) *Handbook of Political Communication*, Sage, Beverly Hills, pp. 476–85.

An expanded framework

The production of political communications is inherently complex. When approached unilaterally, essential features tend to be distorted or ignored. Both in order to overcome the resulting theoretical problems and to structure empirical data derived from many observations of political communicators at work in Britain (Blumler, 1969, 1979; Blumler, Gurevitch, and Ives, 1978), we have developed an alternative analytical framework couched in the following summary terms: media-disseminated political communications derive from interactions between (1) two sets of mutually dependent and mutually adaptive actors pursuing divergent (though overlapping) purposes, whose relationships with each other are typically (2) role-regulated, giving rise to (3) an emergent shared culture, specifying how they should behave toward each other, the ground rules of which are (4) open to contention and conflicting interpretation, entailing a potential for disruption, which is often (5) controlled by informal and/or formal mechanisms of conflict management. The following sections outline some implications of each of these elements in turn.

Dependence and adaptation

Political communication originates in mutual dependence within a framework of divergent though overlapping purposes. Each side of the politician–media professional partnership is striving to realize certain goals *vis-à-vis* the audience; yet it cannot pursue them without securing in some form the cooperation of the other side. Sometimes they share certain goals – for example, addressing, and sustaining credibility with, a large audience. As Fant (1980) pointed out, in televizing American presidential nominating conventions, 'the networks and the parties have a common desire to attract as many television viewers as possible'. Usually the actors' purposes are in some tension as well: journalists are primarily aiming to hold the attention of a target audience through some mixture of alerting, informing, and entertaining them. Politicians are primarily trying to persuade audience members to adopt a certain view of themselves, or of their parties or factions, and of what they are trying to achieve in politics.

Whatever the exact mixture of goals, each side needs the other and must adapt its ways to theirs. Politicians need access to the communication channels that are controlled by the mass media, including the hopefully credible contexts of audience reception they offer. Consequently, they must adapt their messages to the demands of formats and genres devised inside such organizations and to their associated speech styles, story models, and audience images. As a verbal example of such adaptation, it is striking to note that it was a British politician, dedicated to his party's social reform programme (and not a TV newsman), who told us (Blumler *et al.*, 1978):

> Voters formulate their impressions in rather vague terms and the most they can take in is some sort of a nutshell, namely something that some leader has said or done that he has seen on TV. That is about as much as they can take and about as much as they will get. Some of them will even be sick of that. They will be getting much more than they really want. That is because the ordinary person isn't really interested in politics. . . . The ordinary person comes home tired out from work, and all he wants to do is to put his feet up and watch the telly. He has done his stint of hard work from 9 to 6, and after that he wants to forget about the world's problems and does not want to have to exercise his mind.

Likewise, journalists cannot perform their task of political scrutiny without access to politicians for information, news, interviews, action, and comment: 'To be convincing purveyors of reality . . . journalists must get as close as they can to the sources of events' (Polsby, 1980). And as a verbal example of the resulting adaptation, it is striking to note that it was a British broadcasting executive, firmly devoted to the independence of his organization (and not a politician), who extolled the virtues of the party handout to us (Blumler *et al.*, 1978) in these terms:

> There is no great merit in taking a subject, talking to it and then letting some sub-editor get it down to the essentials for you, rather than doing that job yourself. If we were a newspaper with endless columns of print, he might not have to bother. In the case of broadcasting, however, a man who can prepare this kind of comment pithily and concretely will get the coverage he is seeking.

Thus, each side to the prospective transaction is in a position to offer the other access to a resource it values. The mass media offer politicians access to an audience through a credible outlet, while politicians offer journalists information about a theatre of presumed relevance, significance, impact, and spectacle for audience consumption. Because such resources are finite, however, rivals inside each camp compete more or less keenly for them, further strengthening the pressures promoting a mutual adaptation. The scope and terms of politicians' access to the media depend not only on conventional limitations of time and space (a 30-minute news bulletin; a 10-minute interview) but also on the 'threshold of tolerance' a given organ's audience is assumed to exhibit toward political messages. So in competing for favourable attention in the preferred 'slots', politicians adjust to perceived media values and requirements, a process that is illustrated by British campaigners' conviction that at election time 'the essential requirement . . . was to keep the news initiative from one's rivals' by fashioning more catchy 'golden phrases' for newsmen to headline and circulate (Blumler *et al.*, 1978).

But politicians also command scarce resources. Not only is the amount of informational raw material they can supply limited; it may also vary in quality – for example, a strong leak on a headline development is worth more than a speculative rumour about a more technical issue from a lower-placed source. Politicians are therefore in a position, especially when newsworthy, to 'ration the goodies', use them as bargaining counters, and direct reporters' attention to their pet themes. 'Pack journalism', which stems from a subtle mixture of (1) uncertainty about what really counts as political news and (2) anxiety not to miss something the competition will be carrying, intensifies the ensuing adaptations. As Polsby (1980) pointed out:

> Nobody who intends to supply the masses with their daily ration of news can afford to be out on a limb too often, peddling what may come to be viewed as an idiosyncratic version of reality. . . . Competitiveness thus entails snuggling up to news sources.

Of course, many of these factors operate as variables, not constants. Politicians vary in their need for media publicity. Local radio station managers, interviewed in Britain about the broadcasting of Parliament, for example, often equated MPs' efforts to get their debate contributions heard by listeners with the narrowness of their majorities over opponents at the previous general election. Similarly, journalists will be more anxious to cover certain politicians and events than others. As recent American studies have suggested (Ostroff, 1980; Clarke and Evans, 1980), the pressure on them to follow the top politicians and uncritically pass on their initiatives is greater in presidential campaigns than in state-level races. But despite such sources of variation, the forces of mutual dependence, competition, and adaptation will tend most formatively to shape political communication about precisely those personalities and situations that receive the heaviest and most regular coverage in political news.

Role relationships

The recurrent interactions that result in political communication for public consumption are negotiated, not by unsocialized individuals, but by individuals-in-roles – whose working relationships are consequently affected by normative and institutional commitments. In Chittick's (1970) definition:

> The term 'role' refers . . . to the socially prescribed behavior of a position holder.
> . . . Role theory posits that position holders will behave in accordance with both their own role expectations and those of counter position holders.

What theoretical advantages flow from treating political communicators as occupants of roles, the terms of which guide their own behaviour and shape their relationships with and expectations of their counterparts in the message production process? These may be outlined from three perspectives.

First, such an approach explains the behaviour of political communicators by locating them in their respective organizational settings, where their roles are chiefly defined and performed. In the case of political journalists, role-anchored guidelines serve many functions. They provide models of conduct to be observed when contacting politicians or appearing before the public as 'representatives' of their organizations, whose standards they are supposed to display (Kumar, 1975). They steer activity in countless daily routines. In an observation study of BBC current affairs producers at work during the British general election of 1966, for example, certain initiatives taken to improve their campaign coverage were traced to 'the internal role-definitions of their positions to which television journalists subscribe', including responsibilities 'to serve the audience adequately' and 'to the standards of their own profession' (Blumler, 1969). They are a source of support when conflict erupts. When, during the British general election of 1979, a BBC news executive dealt with various party complaints about unfairness, for example, he was observed to handle them confidently partly because he was an institutional figure. He could draw on corporation policy, professional standards, and past precedents both to justify what had been done and to suggest solutions to difficulties. So long as he was true to his role, he was protected. Professional roles may also dictate journalists' reactions to proposed innovations. Changes which are interpreted as enhancing or extending their established roles (such as the broadcasting of Parliament) will tend to be welcomed. Those which are perceived as challenging or denying their roles [such as the Blumler *et al.* (1978) recommendation that election reporting in daily news bulletins be drastically reduced] will tend to be rejected.

In contrast to professional journalists, many practising politicians are only part-time communicators. Even so, their media arrangements are often tended by full-time specialists with corresponding roles to match – press officers, publicity aides, campaign managers, speech writers, and so on. And when functioning as communicators, politicians also act out certain role prescriptions themselves: 'representing' the interests of a party, government, or department of state; responding to the expectations of political colleagues, with whom their reputations can be strengthened or weakened by the quality of their public appearances; and addressing the electoral audience in a certain style. In fact, there may often be a close connection between a politician's public image and his internal communication-role definition. Certainly impressions of politicians' qualities as communicators have become increasingly important features of their public images in recent years – and so, presumably, of their internalized communication roles as well.

Second, a focus on roles as shapers and regulators of behaviour also connects the interactions of media professionals and partisan advocates to the surrounding sociopolitical culture of the society concerned. This helps to explain their patterned continuity over time and their variety across diverse societies. A noteworthy example recently came to light in the formation of broadcasting policy for coverage of the 1979 elections to the European Parliament in the nine member states of the European Community. A team of comparative investigators of the role of broadcasting in those elections concluded: 'In most countries the point of departure for organizing how television would present the campaign to viewers was a set of past principles, conventions, programme formats and practices of *general election* coverage' (Blumler[1]). In each political communication system, cultural influences ensured that politicians' and broadcasters' European election roles would correspond closely to previously formed national election patterns. *In toto* they therefore amounted to nine more or less distinct campaigns instead of a single uniform one. In other words, mass media structures, their organizational and professional ideologies, and their specific work practices are in every society specific to and shaped by its culture. Likewise, the structure and operations of the political institutions of society are products of the same cultural forces. It is not surprising, therefore, that a high degree of fit should be found between those institutions, which is reflected, at the interface between media and political institutions, in a fit between the role-regulated behaviours of the interacting communicators.

Several general features of such interaction are underlined by the considerations spelled out above. For one thing, communication behaviour is *normatively prescribed* involving *legitimated* expectations and actions. This suggests that the capacity of the participants to exchange resources or exercise influence is constrained by the guidelines pertaining to the roles they perform. Thus, political reporters cannot, without great risk, offer politicians any type of news treatment that lies outside the authority of their roles. Likewise, politicians will tend to avoid behaviour *vis-à-vis* media personnel (such as blatant favours or explicit sanctions) that would be construed to breach their role prescriptions. Exchange and the tussles of mutual influence are normatively bounded. In addition, behaviour on both sides is conditioned by expectations of how each will, because they should, behave toward the other. This has important consequences for the structure of the interaction. It underlies and explains the predictability of the behaviour patterns involved and the ability of each side to count on much that the other will do so long as its expectations are met. It also helps to explain the note of outrage that is sometimes sounded during adversarial episodes – reflecting the injured party's conviction, not merely that its interests were damaged, but that supposedly accepted moral boundaries had been over-stepped. And it explains the relative stability of structure of those many joint activities out of which political communication daily emerges.

Third, a reference to role conceptualization clarifies the partial plausibility of the adversary and exchange models and helps to reconcile their apparent opposition. On the one hand, exchange mechanisms are set in motion when performance of role obligations on either side requires the enlisting of cooperation from the other. On the other hand, adversarial relations are triggered when the role obligations of the two sides are such as to bring them into collision course with each other.

An emergent shared culture

Many British television journalists and party publicists, when interviewed by the authors afterwards about their roles in the country's general elections of February and October 1974, often emphasized the need for *mutual trust* in their relations with each other. A party press officer said: 'If I gave the media a bum steer over the significance of a speech about to be made by my leader, they would no longer take my guidance so seriously in the future'. Another concluded a lengthy account of campaign exchanges by baldly asserting: 'Both sides are operating on the basis of news values'. Broadcasters also mentioned special efforts they had made to convince politicians they could be trusted to respect and apply shared norms. A 50-minute discussion programme focused one of its three campaign editions on an issue the parties expected Labour to prefer, another on one plugged by the Conservatives, and yet another on one that both could agree was important. Vox pop interviews with floating voters in a magazine item had to be balanced in respect of their likely eventual leanings. And the senior political correspondent of an evening news bulletin said:

> If Labour material led the election news on the previous night and again on the current night, by golly the next night it would have to be Conservative led.

This was not to imply that uncertainty could be eliminated from the relationship. It was as if the communicators were playing a game with more or less agreed-upon rules, in which one or another participant would sometimes make an unexpected move – or even campaign for revised rules. Several party officials pictured their publicity initiatives as pieces of bait dangled before newsmen. The journalistic fish might not bite, but if the anglers chose the right bait for the conditions, and the political weather did not suddenly change, they stood a good chance of making a catch. In the process, however, each side needed to count on the other's observance of certain rules of conduct to an extent sufficient (1) to allow campaigners to frame publicity strategies that could be coherently unfolded and (2) to enable news executives to give assignments to reporters, camera crews, and OB units without risking a waste of precious resources.

All this reflects an underlying sociological imperative. In any continuing relationship based on mutual dependence and need, a culture, structuring all the areas of behaviour in which both sides regularly interact, tends to emerge. The norms of that culture then (1) regulate the relationship, (2) get embedded in behavioural routines which often assume the status of precedents to be followed in the future, (3) are points of reference when disputes arise over alleged failures to respect existing ground rules or demands to change them, and (4) revert back to and become absorbed into the internal role definitions of the respective actors. This does not mean that all participants will embrace the operative norms equally enthusiastically or without reservation. Cultural differences will persist and be voiced as well. But a shared culture is continually re-established, even in the face of disagreement, because it is indispensable to undergird the relationship.

Such norms of mutual working can govern a wide range of matters. For example, the emergent culture normally includes shared criteria of fairness. In a British election campaign, the two major parties are usually reckoned to deserve equal amounts of air time and the Liberals 60 percent of their share, while minor and new parties merit one five-minute broadcast so long as they put up candidates in a specified minimum number of constituencies. In other countries, quite different principles of fairness are applied – for example, absolutely equal treatment for all political parties regardless of size in Denmark. The Anderson candidacy in the American presidential campaign of 1980 was interesting from this point of view, because there was so little precedent to follow in arranging coverage of his peculiar appeal. An emergent culture had to be hastily cobbled together, and

Anderson's attempt to prize a regular stream of stories from the media may have suffered from his lack of enduring organization (which undermined the expectation of continuing interaction after the election was over).

The shared culture may also include certain criteria of objectivity. The many distancing devices, described by Tuchman (1972) as 'strategic ritual protecting newspapermen from the risks of their trade . . . including critics', owe much of their defensive efficacy to their acceptance by politicians and other news sources as valid marks of an objective approach.

Role relationships are also regulated by criteria of behavioural propriety in interaction. Respect for embargoes, the anonymity of sources, and the confidences of 'off-the-record' disclosures come to mind here. In addition, certain boundaries distinguishing acceptable from impermissible areas of questioning may be well defined in one national news culture while following different lines in another. For example, the state of health of politicians is more searchingly probed by reporters in the United States than in Britain. Harold Wilson's belief that his sources of private income were off-limits to a questioning interviewer triggered a fierce row between the Labour Party and the BBC in 1971, obliging the latter to take many steps to mend the rift-even though Mr Wilson's reaction was widely regarded at the time as overly extreme (Briggs, 1979).

In addition, and perhaps most significantly, interaction is regulated by a to some extent shared framework of news values, indicating both who and what will tend to be treated as newsworthy. As Elliott (1977) pointed out, 'Accepting some sources as official and reliable while questioning or ignoring others is an important part of journalistic routine', and those inside the charmed circle of access will expect its existing boundaries to be maintained more or less intact. Shared substantive definitions of news make it possible for each side to try to manipulate the situation to its own advantage. Politicians, for example, needing exposure but lacking control over it can then so adjust their behaviour to strengthen their chance of winning the most favourable coverage possible in the prevailing news-based definition of the situation.

In all these spheres complex processes and calculations play on the emergence, entrenchment, and revision of the ground rules. First, for each side there is often a mixture of benefit and cost in conforming to the prevailing pattern. Despite their highly privileged access rights, for example, top politicians may occasionally be on the receiving end of extremely unfavourable treatment, due to the access of journalists to other news sources, a pile-up of incidents casting doubt on their competence and power to control events, or even the impact of a 'hoist-with-his-own-petard' syndrome, when a statesman's verbal blunders are flung back into his face. The fact that politicians rarely object to such treatment suggests either that they accept the ruling news-value system or realize that complaining would be counterproductive. Likewise, during the British general election of 1979, some television journalists criticized their own overly receptive response to visual events stage-managed by the party leaders. Yet they continued to present them, even after questioning their newsworthiness, partly because they could not afford unilaterally to suspend a shared convention. Instead, they occasionally salved their reportorial consciences by clothing them in a sceptically toned commentary.

Second, the existing fabric of news values is not solely a media product, which is then imposed on and accepted by politicians as a *fait accompli*. Politicians' definitions of situations may not only differ from those of journalists; at times they may also contribute to what counts as political news. The recent history of election coverage in Britain includes several episodes of attempted news creativity by politicians. The first use of the walkabout as a regular campaign device in the 1970 general election is a case in point. It originated in the need of the Labour leader for a source of daily appearances in a campaign that he wished to play in low-key vein, stirring up no enlivening issues. Yet during the 1979 campaign Leader walkabouts were screened almost daily in TV news (Pilsworth, 1980); broadcasters had come to accept them as a routine feature of their election coverage.

Third, an ever-evolving shared culture emerges from an ever tactically shifting process in which the principal actors strive to influence each other for their own benefit. As Polsby (1980) pointed out, journalistic professionalism demands that 'news media élites establish their own account of day-to-day reality, independent of that propounded by the politicians whom they cover'. In response, politicians can try either to exploit the dominant story lines or challenge their legitimacy. Rather more frequent recourse to the latter strategy has been encouraged in recent years by a growing awareness of the ultimate subjectivity of news judgements, which are relative to certain values and can only be universal in application if there is agreement on such underlying values (Gans, 1979). Barring such an agreement, more and more groups may come to regard the news as it applies to their affairs as wittingly or unwittingly politicized and therefore fit to be pressurized. Hence, the mass media have latterly been urged to assign more understanding reporters to racial beats, to be less strike-fixated in their coverage of industrial relations, and to look differently at feminist concerns. At a given time, then, the dominant system of news values will in part reflect the outcomes of previous tugs of war between journalists and representatives of numerous sectional groups, including politicians.

Fourth, despite much argument and tactical struggle, the influence of certain forces promoting normative integration can be detected in modern political communication systems as well. One is the presence inside media and political institutions of boundary roles, whose occupants are closely familiar with the values and practices of the other camp. The publicity advisors of politicians may convey to their masters an impression of the current news-value system as part of the natural order of things. Likewise, media organizations often appoint to their executive teams one or more individuals who are particularly sensitive to and *au fait* with leading politicians and their publicity problems. Both sides also seem to feel the need to be in a position, when engaged in or anticipating disputes, convincingly to appeal to principles that transcend their purely sectional interests. This strengthens the elements of shared culture by emphasizing their overarching standing. In the previously mentioned observation study of the British general election of 1966, for example, it was noted that 'the appeal of a political party to a principle of fairness which the producers themselves regarded as legitimate . . . helped to remind the broadcasters of considerations that had been overlooked in the hectic conditions of election programming' (Blumler, 1969). For their part, media men also seem motivated to enter potentially tense situations with 'clean hands' – able to say, if a row was to erupt, that they at least had behaved quite properly and responsibly.

Note

1. Blumler, J. G. (1980) Comparative analysis of broadcasting organization policy for the European elections. Paper presented to Conference on the Role of Broadcasting in the European Elections, Brussels, September, 1980.

References

Blumler, J. G. (1969) Producers' attitudes towards television coverage of an election campaign: a case study. In Halmos, P. (ed.) *The Sociology of Mass-media Communicators*, University of Keele, Keele.

Blumler, J. G. (1979) Communication in the European elections: the case of British broadcasting. *Government and Opposition*, Vol. 14, pp. 508–30.

Blumler, J. G., Gurevitch, M., and Ives, J. (1978) *The Challenge of Election Broadcasting: A Role Analysis*, Leeds University Press, Leeds.

Briggs. A. (1979) *Governing the BBC*, BBC, London.

Chittick, W. O. (1970) *State Department, Press, and Pressure Groups*, John Wiley, New York.

Clarke, P. and Evans, S. H. (1980) 'All in a day's work': reporters covering congressional campaigns. *Journal of Communication*, Vol. 30, No. 1, pp. 112–21.

Elliot, P. (1977) Media organizations and occupations: an overview. In Curran, J., Gurevitch, M. and Woollacott, J (eds) *Mass Communication and Society*, Edward Arnold, London in association with The Open University Press.

Fant, C. H. (1980) Televising presidential conventions, 1952–1980. *Journal of Communication*, Vol. 30, pp. 130–39.

Gans, H. J. (1979) Deciding what's news: a study of CBS evening news. NBC nightly news. *Newsweek and Time*, Pantheon, New York.

Kumar, K. (1975) Holding the middle ground: The BBC, the public and the professional broadcaster. *Sociology*, Vol. 9, pp. 67–88.

Ostroff, D. H. (1980) A participant-observer study of TV campaign coverage. *Journalism Quarterly*, Vol. 57, pp. 415–19.

Pilsworth, M. (1980) Balanced broadcasting. In Butler, D. and Kavanagh, D. (eds) *The British General Election of 1979*, Macmillan, London.

Polsby, N. W. (1980) The news media as an alternative to party in the presidential selection process. In Goldwin R. A. (ed.) *Political Parties in the Eighties*, American Enterprise Institute for Public Policy Research, Washington and Kenyon College, Gambier, Ohio.

Tuchman, G. (1972) Objectivity as strategic ritual: an examination of newsmen's notions of objectivity. *American Journal of Sociology*, Vol. 77, pp. 660–79.

Section 3

Media effects

15

The media effects tradition

Chris Newbold

The implication that the media effects tradition has been the motor force behind the development of mass communication research was established and illustrated in Section 1. Indeed, as commentators such as McQuail have noted, 'the entire study of mass communication is based on the premise that the media have significant effects'; however, he adds that, 'yet there is little agreement on the nature and extent of these assumed effects' (McQuail, 1994, p. 327). As this section shows, much of the movement in the effects research tradition has been away from the notion of direct effects (the stimulus–response or magic-bullet premise), towards an interest in mediation and intervention – the filtering or prismatic 'intervening variables', to do with the individual, the physical context of viewing or reading, and the social and cultural context, that lie between the delivery of a 'message' and any influence it may be said to have.

The preoccupation with effects can be related to a wide range of issues and interests. Mass media products were new to the nineteenth century, and have since gone through a variety of transformations, both technological and cultural. They are, almost by definition, designed to attract attention, and have regularly challenged and provoked establishment values in order to do so. Unease about the media, whether popular or establishment in origin, is an under-researched phenomenon, but it is clear that there has always been substantial unease, and a body of opinion which believes that more should be done to study the 'effects' of media. Such concern has typically focused on issues related to violence, sexual behaviour, 'bad language', moral values. There are others whose interest is in measuring more benign, positive, or even 'pro-social' effects, whether these are to do with the 'effects' of media on political behaviour, consumption, levels of information and education, or campaigns against smoking, drug abuse, or AIDS. Media industries and advertisers have an innate interest in questions relating to the audiences for their programmes and advertisements. As both Hardt and Gitlin demonstrated in the first section, the majority of American-based research was, and to an extent still is, based on an administrative model, funded by the media industries themselves and whose goals, at least in relation to the drive for advertising revenue might more narrowly be described as the delivery of audiences to advertisers (see the Smythe extract in Section 4). This too can be seen as requiring that a certain 'effect' be shown to exist, otherwise why should advertisers use the medium?

This section focuses on effects studies themselves, rather than the place of such studies within the field as a whole. Each of the various strands or phases of research has developed in reaction to preceding phases, and the effects tradition itself has a somewhat developmental and linear history (see Lowery and DeFleur, 1988). Over time there is evidence of greater sophistication and critical awareness, even to the point that the term 'effect' is used only sparingly or subject to careful qualification. What they retain in common is an attempt to understand the relationship between media content and its audience, with or without reference to the term 'effect'.

The effects tradition may be traced at least as far back as the 'Payne studies' (Dale, 1933) in the 1930s and Hovland (1949), and perhaps even further back to the mass society theories of the late nineteenth century. Our concern here is with the dynamic expansion of the field in the period following the Second World War, and the generation of awareness at that time of the importance of 'intervening variables'.

The notion of 'intervening variable' connects back to an interest within social theory in the 'rediscovery of the primary group', and to studies such as those of 'Hawthorne' (Roethlisberger and Dickson, 1939) and Stouffer (1949) which recognized that attempts to manipulate human behaviour in hierarchical organizations were often undermined by the resistance of cohesive organizational subcultures. Earlier effects studies had tended to focus on short-term and measurable effects, and the audience was perceived as an aggregate of isolated individuals. The newer generation of studies emphasized the social relations that connected people, the shared values that accounted for group solidarity in small groups or communities, and the relationship of attitudes and behaviour to such close personal groups. Studies of 'the two-step flow' in the 1940s stressed the importance of interpersonal networks in the communication process.

The first extract in this section is drawn from the second of these studies, Katz and Lazarsfeld *Personal Influence*. Published in 1955, and based on 1945 research data, it was sparked off by the first two-step flow study, *The People's Choice* (1948) which had been researched in 1941. The main focus of this first study was on factors that influenced voting behaviour; its 'discovery', as Katz and Lazarsfeld called it, was that mass media played very little part in the process of attitude and opinion formation. The main influence was that of other people. Key people within the primary group were seen to take the role of 'opinion leaders'; these opinion leaders were important 'intervening variables' between media and audience.

The extract from *Personal Influence* contextualizes the two-step flow, and further examines the role of opinion leaders or 'influentials'. Gitlin's criticism notwithstanding (see Section 1), the concept of the 'two-step flow' is important, in that it switched the focus of research from the individual in a laboratory, to the individual as member of one or more primary groups in their social context, and in doing so it invited a broader range of relevant factors into the analysis. In short, its own defects aside, it greatly extended the research imagination.

In his famous statement 'mass communication does not ordinarily serve as a necessary or sufficient cause of audience effects, but rather functions through a nexus of mediating factors' (Klapper, 1960, p. 81), Joseph Klapper moves away from a media-centric approach. In the extract in this section he assesses the state of effects research, considering in particular the uniqueness of mass communication itself as an influence, whilst also assessing the roles of other important influences which contribute to observable change of opinion.

Observable change of opinion in this framework refers to effects which are registered in the short term. Few studies in this tradition have been able to analyse or hypothesize the effects of media consumption over considerably wider time spans. This may in large part be a reflection of the limitations of the favoured quantitative methodologies which dominate effects studies, as well as of demands of industry for immediate feedback and results.

One approach to effects which has grappled directly with the issue of long-term effects is to be found in the work of George Gerbner and his theory of 'media cultivation'. This grew out of 1960s and 1970s research into media violence and society, in the wake of intense public debate. The key to understanding cultivation as 'effects' is its examination of the relationship between television culture and the symbolic environment it creates for the audience, the idea being that television 'cultivates' people's beliefs. The viewer is subject to a slow, cumulative effect, related to the intensity of his or her viewing over long stretches of exposure to the values and world representations of television.

Gerbner's extract in this section focuses on his research model of cultural indicators. Cultural indicators can be understood as similar to economic indicators utilized by economists in the understanding and creating of economic policy. A study of television would serve as an indicator of cultural values. Television is then seen as the predominant contributor to the symbolic environment, taking the place that organized religion held in past centuries. Gerbner's central concern is to show how far viewers' perceptions of society, social structures, gender roles, and so on, are congruent with and modelled on the (highly skewed) representations of these things through television.

Television cultivates consciousness. According to Gerbner it tells us about what is good and bad in our society; it is a symbolic system which cultivates and regulates our perceptions. Thus, methodologically a lot of emphasis is placed on content analysis of television output to unpack the values and beliefs it propagates. Such analysis explores the cultivation of collective perceptions and ideas through the public message system.

One of its consequences for research has been to resurrect the notion of the media, and particularly television, as a source of powerful effects, where television acts as a stimulus, and the audience responds in terms of behaviour, attitude and opinion change, albeit over an elongated period of time and viewing exposure. Thus, whereas in Europe the reconceptualization of the media as powerful came about in the late 1960s and 1970s through the process of highly-abstract, French-inflected, neo-Marxist macro-analysis of media as 'ideological apparatuses' of social reproduction, in the U.S.A. a similar outcome was the product of essentially empirical, content-based analysis. It was open to criticism, however, for its particular focus on television, and its relative insensitivity to patterns of difference in television watching other than along the continuum of 'light' to 'heavy' television viewing.

Where Gerbner is concerned with media as general agents of enculturation through popular perceptions of society, McCombs and Shaw suggest one of the mechanisms through which the media create consensus. Unlike Gerbner's hypothesis, their agenda-setting model attributes to media not a direct influence on attitude formation, but on what it is that people think it is important to be thinking about. Thus the mass media influence people not by telling them what to think, but by telling them what to think about. The basic idea of agenda setting asserts a direct causal relationship between the content of the media agenda and subsequent public perceptions of what the important issues of the day are. Research can establish this relationship by both examining the content of the media agenda and through interviewing audience members in order to explore the extent of congruity between media and audiences in the priorities which they attribute to issues. The salience of an issue in the agenda setting model is important since the model proposes that an issue of high media salience will be also perceived by the audience to be very important, whereas issues of lower media salience will not be highly rated by audiences, and ones of very low salience may never even be registered by audiences.

McCombs and Shaw here report a satisfactory first test of the agenda-setting hypothesis. Subsequent research such as that of Oscar Gandy (1982) has tried to move the analysis away from media definitions of importance to the agendas which are set by those organizations and power groups which enjoy privileged access to the media. None the less the premise remains that the media are sufficiently powerful that they can construct audience perceptions of the social world, yet again swinging research away from the earlier model of limited effects so ably summarized by Klapper (1960).

Asking not what the media do to people, but what people do with the media, the 'uses and gratifications' approach represented here in the extract from Blumler, Katz, and Gurevitch, takes us back from the media to the audiences, not the passive audiences of the stimulus–response model but, in the first of its many guises over the past 20 years, an active audience in control, to some extent, of the ways in which its members choose to be 'affected' by the media. 'Uses and gratifications' shifts the focus of research in the 'effects tradition' away from the persuasive aims of the communicator towards the recognized needs of the audience, to treat these needs as intervening variables in the relationship of media content with audience reception. An updated version of what they describe in the article as a functionalist approach to the media can be stated thus: 'Uses and gratification theory is concerned with the social and psychological origins of needs, which generate expectations of the mass media or other sources which lead to differential patterns of media exposure resulting in need gratification and other unintentional consequences' (Rosengren et al., 1985, p.14.).

The 'uses and gratifications' approach can be traced back to the work of Herzog (1944) in which she examined the use that women listeners made of day-time radio soap operas to escape their mundane lives; indeed a similar approach was taken by Radway in 1984 to examine women's reading of romance novels (see Section 10).

The main thrust of the approach is to examine people's motivations for media use. It has been criticized for an overly functionalist conception, focusing on the role of media in satisfying audience needs, a process understood in purely individualistic terms rather than in relation to the social context of both production and consumption. In its simpler manifestations the media are represented as innately neutral or positive resources at the disposal of individual needs. Media content always serves a function; otherwise it would not exist. Methodologically the theory places possibly undue faith in the ability of people, when asked, to articulate their own needs and gratifications in relation to the media. The search for a finite list of functional categories in aid of quantitative research may be a significant barrier to deeper investigation of the psychologically, socially and culturally contextualized ways in which viewers or readers experience, enjoy, negotiate, reflect upon, fantasize and in many other ways interact with the media.

'Uses and gratifications' was a major influence in the 'effects tradition', and many of its earlier conceptual problems have been engaged and resolved; McQuail (1984), for instance, goes some way towards this. There have also been attempts to unite some of the media-centred approaches with notions of differential audience judgements and opinions. In particular, McCombs and Weaver (1985) suggest a synergy of agenda setting with uses and gratifications to bring together media-centred and audience centred approaches.

The final extract, by Jensen and Rosengren, talks of combining some of the main strands of the field within the 'effects tradition' by emphasizing their common concern with the audience. Effects research, uses and gratifications, literary criticism, cultural studies and reception analysis, each unravels strands that are generally intertwined in the same rope, and which may be rewound. The author calls for cross-cultural and pluri-methodo-logical development. In short, while this tradition shows evidence of antagonism between different theories, there is also some evidence of mutual learning and of a will for convergence.

References and further reading

Cumberbatch, G. and Howitt, D. (1989) *A Measure of Uncertainty: The Effects of the Mass Media*. British Standards Council Research Monograph Series: 1, John Libby.

Dale, E. (1933) *Children's Attendance at Motion Pictures*, Macmillan.

Dale, E. (1933) *Motion Pictures and Youth: A Summary*, Macmillan.

Gandy, O. (1982) *Beyond Agenda Setting*, Ablex, Norwood, NJ.

Herzog, H. (1944) What do we really know about daytime radio listeners? In Lazarsfeld, P. F. (ed.) *Radio Research*, Duell, Sloan and Pearce, New York.

Hovland, C. I., Lumsdane, A. A. and Sheffield, F. D. (1949) *Experiments in Mass Communication*, Princeton University Press, Princeton, NJ.

Klapper, J. T. (1960) *The Effects of Mass Communication*, Free Press, New York.

Lazarsfeld, P. F., Berelson, B. and Gaudet, H. (1948) *The People's Choice*, Columbia University Press.

Lowery, S. A. and DeFleur, M. L. (1988) *Milestones in Mass Communications Research*, 2nd edn, Longman.

McCombs, M. E. and Weaver, D. H. (1985) Towards a merger of gratification's and agenda-setting research. In Rosengren *et al.* (eds) *Media Gratification's: Current Perspectives*, Sage.

McQuail, D. (1984) With the benefit of hindsight: reflections on uses and gratification's research. In *Critical Studies in Mass Communication*, Vol. 1. No. 2.

McQuail, D. (1994) *Mass Communication Theory: An Introduction*, 3rd edn, Sage.

Roethlisberger, F. J. and Dickson, W. J. (1939) *Management and the Worker*, Harvard University Press.

Rosengren, K. E., Palmgreen, P. and Wenner, L. (1985) *Media Gratification Research: Current Perspectives*, Sage.

Stouffer, S. A. *et al.* (1949) *The American Soldier: Studies in Social Psychology in World War*. Princeton University Press.

16

Between media and mass/the part played by people/the two-step flow of communication

Elihu Katz and Paul F. Lazarsfeld

From Katz, E. and Lazarsfeld, P. F. (1955) *Personal Influence: The Part Played by People in the Flow of Mass Communications*, The Free Press, Glencoe, IL, pp. 15–42, 309–20.

Between media and mass

Mass media research: the study of 'campaigns'

Mass media research began, and as it proceeded, it became traditional to divide the field of communications research into three major divisions. Audience research – the study of how many of what kinds of people attend to a given communications message or medium – is, historically, the earliest of the divisions, and still the most prolific. The second division is that of content analysis, comprising the study of the language, the logic and the layout of communications messages. And finally, there is what has been called effect analysis or the study of the impact of mass communications.

For some purposes, this three-way division is useful. For other purposes, however – and, notably, for the purpose at hand – it is misleading because it obscures the fact that, fundamentally, all of communications research aims at the study of effect. From the earliest theorizing on this subject to the most contemporary empirical research, there is, essentially, only one underlying problem – though it may not always be explicit – and that is, 'what can the media "do"?' [. . .]

We have been talking as if effect were a simple concept when, in fact, there are a variety of possible effects that the mass media may have upon society, and several different dimensions along which effects may be classified.[1]

We are suggesting that the over-riding interest of mass media research is in the study of the effectiveness of mass media attempts to influence – usually, to change – opinions and attitudes in the very short run. Perhaps this is best described as an interest in the effects of mass media 'campaigns' – campaigns to influence votes, to sell soap, to reduce prejudice. Noting only that there are a variety of other mass media consequences which surely merit research attention but have not received it, let us proceed with this more circumspect definition clearly in mind: mass media research has aimed at an understanding of how, and under what conditions, mass media 'campaigns' (rather specific, short-run efforts) succeed in influencing opinions and attitudes.

Intervening variables and the study of effect

If it is agreed that the focus of mass media research has been the study of campaigns, it can readily be demonstrated that the several subdivisions of research – audience research, content analysis, etc. – are not autonomous at all but, in fact, merely subordinate aspects of this dominant concern. What we mean can be, readily illustrated. Consider, for example, audience research – the most prolific branch of mass media research. One way of looking at audience research is to see it only as an autonomous research arena, concerned with what has been called fact-gathering or book-keeping operations. We are suggesting, however, that audience research may be viewed more appropriately as an aspect of the study of effect, in the sense that counting up the audience and examining its characteristics and its likes and dislikes is a first step toward specifying what the potential effect is for a given medium or message.

One might say that the intellectual history of mass media research may, perhaps, be seen best in terms of the successive introduction of research concerns – such as audience, content, and the like – which are basically attempts to impute effects by means of an analysis of some more readily accessible intermediate factors with which effects are associated.

However, these factors serve not only as a basis for the indirect measurement or imputing of effects: they also begin to specify some of the complexities of the mass communications process. That is to say, the study of intermediate steps has led to a better understanding of what goes on in a mass media campaign – or, in other words, to an understanding of the sequence of events and the variety of factors which 'intervene' between the mass media stimulus and the individual's response. Thus, each new aspect introduced has contributed to the gradual pulling apart of the scheme with which research began: that of the omnipotent media, on one hand, sending forth the message, and the atomized masses, on the other, waiting to receive it – and nothing in-between.

Four intervening variables in the mass communication process

The four variables we shall consider contribute, under some conditions, to facilitating the flow of communications between media and masses and, under other conditions, to blocking the flow of communications. It is in this sense, therefore, that we call them intervening.[2]

First, there is the variable of 'exposure' (or 'access', or 'attention') which derives, of course, from audience research.[3] Audience research has shown that the original mass communications 'model' is not adequate, for the very simple reason that people are not exposed to specific mass media stimuli as much, as easily, or as randomly as had been supposed. Exposure or non-exposure may be a product of tech... gical factors (as is the case in many pre-industrial countries),[4] political factors (as in the case of totalitarian countries), economic factors (as in the case of not being able to afford a TV set), and especially of voluntary factors – that is, simply not tuning in. In the United States, it is, typically, this voluntary factor that is most likely to account for who is in the audience for a particular communication message. Perhaps the most important generalization in this area – at least as far as an understanding of the process of effective persuasion is concerned – is that those groups which are most hopefully regarded as the target of a communication are often least likely to be in the audience. Thus, educational programmes, it has been found, are very unlikely to reach the uneducated; and good-will programmes are least likely to reach those who are prejudiced against another, group; and so on.[5] It is in this sense that we consider the mere fact of exposure itself a major intervening variable in the mass communications process.

A second focus of mass media research which developed very early was the differential character of the media them selves. The research which falls into this category asks the general question: What is the difference in the effect of message X if it is transmitted via medium A, B or C? The appearance of Cantril and Allport's (1935) book, *The Psychology of Radio*, called attention to a whole set of these 'media comparison' experiments. Here, type-of-medium is the intervening variable in so far as the findings of these studies imply that the process of persuasion is modified by the channel which delivers the message.[6]

Content – in the sense of form, presentation, language, etc. – is the third of the intervening variables on our list. And while it is true that the analysis of communications content is carried out for a variety of reasons, by and large, the predominant interest of mass media research in this area relates to the attempt to explain or predict differences in effect based on differences in content. To be more precise, most of the work in this field imputes differences in intervening psychological processes – and thus, differences in effects – from observed differences in content.[7] Content analysis informs us, for example, of the psychological techniques that are likely to be most effective (e.g. repetition, appeal to authority, band-wagon, etc.); the greater sway of 'facts' and 'events' as compared with 'opinions'; the cardinal rule of 'don't argue'; the case for and against presenting 'one side' rather than 'both sides' of controversial material; the 'documentary' vs the 'commentator' presentation; the damaging effect of a script at 'cross-purposes' with itself; etc. Important techniques have been developed for use in this field, and the controlled experiment has also been widely adopted for the purpose of observing directly the effect of the varieties of communications presentation and content. The characteristic quality of these techniques is evident: they concentrate on the 'stimulus', judging its effectiveness by referring either to more or less imputed psychological variables which are associated with effects or to the actual 'responses' of those who have been exposed to controlled variations in presentation.

A fourth set of mediating factors, or intervening variables, emerges from study of the attitudes and psychological predispositions of members of the audience, insofar as these are associated with successful and unsuccessful campaigns. In this area, mass media research has established very persuasively what social psychologists have confirmed in their laboratories

– that an individual's attitudes or predispositions can modify, or sometimes completely distort, the meaning of a given message. For example, a prejudiced person whose attitude toward an out-group is strongly entrenched may actively resist a message of tolerance in such a way that the message may even be perceived as a defence of prejudice or as irrelevant to the subject of prejudice entirely.[8]

Just as prior attitudes on issues must be studied, so attitudes toward the media themselves must be accounted for if we are fully to understand the role of psychological predispositions in modifying the effectiveness of communications. Here research on predispositions joins with the previous subject of media differences. Thus, many people regard the radio as more trustworthy than the newspaper, and others have the opposite opinion. In the same way, in many of the highly politicized countries abroad, there is a great intensity of feeling about the relative trustworthiness not just of the several media in general but of each newspaper and each radio station.[9] Similarly, attitudes toward the sources to which information and news are credited are likely to affect the acceptance of a mass media message. The very large number of studies which fall under the heading of 'prestige suggestion' bear on this problem.[10]

So far, then, we have examined four intervening factors – exposure and predisposition from the receiving end, media differences and content differences from the transmission end – and each gives a somewhat better idea of what goes on in between the media and the masses to modify the effects of communications.[11] That is, each time a new intervening factor is found to be applicable, the complex workings of the mass persuasion process are illuminated somewhat better, revealing how many different factors have to be attuned in order for a mass communications message to be effective. Thus, the image of the process of mass communications with which researchers set out, that the media play a direct influencing role, has had to be more and more qualified each time a new intervening variable was discovered.

The part played by people

During the course of studying the presidential election campaign of 1940, it became clear that certain people in every stratum of a community serve relay roles in the mass communication of election information and influence.[12]

This 'discovery' began with the finding that radio and the printed page seemed to have only negligible effects on actual vote decisions and particularly minute effects on changes in vote decisions. [. . .]

The opinion leader idea and the two-step flow of communication

To investigate this problem, particular attention was paid to those people who changed their vote-intention during the course of the campaign. When these people were asked what had contributed to their decision, their answer was: other people. The one source of influence that seemed to be far ahead of all others in determining the way people made up their minds was personal influence. Given this clue from the testimony of the voters themselves, other data and hypotheses fell into line. People tend to vote, it seems, the way their associates vote: wives like husbands, club members with their clubs, workers with fellow employees, etc. Furthermore, looked at in this way, the data implied (although they were not completely adequate for this new purpose) that there were people who exerted a disproportionately great influence on the vote intentions of their fellows. And it could be shown that these 'opinion leaders' – as they were dubbed – were not at all identical with those who are thought of traditionally as the wielders of influence; opinion leaders seemed to be distributed in all occupational groups, and on every social and economic level.

The next question was obvious: who or what influences the influentials? Here is where the mass media re-entered the picture. For the leaders reported much more than the non-opinion leaders that for them, the mass media were influential. Pieced together this way, a new idea emerged – the suggestion of a 'two-step flow of communication'. The suggestion basically was this: that ideas, often, seem to flow from radio and print to opinion leaders and from them to the less active sections of the population.

The traditional image of the mass persuasion process must make room for 'people' as intervening factors between the stimuli of the media and resultant opinions, decisions and actions.

We might say, perhaps, that as a result of investigating and thinking about the opinion leader, mass communications research has now joined those fields of social research which, in the last years, have been 'rediscovering' the primary group.[13] And if we are correct, the 'rediscovery' seems to have taken place in two steps. First of all, the phenomenon of opinion leadership was discovered. But then, study of the widespread distribution of opinion leaders throughout the population and analysis of the character of their relations with those for whom they were influential (family, friends, co-workers) soon led to a second idea. This was the idea that opinion leaders are not a group set apart, and that opinion leadership is not a trait which some people have and others do not, but rather that opinion leadership is an integral part of the give-and-take of everyday personal relationships. It is being suggested, in other words, that all interpersonal relations are potential networks of communication and that an opinion leader can best be thought of as a group member playing a key communications role. It is this elaboration – that is the tying of opinion leaders to the specific others with whom they are in contact – that completes the 'rediscovery'. [. . .]

The two-step flow of communication

Formulated first in *The People's Choice*, the hypothesis suggests that 'ideas often flow from radio and print to the opinion leaders and from them to the less active sections of the population'.[14] But since this formulation, and the evidence to substantiate it, were based only upon one kind of opinion leader – people who were influential for others during the course of an election campaign – we do not yet know whether the hypothesis is applicable to opinion leadership in other realms as well. In this chapter, then, we want to compare the media behaviour of opinion leaders and non-leaders to see whether the leaders tend to be the more exposed, and the more responsive group when it comes to influence stemming from the mass media. In general, we shall find that the hypothesis is substantiated in each of the arenas of influence with which we are concerned.

Opinion leadership and exposure to the mass media

[. . .]

It is plain from the table that influentials of every type read a larger number of magazines than those who are not influential. Thus, the non-leader group includes in its ranks many fewer readers of five or more magazines; and this is true, too, the Table 16.1 shows, when education is taken into account.[15] In other words, then, opinion leaders in each arena – whether it be marketing, fashions, politics or movie-going – tend to have greater contact than non-leaders with the features and advertisements in America's magazines.

When we turn from magazines to other media, we find that, as a rule, the same phenomenon holds true that is opinion leaders exceed non-leaders in exposure. [. . .]

Leaders tend to exceed non-leaders in number of hours of radio listening, too, although the differences are quite small and not always consistent. The movie leaders of both educational levels seem to be particularly attentive to radio, together with the lower-educated marketing and fashion leaders. However, the well-educated leaders in the latter two realms, plus the political leaders on both educational levels, do not exceed the non-leaders in time spent listening to the radio.[16] The political leaders, furthermore, are the only group which does not exceed the non-leaders in movie-going; all other leaders do.[17]

In sum, it can safely be stated that the opinion leaders in every realm tend to be more highly exposed to the mass media than are the non-leaders. But while we have begun to talk about these variations, that is, about the different media habits of one kind of leader as compared with another, we have not yet talked explicitly about the relationship between such variations and the different content of the several media.

[. . .]

Table 16.1. Opinion leaders read more magazines than non-leaders

Number of magazines	Low education Marketing leaders	Fashion leaders	Public affairs leaders	Movie leaders	Non-leaders
5 or more	41%	58%	60%	58%	30%
less than 5	59	42	40	42	70
100% =	(91)	(79)	(30)	(64)	(270)
	High education Marketing leaders	Fashion leaders	Public Affairs leaders	Movie leaders	Non-leaders
5 or more	65%	69%	63%	71%	53%
less than 5	35	31	37	29	47
100% =	(75)	(80)	(50)	(58)	(146)

Opinion leadership and mass media effect

So far we have seen that the opinion leaders tend to be both more generally exposed to the mass media, and more specifically exposed to the content most closely associated with their leadership. Presumably this increased exposure then becomes a component – witting or unwitting – of the influence which such influentials transmit to others. As a result of these findings, the idea of the 'two-step flow of communication' gains credence.

That is as far as the idea of the 'two-step flow' takes us. Yet it would seem worthwhile to proceed one step further, to see whether opinion leaders actually make more 'use' of their greater media exposure in their own decisions. We want to see whether opinion leaders are not only more exposed to the media – which is all that the two-step flow hypothesis claims – but, compared with non-leaders, whether they are relatively more *affected* by them as well.

Let us consider this possibility in the case of fashions Specifically, we can assess the relevant influences that went into the making of the opinion leaders' decisions and compare them with those factors which were influential for non-leaders. Thus, Table 16.2 is a comparison of those fashion leaders and non-leaders who, upon reporting some recent change in their clothes, hairdo, make-up style, etc., were asked: 'who or what suggested this change to you?'. For each level of education, the table reports the percentage of all influences named which were personal influences and the percentage which were mass media influences.

On each level of education, Table 16.2 clearly indicates that fashion leaders who recently made some change were more influenced in their decisions by the mass media, and less by other people, than recent changers among the non-leaders. Although not very large, the differences in the table are consistent throughout.[19]

As we expected, the data for marketing and also for movie going are inconclusive; that is, the several channels of influence impinge on the leaders

Table 16.2. Fashion leaders are influenced more by mass media and less by other people than are non-leaders[18]

	Percent of all influences mentioned (recent changers only)			
	Low education		High education	
'Who or what suggested change?'	Fashion leaders	Non-fashion leaders	Fashion leaders	Non-fashion leaders
Heard or saw somebody	40%	56%	37%	47%
Mass media	42	31	42	33
Other	18	13	21	20
Total influences (=100%)	(164)	(308)	(135)	(250)

in much the same way as they do upon the non-leaders. Contrary to our expectations, however, the public affairs leaders do not behave like the fashion leaders either. If anything, these leaders are more likely than non-leaders to report personal influence as the more significant component of their recent opinion changes. In other words, although each of the leader types is more exposed to the media than non-leaders – and, presumably, therefore more likely to incorporate media content into the influences they pass on – nevertheless when it comes to crediting the media with impact on personal decisions, only the fashion leaders significantly exceed the non-leaders in this.

It is interesting to ask why the public affairs leader, whom we expected to make more use of her greater, media exposure in her personal decisions, tends to rely less, not more, on the media than non-leaders. It may be, perhaps, that our sample contains a disproportionately large number of 'local' rather than 'cosmopolitan' leaders, and that the latter – if our data permitted us to examine them separately – would in fact show greater media impact in their decisions. Or, it may be that the effect of the media in public affairs would be more clearly visible if we traced the networks of interpersonal influence further back; in other words, we might find that the next step – that is, the opinion leaders of the opinion leaders – are the ones who form opinions in more direct response to the media. Or, it might be that we would have to go back several steps before we found the link between the interpersonal networks of public affairs opinion and disproportionate mass media effect. Compared with the realm of fashions at any rate, one is led to suspect that the chain of interpersonal influence is longer in the realm of public affairs and that 'inside dope' as well as influencing in specific influence episodes is much more a person-to-person affair. In any event, the different combinations of media and personal influence which go into the several opinion leader roles we have examined, seem to corroborate much that, to date, has been merely speculative as well as pointing to new lines of research on the flow of influence.

In sum, there is need to enquire not only into the media exposure patterns of opinion leaders and the extent to which their own opinions and decisions are shaped by the media, but also into the different kinds of 'uses' to which the media are put by leaders in each realm, as compared with non-leaders.

Notes

1. Lazarsfeld (1948), for example, has distinguished 16 different types of effects by cross-tabulating four types of mass media 'stimuli' and four types of audience 'response'. The responses are classified along a rough time dimension – immediate response, short-term effects, long-term effects and institutional change, This classification makes clear, for example, that an investigation of the effect of Uncle Tom's Cabin on the outbreak of the Civil War calls for particular kinds of concepts and particular research tools and that this kind of effect must be distinguished from a study of the effect of print on Western civilization, on one hand, and a study of the effect of a subway car-card campaign on prejudiced attitudes, on the other. Many of the substantive statements about mass media research findings in this chapter are based on this paper and on Klapper (1950).
2. Our use of this phrase should not be confused with the technical usage in the methodology of survey analysis where 'intervening variable' refers to a 'test'

factor which is introduced to 'interpret' a correlation between two factors to which it (the 'test' factor) is related. See Lazarsfeld and Kendall (1950) for a full discussion of this usage. For a discussion of the widespread usage of this term in psychology, see Tolman (1951), pp. 281–5.

3. For reviews of some of the major findings of audience research in radio, newspapers, movies and television, see Lazarsfeld and Kendall (1948), Minnesota (1949), Schramm and White (1949), Handel (1950), Meyersohn (1953), Lazarsfeld (1948). It is needless perhaps to reiterate that the findings of audience research have an intrinsic value other than the one here discussed, and that the motivation to do audience research is not exclusively to impute effects. Research on, say, the likes and dislikes of an audience may be motivated by a desire to understand what an audience wants in order to pitch a 'campaign' in the right way, and/or by a desire to study the characteristics of audience 'tastes' for the sake of testing some hypothesis in this realm.

4. See Huth (1952) for a discussion of such factors as barriers to international technical assistance and informational programmes.

5. Examples of this phenomenon are documented in Lazarsfeld (1948) and Klapper (1950).

6. In a sense, one of the later sections of this book, *The Impact of Personal Influence* (Part 2, Section 2) contributes to this tradition by comparing the relative effectiveness of personal influence with the influence of radio, newspapers and magazines. See also Lazarsfeld, Berelson and Gaudet (1948, Chapters 14 and 16).

7. The authoritative work in this field outlining the technique of content analysis and the several uses to which it can be put is Berelson (1951); this book also contains an extensive bibliography of content studies. For a report on the most important series of experimental studies to date which, instead of imputing effects from content, attempt to measure the relationship between content variation and variation in effects directly, see Hovland, Lumsdaine and Sheffield (1949). Statements of some of the 'principles' of effective propaganda can be found in the publications of the Institute for Propaganda Analysis, e.g. in Lee and Lee (eds) (1939), etc. For further discussion of 'principles, see Krech and Crutchfield (1948, Chapter 9).

8. This motivated missing-of-the-point is documented in Cooper and Jahoda (1947). For an illustration in the realm of public opinion on international affairs, see Hyman and Sheatsley (1952) where the ineffectiveness of providing favourable information to people with initially unfavourable attitudes is demonstrated. For a purely theoretical treatment of this same theme, see Katz, D. (1949).

9. Attitudes toward the comparative trustworthiness of the media were investigated as part of a study by the Social Science Research Council (1947) and in communications studies in the near and middle East by the Bureau of Applied Social Research (1951).

10. For a review of these studies, see Asch (1952).

11. As has been noted earlier, together with the greater precision and increasing predictive power of mass communications research where it takes account of such factors, there has come an increasing scepticism about the potency of the mass media. As research becomes bolder, it becomes increasingly easy to show that – outside the range of marketing influences – mass media influence-attempts have fallen far short of the expectations of the communicators. This is notoriously the case with regard to persuasion attempts in the civic and political areas. It would be a mistake, however, to generalize from the role of the mass media in such direct, short-run effects to the degree of media potency which would be revealed if some longer-run, more indirect effects were conceptualized and subjected to study.

12. Lazarsfeld, Berelson and Gaudet (1948).
13. The 'rediscovery' of the primary group is an accepted term by now, referring to the belated recognition that researchers in many fields have given to the importance of informal, interpersonal relations within situations formerly conceptualized as strictly formal and atomistic. It is 'rediscovery' in the sense that the primary group was dealt with so explicitly (though descriptively and apart from any institutional context) in the work of pioneering American sociologists and social psychologists and then was systematically overlooked by empirical social research until its several dramatic 'rediscoveries'. As Merton (1948, pp. 66–7) points out, and as we shall demonstrate below, it was essentially the 'latent functions' of primary groups which were 'rediscovered'. For an account of early interest in the primary group as well as some of the stories of rediscovery and of present-day research, see the aforementioned Shils (1951) paper.
14. Lazarsfeld, Berelson and Gaudet (1948, p. 151). It is important to distinguish between the flow of *influence* and of *information*. The roles of media and interpersonal sources in the spread of a news event is considered, for example in Bogart (1950), Larsen and Hill (1954). See Whyte (1954) for an example, paralleling our own, of the role of word-of-mouth in the flow of consumer influence together with suggestions concerning linkages with mass media.
15. 'High education' begins with high school graduates: 'low education' includes all who have less than a complete high school education.
16. The study was completed before the general introduction of television.
17. These tables are not shown here.
18. This table is based only on those who reported a recent fashion change (in clothes, hairdo, makeup, etc.). The base figures under each column represent the total number of influences mentioned by each group in connection with their fashion decisions.
19. Controlling level of interest-that is, comparing equally interested leaders and non-leaders on each level of education – the differences still persist as markedly as when education alone is controlled.

References

Asch, S. E. (1952) *Social Psychology*, Prentice-Hall, New York.

Berelson, Bernard R. (1951) *Content Analysis In Communication Research*, Free Press, Glencoe, IL.

Bogart, Leo (1950) The spread of news on a local event: a case history. *Public Opinion Quarterly*, Vol. 14, pp. 769–72.

Bureau of Applied Social Research, Columbia University (1951) Unpublished series of studies on communications behaviour in the near and middle East.

Cantril, Hadley and Allport, Gordon (1935) *The Psychology of Radio*, Harper & Brothers, New York.

Cooper, Eunice and Jahoda, Marie (1947) The evasion of propaganda. *Journal of Psychology*, Vol. 23, pp. 15–25. Reprinted in Katz, Cartwright *et al.* (1954).

Handel, Leo A. (1950), *Hollywood Looks at its Audience*, University of Illinois Press, Urbana, IL.

Hovland, Carl I., Lumsdaine, Arthur A. and Sheffied, Fred D. (1949) *Experiments in Mass Communications*, (Studies in Social Psychology in World War II, Vol. III), Princeton University press, Princeton, NJ.

Huth, Amo G. (1952) Communications and economic development. *International Conciliation*, No. 477, Carnegie Endowment for International Peace.

Hyman, Herbert H. and Sheatsley, Paul B. (1952) Some reasons why information campaigns fail. In Swanson, Newcomb and Hartley (eds) *Readings in Social Psychology*, Henry Holt, New York.

Katz, Daniel (1949) Psychological barriers to communication. In Schramm, Wilbur (ed.) *Mass Communications*, University of Illinois Press, Urbana, IL.

Klapper, Joseph T. (1950) *The Effects of the Mass Media*, Bureau of Applied Social Research, Columbia University, New York.

Krech, David and Crutchfield, Richard S. (1948) *Theory and Problems in Social Psychology*, McGraw-Hill, New York.

Larsen, Otto N. and Hill, Richard J. (1954) Mass media and interpersonal communication in the diffusion of a news event. *American Sociological Review*, Vol. 19, pp. 426–33.

Lazarsfeld, Paul F. (1948) Communications research and the social psychologist. In Dennis, Wayne (ed.) *Current Trends in Social Psychology*, University of Pittsburgh Press, Pittsburgh, PA.

Lazarsfeld, Paul F., Berelson, Bernard and Gaudet, Hazel (1948) *The People's Choice*, Columbia University Press, New York.

Lazarsfeld, Paul F. and Kendall, Patricia L. (1948) *Radio Listening in America*, Prentice-Hill, New York.

Lazarsfeld, Paul F. and Kendall, Patricia L. (1950) Problems of survey analysis. In Merton and Lazarsfeld (eds) *Continuities in Social Research: Studies in the Scope and Method of 'The American Soldier*. Free Press, Glencoe. IL.

Lee, Alfred M. and Lee, Elizabeth B. (1939) *The Fine Art of Propaganda*, Harcourt, Brace, New York.

Merton, Robert K. (1949) *Social Theory and Social Structure*, Free Press, Glencoe, IL.

Meyersohn, Rolf (1953), Research in television: some highlights and a bibliography. Unpublished memorandum of the Bureau of Applied Social Research, Columbia University.

Minnesota, University of, School of Journalism Research Division (1949) *Newspapers and their Readers* (2 vols) University of Minnesota Press, Minneapolis, MN.

Schramm, Wilbur and White, David M. (1949) Age, education and economic status as factors in newspaper reading. *Journalism Quarterly*, Vol. 26, pp. 155–7.

Shils, Edward A. (1951) The study of the primary group. In Lerner and Lasswell (eds) *The Policy Sciences*, Stanford University Press, Stanford, CA.

Social Science Research Council (1947) *Public Reaction to the Atomic Bomb and World Affairs*, Cornell University Press, Ithaca, NY.

Tolman, Edward C. (1951) A psychological model. In Parsons and Shils (eds) *Toward A General Theory of Action*, Harvard University Press, Cambridge, MA.

Whyte Jr, William H. (1954) The web of word-of-mouth. *Fortune*, November.

17

The effects of mass communication

Joseph T. Klapper

From Berelson, B. and Janowitz, M. (eds) (1966) *Reader in Public Opinion and Communication*, 2nd edn, The Free Press, New York, pp. 473–86.

Twenty years ago, writers who undertook to discuss mass communication typically felt obliged to define that then unfamiliar term. In the intervening years, conjecture and research upon the topic, particularly in reference to the *effects* of mass communication, have burgeoned. The literature has reached that stage of profusion and disarray, characteristic of all proliferating disciplines, at which researchers and research administrators speak wistfully of establishing centres where the accumulating data might be sifted and stored. The field has grown to the point at which its practitioners are periodically asked by other researchers to attempt to assess the cascade, to determine whither we are tumbling, to attempt to assess, in short 'what we know about the effects of mass communication'.

The bases of pessimism

The pessimism, at present, is widespread, and it exists both among the interested lay public and within the research fraternity.

Some degree of pessimism, or even cynicism, is surely to be expected from the lay public, whose questions we have failed to answer. Teachers, preachers, parents, and legislators have asked us a thousand times over these past 15 years whether violence in the media produces delinquency, whether the escapist nature of much of the fare does not blind people to reality, and just what the media can do to the political persuasions of their audiences. To these questions we have not only failed to provide definitive answers, but we have done something worse: we have provided evidence in partial support of every hue of every view. We have claimed, on the one hand, and on empirical grounds, that escapist material provides its audience with blinders and with an unrealistic view of life,[1] and, on the other hand, that it helps them meet life's real problems.[2] We have hedged on the crime and violence question, typically saying, 'Well, probably there is no causative relationship, but there just might be a triggering effect'.[3] In reference to persuasion, we have maintained that the media are after all not so terribly powerful,[4] and yet we have reported their impressive success in promoting such varied phenomena as religious intolerance,[5] the sale of war bonds,[6] belief in the American Way,[7] and disenchantment with Boy Scout activities.[8] It is surely no wonder that a bewildered public should regard with cynicism a research tradition which supplies, instead of definitive answers, a plethora of relevant but inconclusive and at times seemingly contradictory findings.

Considerable pessimism, of a different order, is also to be expected within the research fraternity itself. Such anomalous findings as have been cited above seemed to us at first to betoken merely the need of more penetrating and rigorous research. We shaped insights into hypotheses and eagerly set up research designs in quest of the additional variables which we were sure would bring order out of chaos and enable us to describe the process of effect with sufficient precision to diagnose and predict. But the variables emerged in such a cataract that we almost drowned. The relatively placid waters of 'who says what to whom'[9] were early seen be muddied by audience predispositions, 'self-selection', and selective perception. More recent studies, both in the laboratory and the social world, documented the influence of a host of other variables including various aspects of contextual organization;[10] the audiences' image of the sources;[11] the simple passage of time;[12] the group orientation of the audience member and the degree to which he values group membership;[13] the activity of opinion leaders;[14] the social aspects of the situation during and after exposure to the media,[15] and the degree to which the audience member is forced to play a role;[16] the personality pattern of the audience member;[17] his social class, and the level of his frustrations;[18] the nature of the media in a free enterprise system;[19] and the availability of 'social mechanism[s] for implementing action drives'.[20] The list, if not endless, is at least overwhelming, and it continues to grow. Almost every aspect of the life of the audience member and the culture in which the communication occurs seems susceptible of relation to the process of communication effect. As early as 1948, Berelson, cogitating on what was then known, came to the accurate if perhaps moody conclusion that 'some kinds of *communication* on some kinds of *issues*, brought to the attention of some kinds of *people* under some kinds of *conditions*, have some kinds of *effects*'.[21] It is surely no wonder that today, after another decade at the inexhaustible fount of variables, some researchers should feel that the formulation of any systematic description of what effects are now effected and the predictive application of such principles, are goals which become the more distant as they are the more vigorously pursued.

The bases of hope

This optimism is based on two phenomena. The first of these is a new orientation toward the study of communication effects which has recently become conspicuous in the literature. And the second phenomenon is the emergence, from this new approach, of a few tentative generalizations. [. . .]

The 'phenomenistic' approach

The new orientation, which has of course been hitherto and variously formulated, can perhaps be described, in a confessedly over-simplified way, as a shift away from the concept of 'hypodermic effect' toward an approach which might be called 'situational' or 'functional'.[22] Because of the specific, and for our purposes sometimes irrelevant, connotations attached to these two terms, we will here use a word coined by the present author in an earlier publication and refer to the approach as 'phenomenistic'.[23] Whatever it be called, it is in essence a shift *away* from the tendency to regard mass communication as a necessary and sufficient cause of audience effects, toward a view of the media as influences, working amid other influences, in a total situation. The old quest of specific effects stemming from the communication has given way to the observation of existing conditions or changes, followed by an inquiry into the factors, *including* mass communication, which produced those conditions and changes, and the roles which these factors played relative to each other. In short, attempts to assess a stimulus which was presumed to work alone have given way to an assessment of the role of that stimulus in a total observed phenomenon.

Examples of the new approach are becoming fairly numerous. The so-called Elmira[24] and Decatur[25] studies, for example, set out to determine the critical factors in various types of observed decisions, rather than to focus exclusively on whether media did or did not have effects. The Rileys and Maccoby focus on the varying functions which media serve for different sorts of children, rather than enquiring whether media do or do not affect them.[26] Some of the more laboratory-oriented researchers, in particular the Hovland school, have been conducting ingeniously designed controlled experiments in which the communication stimulus is a constant, and various extra-communication factors are the variables.[27]

It is possible that the phenomenistic approach may so divert our attention to the factors with which mass communication is in interplay, or to the fact that interplay exists, that we forget our original goal of determining the effects of mass communication itself. For example, the effects of mass communication are likely to differ, depending upon whether the communication is or is not in accord with the norms of groups to which the audience members belong. The effects of fantasy and of media depictions of crime and violence are likely to have different effects among children who are primarily oriented toward different types of groups. This is valuable information which contributes greatly to our knowledge of the processes and types of mass communication effect. But if research is to provide socially meaningful answers to questions about the effects of mass communication, it must inquire into the relative prevalence of these different conditions under which mass communication has different effects.

It must be remembered that though mass communication seems usually to be a *contributory* cause of effects, it is often a major or necessary cause and in some instances a sufficient cause. The fact that its effect is often mediated, or that it often works among other influences, must not blind us to the fact that mass communication possesses qualities which distinguish it from other influences, and that by virtue of these qualities, it is unlikely to have characteristic effects. But there seems some danger that attention may at times become too exclusively focused on the other factors to which the phenomenistic approach points, and the dangers of such neglect must be kept in mind.

[. . .]

Concluding note

[. . .]

Sketchy and imperfect as they are, these propositions regarding the process and direction of effect seem applicable to the effects of persuasive communications and to the effects of various kinds of non-persuasive media content upon a wide range of audience orientations and behaviour patterns. Furthermore, the mediating variables such as predispositions, group membership, personality patterns, and the like, seem to play essentially similar roles in all these various kinds of effects.

They do not, for example, cover the residuum of direct effects, such as the creation of moods, except to note that such effects exist. They recognize, but in no way illuminate, the dynamism of the variety of effects stemming from such contextual and presentational variables as order, timing, camera angles, and the like. They are less easy to apply, and are conceivably inapplicable, to certain other broad areas of effect, such as the effect of the media upon each other, upon patterns of daily life, and upon cultural values as a whole. To be sure, we have spoken of cultural values as a mediating factor which in part determines media content, but certainly some sort of circular relationship must exist, and media content must in turn affect cultural values.

Such concepts suggest what is perhaps the greatest danger inherent in the approach to communications research is the tendency to go overboard in blindly minimizing the effects and potentialities of mass communications. In reaping the fruits of the discovery that mass media function amid a nexus of other influences, we must not forget that the influences nevertheless differ. Mass media of communication possess various characteristics and capabilities distinct from those of peer groups of opinion leaders. They are, after all, media of *mass* communication, which daily address tremendous cross-sections of the population with a single voice. It is neither sociologically unimportant nor insignificant that the media have rendered it possible, as Wiebe (1952) has put it, for Americans from all social strata to laugh at the same joke, nor is it insignificant that total strangers, upon first meeting, may share valid social expectations that small talk about Lucy and Desi, or about Betty Furness, will be mutually comprehensible. We must not lose sight of the peculiar characteristics of the media nor of the likelihood that of this peculiar character there may be engendered peculiar effects.

We must remember also that under conditions and in situations other than those described in this volume, the media of mass communication may well have effects which are quite different and possibly more dramatic or extensive than those which have here been documented.

For example, the research here cited which bears upon mass communication of an instrument of persuasion has typically dealt with non-crucial issues and has been pursued either in laboratories or in naturalistic situations within a relatively stable society. Little attention has here been given to the potentialities of persuasive mass communication at times of massive political upheaval or in situations of actual or imminent social unrest. Given the rumblings of serious social malcontent – or, in terms of our current orientation, given individuals with predispositions toward change, unstructured as the envisaged change may be – mass communication would appear to be capable of molding or 'canalizing' the predispositions into specific channels and so producing an active revolutionary movement. Some such process, in miniature, appears to have occurred in the previously cited cases of Nazi and North Korean soldiers who, upon the dissolution of their primary groups, became susceptible to Allied propaganda. A similar process of greater social width may well have occurred in under-developed countries in which the Communist party has recently become a major political force. Mass communication in such areas has of course been deliberately and carefully abetted by personal influence and by the formation and manipulation of reinforcing primary and secondary groups. Although it cannot therefore be said to have been a sufficient cause of the observed social changes, it may well have been an extremely important or even a crucial cause. Its effects may have been largely restricted to the activation and focusing of amorphous unrest, but these appear to have had consequences far beyond those normally associated with the reinforcement of pre-existing and specific attitudes. The fear that a similar activation process may occur, or that the media might actually create new attitudes, presumably lies behind the totalitarian practice of denying media access to voices of the political opposition.[28]

Even within a relatively stable social situation, the media of mass communication may well exercise extensive social effects upon the masses by the indirect road of affecting the élite. Particular vehicles of mass communication (e.g. *The New York Times*) and other vehicles directed toward a more specialized audience (e.g. *The Wall Street Journal* or *U.S. News and World Report*) may reasonably be supposed to affect the decisions and behaviour of policy-making élites. Individual business and political leaders may or may not be 'opinion leaders' in the sense in which the term is used in communications research – i.e. they may or may not critically influence a handful of their peers. But their decisions and their consequent behaviour in themselves affect society at large, and the mere fact of their taking a particular stand frequently serves to make that stand and the issue to which it pertains a topic of media reporting and debate, and a topic in regard to which personal influence, in the more restricted sense of the term, is exercised. The media may, in short, stimulate the élite to actions which affect the masses and which incidentally re-stimulate and so affect both the media and channels of interpersonal influence.

It has also been suggested that the classic studies of how voters make up their minds – e.g., Lazarsfeld, Berelson, and Gaudet (1948) and Berelson, Lazarsfeld, and McPhee (1945) – provide an incomplete picture of the total effects of mass communication because they concentrate only on effects which occur *during* the campaign itself. Lang and Lang (1959), for example, point out that although most of the voters observed in such studies apparently kept to a decision made before the campaign began, shifts in voting behaviour sufficient to produce changes of administration do occur. They suggest that such changes take place slowly *between* the campaigns, as new issues arise and as the images of the parties change or fail to change. Mass communication, they propose, makes these issues salient and builds the party images, and may thus exercise a much more extensive effect than is revealed in the classic voting studies. The Langs call for research designed to investigate the possibility of such effects and of various other types of effect which they believe mass communication may exercise upon political opinion.

Some elections, furthermore, may be more 'critical' than others. Key (1955), for example, notes that there is 'a category of elections,' including those of 1896 and 1928, in which

> ... voters are, at least from impressionistic evidence, unusually deeply concerned, in which the extent of electoral involvement is relatively quite high, and in which the decisive results of the voting reveal a sharp alteration of the pre-existing cleavage within the electorate. Moreover, and perhaps this is the truly differentiating characteristic of this sort of election, the realignment made manifest in the voting in such elections seems to persist for several succeeding elections.[29]

The elections on which the classic voting studies focus are not 'critical' by these criteria, but are rather occasions on which previously manifested alignments held more or less stable. What role mass communication may play in determining voters' decisions before a 'critical' election is not yet known.

Mass media may also have extensive but as yet undocumented effects of various non-political sorts. We have already alluded, for example, to the probable but unmapped interplay between the mass media and cultural values. To look more closely into one aspect of this matter, one might postulate that the media play a particularly important role in the socialization and acculturation of children. Such studies of children as are cited in this volume have dealt with children aged five and older, and have focused on highly specific attitudes or patterns of behaviour. But to what degree do the media structure, even for younger children, the society and the culture which they are entering? The influence of the media in these respects is no doubt modified by the influence of the family, of the school, and of peer groups; but the question of ultimate media effect is complicated, perhaps beyond the possibility of simplification, by the fact that the persons comprising these very sources of extra-media influence are themselves exposed to and affected by the media. The role and the effects of the media in the socialization of the child can perhaps no longer be accurately assessed, but some concept of its possible scope may be obtained by performing the mental experiment of imagining the process of socialization occurring in a society in which mass media did not exist. Our knowledge of primitive cultures and of pre-media years suggests that the present social system and the present culture are at least in part a product of the existence of mass communication, and may be dependent upon such communication for their continued existence.

One may also speculate on the possibility that some of the functions served by mass communication may, perhaps indirectly and perhaps only after a long period, have certain effects both upon the audience as individuals and upon integral elements of the social structure. We have noted, for example, that certain light media material, such as comic strips, serves certain audience members by providing a common ground for social discourse. It is interesting to speculate on what alternative systems of serving the same function may be thereby replaced, may be reduced in importance, or may simply fail to develop for lack of being needed. If no comic strips or other mass media material existed to serve the conversational needs of the adult males observed by Bogart (1955), might they and others like them perhaps be more actively interested in each other's real life goals and problems? Do mass media, by providing an easily available and common ground for chit-chat, perhaps reduce or retard the development of interest in one's fellow men? And to what degree, if any, has the serving of such functions by mass media affected the functions previously served by such institutions as the neighbourhood bar and barber shop?

The phenomenistic approach also has its dangers and limitations. As we have noted, the identification of conditions under which mass communication has different effects is only a step in the direction of answering the basic questions about the incidence of such effects. If the influence of mass communication is to be described in socially meaningful terms, research must also enquire into the relative prevalence of the conditions under which the several effects occur.

Notes

1. For example Arnheim (1944) and Herzog (1944).
2. For example Warner and Henry (1948).
3. This is a typical conclusion of surveys of pertinent literature and comment, e.g. Bogart (1956, pp. 258–74).
4. For example Lazarsfeld and Merton (1948); Klapper (1948).
5. Klapper (1949, pp. II–25, IV–52).
6. Merton (1946).
7. The efficacy as well as the limitations of media in this regard are perhaps most exhaustively documented in the various unclassified evaluation reports of the United States Information Agency.
9. Lasswell proposed in 1946 (Smith, Lasswell and Casey, p. 121) that communications research might be described as an inquiry into 'Who says what, through what channels (media) of communication, to whom, [with] what . . . results'. This now classic formulation was widely adopted as an organizational framework for courses and books of readings in communications research and greatly influenced research orientations as well.
10. For example Hovland (1954); Hovland et al. (1957).
11. For example Merton (1946, p. 61); Freeman, Weeks and Wertheimer (1955); Hovland, Janis, and Kelly (1953, Chapter ii), which summarizes a series of studies by Hovland, Weiss, and Kelman.
12. Hovland, Lumsdaine, and Sheffield (1949) *in re* 'sleeper effects' and 'temporal effects.'
13. For example Kelley and Volkart (1952); Riley and Riley (1951); Ford (1954); Katz and Lazarsfeld (1955) review a vast literature on the subject (pp. 15–133).
14. Katz (1957) provides an exhaustive review of the topic.
15. For example Friedson (1953). For an early insight, see Cooper and Jahoda (1947).
16. Janis and King (1954), King and Janis (1953), and Kelman (1953), all of which are summarized and evaluated in Hovland, Janis and Kelley (1953); also Michael and Maccoby (1953).
17. For example Janis (1954); Hovland, Janis and Kelley (1953, Chapter vi); Janis et al. (1959).
18. For example Maccoby (1954).
19. For example Klapper (1948); Klapper (1949, pp. IV–20–27); Wiebe (1952b).
20. Wiebe (1951).

21. Berelson (1948, p. 172).
22. See Berelson, Lazarsfeld, and McPhee (1954, p. 234), for 'hypodermic effect'.
23. Klapper (1957–8).
24. Berelson, Lazarsfeld, and McPhee (1954, p. 234).
25. Katz and Lazarsfeld (1955).
26. Riley and Riley (1951), and Maccoby (1954).
27. For example the experimental programmes described in Hovland, Janis and Kelley (1953), Hovland *et al.* (1957), and Janis *et al.* (1959).
28. Monopoly propaganda as practised by totalitarian governments, and a kind of unwitting monopoly propaganda practised in democracies in favour of certain cultural values, are believed by some authors to be in themselves very effective procedures. See, for example, Kazarsfeld (1942), Lazarsfeld and Merton (1948), and Klapper (1948) and (1949, IV–20–27). In general, these writers suggest that the monopoly propaganda continually reinforces the attitudes it espouses, while simultaneously handicapping the birth and preventing the spread of opposing views. The argument is logically appealing and has been advanced as a conjectural explanation of various attitude and opinion phenomena, but it has been neither substantiated nor refuted by empirical research.
29. Key (1955, p. 4).

References

Arnheim, Rudolf (1944) The world of the daytime serial. In Lazarsfeld, Paul F. and Stanton, Frank N. (eds) *Radio Research, 1942–43*, Duell, Sloan and Pearce, New York.

Berelson, Bernard (1948) Communications and public opinion. In Schramm, Wilbur (ed.) *Communications in Modern Society*, University of Illinois Press, Urbana, IL.

Berelson, Bernard, Lazarsfeld, Paul and McPhee, William (1954) *Voting: A Study of Opinion Formation in a Presidential Campaign*, University of Chicago Press, Chicago.

Bogart, Leo (1955) Adult talk about newspaper comics. *American Journal of Sociology*, Vol. LXI, pp. 26–30.

Bogart, Leo (1956) *The Age of Television*, Frederick Ungar, New York.

Cooper, Eunice and Jahoda, Marie (1947) The evasion of propaganda. *Journal of Psychology*, Vol. XXIII, pp. 15–25.

Ford, Joseph B. (1954) The primary group in mass communication. *Sociology and Social Research*, Vol. XXIII, pp. 15–25.

Freeman, Howard E., Weeks, H. Ashley, and Wertheimer, Walter I. (1955) News commentator effect: a study in knowledge and opinion change. *Public Opinion Quarterly*, Vol. XIX, pp. 209–15.

Friedson, Eliot (1953) The relation of the social situation of contact to the media of mass communication. *Public Opinion Quarterly*, Vol. XVII, pp. 230–8.

Herzog, Herta (1944) What do we really know about daytime serial listeners. In Lazarsfeld, Paul and Stanton, Frank (eds) *Radio Research, 1942–43*, Duell, Sloan and Pearce, New York.

Hovland, Carl I. (1954) Effects of the mass media of communication. In Lindzey, Gardner (ed.) *Handbook of Social Psychology*, Addison-Wesley, Cambridge, MA, Vol. II, pp. 1062–103.

Hovland, Carl I. *et al.* (1957) *The Order of Presentation in Persuasion*, Yale University Press, New Haven.

Hovland, Carl I., Lumsdaine, Arthur A. and Sheffield, Fred D. (1949) *Experiments on Mass Communication. Studies in Social Psychology in World War II*, Princeton University Press, Princeton, Vol. III.

Hovland, Carl I., Janis, Irving L. and Kelley, Harold H. (1953) *Communication and Persuasion*, Yale University Press, New Haven.

Hovland, Carl I. *et al.* (1959) *Personality and Persuasibility*, Yale University Press, New Haven.

Hovland Carl I. and King, B. T. (1954) The influencing of role-playing on opinion change. *Journal of Abnormal and Social Psychology*, Vol. XLIX, pp. 211–18.

Janis, Irving L. (1954) Personality correlates of susceptibility to persuasion. *Journal of Personality*, Vol. XXII, pp. 504–18.

Katz, Elihu (1957) The two-step flow of communication. *Public Opinion Quarterly*, Vol. XXI, pp. 61–78.

Katz, Elihu and Lazarsfeld, Paul (1955) *Personal Influence*, The Free Press, Glencoe, IL.

Kelley, Harold H. and Volkart, Edmund H. (1952) The resistance to change of group anchored attitudes. *American Sociological Review*, Vol. XVII, pp. 453–65.

Kelman, Herbert C. (1953) Attitude as a function of response restriction. *Human Relations*, Vol. VI, pp. 185–214.

Key, V. O. (1955) A theory of critical elections. *Journal of Politics*, Vol. XVII, pp. 3–18.

King, B. T. and Janis, Irving L. (1953) Comparison of the effectiveness of improvised versus non-improvised role-playing in producing opinion changes. Paper presented before the Eastern Psychological Association.

Klapper, Joseph T. (1948) Mass media and the engineering of consent. *American Scholar*, Vol. XVII, pp. 419–29.

Klapper, Joseph T. (1957–8) What we know about the effects of mass communication: the brink of hope. *Public Opinion Quarterly*, Vol. XXI, No. 4.

Lang, Kurt and Lang, Gladys E. (1959) The mass media and voting. In Burdick, Eugene and Brodbeck, A., *American Voting Behavior*, The Free Press, Glencoe, IL.

Lazarsfeld, Paul F. (1942) The effects of radio on public opinion. In Waples, Douglas (ed.) *Print, Radio and Film in a Democracy*, University of Chicago Press, Chicago.

Lazarsfeld, Paul F., Berelson, Bernard and Gaudet, Hazel (1948) *The People's Choice*, Columbia University Press, New York.

Lazarsfeld, Paul F. and Merton, Robert K. (1948) Mass communication, popular taste and organized social action. In Bryson, Lyman (ed.) *The Communication of Ideas*, Harper and Bros, New York.

Maccoby, Eleanor E. (1954) Why do children watch TV? *Public Opinion Quarterly*, Vol. XVIII, pp. 239–44.

Merton, Robert K. (1946) *Mass Persuasion*, Harper and Bros, New York.

Michael, Donald N. and Maccoby, Nathan (1953) Factors influencing verbal learning from films under varying conditions of audience participation. *Journal of Experimental Psychology*, Vol. XLVI, pp. 411–18.

Riley Jr, John W. and Riley, Mathilda White (1959) Mass communication and the social system. In Merton, Robert K., Broom, Leonard and Cottrell, Leonard S., Jr (eds) *Sociology Today: Problems and Prospects*, Basic Books, New York.

Riley, Mathilda White and Riley Jr, John W. (1951) A sociological approach to communication research. *Public Opinion Quarterly*, Vol. XV, pp. 444–60.

Smith, Bruce L., Lasswell, Harold D. and Casey, Ralph D. (1946) *Propaganda, Communication and Public Opinion*, Princeton University Press, Princeton.

Warner, Lloyd and Henry, William (1948) The radio day time serial: a symbolic analysis. *Genetic Psychology Monographs*, Vol. XXXVII, pp. 3–71.

Wiebe, Gerhardt D. (1952a) Mass communications. In Hartley, Eugene and Hartley, R. E. *Fundamentals of Social Psychology*, A. A. Knopf, New York.

Wiebe, Gerhardt D. (1952b) Responses to the televised Kefauver hearings. *Public Opinion Quarterly*, Vol. XVI, pp. 179–200.

18

Toward 'cultural indicators': the analysis of mass mediated public message systems

George Gerbner

From Allen, W. H. (ed.) (1969) *AV Communication Review*, Department of Audiovisual Instruction, Washington DC, Vol. 17, No. 2, pp. 137–48.

The systematic analysis of message content is a traditional area of study in communication research and related fields. Recent developments led to a revival of interest in the area. But none of the new frameworks and approaches presented consider the analysis of message systems addressed to heterogeneous and anonymous publics, such as mass communications, a source of theoretical development not necessarily generated in other areas of interest. The purpose of this paper is to suggest an approach that justifies such development and can also lead to results of practical policy significance, such as a scheme of social accounting for trends in the composition and structure of mass-mediated public message systems. The approach is based on a conception of these message systems as the common culture through which communities cultivate shared and public notions about facts, values, and contingencies of human existence.

Change in the symbolic environment

The 'Cultural Revolution' is not only a Chinese slogan. It is also a fact of social life whenever a particular political–industrial order permeates the sphere of public message production. A change in the social bases and economic goals of message mass-production leads, sooner or later, to a transformation of the common symbolic environment that gives public meaning and sense of direction to human activity. The need is for a theory that can lead to the development of 'cultural indicators' taking the pulse of the nature and tempo of that transformation.

Our theoretical point of departure, then, is that changes in the mass production and rapid distribution of messages across previous barriers of time, space, and social grouping bring about systematic variations in public message content whose full significance rests in the cultivation of collective consciousness about elements of existence. (It should be noted at the outset that the terms *common*, *shared*, *public*, or *collective* cultivation do not necessarily mean consensus. On the contrary, the public recognition of subcultural, class, generational, and ideological differences and even conflicts among scattered groups of people requires some common

144

awareness and cultivation of the issues, styles, and points of divergence that make public contention and contest possible. The struggles for power and privilege, for participation in the conduct of affairs, for the redistribution of resources, and for all forms of social recognition and justice, are increasingly shifting from the older arenas to the newer spheres of public attention and control in mass-produced communications.)

Selective habits of participation in one's cultural environment limit each of us to risky, and often faulty, extrapolation about the cultural experience of heterogeneous communities. Informed policy making and the valid interpretation of social response increasingly require general and comparative indicators of the prevailing climate of the man-made symbolic environment. But knowledge of a message system, over and above that which we select for our own information or entertainment, and which has significance for a collectivity such as an entire cultural community, cannot be given in the lifetime experience of any single person.

What *can* be given is a representative abstraction from the collectively experienced total texture of messages, relevant to certain investigative purposes. Sampling is not the major problem, and neither is the efficient processing of large quantities of data, although these are important procedural considerations. Nor is great theoretical challenge involved in the analysis of mass media messages for specific critical, control, evaluative, or policy purposes. The outstanding problems are the development of a generalized scheme applicable to the investigation of the broadest terms of collective cultivation in different cultural communities, and making these terms salient to elements of existence represented in public message systems. Philosophers, historians, anthropologists, and others have, of course, addressed themselves to such problems before. But the rise of the institutionalized and corporately managed cultivation of collective consciousness by mass media has given a new urgency and social policy significance to the inquiry.

Cultivation of public consciousness through mass communication

A word on *cultivation*. I use the term to indicate that my primary concern in this discussion is not with information, education, persuasion, etc., or with any kind of direct communication 'effects'. I am concerned with the collective context within which, and in response to which, different individual and group selections and interpretations of messages take place. In that sense, a message (or message system) cultivates consciousness of the terms required for its meaningful perception. Whether I accept its 'meaning' or not, like it or not, or agree or disagree, is another problem. First I must attend to and grasp what it is about. Just how that occurs, how items of information are integrated into given frameworks of cognition, is also another problem. My interest here centres on the fact that any attention and understanding cultivates the terms upon which it is achieved. And to the considerable extent to which these terms are common to large groups, the cultivation of shared terms provides the basis for public interaction.

Public is another word of special significance here. It means both a quality of information and 'an amorphous social structure whose members share a community-of-interest which has been produced by impersonal communication and contact' (Gould and Kolb, 1964, p. 558). As a quality of information, the awareness that a certain item of knowledge is publicly held (i.e. not only known to many, *but commonly known that it is known to many*) makes collective thought and action possible. Such knowledge gives individuals their awareness of collective strength (or weakness), and a feeling of social identification or alienation As an 'amorphous social structure, etc.' a public is a basic unit of and requirement for self-government among diverse and scattered groups The creation of both the consciousness and the social structure called public is the result of the 'public-making' activity approximately named publication. 'Public opinion' is actually the outcome of some sort of eliciting and some private views through their publication – as in the publication of polls.

Publication as a general social process is the creation and cultivation of shared ways of selecting and viewing events and aspects of life. Mass production and distribution of message systems transforms selected private perspectives into broad public perspectives, and brings mass publics into existence. These publics are maintained through continued publication. They are supplied with selections of information and entertainment, fact and fiction, news and fantasy or 'escape' materials which are considered important or interesting or entertaining and profitable (or all of these) in terms of the perspectives to be cultivated.

Publication is thus the basis of community consciousness and self-government among large groups of people too numerous or too dispersed to interact face to face or in any other personally mediated fashion. The truly revolutionary significance of modern mass communication is its 'public-making' ability. That is the ability to form historically new bases for collective thought and action quickly, continuously, and pervasively across previous boundaries of time, space, and culture.

The terms of broadest social interaction are those available in the most widely shared message systems of a culture. Increasingly these are mass-produced message systems. That is why mass media have been called the 'agenda-setters' of modern society Whether one is widely conversant with or unaware of large portions of them, supportive or critical of them, or even alienated from or rebellious of them, the terms of the culture shape the course of the response.

The approach I am suggesting is, therefore, concerned with the overall patterns and boundary conditions within which the processes of individual cognition, message utilization, and social interaction occur. The approach is directed toward answering the most general questions about the broadest terms of collective concept-formation given in mass-produced public message systems. What perspectives and what choices do they make available to entire communities over time, across cultures, and in different societies? With what kinds and proportions of properties and qualities are these choices weighted? What are the underlying structures of association in large message systems that are not apparent in their separate component units?

The need for 'cultural indicators'

We need to know what general terms of collective cultivation about existence, priorities, values, and relationships are given in collectively shared public message systems before we can reliably interpret facts of individual and social response. For example, it means little to know that 'John believes in Santa Claus' until we also know in what culture, at what point in time, and in the context of what public message systems cultivating the reinforcement or inhibition of such beliefs. Similarly, interpretations of public opinion (i.e. responses to questions elicited in specific cultural contexts), and of many social and cultural policy matters, require the background knowledge of general 'cultural indicators' similar to the economic indicators compiled to guide economic policy and the social indicators proposed to inform social policy making.

What distinguishes the analysis of public, mass-mediated message systems as a social scientific enterprise from other types of observation, commentary, or criticism is the attempt to deal comprehensively, systematically, and generally rather than specifically and selectively or *ad hoc* with problems of collective cultural life. This approach makes no prior assumptions about such conventionally demarcated. functions as 'in formation' and 'entertainment,' or 'high culture' and 'low culture'. Style of expression, quality of representation, artistic excellence, or the quality of individual experience associated with selective exposure to and participation in mass-cultural activity are not considered critical variables for this purpose. What is informative, entertaining (or both), good, bad, or indifferent by any standard of quality are selective judgements applied to messages quite independently from the social functions they actually perform in the context of large message systems touching the collective life of a whole community. Conventional and formal judgements applied to selected communications may be irrelevant to general questions about the presentation of what *is*, what is *important*, what is *right*, and what is *related* to what in mass-produced composite message systems.

Non-relevance of some conventional distinctions

Just as we make no *a priori* assumptions about the significance of style, quality, and subjective experience associated with different types of message systems, we do not recognize the validity of conventional distinctions of function attached to non-fictional vs fictional modes of presentation. 'Fact' may be stranger than fiction, and the veracity of 'fiction' greater than that of the presumably factual. Regardless of verisimilitude, credibility, or what is actually 'believed' in a presentation, message systems cultivate the terms upon which they present subjects or aspects of life. There is no reason for assuming that the cultivation of these terms depends in any significant way upon the mode of presentation, upon agreement or disagreement with or belief or disbelief in the presentations involved, or upon whether these presentations are presumably factual or imaginary. This does not mean, of course, that we do not normally attach greater credibility to a news story, a presumably factual report, a trusted source, a familiar account, than to a fairy tale or to what we regard as false or inimical. What it does mean is that in the general process of image formation and cultivation, fact and fable play equally significant and inter-related roles.

There is, however, an important difference between the ways fiction and non-fiction deal with life. Reportage, exposition, explanation, argument – whether based on fact, fancy, opinion, or all of these – ordinarily deal with specific aspects of life or thought extracted from total situations. What gives shape, focus, and purpose to the non-fictional mode of presentation is that it is analytical; it implicitly organizes the universe into classes of subjects and topics, and it devotes primary attention to one or more of these subjects and topics.

The usual purpose of the fictional and dramatic modes of presentation is to present situations rather than fragments of knowledge as such. The focus is on people in action; subjects and topics enter as they become significant to the situations.

From the point of view of the analysis of elements of existence, values, and relationships inherent in large message systems, fiction and drama thus offer special opportunities. Here an aspect of life, an area of knowledge, or the operation of a social enterprise appears imaginatively re-created in its significant associations with total human situations. The requirements that make the treatment of specific subjects secondary to the requirements of telling a 'good story' might make the treatment of those subjects more revealing of the underlying assumptions cultivated in the story-telling process.

It should be stressed again that the characteristics of a message system are not necessarily the characteristics of individual units composing the system. The purpose of the study of a system *as system* is to reveal features, processes, and relationships expressed in the whole, not in its parts. Unlike most literary or dramatic criticism, or, in fact, most personal cultural participation and judgement, this approach to message system analysis focuses on the record of institutional behaviour in the cultural field, and on the dynamics of message-production and image cultivation in a community but not necessarily in selective personal experience and response.

The systems with which we deal contain images and motion as well as words. This places great demands on methods of recording and notation, and challenges the ingenuity of the scientific analyst. Because of the necessity to abstract propositional forms from statements made in a variety of modes, methods of analysis must rely on explicitly formulated rules and procedures. But there is no reason to assume that the system-theoretic notions developed by Rapoport (in press) are not as applicable to these as to other 'large corpuses of verbal data'. Rapoport's description of man's 'ocean of words' provides a vivid rationale for the study of the process in which mass produced messages play a key part:

> Just as all living organisms live in certain specialized environments to which they adapt and which completely determines their lives so do human beings live to a significant extent in an ocean of words. The difference lies in the fact that the human environment is to a large extent man made. we secrete words into the environment around us just as we secrete carbon dioxide and in doing so, we create an invisible semantic environment of words which is part of our existence in quite as important ways as the physical environment. The content of verbal output does not merely passively reflect the complex social, political, and economic reality of the human race; it interacts with it as well. As our semantic environment incorporates the verbal outputs secreted into it, it becomes both enriched and polluted, and these changes are in large measure responsible for the course of human history. It behooves us to study this process.

Terms of the analysis

The approach needed is that capable of abstracting and analysing the most general terms of cultivation given in mass produced public message systems. Generality is necessary to encompass many specific classes of statements and diverse investigative purposes within comparable terms of the same framework. But this kind of generality implies a high level of abstraction and selection which, in turn, arises from a conception of salience to some general investigative purpose. As I have already noted, the present purpose is not governed by direct interest in sources as senders or in interpreters as receivers of messages. It is, however, governed by interest in the cultivation of consciousness of elements of existence inferred from public message systems. Our task is to combine generality with salience to the composition and structure of knowledge given in large-scale message systems addressed to collective social entities.

We begin by defining such knowledge as propositions ex pressed in the images, actions, and language of the most widely shared (i.e. mass-produced and rapidly distributed) message systems of a culture. Elements of existence refer to the assumptions, contexts, points of view, and relationships represented in these message systems and made explicit in the analysis.

A summary of the questions, measures, and terms of general analysis of public message systems appears in Fig. 18.1. The questions relate to the

Questions	Definitions	Measures and terms of analysis	Brief explanations of questions
1. What is?	Public assumptions about existence	Distribution, frequency of attention	What things (or kinds of things) does this message system call to the attention of a community?
2. What is important?	Context of priorities	Ordering, scaling, for *emphasis*	In what context or order of importance are these things arranged?
3. What is right, etc.?	Point of view, affective qualities	Measures of differential *tendency*	In what light or from what point of view are these things presented?
4. What is related to what?	Proximal or logical associations	Contingencies, clustering *structure*	In what structure associations with one another are these things presented?

Fig. 18.1. Questions and terms of public message system analysis

cultivation of collective notions about: (1) 'what is' (i.e. what exists as an item of public knowledge); (2) 'what is important' (i.e. how the items are ordered); (3) 'what is right' (or wrong, or endowed with any qualities, or presented from any point of view); and (4) 'what is related to what' (by proximity or other connection). The corresponding terms of analytical measures are those of: (1) attention; (2) emphasis; and (3) tendency (the first three describing the composition of the system – i.e. what elements compose it and how they are distributed in it); and (4) structure (i.e. how they are put together or related to one another). A brief discussion of each of these terms follows.

1. *Attention* is the result of selection of phenomena to be attended. A measure of attention is an indication of the presence and frequency of subject elements (topics, themes, etc.) in a message system. The significance of attention as an aspect of the process of message-production and image-formation is that it stems from, and, in turn cultivates, assumptions about existence; it provides common conceptions about what 'is' (or at least what is sufficiently common and public knowledge to form a basis for social interaction).

2. *Emphasis* is that aspect of the composition of message systems which establishes a context of priorities of importance or relevance. The context of emphases sets us a field of differential appeal in which certain things stand out. Emphasis 'structures the agenda' of public conception and discourse cultivated in message systems. Measures of emphasis may be based on such indications of size, intensity, or stress as the headlining of topics in news items or the featuring of certain topics or themes as the major points of stories.

3. *Tendency.* The position of a system (as of an individual) in time, space, and in the overall structure of social relations enters into the approach, point of view, or direction from which it deals with aspects of existence. The directionality of presentation, the explicit or contextual judgement of qualities of phenomena expressed in the presentation, is called tendency.

The broadest overall dimension of judgement is a summary evaluation of the goodness or badness, rightness or wrongness of things. A measure of the favourable–unfavourable associations expressed in the comparative study of message systems may be called *critical tendency*; it is based primarily on whether a subject or topic appears in a supportive or critical context.

But judgement is, of course, multidimensional. *Differential* tendency can be used to describe a measure indicating directionality of judgement in several different dimensions.

4. *Structure* is that aspect of context which reveals relationships among components. These may be simply proximal, which we may call clustering, or they may be causal or other logical relationships. In this approach we are primarily interested in explicating the 'logic' implicit in the proximal structuring or clustering rather than in forms of reasoning; the former is more likely to be a property of large systems and thus not easily available to scrutiny. For example, the reasoning employed in the assertion that 'John loves Mary and will marry her' (whether expressed in a sentence, a story, a series of visual images, etc.) is apparent in that single statement. But if we compare two large message systems and find that the proximal occurrences of the words or concepts of 'love' and 'marry' is significantly

more frequent in one than in the other, we have discovered an element of comparative linkage or structure, and a kind of 'logic', that would not be revealed by inspecting propositions separately.

The above terms of analysis are suggested as standard category classes. The specific categories, and other methods of analysis, require considerable elaboration which cannot be attempted here. This approach to message system analysis is itself a part of a larger framework for an institutional approach to mass communications research described elsewhere (Gerbner, 1966c, 1967a). And while many studies cited in this volume and in the literature fit one or more of the general terms sketched above, the only investigation using all of them has been limited to a comparative study of the portrayal of education in the press and mass fiction of ten countries (Gerbner, 1964b).

The reader interested in a specific example of attention analysis may find it in a study of convention press coverage (Gerbner, 1967b). Analyses of trends in attention may be found in a study of 'Psychology, psychiatry and mental illness in the mass media: a study of trends, 1900–1959' (Gerbner, 1961b); or of 'Education about education by mass media' (Gerbner, 1966a). Studies focusing on emphasis include a comparative investigation of UN press coverage (Gerbner, 1961a). Differential tendencies were investigated in the study of ideological perspectives in the French press (Gerbner 1964a), and in a comparative study of characterizations in mass fiction and drama (Gerbner, 1966b). The analysis of message system structure was attempted in the comparative portrayal of education study cited above.

I know of no comprehensive and comparative studies of the kind that might yield the cultural indicators needed for a realistic assessment of the much-debated condition of man in modern 'mass cultures'. One reason might be the paucity of explicit formulations of the theoretical significance and types of inference that might be derived from the analysis of mass mediated public message systems. Another might be the lack of general terms salient to such analysis. The intention of this chapter has been to try to narrow these gaps.

References

Gerbner, G. (1961a) Press perspectives in world communications: a pilot study. *Journalism Quarterly*, Vol. 38, pp. 313–22.

Gerbner, G. (1961b) Psychology, psychiatry and mental illness in the mass media: a study of trends, 1900–1959. *Mental Hygiene*, Vol. 45, pp. 89–93.

Gerbner, G. (1964a) Ideological perspectives and political tendencies in news reporting. *Journalism Quarterly*, Vol. 41, pp. 495–509.

Gerbner, G. (1964b) Mass communications and popular conceptions of education: a cross-cultural study. Cooperative Research Project No. 876, U.S. Office of Education.

Gerbner, G. (1966a) Education about education by mass media. *The Educational Forum*, Vol. 31, 7–15.

Gerbner, G. (1966b) Images across cultures: Teachers and mass media fiction and drama. *The School Review*, Vol. 74, pp. 212–29.

Gerbner, G. (1966c) An institutional approach to mass communications research. In Thayer, L. (ed.) *Communication: Theory and Research*, Charles C. Thomas, Springfield, IL.

Gerbner, G. (1967a) Mass communication and human communication theory. In Dance, F. E. X. (ed.) *Human Communication Theory: Original Essays*, Holt, Rinehart and Winston, New York.

Gerbner, G. (1967b) The press and the dialogue in education: a case study of a national educational convention and its depiction in America's daily newspapers. *Journalism Monograph*, No. 5.

Gould, J. and Kolb, W. L. (1964) *A Dictionary of the Social Sciences*, The Free Press, New York.

Rapoport, A. (in press) A system-theoretic view of content analysis. In Gerbner, G., Holsti, O. R., Krippendorff, K., Paisley, W. J. and Stone, P. J. (eds) *The Analysis of Communication Content: Developments in Scientific Theories and Computer Techniques*. John Wiley, New York.

19

The agenda-setting function of mass media*

Maxwell E. McCombs and Donald L. Shaw

From Roshco, B. et al. (eds) (1972) *The Public Opinion Quarterly*, Vol. 36, No. 2. Columbia University Press, New York, pp. 176–87.

In choosing and displaying news, editors, newsroom staff, and broadcasters play an important part in shaping political reality. Readers learn not only about a given issue, but also how much importance to attach to that issue from the amount of information in a news story and its position. In reflecting what candidates are saying during a campaign, the mass media may well determine the important issues – that is, the media may set the 'agenda' of the campaign.

The authors are associate professors of journalism at the University of North Carolina, Chapel Hill.

In our day, more than ever before, candidates go before the people through the mass media rather than in person.[1] The information in the mass media becomes the only contact many have with politics. The pledges, promises, and rhetoric encapsulated in news stories, columns, and editorials constitute much of the information upon which a voting decision has to be made. Most of what people know comes to them 'second' or 'third' hand from the mass media or from other people.[2]

Although the evidence that mass media deeply change attitudes in a campaign is far from conclusive,[3] the evidence is much stronger that voters learn from the immense quantity of information available during each campaign.[4] People, of course, vary greatly in their attention to mass media political information. Some, normally the better educated and most politically interested (and those least likely to change political beliefs), actively seek information; but most seem to acquire it, if at all, without much effort. It just comes in. As Berelson succinctly puts it: 'On any single subject many "hear" but few "listen" '. But Berelson also found that those with the greatest mass media exposure are most likely to know where the candidates stand on different issues.[5] Trenaman and McQuail found the same thing in a study of the 1959 general election in England.[6] Voters do learn.

They apparently learn, furthermore, in direct proportion to the

*This study was partially supported by a grant from the National Association of Broadcasters. Additional support was provided by the UNC Institute for Research in Social Science and the School of Journalism Foundation of North Carolina.

emphasis placed on the campaign issues by the mass media. Specifically focusing on the agenda-setting function of the media, Lang and Lang observe:

> The mass media force attention to certain issues. They build up public images of political figures. They are constantly presenting objects suggesting what individuals in the mass should think about, know about, have feelings about.[7]

Perhaps this hypothesized agenda-setting function of the mass media is most succinctly stated by Cohen, who noted that the press 'may not be successful much of the time in telling people what to think, but it is stunningly successful in telling its readers what to think about'.[8] While the mass media may have little influence on the direction or intensity of attitudes, it is hypothesized that the mass media set the agenda for each political campaign, influencing the salience of attitudes toward the political issues.

Method

To investigate the agenda-setting capacity of the mass media in the 1968 presidential campaign, this study attempted to match what Chapel Hill voters said were key issues of the campaign with the actual content of the mass media used by them during the campaign. Respondents were selected randomly from lists of registered voters in five Chapel Hill precincts economically, socially, and racially representative of the community. By restricting this study to one community, numerous other sources of variation – for example, regional differences or variations in media performance – were controlled.

Between 18 September and 6 October, 100 interviews were completed. To select these 100 respondents a filter question was used to identify those who had not yet definitely decided how to vote – presumably those most open or susceptible to campaign information. Only those not yet fully committed to a particular candidate were interviewed. Borrowing from the Trenaman and McQuail strategy, this study asked each respondent to outline the key issues as he saw them, regardless of what the candidates might be saying at the moment.[9] Interviewers recorded the answers as exactly as possible.

Concurrently with the voter interviews, the mass media serving these voters were collected and content analysed. A pretest in spring 1968 found that for the Chapel Hill community almost all the mass media political information was provided by the following sources: *Durham Morning Herald*, *Durham Sun*, *Raleigh News and Observer*, *Raleigh Times*, *New York Times*, *Time*, *Newsweek*, and NBC and CBS evening news broadcasts.

The answers of respondents regarding major problems as they saw them and the news and editorial comment appearing between 12 September and 6 October in the sampled newspapers, magazines, and news broadcasts were coded into 15 categories representing the key issues and other kinds of campaign news. Media news content also was divided into 'major' and 'minor' levels to see whether there was any substantial difference in mass media emphasis across topics.[10] For the print media, this major/minor division was in terms of space and position; for television, it was made in terms of position and time allowed. More specifically, *major* items were defined as follows:

1. Television: any story 45 seconds or more in length and/or one of the three lead stories.
2. Newspapers: any story which appeared as the lead on the front page or on any page under a three-column headline in which at least one-third of the story (a minimum of five paragraphs) was devoted to political news coverage.
3. News magazines: any story more than one column or any item which appeared in the lead at the beginning of the news section of the magazine.
4. Editorial page coverage of newspapers and magazines: any item in the lead editorial position (the top left corner of the editorial page) plus all items in which one-third (at least five paragraphs) of an editorial or columnist comment was devoted to political campaign coverage.

Minor items are those stories which are political in nature and included in the study but which are smaller in terms of space, time, or display than major items.

Findings

The overall *major* item emphasis of the selected mass media on different topics and candidates during the campaign is displayed in Table 19.1. It indicates that a considerable amount of campaign news was not devoted to discussion of the major political issues but rather to *analysis of the campaign itself*. This may give pause to those who think of campaign news as being primarily about the issues. Thirty-five percent of the major news coverage of Wallace was composed of this analysis ('Has he a chance to win or not?'). For Humphrey and Nixon the figures were, respectively, 30 percent and 25 percent. At the same time, the table also shows the relative emphasis of candidates speaking about each other. For example, Agnew apparently spent more time attacking Humphrey (22 percent of the major news items about Agnew) than did Nixon (11 percent of the major news about Nixon). The overall minor item emphasis of the mass media on these political issues and topics closely paralleled that of major item emphasis.

Table 19.2 focuses on the relative emphasis of each party on the is sues, as reflected in the mass media. Table 19.2 shows that Humphrey/Muskie emphasized foreign policy far more than did Nixon/Agnew or Wallace/ Lemay. In the case of the 'law and order' issue, however, over half the Wallace/ Lemay news was about this, while less than one-fourth of the Humphrey/ Muskie news concentrated upon this topic. With Nixon/Agnew it was almost a third – just behind the Republican emphasis on foreign policy. Humphrey of course spent considerable time justifying (or commenting upon) the Vietnam War; Nixon did not choose (or have) to do this.

The media appear to have exerted a considerable impact on voters' judgements of what they considered the major issues of the campaign (even though the questionnaire specifically asked them to make judgements without regard to what politicians might be saying at the moment). The correlation between the major item emphasis on the main campaign issues

Table 19.1. Major mass media reports on candidates and issues, by candidates

	Nixon	Agnew	Hum- phrey	Muskie	Wallace	Lemay[a]	Total
The issues							
Foreign policy	7%	9%	13%	15%	2%	–	10%
Law and order	5	13	4	–	12	–	6
Fiscal policy	3	4	2	–	–	–	2
Public welfare	3	4	(*)[b]	5	2	–	2
Civil rights	3	9	(*)[b]	0	4	–	2
Other	19	13	14	25	11	–	15
The campaign							
Polls	1	–	–	–	1	–	(*)[b]
Campaign events	18	9	21	10	25	–	19
Campaign analysis	25	17	30	30	35	–	28
Other candidates							
Humphrey	11	22	–	5	1	–	5
Muskie	–	–	–	–	–	–	–
Nixon	–	–	11	5	3	–	5
Agnew	–	–	(*)[b]	–	–	–	(*)[b]
Wallace	5	–	3	5	–	–	3
Lemay	1	–	1	–	4	–	
Total percent	101%[c]	100%	99%	100%	100%	–	98%[c]
Total number	188	23	221	20	95	11	558

[a]Coverage of Lemay amounted to only 11 major items during the 12 September–6 October period and are not individually included in the percentages; they are included in the total column.
[b]Less than 0.05 percent.
[c]Does not sum to 100% because of rounding.

Table 19.2. Mass media report on issues, by parties

	Republican Nixon/Agnew			Democratic Humphrey/Muskie			American Wallace/Lemay		
Issues	Major	Minor	Total	Major	Minor	Total	Major	Minor	Total
Foreign policy	34%	40%	38%	65%	63%	64%	30%	21%	26%
Law and order	26	36	32	19	26	23	48	55	52
Fiscal policy	13	1	6	10	6	8	–	–	–
Public welfare	13	14	13	4	3	4	7	12	10
Civil rights	15	8	11	2	2	2	14	12	13
Total percent[a]	101%	99%	100%	100%	100%	101%	99%	100%	101%
Total number	47	72	119	48	62	110	28	33	61

[a]Some columns do not sum to 100% because of rounding.

carried by the media and voters' independent judgements of what were the important issues was +0.967. Between minor item emphasis on the main campaign issues and voters' judgements, the correlation was +0.979. In short, the data suggest a very strong relationship between the emphasis placed on different campaign issues by the media (reflecting to a considerable degree the emphasis by candidates) and the judgements of voters as to the salience and importance of various campaign topics.

But while the three presidential candidates placed widely different emphasis upon different issues, the judgements of the voters seem to reflect the *composite* of the mass media coverage. This suggests that voters pay some attention to all the political news *regardless* of whether it is from, or about, any particular favoured candidate. Because the tables we have seen reflect the composite of all the respondents, it is possible that individual differences, reflected in party preferences and in a predisposition to look mainly at material favourable to one's own party, are lost by lumping all the voters together in the analysis. Therefore, answers of respondents who indicated a preference (but not commitment) for one of the candidates during the September–October period studied (45 of the respondents; the others were undecided) were analysed separately. Table 19.3 shows the results of this analysis for four selected media.

Table 19.3 shows the frequency of important issues cited by respondents who favoured Humphrey, Nixon, or Wallace correlated (a) with the frequency of *all* the major and minor issues carried by the media; and (b) with the frequency of the major and minor issues oriented to *each party* (stories with a particular party or candidate as a primary referent) carried by each of the

Table 19.3. Intercorrelations of major and minor issue emphasis by selected media with voter issue emphasis

Selected media	Major items		Minor items	
	All news	News own party	All news	News own party
New York Times				
Voters (D)	0.89	0.79	0.97	0.85
Voters (R)	0.80	0.40	0.88	0.98
Voters (W)	0.89	0.25	0.78	−0.53
Durham Morning Herald				
Voters (D)	0.84	0.74	0.95	0.83
Voters (R)	0.59	0.88	0.84	0.69
Voters (W)	0.82	0.76	0.79	0.00
CBS				
Voters (D)	0.83	0.83	0.81	0.71
Voters (R)	0.50	0.00	0.57	0.40
Voters (W)	0.78	0.80	0.86	0.76
NBC				
Voters (D)	0.57	0.76	0.64	0.73
Voters (R)	0.27	0.13	0.66	0.63
Voters (W)	0.84	0.21	0.48	−0.33

four media. For example, the correlation is 0.89 between what Democrats see as the important issues and the *New York Times'* emphasis on the issues in *all* its major news items. The correlation is 0.79 between the Democrats' emphasis on the issues and the emphasis of the *New York Times* as reflected *only* in items about the Democratic candidates.

If one expected voters to pay more attention to the major and minor issues oriented to their own party – that is, to read or view *selectively* – the correlations between the voters and news/opinion about their own party should be strongest. This would be evidence of selective perception.[11] If, on the other hand, the voters attend reasonably well to *all* the news, *regardless* of which candidate or party issue is stressed, the correlations between the voter and total media content would be strongest. This would be evidence of the agenda-setting function. The crucial question is which set of correlations is stronger.

In general, Table 19.3 shows that voters who were not firmly committed early in the campaign attended well to *all* the news. For major news items, correlations were more often higher between voter judgements of important issues and the issues reflected in all the news (including of course news about their favoured candidate/party) than were voter judgements of issues reflected in news *only* about their candidate/party. For minor news items, again voters more often correlated highest with the emphasis reflected in all the news than with the emphasis reflected in news about a favoured candidate. Considering both major and minor item coverage, 18 of 24 possible comparisons show voters more in agreement with all the news rather than with news only about their own party/candidate preference. This finding is better explained by the agenda-setting function of the mass media than by selective perception.

Although the data reported in Table 19.3 generally show high agreement between voter and media evaluations of what the important issues were in 1968, the correlations are not uniform across the various media and all groups of voters. The variations across media are more clearly reflected in Table 19.4, which includes all survey respondents, not just those predisposed toward a candidate at the time of the survey. There also is a high degree of consensus among the news media about the significant issues of the campaign, but again

Table 19.4. Correlations of voter emphasis on issues with media coverage

	Newsweek	Time	New York Times	Raleigh Times	Raleigh News and Observer
Major items	0.30	0.30	0.96	0.80	0.91
Minor items	0.53	0.78	0.97	0.73	0.93

	Durham Sun	Durham Morning Herald	NBC News	CBS News	
Major items	0.82	0.94	0.89	0.63	
Minor items	0.96	0.93	0.91	0.81	

there is not perfect agreement. Considering the news media as mediators between voters and the actual political arena, we might interpret the correlations in Table 19.5 as reliability coefficients, indicating the extent of agreement among the news media about what the important political events are. To the extent that the coefficients are less than perfect, the pseudo-environment reflected in the mass media is less than a perfect representation of the actual 1968 campaign.

Two sets of factors, at least, reduce consensus among the news media. First, the basic characteristics of newspapers, television, and newsmagazines differ. Newspapers appear daily and have lots of space. Television is daily but has a severe time constraint. News magazines appear weekly; news therefore cannot be as 'timely'. Table 19.5 shows that the highest correlations tend to be among like media; the lowest correlations, between different media.

Second, news media do have a point of view, sometimes extreme biases. However, the high correlations in Table 19.5 (especially among like media) suggest consensus on news values, especially on major news items. Although there is no explicit, commonly agreed-upon definition of news, there is a professional norm regarding major news stories from day to day. These major-story norms doubtless are greatly influenced today by widespread use of the major wire services – especially by newspapers and television – for much political information.[12] But as we move from major events of the campaign, upon which nearly everyone agrees, there is more room for individual interpretation, reflected in the lower correlations for minor item

Table 19.5 Intercorrelation of mass media presidential news coverage for major and minor items

	News-week	Time	New York Times	Raleigh Times	Raleigh News & Ob-server	Durham Sun	Durham Morn-ing Herald	NBC	CBS
					Major items				
Newsweek		0.99	0.54	0.92	0.79	0.81	0.79	0.68	0.42
Time	0.65		0.51	0.90	0.77	0.81	0.76	0.68	0.43
New York Times	0.46	0.59		0.70	0.71	0.66	0.81	0.66	0.66
Raleigh Times	0.73	0.66	0.64		0.85	0.89	0.90	0.72	0.62
Raleigh News and Observer	0.84	0.49	0.60	0.74		0.84	0.93	0.82	0.60
Durham Sun	0.77	0.47	0.47	0.70	0.80		94	0.91	0.77
Durham Morning Herald	0.89	0.68	0.68	0.80	0.93	0.73		0.89	0.76
NBC News	0.81	0.65	0.38	0.87	0.73	0.84	0.75		0.82
CBS News	0.66	0.60	0.83	0.88	0.79	0.76	0.78	0.72	
				Minor items					

agreement among media shown in Table 19.5. Since a newspaper, for example, uses only about 15 percent of the material available on any given day, there is considerable latitude for selection among minor items.

In short, the political world is reproduced imperfectly by individual news media. Yet the evidence in this study that voters tend to share the media's *composite* definition of what is important strongly suggests an agenda-setting function of the mass media.

Discussion

The existence of an agenda-setting function of the mass media is not proved by the correlations reported here, of course, but the evidence is in line with the conditions that must exist if agenda-setting by the mass media does occur. This study has compared aggregate units – Chapel Hill voters as a group compared to the aggregate performance of several mass media. This is satisfactory as a first test of the agenda-setting hypothesis, but subsequent research must move from a broad societal level to the social psychological level, matching individual attitudes with individual use of the mass media. Yet even the present study refines the evidence in several respects. Efforts were made to match respondent attitudes only with media actually used by Chapel Hill voters. Further, the analysis includes a juxtaposition of the agenda-setting and selective perception hypotheses. Comparison of these correlations too supports the agenda-setting hypothesis.

Interpreting the evidence from this study as indicating mass media influence seems more plausible than alternative explanations. Any argument that the correlations between media and voter emphasis are spurious – that they are simply responding to the same events and not influencing each other one way or the other – assumes that voters have alternative means of observing the day-to-day changes in the political arena. This assumption is not plausible; since few directly participate in presidential election campaigns, and fewer still see presidential candidates in person, the information flowing in inter-personal communication channels is primarily relayed from, and based upon, mass media news coverage. The media are the major primary sources of national political information; for most, mass media provide the best – and only – easily available approximation of ever-changing political realities.

It might also be argued that the high correlations indicate that the media simply were successful in matching their messages to audience interests. Yet since numerous studies indicate a sharp divergence between the news values of professional journalists and their audiences, it would be remarkable to find a near perfect fit in this one case.[13] It seems more likely that the media have prevailed in this area of major coverage.

While this study is primarily a sociology of politics and mass communication, some psychological data were collected on each voter's personal cognitive representation of the issues. Shrauger has suggested that the salience of the evaluative dimension – not the sheer number of attributes – is the essential feature of cognitive differentiation.[14] So a content analysis classified respondents according to the salience of affect in their responses to open-ended questions about the candidates and issues.[15] Some voters described the issues and candidates in highly affective terms. Others were much more matter-of-fact. Each respondent's answers were classified by the coders as 'all affect', 'affect dominant', 'some affect but not dominant,' or 'no affect at all'.[16] Regarding each voter's salience of affect as his cognitive style of storing political information, the study hypothesized that cognitive style also influences patterns of information-seeking.

Eschewing causal language to discuss this relationship, the hypothesis states that salience of affect will index or locate differences in the communication behaviour of voters. But a number of highly efficient locator variables for voter communication behaviour already are well documented in the research literature. Among these are level of formal education and interest in politics generally. However, in terms of *The American Voter's* model of a 'funnel' stretching across time, education and political interest are located some distance back from the particular campaign being considered.[17] Cognitive style is located closer to the end of the funnel, closer to the time of actual participation in a campaign. It also would seem to have the advantage of a more functional relationship to voter behaviour.

Examination of the relationship between salience of affect and this pair of traditional locators, education and political interest, showed no significant correlations. The independent effects of political interest and salience of affect on media use are demonstrated in Table 19.6. Also demonstrated is the efficacy of salience of affect as a locator or predictor of media use, especially among persons with high political interest.[18]

Both salience of affect and media use in Table 19.6 are based on the issue that respondents designated as the most important to them personally. Salience of affect was coded from their discussion of why the issue was important. Use of each communication medium is based on whether or not the respondent had seen or heard anything via that medium about that particular issue in the past twenty-four hours.

High salience of affect tends to block use of communication media to acquire further information about issues with high personal importance. At least, survey respondents with high salience of affect do not recall acquiring recent information. This is true both for persons with low and high political interest, but especially among those with high political interest. For example, among respondents with high political interest and high salience of affect only 36 percent reported reading anything in the newspaper recently about the issue they believed to be most important. But among high

Table 19.6 Proportion of media users by political interest and salience of affect

| Media | Low political interest | | High political interest | |
	High affect (N = 40)	Low affect (N = 17)	High affect (N = 25)	Low affect (N = 12)
TV	15.0%	17.7%	20.0%	41.7%
Newspapers	27.5	35.4	36.0	58.3
News magazines	7.5	11.8	24.0	33.3
Radio	12.5	11.8	8.0	33.3
Talk	20.0	17.7	64.0	75.0

political interest respondents with low salience of affect nearly six of ten (58.3 percent) said they acquired information from the newspaper. Similar patterns hold for all the communication media.

Future studies of communication behaviour and political agenda setting must consider both psychological and sociological variables; knowledge of both is crucial to establishment of sound theoretical constructs. Considered at both levels as a communication concept, agenda-setting seems useful for study of the process of political consensus.

Notes

1. See Berelson, Bernard R., Lazarsfeld, Paul F. and McPhee, William N. (1954) *Voting*, University of Chicago Press, Chicago, p. 234. Of course to some degree candidates have always depended upon the mass media, but radio and television brought a new intimacy into politics.
2. Lang, Kurt and Lang, Gladys Engel (1966) The mass media and voting. In Berelson, Bernard and Janowitz, Morris (eds) *Reader in Public Opinion and Communication*, 2nd edn, Free Press, New York, p. 466.
3. See Berelson *et al.*, op. cit. (Note 1), p. 223; Lazarsfeld, Paul F., Berelson, Bernard and Gaudet, Hazel (1948) *The People's Choice*, Columbia University Press, New York, p. xx; and Trenaman, Joseph and McQuail, Denis (1961) *Television and The Political Image*, Methuen, London, pp. 147, 191.
4. See Cohen, Bernard C. (1963) *The Press and Foreign Policy*, Princeton University Press, Princeton, p. 120.
5. Berelson *et al.*, op. cit. (Note 1), pp. 244, 228.
6. Trenaman and McQuail, op. cit. (Note 3), p. 165.
7. Lang and Lang, op. cit. (Note 2), p. 468. Trenaman and McQuail warn that there was little evidence in their study that television (or any other mass medium) did anything other than provide information there was little or no attitude change on significant issues. 'People are aware of what is being said, and who is saying it, but they do not necessarily take it at face value', see op. cit. (Note 3), p. 168. In a more recent study, however, Blumler and McQuail found that high exposure to Liberal party television broadcasts in the British general election of 1964 was positively related to a more favourable attitude toward the Liberal party for those with medium or weak motivation to follow the campaign. The more strongly motivated were much more stable in political attitude. See Blumler, Jay G. and McQuail, Denis (1969) *Television in Politics: Its Uses and Influence*, University of Chicago Press, Chicago, p. 200.
8. Cohen, op. cit. (Note 4), p. 13.
9. See Trenaman and McQuail, op. cit. (Note 6), p. 172. The survey question was: 'What are you most concerned about these days? That is, regardless of what politicians say, what are the two or three main things which you think the government should concentrate on doing something about?'.
10. Intercoder reliability was above 0.90 for content analysis of both 'major' and 'minor' items. Details of categorization are described in the full report of this project. A small number of copies of the full report is available for distribution and may be obtained by writing the authors.
11. While recent reviews of the literature and new experiments have questioned the validity of the selective perception hypothesis, this has nevertheless been the focus of much communication research. For example, see Carter, Richard F., Pyszka, Ronald H. and Guerrero, Jose L. (1969) Dissonance and exposure to arousive information. *Journalism Quarterly*, Vol. 46, pp. 37–42; and Sears, David

O. and Freedman, Jonathan L. (1967) Selective exposure to information: a critical review. *Public Opinion Quarterly*, Vol. 31, pp. 194–213.

12. A number of studies have focused on the influence of the wire services. For example, see Gold, David and Simmons, Jerry L. (1965) News selection patterns among Iowa dailies. *Public Opinion Quarterly*, Vol. 29, pp. 425–30; Stempel III, Guido H. (1964) How newspapers use the Associated Press afternoon A-wire. *Journalism Quarterly*, Vol. 41, pp. 380–84; Casey, Ralph D. and Copeland Jr, Thomas H. (1958) Use of foreign news by 19 Minnesota Dailies. *Journalism Quarterly*, Vol. 35, pp. 87–9; Lewis, Howard L. (1960) The Cuban revolt story: AP, UPI, and three papers. *Journalism Quarterly*, Vol. 37, pp. 573–78; Van Horn, George A. (1952) Analysis of AP news on trunk and Wisconsin state wires. *Journalism Quarterly*, Vol. 29, pp. 426–32; and Cutlip, Scott M. (1954) Content and flow of AP news – from trunk to TTS to reader. *Journalism Quarterly*, Vol. 31, pp. 434–46.

13. Furthermore, five of the nine media studied here are national media and none of the remaining four originate in Chapel Hill. It is easier to argue that Chapel Hill voters fit their judgements of issue salience to the mass media than the reverse. An interesting study which discusses the problems of trying to fit day-to-day news judgements to reader interest is Stempel III, Guido H. (1967) A factor analytic study of reader interest in news. *Journalism Quarterly*, Vol. 44, pp. 326–30. An older study is Griffin, Philip F. (1949) Reader comprehension of news stories: a preliminary study. *Journalism Quarterly*, Vol. 26, pp. 389–96.

14. Shrauger, Sid (1967) Cognitive differentiation and the impression-formation process. *Journal of Personality*, Vol. 35, pp. 402–14.

15. Affect denotes a 'pro/con' orientation, a feeling of liking or disliking something. Cognition, by contrast, denotes the individual's perception of the attitude object, his 'image' or organized set of information and beliefs about a political object.

16. Coder reliability exceeded 0.90.

17. Campbell, Angus, Converse, Philip, Miller, Warren and Stokes, Donald (1960) *The American Voter*, John Wiley, New York, Chapter 2.

18. No statistical analysis is reported for the five separate three-way analysis in Table 19.6 because of small Ns in some cells, but despite these small Ns the pattern of results is consistent across all media.

20

Utilization of mass communication by the individual

*Elihu Katz, Jay G. Blumler and
Michael Gurevitch*

From Blumler, J. G. and Katz, E. (eds) (1974) *The Uses of Mass Communications: Current Perspectives on Gratifications Research*, Sage, Beverly Hills, pp. 21–9.

Some basic assumptions of theory, method and value

Perhaps the place of 'theory' and 'method' in the study of audience uses and gratifications is not immediately apparent. The common tendency to attach the label 'uses and gratifications approach' to work in this field appears to virtually disclaim any theoretical pretensions or methodological commitment. From this point of view the approach simply represents an attempt to explain something of the way in which individuals use communications, among other resources in their environment, to satisfy their needs and to achieve their goals, and to do so by simply asking them. Nevertheless, this effort does rest on a body of assumptions, explicit or implicit, that have some degree of internal coherence and that are arguable in the sense that not everyone contemplating them would find them self-evident. Lundberg and Hulten (1968) refer to them as jointly constituting a 'uses and gratifications model'. Five elements of this model in particular may be singled out for comment:

1. The audience is conceived of as active, that is, an important part of mass media use is assumed to be goal directed (McQuail, Blumler and Brown, 1972). This assumption may be contrasted with Bogart's (1965) thesis to the effect that 'most mass media experiences represent pastime rather than purposeful activity, very often [reflecting] chance circumstances within the range of availabilities rather than the expression of psychological motivation or need'. Of course, it cannot be denied that media exposure often has a casual origin; the issue is whether, in addition, patterns of media use are shaped by more or less definite expectations of what certain kinds of content have to offer the audience member.
2. In the mass communication process much initiative in linking need gratification and media choice lies with the audience member. This places a strong limitation on theorizing about any form of straight-line effect of media content on attitudes and behaviour. As Schramm, Lyle and Parker (1961) said

> In a sense the term 'effect' is misleading because it suggests that television 'does something' to children. . . . Nothing can be further from the fact. It is the children who are most active in this relationship. It is they who use television rather than television that uses them.

3. The media compete with other sources of need satisfaction. The needs served by mass communication constitute but a segment of the wider range of human needs, and the degree to which they can be adequately met through mass media consumption certainly varies. Consequently, a proper view of the role of the media in need satisfaction should take into account other functional alternatives – including different, more conventional, and 'older' ways of fulfilling needs.
4. Methodologically speaking, many of the goals of mass media use can be derived from data supplied by individual audience members themselves – that is, people are sufficiently self-aware to be able to report their interests and motives in particular cases, or at least to recognize them when confronted with them in an intelligible and familiar verbal formulation.
5. Value judgements about the cultural significance of mass communication should be suspended while audience orientations are explored on their own terms. It is from the perspective of this assumption that certain affinities and contrasts between the uses and gratifications approach and much speculative writing about popular culture may be considered.

State of the art: theoretical issues

From the few postulates outlined above, it is evident that further development of a theory of media gratification depends, first, on the clarification of its relationship to the theoretical traditions on which it so obviously draws and, second, on systematic efforts toward conceptual integration of empirical findings. Given the present state of the art, the following are priority issues in the development of an adequate theoretical basis.

Typologies of audience gratifications

Each major piece of uses and gratification research has yielded its own classification scheme of audience functions. When placed side by side, they reveal a mixture of shared gratification categories and notions peculiar to individual research teams. The differences are due in part to the fact that investigators have focused on different levels of study (e.g. medium or content) and different materials (e.g. different programmes or programme types on, say, television) in different cultures (e.g. Finland, Israel, Japan, Sweden, the United Kingdom, the United States, and Yugoslavia).

Unifunctional conceptions of audience interests have been expressed in various forms. Popular culture writers have often based their criticisms of the media on the ground that, in primarily serving the escapist desires of the audience, they deprived it of the more beneficial uses that might be made of communication (McDonald, 1957). Stephenson's analysis (1967) of mass communication exclusively in terms of 'play' may be interpreted as an extension, albeit in a transformed and expanded expression, of this same notion. A more recent example has been provided by Nordenstreng (1970), who, while breaking away from conventional formulations, still opts for a unifunctional view when he claims that 'It has often been documented (e.g. during television and newspaper strikes in Finland in 1966–67) that perhaps the basic motivation for media use is just an unarticulated need for social contact.'

The wide currency secured for a bifunctional view of audience concerns is reflected in Weiss' (1971) summary, which states that 'When . . . studies of uses and gratifications are carried out, the media or media content are usually viewed dichotomously as predominantly fantasist–escapist or informational–educational in significance'. This dichotomy appears, for example, in Schramm's (1949) work (adopted subsequently by Schramm, Lyle and Parker, 1961; Pietila, 1969; Furu, 1971), which distinguishes between sets of 'immediate' and 'deferred' gratifications, and in the distinction between informational and entertainment materials. In terms of audience gratifications specifically, it emerges in the distinction between surveillance and escape uses of the media.

The four-functional interpretation of the media was first proposed by Lasswell (1948) on a macro-sociological level and later developed by Wright (1960) on both the macro- and the micro-sociological levels. It postulated that the media served the functions of surveillance, correlation, entertainment, and cultural transmission (or socialization) for society as a whole, as well as for individuals and subgroups within society. An extension of the four-function approach can also be found in Wright's suggestive exploration of the potential dysfunctional equivalents of Lasswell's typology.

None of these statements, however, adequately reflects the full range of functions, which has been disclosed by the more recent investigations. McQuail, Blumler and Brown (1972) have put forward a typology consisting of the following categories: diversion (including escape from the constraints of routine and the burdens of problems, and emotional release); personal relationships (including substitute companionship as well as social utility); personal identity (including personal reference, reality exploration, and value reinforcement); and surveillance.

An effort to encompass the large variety of specific functions that have been proposed is made in the elaborate scheme of Katz, Gurevitch and Haas (1973). Their central notion is that mass communication is used by individuals to connect (or sometimes to disconnect) themselves – via instrumental, affective, or integrative relations – with different kinds of others (self, family, friends, nation, etc.). The scheme attempts to comprehend the whole range of individual gratifications of the many facets of the need 'to be connected'. And it finds empirical regularities in the preference for different media for different kinds of connections.

Gratification and needs

The study of mass media use suffers at present from the absence of a relevant theory of social and psychological needs. It is not so much a catalogue of needs that is missing as a clustering of groups of needs, a sorting out of different levels of need, and a specification of hypotheses linking particular needs with particular media gratifications. It is true that the work of Schramm, Lyle and Parker (1961) draws on the distinction between the reality and pleasure principles in the socialization theories of Freud and others, but more recent studies suggest that those categories are too broad to be serviceable. Maslow's (1954) proposed hierarchy of human needs may hold more promise, but the relevance of his categories to expectations of communication has not yet been explored in detail. Lasswell's (1948) scheme to specify the needs that media satisfy has proven useful, and it may be helpful to examine Lasswell and Kaplan's (1950) broader classification of values as well.

Alternatively, students of uses and gratifications could try to work backwards, as it were, from gratifications to needs. In the informational field, for example, the surveillance function may be traced to a desire for security or the satisfaction of curiosity and the exploratory drive; seeking reinforcement of one's attitudes and values may derive from a need for reassurance that one is right; and attempts to correlate informational elements may stem from a more basic need to develop one's cognitive mastery of the environment. Similarly, the use of fictional (and other) media materials for 'personal reference' may spring from a need for self-esteem; social utility functions may be traced to the need for affiliation; and escape functions may be related to the need to release tension and reduce anxiety. But whichever way one proceeds, it is inescapable that what is at issue here is the long-standing problem of social and psychological science: how to (and whether to bother to) systematize the long lists of human and societal needs. Thus far, gratifications research has stayed close to what we have been calling media-related needs (in the sense that the media have been observed to satisfy them, at least in part), but one wonders whether all this should not be put in the broader context of systematic studies of needs.

Sources of media gratifications

Studies have shown that audience gratifications can be derived from at least three distinct sources: media content, exposure to the media *per se*, and the social context that typifies the situation of exposure to different media. Although recognition of media content as a source of gratifications has provided the basis for research in this area from its inception, less attention has been paid to the other sources. Nevertheless, it is clear that the need to relax or to kill time can be satisfied by the act of watching television, that the need to feel that one is spending one's time in a worthwhile way may be associated with the act of reading (Waples, Berelson and Bradshaw, 1940; Berelson, 1949), and that the need to structure one's day may be satisfied merely by having the radio 'on' (Mendelsohn, 1964). Similarly, a wish to spend time with one's family or friends can be served by watching television at home with the family or by going to the cinema with one's friends.

Each medium seems to offer a unique combination of (a) characteristic contents (at least stereotypically perceived in that way); (b) typical attributes (print vs broadcasting modes of transmission, iconic vs symbolic representation, reading vs audio or audio-visual modes of reception); and (c) typical exposure situations (at home vs out-of-home, alone vs with others, control over the temporal aspects of exposure vs absence of such control).

The issue, then, is what combinations of attributes may render different media more or less adequate for the satisfaction of different needs (Katz, Gurevitch and Haas, 1973).

Gratifications and media attributes

Much uses and gratifications research has still barely advanced beyond a sort of charting and profiling activity: findings are still typically presented to show that certain bodies of content serve certain functions or that one medium is deemed better at satisfying certain needs than another. The further step, which has hardly been ventured, is one of explanation. At issue here is the relationship between the unique 'grammar' of different media – that is, their specific technological and aesthetic attributes – and the particular requirements of audience members that they are then capable, or incapable, of satisfying. Which, indeed, are the attributes that render some media more conducive than others to satisfying specific needs? And which elements of content help to attract the expectations for which they apparently cater?

It is possible to postulate the operation of some kind of division of labour among the media for the satisfaction of audience needs. This may be elaborated in two ways: taking media attributes as the starting point, the suggestion is that those media that differ (or are similar) in their attributes are more likely to serve different (or similar) needs; or, utilizing the latent structure of needs as a point of departure, the implication is that needs that are psychologically related or conceptually similar will be equally well served by the same media (or by media with similar attributes).

To illustrate the first approach, Robinson (1972) has demonstrated the interchangeability of television and print media for learning purposes. In the Israeli study, Katz, Gurevitch and Haas (1973) found five media ordered in a circumplex with respect to their functional similarities: books–news-papers–radio–television–cinema–books. In other words, books functioned most like newspapers, on the one hand, and like cinema, on the other. Radio was most similar in its usage to newspapers, on the one hand, and to television, on the other. The explanation would seem to lie not only with certain technological attributes that they have in common, but with similar aesthetic qualities as well. Thus, books share a technology and an informational function with newspapers, but are similar to films in their aesthetic function. Radio shares a technology, as well as informational and entertainment content, with television, but it is also very much like newspapers – providing a heavy dose of information and an orientation to reality.

An illustration of the second aspect of this division of labour may also be drawn from the same study. Here, the argument is that structurally related needs will tend to be serviced by certain media more often than by others. Thus, books and cinema have been found to cater to needs concerned with self-fulfilment and self-gratification: they help to 'connect' individuals to themselves. Newspapers, radio, and television all seem to connect individuals to society. In fact, the function of newspapers for those interested in following what is going on in the world may have been grossly under-estimated in the past (Edelstein, 1973; Lundberg and Hulten, 1968). Television, however, was found to be less frequently used as a medium of escape by

Israeli respondents than were books and films. And a Swedish study of the 'functional specialities of the respective media' reported that 'A retreat from the immediate environment and its demands – probably mainly by the act of reading itself – was characteristic of audience usage of weekly magazines' (Lundberg and Hulten, 1968).

Media attributes as perceived or intrinsic

When people associate book-reading, for example, with a desire to know oneself, and newspapers with the need to feel connected to the larger society, it is difficult to disentangle perceptions of the media from their intrinsic qualities. Is there anything about the book as a medium that breeds intimacy? Is there something about newspapers that explains their centrality in socio-political integration? Or, is this 'something' simply an accepted image of the medium and its characteristic content?

In this connection, Rosengren (1972) has suggested that uses and gratifi-cations research may be profitably connected with the long-established tradition of enquiry into public perceptions of the various media and the dimensions according to which their respective images and qualities are differentiated [cf. especially Nilsson (1971) and Edelstein (1973) and the literature cited therein]. A merger of the two lines of investigation may show how far the attributes of the media, as perceived by their consumers, and their intrinsic qualities are correlated with the pursuit of certain gratifications. So far, however, this connection has only been partially discussed in the work of Lundberg and Hulten (1968).

The social origins of audience needs and their gratifications

The social and environmental circumstances that lead people to turn to the mass media for the satisfaction of certain needs are also little understood as yet. For example, what needs, if any, are created by routine work on an assembly line, and which forms of media exposure will satisfy them? What motivates some people to seek political information from the mass media and others to actively avoid it? Here one may postulate that it is the combined product of psychological dispositions, sociological factors, and environmental conditions that determines the specific uses of the media by members of the audience.

At certain levels it should not prove unduly difficult to formulate discrete hypotheses about such relationships. For example, we might expect 'substitute companionship' to be sought especially by individuals with limited opportunities for social contacts: invalids, the elderly, the single, the divorced or widowed living alone, the housewife who spends much time at home on her own, and so on.

At another level, however, it is more difficult to conceive of a general theory that might clarify the various processes that underlie any such specific relationships. A preliminary structuring of the possibilities suggests that social factors may be involved in the generation of media-related needs in any of the following five ways (each of which has attracted some comment in the literature):

1. social situation produces tensions and conflicts, leading to pressure for their easement via mass media consumption (Katz and Foulkes, 1962);
2. social situation creates an awareness of problems that demand attention, information about which may be sought in the media (Edelstein, 1973);
3. social situation offers impoverished real-life opportunities to satisfy certain needs, which are then directed to the mass media for complementary, supplementary, or substitute servicing (Rosengren and Windahl, 1972);
4. social situation gives rise to certain values, the affirmation and reinforcement of which is facilitated by the consumption of congruent media materials (Dembo, 1972);
5. social situation provides a field of expectations of familiarity with certain media materials, which must then be monitored in order to sustain membership of valued social groupings (Atkins, 1972).

The versatility of sources of need satisfaction

Before becoming too sanguine about the possibility of relating social situations to psychological needs to media/content gratifications, it is important to bear in mind that gratifications studies based on specific media contents have demonstrated that one and the same set of media materials is capable of serving a multiplicity of needs and audience functions. Presumably, that is why Rosengren and Windahl (1972) have drawn attention to 'a growing consensus that almost any type of content may serve practically any type of function'. For example, Blumler, Brown and McQuail (1970) have found that the television serial *The Saint* serves functions of personal reference, identification with characters, and reality-exploration, in addition to its more obvious diversionary function. Similarly, their study of the gratifications involved in news viewing referred not only to the expected surveillance motive but also to functions of social utility, empathy, and even escape. In summarizing the implications of their evidence, McQuail, Blumler and Brown (1972) point out that:

> the relationship between content categories and audience needs is far less tidy and more complex than most commentators have appreciated. . . . One man's source of escape from the real world is a point of anchorage for another man's place in it.

Gratifications and effects

Pioneers in the study of uses and gratifications were moved chiefly by two aspirations. The first, which has largely been fulfilled, was to redress an imbalance evident in previous research: audience needs, they said, deserved as much attention in their own right as the persuasive aims of communicators with which so many of the early 'effects' studies had been preoccupied. The second major aim of uses and gratifications research, however, was to treat audience requirements as intervening variables in the study of traditional communication effects. Glaser's (1965) formulation offers a typical expression of the rationale behind this prospect:

> Since users approach the media with a variety of needs and predispositions
> ... any precise identification of the effects of television watching ... must identify
> the uses sought and made of television by the various types of viewers.

Despite this injunction, hardly any substantial empirical or theoretical effort has been devoted to connecting gratifications and effects. Some limited evidence from the political field suggests that combining functions and effects perspectives may be fruitful (Blumler and McQuail, 1968). But there are many other foci of traditional effects studies for which no detailed hypotheses about gratifications/effects interactions have yet been framed.

One obvious example is the field of media violence. Another might concern the impact on inhabitants of developing countries of exposure to television serials, films, and popular songs of foreign (predominantly American) origin. Yet another might relate to the wide range of materials, appearing especially in broadcast fiction, that purport simultaneously to entertain and to portray more or less faithfully some portion of social reality, e.g. the worlds of law enforcement, social work, hospital life, trade unionism, working-class neighbourhoods, and ways of life at the executive level in business corporations and civil service departments.

Hypotheses about the cumulative effects of exposure to such materials on audience members' cognitive perceptions of these spheres of activity, and on the individuals engaged in them, might be formulated in awareness of the likely fact that some individuals will be viewing them primarily for purposes of escape, while others will be using them for reality-exploring gratifications. In these circumstances should we expect a readier acceptance of portrayed stereotypes by the escape seekers – the thesis of Festinger and Maccoby (1964) on persuasion via distraction might be relevant here – or by those viewers who are trusting enough to expect such programmes to offer genuine insights into the nature of social reality?

A similar body of recently analysed materials may be found in the television soap opera, with its postulated capacity to 'establish or reinforce value systems' (Katzman, 1972). In fact one cluster of gratifications that emerged from an English study of listeners to a long-running day-time radio serial (The Dales) centred on the tendency of the programme to uphold traditional family values (Blumler, Brown and McQuail, 1970). This suggests that an answer to Katzman's 'key question' ('to what degree do daytime serials change attitudes and norms and to what extent do they merely follow and reinforce their audience?') might initially be sought by distinguishing among the regular followers of such programmes those individuals who are avowedly seeking a reinforcement of certain values from those who are not.

In addition, however, the literature refers to some consequences of audience functions that conventional effects designs may be unable to capture. First, there is what Katz and Foulkes (1962) have termed the 'feedback' from media use to the individual's performance of his other social roles. Thus, Bailyn (1959) distinguished child uses of pictorial media that might 'preclude more realistic and lasting solutions' to problems from those that, at one level, were 'escapist' but that should more properly be categorized as 'supplementation'. Similarly, Schramm, Lyle and Parker (1961) maintained that child uses of the mass media for fantasizing might either drain off discontent caused by the hard blows of socialization or lead a child into withdrawal from the real world. And Lundberg and Hulten (1968) have suggested that for some individuals the substitute companionship function may involve use of the media to replace real social ties, while for others it may facilitate an adjustment to reality.

Second, some authors have speculated on the connection between functions performed by the media for individuals and their functions (or dysfunctions) for other levels of society. This relationship is particularly crucial for its bearing on evaluative and ideological controversies about the role of mass communication in modern society. Thus, Enzenberger (1972) suggests that the 8-millimetre camera may satisfy the recreational and creative impulses of the individual and help to keep the family together while simultaneously atomizing and depoliticizing society. Or news viewing may gratify the individual's need for civic participation; but if the news, as presented, is a disjointed succession of staccato events, it may also leave him with the message that the world is a disconnected place. Similarly, many radical critics tend to regard television as part of a conspiracy to keep people content and politically quiescent – offering respite, para-social interaction with interesting and amusing people, and much food for gossip – while propagating a false social consciousness.

References

Atkin, C. K. (1972) Anticipated communication and mass media information-seeking. *Public Opinion Quarterly*, Vol. 36.

Bailyn, L. (1959) Mass media and children. *Psychological Monographs*, Vol. 71.

Berelson, B. (1949) What 'missing the newspaper' means. In Lazarsfeld, P. F. and Stanton F. N. (eds) *Communications Research, 1948–9*, Duell, Sloan & Pearce, New York.

Blumler, J. G., Brown, J. R. and McQuail, D. (1970) The social origins of the gratifications associated with television viewing. The University of Leeds, Leeds (mimeo).

Blumler, J. G. and McQuail, D. (1969) *Television in Politics*, University of Chicago Press, Chicago.

Bogart, L. (1965) The mass media and the blue collar worker. In Bennet, A. and Gomberg, W. (eds) *Blue-collar World: Studies of the American Worker*, Prentice-Hall, Englewood Cliffs, NJ.

Dembo, R. (1972) Life style and media use among English working-class youths. *Gazette*, Vol. 18.

Edelstein, A. (1973) An alternative approach to the study of source effects in mass communication. *Studies of Broadcasting*, Vol. 9.

Enzenberger, H. M. (1972) Constituents of a theory of the media. In McQuail, D. (ed.) *Sociology of Mass Communications*, Penguin, Harmondsworth.

Festinger, L. and MacCoby, N. (1964) On resistance to persuasive communication. *Journal of Abnormal and Social Psychology*, Vol. 60.

Furu, T. (1971) *The Function of Television for Children and Adolescents*, Sophia University, Tokyo.

Glaser, W. A. (1965) Television and voting turnout. *Public Opinion Quarterly*, Vol. 29.

Katz, E. and Foulkes. D. (1962) On the use of the mass media for 'escape': clarification of a concept. *Public Opinion Quarterly*, Vol. 26.

Katz, E., Gurevitch, M. and Haas, H. (1973) On the use of mass media for important things. *American Sociological Review*, Vol. 38.

Katzman, N. (1972) Television soap operas: what's been going on anyway? *Public Opinion Quarterly*, Vol. 36. Lasswell, H. (1948) The structure and function of communications in society. In Bryson, L. (ed.) *The Communication of Ideas*, Harper, New York.

Lasswell, H. and Kaplan, A. (1950) *Power and Society*, Yale University Press, New Haven.

Lundberg, D. and Hulten, O. (1968) *Individen och Massmedia*, EFI, Stockholm.

McDonald, D. (1957) A theory of mass culture. In White, D. M. and Rosenberg, B. (eds) *Mass Culture: The Popular Arts in America*, Free Press, Glencoe.

McQuail, D., Blumler, J. G. and Brown, J. R. (1972) The television audience: a revised perspective. In McQuail, D. (ed.) *Sociology of Mass Communications*, Penguin, Harmondsworth.

Maslow, A. H. (1954) *Motivation and Personality*, Harper, New York.

Mendelsohn, H. (1964) Listening to radio. In Dexter, L. A. and White, D. M. (eds) *People, Society and Mass Communications*, Free Press, Glencoe.

Nilsson, S. (1971) Publikens upplevelse av- tv-program. Sveriges Radio PUB., Stockholm (mimeo).

Nordenstreng, R. (1970) Comments on 'gratifications research' in broadcasting. *Public Opinion Quarterly*, Vol. 34.

Pietila, V. (1969) Immediate versus delayed reward in newspaper reading. *Acta Sociologica*, Vol. 12.

Robinson, J. P. (1972) Toward defining the functions of television. In *Television and Social Behavior*, National Institute of Mental Health, Rockville, MD, Vol. 4.

Rosengren, K. E. (1972) Uses and gratifications: an overview. University of Lund, Sweden (mimeo).

Rosengren, K. E. and Windahl, S. (1972) Mass media consumption as a functional alternative. In McQuail, D. (ed.) *Sociology of Mass Communications*, Penguin, Harmondsworth.

Schramm, W. (1949) The nature of news. *Journalism Quarterly*, Vol. 26.

Schramm, W., Lyle, J. and Parker, E. B. (1961) *Television in the Lives of Our Children*, Stanford University Press, Stanford.

Stephenson, W. (1967) The play theory of mass communication. University of Chicago Press, Chicago.

Waples, D., Berelson, B. and Bradshaw, F. R. (1940) *What Reading Does to People*, University of Chicago Press, Chicago.

Weiss, W. (1971) Mass communication. *Annual Review of Psychology*, Vol. 22.

Wright, C. (1960) Functional analysis and mass communication. *Public Opinion Quarterly*, Vol. 24.

21

Five traditions in search of the audience

Klaus Bruhn Jensen and Karl Erik Rosengren

From Blumler, J. G. *et al.* (1990) *European Journal of Communication*, Sage, London, Vol. 5, Nos 2–3.

This article is an attempt to explicate, in terms of a number of basic characteristics of the various approaches, the confluences which have recently taken place in research on the reception, uses and effects of mass media content, while at the same time identifying the controversies arising from different theoretical and political orientations. Coming from different traditions, the authors wish to suggest that the process of dialogue and *détente* may lead to a dynamic state of coexistence, rather than final unification.

For analytical purposes, we note five main traditions of research in this area: (1) effects research, (2) uses and gratifications research, (3) literary criticism, (4) cultural studies, (5) reception analysis. [. . .]

Systematics

Theories

Theories about mass-media audiences are being developed in all five traditions discussed in this article. In simplified terms, the sets of theories available in the area may be divided into the humanistic type and the social-science type, which are the legacy of 'arts' and 'science', respectively.

The social-science type theories have been developed mainly within the traditions of effects research and U&G research, often on the basis of more general psychological, social–psychological and sociological theories. They are usually transformed into graphical and statistical models of processes of influence whose elements and inter-relations may be tested by formalized procedures. The humanistic type theories, in their turn, derive mainly from the traditions of literary criticism and cultural studies. They are systematic but as a rule not formalizable descriptions of how content structures – media discourses – come to carry specific meanings for recipients in a particular social context. In reception analysis, attempts are being made to combine the two types of theories.

Substantively, theories in the area may be thought of as specific conceptualizations of mass communication processes within the message/audience nexus. Three constituents of such processes are of particular relevance for audience studies: message, audience and social system, or – in the terminology of the humanities – text/discourse, recipient and context.

Typically, the tradition of *effects research* tends to conceive of media messages

as symbolic stimuli having recognizable and measurable physical characteristics. While originally the interest was often focused on isolated, undifferentiated stimuli – for example, an act of violence or a programme classified
as 'violent' – the insight has gradually grown stronger that what must be
studied is configurations of stimuli and stimuli differentiated according to
context-oriented theory. [. . .]

The *U&G* tradition right from its beginning stressed the differential needs,
orientations and interpretive activities of members of the audience
possessing differential social and/or individual characteristics (Blumler and
Katz, 1974; Rosengren *et al.*, 1985). On the content side, there has been a
discrepancy, however, between, on the one hand, the tendency to theorize
about media content in terms of subjectively felt needs and perceptions of
audience members and, on the other hand, the tendency to study empirically
the use of media content categorized in terms of 'objectively given', traditional
content categories (cf. Rosengren, 1974, p. 277). The incorporation of
expectancy-value theory into U&G research offers one solution to this
problem (Palmgreen and Rayburn, 1985). [. . .]

The majority of studies within *literary criticism* have focused on the structure
of literary messages, or works. Traditionally, the literary work is seen as a
rule-governed configuration of linguistic and rhetorical structures which in
the aggregate make up genres as defined in aesthetics or hermeneutics (Frye,
1957; Eagleton, 1983). It is interesting to note that – for literary criticism as
well as for effects research – meaning is taken to be immanent in content
structures. While both specific texts and genres may give rise to different
interpretations, literary analysis may be said to provide the appropriate
response according to literary tradition or, alternatively, it may suggest a new,
more insightful reading, sometimes from the viewpoint of an implied reader.
Hence, the reader is most often a critical construct to be deduced from literary
discourse or tradition. When empirical readers are studied, attention is
frequently focused on individual readings or general sociological or
psychological aspects of literary meaning rather than historically or
demographically specific recipients. The social system in which literature is
produced, then, is most often present as an abstract framework of the analysis,
or sometimes as 'historical background' provided in an introductory section.

Work in *cultural studies*, similarly, focuses on the actual message or discourse
of communication. Like literary criticism it also pays special attention to the
genre in question, its implied reader positions and associated social uses.
Unlike literary criticism, however, cultural studies are not centred on just
high culture, but on popular cultural discourses as well. Thus, media
messages are conceived of as generically structured discourses which are
relevant for audiences in different cultural and social practices.
[. . .]

Reception analysis has drawn the components of its theoretical
framework from both the humanities and the social sciences. Like cultural
studies, reception analysis speaks of media messages as culturally and
generically coded discourses, while defining audiences as agents of meaning
production. Like U&G research, reception analysis conceives of recipients
as active individuals who can do a variety of things with media in terms
of consumption, decoding and social uses. What characterizes reception

analysis is, above all, an insistence that studies include a comparative empirical analysis of media discourses with audience discourses – content structures with the structure of audience responses regarding content. [. . .]

Trying to sum up present theoretical developments in the five research traditions discussed, we note, first of all, how in all five traditions the audience members have come to stand out as increasingly active and selective in their use and interpretation of mass-media messages. In metaphorical terms, we could say that audiences, rather than 'reading out' messages from media, are seen to 'read in' quite diverse meanings into mass-mediated texts. In classical terms, *eisegesis* may be a more important aspect of audience activities than *exegesis*. At the same time the social context has also come to appear as ever more important in shaping both audience, mass-media genres and institutions, as well as the interaction between media and recipients.

Despite such conceptual differentiations within each tradition, however, the scope of each one of the two main types of theories – oriented towards the humanities and social science, respectively – stands out as somewhat limited when regarded in the light of the other. One basic reason for this state of affairs is that there are major differences not only in the extent to which our five traditions specify three constituents of communication processes fundamental to all audience research (message, audience and social context), but also in the mode in which this is being done.

Social science-oriented audience research has succeeded in differentiating, to varying degrees, the conception of the macro social system, the media-institutional environment and the audience as social–psychological entities. It is on this foundation that social science successfully performs replicable studies of representative samples from well-defined populations of audiences. Conversely, humanistically-oriented audience studies have offered elaborate theories of meaning and representation to account for the sense which audiences attribute to media content and which may serve to explain cognitive and behavioural effects of media use. Recent reception studies have also successfully examined empirical recipients as social and psychological entities who think, feel and act in ways similar to those of characters represented in textual discourse.

Methodologies and modes of analysis

Just as one may find two main types of theories in the area of audience research, one may distinguish between two forms of methodologies and modes of analysis. Social-scientific work puts great weight on establishing explicitly operationalized categories of analysis, and on keeping – in principle at least – the phases of theory and hypothesis formation, observation, analysis, interpretation and presentation of results separate from each other. Moreover, the assumption is that the researcher's role in the act of data collection and analysis can and should be minimized. The humanistic tradition, in contrast, assumes that in principle, no distinction can be made between the collection, analysis and interpretation of 'data'. The best a researcher can offer is said to be a reflexive accounting of the contexts, purposes and participant roles through which a piece of research is constituted

(Lindlof and Anderson, 1988). Like other forms of science, however, humanistic scholarship generally is required to abide by the systematic procedures and explicit levels of enquiry which facilitate meaningful inter-subjective agreement and/or disagreement.

These two mainstreams of general methodology are often referred to in terms of the distinction between quantitative and qualitative approaches.

Effects and U&G research – in parallel with their theoretical orientations – rely primarily on the social-science type of methodologies. Literary criticism and cultural studies rely primarily on the humanist type, while in reception analysis both types may be found.

Within a general social-science methodology, in both *effects research and U&G research* a number of specific methods and techniques have been used, including laboratory experiments, natural and field experiments, survey studies by means of questionnaires and standardized interviews, participant observations, in-depth interviews, etc. The main difference between the two traditions is probably that effects research as a rule tends to prefer highly structured and standardized techniques, while U&G research seems to have been relatively more open towards less structured, 'naturalistic' techniques such as in-depth interviews and participant observation.

In general, and regardless of the specific methods applied, in both traditions today there is a tendency for researchers to try to apply a holistic perspective, locating media use and effects within as broad a psychological, social–psychological, and sociological framework as possible. Methodologically, this tendency gives rise to at least two types of efforts.

In the first place, researchers try to use in just one study more than one specific research technique, combining, for example, surveys by means of highly structured and standardized questionnaires with more or less unstructured, conversational, in-depth interviews (Jarlbro, 1986; Rosengren, 1989). Second, there is a clear tendency to follow over time the phenomena studied – sometimes over considerable periods of time (Milawsky *et al.*, 1982; Singer *et al.*, 1984; Sonesson, 1989; cf. Rosengren, 1990). This applies both at the individual level and at aggregated levels (panel versus cohort studies). Sometimes, cross-sectional and longitudinal studies are combined, and occasionally such temporal comparative studies are combined with comparisons over space, generating quite complicated research designs (Huesman and Eron, 1986; Rosengren and Windahl, 1989). In this way, it is hoped, it becomes possible to distinguish between two pairs of otherwise almost indistinguishable determinants of media use and effects: finalistic and causal, individual and structural determinants. [. . .]

A major difference between communication research of the social science type and the mainstream of literary studies is their conception of analysis and interpretation. Except for the social science-oriented literary research, *literary criticism* does not normally make a methodological distinction between the analysis of 'data' and the subsequent interpretation of aggregated 'findings'. Instead, relying on a variety of text-critical methods developed within linguistics, literary theory and rhetoric, it aims at performing what may be regarded as analysis-cum-interpretation, in order to substantiate one, sometimes more, possible and reasonable readings.

The tool of research is the interpretive capacity of the scholar and the categories of analysis are grounded primarily in the literary works being examined. The meaning of each constitutive element is established with reference to the context of the work as a whole. Its wider significance may be assessed by considering the social context of historical and psychoanalytic factors, which offer cues to understanding particular authors, readerships or origins of literary themes. The role of the empirical reader, however, has rarely been operationalized or posed as an explicit methodological issue in literary studies, except in recent work which, by and large, has drawn its research designs from sociology, social psychology and psychology (cf. Schmidt, 1980–2; Svensson, 1985; Groeben and Vorderer, 1988).

While growing out of literary criticism, *cultural studies* perform their analysis-cum-interpretation through methods which refer explicitly to extra-textual frameworks of explanation. The discourses of literature and media are said to be inscribed in broader social and cultural practices. The categories of analysis, consequently , are grounded not only in literary theory but in theories of social structure and subjectivity as well – granting the fact that the primary tool of research still remains the interpreting scholar.

More specifically, a variety of cultural forms – from oral storytelling, to graffiti, to particular modes of everyday conversation – may be interpreted as the popular expression and maintenance of social and cultural identi-ties which are based in interpretive communities. These communities, in their turn, are formed in processes of gendered, ethnic and sub-cultural socialization, which to no small extent feed on the mass media. While audience publics are thus seen as active participants in the social product-ion of meaning, often challenging media constructions of reality, the focus of analysis has tended to be the over-arching discourses of culture, rather than their local, empirical producers and recipients.

Drawing on methods of analysis-cum-interpretation from the literary tradition and the conception of communication and cultural processes as socially situated discourses from cultural studies, *reception analysis* can be said to perform a comparative reading of media discourses and audience discourses in order to understand the processes of reception. Audience discourses are generated within small-scale empirical designs relying particularly on in-depth interviewing and participant observation. Comparing these discourses with the structure of media content, reception studies have indicated how particular genres and themes may be assimilated by specific audiences. With reference, moreover, to the social context of audience background variables as well as to other cultural and political institutions, reception analysis has explored how audiences may contribute to social meaning production and cultural patterns generally through their membership of socially specific interpretive communities. How mass mediated meaning comes to orient social action and cognition, however, remains a question for more comprehensive audience studies.

One methodological difficulty of reception analysis in its current form is that, while it offers a theoretically informed, empirical examination of com-munication processes, its findings are not easily replicable. In fact they can only seldom be generalized beyond the small groups of individuals studied. The same difficulty besets cultural studies and literary criticism (except for most of the social science-oriented variants already mentioned). Generalizability, of course, is a widely accepted demand in audience research of the effects and U&G types, both of which aim at producing replicable studies of representative samples from well-defined populations. This basic difference between effects and U&G research and literary criticism, cultural studies and reception analysis points to a general issue for audience research brought to the fore also in our theoretical considerations. If each tradition contributes a perspective which is thought to have relevance and explanatory value in itself, the question is how the field might arrive at terms of co-operation that would serve the interests of further research and, perhaps, those of the audience.

Trying to sum up the methodological similarities and dissimilarities between our five research traditions, one is struck by the parallel between, on the one hand, the functions of experimental research in effects and U&G studies, and on the other the empirical–qualitative approach of literary, cultural and reception studies.

In both cases, through intensive and careful observation of a small number of selected cases, new knowledge is produced about what happens under specified conditions. What 'happens' is audiences attributing particular meanings to a given media content; these meanings, in turn, may come to inform and affect the cognition and behaviour of particular audience members. These are forms of impact which can be established, for example, through experimental designs or participant observation in family settings. Quantitative survey research, however, using representative samples drawn from strictly defined populations, gains knowledge about what happens in these populations with a precise measure of probability. The survey methodology is, of course, designed with a view to recreate, so far as possible, a set of specified and uniform conditions under which the respondents can address, in a theoretically grounded and valid manner, the kind of audience response under examination. The verbal response by which an interviewee addresses an aspect of media and related attributes is thus the fundamental constituent of such methodologies. The correlation of such responses in terms of statistical procedures establishes the different forms of impact.

Eventually, survey research and experiments in the laboratory as well as empirical qualitative studies are interdependent. Not only do they represent complementary forms of evidence, reminiscent of the classical *in vitro* versus *in vivo* distinction. They also enter into a system of theoretical checks and balances in which the explanatory value of each mode of analysis – independently and in combination with other analytical modes – may be examined. This type of theory and methodology development is, indeed, one of the most important tasks for further research in the area of audience studies.

The main results of our overview of the theoretical and methodological characteristics of the five research traditions under discussion are schematically summarized in Table 21.1.

Before offering some suggestions about further research, we shall take up the major social and political implications which audience studies have raised in the past and are likely to raise also in the future.

Table 21.1. Main characteristics of five audience research traditions

| | Research tradition | | | | |
	Effects research	Uses and gratifications	Literary criticism	Cultural studies	Reception analysis
Type of theory	Semi-formalized	Semi-formalized	Verbal	Verbal	Verbal
Focus of theory					
Message	Less central	Less central	Central	Central	Central
Audience	Central	Central	Peripheral	Less central	Central
Social system	Less central	Central	Less central	Less central	Less central
Type of methodology	Social science	Social science	Humanist	Humanist	Mainly humanist
Approaches					
Experimental	Often	Seldom	Seldom	Almost never	Almost never
Survey	Often	As a rule	Seldom	Seldom	Seldom
In-depth interview	Sometimes	Sometimes	Seldom	Often	As a rule
Message analysis	Seldom	Seldom	As a rule	As a rule	As a rule
Techniques of analysis					
Statistical	As a rule	As a rule	Seldom	Seldom	Seldom
Interpretive	Seldom	Sometimes	As a rule	As a rule	As a rule
Modes of presentation					
Numerical, tabular	As a rule	As a rule	Almost never	Seldom	Sometimes
Verbal, analytical	As a rule	As a rule	Sometimes	Often	As a rule
Verbal, narrative	Sometimes	Sometimes	As a rule	As a rule	As a rule

Pragmatics

[. . .]

Further research

It is unrealistic to hope to completely reconcile the differential legacies of arts and sciences which inform the five traditions of audience research outlined in this article, and as stated this is not our ambition. Yet we do maintain that there are further possibilities of convergence at several levels of analysis, not least in terms of interdisciplinary *theory development*.

Substantively, our systematics suggest that a comprehensive theoretical framework for audience research requires at least three components: (1) a theory of the social structures in which media and audiences are embedded; (2) a theory of discourse or communication which accounts for the nature of media representation (print, aural, visual); and (3) a theory of socio-cultural and social–psychological dispositions with which individuals approach and interact with media content. Each of these three components, of course, needs further clarification and differentiation. A social structure theory, for instance, must encompass the macro (societal), the mezzo (institutional) and the micro (individual) level.

In general it may be said that, whereas the traditions coming from the social sciences offer highly differentiated and specific models of the social context of media, textual research based in the humanities provides theories of representation which consider, among other things, the specific nature of the medium and its modes of addressing the audience. The third component – the status of the audience as social–psychological agents – has been given a variety of formulations within social psychology and psychoanalysis, emphasizing either the material, biological and social base, or its cognitive, cultural character (cf. for instance, McQuail and Windahl, 1981). A substantive theory of mass communication will require a conceptual and terminological apparatus incorporating psychological, social and cultural aspects of mass communication.

In terms of *methodology*, this implies that studies in the area should combine elements of content analysis with audience research in one design. Too often, research based in the humanities has neglected standard demographic classifications of the populations which it sets out to examine. Similarly, much social science research has tended to think of content in technical terms, as isolated bits of information rather than as culturally coded vehicles of meaning. Reconciling this split may be more important for the development of truly interdisciplinary methodologies than a routine examination of quantitative/ qualitative and/or administrative/critical distinctions. [. . .]

Several types of empirical projects suggest themselves as concrete examples of inter-disciplinary studies in the area. We are content to mention briefly three such projects.

First, a type of multi-method research which may be rather easy to carry out, is the combination of an experimental design and reception studies of the audience-cum-content analysis type. Studies building on systematic variations in the media content received by systematically varied audience categories have proved useful in much commercial research (the results of which are more often than not closed to the academic community). It may be about time for this promising combination to be brought to bear on theoretically more relevant problems than those of marketing research. The challenging task lying before us is to open up the black box hiding the specific social–psychological processes behind and below the general process of reception. As a matter of fact, attempts in this direction are already being undertaken, especially by psychologically- and humanistically-oriented communication researchers (Hawkins *et al.*, 1988; Höijer, 1989; Sypher and Higgins, 1989). An intriguing question concerns the extent to which such (and other) empirical and theoretical results would be stable over time and social space (Rosengren, 1990). That question brings us to our second suggestion about inter-disciplinary research in the field.

We believe that comparative studies across cultures would lend themselves very well to further developments in multi-method empirical research. As suggested by ethnographies both within anthropology and in recent media research (Lull, 1988), various forms of in-depth, naturalistic observation and interaction with audience respondents may be necessary in order to characterize and delimit the context of data gathering. At the same time, survey techniques may be used to examine particular issues which emerge in the course of the study, specifying in turn, the purposes of further observation or interviewing and providing an opportunity to assess comparatively two sets of findings regarding the same object of study. Contributing to an important and relatively under-researched area of international communication research, such studies would fit the recent strong trend towards an increased interest in comparative studies in communication. They would also be able to explore the extent to which current research methodologies, most of which embody a specific form of western rationality, apply to the reception and impact of media across cultures (cf. Liebes and Katz, 1986; Lull, 1988).

Third, audience research may return to community studies, as carried out by some early work in the field, in order to assess the explanatory value of different traditions (Lynd and Lynd, 1929; cf. Caplow and Bahr, 1983). Case studies of the cultural and communicative practices of specific communities represent an opportunity to examine in detail the kinds of micro- and macro-social contexts in which most media use takes place. Case studies also lend themselves specifically to the combination of several modes of empirical analysis. They thus offer excellent opportunities to complement the limitations naturally inherent in each and every single research tradition.

In the long term, of course, the combined approaches suggested above must in their turn be combined. In comparative studies based on the combination of several methodologies we may at last find the audience.

References

Blumler, J. and Katz, E. (eds) (1974) *The Uses of Mass Communications: Current Perspectives on Gratifications Research*, Sage, Beverly Hills, CA.

Caplow, T. and Bhar, H. M. (1983) *Middletown Families*, University of Minnesota Press, Minneapolis, MN.

Eagleton, T. (1983) *Literary Theory: An Introduction*, University of Minnesota Press, Minneapolis, MN.

Frye, N. (1957) *Anatomy of Criticism*, Princeton University Press, Princeton, NJ.

Groeben, N. and Vorderer, P. (1988) *Leserpsychologie: Lesemorivation – Lekturedrewirkung*, Aschendorff, Munster.

Hawkins, R., Wiemann, J. M. and Pingree, S. (eds) (1988) *Advancing Communication Science: Merging Mass and Interpersonal Processes*, Sage, Newbury Park, CA.

Höijer, B. (1989) Reliability, validity and generalizability: three questions for qualitative reception research. Paper presented to the IX Nordic Mass Communication Research Conference, Bergby, Sweden, 20–23 August.

Huesman, L. R. and Eron, L. D. (eds) (1986) *Television and the Aggressive Child: A Cross-national Comparison*, Erlbaum, Hillsdale, NJ.

Jarlbro, G. (1986) Family communication patterns revisited: reliability and validity. In *Lund Research Papers on the Sociology of Communication*, Department of Sociology, Lund, Vol. 4.

Liebes, T. and Katz, E. (1986) Patterns of involvement in television fiction: a comparative analysis. *European Journal of Communication*, Vol. 2, pp. 151–72.

Lindlof, T. and Anderson, J. (1988) Problems in decolonizing the human subject in qualitative audience research. Paper presented to the Congress of the International Association for Mass Communication Research, Barcelona, Spain, 24–29 July.

Lull, J. (ed.) (1988) *World Families Watch Television*, Sage, Newbury Park, CA.

Lynd, R. S. and Lynd, H. M. (1929) *Middletown: A Study in American Culture*, Harcourt, New York.

McQuail, D. and Windahl, S. (1981) *Communication Models for the Study of Mass Communications*, Longman, London.

Milawsky, J. R., Stipp, H. H., Kessler, R. C. and Rubens, W. S. (1982) *Television and Aggression: A Panel Study*, Academic Press, New York.

Palmgreen, P. and Rayburn, J. D. (1985) An expectancy-value approach to media gratifications. In Rosengren, K. E., Wenner, L. A. and Palmgreen, P. (eds) *Media Gratifications Research: Current Perspectives*, Sage, Beverly Hills, CA.

Rosengren, K. E. (1974) Uses and gratifications: a paradigm outlined. In Blumler, J. G. and Katz, E. (eds) *The Uses of Mass Communications: Current Perspectives on Gratifications Research*, Sage, Beverly Hills, CA.

Rosengren, K. E. (1989) Paradigms lost and regained. In Dervin, B., Grossberg, L., O'Keefe, B. J. and Wartella, E. (eds) *Rethinking Communication*, Sage, Newbury Park, CA, Vol. 1.

Rosengren, K. E. (1990) Media use in childhood and adolescence: invariant change? *Communication Yearbook*, Vol. 14.

Rosengren, K. E. and Windahl, S. (1989) *Media Matter: TV Use in Childhood and Adolescence*, Ablex, Norwood, NJ.

Rosengren, K. E., Wenner, L. A. and Palmgreen, P. (eds) (1985) *Media Gratifications Research: Current Perspectives*, Sage, Beverly Hills, CA.

Schmidt, S. J. (1980–82) Grundriss der empirischen Literaturwissenschaft, Vieweg, Braunschweig/Wiesbaden, Vols 1–2.

Singer, J. L., Singers, D. G. and Rapaczynski, W. S. (1984) Family patterns and television viewing as predictors of children's beliefs and aggression. *Journal of Communication*, Vol. 34, No. 2, pp. 73–89.

Sonesson, I. (1989) *Vem fostrar våra barn – videon eller vi?* Esselte Stadium, Stockholm.

Svensson, C. (1985) *The Construction of Poetic Meaning*, Liber, Malmö.

Sypher, H. E. and Higgins, E. T. (1989) Social cognition and communication: an overview. *Communication Research*, Vol. 16, pp. 309–13.

Section 4

Political economy

22

The political economy approach

Oliver Boyd-Barrett

The term 'political economy' in media research has a broadly 'critical' signification, often associated with macro-questions of media ownership and control, interlocking directorships and other factors that bring together media industries with other media and with other industries, and with political economic and social élites. It commonly looks at processes of consolidation, diversification, commercialization, internationalization, the working of the profit motive in the hunt for audiences and/or for advertising, and its consequences for media practices and media content.

In his history of the political economy tradition Mosco (1995) argues that despite this 'critical' signification, classical economics belonged to precisely this tradition, whereas the later development of 'orthodox' or 'neo-classical' economics followed a reductionist trajectory of identifying economic 'laws' or formulae to explain the relationship between individuals and markets, in isolation from broader historical and socio-political contexts.

Mosco offers both a narrow and a more ambitious definition of political economy. In its narrow sense, 'political economy is the study of the social relations, particularly the power relations, that mutually constitute the production, distribution, and consumption of resources, including communication resources'. But in its more ambitious form it is 'the study of control and survival in social life'.

Mosco identifies three essential features of political economy. First of all, it foregrounds the study of social change and historical transformation. It is in this sense, particularly, that some of the 'founding fathers' of economics who studied the transition from agricultural to industrial society, such as Smith, Ricardo and Mill as well as Marx, may be regarded as political economists. 'Political economy' theories encompass conservatives, socialists, Marxists, feminists and environmentalists according to whether they give central place to tradition, community, labour, gender or the organic environment. Secondly, political economy also has an interest 'in examining the social whole or the totality of *social relations* that constitute the economic, political, social and cultural fields'. Thirdly, it is committed to moral philosophy, having an interest in social values and moral principles. To these may be added a fourth feature, suggested by Golding and Murdock (1991) who, in describing a 'critical' political economy include a central concern with 'the balance between capitalist enterprise and public intervention', although arguably this is subsumed within social praxis as a way of addressing issues of value.

Political economy explanations distrust reductionism and linear causality; they are 'critical' in the sense, for example, that they assess knowledge in relation to values (such as participation and equality), and they focus on processes more than on institutions. Mosco offers three 'entry' concepts for the application of political economy to communication: 'commodification' (the process of taking goods and services which are valued for their use, and transforming them into commodities which are valued for what they can earn in the market place); 'spatialization' (the process of overcoming the constraints of space and time in social life); 'structuration', which incorporates the ideas of agency, social process and social practice into the analysis of structures. Even though the most powerful contributions of political economy to communication studies have been the analyses of media institutions and their contexts, Mosco's concepts are relevant to enquiries across the entire range of media activity, and have the potential to address in one holistic model the entire cycle from production (and its contexts) to reception (and its contexts). They provide a basis on to which can be mapped the identification by Golding and Murdock (1991) of four historical processes that are central to a critical political economy of culture: the growth of the media; the extension of corporate reach; commodification; and the changing role of state and government intervention, each of which also lends itself to analysis in terms of commodification, spatialization and structuration.

The late-1960s was a period in which radical thinkers increasingly questioned the extent of intellectual specialization in the social sciences and, more specifically, the narrowing of research questions to phenomena which could be interrogated through the empirical methods and 'truth' criteria of the natural sciences. Criteria of 'reliability' were privileged above criteria of 'validity', often at the expense of marginalizing powerful explanatory forces. The supremacy of 'administrative research' and of survey and experimental method in media studies in the 1950s illustrated these dangers. The rediscovery of 'critical' traditions during the 1960s, and the influence of radical economics (e.g. Baran and Sweezy, 1966) helped to introduce the concept of 'political economy' to media study. This was not the first time that a media theory located media within broader social and historical contexts – this had already been attempted, for example, by the Frankfurt school and in the media histories of Harold Innis (1972) and McLuhan (1964).

Dating from 1971 the Schiller extract in this section illustrates the radicalizing potential of political economy, in this case applied to international communication at a time when much of the work in this particular field was addressed to the 'modernizing' potential of the media in 'Third World' countries with little or no reference to questions of media ownership, control, nor even to content, and still less to broader issues of dominance and dependency, tied aid, super-power conflict, and media commercialization. There had previously been much interest in the relationship between different indices of 'modernization', including industrialization and urbanization. It was not that there was no interest at all in broader social contexts or in social change; but questions about who was setting this research agenda, to whose benefit, informed by which ideologies and discourses, were neglected.

Schiller's analysis was and continues to be endorsed by subsequent events. Acceleration of media privatization and commercialization which in 1971 he predicted for Western Europe and Asia were amply demonstrated throughout the 1980s and 1990s. Schiller locates these processes with reference to both the needs of capital for expansion beyond domestic markets in order to maintain sales growth, and the vital role of advertising in facilitating the penetration of overseas markets, reflected in the power of advertiser lobbies (through subversion where necessary, as in the case of the 'radio pirates') in bringing about changes in national media regulation likely to enhance the scope and opportunities for advertising and its influence (direct or indirect) on surrounding programme content. Such changes are even more crucially reflected in general business practices, so that it is not the export of media products that is significant in international communication so much as the export of business practice. Schiller's work set the stage for studies of media contributions to processes of cultural or media 'imperialism'. There has been a tendency here to focus almost exclusively on the negative implications of such processes, and to marginalize the significance of international media influences other than those which could be located within a framework of dominance and dependency.

Schiller illustrates two of the three key features which Mosco attributes to political economy analysis: historical dimension, and emphasis on the totality of social relations. There is also recognition of processes of human agency, (for example in the role attributed to lobbyists and pirate broadcasters) although arguably there is insufficient interest in counter-trends. Such interest might have helped identify the further development of non-U.S. exports and the growing internationalization of capital itself which has gradually undermined the global–national dichotomy that is key to much of Schiller's work. In his perspective on the power of advertising, human beings are much of the time 'consumerized' by manipulated needs. While this view may be contested by the (re-)discovery in 'new audience research' of the multiplicity of ways in which texts are used and read, it still requires exploration given the continuing massive scale of advertising investment. The model of media influence presented by Schiller also tends to assume a one-to-one relationship between macro-economic needs and media content, and thus clearly pre-dates 1970s' discussion in cultural studies of the scope for and influence of 'autonomous spaces' within the media, that is to say, opportunities for expression that are autonomous of or at least distanced from basic economic determinants, even if such opportunities arise only in the Gramscian interstices of struggle for hegemony among rival social élites.

The Murdock and Golding contribution to the 1973 Socialist Register in this section was a very early application of the title 'political economy' to media study in the U.K. In their introduction the authors refer to contemporary discussions of the reproduction and legitimation of class relations in reference to education (e.g. Bernstein, 1971), and they note the absence of reference to media in such discussions. The article makes good this deficiency and signals the revival of critical media theory in the U.K. A political economy of mass media, they argue, starts with the recognition that the media are 'first and foremost industrial and commercial organizations which produce and distribute commodities'. The different media sectors cannot be studied in isolation, as they are already interlinked through corporate control, and their activities can only be understood with reference to the broad economic context. Analysis must extend also to the ideological work of the media, in their dissemination of ideas about economic and political structures. A political economy of the media cannot focus only on the production and distribution of commodities but must also take full account of the peculiar nature of these commodities and the ideological work that they do.

The extract chosen here discusses the dynamics of change in media industries, with particular reference to processes of concentration in the control of media by a few large companies. Concentration occurs both internally among the media themselves, and externally, between media and non-media companies. Concentration results from processes of integration (horizontal and vertical), diversification of interests, and internationalization – providing further illustration of processes identified by Schiller. The economic concepts which are used to marshall the data collated here have proven powerful tools of analysis. As in the case of the Schiller article, they bring to light processes that have only accelerated over the intervening 20–25 years even if the details of their manifestation have changed in surprising ways.

Murdock and Golding discussed the implications of this evidence with reference to questions of reduced choice in leisure and entertainment, use of non-work time, and the ideological work of media in consolidating the 'consensus'. Media contribution to 'consensus' (a central but problematic term throughout radical left-wing debates of the 1970s) occurs in a variety of ways: representation of opposition to the status quo as either illegitimate and punishable or, alternatively, as ephemeral and therefore not threatening; constant invocation of a 'national interest' as more important than 'sectional' interests; representation of public debate as about the means towards ends which are assumed to be agreed; the claim that any residual dissent can be successfully articulated through existing channels; the representation of society as open to widespread social mobility; and through the assertion of 'we-ness' between audience and medium, reinforcement of the notion of a uniform moral community. A significant problem of this approach was the relative absence of research to show that audiences did indeed respond to media content in the way that the theory suggested they would and research, when it came, was less supportive of the thesis than had been assumed – a problematic which has shaped the course of political economy into the 1990s.

Political economy was one response to the prevailing directions of earlier media effects studies. These shared a psychologistic concentration on the individual, were often financed by the industry, and yielded inconclusive findings. Political economy theorists argued that the significance of media went much further than questions of individual effects, uses and gratifications, and had to do with the relationship of media to other social institutions, to the economy, to the formation of social ideologies. The importance of media could not be reduced to linear, causal, stimuli–response theories. There was a tension between this position and the classic Marxist formulation of a base/superstructure model of society wherein the ruling ideas are the ideas of the ruling élite and whose purpose is to reproduce, through the formulation of 'false consciousness' of the proletariat, existing inequalities between the social classes. The classic Marxist position, therefore, did assume a very direct process of 'media effect'.

The extract from Garnham in this section provides a flavour of the complexity of late 1970s' thinking around this very issue. A number of positions are outlined: the classic Marxist base/superstructure dichotomy; collapse of the superstructure into the base as a result of the industrialization of culture (Adorno and Horkheimer); media as relatively autonomous 'ideological apparatuses' in control of symbolic codes (Hall, 1980); media as the sale of audiences to advertisers (Smythe, 1980). In Garnham's model the media are significant both directly as creators of surplus value (entertainment products), and indirectly, through advertising, as creators of surplus value within other sectors.

The work of Dallas Smythe in this section centres on a different feature: the media as producers not only of entertainment commodities, but of audiences. Audiences-as-commodities are sold on to advertisers. Audiences produce surplus value for advertisers by devoting their time ('working') to consumption of advertising messages and to the purchase of other commodities. This thesis has the merit of highlighting the triangular relationship between media, audiences and advertisers. But it is, by implication, a regression to the stimulus–response model of media effect. Like the Frankfurt school, it so economizes the role of the media (perhaps reflecting the media context of North America more than that of Europe) that it undermines the base/superstructure dichotomy of Marxist analysis within which it operates. It presumes that programming is only there to support advertising, and that advertising works (even if only on the basis of statistically-predictable 'hits'). More significantly, as noted in the Garnham extract, Smythe's somewhat reductionist thesis tends to marginalize other important questions about the political economy of media.

There may be less interest in the 1990s in establishing specific links between political economy and particular features of classic Marxist analysis; but application of political economy analysis remains vigorous and relevant – one might say it is demanded by the need to understand the pace of real-world events (as illustrated in how the 'élite' press covers changes in the media industries, often framed within parameters not dissimilar to those of political economy). While this may seem ironical in the post-communist world, it is an outcome of the removal of many of the previous constraints on the operation of monopoly capital.

Political economy in the 1990s shows greater awareness of the need to demonstrate precisely how the political–economic formation of the media is related to media content, and to the discourses of public debate and private consciousness. Golding and Murdock (1991, p. l5) outline a critical political economy which focuses 'on the interplay between the symbolic and economic dimensions of public communication' and which 'sets out to show how different ways of financing and organizing cultural production have traceable consequences for the range of discourses and representations in the public domain and for audiences' access to them'. Such analysis gives greater weight to the contradictions within the system, to the constraints and not only the opportunities which influence how powerful interests use the media and offers a more sophisticated understanding of how meaning is made and re-made through the concrete activities of producers and consumers. Economics may define the key features of communicative activity of the media, but it does not provide a complete explanation for all aspects of such activity.

Political economy in the 1990s continues to chart the extent to which cultural production is controlled or influenced by large corporations. Hamelink (1994) argues that there are four key trends in world communication: digitization, consolidation, deregulation, and globalization. Schiller, in 1969, had begun to chart the course of globalization. Murdock and Golding established the study of media consolidation in their 1973 article. A relatively new feature of political economy is its concern to understand the causes and implications of privatization, which is to say, the processes by which governments since the early 1980s have sought to reduce support for publicly-owned media and at the same time to dismantle and reformulate the regulatory frameworks governing the private control of media, processes which were further accelerated by the collapse of the communist block in the late 1980s. Digitization refers to the extension of the binary language of computer communication to all electronic communication, and this too is a process which began to acquire strong public visibility from the early 1980s.

Hamelink sees the four processes as inter-related. Digitization facilitates technological integration and institutional consolidation; these processes enhance the drive to larger and larger conglomerates – globalization – which, in order to sustain their power and their rate of growth through acquisition and market penetration, increase the pressure for national deregulation and privatization of media. Governments define it as in their interest to facilitate the international expansion of domestic media industries, while international conglomerates urge upon governments the 'advantages' of privatization, namely: the dismantling of cumbersome media bureaucracies often protective of 'socialist' ideologues, less government expenditure on subsidy, more tax revenue, promotion of business through advertising, promotion of an entrepreneurial culture. As privatized media typically reduce the proportion of time devoted to news and public affairs, they may also appear less challenging and more politically compliant.

Political economy has always been critical, if perhaps not quite as critical, of the public as of the privately controlled media (Curran, 1991). It has identified the links between state and public media – even of public media supposedly protected from direct state interference – and the opportunities for indirect state intervention in the control and operation of public media. The survival and operation of public media is greatly influenced by the competition they face from private media for talent, revenues, and audiences. The state is not seen as neutral but as a forum within which major economic interests exercise considerable power and influence, not least power and influence over the regulation of public and private media. Nonetheless, it is widely recognized that the undermining of public media by processes of privatization has important implications for the quality of public debate, and this, together with the practical problems which have confronted the newly democratic states of Eastern Europe in reformulating their media systems, has contributed to the vitality of interest within the communications academy in the application and adaptation of Habermas' concept of the 'public sphere' to media analysis (see Section 5).

References and further reading

Adorno, T. and Horkheimer, M. (1944) *The Dialectics of Enlightenment*, Herder and Herder, New York.

Baran, Paul A. and Sweezy, Paul M., *Monopoly Capital: An Essay on the American Economic and Social Order*, Monthly Review Press, New York.

Bernstein, B. (1971), *Class, Codes and Control*, Routledge and Kegan Paul, London, Vol. 1.

Curran, James (1991) Mass media and democracy: a reappraisal. In Curran, James and Gurevitch, Michael (eds) *Mass Media and Society*, Edward Arnold, London, pp. 82–117.

Golding, Peter and Murdock, Graham (1991) *Culture, Communications, and Political Economy*. In Curran, James, and Gurevitch, Michael (eds) *Mass Media and Society*, Edward Arnold, London, pp. 15–32.

Hall, S. (1980) *Encoding and Decoding in the Television Discourse*. In Hall, S. *et al.* (eds) *Culture, Media, Language*, Hutchinson, London, pp. 197–208.

Hamelink, Cees J. (1994) *Trends in World Communication. On Disempowerment and Self-empowerment*, Southbound, Penang.

Innis, Harold (1972) *Empire and Communications*, University of Toronto Press, Toronto.

McLuhan, Marshall (1964) *Understanding Media*, Routledge Kegan and Paul, London.

Mosco, Vincent (1995) The political economy tradition of communication research, Unit 4 of the MA in Mass Communications (by distance learning), Centre for Mass Communications Research, University of Leicester.

Smythe, Dallas (1980), *Dependency Road*, Ablex, Norwood, NJ.

23

The international commercialization of broadcasting

Herbert I. Schiller

From Schiller, Herbert I. (1971) *Mass Communications and American Empire*, Beacon Press, Boston MA, pp. 94–103.

The global commercialization of communications systems

In the pre-television era, the United States stood alone amongst advanced industrialized nations in having its radio broadcasting unabashedly commercial. In no other society did advertisers pay the bill and direct the destinies of the medium so completely. State broadcasting authorities in Europe were the rule and the American arrangement was the exception.

With the advent of television, but not because of it, many national broadcasting structures adopted one or another variants of the American style. Dizard, author of *Television: A World View*, has written about this shift:

> Television has developed primarily as a commercial medium. This was to be expected in the United States and a few other countries, notably in Latin America, where broadcasting was traditionally a private venture. Elsewhere, however, broadcasting was a state monopoly without commercial connections. Theoretically, television should have followed in the established pattern; significantly it did not . . . At present, television systems in over fifty countries are controlled, in whole or in part, by private interests under state supervision. Commercial advertising is carried by all but a handful of the world's ninety-five television systems.[1]

For the new countries the emerging pattern is the same. Dizard notes 'the virtual domination of local television in developing nations by commercial interest'.[2] UNESCO reports the same finding. A 1963 study concludes, after presenting evidence that television has been less subject to state control than radio that 'this might seem to show that the tendency towards commercial operation is becoming more accentuated in television services than in radio broadcasting.'[3]

Even strong, industrialized nations have been forced to modify their long-time stabilized broadcasting services and accept commercial operations. Britain yielded in 1954. France teetering on the edge of advertising-sponsored support for years has just moved across the line. The Russians, a special case to be sure, advertise in American newspapers their willingness to accept commercial material over their state-owned TV system.[4]

What has powered this almost universal push toward commercialization in the electronics communications media? Its advocates claim that commercial broadcasting is the most satisfactory method of meeting the financial and programmatic needs of the new media. Dizard, for instance, asserts that 'The change [to commercialization] confirmed the effectiveness of American-style broadcasting both as a revenue producer and as a highly acceptable form of entertainment and persuasion'.[5]

The revenue-producing capabilities of commercial broadcasting cannot be disputed. The acceptability of the entertainment offered is another matter that will be considered further along. But neither reason faintly suggests the more fundamental forces that are operating. *Nothing less than the viability of the American industrial economy itself is involved in the movement toward international commercialization of broadcasting.* The private yet managed economy depends on advertising. Remove the excitation and the manipulation of consumer demand and industrial slowdown threatens. *Broadcasting* magazine puts it this way: 'In this country, where production capacity exceeds consumer demand, advertising has become more than an economic force – it is an influence on our quality of life.'[6]

The continuing and pressing requirements of U.S. manufacturers to reach annually higher output levels to sustain and increase profit margins activate the process that is relentlessly enveloping electronic (and other) communications in a sheath of commercialization. What happens, of course, is a continuing interaction. The direct intrusion of American influence catalyses developments in the affected nations. Also, those countries with similar industrial structures and organization feel corresponding, if at first weaker, impulses themselves in the same direction.

The international dynamics resulting from the explosive force of private enterprise industrialism's market requirements find expression in ordinary trade accounts. *Television Magazine*, for instance, describes the interconnections between the advertising, manufacturing and broadcasting industries:

> About 1959 a gentle curve representing the expansion of American advertising agencies overseas started an abrupt climb which hasn't yet levelled off . . . The growth of television abroad had something to do with this upsurge, since the head-start American agencies had in dealing with the medium commercially has given them a highly exportable know-how. But television wasn't the prime mover. *That role belongs to the client: The American consumer goods industry.*

The magazine explained this process with a simple illustration:

> Take a giant corporation like Proctor and Gamble with sales over $2 billion a year. Its position on the open market is based partly on the corporation's growth rate. But to add, say, 10% in sales each year becomes increasingly difficult when already over the two billion mark. *Where do you find that additional $200 million? The answer, for more and more American corporations, is overseas.*

American companies have been crossing the oceans regularly, either through direct acquisition or new plant expansion or leasing arrangements or combinations thereof. U.S. private direct investments in manufacturing across the globe have spurted in the 24 years beginning in 1943, from $2276 millions to $22,050 millions. In this period in Western Europe alone, manufacturing investments have increased from $879 millions to $8879 millions. To assist in marketing the output of their expanding foreign facilities,

U.S. advertising agencies have been accompanying the industrial plants overseas. McCann–Erickson has 70 offices employing 4619 persons in 37 countries. J. Walter Thompson, 'The grand-daddy of international operations', has 1110 people employed in its key London office alone. England has 21 American-associated ad agencies, West Germany has 20 and France 12. In Latin America, Brazil has 15 American ad agencies and Canada has more U.S. agencies than any other nation. Even the developing world has begun to be penetrated. 'Three enterprising U.S. agencies have tackled the huge market of India . . . [and] Africa, too, may be part of a future wave of agency expansion overseas'.[8]

The advertising agencies rely on the communications media to open markets for their patrons – the Americans and Western European consumer goods producers. The state-controlled broadcasting structures which resist commercialization are under the continuous siege of the ad-men and their cohorts in public relations and general image promotion.

Once the privately-directed manufacturing enterprises have begun their goods production, all energies are concentrated on securing the public's ever-widening acceptance of the outpouring commodity streams. The insistence of powerful American sellers, temporarily allied with their local counterparts, on obtaining advertising outlets abroad is overwhelming state broadcasting authorities, one after another. The successful campaign to introduce commercial television in England was largely a matter of industry ad-men manipulating complex political wires. The former director of the BBC's television explained with some understatement, what happened in Britain:

> . . . there was an unusually strong demand from large sections of British industry in the early nineteen fifties for more opportunities for advertising their goods. Wartime restrictions especially on paper had only recently been lifted, and a real boom in consumer goods was developing, but industry felt that there were insufficient opportunities for telling the public about the large range of new goods which were becoming available. Television was obviously an excellent medium for this, and industry was not averse to harnessing the television horse to the industrial chariot.'

Raymond Williams, also generalizing from the British experience, writes that 'It is almost a full-time job to work for democratic communications against the now fantastic economic and political pressures of managed capitalism.'[10]

What is emerging on the international scene bears striking resemblance to the routine in the United States, of uncoordinated expansion of goods production, their promotion through the communications media, higher sales, further plant expansion and then the cycle's repetition. The symptoms that Fromm finds endemic in America are spreading across oceans and continents. Industrial society's troubled individual who seeks release in goods consumption is appearing throughout the expanding orbit of the international free market. According to Fromm

> Twentieth century industrialism has created this new psychological type, *homo consumens*, primarily for economic reasons, i.e. the need for mass consumption which is stimulated and manipulated by advertising. But the character type, once created, also influences the economy and makes the principles of ever-increasing satisfaction appear rational and realistic. Contemporary man, thus, has an unlimited hunger for more and more consumption.'[11]

The man in the market economy has become a message receiver beyond all imagination. This individual is the target of the most effective communications media devised by modern technology. Bombarded in the United States by an estimated 1500 advertising messages a say,[12] and exposed to 4000 hours of TV viewing before arriving in grade school[13] 'contemporary men' are multiplying rapidly in the North Atlantic community. In fact, *homo consumens* is beginning to be discovered as well as in Africa, Latin America and Asia. In 14 industrial private enterprise countries in 1964, $21 billion were spent on advertising, two-thirds of which were expanded in the United States.[14] Financing much of this staggering budget for global commercial message-making are the powerful multi-national corporations whose plants and service installations are spread over several countries. The major United States advertisers are, as might be expected, the most prominent consumer goods producers. Tobacco, drugs, cosmetics, beer, automobiles, gasoline, and food products are the chief sponsoring industries of commercial television in the United States. Table 23.1 is an abbreviated listing of the largest American TV advertisers in 1966.

The engines of commercialization in the West are these 'big spenders'. Long ago they captured the radio spectrum in the United States. Now they are waging successful campaigns to extend their conquests to Europe, Africa and Asia. One advertising agency predicts that in 1976, American advertisers will be spending as much abroad as they do in the United States.[16] *Television Age*'s annual survey of television around the world, offers country by country progress reports of the multi-national companies' advertising penetration. For example, in Argentina, 'gasolines and automobile manufacturers, such as Shell, Esso, General Motors, Ford . . . are major advertisers . . . Ponds, Philips, Gillette, Nestle and Colgate are also heavy advertisers . . .'. In Australia, 'Coca-Cola and Chemstrand are major advertisers along with Ford, Lever Brothers, Alcoa, Ansett Airlines, The Australian Biscuit

Table 23.1. Television advertising expenditures of U.S. companies, 1966[15]

1. Proctor & Gamble	$179.2 million
2. Bristol-Myers	$93.6
3. General Foods	$93.3
4. Colgate–Palmolive	$67.1
5. Lever Brothers*	$58.0
6. American Home Products	$57.1
7. R. J. Reynolds	$49.8
8. Gillette	$41.9
9. Warner–Lambert	$41.3
10. American Tobacco	$40.8
11. General Mills	$39.1
12. Sterling Drug	$39.0
13. Coca-Cola Co./Bottlers	$38.8
14. General Motors	$38.4
15. Kellogg	$35.1

*Lever Brothers is British-owned.

Co., Beecham Products and Bristol-Myers'. In Finland, 'Ford, Coca-Cola and General Motors are about as active here as they are in the U.S.'.[17] Wherever big company influence penetrates, electronic communications are subverted to salesmanship.

'Three soap companies', Fred Friendly notes, 'Proctor & Gamble, Colgate–Palmolive, and Lever Brothers, account for about 15 percent of the nation's total television sales. This is one reason why Americans know more about detergents and bleaches than they do about Vietnam or Watts. The three great printing presses in their seven-day-a-week continuous runs are so oriented to advertising and merchandise that after a single day of viewing television, a visitor from another planet could only infer that we are bent on producing a generation of semiliterate consumers'.[18]

It is not only a matter of the ubiquitous, jarring commercial. The entire content that illuminates the home screen is fitted to the marketeer's order. 'TV is not an art form or a culture channel; it is an advertising medium,' states an American TV writer. Therefore, '. . . it seems a bit churlish and un-American of people who watch television to complain that their shows are so lousy. They are not *supposed* to be any good. They are *supposed* to make money . . . [and] in fact, "quality" may be not merely irrelevant but a distraction'.[19]

Admittedly, the situation of radio–television in the United States is the extreme case. In Western Europe, the tradition of state broadcasting authorities exercising some social responsibility has not yet been demolished. But the striving of the consumer goods producers to gain the attention of large audiences is unrelenting, and as Fromm observes, once the contact is made, the audience itself searches out further stimuli. If commercials are still controlled and compressed into special slices of the viewing time in some national systems abroad, the shows themselves often follow the dictates, directly or indirectly, of their sponsors. Certainly, this is the case in the popular and widely shown American productions where the advertising agency may have sat in at each stage of a script's development. Consider this account of a show's gestation: 'The writing of a half-hour script takes approximately three weeks. As a first step, Baer (responsible for such shows as 'Petticoat Junction', 'The Munsters', and 'Bewitched') submits several basic ideas for the plot to the producer. If the latter likes one of them, he gives the signal to go ahead. The next step is a five- or six-page outline. This is read by the producer, the story editor and sometimes representatives from the advertising agency. On some shows the advertising people only read the finished script.'

Whether in at the beginning of the 'creative' process or at its conclusion, the advertiser's influence in American programming is paramount. Inevitably, 'the writer feels that some of his best and most meaningful ideas have not reached the air because they were not considered commercial enough. Sponsors and producers do not want too radical a departure from what has been done before. Since the financial stake is so large, they want to play it safe'.[20]

All the same, American shows, written exclusively to serve the ends of goods producers, are gobbling up the international TV market. ABC, NBC and CBS send their packaged programming to all continents, charging what the freight will bear. In low-income areas in Africa and Asia, old U.S. films and shows are dumped at low prices to secure a foothold in emerging markets, regardless of the relevance or appropriateness of the 'entertainment'.

In Western Europe, the most stable non-commercial broadcasting structures of sovereign states are unable to resist the forces that are arrayed against them. Here is one description of how 'commercials' defy national boundaries, especially in the geographically compact North Atlantic region:

> Of course, the continued expansion of commercial television, despite powerful opposition, is playing a major role in making unity of diversity. Although many important countries, particularly in Europe, still forbid TV advertising, there is a certain 'spillover' effect that tends to spread commercials even to those countries that originally were adamant. Only this year did the 11-year-old government-controlled Swiss TV service permit commercials on its three regional networks. The move was in large part prompted by the concern of Swiss manufacturers who knew their customers were viewing Italian and German TV across the border. The same process is expected to unfold in the Netherlands, a large part of which is also open to German programming and advertising messages. If Netherland TV goes commercial, then Belgium is expected to follow shortly thereafter. Then France and Scandinavia will be the last big holdouts . . . If French television goes commercial, an executive at J. Walter Thompson remarks, then there truly will be a common market for the TV advertiser.[21]

The pressure on the non-commercial European TV networks to incorporate private programming and commercials is mounting and the same forces are at work in radio broadcasting. France was compelled to shift the programming patterns on one of its biggest radio networks, France-Inter, because of the competition of foreign stations close to the border. 'The change was forced on the non-commercial network when it realized that it was losing its young listeners to the Luxembourg Radio and European Number One, two stations situated on the borders of France that adhere to the American-style diet of pop music interspaced with commercials and newscasts'.[22]

If 'legitimate' infiltration and demolition of non-commercial state systems of broadcasting is inapplicable for one reason or another, less sophisticated techniques are available. Consider the bizarre charades of the pirate radio stations which were located off the coast of England and some even in the Thames estuary. These illegal transmitters completely disregarded international frequency allocation agreements. They broadcast pop music interlaced with commercials to European and English audiences who are apparently hungering for the entertainment and not at all displeased with the accompanying consumer messages. Though the pirates were small-scale broadcasters, behind them stood large-scale interests. In England, until the government actively intervened, both the Institute of Practitioners in Advertising and the Incorporated Society of British Advertisers lent indirect support to the pirates. A director of the ISBA stated: 'We recognize they fulfil a need. We would be happier, though, if they were on-shore and permanent'.[23]

Reacting to an impending governmental regulatory bill, one of the pirates, Radio London, commented: 'We expect to get sufficient advertising from overseas to enable us to continue. We have four million overseas listeners, *and much of our revenue is from international companies who would not be affected by British legislation'*.[24] Even after Parliament acted against the offshore broadcast facilities, national companies, their advertising agencies, wealthy free-booters, and broadcast and record companies – continued to support the pirates in their efforts to weaken the state broadcasting authority.

Piracy apart, programming cannot be contained under present *laissez-faire* conditions within national frontiers. The flashy show with its lowest common denominator emotional features, styled expressly by commerce for the mass audience, cannot be kept out of one country if presented in another nearby. However questionable the 'domino theory' may be in analysing political developments in South-east Asia, it is certainly an apt explanation for the march of commercial radio and television in Western Europe. Once a commercial inroad has been made electronically, technology and geography can be relied upon to exploit the advantage in depth.

A similar progression is beginning to appear in Asia. All-India Radio, reversing a 30-year policy, has acceded, with governmental approval, to commercial advertising. The explanations for the decision are familiar. The government needed revenue, and, more persuasive, 'Indian companies have been placing advertisements on the Ceylon Radio, whose light, commercial-studied programmes can be heard throughout India'. The parallel is striking 'Ceylon, an island a few miles off India's southern coast, has been compared in this respect to the pirate radio stations that beam commercial programmes to Britain . . . '.

Notes

1. Dizard, Wilson P. (1966) *Television a World View*, Syracuse University Press, Syracuse, New York, pp. 12–13.
2. Dizard, op. cit. (Note 1), p. 239.
3. UNESCO (1963) *Statistics on Radio and Television, 1950–1960*, Paris, France, p. 20.
4. *The New York Times*, 16 January 1967.
5. Dizard, op. cit. (Note 1), p. 13.
6. *Broadcasting*, 26 June 1967.
7. Ralph Tyler (1965) Agencies abroad: new horizons for U.S. advertising. *Television Magazine*, September, p. 36 (italics added).
8. Ibid., p. 65. In 1967, according to *Printers Ink*, there were 'at least 46 U.S.-based ad agencies abroad, with a total of 382 branch offices beyond the U. S. boundaries'. Forty of these agencies, reported *Advertising Age*, claimed overseas billings of $1138 millions.
9. Beadle, Gerald (1963) *Television: A Critical Review*, George Allen and Unwin, London, p. 82.
10. Raymond Williams (1967) Britain's press crisis. *The Nation*, 10 April, p. 467.
11. Fromm, Erich (1966) The psychological aspects of the guaranteed income. In Robert Theobold (ed.) *The Guaranteed Income*, Doubleday, New York, p. 179.
12. *The Wall Street Journal*, 3 November 1965.
13. *Television Magazine*, July 1967, p. 37.
14. Advertising investments around the world. *International Advertising Association*, October 1965.
15. *Broadcasting*, 17 April 1967, p. 38.
16. Ibid., 19 December 1966, p. 23.

17. *Television Age*, 3 July, 1967, pp. 33 and 61.
18. Friendly, Fred (1967) *Due to Circumstances Beyond Our Control*, Random House, New York, pp. 294–5.
19. Karp, Daniel (1966) TV shows are not supposed to be good. *The New York Times Magazine*, 23 January.
20. *The New York Times*, 12 December 1965.
21. *Television Magazine*, September 1965.
22. *The New York Times*, 26 February 1967. See also, Rising tide of monied interests may yet swing 3rd French TV web. *Variety*, 15 February 1967, p. 38.
23. *The Sunday Times*, London, 19 June 1966.
24. *The Times*, London, 2 July 1966 (italics added).
25. *The New York Times*, 29 January 1967.

24

For a political economy of mass communications

Graham Murdock and Peter Golding

From Miliband, R. and Saville, J. (eds) (1973) *The Socialist Register*, The Merlin Press, London, pp. 207–23.

The industrialization of mass communications

From differentiation to concentration

The present concentrated structure of the media industries is the latest stage in a sequence of organizational changes reflecting their changing economic base. Schematically all the media have gone through a similar cycle. Firstly, small-scale or personalized production of a cultural product expands. Distribution and selling become separated and commercialized. As new technology enters the medium, production becomes industrialized and consumption becomes large scale and impersonal. This process of differentiation is succeeded by a period in which the growth of the industry reaches saturation and is hit by a series of pressures due to rising costs, declining revenue, and a changing pattern of demand. This is the process of concentration which we consider below. The final stage in this sequence involves a developing tension between new technological potentialities on the one hand and economic concentration on the other. Both book and newspaper publishing began as small personalized activities; until the eighteenth century publisher–printers were responsible for both. Newspapers indeed began in the form of personal handwritten newsletter services, while book production preceded printing as a handwritten activity in ecclesiastical education. As authors established greater autonomy from publishers so too the eighteenth century saw the separation of bookseller from printer. Grub Street was born and writing, as Goldsmith complained, 'converted to a mechanic trade'. After 1750 newspaper publisher–printers were replaced by joint-stock companies.

The cinema split even more distinctly after its early fairground origins in the 1890s. Exhibition, based initially on the stockpiling of films by early showmen, became a differentiated arm of the industry. As film makers competed for the favours of the exhibitors the open sale of films declined, to be replaced by a hiring system, bringing with it the middle-men or renters.

Growing industrialization of the media – the introduction of new technology and mass production – brings with it a demand for greater financial underpinning. Through the nineteenth century the mechanization of paper-production, the steam-printing press, and later Linotype greatly advanced the industrialization of the print industries. For books this meant the growth of differentiated distribution through the circulating libraries, and finally the penny book and widespread marketing.

For newspapers rapid industrialization combined with decreasing prices when stamp tax ended facilitated rapidly rising circulations as individual purchases replaced collective subscriptions. Gradually the press became part of that embryonic entertainment industry which included professional sport and the music hall. The 'new journalism' as Arnold labelled it drew on American typographical and photographic techniques, headlines, interviews, the factual 'reporting' of the news agencies, and sports news to attract a new public. The so-called Northcliffe revolution was the recognition that the members of this public were also the consumers in the retail revolution. The bigger companies produced by the 1873–94 depression recognized the enlarged national press as the ideal advertising medium for the competitive selling of branded goods. The *Mail*, *Mirror* and *Express* all started in the period around 1900 on this new economic base.

Expansion and technological sophistication attracted capital into each medium. As exhibition boomed in the cinema, capital in the industry rose from £110,000 in 1908 to over £3 million in 1910.[1] Between the wars the cinema attracted a vast new audience. High and rising rental prices and a massive growth in the number of cinemas brought, as Lord Burnham observed in 1920, 'the high financiers of the world . . . flocking into the cinema industry'.[2] Nearly 1000 cinemas were built between 1924 and 1932 and capital in the industry rose from £15 million in 1914 to £70 million in 1929. As exhibition flourished so did the chains controlling it. By 1944 a third of the cinema seats were owned by three chains, ABC (which started as a production company in 1928), Gaumont-British, and Odeon. The latter two companies were taken over by Rank in 1941, and the new chain and ABC (now part of EMI) have dominated post-war film exhibition.

In the same way the expanded press attracted the attention of financiers, and by 1929 four of them, Inveresk, Rothermere, the Berry brothers, and Cowdray controlled roughly half the daily circulation. The ensuing battle for readers in the 1930s and the massive marketing operation it generated in effect created the mass popular daily press, doubling the national daily circulation between 1920 and 1939.

Broadcasting necessarily began as an industry requiring expensive technology and financial backing. Arriving after the industrialization of the economy the cycle of industrialization → commercialization → saturation → crisis has been a comparatively contracted one. The six companies which formed the British Broadcasting Company in 1922 appointed Reith as General Manager later in the same year. He spent the next four years demonstrating, as he was later to put it in his autobiography, that 'whatever was in the interests of broadcasting must eventually be in the interests of the wireless trade'.[3]

Television did not develop substantially until the post-war period, and it did not take long for financial backing to perceive the potential of the new medium. After war-time introduction to lighter styles of broadcasting the not uncommon opposition to the BBC in the Conservative Party, allied with advertising and equipment manufacturing interests produced 'perhaps the most remarkable exhibition of political lobbying this country has ever seen'.[4]

Commercial television opened in 1954, and licences climbed from three million in that year to eight million in 1958, arriving at virtual saturation in 1968. The resulting massive change in leisure patterns produced a decline in the cinema and popular press from their peak years (in 1946 for the cinema and about 1960 for the popular press), and was a major factor in the resulting stage of consolidation and concentration.

Consolidation

Concentration has taken different forms in each of the media industries, but the pattern of their increasing involvement with each other and with broader industrial enterprises is a universal response to the general problems outlined above. This latest stage is worth examining in closer detail.

Publishing. Most books read today are borrowed from libraries or from other people. The growth of public libraries since 1919 has been a major source of income for publishers. While 312 million library issues were registered in 1948/9, 20 years later the figure was over 600 million.[5] But as book prices have risen rapidly library budgets have failed to keep up and only account for about 10–15% of book sales; thus libraries are contributing proportionately more to book reading and less to sales.

Rising costs have terrorized the industry. Between 1966 and 1972 paper, printing, and binding costs rose by between 73 and 80%.[6] Hardback prices consequently doubled in price between 1963 and 1970, and the overall price of books rose 112% between 1965 and 1971.[7] The proportion of hardback sales has not surprisingly fallen before the advance of the 'paperback revolution'. In the decade from 1960 to 1970 the number of paperback titles in print rose from under 6000 to over 37,000. For a large part of the publishing industry paperback and other rights (book clubs, films, serialization) have become the main hope for profitability. Paperback publishing provides the financial cornerstone of the whole industry, and by 1972 accounted for 45% of sales revenue.[8] Yet, because paperback publishing, relying on large print runs and extensive promotion and distribution, requires large-scale finance, small traditional craft-like publishers have been coalesced into groups (like Associated Book Publishers comprising Methuen, Tavistock, Eyre and Spottiswoode, Chapman and Hall, *inter alia*), and into the multi-media combines who control paperback publishing (Granada, Thomson, Pearson Longman, etc.).

The other growth field in publishing is in educational textbooks, whose sales jumped by 65% in the period 1969 to 1972 alone. Yet here again, this is precisely a field requiring large financial backing and, increasingly, export organization. Thus publishing has quite clearly responded to pressures with massive consolidation and industrialization. The proliferation of titles in the desperate search for large-scale successes have sucked the industry into a financial expansion that has totally changed its character.

The press. The period since 1945 has been one of perpetual crisis for the press, littered with commissions, enquiries, and obituaries for dead newspapers. For a few years after the war, newsprint rationing kept costs low and advertising was a seller's market. But costs rose by between 70 and 140% from 1957 to 1965, especially newsprint and labour. This rise in fixed costs led to a rise in the break-even point (the recovery of 'first-copy' costs) putting a premium on high circulation to spread costs.[9]

Inevitably prices reflected this cost inflation, and many national dailies doubled, or even trebled their cover price between 1959 and 1971. The resulting decline in circulations reflects both a decreasing willingness to buy two newspapers, and a growing use of television as a primary source of information and entertainment.   However, the overall circulation decline (of 11% between 1961 and 1971) disguises variation within the press. While 'popular' dailies have lost most sales the 'qualities' have in fact steadily risen in circulation, though remaining a small absolute part of the market. The problem for the populars is their high survival threshold, given that roughly two-thirds of their income is sales revenue, while the qualities get nearly three-quarters of their income from advertising. Thus a newspaper like the *News Chronicle* can disappear with a circulation of well over a million.

These problems are reinforced by the problematic nature of advertising. The advertising industry grew comparatively slowly through the 1960s and its proportional contribution to newspaper revenue in fact declined. In addition, commercial television, though largely creating its own new advertising revenue, reduced the share of advertising going to the national press from 34% in 1956 to 18% in 1971 (though newspapers more or less held their own through the 1960s by keeping rates very low).[10] The variations within advertising reinforced the revenue pattern. While the advertisers of consumer goods, food, and drink switched from the national populars to television, classified advertising of jobs, property and services expanded and contributed to the comparative vigour of the quality and provincial press. Thus only three or four of the national dailies are profitable and the spectre of closure haunts Fleet Street despite occasional bouts of optimism and the recent surge of the *Sun*. The response has been two-fold. Firstly, newspapers have merged into groups, with each other, with provincial chains, or with other publishing interests. Secondly, in order to stay alive, they have joined diversified industrial groups able and willing for whatever reason to support loss-making newspapers.

Broadcasting. Despite the golden age when commercial television, in Lord Thomson's immortal phrase, was 'a licence to print money', broadcasting has more recently foundered in the same sea of pressures as the other media. Advertising revenue has been uneven and unpredictable, rising only slowly through the 1960s and hardly at all in 1969–71. Depressed profits in some of those industries providing the bulk of television advertising in the late 1960s (like food manufacturing, hit by the power of the chain supermarkets) lay behind this uncertainty.

At the same time the levy on television advertising revenue was beginning to bite. Introduced in 1965 the levy immediately represented over 25% of the costs of network companies. By 1969 the levy was extracting over £25 million and represented nearly 40% of costs of the big five network companies.[11] The levy was reduced by the Conservative government in 1971 by £10 million.

The problem of revenue was exacerbated by the spread of television ownership. By 1968 virtual saturation point had been reached with over 15 million licences in operation. If there is no increase in the audience there can be no increase in advertising revenue, especially in view of the growing power of agencies to keep rates down and enforce discounts. The option is to increase broadcasting time, as duly occurred in 1972 after a resurgence in the advertising industry, increasing the demand for an extra commercial channel.

The ITV audience has not just remained static, however, it has actually declined since the arrival of BBC2 in 1964 enabled BBC1 to compete aggressively for ratings. Where ITV had something over two-thirds of the audience in the early 1960s this figure gradually dropped to 54% by 1972.[12]

The final factor in this catalogue of pressures was the rapid rise in costs created by the introduction of colour, and the increased production of expensive programmes for the American market. Total costs rose by about 50% between 1965 and 1970.

The BBC has been far from immune from pressures. Increased costs with the expansion of the second service, and the spread of colour have created a situation which the annual report coyly described as 'financial inhibition'.[13] Despite licence fee increases in 1965, 1969 and 1971, by 1971 the BBC's accumulated deficit was over £6 million, and despite the recent drop in this figure as more colour licences are bought, the bailing out of the BBC is now a permanent feature of its political environment.

Cinema. The cinema has been a major victim of changing leisure patterns. Since the peak of admissions in 1946 of 1635 millions they have shrunk steadily and dramatically to 182 million in 1972. In the same period the number of cinemas has contracted from 4703 to 1510. The major villain, of course, is television, particularly after the rapid expansion of set ownership in the late 1950s. The result has been government assistance, contraction, and a reliance on American finance, as well as the concentration which we consider later.

Government aid has been by legislation in the form of quotas against foreign films, by a statutory levy on seat prices, redistributed among British film producers according to box-office success, and through the National Film Finance Corporation which provided funds for domestic production, particularly by support of British Lion. However, the failure of the latter had, by 1971, prompted the Corporation to withdraw from independent support of films and instead to concentrate on financing strictly commercial films in conjunction with a private consortium.[14]

The other response to contraction was the acceptance of massive American backing as the domestic market in the U.S.A. sank in the wake of television. The proportion of feature films on the two dominant circuits which were American-financed doubled from 43% in 1962 to 88% in 1968. However, problems in the American film industry have depleted much of this support and the proportion has fallen steadily over the last five years.

Records. Unlike the cinema, the record industry has been a beneficiary rather than a victim of changing leisure patterns. Whereas the profitability of almost all the other media sectors declined between 1967 and 1971, the record market expanded at an annual rate of 11%.[15] This growth is due largely to the increasing importance of the youth market for pop music. In fact, the various sorts of pop account for just over 90% of the total record market.[16] Undoubtedly, the most significant recent trend in the record industry has been the rise of the long-playing record (LPs). LPs, which now account for over 60% of record production and sales, have become the industry's principal financial prop. The period since 1967 has seen some reduction in the dominance of the two 'major' companies – EMI and Decca. Whereas in 1967 their joint share of the LP market was 58%, by 1970 the figure had dropped to 32% and by the end of 1972 to 27%.[17] However, this vacuum has been filled not by the independents but by other major companies.

The dimensions of concentration

The increasing concentration of control and influence in the hands of a few large companies is the outcome of three interlinked but analytically distinct processes: integration; diversification; and internationalization.

Integration. There are two main types of integration: horizontal integration, where firms acquire additional units at the same level of production, and vertical integration where they acquire units at different levels. Both types of integration are accomplished by the familiar mechanisms of mergers and take-overs. The period 1967–70 saw a boom in both mergers and take-overs. In those four years, commercial and industrial companies spent almost £5000 million on acquisitions – considerably more than the total for the whole of the preceding 16 years.[18] Media companies were part of this general trend. Horizontal integration enables companies to consolidate and extend their control within a particular sector of media production and to maximize the economies of scale and shared resources. The most notable example within publishing was the acquisition by reverse take-over of Penguin Books, the world's largest paperback house, by Pearson Longmans, one of Britain's largest publishing corporations. An important instance within the newspaper industry was the acquisition of two leading 'qualities', *The Times* and *The Sunday Times*, by the Thomson Organization, which at that time was already the world's leading newspaper corporation with almost 90 newspapers in the U.S.A. and Canada, and over fifty provincial and local papers in the United Kingdom.

Vertical integration occurs when a company with interests in one stage of the production process extends its operations to other stages such as the supply of raw materials, the provision of capital equipment, and the organization of distribution and retailing. This considerably reduces the company's vulnerability to fluctuations in the supply and cost of essential materials and services and enables it to regulate and rationalize production more precisely and to increase its control over the market. The most significant instance of vertical integration occurred in 1970 when the leading British newspaper and magazine publishers IPC merged with the Reed

Group Limited, an international corporation with interests in wood, pulp, papers and newsprint. The resulting company, Reed International Limited, has interests in most stages of newspaper publishing, from raw materials to retailing. Another notable example of vertical integration occurred in the film industry when Electrical and Musical Industries Ltd (EMI) acquired the Associated British Picture Corporation in 1969. This gave the corporation a substantial interest in both film production and exhibition. Then, in 1970, EMI acquired Anglo Amalgamated Film Distributors Ltd, which gave the group an interest in every stage of film production, from finance through production to distribution and exhibition. These, and other less spectacular moves towards vertical integration, have considerably accelerated the shift from differentiation to concentration.

The overall result of these twin integrative processes has been to consolidate the control of the four or five leading companies within each media sector. Table 24.1 summarizes the current situation in selected sectors.

Although incomplete, the above table clearly indicates that the ownership and control of the British mass media tends to be highly concentrated, with the five leading companies in each sector accounting for 69% or more of the market.

Concentration of ownership is most marked in the national press, with the 'Big Five' accounting for well over 80% of the circulation of both the national dailies and the Sundays. A more detailed account of the breakdown of market shares is given in Table 24.2.

The national 'daily' market is dominated by the four leading 'populars'. Heading the list and still well out in front is Reed International's *Daily Mirror*, followed by Beaverbrook's *Daily Express*, News International's *Sun*, and Associated's *Daily Mail*. The 'quality' end of the spectrum is dominated by *The Telegraph* with 10% of the total 'daily' circulation. *The Times* and *The Guardian* come a poor second and third with just over 2% of the circulation each. Pearson's *Financial Times* accounts for just over 1%. The national Sunday market is even more concentrated, with the leading three companies taking just over 80% of the circulation. Half of this is accounted for by the two Reed papers, the *Sunday People* and *Sunday Mirror*, followed by News International's *News of the World* and Beaverbrook's *Sunday Express*. The 'quality' sector is convincingly headed by Thomson's *Sunday Times* with just under 7% of the total circulation, the remainder being split almost equally between the *The Observer* and the *Sunday Telegraph*.

Table 24.1 Proportion of the total market accounted for by the five leading companies in selected mass media sectors[19] (percentages are rounded off to the nearest whole number)

National morning newspaper: % of circulation	86%
National Sunday newspaper: % of circulation	88%
Network television: % of television homes served	73%
Paperbacks: % of domestic production (1971)	86%*
Mid-price long playing record:† % of market	69%
Cinema exhibition: % of admissions‡	78%

*Denotes estimate. †Mid-price = 99p to £1.98p. ‡Top four companies.

Table 24.2 Proportion of national newspaper circulation accounted for by the leading five companies (June 1972)[20]

	Morning daily	Sunday	All newspapers*
Reed International	30.0	40.5	30.3
News International	18.0	24.6	17.6
Beaverbrook	23.3	16.1	16.5
Associated Newspapers	11.9	–	7.3
Thomson Organization	2.4	6.8	7.3
Total market share	85.6	88.0	79.0

*Includes provincial press.

Concentration in the provincial daily press is less marked. Nevertheless, the five leading companies in this sector still account for 60.7% of the evenings' circulation and 39.9% of the mornings'. Of the major national groups only two have a substantial share: Thomsons with a fifth of both the mornings and evenings, and the Daily Mail group with 13.9% of the evenings and 3.3% of the mornings. The other leading provincial daily groups are United Newspapers, and the family concerns controlled by the Iliffes and the Cowdrays (Viscount Cowdray is also chairman of Pearson whose publishing subsidiaries include the *Financial Times* and Pearson Longmans.)

The initial allocation of commercial television contracts concentrated control in the hands of the four companies serving the major population centres. Associated-Rediffusion provided weekday programming in the London area, ATV served London at weekends and the Midlands during weekdays, Granada provided weekday television in the North, while ABC filled the weekend slots in the North and Midlands. The remainder of the country was divided into ten regions each served by its own company. The primary task of these smaller regional companies was to produce local news bulletins and other programmes of local interest. The rest of their air-time was filled by programmes produced by the four network companies. When the commercial television franchises were re-allocated in 1967, the number of network companies was increased from four to five. Weekday London programming was awarded to Thames and the weekend slot to London Weekend; ATV served the Midlands, while the North was split between Granada and Yorkshire Television. These five network companies together served 73.2% of the television homes in Britain and received around two thirds of ITV's gross revenue. In theory the pattern of contractors was originally 'designed to spread responsibility for making programmes over as many companies as the expected advertising revenues would support and to provide (very roughly) equal revenue potential for each company'.[21] In practice, however, network programme planning provides a functional equivalent to integration, and the five network companies produce all but a tiny handful of prime-time output. The recurrent problems of the ITA with regard to franchise allocation and the like reflect the permanent contradiction of a state regulatory agency attempting to control a commercial system.

Integration in publishing has gradually split the industry into two groups. Old independent publishing houses like Faber and Faber, or Routledge and Kegan Paul, maintain their independence and survive on small steady returns on capital. Meanwhile many firms have been forced along the several dimensions of concentration to cope with the mass marketing and export methods now the lifeblood of British publishing.

Associated Book Publishers area major example of a group of medium sized publishers taking advantage of joint operations, though, like many general publishers they are glad to get a return on sales of 4 or 5%.[22] The group includes Methuen, Eyre and Spottiswoode, Sweet and Maxwell, and Chapman and Hall. The major university presses remain secluded havens of indeterminate profitability. Concentration in publishing is generally difficult to calibrate, especially in the hardback market where it is not yet particularly important anyway. But as early as 1949 Sir Stanley Unwin estimated that 'about 85% of the total book turnover is represented by the sales of at most 50 firms'.[23] *The Economist* in 1958 estimated that the ten largest publishers issued 23% of all new titles that year. Luckham in 1969 modified this to the six largest producing nearly 30%.[24] These six were Hamlyn (purchased by IPC, itself now part of Reed International), Collins, Penguin (part of the Pearson Longman empire), ABP, Hutchinson, and Routledge and Kegan Paul. At the same time bookselling had also become highly concentrated; by 1965 80% of the trade was going to 10% of the booksellers.[25]

The paperback publishers are integrated into groups with parent diversified companies. Pearson Longman control Longman hardbacks as well as Penguin, and Ladybird books. Granada Publishing comprises Adlard Coles, Crosby Lockwood Staples, and Hart-Davis MacGibbon, as well as Mayflower, Panther, Paladin and a substantial holding in Chatto and Windus, and Cape. Lord Thomson controls, among others, Thomas Nelson, Michael Joseph, Hamish Hamilton, Rainbird, and Sphere. Of the other major paperback imprints Pan is jointly controlled by Macmillan and Heinemann, Corgi by the American publishers Bantam (themselves part of the National General Film Corporation), and Fontana by the giant Collins publishing house.

In 1968 British film production was dominated by American companies. Then in 1969 Hollywood experienced a crisis as five of the seven major companies lost a total of $180 million, and as part of the resulting rationalization, investment in the British film industry was cut back by 40%. Because of the sums required, only the large companies such as EMI and Rank were in a position to step into this vacuum. The American film industry has recently undergone something of a resurgence, but in 1972 EMI continued to lead British production with nine films, followed by the Rank Organization and the Laurie Marsh group with six each. The other notable feature of the present situation is the rapid growth of independent producers, a point we shall return to later. The main trends in British film production are summarized in Table 24.3.

Between the film producer and the public stand the intermediary stages of distribution and exhibition. At the level of distribution the influence of the reciprocal arrangements and combines of the dominant groups is decisive. In 1972 for example, 16 of the top 20 box office films in Britain were distributed

Table 24.3 British film production in selected years[27]

Number of films produced by:	1968	1972
Leading American companies	54%	23%
Leading British companies	14%	31%
Independents	13%	30%
Total number of films produced	81	84

by the three major coalitions; seven by the Columbia–Warner group, six by the EMI–MGM combine, and three by the Fox-Rank group.[26] At the exhibition level, only the large companies have the capital required to undertake the extensive alterations to cinemas necessary to attract the declining audiences. This had the effect firstly of consolidating the duopolistic domination of the EMI and Rank chains, and secondly of driving the smaller chains into the hands of large companies such as Granada and the Laurie Marsh group, who have interests in a wide range of leisure facilities. The only other significant cinema chain is the Star group [in 1972 Rank accounted for 27% of cinema admissions, EMI for 25%. The Marsh Group for 14%, Star for 12% (*Retail Business*, No. 177)].

Since 1968, when they accounted for half the records produced, LPs have rapidly increased in importance until they now constitute over 60% of total record production and contribute the bulk of the record industry's profits. LPs can be divided into three main types on the basis of selling price; budget record (selling for under £1) mid-price (£1–2) and full price (£2+). The budget market is dominated by two companies – the Minnesota-based Pickwick International and EMI'S Music for Pleasure. Pickwick currently claim to be running just ahead of MFP with 40% of the market. The mid-price market is dominated by the two leading British 'majors', EMI and Decca, whose joint market share stood at 50.6% in the last quarter of 1972.[28] At the full price range, however, their joint share drops to just over a quarter (25.6%). However, this gap is filled not by the independents but by the other leading companies, most notably CBS and RCA, the two giant American corporations, and Polydor, the record subsidiary of Siemens, the German electronics combine. Recently the American marketing firms of K-Tel and Ronco have been making a significant impact, re-releasing material leased from the majors on records backed by extensive TV promotion. At the end of 1972, K-Tel's share of the full price market stood at 10.3%. Despite this increasing complexity, however, taken overall, the record market continues to be dominated by EMI.

Diversification. In addition to consolidating their position within a particular medium through mergers and take-overs, the larger companies have increasingly diversified their interests and acquired holdings in a range of leisure and information-providing facilities. Diversification enables companies to hedge their bets and to cushion the effects of recession in a particular sector. The Associated Television Corporation Limited (ATC) provides a good illustration of how this works in practice. ATC's operations are split into two main divisions; network television represented by ATV which serves the Midlands, and the 'diversified interests'. These include a film-making subsidiary ITC, Pye records, Northern Songs (which holds the rights to 200 of the Beatles' most popular songs), the Stoll Theatre group which includes the London Palladium and ten other West End theatres, Planned Music Limited, and a merchandising company, Century 21 Enterprises. In July 1969, the levy on the turnover of the commercial television companies was increased, and in the words of ATC's Chairman, Lord Renwick, 'This . . . immediately produced a crisis which changed the whole financial structure of Independent Television and endangered the very existence of some companies not protected by diversified operations'.[29] The post-tax profits of Westward TV which serves the south-west of England, for example, dropped from £139,000 in 1969 to £64,000 in 1970.[30] ATC however, was 'protected by diversified operations' most notably its film and music interests, as Table 24.4 below clearly shows, and these cushioned the effects of the levy on the company's profitability.

During the period of financial stringency in the television industry, the share of profits attributable to ATV dropped from around a half to under a fifth, and the gap was filled by the expansion of the record and film interests. During the summer of 1969 for example, more ATC productions were screened in 'prime time' on American networks than any other single producing company with the exception of MCA Universal. The success of the diversified activities was not entirely sufficient to maintain profits but it certainly cushioned the effects of the levy. Then, as the domestic television situation improved, the balance of profits attributable to network operations and to the diversified activities evened out again to around 50–50 and overall profitability increased substantially.

As well as providing a cushion against recession in a particular sector, diversification (whether through direct acquisition, investment or reciprocal arrangements) enables a company to capitalize on a commodity's success in one sector by marketing spin-offs in a number of other sectors. Here, for example, is ATC's write-up of the success of 'The Persuaders'.

'The Persuaders', featuring Tony Curtis and Roger Moore, has been sold to more than 62 countries. American Broadcasting has scheduled the re-run of 13

Table 24.4 Proportion of ATCs pre-tax profits accounted for by selected activities: 1969–1972

	1969	1970	1971	1972
Network TV (ATV)	49%	11%	17.5%	51.5%
Film production and distribution	22%	41%	32%	21%
Records and music	12%	32%	38%	24%
Pre-tax profit (£millions)	5.6	5.3	4.9	6.2

episodes . . . the theme composed and recorded by John Barry, has sold more than 116,000 records in the U.K. Pan Books have sold 180,000 paper-backs based on the series.[32]

Diversified activities are becoming increasingly important, and in several leading media companies they already account for more than half the annual turnover.[33] For example, although IPC is the country's leading newspaper publisher with 30.3% of the total circulation, IPC only accounted for 30% of Reed International's 1972 turnover. Similarly, in 1972 over half the turnover of the Thomson Organization was attributable to activities other than newspaper publishing. They included book and magazine publishing and trade exhibitions (24.6%) and package holidays (27.6%). Granada and Rank provide other prominent examples of media companies with diversified leisure interests. In 1972 for example, 40% of Granada's turnover came from TV set rental, 36.2% from network TV operations, 7.9% from motorway services, 6.2% from cinemas and bingo, and 5.6% from publishing. Similarly, 28.4% of Rank's 1972 turnover came from TV and radio-set manufacture, 19.9% from film exhibition, 15% from audio-visual equipment manufacture (notably Leak Wharfdale hifi sets), 7.7% from hotels, restaurants and motor ports, and 7.2% from dancing and bingo. Rank also hold 37.6% of the ordinary shares of Southern TV, one of the main regional TV companies. However, undoubtedly the most spectacular example of diversification is provided by EMI, which in addition to heading the record industry and having a substantial stake in all levels of the cinema industry, holds just over 50% of the voting shares in Thames TV, the most successful network company. In 1972, records and tapes accounted for 55% of EMI's turnover, film interests for 15%, TV interests for 7%, and electronics and TV manufacture for 23%. Recently EMI have extended their diversification policy even further with the acquisition of the 'Golden Egg' restaurant chain, and investments in the Swindon Cable TV station and in the Brighton Marina complex.

In addition to consolidating and extending their control within and across the various media sectors, the big companies are also becoming increasingly intermeshed through joint investments, reciprocal share holdings and interlocking directorships. The pattern is immensely complex, but the following instance provide a simple illustration of the emerging network. Among the EMI directors is Lord Shawcross, who is a director of Times Newspapers in the Thomson Organization, and Chairman of Thames TV. Similarly, the ATC board includes representatives of the two leading newspaper groups, Sir Hugh Cudlipp, Deputy Chairman of Reed International, and Sir Max Aitken, Chairman of Beaverbrook. In addition EMI and ATC are linked through the Grade family. After the Second World War, the two Grade brothers, Lew and Leslie, established an actors' and artists' agency, while their half-brother, Bernard Delfont, built up his own agency business. The two companies later merged to form the Grade Organization under the direction of Leslie Grade and Bernard Delfont. In 1967 the Grade Organization was acquired by EMI, but Delfont continued as chairman and the Grade family retained its interests. Currently, Bernard Delfont is Chairman of the EMI Film and Theatre Corporation Ltd. and Lew Grade is Deputy Chairman and Chief Executive of ATC.

Internationalization. The third aspect of concentration is the inter-nationalization of the media, embracing export and foreign investment as well as foreign ownership of British media companies. Exports play an increasingly important role for all media industries and most of all in publishing. Book exports rose from 29% of total sales in 1949 to 47% in 1969. Educational texts flow in growing profusion to the Third World and in 1972 made up over 20% of British book exports (a proportion nearly doubling in four years).[34] The old slogan that 'trade follows the book' has been outmoded by the book becoming the trade.

Similarly the export of TV programmes is an ever-more important source of income for both the BBC and the larger independent companies. ATC derived 31% of its sales revenue from overseas in 1971–72 and has been a leader in the growth of the British programme export drive under the inspired control of Sir Lew Grade. The potential of TV film exports was healthy enough to encourage ATC's chairman, Lord Renwick, to announce last year an investment programme of £7 million to back it up.[35] Production for the foreign market encourages mid-Atlantic innocuity and expensively superficial slickness, as well as feeding back onto domestic production styles and resources.

This is not a development that has left the BBC untouched, suffering as it has been from the permanent nightmare of 'financial inhibition' and the impending reorganization of broadcasting. In 1971–72 the income of BBC Enterprises, the marketing wing of the Corporation, rose by 11% and contributed about a fifth of the total surplus on the year's working.[36] Total programme sales to nearly 100 countries amount to about £2.5 million. The success of BBC programme sales is a rare glimmer in a preponderantly gloomy financial atmosphere. It joins merchandising, and record sales (over 150 titles in 1972) among the extensions of the BBC's commercial activities. Co-production with Time-Life and other organizations adds to this growing nexus.

Internationalization also involves overseas investment by media companies. The participation of news media in imperial expansion was crucial both as the communications arm of the empire and as a source of revenue for the media. In most colonial countries local indigenous newspapers were either started by British companies or later succumbed to competition from them (the chain of IPC newspapers in West Africa is a good example of this). Most television stations in colonial territories have been set up by British companies who continue to service them with programme material, training, and equipment.[37]

Direct investment in Europe is a more recent and growing form of inter-nationalization. The Thomson Organization have considerable interests in German newspapers, and like many media firms are preparing for the impact of entry into Europe. EMI own record companies in virtually every European country, and indeed all over the world, while Ranks have film exhibition interests in Holland and laboratories in Italy.

Foreign, mainly American, ownership of British media has further con-solidated the monolithic character of the industry, though with the flight of American capital from the ailing film industry, the frequent lack of success of American publishing interests in taking over British firms and the enduring insularity of most of the press (despite the Australian Murdoch and the Canadian Thomson) this aspect of internationalization is frequently overstated at the expense of other more subtle relationships.

The complexity of these relationships is in part a facet of the wider face of what is frequently stigmatized as 'cultural imperialism' or 'the cultural offensive', in which British media are but part of a global marketing system as yet incompletely documented. American television film series dominate international programme sales, amounting to nearly 200,000 programme hours in 1971, and providing a revenue that year of approximately $85 million.[38] For all but a very few non-Communist nations television is an American medium. On the other hand the two dominant news films agencies, Visnews and UPITN, are British-based (the latter being half American). The international traffic in newsfilm (and in a visual medium this dominates news selection) is a major part of the export of cultural material from the developed countries to the Third World, and is a more concentrated version of a similar one-way flow through the news agencies.

Internationalization, then, shares with other aspects of concentration the effect of consolidating the necessary commercial constraints on cultural production. As an increasingly evident response of the media to domestic economic pressures involvement in the international market is an inevitable development of later media industrialization.

Notes

1. Low, R. (1949) *The History of the British Film 1906–1914*, Allen and Unwin, London.
2. Low, R. (1971) *The History of the British Film 1918–1929*, Allen and Unwin, London.
3. Reith, J. W. C. (1949) *Into the Wind*, Hodder and Stoughton, London.
4. Wilson, H. H. (1961) *Pressure Group*, Secker and Warburg, London.
5. Figures from the *Municipal Yearbook*, annually.
6. Report by Educational Publishers' Council, London, September 1972. See summary in *The Author*, Vol. 83, No. 4, Winter, 1972, pp. 187–8.
7. Department of Education and Science (1972) Library Information Series, No. 1, *The Purchase of Books by Public Libraries*, HMSO, London.
8. Calculated from Board of Trade Business Monitor, Production Series, p. 75, *General Printing and Publishing*, HMSO, London, quarterly.
9. See National Board for Prices and Incomes (1970/1) Report No. 141, *Costs and Revenues of National Daily Newspapers*, Cmnd 4277 sess., HMSO, London.
10. See annual reports of The Press Council, and The Printing and Kindred Trades Federation, *National Newspaper Industry*, London, December, 1972.
11. National Board for Prices and Incomes (1970/1) Report No. 156, *Costs and Revenues of Independent Television Companies*, Cmnd. 4524 sess. HMSO, London.
12. See BBTA Bulletins.
13. *BBC Annual Report and Accounts*, Cmnd. 5111, sess. 1971/2, HMSO, London.
14. *National Film Finance Corporation, Annual Report 1971*, Cmnd. 4761, sess. 1970/1, HMSO, London, para. 13.
15. Special Report No. 1: Gramophone Records, *Retail Business*, No. 159, May 1971, p. 18.
16. Ibid., p. 28.
17. 1967 figures from *The Times*, 29 November, 1968, p. iv; 1970 figures from *Retail Business*, op. cit. (Note 15), p. 26; 1972 figures from *Music Week*, 27 January, 1973.
18. Glyn, Andrew and Sutcliff, Bob (1972) *British Capitalism, Workers and the Profits Squeeze*, Penguin Books, p. 143.

19. Newspaper figures from the *19th Annual Report of The Press Council 1972* ,pp. 11921; TV figures from *Independent Televison Authority Annual Report and Accounts 1971/2* (House of Commons paper 1, sess 1972/3), HMSO, London; paperback figures are calculations from the estimates given in Blond, A. (1971) *The Publishing Game*, Jonathan Cape, London; record figures from *Music Week*, 17 January, 1973. Cinema figures from *Retail Business* No. 177, November, 1972, p. 37.
20. Figures from Press Council 1972, op. cit.
21. PIB Report No. 156, op. cit.
22. Annual Report and Accounts 1972.
23. Letter to the *Economist*, 15 October 1949.
24. Luckham, B. (1969) The market for books. In Astbury, R. (ed.) *The Writer in the Market Place*, Clive Bingley, London, pp. 153–76.
25. Harris, G. E. (1968) The book trade. In Collison, R. L. (ed.) *Progress in Library Science*, Butterworth, London.
26. *Cinema TV Today*, 30 December 1972.
27. Calculated on the basis of figures given in *Cinema TV Today*, 6 January 1973.
28. *Music Week*, op. cit.
29. *Associated Television Corporation Limited Annual Report and Accounts 1970*, p. 4.
30. *Westward TV Report and Accounts 30 April 1970*, p. 7.
31. This table is derived from the figures given in the ATC Annual Reports for the respective years.
32. *Associated Television Corporation Ltd. Annual Report and Accounts 1972*, p. 11.
33. The figures for the proportion of turnover are calculated from figures given in the 1972 Annual Reports of the respective companies.
34. See Deane, M. (1951) United Kingdom publishing statistics. *Journal of the Royal Statistical Society*, Vol. 114, Series A, pp. 468–89; and Board of Trade Business Monitor Production Series, p. 75. *General Printing and Publishing*, quarterly returns, from which our figures are calculated.
35. Annual Report, 1972, p. 4.
36. *BBC Annual Report and Accounts 1971/2*. Cmnd. 5111, sess. 1971/2, HMSO, London, pp. 17–19.
37. See Elliott, P. and Golding, P., *Mass Communications and Social Change*, paper given to 1972 British Sociological Association conference, forthcoming in conference anthology.
38. Varis, T., *International Inventory of Television Programme Structure and the Flow of TV Programmes Between Nations*, Research Institute, University of Tampere, 1973.

25

Contribution to a political economy of mass communication

Nicholas Garnham

From Garnham, N. (ed.) (1979) *Media, Culture and Society*, Vol. 1, No. 2, Academic Press, London, pp. 130–4.

The inadequacies of existing Marxist theory

From this perspective available historical materialist theories are inadequate to deal with the real practical challenges they face largely because they offer reductionist explanations which favour either a simple economic determinism or an ideological autonomy, thus failing to analyse and explain precisely that which makes the object of analysis centrally significant, namely the relationship between the economic and the ideological. Thus we are offered the following.

(a) An unproblematic acceptance of the base/superstructure model drawn from a partial reading of the German ideology which, unargued, simply states that the mass media are ideological tools of ruling-class domination either through direct ownership or, as in the case of broadcasting, via ruling class control of the state. Such a position neglects both the specific effects of subordinating cultural production and reproduction to the general logic of capitalist commodity production and the specificities of the varying and shifting relationships between economic, ideological and political levels within actual concrete historical moments. Miliband in *Marxism and Politics* expresses a classic version of this theory:

> Whatever else the immense output of the mass media is intended to achieve, it is *also* intended to help prevent the development of class-consciousness in the working class and to reduce as much as possible any hankering it might have for a radical alternative to capitalism. The ways in which this is attempted are endlessly different; and the degree of success achieved varies considerably from country to country and from one period to another – there are other influences at work. But the fact remains that 'the class which has the means of material production at its disposal' does have, 'control at the same time of the means of mental production': and that it does seek to use them for the weakening of opposition to the established order. Nor is the point much affected by the fact that the state in almost all capitalist countries 'owns' the radio and television – its purpose is identical (Miliband, 1977, p. 50).

It should be noted here that for all its philosophical sophistication the Althusserian position on ISA represents little if any advance on this position, as indeed Simon Clarke (1977) has correctly noted with respect to the Miliband/Poulantzas controversy.

(b) Secondly, and in partial reaction against this classic Marxist explanation of the role of the mass media, we are offered an elaboration of the relative autonomy of the superstructure and within the superstructure of the ideological and political levels. All such theories in their effort to reject economism or, as Althusser puts it, 'the idea of a "pure and simple" non-overdetermined contradiction', to a greater or lesser extent have also removed economic determinacy, i.e. as Althusser again puts it, in such theories 'the lonely hour of the "last instance" never comes' (Althusser, 1969, p. 113). This general position has rightly developed the insights of the Frankfurt school into the importance of the superstructure and of mediation, while damagingly neglecting a crucial component of the Frankfurt school's original position, namely the fact that under monopoly capitalism the superstructure becomes precisely industrialized; it is invaded by the base and the base/superstructure distinction breaks down but via a collapse into the base rather than, as is the tendency with the post-Althusserian position, via the transformation of the base into another autonomous superstructural discourse.

> In our age the objective social tendency is incarnate in the hidden subjective purpose of company directors, the foremost among whom are in the most powerful sectors of industry – steel, petroleum, electricity and chemicals. Culture monopolies are weak and dependant in comparison. They cannot afford to neglect their appeasement of the real holders of power if their sphere of activity in mass-society is not to undergo a series of purges (Adorno and Horkheimer, 1977, p. 351).

The truth of this original insight is demonstrated monthly as firms in the cultural sector are absorbed into large industrial conglomerates and brought under the sway of their business logic. Indeed, the real weakness of the Frankfurt school's original position was not their failure to realize the importance of the base or the economic, but insufficiently to take account of the economically contradictory nature of the process they observed and thus to see the industrialization of culture as unproblematic and irresistible. Those who have come after, while rightly criticizing the Frankfurt school for its absence of concrete class analysis, an absence stemming precisely from their insufficiently nuanced analysis of the economic level, in developing their theories of the effectivity of the superstructure have, ironically, massively compounded the original error.

'The most distinguished exponent of the post-Althusserian position in Britain, Stuart Hall, in his essay 'Culture, the media and the ideological effect' (Curran *et al.*, 1977), recognizes that there is a decisive relationship between the growth of the mass media and 'everything that we now understand as characterizing "monopoly capitalism" ', but at the same time refuses an analysis of this decisive relationship claiming that 'these aspects of the growth and expansion of the media historically have to be left to one side by the exclusive attention given here to media as "ideological apparatuses" '. Murdoch and Golding (1979) rightly criticize Hall and claim that 'on the contrary the ways in which the mass media function as "ideological apparatuses" can only be adequately understood when they are systematically related to their position as large scale commercial enterprises in a capitalist economic system and if these relations are examined historically'. Hall's failure to do this leads him to explain the ideological effect in terms of pre-existent and ideologically predetermined communicators or encoders choosing from a pre-existent and ideologically predetermined set of codes so that there is a systematic tendency of the media to reproduce the ideological field of society in such a way as to reproduce also its structure of domination. That is to say he offers the description of an ideological process, but not an explanation of why or how it takes place, except in tautological terms. Moreover, he is led by his mode of analysis, as again Murdoch and Golding rightly point out, to favour a specific and atypical instance of media practice, namely public service broadcasting and indeed within that, an atypical form, namely informational broadcasting. While stressing that the production of the ideological effect requires work and struggle, his mode of analysis does not allow him to deal, for instance, with an important and developing moment in that struggle within the Press caused by a contradiction between the crucial underpinning idea of a 'free press' and the economic pressures towards monopoly or the relationship precisely between the ideological effect of broadcasting and the fact that it is perceived by its audience to be under state control as opposed to the biased privately owned press.

(c) A further elaboration of the post-Althusserian position, popular within film studies leads in its elaboration of a theory of autonomous discourses effectively to an evacuation of the field of historical materialism, whatever its materialistic rhetoric, placing its determinacy in the last instance on the unconscious as theorized within an essentially idealist, indeed Platonist, problematic. Such idiocies need detain us no further.[1]

(d) Finally, Dallas Smythe, identifying the excessive stress on the autonomy of the ideological level within Western Marxism as its 'blind-spot', rightly redirects our attention away from the mass media as ideological apparatuses and back to their economic function within capitalism. But in so doing, he proposes an extreme reductionist theory. For Smythe, any political economy of mass media must be based upon an analysis of its commodity form and for him the commodity form specific to the mass media is the 'audience', that is to say, for Smythe, the crucial function of the mass media is not to sell packages of ideology to consumers, but audiences to advertisers. Now it is undoubtedly important to focus attention upon the ways in which the mass media manufacture and sell audiences as one moment in the complex circuit of capital that structures the operation of the mass media economically. Moreover, to stress this moment as the crucial one and to concentrate on the mass media's directly functional role for capital as advertising vehicles is undoubtedly a more plausible reflection of reality in the North American context than it would be in Europe. However, Smythe's theory misunderstands the function of the commodity form as an abstraction within Marxist economic theory and thus neglects the relationship between specific forms of the commodity, in this case the audience, and the commodity form in general. As a result, his theory lacks any sense of contradiction, failing to account for the function of those cultural commodities directly exchanged, failing to account for the role of the state, failing sufficiently to elaborate the function for capital of advertising itself and, perhaps most crucially of all, failing to relate the process of audience production by the mass media to determinants of class and to class-struggle.[2]

The ideological level

What problems is it, then, that a political economy of mass-communication attempts to analyse. The research perspective, whose theoretical and historical basis I have briefly outlined, attempts to shift attention away from the conception of the mass media as ISAs and sees them first as economic entities with both a direct economic role as creators of surplus value through commodity production and exchange and an indirect role, through advertising, in the creation of surplus value within other sectors of commodity production. Indeed, a political economy of mass-communication in part chooses its object of study precisely because it offers a challenge to the Althusser/Poulantzas theorization of the social formation as structured into the relatively autonomous levels of the economic, the ideological and the political. For the major institutions of mass-communication, the press and broadcasting, although, as will be analysed later, displaying notable differences of articulation, both at the same time display the close inter-weaving within concrete institutions and within their specific commodity forms of the economic, the ideological and the political. When we buy a newspaper we participate simultaneously in an economic exchange, in subjection to or reaction against an ideological formation and often in a quite specific act of political identification or at least involvement. We also know from historical analysis of the development of the press that the nature of the political involvement is quite specifically economically conditioned. Similarly, TV news is economically determined within commodity production in general, performs an ideological function and explicitly operates within politics, in terms of balance, etc.

While accepting that the mass media can be and are politically and ideologically over-determined within many specific conjunctures, a political economy, as I understand it, rests upon ultimate determination by the economic (a level that itself always remains problematic and to be defined in the process of analysis).

Indeed, one of the key features of the mass media within monopoly capitalism has been the exercise of political, and ideological domination through the economic.[3] What concerns us in fact is firstly to stress, from the analytical perspective, the validity of the base/superstructure model while at the same time pointing to and analysing the ways in which the development of monopoly capitalism has industrialized the super-structure. Indeed Marx's own central insight into the capitalist mode of production stressed its generalizing, abstracting drive; the pressure to reduce everything to the equivalence of exchange value. Before going on to examine the economic level and its specific articulations within the cultural sphere, let us look at the relationship between the material conditions of produc-tion (not, as we have seen, to be confused with the economic far less the capitalist modes of such production, which are specific forms) on the one hand and ideological forms on the other. That is to say how do we relate Williams' correct stress, within the limits indicated, upon the materiality of cultural production, to Marx's famous distinction 'between the material transformations of the economic conditions of production, which can be determined with the precision of natural science, and the legal, political, aesthetic or philosophic – in short – ideological – forms in which men become conscious of this conflict and fight it out' (Marx, 1859).

What the quotation from Marx underlines is the importance of the distinction between the two levels, a distinction focused upon the difference between the *unconscious* forces governing material production 'beyond our will', etc. and the conscious form of ideology. If we follow the Althusserians and make ideology an unconscious process this crucial distinction is lost.

As far as the mass media specifically are concerned this distinction points to the need to distinguish between the media as processes of material production (whether capitalist or not is precisely a question for analysis) on the one hand, and as sites of ideological struggle on the other and the relationship between those two levels or instances.

There are here two distinctions to be made. I think we can liken ideological practice to what Marx called the 'real labour process'.

> Looking at the process of production from its real side, i.e. as a process which creates new use-values by performing useful labour with existing use values, we find it to be a real labour process. As such its element, its conceptually specific components, are those of the labour process itself, of any labour process, irrespective of the mode of production or the stage of economic development in which they find themselves (Marx, 1976).

That is to say the process of consciousness and of representation, for instance, language, are real processes by which human beings socially appropriate their environment (nature) which pre-exist and continue to exist within specifically capitalist modes of ideological production and indeed upon which these capitalist modes rest.

The materiality of such ideological production *qua* ideology rests upon the fact that consciousness is a human transformation of 'real' experience, it is in that sense 'practical knowledge'. Clearly therefore, the relationship of any particular instance of ideological production to the totality of social experience will depend upon an analysis of the experiential position of the human consciousness in question, e.g. the conventional and simple definition of class consciousness as based upon the direct experience of a given position within the capital/labour relationship. Of course in any complex society such direct experience becomes highly mediated both diachronically and synchronically. But its translation into forms of representation is nonetheless a process of consciousness which is different from and in its forms has no necessary correspondence with, the economic processes to which it relates or of which it is a representation. Indeed as a representation it is precisely by definition distinct from those processes which it represents.   Moreover ideological forms can never be simply collapsed into a system of exchange values, i.e. the specifically capitalist mode of production, precisely because ideological forms, forms of consciousness, are concerned with difference, with distinction; they are by definition heterogeneous (as Marx himself remarked when discussing the limited possibilities for the subsumption of ideological production under capitalism, 'I want the doctor and not his errand boy'). Whereas exchange value is precisely the realm of equivalence.

Notes

1. We intend to publish a detailed critique of this position in a forthcoming issue. In the meantime, see Thompson (1978), Williams (1977) and Corrigan and Singer (1978).
2. See Smythe (1977), Murdoch (1978) and Levant (1978).
3. See Curran, J., Capitalism and control of the press 1800–1979, in Curran *et al.* (1977).
4. For a detailed discussion of this problem see Baudrillard (1972–5).

References

Adorno, T. and Horkheimer, M. (1977) The culture industry (abridged). In Curran, J. *et al.* (eds) *Mass Communication and Society*, Edward Arnold, London.

Althusser, L. (1969) *Contradiction and Over-determination*, Allen Lane, London.

Baudrillard, J. (1972) *Pour une Critique de l'Economic Politique du Signe*, Gallimard, Paris.

Baudrillard, J. (1975) *The Mirror of Production*, Tela Press, St. Louis.

Clarke, S (1977) Marxism, sociology and Poulantzas's theory of the state. *Capital and Class*, No. 2, Summer.

Corrigan, P. and Singer, D. (1978) Hindess and Hirst: a critical review. *Socialist Register*, Merlin, London.

Curran, J. *et al.* (eds) (1977) *Mass Communication and Society*, Edward Arnold, London.

Financial Times (1978) Electronic rentals ups its ratings, 19 December.

Levant, P. (1978) The audience commodity: on the blindspot debate. *Canadian Journal of Political and Social Theory*.

Marx, K. (1859) Preface to a contribution to a critique of political economy. In Marx, K. and Engels, F. (eds) (1962) *Selected Works*, Vol. 1, p. 364, Lawrence and Wishart, London.

Marx, K. (1976) Results of the immediate process of production. In *Capital*, Pelican, Vol. 1.

Miliband, R. R. (1977) *Marxism and Politics*, OUP, p. 50.

Murdoch, G. (1978) Blindspots about Western Marxism: a reply to Dallas Smythe. *Canadian Journal of Political and Social Theory*, Vol. 2, No. 2.

Murdoch, G. and Golding, P. (1979) Ideology and the mass media: the question of determination. In Barrett, M. *et al.* (eds) *Ideology and Cultural Production*, Croom-Helm, London.

Symthe, D. (1977) Communication: blindspot of Western Marxism. *Canadian Journal of Political and Social Theory*, Vol. 1, No. 3.

Symthe, D. (1978) Rejoinder to Graham Murdoch. *Canadian Journal of Political and Social Theory*, Vol. 2, No. 2.

Thompson, E. P. (1978) *The Poverty of Theory*, Merlin, London.

Williams, R. (1977) *Marxism and Literature*, OUP.

26

On the audience commodity and its work

Dallas Smythe

From Smythe, D. (1981) *Dependency Road: Communications, Capitalism, Consciousness, and Canada*, Ablex, Norwood, NJ, pp. 39–47.

What is the nature of the service performed for the advertiser by the members of the purchased audience? In economic terms, the audience commodity is a non-durable producers good which is bought and used in the marketing of the advertiser's product. The work which audience members perform for the advertiser to whom they have been sold is learning to buy goods and to spend their income accordingly. Sometimes, it is to buy any of the class of goods (e.g. an aircraft manufacturer is selling air transport in general, or the dairy industry, all brands of milk) but most often it is a particular 'brand' of consumer goods. In short, they work to create the demand for advertised goods which is the purpose of the monopoly-capitalist advertisers. Audience members may resist, but the advertiser's expectations are realized sufficiently that the results perpetuate the system of demand management.

People in audiences, we should remember, have had a rich history of education for their work as audience members. As children, teenagers, and adults they have observed old and new models of particular brands of products on the street, in homes of friends, at school, at the job front, etc. Much time will have been spent in discussing the 'good' and 'bad' features of brands of commodities in hundreds of contexts. A constant process of direct experience with commodities goes on and blends into all aspects of people's lives all the time. Advertisers get this huge volume of audience work (creation of consumer consciousness) as a bonus even before a specific media free-lunch–advertising programme appears on the tube face and initiates a new episode in audience work. While people do their work as audience members they are simultaneously reproducing their own labour power. In this respect, we may avoid the trap of a manipulation-explanation by noting that if such labour power is, in fact, loyally attached to the monopoly-capitalist system, this would be welcome to the advertisers whose existence depends on the maintenance of that system. But in reproducing their labour power, workers respond to other realistic conditions which may on occasion surprise and disappoint the advertisers.

The nature of audience work may best be approached through successive approximations. At a superficial level it looks like this: 'Customers do not buy things. They buy tools to solve problems', according to Professor T. N. Levitt (1976, p. 73) of Harvard Business School. The nature of the work done by audience power thus seems to be to use the advertising–free-lunch combination of sensory stimuli to determine whether s/he (1) has the 'problem' the advertiser is posing (e.g. loneliness, sleeplessness, prospective economic insecurity for loved ones after the breadwinner's death, etc.), (2) is aware that there is a class of commodities which, if purchased and used will 'solve' that problem (e.g. shampoo, non-prescription sleeping drugs, life insurance) and that people like him/her use this class of commodity for this purpose, (3) ought to add brand X of that class of commodities to the mental or physical shopping list for the next trip to the store. This is the advertisers' rational basis. For audience members, however, their work is not so rational.

There is an *ever-increasing* number of decisions forced on audience members by new commodities and their related advertising. In addition to the many thousand of different items stocked by a typical supermarket at any one time, more than a thousand new consumer commodities appear each year. Literally millions of possible comparative choices face the audience member who goes shopping. As a long line of books stretching back to the 1920s has argued (for example, Chase and Schlink, 1927), the consumer is totally unable to *know* either the craftsman's sense of quality or the 'scientific' basis of quality as built into consumers goods by modern mass production techniques. Imagine yourself entering a toilet goods section of a modern department store in which every product was in a similar glass container and the containers bore only the chemical description of the contents and the price. Unless you were a very experienced chemist specializing in cosmetics and other toiletries (and even then you would have to do a lot of thinking), how could you know which was a 'best buy', or even what the product was intended to do: be a shampoo, deodorant, skin-care cream, or what? Lacking the product brand name, the shape and symbolic decoration of the package, you would be helpless.[1]

It must be assumed that when most people go shopping, even for H.P.G., there is real necessity moving them. The refrigerator needs re-stocking. Soap is needed for washing, and so on. And that they are increasingly aware of the squeeze of increasing cost of living versus inadequate income. The recent appearance of 'no-name brand' commodities is a response of monopoly capitalism to consumer resistance to the usual brand pricing practice. In the 1950s there was a flurry of 'discount stores' where 'standard' brand merchandise (acquired from bankrupt stores, from usual sources, or from thieves) was sold at substantial discounts. This was a tactical response of the system to consumer resistance. And with the artificial prosperity of the Vietnam war period these stores disappeared. It is probable that 'no-name brand' merchandise is a similar, temporary tactical concession. In any event, 'no-name brands' amount in fact to new 'house brands' with, for the present, reduced prices.

Your work, as audience member, has to do with how your life's problems interact with the advertising–free-lunch experience. But how? How, in light of that experience do you decide whether you really have the 'problem' to which the advertiser has sought to sensitize you? And if the answer to this question be affirmative, how do you decide that the class of commodities which have been produced to cope with that problem will really serve their advertised purpose? And if the answer to that question be affirmative, how do you decide whether to buy brand A, B, or n? *The process contains a monstrous contradiction. It is totally rational from the advertisers' perspective and totally irrational from the audience members'.*

Faced with the necessity to make some decisions as to what classes and what brands of commodities to put on the shopping list (if only to preserve a shred of self-respect as one capable of making one's own decisions), it seems that Staffen B. Linder (1970, p. 59) may be correct in saying that the most important way by which consumers can cope with commodities and advertising is to limit the time spent per purchase in thinking about what to buy:

> Reduced time for reflection previous to a decision would apparently entail a growing irrationality. However, since it is extremely rational to consider less and less per decision there exists a rationale of irrationality.

'Impulse purchasing' has increasingly become the practice of Consciousness Industry, as market researchers have studied the effect of store layout, shelf-level display, and commodity package design and artwork on customers pushing their basket-carts through supermarket aisles. Studies of eye-blink rates indicate that a semi-hypnotic condition of the customer results in impulse purchases for which no rationale can be remembered when the customer returns home. 'Consumers' produced and delivered by Consciousness Industry are in the position of trying to cope with a giant con game. They know that they do not really have all the problems which advertisers press them to solve by buying their products. Placed in a time- and income-spending bind, the impossibility of making rational shopping decisions forces consumers to 'take a chance'. The lottery is perhaps the best model for explaining what happens at the moment of truth when the customer reaches for the package from the shelf. And it is perhaps significant that lotteries, so long excluded from socially sanctioned practice, have recently become legal and generally used in North America. For consumers accustomed to taking a chance on a $9.99 item on the supermarket shelf, the option of a statistically sheer random 'chance' to win a million dollars can be very attractive and compelling. Yet the rationale of irrationality (Linder's) is unsatisfactory as an explanation of audience work. It may serve as a first approximation to an explanation. But we must dig deeper into the process of which audience work is a part.

How can audience power be 'work' when it takes place in 'free' or 'leisure' time? What becomes of the labour theory of value if audiences are working? Is it not true that what people do when not working at the job front (where they are paid money for their work) is their free or leisure time *by definition*? Is it not true that 'you can do as you please' in this 'free' time? Have not 'modern' household appliances relieved women of household work?

At the outset it is important to note that the idea of such free or leisure time is a hand-me-down from the upper classes in bourgeois society. It derives from the upper-class notion of leisure for the enjoyment of 'official culture' (see Chapter 9). At the height of imperialist power toward the end of the nineteenth century, it took the form of emulating the conspicuous consumption of the rich and powerful, as Veblen so bitingly revealed in *The Theory of the Leisure Class* (1899). As transformed by monopoly capitalism, it meant the imitation of *expensive* consumption, for, as Veblen also pointed out, the policy of monopoly capitalism was to be 'a competition in publicity and scarcity'. David Riesman (1950) and Stuart Ewen (1976) focused on the illusory semblance of reality in such 'leisure' and 'free time'.

It is necessary to state clearly that just as people are rarely totally controlled by Consciousness Industry, so marketed commodities rarely have absolutely no use value. Repeatedly, in different ways I emphasize that most people embody a dialectical tension: they feel it necessary to cooperate with the monopoly-capitalist system in a variety of ways and for a variety of reasons; yet at the same time, as human beings they resist such cooperation in a variety of ways, for a variety of reasons. An analogous internal dialectical tension seems to exist *within* most commodities under capitalism. The gas-guzzling, overpowered, dangerous private automobile *also* transports you from home to work and back again; when suitably 'hotted up', it may even lure into a lasting relationship a commoditized person of the opposite sex, just as the advertisements promise. The relative strength of the repressive and emancipatory ingredients in a commodity obviously differs greatly as between different commodities, e.g. an adulterated drug as against ordinary packaged milk. This dialectical conflict within commodities exists within producer goods as well as consumer goods, which is the reason that the term *technology*, with its assumed neutral quality, is dangerously misleading. For most people in the core area today, leisure or free time, like technology, are propaganda devices which obscure and confuse the real contradictions between the respects in which people cooperate with and resist the monopoly-capitalist system and its commodities.

Except for those people who have been so rich that they did not have to work, all people have always had to work – one way or another – when not at the job in order to prepare themselves to work *tomorrow*. *Before* the mass production of consumer goods – roughly before 1875 – in capitalist core countries, people's work to prepare themselves to work tomorrow (e.g. to reproduce their labour power) was done under conditions of cottage industry. For example they baked their own bread using flour which they might have ground themselves and yeast which they cultured for themselves. But with the mass production of consumer goods, their work to reproduce their labour power depends on buying and using consumer goods *in end-product form*. They have become dependent on factory-baked bread. And if sophisticated durable goods, e.g. vacuum cleaners, have relieved them of the necessity to sweep with brooms, it has required them to spend time buying filters and other equipment and arranging for maintenance of such equipment by 'service men'. And the endless proliferation of new commodities which clamour for their place in household consumption (e.g. electric can openers, electric carving knives, power lawn mowers, etc.) demands so much of so-called free time to buy, use, and maintain them that the idea of 'free time' has become ridiculous. Consider what has happened to the time available to workers and the way it is used in the past century.

In 1850, under conditions of cottage industry, i.e. unbranded consumer goods, the average work week of employed men was about 70 hours per week in the United States.[2] The average worker could devote about 42 hours per week to such cottage industry types of reproduction of his labour power. By 1960, the time spent on the job was about 39.5 hours per week – an apparent reduction in time spent on the job of about 30 hours per week (to which should be added 2.5 hours as a generous estimate of the weekly equivalent of paid vacations).

Advertisers and home economists regularly argued that the apparent reduction in 'work' hours created new leisure time for workers and housewives between 1910 and 1940, as Stuart Ewen's *Captains of Consciousness* (1976) demonstrated. Consumer durable goods like washing machines, vacuum cleaners, etc., were said to free housekeepers from work. Some time was indeed freed from drudgery in this way, but the illusion that most people had large blocks of free time was a myth created by Consciousness Industry. Upon close inspection, as we shall argue, leisure time for most people is work time. As Marylee Stephenson (1977, p. 32) puts it 'over 90% of 51% of the adult population is engaged in ... wageless labour (known as housework) for their entire adult life. ...'.

In fact, the meaning of the almost 30 hours per week by which the *job* work week shrank between 1850 and 1960 was transformed doubly by monopoly capitalism. One transformation removed huge chunks of people's time from their discretion by metropolitan sprawl and by the nature of unpaid work which workers were obligated to perform. For example, recently travel time to and from the job has been estimated at 8.5 hours per week; 'moonlighting' employment at a minimum of one hour per week; repair work around the home at another five hours per week; and men's work on household chores and shopping at another 2.3 hours per week. As I write this the postman drops through the slot a piece of direct mail advertising for a *Do-It-Yourself* manual. It tells me that owning this manual:

> ... is like having the experts at your side ... but without having to pay for them! You can save the expense of countless calls for cabinetmaker, carpenter, decorator, electrician, heating expert, locksmith, mason, painter, paperhanger, plasterer, plumber, roofer, rug cleaner, tile layer.

And it lists more than 50 'projects you can build for your home or garden' with the manual.

A total of 16.8 hours per week of the roughly 32 hours of time supposedly 'freed' as a result of 'modernization' is thus anything but free. A further 7 hours of the 32 hours of 'freed' time disappears when a correction for part-time female employment is made in the reported hours per week in 1960.[3]

A second transformation involved the pressure placed by the system on the remaining hours of the week. If sleeping is estimated at eight hours a day, the remainder of the 168 hours in the week after subtracting sleeping time and the unfree work time identified earlier was 42 hours in 1850 and 49 hours in 1960. The apparent increase in 'free' time has thus shrunk to seven hours per week (instead of about 30 hours). We lack systematic information about the use of this increased free time for both dates. We do know that certain types of activities were common to both dates: personal care, making love, visiting with relatives and friends, preparing and eating meals, attending union, church, and other associative institutions, including saloons. We also know that in 1960 (but not in 1850) there was a vast array of *branded* consumer goods and services pressed on workers through advertising, retail establishment displays, and peer group influence. Attendance at spectator sports and participation in such activities as little leagues, bowling, camping, and 'pleasure driving' of the automobile or snowmobile – all promoted for the sake of equipment and energy sales by the Consciousness Industry – now takes time that was devoted to non-commercial activities in 1850. In-house time must now be devoted to deciding whether to buy and to use (by whom, where, under what conditions, and why) an endless proliferation of goods for personal care, household furnishings, clothing, music reproduction equipment, etc. And thus far we have not mentioned mass media *use*, although it should be noted that workers are guided in all income and time expenditures by the mass media – through the blend of explicit advertising and advertising implicit in the programme content.

Let us now introduce mass media use as it relates to the seven hours of 'free' time thus far identified (ignoring the pressures on the audience to use its time and income referred to in the preceding paragraph). How much time do most people spend as part of the audience product of the mass media – their time which is sold by the media to advertisers? David Blank, economist for the Columbia Broadcasting System, found in 1970 that the average person watched television for 3.3 hours per day (23 hours per week) on an annual basis, listened to radio for 2.5 hours per day (18 hours per week), and read newspapers and magazines for one hour per day (seven hours per week) (Blank, 1970). Recent years show similar magnitudes. If we look at the audience product in terms of families rather than individuals, we find that in 1973 advertisers in the United States purchased television audiences for an average of a little more than 43 hours per home per week.[4] By industry usage, this lumps together specialized audience commodities sold independently as 'housewives', 'children' and 'families'. In the prime time evening hours (7:00 p.m. to 11:00 p.m.), the television audience commodity consisted of a daily average of 83.8 million people, with an average of two persons viewing per home. Women were a significantly higher proportion of this prime time audience than men (42% as against 32%; children were 16%; teenagers 10%).

Let us sum up these figures. Television, radio, and newspapers plus magazines take up 48 hours per week, for the average American! And they have only seven hours more free time than in 1850! Obviously some doubling up takes place. So let us estimate that half of the radio listening takes place while travelling to or from work; perhaps another quarter while doing the personal care chores at the beginning and end of the day. As for television, perhaps a fourth of it (on average) is glimpsed while preparing meals, eating, washing dishes, or doing other household tasks or repair/construction work. Estimate half of newspaper and magazine reading as taking place while travelling between home and job, while eating, etc. Our reduced exclusive audience time with the four commercial media is now down to 22 hours per week. Obviously more doubling takes place between audience time and other activities, and the reader is invited to make more precise estimates based on (perhaps) some empirical research. On television broadcasts of commercial sports events in the United States one sees some spectators *in the stadia* who are simultaneously watching the live event and portable television sets (for the 'instant replay' in stadia not blessed with huge overhead television screens for that purpose), or listening to the radio (for the sportscaster's instant comments on the play just completed).

Perhaps the only conclusion to be drawn at this time on this point is that there is no free time devoid of audience activity which is not pre-empted by other activities which are market-related (including sleep which is necessary if you are to be fit to meet your market tests on the morrow). In *any* society, sleep and other non-work activities are necessary to restore and maintain life and labour power. Work itself is not intrinsically oppressive. It is the inclusion in so-called leisure time of commodity producing work under monopoly capitalism which creates the contradiction between oppressive and liberating activity in time for which people are not paid.

Notes

1. I am indebted to William Leiss for this hypothetical and chastening idea. See his *The Limits to Satisfaction* (1976, p. 81).
2. The following analysis of time use is based on de Grazia (1964).
3. Part-time workers (probably more female than male) amounted in 1960 to 19% of the employed labour force in the United States and they worked an average of 19 hours weekly. If we exclude such workers in order to get a figure comparable to the 70 hours in 1850, we consider the weekly hours worked by the average American male who worked at least 35 hours per week. We then find that they averaged 46.4 hours (as against 39.5 hours for all workers). For the sake of brevity, I omit the counterpart calculation of 'free time' for women jobholders. No sexist implications are intended.
4. *Broadcasting Yearbook*, 1974, p. 69.

References

Blank, David M. (1970) Pleasurable pursuits – the changing structure of leisure time spectator activities. National Association of Business Economists, Annual Meeting September 1970. (Unpublished paper.)

Chase, Stuart and Schlink, F. J. (1927) *Your Money's Worth: A Study in the Waste of the Consumer's Dollar*, Macmillan, New York.

de Grazia, Sebastian (1964) *Of Time, Work and Leisure*, Anchor, New York.

Ewen, Stuart (1976) *Captains of Consciousness*, McGraw-Hill, New York.

Levitt, T. N. (1976) The industrialization of service. *Harvard Business Review*, September–October, pp. 63–74.

Linder, Staffen B. (1970) *The Harried Leisure Class*, Columbia University Press, New York.

Riesman, David (1950) *The Lonely Crowd*, Yale University Press, New Haven.

Stephenson, Marylee (1977) Never done, never noticed: women's work in Canada. *This Magazine*, Vol. 11, No. 6, December, pp. 31–3.

Veblen, Thorstein (1927) *The Theory of the Leisure Class*, Macmillan, New York, 1899.

Section 5

The public sphere

27

Conceptualizing the 'public sphere'

Oliver Boyd-Barrett

The concept of 'public sphere' derives from a 1962 work by Jürgen Habermas. Amongst other things his book is the history of a social, political and cultural practice namely, the practice of open exchange of views and discussion about issues of general social importance. It is about the formation of a sense of the 'public', not as an abstract principle, but as a *culturally-embedded social practice*. The influence of this work rests in part on this social and cultural dimension, given that historical analysis of media until recently conformed to orthodox historical narrative, characterized by a focus on institutional chronologies, their relations with the state and with élites. The work of Scannell and Cardiff (1989), also represented in this volume, has decisively exposed the limitations of orthodox historical narrative in the context of British broadcasting, looking among other things at how broadcasting created new 'publics' for sporting, cultural and other events, the formulation of new meanings of nation and national identity, the meanings of broadcasting in the everyday lives of different social groups, its (differential) insertion into life routines or what Habermas has called the 'lifeworld', and its impact on the horizons of spatial and temporal consciousness.

Habermas elevates the eighteenth century coffee house as a bourgeois 'public sphere', an ideal forum within which newspapers and journals were read and discussed in face-to-face groups, whose discussions were framed with reference to and on behalf of broader social interests than merely the interests of those who were physically present, and which helped to transform the relationship between aristocracy and the business classes. This public sphere, as Garnham (in this section) argues, was independent of church and state and in principle, if not in fact, open to all. Habermas argues that at first the media (of the eighteenth century) formed an integral part of this public sphere but later, when commodified through mass distribution and the acquisition of mass audiences for sale to advertisers, the media distanced themselves from this role. The theory has been criticized (see Thompson in this section) for idealizing and perhaps romanticizing what was in fact not only a very élite world (engaging principally those with enough leisure to sit around talking in coffee houses, and those with enough connections to lend influence to such talk), but also a male world. It overlooks the history of the radical working-class press (Curran and Seaton, 1988). But it is also over-pessimistic in its assessment of the rise of the mass media. Newspapers, radio and television – some media, some of the time – clearly do still serve as a forum for discussion of issues of public interest among people who are knowledgeable, interested, able to speak on behalf of broader social interests, and whose discussions have the potential of being of political influence. There is considerable participation by politicians in the media, even if politicians are not always able to dominate the terms of discussion. The modern media, it may be argued, while they no longer feed in directly to face-to-face group discussions of public affairs in the manner described by Habermas have instead invented their own publics and public forums for discussion. The view that any such programmes only function to 'consolidate the consensus' (as in the original political economy model proposed by Golding and Murdock in 1973 – see this volume) is today commonly rejected as far too simplistic. It is true that the mass media of the late nineteenth and twentieth centuries were influenced by commercial forces of a range and magnitude not in evidence before that time. But the smaller media which oiled the conversations of the bourgeois coffee house public sphere were tied to the interests of a relatively privileged élite in defining what were the issues most worth talking and thinking about at that time. Furthermore, Habermas privileges political news in the bourgeois public sphere, while he exaggerates the 'corruption' of commercialization in the mass media of the late nineteenth and twentieth centuries.

For all its defects, one may enquire why such a theory continues to be influential. I have suggested that the weight it gives to the everyday culture of a social class and its use of the media gives it a sociological, not to say ethnographic, authenticity which is impressive and which underlines the dearth of equivalent work for other media in other historical and social contexts. Its influence also relates to the relative length of time it has taken for the theory to be fully published in English (the extract in this section is from the 1989 translation), so that it reached the high point of its influence during the period of *glasnost*, the subsequent collapse of the Soviet Union and of communism in Eastern Europe. For some considerable time, the trajectory of Reaganite and Thatcherite policies in the U.S. and in the U.K. respectively, their diffusion throughout the world and their widespread application to public bureaucracies amounted to a revitalization and energizing of capitalist ideology and practice, which has both accentuated the conditions that could be expected to provoke radical oppositional analysis while paradoxically undermining the very legitimacy and opportunities for such analysis. The toppling of communism precisely at the peak of a capitalist economic boom threatened any claims to relevance on the part of older schools of critical media study which had always assumed, explicitly or implicitly, that there was a meaningful alternative to capitalism. The practical urgent necessity for research to help re-define and re-regulate the role of the media in the East, coupled with the equally urgent need for the West to come to terms with the consequences of a decade of privatization of public media and of more intensive commercialization of private media, and the political advantages for media scholarship to establish fresh dialogue with the world beyond academe, have all highlighted the potential usefulness of the discourse of the 'public sphere' (a discourse which is not as strongly marked by right/left wing political associations as the discourses of political economy) in application to a range of issues to do with the relationship of the media to the state, to the people, and to business.

In this discussion we find a reformulation of the thesis of the decline of the public sphere. Explanations for decline are no longer related specifically to the commodification of the media as Habermas argued, but, as Elliott argues in this section, to the commercialization of society in general and to the elevation, through Reaganite and Thatcherite politics, of market forces as the best arbiter of the relationship between providers and consumers of goods and services, even services like education and information which had previously been furnished as of right to all citizens. The 1980s' resurgence of capitalism was facilitated by the rapid development of computer and communication electronics, which have now transformed and weakened the labour market, promoted a wide new range of information goods and services (for both consumption and production purposes, e.g. videotext television *and* home video cameras), accented hedonistic pleasure but marginalized political content, while constricting still further the control of monopoly capital over access to mass markets. The supposed public benefits of 'the free operation of the market', so central to Republican and Conservative ideology, are a mirage – for reasons that have been known for well over a century, and which are rehearsed yet again in the extract here from Garnham. Left to themselves, 'free' markets become monopoly markets where one or a few suppliers determine the range and quality of services to suit their own interests. Access to such markets for new providers is prohibitively expensive, and barely possible even after considerable compromise, while customers must adjust their consumption habits to the goods and services which are available. Not only is 'choice' in the 'free' media market a restricted choice, but enthusiasm for the free market is in part an evasion of the difficult choices that would otherwise be necessary between competing ways of balancing economic and political imperatives. Murdock puts this more broadly, linking media privatization to consumerist ideology which 'encourages people to seek private solutions to public problems by purchasing a commodity. It urges them to buy their way out of trouble rather than pressing for social change and improved social provision' (Murdock, 1992, p. 19).

Within the media industry the most effective protection so far devised, while itself seriously flawed (see Keane in this section) has been state-protected public monopoly, operating according to principles of the public good; whatever its faults, this model invites positive re-evaluation once the implications of unfettered private expansion become apparent. Keane, in this section, argues for a plurality of non-state media of communication, together with the creation of politically-accountable, supranational regulatory bodies, and the attribution of common carrier responsibilities to large media corporations. Curran (1991) proposes a mixed model of core public service television with peripheral private, professional, social, civic sectors. These architectures of the ideal configuration, however, mask a myriad of very complex regulatory and operational practicalities, and may also prove short-sighted in the light of technological developments. Murdock (1992) prefers to establish basic principles: the need in a democratic society for citizens to have access to information, advice and analysis that will enable them to know what their personal rights are and to pursue them effectively; access to the broadest possible range of information, debate, etc. on areas that involve public political choices; the facility for people to recognize themselves and their aspirations in the range of representations on offer within the media, and to contribute to the development of these. A broad, alternative strategy, however, might focus on the praxis of lobbying, debate, intervention and development of alternative sources of production with a view to reforming or developing specific features of current structures so as to achieve limited but realizable social and political goals. Such a strategy will encounter the tension identified by Livingstone and Lunt (1994) between confining open discussion only to include positions that have already acquired social consensus, and the alternative process of using public debate for opening up issues at the point of contest and opinion formation which, they believe, does happen in some genres, notably the audience discussion programme. This genre, amongst other things, undermines the distinction between expert or élite, and the public (but does not undermine the power of the 'mediator', who anchors the show to one of three generic constructions – debate, romantic narrative or 'therapy session').

No re-evaluation can afford to minimize the dangers, however, of a public agenda that is determined by unelected and unaccountable journalists. The powerful mediation of journalists has worked against politicians, argues Garnham, and has weakened and undermined the authority of political parties, whereas a media structure which allowed them direct representation, albeit in competition, would have strengthened the political process. The public media, Keane observes, distribute entitlements to speak and to be heard unevenly. Instead, they rely on a cast of professionals or 'regulars' appointed solely by the media to speak on behalf of the public. Murdock refers to the failure of public broadcasting to 'keep pace with the proliferation of political and social discourses' (Murdock, 1992, p. 31). A responsible nation-wide democratic system requires a media system which is coterminous with it and which can generate discussion of issues of public concern in a way which does not favour partisan interests, whether these be the interests of particular political parties, the interests of media bosses or media professionals. There are not too many existing examples – Holland is often cited – and even here it looks increasingly difficult for such systems to withstand the pressures which are created by private commercial competitors, linked as many of these are to powerful international networks and devoted to substantial doses of international (much of it American) entertainment. Garnham identifies the tendencies towards internationalization of media as a further threat to his ideal public service model, and this observation highlights the paradox that while media ownership, control and (entertainment) content become increasingly internationalized it cannot be said that the media (yet) function to develop an *international* public(s) nor even a European public in the way that the BBC once created a national public for the United Kingdom. That is to say, the media public affairs agendas are not dominated by a systematically organized calendar of rituals and events appropriate to the nurture of international audience identification of themselves as 'members' of such a public, nor are they far advanced in the development of an appropriate or coherent sense of international or European 'we-ness' similar to that which was constructed for the United Kingdom by the BBC in its first three decades of broadcasting, although there are embryonic steps in this direction.

Caveats about public broadcasting notwithstanding, then, the crisis of broadcasting induced by privatization has led to salutary recall of the achievements of a previous era. Murdock identifies four key roles played by the BBC in organizing a 'new system of representation that emerged to service the extension of citizenship rights': it provided a public forum for legitimated interest groups; it probed into popular thinking, providing a new source of surveillance and feedback for power-holders; it cemented the dominant definitions of citizenship, nation and culture; and it redrew the line between private and public spheres. Each of these roles depended on a vigorous balance between what may loosely be called 'public service' functions of news and documentary, and 'entertainment' functions (which does not mean that 'public service' functions cannot also entertain or that 'entertainment' cannot also inform).

It is clear that the decline of public broadcasting is a threat to the 'public service' functions of broadcasting, against which it may seem that the only remedy is the reintroduction of strong state-regulated controls on private suppliers – and such control is by definition disliked by governments which have dismantled or weakened public broadcasting. Livingstone and Lunt warn that 'because market models of broadcasting are partly legitimated through a critique of the elitist and patronizing aspects of the public service ethic, an emancipatory rather than an oppressive conception of the public service ethic is needed to counter the arguments for a market-led broadcasting system' (Livingstone and Lunt, 1994, p. 17).

References and further reading

Curran, James and Seaton, Jean (1988) *Power Without Responsibility*, 3rd edn, Fontana, London.

Curran, James (1991) Mass media and democracy: a reappraisal. In Curran, James and Gurevitch, Michael (eds) *Mass Media and Society*, Edward Arnold, London, pp. 82–117.

Keane, John (1993) Democracy and media: without foundations. In Keane, John (ed.) *Media in Transition: From Totalitarianism to Democracy*, Kyiv Abris, pp. 3–24

Livingstone, Sonia and Lunt, Peter (1994) *Talk on Television*, Routledge, London.

Murdock, Graham (1992) Citizens, consumers and public culture. In Schroder, Kim Christian and Skovmand, Michael (eds) *Media Cultures*, Routledge, London, pp. 17–41.

Scannell, Paddy and Cardiff, David (1989) *The Social History of British Broadcasting*, Blackwell, Oxford.

28

Institutions of the public sphere

Jürgen Habermas

From Habermas, J. (1989) *The Structural Transformation of the Public Sphere*, (translated by Burger T.), Polity Press, Cambridge, pp. 31–8, 41–3.

Institutions of the public sphere

In seventeenth century France *le public* meant the *lecteurs, spectateurs*, and *auditeurs* as the addressees and consumers, and the critics of art and literature,[1] reference was still primarily to the court, and later also to portions of the urban nobility along with a thin bourgeois upper stratum whose members occupied the loges of the Parisian theatres. This early public, then, comprised both court and 'town'. The thoroughly aristocratic polite life of these circles already assumed modern characteristics. With the Hôtel de Rambouillet, the great hall at court in which the prince staged his festivities and as patron gathered the artists about him was replaced by what later would be called the *salon*.[2] The hotel provided the model for the *ruelles* (morning receptions) of the *precieuses*, which maintained a certain independence from the court. Although one sees here the first signs of that combination of the economically unproductive and politically functionless urban aristocracy with the eminent writers, artists, and scientists (who frequently were of bourgeois origin) typical of the salon of the eighteenth century, it was still impossible, in the prevailing climate of honnêteté, for reason to shed its dependence on the authority that turns conversation into criticism and *bons mots* into arguments. Only with the reign of Philip of Orleans, who moved the royal residence from Versailles to Paris, did the court lose its central position in the public sphere, indeed its status *as* the public sphere. For inasmuch as the 'town' took over its cultural functions the public sphere itself was transformed.

The sphere of royal representation and the grand *goût* of Versailles became a facade held up only with effort. The regent and his two successors preferred small social gatherings, if not the family circle itself, and to a certain degree avoided the etiquette. The great ceremonial gave way to an almost bourgeoisie intimacy:

> At the court of Louis XVI the dominant tone is one of decided intimacy, and on six days of the week the social gatherings achieve the character of a private party. The only place where anything like a court household develops during the Régence is the castle of the Duchess of Maine at Sceaux, which becomes the scene of brilliant, expensive and ingenious festivities and, at the same time, a new centre of art, a real Court of the Muses. But the entertainments arranged

by the Duchess contain the germ of ultimate dissolution of court life They form the transition from the old-style court to the *salons* of the eighteenth century – the cultural heirs of the court.[3]

In Great Britain the Court had never been able to dominate the town as it had in the France of the Sun King.[4] Nevertheless, after the Glorious Revolution a shift in the relationship between court and town can be observed similar to the one that occurred one generation later in the relationship between *cour* and *ville*. Under the Stuarts, up to Charles II, literature and art served the representation of the king. 'But after the Revolution the glory of the Court grew dim. Neither the political position of the Crown, nor the personal temperament of those who wore it was the same as of old. Stern William, invalid Anne, the German Georges, farmer George, domestic Victoria, none of them desired to keep a Court like Queen Elizabeth's. Henceforth the Court was the residence of secluded royalty, pointed out from afar, difficult of access save on formal occasions of proverbial dullness.'[5] The predominance of the 'town' was strengthened by new institutions that, for all their variety, in Great Britain and France took over the same social functions: the coffee houses in their golden age between 1680 and 1730 and the *salons* in the period between regency and revolution. In both countries they were centres of criticism – literary at first, then also political – in which began to emerge, between aristocratic society and bourgeois intellectuals, a certain parity of the educated. Around the middle of the seventeenth century, after not only tea – first to be popular – but also chocolate and coffee had become the common beverages of at least the well-to-do strata of the population, the coachman of a Levantine merchant opened the first coffee house. By the first decade of the eighteenth century London already had 3000 of them, each with a core group of regulars.[6] Just as Dryden, surrounded by the new generation of writers, joined the battle of the 'ancients and moderns' at Will's, Addison and Steele a little later convened their 'little senate' at Button's; so too in the Rotary Club, presided over by Milton's secretary, Marvell and Pepys met with Harrington who here probably presented the republican ideas of his *Oceana*.[7] As in the *salons* where 'intellectuals' met with the aristocracy, literature had to legitimate itself in these coffee houses. In this case, however, the nobility joining the upper bourgeois stratum still possessed the social functions lost by the French; it represented landed and moneyed interests. Thus critical debate ignited by works of literature and art was soon extended to include economic and political disputes, without any guarantee (such as was given in the *salons*) that such discussions would be inconsequential, at least in the immediate context. The fact that only men were admitted to coffee-house society may have had something to do with this, whereas the style of the *salon*, like that of the rococo in general, was essentially shaped by women. Accordingly the women of London society, abandoned every evening, waged a vigorous but vain struggle against the new institution.[8] The coffee house not merely made access to the relevant circles less formal and easier; it embraced the wider strata of the middle class, including craftsmen and shopkeepers. Ned Ward reports that the 'wealthy shopkeeper' visited the coffee house several times a day,[9] this held true for the poor one as well.[10]

In contrast, in France the *salons* formed a peculiar enclave. While the bourgeoisie, for all practical purposes excluded from leadership in state and church, in time completely took over all the key positions in the economy, and while the aristocracy compensated for its material inferiority with royal privileges and an ever more rigorous stress upon hierarchy in social intercourse, in the *salons* the nobility and the *grande bourgeoisie* of finance and administration assimilating itself to that nobility met with the 'intellectuals' on an equal footing. The plebeian d'Alembert was no exception; in the *salons* of the fashionable ladies, noble as well as bourgeois, sons of princes and counts associated with sons of watchmakers and shopkeepers.[11] In the *salon* the mind was no longer in the service of a patron; 'opinion' became emancipated from the bonds of economic dependence . Even if under Philip the *salons* were at first places more for gallant pleasures than for smart discourse, such discussion indeed soon took equal place with the *diner*. Diderot's distinction between written and oral discourse[12] sheds light on the functions of the new gatherings. There was scarcely a great writer in the eighteenth century who would not have first submitted his essential ideas for discussion in such discourse, in lectures before the *académies* and especially in the *salons*. The *salon* held the monopoly of first publication: a new work, even a musical one, had to legitimate itself first in this forum. The Abbé Galiani's *Dialogues on the Grain Trade* give a vivid picture of the way in which conversation and discussion were elegantly intertwined, of how the unimportant (where one had travelled and how one was doing) was treated as much with solemnity as the important (theatre and politics) was treated *en passant*.

In Germany at that time there was no 'town' to replace the courts' publicity of representation with the institutions of a public sphere in civil society. But similar elements existed, beginning with the learned *Tischgesellschaften* (table societies), the old *Sprachgesellschaften* (literary societies) of the seventeenth century. Naturally they were fewer and less active than the coffee houses and *salons*. They were even more removed from practical politics than the salons; yet, as in the case of the coffee houses, their public was recruited from private people engaged in productive work, from the dignitaries of the principalities' capitals, with a strong preponderance of middle-class academics. The *Deutsche Gesellschaften* ('German Societies'), the first of which was founded by Gottsched in Leipzig in 1727, built upon the literary orders of the preceding century. The latter were still convened by the princes but avoided social exclusiveness; characteristically, later attempts to transform them into knightly orders failed. As it is put in one of the founding documents, their intent was 'that in such manner an equality and association among persons of unequal social status might be brought about'.[13] Such orders, chambers, and academies were preoccupied with the native tongue, now interpreted as the medium of communication and understanding between people in their common quality as human beings and nothing more than human beings. Transcending the barriers of social hierarchy, the bourgeois met here with the socially prestigious but politically uninfluential nobles as 'common' human beings.[14] The decisive element was not so much the political equality of the members but their exclusiveness in relation to the political realm of absolutism as such: social equality was possible at first only as an equality outside the state. The coming together of private people into a public was therefore anticipated in secret, as a public sphere still existing largely behind closed doors. The secret promulgation of enlightenment typical of the lodges but also widely practised by other associations and *Tischgesellscllaften* had a dialectical character. Reason, which through public use of the rational faculty was to be realized in the rational communication of a public consisting of cultivated human beings, itself needed to be protected from becoming public because it was a threat to any and all relations of domination. As long as publicity had its seat in the secret chanceries of the prince, reason could not reveal itself directly. Its sphere of publicity had still to rely on secrecy; its public, even as a public, remained internal. The light of reason, thus veiled for self-protection, was revealed in stages. This recalls Lessing's famous statement about Freemasonry which at that time was a broader European phenomenon: it was just as old as bourgeois society – 'if indeed bourgeois society is not merely the offspring of Freemasonry'.[15]

The practice of secret societies fell prey to its own ideology to the extent to which the public that put reason to use, and hence the bourgeois public sphere for which it acted as the peacemaker, won out against state-governed publicity. From publicist enclaves of civic concern with common affairs they developed into 'exclusive associations whose basis is a separation from the public sphere that in the meantime has arisen'.[16] Other societies, in contrast (especially those arising in the course of the eighteenth century among bourgeois dignitaries), expanded into open associations access to which (through co-optation or otherwise) was relatively easy. Here bourgeois forms of social intercourse, closeness (*Intimität*), and a morality played off against courtly convention were taken for granted; at any rate they no longer needed affirmation by means of demonstrative fraternization ceremonies.

However much the *Tischgesellschaften, salons*, and coffee houses may have differed in the size and composition of their publics, the style of their proceedings, the climate of their debates, and their topical orientations, they all organized discussion among private people that tended to be ongoing; hence they had a number of institutional criteria in common. *First*, they preserved a kind of social intercourse that, far from presupposing the equality of status, disregarded status altogether. The tendency replaced the celebration of rank with a tact befitting equals.[17] The parity on whose basis alone the authority of the better argument could assert itself against that of social hierarchy and in the end can carry the day meant, in the thought of the day, the parity of 'common humanity' ('*bloss Menschliche*'). *Les hommes*, private gentlemen, or *die Privatleute* made up the public not just in the sense that power and prestige of public office were held in suspense; economic dependencies also in principle had no influence. Laws of the market were suspended as were laws of the state. Not that this idea of the public was actually realized in earnest in the coffee houses, the *salons*, and the societies; but as an idea it had become institutionalized and thereby stated as an objective claim. If not realized, it was at least consequential.

Secondly, discussion within such a public presupposed the problematization of areas that until then had not been questioned. The domain of 'common concern' which was the object of public critical attention remained a preserve in which church and state authorities had the monopoly of interpretation not just from the pulpit but in philosophy, literature, and art, even at a time when, for specific social categories, the development of capitalism already demanded a behaviour whose rational orientation required ever more information. To the degree, however, to which philosophical and literary works and works of art in general were produced for the market and distributed through it, these culture products became similar to that type of information: as commodities they became in principle generally accessible. They no longer remained components of the Church's and court's publicity of representation; that is precisely what was meant by the loss of their aura of extraordinariness and by the profaning of their once sacramental character. The private people for whom the cultural product became available as a commodity profaned it inasmuch as they had to determine its meaning on their own (by way of rational communication with one another), verbalize it, and thus state explicitly what precisely in its implicitness for so long could assert its authority. As Raymond Williams demonstrates, 'art' and 'culture' owe their modern meaning of spheres separate from the reproduction of social life to the eighteenth century.[18]

Thirdly, the same process that converted culture into a commodity (and in this fashion constituted it as a culture that could become an object of discussion to begin with) established the public as in principle inclusive. However exclusive the public might be in any given instance, it could never close itself off entirely and become consolidated as a clique; for it always understood and found itself immersed within a more inclusive public of all private people, persons who – insofar as they were propertied and educated – as readers, listeners, and spectators could avail themselves via the market of the objects that were subject to discussion. The issues discussed became 'general' not merely in their significance, but also in their accessibility: everyone had to *be able* to participate. Wherever the public established itself institutionally as a stable group of discussants, it did not equate itself with the public but at most claimed to act as its mouthpiece, in its name, perhaps even as its educator – the new form of bourgeois representation. The public of the first generations, even when it constituted itself as a specific circle of persons, was conscious of being part of a larger public. Potentially it was always also a publicist body, as its discussions did not need to remain internal to it but could be directed at the outside world – for this, perhaps, the *Diskurse der Mahlern*, a moral weekly published from 1721 on by Bodmer and Breitinger in Zurich, was one among many examples.

In relation to the mass of the rural population and the common 'people' in the towns, of course, the public 'at large' that was being formed diffusely outside the early institutions of the public was still extremely small. Elementary education, where it existed, was inferior. The proportion of illiterates, at least in Great Britain, even exceeded that of the preceding Elizabethan epoch.[19] Here, at the start of the eighteenth century, more than half of the population lived on the margins of subsistence. The masses were not only largely illiterate but also so pauperized that they could not even pay for literature. They did not have at their disposal the buying power needed for even the most modest participation in the market of cultural goods.[20] Nevertheless, with the emergence of the diffuse public formed in the course of commercialization of cultural production, a new social category arose.

[. . .]

In the institution of art criticism, including literary, theatre, and music criticism, the lay judgement of a public that had come of age, or at least thought it had, became organized. Correspondingly, there arose a new occupation that in the jargon of the time was called *Kunstrichter* (art critic). The latter assumed a peculiarly dialectical task: he viewed himself at the same time as the public's mandatary and as its educator.[21] The art critics could see themselves as spokesmen for the public – and in their battle with the artists this was the central slogan – because they knew of no authority beside that of the better argument and because they felt themselves at one with all who were willing to let themselves be convinced by arguments. At the same time they could turn against the public itself when, as experts combating 'dogma' and 'fashion,' they appealed to the ill-in formed person's native capacity for judgement. The context accounting for this self-image also elucidated the actual status of the critic: at that time, it was not an occupational role in the strict sense. The *Kunstrichter* retained something of the amateur; his expertise only held good until countermanded; lay judgement was organized in it without becoming, by way of specialization, anything else than the judgement of one private person among all others who ultimately were not to be obligated by any judgement except their own. This was precisely where the art critic differed from the judge. At the same time, however, he had to be able to find a hearing before the entire public, which grew well beyond the narrow circle of the *salons*, coffee houses, and societies, even in their golden age. Soon the periodical (the handwritten correspondence at first, then the printed weekly or monthly) became the publicist instrument of this criticism.

As instruments of institutionalized art criticism, the journals devoted to art and cultural criticism were typical creations of the eighteenth century.[22] 'It is remarkable enough', an inhabitant of Dresden wrote in justified amazement, 'that after the world for millennia had gotten along quite well without it, toward the middle of the eighteenth century art criticism all of a sudden bursts on the scene'.[23] On the one hand, philosophy was no longer possible except as critical philosophy, literature and art no longer except in connection with literary and art criticism What the works of art themselves criticized simply recalled its proper end in the 'critical journals'. On the other hand, it was only through the critical absorption of philosophy, literature, and art that the public attained enlightenment and realized itself as the latter's living process.

In this context, the moral weeklies were a key phenomenon. Here the elements that later parted ways were still joined. The critical journals had already become as independent from conversational circles as they had become separate from the works to which their arguments referred. The moral weeklies, on the contrary, were still an immediate part of coffee-house discussions and considered themselves literary pieces – there was good reason for calling them 'periodical essays'.[24]

When Addison and Steele published the first issue of the *Tatler* in 1709, the coffee houses were already so numerous and the circles of their frequenters already so wide,[25] that contact among these thousand-fold circles could only be maintained through a journal.[26] At the same time the new periodical was so ultimately interwoven with the life of the coffee houses that the individual issues were indeed sufficient basis for its reconstruction. The periodical articles were not only made the object of discussion by the public of the coffee houses but were viewed as integral parts of this discussion; this was demonstrated by the flood of letters from which the editor each week published a selection When the *Spectator* separated from the *Guardian* the letters to the editor were provided with a special institution: on the west side of Button's coffee house a lion's head was attached through whose jaws the reader threw his letter.[27] The dialogue form too, employed by many of the articles, attested to their proximity to the spoken word. One and the same discussion transposed into a different medium was continued in order to re-enter, via reading, the original conversational medium. A number of the later weeklies of this genre even appeared without dates in order to emphasize the trans-temporal continuity, as it were, of the process of mutual enlightenment. In the moral weeklies,[28] the intention of self-enlightenment of individuals who felt that they had come of age came more clearly to the fore than in the later journals What a little later would become specialized in the function of art critic, in these weeklies was still art and art criticism, literature and literary criticism all in one. In the *Tatler*, the *Spectator*, and the *Guardian* the public held up a mirror to itself it did not yet come to a self-understanding through the detour of a reflection on works of philosophy and literature, art and science, but through entering itself into 'literature' as an object. Addison viewed himself as a censor of manners and morals; his essays concerned charities and schools for the poor, the improvement of education, pleas for civilized forms of conduct, polemics against the vices of gambling, fanaticism, and pedantry and against the tastelessness of the aesthetes and the eccentricities of the learned. He worked toward the spread of tolerance, the emancipation of civic morality from moral theology and of practical wisdom from the philosophy of the scholars The public that read and debated this sort of thing read and debated about itself.

Notes

1. Auerbach, E. finds the word, in the sense of a theatre audience, documented as early as 1629; until then, the use of 'public' as a noun referred exclusively to the state or to the public welfare. See *Das französische Publikum des 17. Jahrhunderts*, München, 1933, p. 5.
2. At that time it still referred to the state room in the sense of the Italian Renaissance, and not to the cabinet, the circle, the reduite, etc.
3. Hauser, A. *The Social History of Art*, Vol. 2, pp. 505–6.
4. Unlike Paris, London was never directly subject to the king. The city, which administered itself by means of elected councillors and maintained public order through its own militia, was less accessible to the court's and Parliament's administration of justice than any other town in the country. Around the turn of the eighteenth century its approximately 12,000 taxpayers, almost all of whom were members of the 89 guilds and companies, elected 26 councillors and 200 council members – a broad, almost 'democratic' base without equal during this period. Nevertheless, after the Glorious Revolution a shift occurred in the relationship between court and town that was comparable, say, to the development under the regency.

5. Trevelyan, G. M. (1944) *English Social History: A Survey of Six Centuries from Chaucer to Queen Victoria*, London, p. 338.
6. Stephen, L. (1903; most recently, 1947) *English Literature and Society in the 18th Century*, London, p. 47. See also Reinhold, H. (1958) Zur Sozialgeschichte der Kaffees und des Kaffeehauses, *Kölner Zeitschrift für Soziologie und Sozialpsychologie*, Vol. 10 (review of a group of works).
7. Westerfrölke, H. (1924) *Englische Kaffeehäuser Sammelpunkte der literarischen Welt*, Jena.
8. As early as 1674 there appeared a pamphlet, 'The women's petition against coffee, representing to public consideration of the grand inconveniences according to their sex from the excessive use of that drying, enfeebling liquor'.
9. Trevelyan, *English Social History*, p. 324, footnote.
10. See 'The clubs of London', *National Review*, Vol. 4, No. 8, April, 1857, p. 301. 'Every profession, trade, class, party, had its favourite coffee-house. The lawyers discussed law or literature, criticised the last new play, or retailed the freshest Westminster-Hall "bite" at Nando's or the Grecian, both close on the purlieus of the Temple .... The cits met to discuss the rise and fall of stocks, and to settle the rate of insurances at Garraway's or Jonathan's; the parsons exchanged university gossip, or commented on Dr Sacherverell's last sermon at Truby's or at Child's in St. Paul's Churchyard; the soldiers mustered to grumble over their grievances at Old or Young Man's, near Charing Cross; the St James's and the Smyrna were the head-quarters of the Whig politicians, while the Tories frequented the Cocoa-Tree or Ozinda's, all in St James's Street; Scotchmen had their house of call at Forrest's, Frenchmen at Giles's or old Slaughter's in St. Martin's Lane; the gamesters shook their elbows in White's, and the Chocolate houses, round Covent Garden; the *virtuosi* honoured the neighbourhood of Gresham College; and the leading wits gathered at Will's, Button's, or Tom's, in Great Russell Street, where after the theatre, was playing at piquet and the best of conversation till midnight.'
11. Hauser, *The Social History of Art*, Vol. 2, pp. 506–7.
12. Nos écrits n'opèrent que sur une certaine classe de citoyens, nos discours sur toutes' (Our writings have an impact only on a certain class of citizens, our speech on all).
13. Manheim, E. (1923) *Die Trägers der öffentlichen Meinung*, Wien, p. 83.
14. Language is considered 'the organ of a transcendental communal spirit' and 'the medium of a public consensus'; see Manheim, *Die Träger der öffentlichen Meinung*, pp. 88 and 92.
15. Lessing, Ernst, and Falk (1778) *Gespräche für Freimaurer*. On the entire complex, see Lennhoff, E. and Posner, O. (1932) *Internationales Freimaurerlexikon* Zürich; also Fay, B. (1935) *La Franc-maçonnerie et la révolution intellectuelle du XVIIIe siécle*, Paris.
16. Manheim, *Die Träger der öffentlichen Meinung*, p. 11.
17. H. Plessner, admittedly in a different context, defines the public sphere as the 'sphere in which tact rules'. Diplomatic relations arise between role bearers, relationships of tact between natural persons; see his *Grenzen der Gemeinschaft*, Bonn, 1924, esp. p. 100.
18. Williams, R., *Culture and Society 1870–1950*, London, 1958, pp. xv, xvi: 'An *art* had formerly been any human skill [art in the sense of artfulness, ability. J.H.]; but *Art*, now, signified a particular group of skills, the 'imaginative' or 'creative' arts. . . . From . . . a 'skill,' it had come . . . to be a kind of institution, a set of body activities of a certain kind.' To this corresponded the change in the meaning of 'culture': '. . . it had meant, primarily, the 'tending of natural growth' [culture in the sense of the cultivation of plants. J.H.], and then, by analogy, a process of human training [e.g. a 'man of culture.' J.H.]. But this latter use, which had usually been a culture *of* something, was changed . . . to *culture* as such, a thing in itself.'

Also Wittram, R. (1958) *Das Interesse an der Geschichte*, Göttingen, who offers several observations on the history of the concept of culture.

19. See Altick, R. D. (1957) *The English Common Reader: A Social History of the Mass Reading Public*, Chicago, especially the first chapter, the results of which are summarized on p. 30. 'If, speculating from such little information as we have, we tried to chart the growth of the reading public in the first three centuries after Caxton, the line would climb slowly for the first hundred years. During the Elizabethan period its rate of ascent would considerably quicken. The line would reach a peak during the Civil War and Commonwealth, when interest in reading was powerfully stimulated by public excitements. But during the Restoration it would drop, because of the lessening of popular turmoil, the damage the war had done to the educational system, and the aristocratic domination of current literature in the age of Dryden. A fresh ascent would begin in the early eighteenth century, the time of Addison and Steele, *and thereafter the line would climb steadily.*'

20. Watt, I. (1957) 'The reading public'. *The Rise of the Novel*, London.

21. In principle anyone was called upon and had the right to make a free judgement as long as he participated in public discussion, bought a book, acquired a seat in a concert or theatre, or visited an art exhibition. But in the conflict of judgements he was not to shut his ears to convincing arguments; instead, he had to rid himself of his 'prejudices'. With the removal of the barrier that representative policy had erected between laymen and initiates, special qualifications – whether inherited or acquired, social or intellectual – became in principle irrelevant. But since the true judgement was supposed to be discovered only through discussion, truth appeared as a process, a process of enlightenment. Some sectors of the public might be more advanced in this process than others. Hence, if the public acknowledged no one as privileged, it did recognize experts. They were permitted and supposed to educate the public, but only inasmuch as they convinced through arguments and could not themselves be corrected by better arguments.

22. As soon as the press assumed critical functions, the writing of news letters developed into literary journalism. The early journals, called *Monthly Conversations, Monthly Discussions*, etc. had this journalism's origin in convivial critical discussion written all over them. Their proliferation may be observed in exemplary fashion in Germany. The beginning was made clear with the *Gelehrte Anzeigen* which, developing out of the Thomasian journals, through articles and reviews submitted philosophy and the sciences to public discussion. After 1736 the well-known *Frankfurtische Gelehrte Zeitungen* too concerned themselves with the 'fine arts and sciences'. Following upon Gottsched's efforts, the journals devoted to literary criticism reached their point of fullest development with the *Bibliothek der schönen Wissenschaften und der freyen Künste*, founded in Berlin in 1757 by Nicolai. Beginning with Lessing's and Mylius's *Beiträge zur Historie und Aufnahme des Theaters* in 1750 a journalistic theatre criticism arose. Journals for music criticism were also founded, although less frequently than those dealing with the stage, once Adam Hiller in Leipzig had created the model with his *Wöchentliche Nachrichten und Anmerkungen die Musik betreffend* in 1767.

23. Dresdner, *Die Entschung der Kuntskritik*, p. 17.

24. Stephen, L., *English Literature and Society*, p. 76. 'The periodical essay represents the most successful innovation of the day . . . because it represents the mode by which the most cultivated writer could be brought into effective relation with the genuine interests of the largest audience.'

25. The *Tatler* expressly addressed the 'worthy citizens who live more in a coffee house than in their shops' *Tatler*, 17 May, 1709.

26. The *Tatler* immediately reached an edition of 4000. How strong the interest was

is demonstrated by the universal regret expressed when the *Tatler* suddenly ceased publication in 1711. For details, see Westerfrölke, *Englische Kaffeehäuser*, p. 64.

27. From then on the submitted letters were published weekly as the 'Roaring of the Lion'.

28. The British models remained valid for three generations of moral weeklies on the continent, too. In Germany *Der Vernünftler* was published in 1713 in Hamburg. Later on the *Hamburger Patriot* was much more successful, lasting from 1724 until 1726. In the course of the entire century the number of these journals grew to 187 in Germany; during the same period in Great Britain the number is reported to have been 227; in France, 31.

29

The media and the public sphere

Nicholas Garnham

From Golding, P., Murdock, G. and Schlesinger, P. (eds) (1986)
Communicating Politics, Leicester University Press, pp. 45–53.

The great strength of the public service model, to which we need to hang on through all the twists and turns of the argument that has raged around it, is the way it (a) presupposes and then tries to develop in its practice a set of social relations which are distinctly political rather than economic, and (b) at the same time attempts to insulate itself from control by the state as opposed to, and this is often forgotten, political control. Reith's original version was undoubtedly drawn from the tradition of the Scottish enlightenment and, within the very narrow limits within which the economic and political forces of the time allowed him to operate, the early practice of the BBC, as Scannell and Cardiff's recent research shows, made a noble effort to address their listeners as rational political beings rather than as consumers (Scannell, 1980; Cardiff, 1980). It is easy to argue that the agenda for debate and the range of information considered important was hopelessly linked to a narrow class-based definition of the public good and that it was doomed to failure, because public aspirations were already so moulded by the consumerist ideology secreted by the dominant set of social relations in society, that this alternative set, as the experience of Radio Luxembourg demonstrated, could only be imposed on listeners by the brute force of monopoly. But this is to miss the point of the enterprise and its continuing importance as both historical example and potential alternative. After all, one could use the same argument (indeed people are already using this argument in relation to the power of local government) that because of declining voter turn-out one should simply abolish elections.

The economic and the political

For the problem with liberal free press theory is not just that the market has produced conditions of oligopoly which undercut the liberal ideal nor that private ownership leads to direct manipulation of political communication, although it does, but that there is a fundamental contradiction between the economic and the political at the level of their value systems and of the social relations which those value systems require and support. Within the political realm the individual is defined as a citizen exercising public rights of debate, voting, and so on, within a communally agreed structure of rules and towards communally defined ends. The value system is essentially social and the legitimate end of social action is the public good.

Within the economic realm, on the other hand, the individual is defined as producer and consumer exercising private rights through purchasing power on the market in the pursuit of private interests, his or her actions being co-ordinated by the invisible hand of the market. This contradiction produces two clashing concepts of human freedom. On the one hand, as expressed for instance by Hayek and in some versions of Thatcherism and Reaganism, human freedom is defined in economic terms as the freedom to pursue private interest without political constraint. On the other hand, the socialist and Marxist traditions define freedom in political terms and advocate political intervention in the workings of the market in order to liberate the majority from its constraints. Both traditions assume that the contradiction is resolvable by suppressing either the political or the economic. These clashing concepts of freedom are reflected in debates about the media's political role. On one side the market is seen as a bulwark against the great enemy, state censorship. Thus private ownership of the means of communication is at best a positive good and at worst the lesser of two necessary evils. On the other side capitalist control of the media is seen as an obstacle to free political communication and as the explanation of the media's role in maintaining capitalist class hegemony. In both traditions politics is equated with state power.

I want to argue that this contradiction is irresolvable because in social formations characterized by an advanced division of labour, both function-ally and spatially, only the market is capable of handling the necessary scale of allocative decision-making across wide sectors of human productive activity, while at the same time there is a range of social decisions which no democratic society will be prepared to leave to the market, or rather if it does leave them to the market, it forfeits all claims to democracy. These include the control of social violence, the provision of a basic level of health and material well-being and above all includes control over the develop-ment of the market itself, both in its internal structure, for example, the problem of monopoly, and its externalities, such as environmental questions.

Once we recognize this irresolvable contradiction then the analytical task becomes one of mapping the interactions between the two spheres and the political task, one of working out the historically appropriate balance between recognizing, on the one hand, that pursuit of political freedom may over-ride the search for economic efficiency, while on the other the extent of possible political freedom is constrained by the level of material productivity.

The field of the mass media is a key focus for examining this contradiction because they operate simultaneously across the two realms. Thus a newspaper or a TV channel is at one and the same time a commercial operation and a political institution. The nature of the largely undiscussed problems this creates can be illustrated if one points to the elaborate structure of law and convention which attempts to insulate politicians, public servants and the political process from economic control – rules against bribery, laws controlling election expenditure, the socially validated view, however often it may actually take place, against the use of public office for private gain. And yet at the same time we allow what we recognize as central political institutions, such as the press and broadcasting, to be privately operated.

We would find it strange now if we made voting rights dependent upon purchasing power or property rights and yet access to the mass media, as both channels of information and fora of debate, is largely controlled by just such power and rights.

But the incompatibility between the commercial and political functions of the media is not just a question of ownership and control, important as such questions are. It is even more a question of the value system and set of social relations within which commercial media must operate and which they serve to reinforce. For it is these that are inimical, not just to one political interest group or another, but to the very process of democratic politics itself. Thus political communication which is forced to channel itself via commercial media – and here I refer not just to the press but to public service broadcasting so far as it competes for audiences with commercial broadcasting and on its dominant terms – becomes the politics of consumerism. Politicians relate to potential voters not as rational beings concerned for the public good, but in the mode of advertising, as creatures of passing and largely irrational appetite, to whose self-interest they must appeal. Politics, as Reagan so strikingly demonstrates, becomes not a matter of confronting real issues and choices, but of image. Appeal to people's dreams and fantasies and reality will take care of itself. Politics becomes no longer a matter of balancing priorities or choosing between desirable but incompatible ends within a political programme, but of single issues which can be packaged in easily consumable and sellable form, like soap powder, and to which the response, like that of the decision to purchase, is a simple and immediate yes or no, not the 'just a moment' of debate. The contemporary prevalence of this model of politics among voters is well illustrated by H. Himmelweit *et al.*'s recent book *How Voters Decide* where what the authors identify as the consumer model of voting appears to best explain actual voting behaviour. Following this model, as the authors put it, 'what matters is that the act of voting, like the purchase of goods, is seen as simply one instance of decision making, no different in kind from the process whereby other decisions are reached' (Himmelweit *et al.*, 1985). Unfortunately, however, there is no mechanism in the political realm like that of the invisible hand of the market, to ensure that individual responses to distinctly presented political issues result in coherent political action. It is a form of politics and political communication which enables both citizens and politicians to live in an essentially apolitical world where all our desires can be satisfied, where we can have higher welfare benefits, higher defence expenditure and lower taxes, where we can strengthen the rights of women without challenging the rights of men, where we can appeal to the majority but at the same time protect minorities. Such a politics is forced to take on the terms of address of the media it uses and to address its readers, viewers and listeners within the set of social relations that those media have created for other purposes. Thus the citizen is appealed to as a private individual rather than as a member of a public, within a privatized domestic sphere rather than within that of public life. For instance, think of the profound political difference between reading a newspaper in one's place of work or in a cafe and discussing it with those who share that concrete set of social relations on the one hand, and watching TV within the family circle or listening to radio or watching a video-cassette on an individual domestic basis on the other. Think of the Sony Walkman as a concrete embodiment of social isolation, as opposed to participation at a rock concert.

Public service and knowledge-broking

However, while I want to argue that the public service model of the media has at its heart a set of properly political values and that its operation both requires and fosters a set of social relations distinct from and opposed to the economic values and relations which are essential to an operating democracy, at the same time in its actual historical operation it has so far shared with the Habermasian concept of the Public Sphere a crucial failure to recognize the problem of mediation within the Public Sphere and thus the role of knowledge-brokers within the system. In particular the public service model has failed to come to terms with the proper and necessary social function of both journalists and politicians. In relation to both groups there is a failure sufficiently to distinguish between two communicative functions within the Public Sphere, on the one hand the collection and dissemination of information and on the other the provision of a forum for debate.

Journalists within public service broadcasting, under the banner of balance and objectivity, claim to carry out both functions and to do so in the name of the public. However, this produces a contradiction. On the one hand, the function of information search and exposition, that carried out at its best, for instance, by teachers, cannot simply be equated with political advocacy. Here Jay Blumler is right (Blumler *et al.*, 1978). On the other hand, journalists are not in any way accountable to the public they claim to serve and themselves constitute a distinct interest. How then are we to ensure that this function is carried out responsibly? It clearly needs to be accompanied by a structure of Freedom of Information, and so on. It also needs much better trained journalists. It also, because of its expense, quite clearly depends upon a public service structure of provision, since otherwise high quality information will become not a public good but an expensive private asset. But it still remains that the function cannot simply be left to unaccountable journalists. It needs a public accountability structure of its own and a quite distinct code of professional values separate from the political debate function. Within such a structure much greater direct access needs to be given to independent fields of social expertise. It is a perennial and justifiable criticism of journalists by experts that journalists themselves decide the agenda of what is relevant and at the same time too often garble the information for presentational purposes. Perhaps bodies such as the Medical Research Council, the Economic and Social Research Council, Greenpeace, Social Audit, and one could list many others, should have regular access to broadcasting and print channels and employ their own journalists to clarify current issues for the general public as a background to more informed political debate.

On the other hand, the debate function needs to be more highly politicized, with political parties and other major organized social movements having access to the screen on their own terms rather as was the case until recently in Holland, although that model is itself in the process of being undermined by the very economic forces to which I pointed at the outset. Here one might envisage a situation where any group that could obtain a membership of over a certain size would be eligible for regular access to air time and national newspaper space. Indeed Habermas himself seems to envisage some such arrangement when he argues that the Public Sphere today requires that 'a public body of organized private individuals take the place of the now defunct public body of private individuals'. Such organizations would themselves, he argues, have to have democratic internal structures. The Public Sphere, he writes, 'could only be realized today, on an altered basis, as a rational reorganization of social and political power under the mutual control of rival organizations committed to the public sphere in their internal structure as well as in their relations with the state and each other' (Habermas, 1979, p. 201).

Public service and the political party

To date, the operation of public service broadcasting has tended to reinforce the apoliticism of consumerism by pitting broadcasting, not just against the state, but against politicians. It is politicians that are seen as inherently untrustworthy, as having to be criticized, as trying to interfere in and control broadcasting. Furthermore, as it has operated within the confines of a tradition of critical journalism and of balance and objectivity, broadcasting has contributed to the observable decline of the political party. It has done so by pre-empting its role as a communicator of politically relevant information and as a structurer of political debate. As the press has become steadily more depoliticized, politicians and political parties have been forced to communicate to the electorate via TV on terms largely dictated by journalists. The parties are unable to expound a coherent position, but are forced to respond issue by issue. By concentrating on personalities TV has at the same time enhanced the position of political leaders at the expense of party organizations. This decline of the political party matters because, in societies split by conflicts of interest (in my view all conceivable societies), parties represent the rationalist and universalist moment of the Hegelian state. That is to say, they are the indispensable institutional form by which the views of the individuals are shaped into that necessary hierarchy of interlocking, mutually interdependent ends and means that we call a political programme, without which rational political action in terms of some version of the public good is impossible. That is not to say that the present pattern of parties is optimal. But the current fashion for movement politics, CND, the women's movement, and so on, which is in itself in part a response to the decline of political parties induced by existing patterns of media dominance, in part a product of that very consumerist ideology I am concerned to critique, in part an expression of dissatisfaction with the programmes of existing parties, in no way provides an alternative to the political party, as indeed these movements are discovering. You cannot develop a realistic and realizable movement towards disarmament or women's rights unless it is integrated with other social and economic objectives into some structure and universal programme of political priorities.

A similar argument holds against the other alternative posed to the public service model, that of some version of pluralism, however the material base of that pluralism might be decided. But in general such visions, such yearnings for a return to a golden age of press freedom, are attempts precisely to avoid the crunch of political choice. Indeed, that is perhaps the main unconscious attraction of the free press model and indeed of the market model, that it removes the weight of conscious social choice.

Public service, universalism and an international public sphere

One of the strengths of the public sphere concept which I would want to stress and which I would want to link to any revitalized notion of public service is that of universalism. I mean by this the notion that the scope of a political decision structure must be conterminous with the scope of the powers it aims to control. In recent tradition this has in general meant within the boundaries of the nation-state, so that citizenship of such states is defined in terms of certain nationally universal rights and obligations. The principle of tying voting to property rights was an important expression of this because it recognized the importance of the relationship between the right to participate in decision making and a not easily avoidable involvement in the consequences of those decisions. It is precisely for this reason that capital, so long as it can flow internationally with ease, should not be accorded such rights. Within this envelope of rights and obligations all citizens, whether they are on the winning or losing side of a political debate, are forced to live with its consequences. Thus proper democratic participation cannot be irresponsible by definition. In some countries this important truth is embodied in laws requiring all citizens to vote. Now, while it would clearly be both impossible and undesirable to require all citizens to participate in a minimum amount of political information consumption and debate or to make electoral participation dependent upon such participation, in principle it is a mere corollary of a requirement to vote. Indeed this is the principle which trade unions correctly mobilize against the institution of mandatory postal ballots. However, public policy should, if democracy is to be taken seriously, favour citizen participation in such debate. If that is the case debate must include as many of the existing views in a society on the relevant issues as possible. This cannot, by definition, be provided by sectionalized, ghettoized media talking only to a particular interest group or the party faithful. In terms of national issues it must take place at a national level and is undercut by a multiplication of simultaneous viewing and listening options. It is this that is the rational core of the argument mobilized in favour of the existing public service broadcasting duopoly in Britain: namely, that the existence of a national focus for political debate and information is important to the national political process. The problem of the relations of scale needed between communication channels and political power then takes on a different dimension when we consider the transnational aspect of current media developments.

If we see media structures as central to the democratic polity and if the universalism of the one must match that of the latter, clearly the current process by which national media control is being undercut is part of that process by which power is being transferred in the economy to the international level without the parallel development of adequate political or communication structures. This is already apparent from the problem facing European governments, in the face of satellite broadcasting, of trying to match their different systems of advertising control and indeed, although so far as I know this has not yet been discussed, systems of political access.

Let us be clear. It is in the interest of the controllers of multinational capital to keep nation-states and their citizens in a state of disunity and disfunctional ignorance unified only by market structures within which such capital can freely flow, while at the same time they develop their own private communication networks. The development of the *Financial Times* and the *Wall Street Journal* and of private, high-cost, proprietary data networks and services on an international scale to serve the corporate community and its agents is a clear sign of this trend. Thus not only do we face the challenge of sustaining and developing the public sphere at a national level. Such a development will simply be bypassed, if we do not, at the same time and perhaps with greater urgency, begin to develop a public sphere where at present one hardly exists, namely, at the international level. It is here that current threats, led by the US government, but supported and abetted by the UK, to UNESCO and the ITU, need to be seen for what they are, attempts to destroy what little public sphere actually exists at an international level. It is significant that the crime of which these institutions stand accused is 'politicization'.

In conclusion, I have tried to argue here that the necessary defence and expansion of the public sphere as an integral part of a democratic society requires us to re-evaluate the public service model of public communication and, while being necessarily critical of its concrete historical actualization, defend it and build upon the potential of its rational core in the face of the existing and growing threats to its continued existence.

References

Blumler, J. G., Gurevitch, M. and Ives, J. (1978) *The Challenge of Election Broadcasting*, Leeds University Press.

Cardiff, D. (1980) The serious and the popular: aspects of the evolution of style in the radio talk, 1928–1939. *Media, Culture and Society*, Vol. 12, No. 1.

Habermas, J. (1979) The public sphere. In Matterlart, A. and Siegelaub, S. (eds) *Communication and Class Struggle*, Vol. 1, International General, New York.

Himmelweit, H. *et al.* (1985) *How Voters Decide*, Academic Press, London.

Scannell, P. (1980) Broadcasting and the politics of unemployment, 1930–1935. *Media, Culture and Society*, Vol. 12, No. 1.

30

The theory of the public sphere

John B. Thompson

From Featherstone, M. (ed.) (1993) *Theory, Culture and Society*, Sage, London, Vol. 10, No. 3, pp. 179–87.

Note: in this extract, *Structural Transformation* refers to Habermas, J. (1989) *The Structural Transformation of the Public Sphere* (translated by Burger, T.), MIT Press, Cambridge, MA; Polity Press, Cambridge. Also, *Habermas and the Public Sphere* refers to Calhoun, C. (ed.) (1992) *Habermas and the Public Sphere*, MIT Press, Cambridge, MA.

I

Structural Transformation offers an historical narrative of the changing forms of public life which is, in many ways, quite compelling. It combines a perceptive historical account of the political culture of early modern Europe with a sharp critical perspective on the degradation of public life in our societies today. But how good are Habermas' arguments, both in historical terms and at a more general theoretical level? If we re-examine these arguments today, with the benefit of hindsight and in the light of work that has been done over the last few decades, how well do the arguments hold up?

Undoubtedly part of the rhetorical force of *Structural Transformation* stems from the way that Habermas weaves together historical analysis and normative critique – a feature that has bothered some commentators over the years. I shall not object in principle to this aspect of Habermas' work, but I will try to distinguish the substantive issues from the normative ones and to deal with each separately. In this section I shall focus on four problems (or sets of problems). All of these are now reasonably well discussed in the critical literature – both in *Habermas and the Public Sphere* and elsewhere – and I shall be drawing on this literature here.

1. Let us begin by considering, from an historical point of view, the adequacy and plausibility of Habermas' account of the emergence of the bourgeois public sphere in early modern Europe. One of the criticisms that has been made most frequently of this account is that, by focusing attention on the *bourgeois* public sphere, Habermas tends to neglect the significance of other forms of public discourse and activity which existed in seventeenth, eighteenth- and nineteenth-century Europe, forms which were not part of, and in some cases were excluded from or opposed to, the forms of bourgeois sociability. This point is made very effectively by Geoff Eley in the Calhoun collection, though somewhat similar criticisms can be found in earlier German

literature.[1] As Eley remarks, the work of E. P. Thompson, Christopher Hill and others has highlighted the significance of a variety of popular social and political movements in the early modern period, and it cannot be assumed that these movements were either derivative of, or organized along similar lines to, the activities which took place in the bourgeois public sphere. On the contrary, argues Eley, the relation between the bourgeois public sphere and popular social movements was often a conflictual one. Just as the emerging bourgeois public sphere defined itself in opposition to the traditional authority of royal power, so too it was confronted by the rise of popular movements which it sought to contain. The bourgeois public sphere was, from the outset, embedded in a field of conflictual social relations which shaped its formation and development.

This is a forceful line of criticism. In the preface to *Structural Transformation*, Habermas had explained that his account would be limited to, as he put it, 'the liberal model of the bourgeois public sphere', and that he would leave aside that 'variant' of the liberal model – what he called 'the plebeian public sphere' – which had briefly appeared on the stage of the French Revolution but which was subsequently suppressed in the historical process. But it seems clear that this schematic way of characterizing popular social and political movements was not satisfactory. Returning to these issues thirty years later, Habermas concedes that his earlier account would have to be substantially revised today. Not only were popular movements much more important in the early modern period than he had previously allowed, but it is also clear that they cannot be adequately understood as mere variants of the liberal model of the bourgeois public sphere (any more than popular culture can be understood as a derivative of dominant cultural forms). Habermas acknowledges that we need a more flexible approach to popular social movements and popular cultural forms, an approach which does not pre-judge their character and which allows for the possibility that they may have a shape and dynamic of their own.

2. Let us now focus on the model of the bourgeois public sphere itself, quite apart from the question of whether this model provided a satisfactory way of thinking about the character of non-bourgeois social movements. It is clear that this model was regarded by Habermas as an idealization of actual historical processes. Although the bourgeois public sphere was based on the principle of universal access, in practice it was restricted to those individuals who had the education and the financial means to participate in it. What does not emerge very clearly from Habermas' account, however, is the extent to which the bourgeois public sphere was not only restricted to educated and propertied élites, but was also a predominantly *male* preserve. Habermas was not unaware of the marginalization of women in the bourgeois public sphere and of the patriarchal character of the bourgeois family; but it could be argued very plausibly that, at the time of writing *Structural Transformation*, he did not appreciate the full significance of this issue.

In recent years a number of feminist scholars have examined the gendered character of the public sphere and political discourse in the early modern period, and have brought sharply into focus a set of issues which remained rather blurred in Habermas' account. Particularly interesting in this regard is Joan Landes' (1988) *Women and the Public Sphere in the Age of the French Revolution.*[2] Landes is concerned with the relation of women to the public sphere in France in the period from 1750 to 1850. Her central argument is that the exclusion of women from the public sphere was not simply a contingent historical circumstance, one of the many respects in which the public sphere in practice fell short of the ideal; rather, the exclusion of women was constitutive of the very notion of the public sphere. For the notion of the public sphere, as it was articulated in the political discourse of the time, was juxtaposed to the private sphere in a gender-specific way. The public sphere was generally understood as a domain of reason and universality in which men were uniquely well equipped to participate, while women, being inclined (supposedly) to particularity and to mannered, frivolous talk, were commonly thought to be better suited to domestic life. Hence the masculine character of the bourgeois public sphere was not an incidental aspect: it was a fundamental feature of a public sphere which, in its very conception, was shaped by a deeply rooted set of assumptions about gender differences.

It is to Habermas' credit that, in reconsidering these issues today, he is swayed by the force of this line of argument. He accepts that, while workers and peasants as well as women were largely excluded from the bourgeois public sphere, the exclusion of women needs to be thought about differently, precisely because this exclusion had, as Habermas now puts it, 'structuring significance'. This shift in Habermas' approach is important, but one might reasonably remain a little sceptical about the extent to which Habermas has taken account of gender issues. For, as Nancy Fraser (1989) has shown, a somewhat similar line of argument can be developed with regard to Habermas' more recent work. It may be that, while Habermas is certainly sympathetic to the issues raised by feminist critics, these issues remain somewhat tangential to the basic assumptions and priorities that shape his way of conceptualizing the social world.

3. The weakest parts of *Structural Transformation* are probably not the sections concerned with the emergence of the bourgeois public sphere, but rather the sections concerned with its alleged decline. Surprisingly, Habermas' arguments concerning the transformation of the public sphere in the nineteenth and twentieth centuries are not addressed in any detail by the contributors to *Habermas and The Public Sphere*, though they are reconsidered by Habermas himself in his reply. If one re-reads today Habermas' account of the changes which have occurred over the last two centuries, one will find many details to dispute and some empirical material which is now well out of date. But the important question is whether Habermas was right to interpret these changes broadly in the way that he did – as a sign that the public sphere of debating citizens had collapsed into a fragmented world of consumers who are enthralled by the media spectacles unfolding before them and manipulated by media techniques. Is there any substance to this interpretation and, more specifically, to the thesis of the refeudalization of the public sphere?

I doubt it. Certainly this account has some *prima facie* plausibility. One need only watch a few party political broadcasts to remind oneself of the extent to which the conduct of politics today has become inseparable from the activity of public relations management. But if we press beyond the level of initial observations, it is clear that there are serious deficiencies to Habermas' account. Let me highlight two. In the first place, it is very doubtful whether the recipients of media products can plausibly be regarded as enthralled and manipulated consumers. In developing this argument, Habermas was betraying his debt to the work of Horkheimer and Adorno, whose theory of mass culture provided part of the inspiration for his own account. Today it is clear, however, that this kind of argument exaggerates the passivity of individuals and takes far too much for granted concerning the process of reception; a more contextualized and hermeneutically sensitive approach would show that the process of reception is a much more complicated and creative activity than the Frankfurt school theorists supposed (this point has been developed in more detail in Thompson, 1990, Chapter 2). Habermas now accepts the force of this criticism and acknowledges that, if he were to rework his account of the transformation of the public sphere, he would have to give more attention to recent work on the reception of media products.

A second problem in Habermas account concerns the thesis of the refeudalization of the public sphere. It is not difficult to see why Habermas had argued that the public sphere was being 'refeudalized': the showiness characteristic of mediated politics today, and its concern to cultivate personal aura rather than to stimulate critical debate, does seem, at least at first glance, to resemble the kind of representative publicness typical of the Middle Ages. But the similarity here is more apparent than real, and the fact that Habermas could seriously make this comparison suggests that he had not really appreciated the quite profound impact that the mass media have had on the modern world. For the development of the media – and especially of the various types of electronic communication – has created new forms of social interaction and information diffusion which exist on a scale and are organized in a manner that preclude any serious comparison with the theatrical practices of feudal courts. Whereas courtly behaviour in the Middle Ages was largely oriented towards individuals who shared the same spatial-temporal context, today it is common for political leaders to appear before millions of recipients who are widely dispersed in space (and perhaps also in time); and the kinds of relationship established through mediated communication are quite different from the face-to-face interaction which takes place in a shared locale. I shall return to these issues below. Here it will suffice to say that, if we wish to understand how public life in the modern world has been reshaped by the development of the media (among other things), we would be well advised to put aside the thesis of the refeudalization of the public sphere and to think about these issues in a different way.

4. I mentioned earlier that *Structural Transformation* could be viewed as an initial attempt to outline a theory of democracy that would be relevant to the conditions of twentieth-century Western societies. Although the bourgeois public sphere has long since declined, the critical principle of publicity retains some relevance as a normative ideal and could be used to guide institutional change. In the closing pages of *Structural Transformation*, Habermas put forward a few ideas about how the critical principle of

publicity could be implemented within the organizations and interest groups which had assumed an ever-increasing role in political affairs. In sketching these proposals for a kind of 'intra-organizational democratization', Habermas was indebted to the work – little known in the English-speaking world – of Wolfgang Abendroth. (Habermas' *Habilitationschrift*, having apparently been received unfavourably by Horkheimer and Adorno, was submitted to Abendroth at Marburg, and the book was subsequently dedicated to him.) But the proposals put forward by Habermas were, at best, exceedingly vague; and Habermas himself gradually came to the view that, given the complexity of modern, internally differentiated societies, such proposals would be largely unworkable in practice.

In recent decades Habermas has continued to pursue the question of how a theory of democracy, informed by the ideas once embodied in the bourgeois public sphere, could be developed and applied to the conditions of modern societies. This has involved two parallel lines of argument. In the first place, Habermas has tried to show that the notion of a discursive formation of the will through a process of reasoned debate can be given a firmer foundation than it had in *Structural Transformation*, and that this notion forms the core of a discourse-centred theory of democracy in which questions of a moral-practical character can be resolved in a rational manner (see Habermas, 1990, 1992). Certainly this line of argument has not won universal assent. Even Habermas' most sympathetic critics find much with which to disagree in his account of practical discourse (see the fine essays by McCarthy, Benhabib and Fraser in *Habermas and the Public Sphere*); and many have doubted whether, in view of the plurality of evaluative and interpretative standpoints characteristic of modern societies, it makes sense to try to build a political theory based on the possibility of rational consensus. Habermas' arguments concerning the theory of practical discourse and its political application have given us a great deal to think about and will, no doubt, continue to generate much debate. But it seems to me that, at least in some respects, his critics are justified, and it would probably be sensible for Habermas to tone down some of his stronger claims in favour of a more modest approach.

The second line of argument developed by Habermas has involved a substantial revision of his theory of society, culminating in the distinction between system and lifeworld elaborated in *The Theory of Communicative Action* (Habermas, 1987). This distinction has major implications for Habermas' theory of democracy. He now accepts that the state and economy are systematically organized fields of action which can no longer be transformed democratically from within: to attempt to do so would be to threaten their capacity to function according to their distinctive logic, with potentially disastrous consequences. The task today of a radical programme of democratization should be, instead, to push back the colonizing intrusion of system imperatives into the lifeworld and to achieve thereby a new balance between forms of societal integration, so that the practically oriented demands of the lifeworld can prevail over the exercise of economic and administrative power.

Not everyone will be convinced that, with the notions of system and lifeworld, Habermas has found the most compelling way to reformulate the political programme of radical democratization. Some will doubt whether the state and economy should be insulated from democratic processes in the manner proposed, and many will wonder what all of this amounts to in practice. Moreover, in developing his theory of society in recent years, Habermas seems largely to have lost sight of a theme that concerned him in his earlier work – namely, the importance of communication media and their structuring impact on social and political life. I want to conclude by returning briefly to this theme and asking whether it can be reformulated in a way that does justice to the forms of mediated communication which are increasingly common in the world today.

II

In the previous section I have considered some of the criticisms that have been made of Habermas' early writings on the public sphere and some of the reasons why Habermas subsequently modified his views. However, there is one issue which has not figured prominently in the debate sparked off by Habermas' work, and yet which is, in my view, of considerable significance for any attempt to rethink the changing character of public life. The issue, put simply, is this: Habermas' conception of the public sphere – whether in the form of the bourgeois public sphere which emerged in the eighteenth century, or in the form of his own, philosophically more elaborate model of practical discourse – is essentially a *dialogical* conception. That is, it is based on the idea that individuals come together in a shared locale and engage in dialogue with one another, as equal participants in a face-to-face conversation. The problem, however, is that this conception bears little resemblance to the kinds of communication established by and sustained through the media, and hence bears little resemblance to the kind of public sphere which the media have helped to create.[3] Let us consider this problem further by returning for a moment to the arguments of *Structural Transformation*.

Many commentators have noted that, in accounting for the formation of the bourgeois public sphere, Habermas attributes a significant role to print. But if we re-read *Structural Transformation* carefully, we will find, I think, that Habermas was not interested in print as such, in the distinctive characteristics of this communication medium and in the kinds of social relations established by it. His way of thinking about print was shaped by a model of communication based on the spoken word: the periodical press was part of a conversation begun and continued in the shared locales of bourgeois sociability. The press was interwoven so closely with the life of clubs and coffee houses that it was inseparable from it: 'One and the same discussion transposed into a different medium was continued in order to re-enter, via reading, the original conversational medium' (*Structural Transformation*, p. 42). So while the press played a crucial role in the formation of the bourgeois public sphere, the latter was conceptualized by Habermas not in relation to print, but in relation to the face-to-face conversations stimulated by it. In this respect, Habermas' account of the bourgeois public sphere bears the imprint of the classical Greek conception of public life: the salons, clubs and coffee houses of Paris and

London were the equivalent, in the context of early modern Europe, of the assemblies and market places of ancient Greece. As in ancient Greece, so too in early modern Europe, the public sphere was constituted above all in speech, in the weighing up of different arguments, opinions and points of view in the dialogical exchange of spoken words in a shared locale.

It is not difficult to see why, with this conception of the public sphere in mind, Habermas was inclined to interpret the impact of newer communication media, like radio and television, in largely negative terms. It was not only because the media industries had become more commercialized and harnessed to particular interests; it was also because the kind of communication situation they created, in which the reception of media products had become a form of privatized appropriation, was a far cry from the dialogical exchange that took place among individuals who gathered together in the clubs and coffee houses of early modern Europe (see *Structural Transformation*, pp. 163–5). Habermas recognizes, of course, that radio and television create new forms of conversation – the TV chat shows, panel discussions, and so on. But these new forms of conversation, he argues, are in no way comparable to the critical rational debate that was constitutive of the bourgeois public sphere. 'Today the conversation itself is administered' (*Structural Transformation*, p. 164), and active debate among informed citizens has been replaced by the privatized appropriation of a conversation carried out in their name. However, we shall not arrive at a satisfactory understanding of the nature of public life in the modern world if we remain wedded to a conception of publicness which is essentially dialogical in character, and which obliges us to interpret the ever-growing role of mediated communication as an historical fall from grace. We should, instead, recognize from the outset that the development of communication media – beginning with print, but including the more recent forms of electronic communication – has created a new kind of publicness which cannot be accommodated within the traditional model. With the development of communication media, the phenomenon of publicness has become detached from the sharing of a common locale. It has become de-spatialized and non-dialogical, and it is increasingly linked to the distinctive kind of visibility produced by, and achievable through, the media (especially television).

Notes

1. Earlier versions of this kind of criticism can be found in Negt and Kluge (1972) and Lottes (1979). Eley (in *Habermas and the Public Sphere*) draws on Lotte's work and discusses it in some detail.
2. See also Carole Pateman (1988), Mary P. Ryan (1990) and Catherine Hall (1992). Issues of gender are addressed by several of the authors in *Habermas and the Public Sphere*; see especially the contributions by Seyla Benhabib, Nancy Fraser, Keith Baker, Mary Ryan and Geoff Eley.
3. For a more detailed discussion of this issue, see Thompson (1990, pp. 119–20 and 238–48); see also Thompson (forthcoming). The question of whether Habermas' conception of the public sphere is suitable for analysing mediated communication is raised by one or two contributors to *Habermas and the Public Sphere* (see especially the essay by Nicholas Garnham), but it is not taken up by Habermas.

References

Fraser, Nancy (1989) What's critical about critical theory? The case of Habermas and gender. In *Unruly Practices. Power, Discourse and Gender in Contemporary Social Theory.* Polity Press, Cambridge, pp. 113–43.

Habermas, Jurgen (1987) *The Theory of Communicative Action, Vol.2, Lifeworld and System: A Critique of Functionalist Reason*, Polity Press, Cambridge.

Habermas, Jurgen (1990) *Moral Consciousness and Communicative Action*, Polity Press, Cambridge.

Habermas, Jurgen (1992) *Fakizitat und Geltung. Beitrage zur Diskurstheorie des Rechts und des demokratischen Rechtsstaats*, Suhrkamp, Frankfurt.

Hall, Catherine (1992) *White, Male and Middle Class: Explorations in Feminism and History*, Polity Press, Cambridge.

Landes, Joan (1988) *Women and the Public Sphere in the Age of the French Revolution*, Cornell University Press, Ithaca, NY.

Lottes, Gunther (1979) *Politische Aufklarung und plebejisches Publikum. Zur theorie und Praxis des englischen Radikalismus im spaten 18. Jahrhundert*, Oldenbourg, Munich.

Negt, Oskar and Kluge, Alexander (1972) *Offentlichkeit und Erfahrung. Zur Organisationsanalyse von burgerlicher und proletarischer Offenlichkeit*, Suhrkamp, Frankfurt.

Pateman, Carole (1988) *The Sexual Contract*, Polity Press, Cambridge.

Ryan, Mary P. (1988) *Women in Public: Between Banners and Ballots, 1825–1880*, Johns Hopkins University Press, Baltimore.

Thompson, John B. (1990) *Ideology and Modern Culture; Critical Social Theory in the Era of Mass Communication*, Polity Press, Cambridge.

Thompson, John B. (forthcoming) Social theory and the media. In Crowley, David and Mitchell, David (eds) *Communication Theory Today*, Polity Press, Cambridge.

31

Intellectuals, the 'information society' and the disappearance of the public sphere

Philip Elliott

From Schlesinger, P. and Sparks, C. (eds) (1982) *Media, Culture and Society*, Academic Press, London, Vol. 4, No. 3, pp. 244–6.

The thesis I wish to advance is that what we are seeing and what we face is a continuation of the shift away from involving people in society as political citizens of nation states towards involving them as consumption units in a corporate world. The consequence of this for the culture is a continuation of the erosion of what Habermas called the public sphere or C. Wright Mills the community of publics. The hallmark of both these types of polity were contests between politically expressed demands based on knowledge, information and association in democratic, nation states – a type of society which Habermas sees as typical of the bourgeois moment of capitalism. Instead a mass society develops founded on an acceptable level of comfort, pleasure and control in which people participate as members of the market.

The consequence of relying on the market, as Nora and Minc (1978) argue, is to set very real limits on what people can hope to achieve. The market provides not for participation but for consumption. In other words, there is a sleight of hand in the arguments of Daniel Bell (1976, 1980) and others who look forward to an explosion of information and communication such as will create an information-based society with a more rational form of culture than we now enjoy. The sleight of hand lies in the assumption that new technologies will increase general access to information and open up new possibilities of two-way communication

The first problem is one of access; the second, what we mean by information and communication. Access is not just a matter of physical means. It also involves having the rights and resources to make use of them. The analogy of a library is appealing because it suggests an open store of knowledge simply waiting for us to bumble around in. Moreover, the public library system is another of those services like public education, established in the nineteenth and twentieth centuries, in recognition of a general right to knowledge. However poorly the ideal has been realized in practice, the library system has been inspired by the aim of an informed citizenry.

The weakness of the analogy between the old and the new becomes apparent however as soon as we consider the aims of the new controllers of information. What is in prospect, as Herbert Schiller (1981) has pointed out, is the privatization of information. The new information producers are commercial corporations who have a primary interest in keeping information secret to protect their commercial secrets. Their secondary interest is to produce a commodity for sale in the market. In the pursuit of this end, the American information industry is already putting pressure on the sources of public information, of which the main one is the government, to commercialize its operations. Information which was once available to the public as of right will, in future, be available at a price. As Schiller argues, there is likely to be a knock-on effect. Information for which there is not a market will not be produced. In Britain there is a neat illustration of the coincidence between political convenience and market forces in the gradual disappearance of the poverty statistics.[1]

There are other problems with the library analogy. Even libraries have catalogues – catalogues designed to make it easy to answer some questions and so inevitably more difficult to answer others. Who will be writing the catalogues? Who will be setting the questions and the range of possible answers? Indeed, who will have accumulated the stock of knowledge? Not, I submit, the myriad of individual subscribers at their computer terminals and yet, another characteristic of the technological Utopia will be a further domestication of living functions and privatization of social life.

Privatization in this sense is one of the key processes associated with the Frankfurt school's analysis of the media and their effect on social relationships, not through the messages they carry but the type of interaction they encourage. By concentrating activities within the home, the broadcast media of radio and television set up a type of human group which has no other connection with each other than their common use of the same service. The strong version of the Frankfurt school argument is that this opens up the possibility of manipulation, an argument which has been severely questioned by 'effects' research. A weak version of the argument is that this process of privatization deprives people of the possibility of answering back because it deprives them of the opportunities for association in which common needs might be recognized and demands formulated. [. . .]

The second problem of Bell's vision of a rational, information-rich society is that much of what we now take as information and as an informative process of communication based on a rational model are anything but, having a high level of symbolic, mythical content and passive, entertainment value. The importance attached to the concept of information owes much to the resilience of the ideal of society as a rational, democratic polity and to the success of intellectuals in promoting the equation information plus rational choice equals social progress. It is an equation which has been much disputed by conservative intellectuals. 'Hayek's law' for example claims that attempts at legislative reform always have opposite effects from those intended. It is only recently, however, that such arguments have begun to carry weight against the interventionist intellectuals of Gouldner's (1979) 'New Class' who had insinuated themselves into the machinery of national government as the providers and processors of the information on which the government should act. While the Labour Party and the SDP dispute their right to Tawney's name for a new interventionist, intellectual society, the intellectual initiative has passed to various right-wing societies and institutes. These are able to attract private funds whereas the financial and occupational base of interventionist intellectualism in public sector research and educational institutions is being put under increasing pressure.

Nevertheless, the persistence of the Fabianesque concept of information as a necessary social resource can also be seen in discussions of the mass media. The growth of the press was based on two processes, the provision of useful information, mainly commercial and financial intelligence to interested parties, and political controversy. Print was the medium which underpinned the concept of the public sphere by providing an arena for political debate. Over time, both these functions have been transformed. From its original base in élite information, the commercial function has expanded beyond all recognition and with the transformation of news into a commodity, the political function has been eclipsed. Nevertheless, debates about the press are still carried on in terms of the argument for a free press able to supply the information and reflect the opinions necessary to foster decision-making in a democracy. The recent introduction of a new daily newspaper in Britain, the *Daily Star*, shows clearly that the mass market daily papers are a very different sort of animal. The lead features in the three tabloids on the day on which the *Daily Star* started in publication showed a quite explicit concern with irrationality, magic, extra scientific potential and play on the sacred and profane dimensions. One featured a round-the-world-yachtswoman and a sex-change witch, the second organized an experiment among its readers to show that metal could be bent by mental power and the third discovered a vicar who painted nudes *à la* Gaugin.

Notes

1. Thus, for example, figures on the take-up rate of means-tested benefits are no longer available and the number below the 'poverty-line' is now calculated biennially instead of annually.
2. On the dispute over Tawney's inheritance see Raphael Samuel's Socialist Society pamphlet, published by *The Guardian* (29 March and 5 April 1982). Examples of bodies which have begun to make more of the ideological running are the Institute for the Study of Conflict, the Institute for Economic Affairs, which now includes within it a Unit for Social Affairs, the Freedom Association, the Adam Smith Institute and the Centre for Policy Studies.

References

Bell, D. (1976) *The Cultural Contradiction of Capitalism*, Heinemann, London.
Bell, D. (1980) The social framework of the information society. In Forrester, T (ed.) *The Microelectronics Revolution*, Blackwell, Oxford.
Gouldner, A. (1979) *The Future of the Intellectuals and the Rise of the New Class*, Macmillan, London.
Nora, S. and Minc, A. (1978) *L'Information de la Societe*, La Documentation Francaise, Paris.
Schiller, H. (1981) *Who Knows: Information in the Age of the Fortune 500*. Ablex, Norwood, NJ.

32

Democracy and media: without foundations

John Keane

From Manaev, O. and Pryliuk, Y. (eds) (1993) *Media in Transition: From Totalitarianism to Democracy*, Abris, Kyiv, pp. 4–12.

There are difficulties in the argument that existing public service media are a bulwark of democratic freedom and equality. It underestimates the ways in which technological change – the advent of cable, satellite, television, community radio – has slowly but surely destroyed the traditional argument that the scarcity of available spectrum frequencies blesses public service broadcasting with the status of a 'natural monopoly' within the boundaries of a given nation-state. Defenders of existing public service media also understate the ways in which the alleged 'balance', 'equality' standards and universalism of existing public service media are routinely perceived by certain audiences as 'unrepresentative'. The repertoire programmes channelled through existing public service media cannot exhaust the multitude of opinions in a complex (if less than fully pluralist) society in motion. The public service claim to representativeness is a defence of *virtual* representation of a fictive whole, a resort to programming which *simulates* the actual opinions and tastes of only *some* of those to whom it is directed.

Music is a pertinent example. Although, for obvious reasons, music has always occupied the bulk of radio time, it has proved impossible in the long term to provide programming with general appeal on public service radio because a shared national musical culture has never existed. Different music appeals to different publics, whose dislikes are often as strong as their likes, and that is why the twentieth century history of radio has resulted in a gradual fragmentation of mass audiences into different taste publics. Public service media corset audiences and violate their own principle of equality of access for all to entertainment, current affairs and cultural resources in a common public domain. For reasons of a commitment to 'balance', government pressures and threatened litigation, the public service representation of such topics as sexuality, politics and violence also tends to be timid. Certain things cannot be transmitted, their disturbing, troublesome or outrageous implications are often closed off. And public service media – here they are no different from their commercial competitors – distribute entitlements to speak and to be heard and seen unevenly. They too develop a cast of regulars – reporters, presenters, commentators, academic experts, businesspeople, politicians, trade unionists, cultural authorities – who appear as accredited representatives of public experience and taste by virtue of their regular appearance on the media.

All that is grist for the mill of those favouring 'deregulation', for whom market competition is the key condition of press and broadcasting freedom, understood as freedom from state interference. That is why defenders of the public service model who talk only about preserving the 'quality' and 'balance' of the existing system make a crucial strategic mistake. 'Save the public service model' is a self-defeating position in the fight against those who consider market-driven media as a necessary condition of democracy. It concedes too much. Market liberals are attempting to rewrite history. They aim to brand the public service model as paternalistic, as timocratic, as an assault on the old European heritage of liberty from state control. Their fight to rewrite history from above serves as an important reminder that those who control the production of traditions, who dominate the present and manipulate the past, are likely also to control the future. And it reminds us that the debate over who shall inherit the old European vocabulary of 'liberty of the press' is long overdue, and that gaining the upper hand in these controversies is imperative for the survival and development of a public service communications system which resolves the flaws of market liberalism, and which, consequently, is more genuinely open and pluralistic, and therefore accessible to citizens of all persuasions.

But what would a redefined, broadened, and more accessible and accountable public service model look like in practice? What would be its guiding principles? In *The Media and Democracy* I argued that public service media could be built on the decommodifying achievements of the original public service model, all the while acknowledging that it has now slipped into a profound and irreversible crisis. A fundamentally revised public service model would aim to facilitate a genuine commonwealth of forms of life, tastes and opinions, to empower a plurality of citizens who are governed neither by despotic states nor by market forces. It would circulate to them a wide variety of opinions. It would enable them to live within the framework of multi-layered constitutional states which are held accountable to their citizens who work and consume, live and love, quarrel and compromise within independent, self-organizing civil societies which underpin and transcend the narrow boundaries of state institutions.

In practice, the redefinition of the public service model requires the development of a plurality of *non-state* media of communication which both function as permanent thorns in the side of political power (helping thereby to minimize political censorship) and serve as the primary means of communication for citizens situated within a pluralistic civil society. It also requires the adoption of measures which protect civil society from the self-paralysing effects of market-based media. It necessitates the regulation and maximum feasible reduction of private corporate power over the means of communication. It is unlikely, of course, that market transactions could ever be eliminated from the heart of a complex, pluralistic civil society. Market transactions can function as useful accessories of social life, enhancing its productiveness, flexibility and efficiency. Market-influenced media can also function as important countervailing forces in the process of producing and circulating opinions; they are not only economic phenomena but sites of signification that often run counter to opinion-making monopolies operated by churches, states and professional bodies. But, contrary to the claims of market liberalism, that does not mean that civil society and its media must be ruled by 'market forces'. There is nothing 'natural' or 'necessary' about profit-seeking, privately owned and controlled communications media. There are in fact many different types of markets which, contrary to the slogan, 'Leave it to the market' – do not crystallize spontaneously. A self-regulating market is utopian as; Karl Polanyi pointed out,[1] it cannot exist for long without paralysing itself and annulling its *social* preconditions. The actual or optimal shape of a market transaction must therefore always be crafted by political and legal regulations. It never emerges spontaneously or grows without the benefits of *non-market* support mechanisms provided by other institutions of civil society and through the state itself. And it always exists in a condition of political uncertainty, either recovering from a reform, wriggling against or cuddling up to existing regulations, or awaiting the next round of regulation.

It is difficult to be precise about which market-regulating and market-suspending strategies can maximize freedom of communication, since their actual shape and effectiveness will vary from context to context, and from time to time. One thing is nevertheless clear: the maximum feasible *decommodification* and 're-embedding' of communications media in the social life of civil society is a vital condition of freedom from state and market censorship. The recent attempts to restrict advertising *aimed at children* (in Italy), to ban unsolicited faxed junk mail (in the United States) and the widening concern everywhere about sexism and racism in the commercial media exemplify and foreshadow the general principle: the communications media should not be at the whim of 'market forces' but rather placed within a political and legal framework which specifies and enforces tough minimum safeguards in matters of ownership structure, regional scheduling, programme content and decision-making procedures.

Such public intervention into the marketplace must avoid slipping into the reductionist demonology of the evil press baron. The obsession with media magnates has little in common with a politics of maximizing freedom and equality of communication. It understates the complexity of issues in the field of media politics and whets old-fashioned appetites for 'nationalizing' the media and placing them under centralized state control. As far as possible, censorious and bureaucratic forms of regulation should be avoided. Public intervention into the market should be open, accountable and positively enabling. It must use publicity to fight against the lack of publicity. It should seek to rely upon the techniques of 'eyebrow lifting', informal and visible pressures which encourage the media to develop programming policies in support of decommodification. When that fails, or is likely to fail, public regulation should aim to entangle capitalist media in a carefully spun spider's web of financial and legal obligations and public accountability. Public intervention in the media marketplace should always attempt to 'level up' rather than 'level down' citizens' non-market powers of communication. It should seek the creation of a genuine variety of media which enable little people in big societies to send and receive a variety of opinions in a variety of ways. It should aim to break down media monopolies, lift restrictions upon particular audience choices and to popularize the view that the media of communication are a public good, not a privately appropriable commodity whose primary function is to produce and circulate corporate speech for profit.

In practical terms, the maximization of freedom and equality of communication requires efforts to 'de-concentrate' and publicly regulate privately owned media and to restrict the scope and intensity of corporate speech. The creation of politically accountable, supranational regulatory bodies, skilled at dealing with such matters as ownership, advertising, tariffs and network access conditions is imperative.[2] Such bodies must be backed by national initiatives which restrict the media power of private capital by forcing such large corporations as News Corporation, Axel Springer Verlag AG and Fininvest to submit to tough legislation which specifies programme quotas and restrictions upon advertising and cross-media ownership. Large media corporations should be treated as *common carriers*. They should be forced by law to carry various citizens' messages if indeed they agree to carry anyone's messages (which they must do in order to survive financially). For example, legal and financial encouragement could be given to efforts to guaranteeing rights of access during certain hours on radio and television to individuals, groups and independent programme makers. Such encouragement would help to build the electronic equivalent of Speakers' Corner and add a much-needed new element of spontaneous drama, fun and intellectual vitality to the media. The absolute powers of private media corporations to construct reality for others could also be broken down by the introduction of democratic decision-making procedures, including experiments (such as those pioneered at *Le Monde*[3]) with worker participation and the formation of 'management teams' (*equipes de direction*).

Freedom and equality of communication also requires the drastic loosening of libel laws in favour of small producers of opinion, which find themselves unable to risk or to survive a libel claim against them by large corporations and professional bodies. It further presupposes the establishment of media enterprise boards to fund alternative ownership of divested media. Freedom of communication requires public support for new enterprises, particularly in areas (such as videotex, interactive television and electronic mail facilities) where entry costs and risks to potential investors are prohibitively high. Freedom of communication undoubtedly requires the establishment of publicly owned printing and broadcasting enterprises which utilize funds raised by an advertising revenue tax or a spectrum usage fee to facilitate new and innovative start-ups which test the market. Greater public support is needed for small production companies which operate within a regulated market and work to distinctive programming remits (as in the Channel 4 model in Britain). And, especially in the transition towards a more democratic order, freedom from state and market censorship necessitates preferential treatment of information publishers with a pluralistic cutting edge – of iconoclastic, independent and rigorous media such as *El Pais*, founded a few months after Franco's death, 'Radio Alice', Bologna's former experimental radio station, which denied 'reality' and rejected the idea of schedules, and the courageous Czechoslovak newspaper, *Ludove Noviny*, all of which have played a critical role in the struggle for democratic procedures.

Inevitably, stricter limits upon the production and circulation of opinions by means of market transactions would imply greater state hectoring of civil society. This is why a new constitutional settlement which ensures that political power is held permanently accountable to its citizens is so important. It is also the reason why the undermining of both state power and market power from below requires the development of a dense network or 'heterarchy' of communications media which are controlled neither by the state nor by commercial markets. Publicly funded, non-profit and legally guaranteed media institutions of civil society, some of them run voluntarily and held directly accountable to their audiences through democratic procedures, are an essential ingredient of a revised public service model.

Numerous examples come to mind. The BBC model of broadcasting institutions, funded by a licence fee, could remain a leading symbol of the non-market non-state sector, but only at the price of the abolition of the present system of government appointment of its management, at the price of the acknowledgement that their original (Reithian) brief is not fully attainable, and of their internal democratization (perhaps along the lines of the system adopted in the Federal Republic of Germany, where representatives of 'socially relevant groups', including political parties, exercised some measure of influence over such matters as programming schedules, personal budgets and organizational structure). Other examples of this sector include the development of local independent cinemas and recording studios and leased-back broadcasting facilities. Political newspapers could be publicly subsidized. A dense and user-friendly network of community libraries equipped with the latest information technologies could be strengthened. Cooperatively run publishers and distributors, community radio stations and other conventional non-profit media would continue to play an important role in strengthening the foundations of a pluralist civil society. More versatile interpersonal communication could be ensured through public funded and equitably distributed telefaxes, videotex systems and electronic mail facilities. The development of publicly funded teleshopping facilities, which are most useful to housebound and senior citizens would also have priority. And support could be provided for the development of new types of equipment – interactive televisions, digital copiers, camcorders and music synthesizers – capable of supporting the communication of opinions among various groups of citizens.

As far as possible, these non-market, non-state media would feed upon the increased flexibility and power and reduced costs of information processing provided by the new microelectronic technologies. These technologies, as market liberals have been quick to point out, have profound implications for a revised public service model. They are revolutionary heartland technologies, whose cost-reducing effects, and ever-widening applicability throughout civil society and the state enable citizens to communicate in previously unthinkable ways. They are potentially a species of 'democratic technics' (Mumford). Improvements in their performance are not yet complete. Optical fibre channel capacity, software quality, random access memory (RAM) capacity, chip density and processing speeds continue to undergo rapid improvement. Nevertheless, these technologies have several unique characteristics in common. They treat all kinds of information (speech, text, video, graphics) in digital form, thus facilitating the transfer of the same data between different media. The new technologies decrease the relative cost of information processing; bulk operations that would previously have been unthinkable can now be carried out. The decreasing size of equipment and the speedier information processing and error-checking capacities also enable smaller scale, decentralized and user-friendly operations within a framework of greater coordination and strategic control which links operations over vast distances. And – this feature is crucial – the new information technologies rupture the traditional television and radio pattern of offering a continuous sequence of programmes to mass audiences. Instead, the new electronic services strengthen the hand of 'narrowcasting' against broadcasting. They offer information on a more individualized basis: at any given moment, the 'receiver' is required to choose or to process the specific information she or he wants.[4]

Notes

1. Polanyi, K. (1945) *The Origins of Our Time*, London.
2. See Garnham, N. (1988) *European Communications Policy*, CCIS, London, October.
3. See Freiberg, J. W., *Class, State, and Ideology*, The French Press, Chapter 3.
4. Miles I. (1988) *Information Technology and Information Society: Options for the Future*, Brighton.

Section 6

Media occupations and professionals

33

The analysis of media occupations and professionals

Oliver Boyd-Barrett

Sociological interest in media occupations and professionals has been driven mainly by a concern to answer the first of Lasswell's (1948) questions in the communication cycle: *who* says what to whom . . . ? The objective has been to identify processes and rationales informing the selection of media content. Articulation of rationales is problematic. In the first place, they become institutionalized into routine practices so that practitioners themselves are not necessarily aware of them. Secondly, the rationales do not correspond altogether, if at all, with the articulations that professionals do provide. Professionals will be inclined to stress the norms and values of their particular occupational specialization, but these perceptions of what they do and why they do it typically omit reference to some of the parameters to do with the economic (or, for that matter, the political) interests of owners, managers or shareholders. Processes of production, thirdly, can be long and complex, both synchronically (in the sense that several chains of people may be involved in the compilation of a television news broadcast, for instance), and diachronically in the sense that media practices often involve the re-working of other, existing texts, such as archive footage or recordings of source statements, or public relations handouts. Fourthly, media practices are integrated with media genres, such that it can be said that practitioners are 'spoken by' genres as much as they develop them, and while genres do change, adjust and evolve over time, there is unlikely to be a simple one-to-one correspondence between the evolution of genres and the evolution of rationales for media practice. In other words, the 'practical–rational–functional' is always likely to be diluted to some extent by the 'historical–traditional' in the explanations for why media operations are the way that they are. The fluid symbiosis of practice and genre, finally, is also a function of broader organizational constraints, as well as of cultural values and expectations.

Analyses of media practice, as one would expect from the foregoing, represent a range of different foci, methodologies and theoretical frameworks. The sociological agenda has tended sometimes to marginalize certain themes – such as ethical and management issues formulated by media professionals and institutions themselves – as 'administrative' rather than 'critical' research. Although media interests have by definition played a significant role in developing 'administrative' research in some fields such as audience research, and have provided funds to academe for so doing, there has been less industry infusion of funds for other areas of media study. In a period during which many sociologists of media concentrated on unpacking the 'hegemonic consensus', as represented by mainstream media, and its construction through political economy and cultural hegemony models (see Chibnall 1977, for example, for one of the best attempts at unpacking this in detail), there was no academy addressing questions posed by the media establishment in areas such as media production. Arguably this has been a loss to the field and to the industry. The rivalry between 'administrative' and 'critical' traditions in audience research may be said to have had the beneficial and unintended function of developing and sharpening awareness of many of the methodological, conceptual, and epistemological issues which each camp had touched upon in its own way. Even if the media industry and 'critical' researchers rarely had anything to talk about with each other, they were at least operating in the same hemisphere and generating research findings which could occasionally, through the natural dialectics of the formation of ideas, be of mutual influence. In the field of organizations and professionals, however, even this small degree of common interest has been lacking and sociological work has generally not been of a kind that would help open doors for further research, or which policy-makers or media themselves would have been much inclined to draw upon or to promote, (witness the reaction of the television establishment to the Glasgow Media Group's *Bad News* studies) or which could be seen to have 'insider' use value. One much-cited potential instance – the conceptualization within UNESCO during the 1970s of the New World Information and Communication Order (NWICO), and research related to this – sunk itself (and almost sunk UNESCO) in a futile effort to fuse together, in the 1978 'Mass Media Declaration', the two incompatible discourses of right-wing, U.S. backed media defence of a 'free flow' of information, and that of protagonists of a 'balanced flow', whose advocates were drawn from an alliance of left-bank UNESCO bureaucrats, academics, and government (as much as or more than media) spokesmen from the Third World (Nordenstreng, 1984). In another area of potential collaboration – educational television – broadcasters who dared to incorporate researchers and evaluators into production teams discovered that resources, time and production culture did not favour the responsiveness of production executives to the findings of formal evaluation (Bates, 1984).

This section begins with Snider's 1969 revisit to an earlier and classic 'gatekeeper' 1950 study by David Manning White. The premise underlying 'gatekeeper' studies was that to understand the selection of news it was necessary to identify those individuals within a news organization who have key roles in reviewing and selecting from incoming news. Given this premise, choice of the 'wire news editor' was a natural one in the context of small- to medium-sized metropolitan dailies in the U.S. which depended and still do depend heavily on the wire services or news agencies for their diet of international, national and even local news. The gatekeeper focus seems to have assumed that such individuals were likely to have personal views, attitudes and idiosyncrasies which could help explain the selections they made. While it is not unreasonable to want to know about the individuals who have responsibility for this kind of selection, as part of the process of developing our overall understanding of news construction and distribution, it is very important that such an approach does not marginalize the contexts within which the selection occurs. Such contexts include those that determine the profile and style of news that is made available to a newspaper (Snider, for example, does refer to broader changes in the competitive environment, including the reduction in the number of competing titles, and in the number of available news agency suppliers), and the degree of dependence of a newspaper on external as opposed to its own internal resources. Other contexts include: the immediate working environment (including factors of socialization which are explored by Warren Breed's classic newsroom study, in this section); the environment of news production as a whole – which includes the news-selection processes of the major news agencies, their competitors and other clients; professional ideologies, which define news values and news-gathering procedures; the symbiotic relationships between news sources and news media (already explored in yet an earlier classic, Rosten's 1937 study of Washington correspondents); the political economy of news media; and the general social and cultural environment.

Many studies suggest that such contexts have more explanatory power than is achieved by focusing solely on the work routines of individuals. Studies of the operations of news agencies (e.g. Boyd-Barrett, 1980), suggest very durable constancies in the profile and style of news supplied to different world-regions. Studies of news values, notably the classic study of Galtung and Ruge (1965), have identified underlying principles of news selection, shown to hold across many different media, different countries and different times. Galtung and Ruge hypothesized that news values would privilege negativity, recency, proximity, consonance (with the cultural values of readers), unambiguity, superlativeness (e.g. the bigger the better), personalization (i.e. news *people* matter more than news *issues*), élite persons, attribution (i.e. availability of a direct source for what is reported), facticity (e.g. events rather than processes or ideas). Bell (1991) has added to this list: continuity (i.e. an event which develops from stories that have already been reported and are therefore familiar to readers is more likely to be reported), competition (a news story has more value if other media also define it as news), co-option (e.g. a story from the national capital of a small country is more likely to be reported if there are already journalists visiting the capital to cover some larger story with more evident international implications), composition (e.g. a story is more likely to be chosen if it fits the overall style and genre-mix of a particular newspaper or news programme), predictability (which refers to the ease with which a story can be covered through established routines and sources), prefabrication (which refers to the availability of existing textual sources, whether printed or electronic, which will make a story easier to develop). Such hypotheses are relatively easy to test and offer powerful predictive yield.

But news values have to be explained as well as identified, both in terms of the immediate pragmatics of news coverage (several of Bell's news values are of this kind) or through analysis of the social and intellectual history of news and news gathering. Gans (1979) for example identifies the origins of (western) news values in small-town rural early nineteenth century America, background source of most big city journalists during the development of the U.S. mass circulation press. Other studies explore the influence of scientism (Schudson, 1978), the influence of the telegraph (Shaw, 1967) and other factors.

The 'gatekeeper' tradition has acquired a certain notoriety for its lack of attention to these broader and more powerful contextual factors. In common with many content analysis studies of its period, news is defined in terms of categories which, while they may be broadly meaningful are also deeply problematic. Not least of the problems is that of 'human interest', something of a residual category which nonetheless spans profound narratives, chronicling and symbolizing movements of taste, fashion and value, particularly related to family life, entertainment and consumption.

Breed's 1954 study of the newsroom was an important development from White's initial gatekeeper study, although it addressed a rather different set of questions, to do with apparent discrepancies between journalistic values and practices, and actual editorial policy. In explaining journalistic conformity in the absence of overt compulsion, Breed's approach was greatly influenced by Merton's (1957) functionalist, role-based sociology: individual behaviour is determined in large measure by group membership, learning of appropriate role-behaviour on entry to groups, and the continuing pressure of the expectations of fellow group-members. Breed looks at processes of socialization and at the factors which help to ensure that once they are socialized, journalists continue to fall in line: institutional authority and sanctions, feelings of obligation to and esteem for superiors, ambition, absence of conflicting group allegiances, intrinsic pleasure of the job, instrumentalist attitude to news. The study is based on interviews with journalists from different newspapers (as well as Breed's own newspaper experience). A study of this kind in the 1990s would be more likely to opt for an ethnographic approach, studying the everyday life of the newsroom through meticulous observation (much as Schlesinger did in his 1979 study of BBC news). Access to news organizations, however, can be difficult to achieve (many media organizations regretted their flirtations with researchers in the 1970s), and Breed's approach was at least do-able. One may query the extent to which such interviews, de-contextualized from actual newsrooms, without the support of observations or of interviews with senior managers, were subject to any inherent tendentiousness arising from Breed's application of a Mertonian functionalist framework and interpretation.

The work of Tunstall in this volume represents quite a different order of conceptual and methodological sophistication. Indeed, there is very little if anything to compare with it to this day in studies of media professionals, with the possible exceptions of the work of Cantor or of Tuchman, although these latter sources are not as daring, either in scope or in their application of theoretical frameworks.

Tunstall draws on the tradition of political communication introduced by Rosten, extending this to a range of different journalistic specialisms, retaining Mertonian functionalism but going further with it in looking at how specialist roles are influenced not just by their own 'reference groups' of fellow specialists (characterized by intriguing competitor–colleague ambivalencies) and their respective networks of news sources, but also by the different cultures of different news media, the different kinds of contribution which different specialisms make to news media (in terms of their relative importance to media for sales revenue, advertising revenue, or for 'prestige' goals) and by their part in a wider journalistic culture with common understanding of the relative status of different specialist groups within that culture. A significant revelation of the Tunstall study, by contrast with generations of journalistic memoirs which had preceded it, was the extent to which news was not an unpredictable and chaotic universe of events but was the steady and reliable prediction, preparation and routine management of 'institutionalized' news, a finding which has been confirmed in a number of succeeding studies (including Tuchman in this section; Schlesinger, 1978; Boyd-Barrett, 1980). The study by Elliott and Golding (1979) in this section, explored such processes of routinization comparatively, looking at broadcast news in three different countries. Among other things, this study locates news within its broader institutional contexts, here focusing particularly on the struggle of news departments against other claimants within media organizations for scarce resources.

In many ways, Tunstall's work on specialist correspondents prefigures that of Tuchman in this section whose concept of the 'news net' aptly systematized general features of news-gathering practice that could explain how news organizations, in collaboration with news sources, managed to 'routinize' the news, through such devices as the routine location of correspondents on key 'beats' and through territorial and organizational distribution of responsibilities. Tunstall (and Tuchman) were more concerned about news gathering, journalistic roles, and perceptions of the contributions of different kinds of news to news media, than about the detailed content of the news itself. Other sociological analysis tended to focus more on critiques of news and news gathering, and the chosen vehicle for analytical sophistication was increasingly that of critical theory. A seminal study by Halloran *et al.* (1970) looked at how newsmen's expectations of a news event framed their reporting and interpretation of the event, even though their initial expectations had not in fact been realized. This highlighted the importance of journalistic 'frames': events are interpreted in the light of previous events that are assumed to be comparable. The work of the Glasgow Media Group (1976) tended to focus yet more directly on the presentation and content of the news itself, demonstrating how the verbal and visual language of news events are framed by ideologies that favour the interests of the powerful and marginalize or render invisible the less powerful.

The work of Cantor extends from news studies such as those of Tunstall or Tuchman in this section, in as much as it reveals for the first time, on this scale [more recently Tunstall (1993), has completed a substantial study of television producers in the U.K.] how the creative forces that lie behind entertainment television are also the result of considerable (though flexible, and evolving) role-specialization, where roles have different degrees of power and are heavily but not absolutely constrained by the perceived discipline of commercial goals. Indeed, Cantor explores not only the constraints but also the opportunities which arise sometimes unexpectedly or from the accumulation of influence in the wake of earlier successes to allow for more 'creative' expression.

Just as in audience research, however, there is a clear trend in 1990s' production research away from the application of formal or abstract frameworks towards greater emphasis, through ethnographic method, on the perceptions of the participants themselves. This goes along with a reluctance to analyse the world through the ready-made categories of traditional sociological empiricism. The difference between Tunstall's work on journalists in 1971, and his work on television producers in 1993 is precisely this – the abandonment of Mertonian functionalism in favour of an approach which develops its categories largely in terms which the participants themselves would recognize, and which are grounded in the evidence of interview and observation. This new approach is particularly well represented in the work shown here of Morrison and Tumber on the coverage by U.K. journalists of the Falklands War, a study which is notable for the richness and depth of interview evidence from its journalist respondents. The extract here adopted is the introduction to the book, in which the authors indicate that they do not trust orthodox sociological analysis to depict the world in a manner which is both sensitive to structural determinants yet can come to terms with the world as it is lived and understood by the participants themselves. The motive is partly humanistic, but it has also a serious scientific purpose. This could be expressed as a return to more 'grounded' analysis, perhaps as a way of testing the validity of the thesis of 'news as the reproduction of dominant ideology' against the richness of everyday working life. It is difficult to contest the authors' argument that if we really want to understand news, then we have to look at news construction through the day-to-day minutiae of news gathering. Much the same message emerges from Bell's work (1991). Where Morrison and Tumber focus on the minutiae of news gathering in the context of a specific event, Bell focuses on the minutiae of news writing. The micro approach is fully vindicated by both studies, not so much because it challenges previous structural theories, but because it raises new and different kinds of question, and because it is scarcely possible for a reader to give these books serious attention without coming away from them with a sense of greatly enriched understanding.

As in the study of news and entertainment, so in the study of media history the 'ethnographic turn' has taken root, and what is increasingly seen to be important are not the orthodox histories of particular institutions and their regulatory environment (histories which are probably easier to relate because the relevant knowledge is well preserved), but the ways in which the working practices of media people were politically, socially, and culturally embedded, and how they interacted with the wider environment of sources and audiences. Scannell and Cardiff in this section look at the ways in which the early BBC broadcasters invented or developed practices from earlier traditions which contributed significantly, through the interweaving of events in programme schedules into a national clock and a national calendar, to both the cultural life of ordinary people on a day-to-day basis, and to the popular 'imagining' of the 'nation', an analysis which more convincingly than most establishes the contribution of media to national identity.

References and further reading

Bates, A. (1984) *Broadcasting in Education: an Evaluation*, Constable, London.

Bell, A. (1991) *The Language of News Media*, Basil Blackwell, Oxford.

Boyd-Barrett, O. (1980) *The International News Agencies*, Constable, London

Chibnall, S. (1977) *Law-and-Order News. An Analysis of Crime Reporting in the British Press*, Tavistock Publications, London.

Galtung, J. and Ruge, M. (1965) The structure of foreign news. *Journal of Peace Research*, Vol. 2, No. 1, pp. 64–91.

Gans, H (1979) *Deciding What's News*, Vintage Books, New York.

Glasgow Media Group (1976) *Bad News*, Routledge and Kegan Paul, London.

Halloran, J., Elliott, P. and Murdock, G. (1970) *Communications and Demonstrations*, Penguin, Harmondsworth.

Lasswell, H. (1948) The structure and function of communication in society. In Bryson (ed.) *The Communication of Ideas*, Harper, New York, pp. 32–51,

Merton, R. K. (1957) *Social Theory and Social Structure*, Free Press, Glencoe, IL.

Nordenstreng, K. (1984) *The Mass Media Declaration of UNESCO*, Ablex, Norwood, NJ.

Rosten, L. C. (1937) *The Washington Correspondents*, Harcourt Brace, New York.

Shaw, D. L. (1967) News bias and the telegraph. *Journalism Quarterly*, Vol. 44, No. 1, pp. 3–12

Schudson, M. (1978) *Discovering the News: A Social History of the News*, Basic Books, New York.

Schlesinger, Philip (1978) *Putting Reality Together*, Constable, London

Tunstall, Jeremy (1993) *The Television Producers*, Routledge, London.

White, David Manning (1950) The 'gate keeper': a case study in the selection of news. *Journalism Quarterly*, Vol. 27, pp. 383–90, Fall.

34

Social control in the newsroom: a functional analysis

Warren Breed

From Blackwell, G. and Jocher, K. (eds) (1955) *Social Forces*, The Williams and Wilkins Co. (for the University of North Carolina Press), Vol. 33, Nos 1–4, pp. 329–32, 335.

Reasons for conforming to policy

There is no one factor which creates conformity-mindedness, unless we resort to a summary term such as 'institutionalized statuses' or 'structural roles'. Particular factors must be sought in particular cases. The staffer must be seen in terms of his status and aspirations, the structure of the newsroom organization and of the larger society. He also must be viewed with reference to the operations he performs through his workday, and their consequences for him. The following six reasons appear to stay the potentially intransigent staffer from acts of deviance – often, if not always.[1]

1. Institutional authority and sanctions

The publisher ordinarily owns the paper and from a purely business standpoint has the right to expect obedience of his employees. He has the power to fire or demote for transgressions. This power, however, is diminished markedly in actuality by three facts. First, the newspaper is not conceived as a purely business enterprise, due to the protection of the First Amendment and a tradition of professional public service. Secondly, firing is a rare phenomenon on newspapers. For example, one editor said he had fired two men in 12 years; another could recall four firings in his 15 years on that paper. Thirdly, there are severance pay clauses in contracts with the American Newspaper Guild (CIO). The only effective causes for firing are excessive drunkenness, sexual dalliance, etc. Most newspaper unemployment apparently comes from occasional economy drives on large papers and from total suspensions of publication. Likewise, only one case of demotion was found in the survey. It is true, however, that staffers still fear punishment; the myth has the errant star reporter taken off murders and put on obituaries – 'the Chinese torture chamber' of the newsroom. Fear of sanctions, rather than their invocation, is a reason for conformity, but not as potent a one as would seem at first glance.

Editors, for their part, can simply ignore stories which might create deviant actions, and when this is impossible, can assign the story to a 'safe' staffer. In the infrequent case that an anti-policy story reaches the city desk, the story is changed; extraneous reasons, such as the pressure of time and space, are given for the change.[2] Finally, the editor may contribute to the durability of policy by insulating the publisher from policy discussions. He may reason that the publisher would be embarrassed to hear of conflict over policy and the resulting bias, and spare him the resulting uneasiness; thus the policy remains not only covert but undiscussed and therefore unchanged.[3]

2. Feelings of obligation and esteem for superiors

The staffer may feel obliged to the paper for having hired him. Respect, admiration and gratitude may be felt for certain editors who have perhaps schooled him, 'stood up for him', or supplied favours of a more paternalistic sort. Older staffers who have served as models for newcomers or who have otherwise given aid and comfort are due return courtesies. Such obligations and warm personal sentiments toward superiors play a strategic role in the pull to conformity.

3. Mobility aspirations

In response to a question about ambition, all the younger staffers showed wishes for status achievement. There was agreement that bucking policy constituted a serious bar to this goal. In practice, several respondents noted that a good tactic toward advancement was to get 'big' stories on page one; this automatically means no tampering with policy. Further, some staffers see newspapering as a 'stepping stone' job to more lucrative work: public relations, advertising, freelancing, etc. The reputation for troublemaking would inhibit such climbing.

A word is in order here about chances for upward mobility. Of 51 newsmen aged 35 or more, 32 were executives. Of 50 younger men, six had reached executive posts and others were on their way up with such jobs as wire editors, political reporters, etc. All but five of these young men were college graduates, as against just half of their elders. Thus there is no evidence of a 'break in the skill hierarchy' among newsmen.

4. Absence of conflicting group allegiance

The largest formal organization of staffers is the American Newspaper Guild. The Guild, much as it might wish to, has not interfered with internal matters such as policy. It has stressed business unionism and political interests external to the newsroom. As for informal groups, there is no evidence available that a group of staffers has ever 'ganged up' on policy.

5. The pleasant nature of the activity

(a) *In-groupness in the newsroom.* The staffer has a low formal status *vis-à-vis* executives, but he is not treated as a 'worker'. Rather, he is a co-worker with executives; the entire staff cooperates congenially on a job they all like and respect: getting the news. The newsroom is a friendly, first-namish place. Staffers discuss stories with editors on a give-and-take basis. Top executives with their own offices sometimes come out and sit in on newsroom discussions.[4]

(b) *Required operations are interesting.* Newsmen like their work. Few voiced complaints when given the opportunity to gripe during interviews. The operations required – witnessing, interviewing, briefly mulling the meanings of events, checking facts, writing – are not onerous.

(c) *Non-financial perquisites.* These are numerous: the variety of experience, eye-witnessing significant and interesting events, being the first to know, getting 'the inside dope' denied laymen, meeting and sometimes befriending notables and celebrities (who are well advised to treat newsmen with deference). Newsmen are close to big decisions without having to make them; they touch power without being responsible for its use. From talking with newsmen and reading their books, one gets the impression that they are proud of being newsmen.[5] There are tendencies to exclusiveness within news ranks, and intimations that such near out-groups as radio newsmen are entertainers, not real newsmen. Finally, there is the satisfaction of being a member of a live-wire organization dealing with important matters. The newspaper is an 'institution' in the community. People talk about it and quote it; its big trucks whiz through town; its columns carry the tidings from big and faraway places, with pictures.

Thus, despite his relatively low pay, the staffer feels, for all these reasons, an integral part of a going concern. His job morale is high. Many newsmen could qualify for jobs paying more money in advertising and public relations, but they remain with the newspaper.

6. News becomes a value

Newsmen define their job as producing a certain quantity of what is called 'news' every 24 hours. This is to be produced even though nothing much has happened. News is a continuous challenge, and meeting this challenge is the newsman's job. He is rewarded for fulfilling this, his manifest function. A consequence of this focus on news as a central value is the shelving of a strong interest in objectivity at the point of policy conflict. Instead of mobilizing their efforts to establish objectivity over policy as the criterion for performance, their energies are channelled into getting more news. The demands of competition (in cities where there are two or more papers) and speed enhance this focus. Newsmen do talk about ethics, objectivity, and the relative worth of various papers, but not when there is news to get. News comes first, and there is always news to get.[6] They are not rewarded for analysing the social structure, but for getting news. It would seem that this instrumental orientation diminishes their moral potential. A further consequence of this pattern is that the harmony between staffers and executives is cemented by their common interest in news. Any potential conflict between the two groups, such as slowdowns occurring among informal work groups in industry, would be dissipated to the extent that news is a positive value. The newsroom solidarity is thus reinforced.

The six factors promote policy conformity. To state more exactly how policy is maintained would be difficult in view of the many variables contained in the system. The process may be somewhat better understood, however, with the introduction of one further concept – the reference group.[7] The staffer, especially the new staffer, identifies himself through the existence of these six factors with the executives and veteran staffers. Although not yet one of them, he shares their norms, and thus his performance comes to resemble theirs. He conforms to the norms of policy rather than to whatever personal beliefs he brought to the job, or to ethical ideals. All six of these factors function to encourage reference group formation. Where the allegiance is directed toward legitimate authority, that authority has only to maintain the equilibrium within limits by the prudent distribution of rewards and punishments. The reference group itself, which has as its 'magnet' element the élite of executives and old staffers, is unable to change policy to a marked degree because first, it is the group charged with carrying out policy, and second, because the policy maker, the publisher, is often insulated on the delicate issue of policy.

In its own way, each of the six factors contributes to the formation of reference group behaviour. There is almost no firing, hence a steady expectation of continued employment. Subordinates tend to esteem their bosses, so a convenient model group is present. Mobility aspirations (when held within limits) are an obvious promoter of inter-status bonds as is the absence of conflicting group loyalties with their potential harvest of cross pressures. The newsroom atmosphere is charged with the related factors of in-groupness and pleasing nature of the work. Finally, the agreement among newsmen that their job is to fasten upon the news, seeing it as a value in itself, forges a bond across status lines.

As to the six factors, five appear to be relatively constant, occurring on all papers studied. The varying factor is the second: obligation and esteem held by staffers for executive and older staffers. On some papers, this obligation–esteem entity was found to be larger than on others. Where it was large, the paper appeared to have two characteristics pertinent to this discussion. First, it did a good conventional job of news getting and news publishing, and second, it had little difficulty over policy. With staffers drawn toward both the membership and the reference groups, organization was efficient. Most papers are like this. On the few smaller papers where executives and older staffers are not respected, morale is spotty; staffers withhold enthusiasm from their stories, they cover their beats perfunctorily, they wish for a job on a better paper, and they are apathetic and sometimes hostile to policy. Thus the obligation–esteem factor seems to be the active variable in determining not only policy conformity, but morale and good news performance as well.
[. . .]

Summary

The problem, which was suggested by the age-old charges of bias against the press, focused around the manner in which the publisher's policy came to be followed, despite three empirical conditions: (1) policy sometimes contravenes journalistic norms; (2) staffers often personally disagree with it; and (3) executives cannot legitimately command that policy be followed. Interview and other data were used to explain policy maintenance. It is important to recall that the discussion is based primarily on study of papers of 'middle' circulation range, and does not consider either non-policy stories or the original policy decision made by the publishers. The mechanisms for learning policy on the part of the new staffer were given, together with suggestions as to the nature of social controls. Six factors, apparently the major variables producing policy maintenance, were described. The most significant of these variables, obligation and esteem for superiors, was deemed not only the most important, but the most fluctuating variable from paper to paper. Its existence and its importance for conformity led to the sub-hypothesis that reference group behaviour was playing a part in the pattern. To show, however, that policy is not iron clad, five conditions were suggested in which staffers may by-pass policy.

Thus we conclude that the publisher's policy, when established in a given subject area, is usually followed, and that a description of the dynamic socio-cultural situation of the newsroom will suggest explanations for this conformity. The newsman's source of rewards is located not among the readers, who are manifestly his clients, but among his colleagues and superiors. Instead of adhering to societal and professional ideals, he re-defines his values to the more pragmatic level of the newsroom group. He thereby gains not only status rewards, but also acceptance in a solidary group engaged in interesting, varied, and sometimes important work. Thus the cultural patterns of the newsroom produce results insufficient for wider democratic needs. Any important change toward a more 'free and responsible press' must stem from various possible pressures on the publisher, who epitomises the policy making and coordinating rôle.

Notes

1. Two cautions are in order here. First, it will be recalled that we are discussing not all news, but only policy news. Secondly, we are discussing only staffers who are potential non-conformers. Some agree with policy; some have no views on policy matters; others do not write policy stories. Furthermore, there are strong forces in American society which cause many individuals to choose harmonious adjustment (conformity) in any situation, regardless of the imperatives. See Fromm, Erich (1941) *Escape From Freedom*, Farrar and Rinehart, New York, and Riesman, David (1950) *The Lonely Crowd*, Yale, New Haven.
2. Excellent illustration of this tactic is given in the novel by an experienced newspaperwoman: Long, Margaret (1953) *Affair of the Heart*, Random House, New York, Chapter. 10. This chapter describes the framing of a Negro for murder in a middle-sized southern city, and the attempt of a reporter to tell the story objectively.
3. The insulation of one individual or group from another is a good example of social (as distinguished from psychological) mechanisms to reduce the likelihood of conflict. Most of the factors inducing conformity could likewise be viewed as social mechanisms. See Parsons, Talcott and Shils, Edward A. (1951) Values, motives and systems of action. In Parsons and Shils (eds) *Toward a General Theory of Action*, Harvard University Press, Cambridge, MA, pp. 223–30.
4. Further indication that the staffer–executive relationship is harmonious came from

answers to the question, 'Why do you think newspapermen are thought to be cynical?'. Staffers regularly said that newsmen are cynical because they get close enough to stark reality to see the ills of their society, and the imperfections of its leaders and officials. Only two, of 40 staffers, took the occasion to criticize their executives and the enforcement of policy. This displacement, or lack of strong feelings against executives, can be interpreted to bolster the hypothesis of staff solidarity. (It further suggests that newsmen tend to analyse their society in terms of personalities, rather than institutions comprising a social and cultural system.)

5. There is a sizeable myth among newsmen about the attractiveness of their calling. For example, the story: 'Girl: "My, you newspapermen must have a fascinating life. You meet such interesting people". Reporter: "Yes, and most of them are newspapermen" '. For a further discussion, see Breed, Warren (1952) The newspaperman, news and society, Ph.D. dissertation, Columbia University, Chapter 17.

6. This is a variant of the process of 'displacement of goals', newsmen turning to 'getting news' rather than to seeking data which will enlighten and inform their readers. The dysfunction is implied in the nation's need not for more news but for better news – quality rather than quantity. See Merton, Robert K. (1949) Bureaucratic structure and personality. In *Social Theory and Social Structure*, Free Press, Glencoe, pp. 151–5.

7. Whether group members acknowledge it or not, 'if a person's attitudes are influenced by a set of norms which he assumes that he shares with other individuals, those individuals constitute for him a reference group'. Newcomb, Theodore M. (1950) *Social Psychology*, Dryden, New York, p. 225. Williams states that reference group formation may segment large organizations; in the present case, the reverse is true, the loyalty of subordinates going to their 'friendly' superiors and to the discharge of technical norms such as getting news. See Williams, Robin M. (1951) *American Society*, Knopf, New York, p. 476.

35

'Mr Gates' revisited: a 1966 version of the 1949 case study

Paul B. Snider

From Emery, E. (ed.) (1967) *Journalism Quarterly*, Association for
Education in Journalism, Iowa City, Vol. 44, No. 3 pp. 419–21, 425–7.

In probably the first study of its kind, 'The "gate keeper": a case study in
the selection of news' (*Journalism Quarterly*, Vol. 27, pp. 383–90, Fall, 1950),
David Manning White asked the telegraph editor of a mid-west morning
newspaper to save unused wire copy for a week and to indicate on each
story why it was not used. The results were then measured and analysed
by White in 'terms of certain basic questions which presented themselves'.

That pioneer investigation has posed more questions than it has answered.

It was our purpose to replicate the White study as faithfully as possible
in an attempt to determine whether 17 years has changed Mr Gates' attitude
toward news.

There have been several changes in the production of Mr Gates' newspaper
which have injected limitations into this study.

Unchanged is the fact that Mr Gates is still the telegraph editor of the same
morning newspaper. The circulation of the morning edition has increased
about 10,000 to approximately 40,000, and the population of what White terms
the 'highly industrialized mid-west city' has increased from 100,000 to 130,000.

One of the major limitations stems from the fact that the two daily
newspapers in the city merged into a single ownership when the evening
paper ownership assumed control in 1954, five years after White's study.
About 1957 the Saturday morning and evening editions were combined into
a single Saturday morning edition and some time later it was decreed that
stories which had been played in the Friday evening paper were not to be
carried in the Saturday morning combined edition unless there was a new
lead or a second day story. As Mr Gates told the author, 'This gimmick
prevents duplication for p.m. readers but doesn't help those a.m.
subscribers'. Therefore Mr Gates was able only to comment upon four
editions in this study since his use or non-use of Saturday stories was predetermined by the evening edition telegraph editor.

The morning edition now receives only the Associated Press. At the time
of the original study, Mr Gates had the full services of International News
Service, United Press and Associated Press from which to choose.

The paper has a smaller news hole today, running consistently with a
65–35% to 68–32% ratio of advertising to news content as compared to a
60–40% ratio during the initial study. In addition; during the period of this

study Mr Gates 'lost' about 35 column inches on page one daily to a camera feature which showed area soldiers on duty in Vietnam. The pictures were made in Vietnam by a staff photographer.

Another limitation is evident in that there are fewer editions today and therefore there are fewer opportunities for Mr Gates to replace and to substitute stories. During the initial study there were five editions daily of the morning newspaper; today there are three daily morning editions. Mr Gates also has fewer assistants today and does more of the work himself.

In 1949 the opposing newspaper presented the major competitive threat; radio and television news were just not considered serious competition. Today there still is some competition between the staffs of the morning and evening editions, but in many news areas one 'beat' reporter covers stories for both the morning and evening newspapers. Recognizing that broadcast news has greater immediacy, Mr Gates strives to produce a product which tells more of the story. Television news still is not considered real competition.

There are later deadlines and faster processes today which enable Mr Gates to insert more up-to-the-minute stories than in 1949.

A contradiction and a limitation are evident in comparing figures from the five issues put out by Mr Gates in 1966 with the figures for seven days' issues in 1949. Mr Gates says he worked six days a week during 1949, yet White implies Mr Gates worked and saved copy for seven days in 1949.

That there was a three-month strike in 1957 to obtain a contract between the American Newspaper Guild and the newspaper must be considered a limitation. A paring down of editorial personnel followed the settlement. Mr Gates was not affected materially but he is an ardent Guildsman; if there is any effect of his unionism upon his news judgement, it must be considered out of the scope of this study.

And the final limitation must be obvious: Mr Gates is 17 years older, and his ulcer 'acts' up a bit more; undoubtedly some of his views have changed over the years. His newspaper is under different management, the community has changed, and the whole outlook of the world is different – how much is not known.
[. . .]

In keeping with the concept of replicating the original study, Mr Gates was asked the same questions posed by White upon completion of his study. When Mr Gates heard White's first question – he did not recall them – he asked for a clarification. Mr Gates wanted to know what White meant by 'categories' in the question 'Does the category of news affect your choice of news stories?'. The author of this study attempted to describe the system used by White, as he understood it. Mr Gates said he'd never thought about news in those categories. His question and comment appear significant in that White asked that subsequent studies seek to answer the question 'Does the category really enter into the choice? That is does the wire editor try to choose a certain amount of crime news, human interest news, etc.?'. Mr Gates' response to the question would seem to indicate that categorizing the news in such a fashion was a foreign concept, at least to him.

White's four original questions were re-submitted to Mr Gates and his answers sought. One additional question was added to the list, i.e. 'How would you define "news"?'. His answers follow:

1. *Does the category of news affect your choice of news stories?*
A. 'Assuming the category of news means classification or grouping of news, I would say that there is an effect on the choice of news stories. It permits one to skim off the cream, and to select stories that relate to local situations. However, wire services do not classify news generally. This is done by the wire editor. The only grouping is in the case of elections, and here again, the wire editor uses only the top stories with others of interest thrown in as back up for an election edition. Classification of news by the editor permits the merger of stories as well as the combination of news through use of inserts and follows.'

(Parenthetically the author must note that Mr Gates has his wire news grouped in broad subject areas on his desk with like stories and related side-bars all together. This may mean 'categories' ' to him.)

2. *Do you feel that you have any prejudices which may affect your choice of news stories?*
A. 'Prejudice in news is a constant battle and I feel I have it won as long as I can come up with 'equal space' and 'play.' I have had to overcome some personal feelings as far as politics and religion are concerned by the 'equal' treatment. One should be strictly neutral and I feel that I am neutral.'
3. *What is your concept of the audience for whom you select stories and what sort of person do you conceive the average person to be?*
A. 'The audience for which I select stories is as varied as the areas the paper reaches. There are business people, professional people, educators and the educated, church people and partisans. In the whole there are those with limited education, headline readers, and those who can't repeat what they've read. I would hope the average person has a high school education and is able to read and understand what is going on.'
4. *Do you have any specific tests of subject matter or way of writing that help you determine the selection of any particular news story?*
A. 'One specific test in the selection of news is that old yardstick of "does the story hit the reader in the stomach or pocketbook?". Another test is timeliness of news. I do not apply tests as such to news selections but do heed timeliness because of competition and the need for 'new' news. Selections seem to be automatic because I am not conscious of a "test".'
5. *How would you define 'news'?*
A. 'News is the day by day report of events and personalities and comes in variety which should be presented as much as possible in variety for a balanced diet.'

Conclusions

How has Mr Gates changed since 1949, if indeed he has changed?

In 1949 Mr Gates used more human interest material (23.2%) than any other type of story followed by national politics (15.8%), international politics

(13.6%), state politics (6.8%), national farm (6.0%) and international war (5.6%). These six categories accounted for 71% of all stories used.

In 1966 Mr Gates' leading category was international war (17.7%), followed by crime (16.8%), national economics (13.6%), human interest (13.6%) and disaster (10.3%). In this year, five categories accounted for 72% of all the stories used. There would appear to be a more even spread of usage among the various categories in the second study than in the first.

The only two categories to be represented in the top 71% of both studies are 'human interest' and 'international war', although their positions vary greatly from one study to the other. It would be the opinion of the author that the position of 'crime' as number two in the second study was a transient thing brought about by the appearance of two top crime stories of the week studied – the Dr Sheppard case and the Valerie Percy inquest.

The question must be asked, however, whether the positions of 'crime' and 'international war' in any fashion reflect the spate of violence being thrust upon the American public primarily through the medium of television. Obviously the 'international war' category results from the Vietnam news; in 1949 the United States was not involved in a shooting war. Mr Gates is not exposed to as much visual violence as many other Americans because he is at work from 6 p.m. until 2 a.m. five nights a week; however, he does not work Saturday and Sunday nights and on those evenings there are still many television programmes on which bodies abound. Mr Gates does not read many books and attends few movies.

Further study is recommended of the old, familiar news factors of proximity, timeliness. prominence, etc., to determine whether they are in fact still valid or whether they are anachronisms of the Pulitzer–Hearst era of journalism. In other words, what convenient pedagogical concepts of telegraph news, indeed of all news, long since discarded by practising newsmen, are still retained as good tools by journalism researchers?

The intervening years and the effect of these years on Mr Gates and upon his newspaper, plus the differences between the interviewers, may have indicated or at least confirmed some trends in today's newspapers.

Mr Gates still picks the stories he likes and believes his readers want. By and large, his 1949 answers to the questions asked are consistent with his 1966 answers. He likes to gather the wire copy in broad classifications as a convenient method of scanning, selecting and consolidating; he does not consciously try to fill any quota, real or imagined, for any particular category. Where in 1949 he chose the best written story from one of the three wire services, today he has but one choice and must do more editing if he dislikes the copy he receives and wants to use the story.

The press of today, if this gatekeeper is any gauge, generally is more concerned with 'hard' news than it was 17 years ago. Today Mr Gates uses fewer human interest stories than he did in 1949 but such stories still rank high with him, being tied for third place in percentage of usage. He uses more international war news.

Both the wire service and Mr Gates produce better balanced products in 1966 than they did in 1949.

36

Specialist correspondents: goals, careers, roles

Jeremy Tunstall

From Tunstall, J. (1971) *Journalists at Work*, Constable, London, pp. 106–14.

Roles and goals: autonomy and control

Work roles, status and tension

A number of factors already discussed might be expected to produce differences in self-perceived status – not only as between the work role and life outside work, but also between different roles within the specialist's working life. Firstly, career insecurity is likely to differ between fields. Secondly, the different goals predominating within different specialist fields can be expected to carry strong status implications. Thirdly, each specialist operates at work within a tripartite division of work roles. Each specialist is:

1. an *employee* (of an organization which itself has advertising, audience and non-revenue goals);
2. a *specialist gatherer* of news from news sources;
3. a *competitor–colleague* within a group of specialists covering the same field for other news organizations.

When specialists are asked about their own status, they do recognize differences between their status in different work roles. All the selected specialists collectively say they see themselves as having their highest status (2.24 or just above 'fairly high') in the specialist news-gatherer role; they see their next highest status in the role of employee of their own news organization (1.97); next comes their status within British national journalism (1.87); and lowest by a substantial margin is their status as a private citizen (1.53). There is also a remarkable consistency through nearly all the fields in seeing the specialist *news-gatherer* role as conferring the highest status, and the private *citizen role* as the lowest.[1]

Specialists say that they experience only fairly low levels of tension; the main finding for all fields combined is:

1. most tension is experienced by specialists in dealings with *news executives* and desks[2] (0.85);
2. second, come dealings with *sources and contacts* (0.62);
3. least tension is experienced in dealing with *competitor–colleagues* in the same field (0.46).

The specialists indicate that the strongest tensions come not from dealings with important news sources, and not from face-to-face and day-to-day competition with competitor–colleagues, but from the way in which competitive and other pressures are channelled through the news organization. Some of these are normal news pressures of time and space; others depend on personalities and processing:

> Very few middle range executives have any useful recent practical experience.

> There is an alarming lack of team work inside newspaper offices in the Street. Everybody seems too concerned with protecting his own interests all the time.

> Tension with news executives results from an indeterminate power structure and different news interests; with sources and contacts because one's interests are different and sometimes opposed.

> The answer here clearly depends upon which executive one is dealing with. I have no problems (and therefore no tension) with some; but with less competent executives tension arises depending on their rank.'

> The editor is a fascist bastard.

All three roles potentially involve specialists in conflict. Loyalty to a news executive may involve a specialist in conflict with a news source or a competitor–colleague; loyalty to a news source may involve conflict with the news desk – and so on. However, within the competitor–colleague role specialists may be able, to some extent, to defend themselves from, and to cushion themselves against, the conflicting interests of news executives and news sources.

Specialists were asked whether they regarded themselves 'primarily as a specialist covering this field' or 'primarily as a journalist working for my present organization'. The following percentages chose the *specialist* alternative:

Foreign specialists	28
Political	66
Mixed	42
Audience	54
Advertising	46
All selected specialists	46
($N = 192$)	

The foreign correspondents tended to interpret the question in terms of their present foreign posting rather than of foreign correspondence in general. But between other fields there are noticeable differences; in particular the high status political lobby correspondents are especially likely to see themselves as *political* first and journalists second.

Status of particular specialist fields

The occupational pecking order is inversely related to the revenue goal emphasis in particular fields. When specialists are asked about other specialist fields, they do indeed have the lowest opinion of motoring specialists (Table

36.1). Labour correspondents come out well above the other mixed goal fields; below these in the opinion of other specialists are the audience goal fields. Table 36.2 lists (using the same scoring system as in Table 36.1) the opinions of the field in capital letters about the other fields. There is great consistency in the foreign and political correspondents being most highly thought of; moreover, motoring correspondents are the least highly thought of by every other specialist field.

The specialists in general push their own fields up a few places in the pecking order. Motoring and football correspondents push themselves up two places; crime correspondents immodestly push themselves up five places; labour and education both up two places; aviation goes up from fourth equal to third; political lobby up one place. The Washington men are unusual in placing foreign correspondents in only fourth place (possibly on the assumption that they themselves are superior to the general run of foreign correspondents); but all the foreign correspondents collectively place themselves second to the political lobby men.

Despite a certain amount of immodesty about themselves, the specialists still acknowledge a status order which accords the highest status to non-revenue foreign correspondence, followed by the political lobby, the

Table 36.1. Specialists' opinions about other specialist fields

Opinion held about these fields	Opinion held by these specialists					
	Foreign	Political	Mixed	Audience	Advertising	All
Foreign	—	2.2	2.1	2.5	2.2	2.27
Political lobby	2.1	—	2.3	2.2	2.1	2.20
Mixed:						
Aviation	1.6	1.5	—	1.6	1.8	1.61
Education	1.7	1.3	—	1.6	2.1	1.61
Labour	2.0	2.4	—	2.1	2.0	2.14
Audience:						
Crime	1.6	1.2	1.3	—	1.7	1.44
Football	1.6	1.2	1.2	—	1.7	1.40
Advertising:						
Motoring*	1.2	0.8	0.8	1.0	—	0.96 (N = 171)

*Unfortunately no question about fashion correspondents was included in the questionnaire.

Note: This table is based on the mean for each field using this scoring system:

Low opinion	0
Medium opinion	1
Fairly high opinion	2
High opinion	3

Table 36.2

WASHINGTON		NEW YORK		BONN/ROME	
Pol. lobby	(1.9)	*Foreign*	(2.3)	Pol. lobby	(2.2)
Education	(1.9)	Pol. lobby	(2.2)	*Foreign*	(2.0)
Labour	(1.9)	Labour	(2.2)	Labour	(2.0)
Foreign	(1.7)	Crime	(1.8)	Crime	(1.6)
Aviation	(1.5)	Aviation	(1.7)	Aviation	(1.5)
Football	(1.5)	Education	(1.7)	Education	(1.5)
Crime	(1.3)	Football	(1.7)	Football	(1.5)
Motoring	(0.9)	Motoring	(1 4)	Motoring	(1.2)

POL. LOBBY		AVIATION		EDUCATION	
Pol. lobby	(2.4)	Pol. Lobby	(2.4)	Foreign	(2.3)
Labour	(2.2)	Labour	(2.2)	Pol. lobby	(2.2)
Foreign	(2.2)	*Aviation*	(2.0)	*Education*	(2.2)
Aviation	(1.5)	Foreign	(1.9)	Labour	(2.0)
Education	(1.3)	Education	(1.9)	Aviation	(1.8)
Crime	(1.2)	Crime	(1.4)	Crime	(1.3)
Football	(1.2)	Football	(1.2)	Football	(1.2)
Motoring	(0.8)	Motoring	(0.8)	Motoring	(0.6)

LABOUR		CRIME		FOOTBALL	
Labour	(2.6)	*Crime*	(2.6)	Foreign	(2.5)
Pol. lobby	(2 3)	Pol. lobby	(2.5)	Pol. lobby	(2.1)
Foreign	(2.2)	Foreign	(2.4)	Labour	(2.0)
Crime	(2.2)	Labour	(2.4)	Crime	(2.0)
Football	(2.2)	Aviation	(1.7)	*Football*	(1.9)
Education	(2.0)	Education	(1.6)	Education	(1.6)
Aviation	(1.9)	Football	(1.5)	Aviation	(1.5)
Motoring	(1.0)	Motoring	(1.0)	Motoring	(1.0)

FASHION		MOTORING	
Foreign	(2.7)	Foreign	(2.1)
Education	(2.7)	Pol. Lobby	(2.1)
Pol. Lobby	(2.0)	Labour	(2.1)
Crime	(2.0)	Aviation	(1.9)
Football	(1.8)	Education	(1.9)
Labour	(1.6)	*Motoring*	(1.8)
Aviation	(1.5)	Crime	(1.6)
Motoring	(1.2)	Football	(1.6)

mixed fields, then the audience fields; the motoring correspondents have a lower relative opinion of themselves than does any other field about itself.

Fields by goal type

The non-revenue goal of foreign correspondence is reflected in the opinion of other specialists – who see this field as very low on both advertising and audience interest. Foreign correspondents are concentrated in the news agency

(Reuters) and quality newspapers. This field provides both the longest career ladder of all the selected fields, and also the most precocious careers; foreign correspondents have finished formal education later and started national specialization earlier. They have also worked for unusually few news organizations both before and after specialization. A foreign correspondent's career often started by his being sent in his mid- or late-twenties to cover a war. Next a typical posting is to a junior job in one of the bigger bureaux, such as New York or Paris.

Foreign correspondents in general were highly thought of by other specialists. They seem securely entrenched in their careers. There is a definite career ladder leading from one capital to another and there are jobs in London on the Foreign desk. Yet the very presence of a career ladder induces insecurity among foreign correspondents because moves on the ladder mean moving house, wife, children's schools, local language, and entire way of life. The risk of marriage breakdown was quoted by many foreign correspondents. The danger of losing touch with the British audience is known to be discussed by news executives in London. Some foreign correspondents seem slightly forlorn, aware that they are in a much desired job, which can be another source of insecurity – a sense that able younger men are waiting in the wings. The approach of retirement may also present special problems for foreign correspondents who have lived most of their adult lives abroad.

The political lobby correspondents are similar to the Foreign specialists in present age, long duration in the field and high esteem in the eyes of other specialists; but lobby men overall differ in having had substantially shorter formal education, much more provincial newspaper and non-London early careers, and much higher job mobility both before and after specialization. Lobby correspondents are the only specialists to see their status as equally high in the news-gatherer and employee roles; also reflecting the unusual status and delicacy of lobby correspondence, these specialists emphasize that they are political correspondents first and journalists only second. Two types of contrasted lobby careers might be: (1) the non privileged career: leave school at 15; messenger boy; reporter on provincial daily; Press Association debate notetaker, and then number three national lobby correspondent; (2) the privileged career: Oxford degree; reporter on national; foreign correspondent; and then number one national lobby correspondent. In practice many lobby careers are a mixture of the two types.

The lobby is unusual in that its high status and the value placed by editors on scarce access to the lobby lead to a high proportion of correspondents having had other previous specialist experience. It is also unusual in providing a relatively long career ladder – from lobby man on a small provincial to the chief political correspondent of a national news organization. Lobby men see their work as especially demanding in terms of energy and the long late hours at Westminster. It is the great volume of detail and the pace of lobby work which produces unease – and leads some lobby men to think that almost any other sort of journalism including television work, with its much shorter stories and less detail, would be less demanding.

Consistent with the classification of *aviation, education and labour as mixed goal fields*, the background characteristics of correspondents in these three fields exhibit overall a pattern similar to that of all the selected specialists combined. *Aviation* correspondence is seen by other specialists as having a stronger element of advertising goal than the other mixed fields. Aviation correspondents, indeed, are similar to the motoring men in lowish formal education, and an unusually long time-gap between entry to journalism and ultimate national specialization. *Education* correspondents are much younger and have had more precocious careers. More education correspondents are university educated and more started on *daily* newspapers; in the shorter period of time they also made more job moves before specialization. Education is extreme in the short average duration of specialists in the field; the field is relatively new and of lowish status. Some young education correspondents see this field as a stepping stone to higher things. *Labour* correspondents are another relatively highly educated group. They also have a solid background on weekly papers – but some jumped straight from this to a much bigger news organization. Labour is a youngish field, but a third of the specialists have specialized in another field previously – a further indication of the fairly high status of this field.

Collectively these fields in the estimation of specialists in general occupy an intermediate level of status, below foreign and political correspondents but superior in esteem to the revenue fields. Of the three mixed goal fields labour is held in the highest esteem. Among the mixed goal fields, education, the most junior, is also the one with the most secure and comfortable feeling of riding on a growing wave. The highest status of the mixed fields, labour, whilst believed to be a passport to higher things in journalism, is regarded by the specialists in it (as well as by some news executives) as the physically most demanding and uncomfortable of all the specialist fields. There is a widespread attitude among labour correspondents that this is not something to make a lifetime's work.

Audience goal: Crime and Football. Among *Football* correspondents a few have previously been professional footballers. Three sorts of journalism experience are found to a greater extent here than in any other specialist field; these are experience as news executives often as sports editor of a London suburban paper; secondly experience in a news agency; thirdly these specialists often have had national sub-editing experience. Just as Football correspondents have had an especially close connection with their subject-matter, so also have *crime* correspondents; it is not unusual for a crime specialist to have a close relative who is a policeman. In the careers of both crime and football men specialized Fleet Street news agencies have been especially important. Both are extreme in low formal education; both were especially likely to have started in the south of England. Both crime and football specialisms are unlikely to lead on to any other kind of specialist journalism. Both crime and football are held in low esteem by specialists in other fields. Both fields regard their news sources as exceptionally unhelpful and both are pessimistic about the future. Football correspondents worry about growing older and out of touch with the young players, they believe that a number of the previous generation of football writers became alcoholics, and they do not welcome the prospect of sports executive jobs. The crime correspondents also profess much gloom about the decline of Crime news, the difficulty of getting young men into the field, and the lack of graduate crime correspondents.

Advertising goal: Fashion and Motoring. The representative fashion correspondent is a woman, who started extremely young in fashion specialization and has never worked in the British provinces. In contrast to all other specialists in the present study, the fashion correspondent typically not only started her career in London but also in a specialized job. The career beginnings of the motoring correspondents could scarcely have been more different. Most motoring correspondents had followed a very non-precocious provincial career route – low formal education and early age of entry to journalism, usually on a weekly paper; Motoring correspondents had also experienced considerable job mobility before unusually late specialization.

Nevertheless the two fields have much else in common. They both, at least partially, acknowledged the existence of the advertising goal. Both sets of specialists report unusually low levels of tension with news sources. In both cases the general view of their future prospects is much different from the audience goal fields. Both fashion and motoring correspondents have been in their fields for an unusually brief time, and both have the prospect of being offered public relations jobs with former news sources.

Implications for autonomy and control

Four general points emerge from this chapter. Firstly one cannot assume all specialists to be working under the same constraints. Secondly career patterns and previous experience of specialist journalists differ considerably between individuals and between fields. Thirdly a specialist journalist operates within three distinct work roles. Fourthly, specialists are attributed differing status according to their field, and specialists see themselves as having differing statuses within their different work roles.

Notes

1. These are means for all selected specialists ($N = 192$) based on this scoring system: Low status = 0; medium = 1; fairly high = 2; high = 3.
2. These are means for all specialists ($N = 190$) based on this scoring system: None = 0; a little = 1; a certain amount = 2; much tension = 3.

37

The news net

Gaye Tuchman

From Mack, A. (ed.) (1978) *Social Research*, New School for Social
Research, New York, Vol. 45, No. 2, pp. 256–66.

News blanket or news net?

There is a significant difference between the ability of a blanket and that
of a net to gather fodder for daily newspaper columns and television air
time. Each arrangement may capture fresh information daily, thus confirming
and reinforcing the old adage 'old news is no news'. But a net has holes.
Its ability to trap is dependent upon the amount invested in intersecting
fibre and the tensile strength of that fibre. The narrower the intersections
between the mesh – the more blanket-like the net – the more can be captured.
Of course, designing a more expensive narrow mesh presupposes a desire
to catch small fish, not a wish to throw them back into the flow of amorphous
everyday occurrences.

Today's news net is intended for big fish. Today's news media place
reporters at legitimated institutions where stories supposedly appealing to
contemporary news consumers may be expected to be found. In New York,
these locations include Municipal Court, police headquarters, the Federal
Court, and City Hall, where reporters' daily rounds bring them into contact
with official meetings, press releases, and official documents such as the
calendar of the Board of Estimate. The gleanings of reporters stationed there
and at similar locations are supplemented by monitoring the police and fire
department's radio dispatches and by assigning other reporters, based in
the main office, to follow activities of such legitimated organizations as the
Board of Education, the Welfare Department, and the Metropolitan Transit
Authority. Significantly, all these organizations maintain files of centralized
information at least partially assembled for reporters' use. Equally
significant, placement of reporters at these locations and assignment of these
responsibilities reaffirm and reinforce these organizations' public legitimacy:
Occurrences are more likely to be defined as news when reporters witness
them or can learn of them with little effort.[1]

The news net is refined by attenuating reportorial responsibility and
economic reward. The metropolitan media hire stringers to alert them to
occurrences in more specialized organizations, such as local colleges, and
in geographic areas of limited but clear circulation value, such as suburbs.[2]
The name 'stringer' connotes an attenuated relationship to the news net,
even as it reaffirms the imagery of the net or web. Finally, the net is
electronically augmented. The wire services link the newsroom to other

geographic areas. Telephone cables link affiliates to a network's newsroom and nightly supplies of fresh stories (called 'feeds') that will not be aired on the network's evening news. Telephone cables also link far-flung bureaux to the newsroom, enabling instant transmission of typed and edited copy. (The actual transmission time is three minutes per page.) The linkages may overlap. For instance, New York dailies maintain Washington bureaux whose work is supplemented by wire-service reports.

Supposedly, this arrangement of intersecting fine mesh (the stringers), tensile strength (the reporters), and steel links (the wire services) provides a news blanket, insuring that all potential news will be found. But the wire services and the news media duplicate one another's efforts rather than offer substantive alternatives. News media send reporters to occurrences they have learned of through wire service accounts.[3] They send a reporter to develop the local angle at a national event for which there is wire-service coverage.[4] By complementing the wire services, they reaffirm the sagacity of the wire services' initial identification of the occurrence as a news event. Additionally, they fan their reporters through institutions in the same pattern used by the wire services.[5] Instead of blanketing the world by their joint efforts, the news media and the news services leave the same sorts of holes in the news net, holes justified by a professionally shared notion of news judgement.[6] Finally, the probability of duplication is enhanced by a common practice of reporters: at bureau, beat, and story-site, they commonly share information with colleagues from competing news organizations.[7] The net-like formation of the dispersion of reporters is of theoretic importance, for it is a key[8] to the constitution of news. The spatial anchoring of the news net at centralized institutional sites is one element of the frame delineating strips of everyday reality as news.

Space and the constitution of news

The news net imposes order on the social world because it enables news events to occur at some locations but not at others. Obviously, reporters cannot write about occurrences hidden from view by their social location – that is, either geographic location or social class. For instance, the assignment of a salaried reporter to City Hall means that stories generated there may be favoured over occurrences at uncovered locations, such as issue-oriented debates among working-class members of an unassigned social movement.

Equally important, the news net is a hierarchical system of information-gatherers. And so the status of reporters in the news net may determine whose information is identified as news. Editors prefer stories by salaried reporters to those by stringers, paid less well and on a piecework basis, simply because the news organization has a financial investment in the former. For instance, when the education editor of a New York daily sent a stringer from a city college to cover a news conference at City Hall, the daily's City Hall bureau chief fumed because (among other reasons) he had a reporter available to do the story. The bureau chief announced to the education editor, 'I have nine reporters down here' for the explicit purpose of writing copy 'like this story'. Generally, though, avoiding stringers means discarding items regarded as 'small fish'. And so this practice reinforces the legitimacy of institutions that host beats and bureaux. Similarly, editors prefer to publish or telecast material prepared by their staff rather than by centralized news services. Barbara Rosenblum reports this pattern in the selection of news photographs.[9] Her participant observation at three major New York City newspapers yielded the finding that their photography editors rarely accept the work of stringers. Faced with a choice of two pictures of the same event, one taken by a staff photographer and the other provided by a wire service, they invariably elected to print their staff member's shot – even if the wire service's picture was photographically superior.

I observed the same patterns in the newsroom of a television station. Somewhat better footage of a story from a centralized service – the news department of the network with which the station was affiliated – was not used when one of the station's crews had covered the story. Rather, the superior network footage was used as an opportunity to chastise the crew for inferior work.[10] Similarly, the station hired stringers only in circumstances of dire need. For instance, when a riot-like disturbance unexpectedly occurred in the middle of the night, they purchased footage from a stringer, since they had not assigned a crew to the story. But whenever the station could plan coverage in advance, it avoided hiring a stringer.

Finally, the news net imposes a frame upon occurrences through the operation of the complex bureaucracy associated with the dispersion of reporters. Interactions among the bureaucratic hierarchy – reporters and editors jockeying with one another – may determine what is identified as news. Reporters compete for assignments. Editors compete to get assignments for their reporters and negotiate to get their reporters' stories in the paper or on the air. As one City Hall bureau chief put it, 'My reporters want to see their by-lines in the paper, and I want to see them there'. Friendly but fierce competitors, editors wheel and deal with one another as representatives of self-interested fiefdoms, nonetheless sharing a common purpose – to produce news for their organization. To understand the impact of these competitive negotiations upon the constitution of news, one must examine the news net in greater detail.

Originally designed to attract readers' interest by catching appropriate stories available at centralized locations, the news net incorporates three assumptions about readers' interests: (1) readers are interested in occurrences at specific localities; (2) they are concerned with the activities of specific organizations; (3) they are interested in specific topics.[11]

Accordingly, the news net is flung through space, focuses upon specific organizations, and highlights topics. Of these three methods of dispersing reporters, geographic territoriality is most important.[12]

Geographic Territoriality. First, the news media divide the world into areas of territorial responsibility. The actual divisions used by any specific news organization replicate the organization's notion of its news mission – what it believes its particular readers want to know[13] and what it is financially prepared to bring them. For instance, both the *New York News* and the *Times* have Washington bureaux. Each also has a metropolitan desk whose territorial prerogatives stretch as far as the state capital in Albany. Conceiving of itself as a local paper, the *News* has a more extensive system of reporters in boroughs and neighbouring states, such as New Jersey, than does the *Times*. Conversely, a self-defined national paper, the *Times* has an extensive system of national and international bureaux; the *News* does not. At the *News*, local reporters are ultimately responsible to the metropolitan editor, and most national and international news is channelled to a wire-service editor. the *Times* has established three coequal desks, a metropolitan desk, a national desk, and a foreign desk, each headed by a senior editor who seeks to place his reporters' stories at good locations in the paper.

Local news programmes use a similar system. With the managing editor of the six o'clock News and the local editor of the eleven o'clock news, the assignment editor of *News* arranged the dispersion of filming crews and reporters throughout Seaboard City. A selection of national and international stories was jointly handled by the managing editor and the 'feed editor' of the eleven o'clock news. Little, if any, national and international news was presented on the six o'clock programme since it was directly followed by the network's evening news, a programme specializing in national and foreign affairs

Organizational specialization. A second method of dispersing reporters is to establish beats and bureaux at organizations associated with the generation of news and holding centralized information. For instance, one or more New York dailies have reporters responsible for covering the United Nations, the City Council, the Mayor's office, the police, the Board of Corrections, and the state government. Reporters may be assigned to these locations by being physically located in the building where that organization's activities are centred or by keeping track of occurrences from their own desks in the city room. For example, at the *News*, some reporters cover politics from the city room, others from the press room at City Hall. The former are directly supervised by the metropolitan editor and assistant city editors; the latter, by the City Hall bureau chief, who is in turn supervised by the metropolitan editor. Still other *News* reporters, located in City Hall's press room, keep tabs on borough politics and are responsible to the City Hall bureau chief and a borough chief located in the main newsroom. Both 'chiefs' are under the metropolitan editor. As is the case with the geographic delineation of responsibility, the coding of stories as "belonging" to one bureau or another is not always clear-cut. The ways in which conflicts are resolved indicate both the priority of territoriality over geographic specialization and how decisions are embedded in bureaucratic distinctions, as the following field data indicate. *New York Times* reporters who do not report to special-ized topical departments (such as the sports, financial or family/ style department) are ultimately responsible to the metropolitan editor with one exception: the United Nations reporter, who works under the aegis of the national desk. That this man reports to the national desk, not the international desk, reveals the power of bureaucratic solutions. The international desk is responsible for foreign correspondents, maintained by funds provided by that desk's budget; and because of time-zone differences between New York and Europe, Africa, and Asia, special bureaucratic provision is made for handling foreign copy. Until the mid-1970s, copy from Europe and Africa was funnelled through London, where, because of the five-hour difference in time zones, it could be edited earlier in the New York day. However, whenever the United Nations reporter or any other reporter travels outside the territorial United States, his or her copy is sent to the international desk, since it alone has an international travel budget. It is not sent to the editor who routinely supervises that reporter's work. For instance, when a *Times* music critic toured European opera houses, copy was relayed to the international editor.

Topical specialization is the third method of dispersing reporters. Formally introduced during the circulation wars of the late nineteenth century, this method is constituted in independent departments with their own budgets. Their editors report directly to a managing editor or executive editor, bypassing the territorial desks. Topical specialities include finance, sports, and family/style or so-called women's departments, as well as culture and education.[14] Since these departments bypass the territorial desks each day, their editors are told how many columns or pages they are expected to fill, and in the case of the women's pages, sports department, and financial department of the *Times*, they may select their own pictures (rather than having them chosen by the photograph editor who selects pictures for territorial desks) and determine their own 'display' or make-up. Finally, when the assistant managing director maps out ('mocks-up') the news product, a culture editor may inform him of the amount of space needed for the cultural copy. For instance, every evening the TV editor of *Seaboard City Daily* emerged from her office, set apart from the city room like the offices of all topical specialists, to tell the assistant managing editor the length of her column.

Notes

1. Snyder and Kelly try to locate objective characteristics of violent events that lead to news coverage. They find that papers in small towns are more likely to cover bar brawls and that a city that has experienced a riot will be less likely to cover stories of riots in other towns [Snyder, David and Kelly, William R. (1977) Conflict intensity, media sensitivity and the validity of newspaper data. *American Sociological Review*. Vol. 42, pp. 105–23]. Unfortunately, like Danzger, these authors do not come to terms with how news organizations transform occurrences into news events and stories [Danzger, M. Herbert (1975) Validating conflict data. *American Sociological Review*, Vol. 40, pp. 570–584; and Reply to Tuchman. Ibid., Vol. 41, pp. 1067–71; cf. Tuchman, Gaye (1976) The news' manufacture of sociological data: a comment on Danzger. Ibid., Vol. 41, pp. 1065–7].
2. At one point, the governor of New Jersey threatened to challenge the licences of New York City television stations because they did not carry a sufficient amount of news about New Jersey. The challenge was based on the lack of commercial stations in New Jersey and the large audience New Jersey contributes to New York stations. The city stations responded by increasing their coverage of New Jersey politics and other sorts of occurrences as well. I use the term 'limited value' to describe suburban readers, such as New Jersey residents, because suburban newspapers are growing while metropolitan papers are declining. Actively competing with *Newsday* for suburban Queens readers, the *Daily News* has a Queens bureau and a complex system of suburban stringers.
3. Danzger, 'Validating conflict data'; Sigal, Leon V. (1973) *Reporters and Officials: The Organization and Politics of Newsmaking*, D. C. Heath, Lexington, MA.
4. Described by David Altheide, *Creating Reality* (Sage Publications, Beverly Hills, 1977).
5. *New Yorker*, 1 March, 1976, pp. 23–4.
6. See Tuchman, *Making News*, Chapters 4 and 7.

7. Ibid., Chapter 4; Tunstall, Jeremy (1971) *Journalists at Work: Specialist Correspondents, Their News Organizations, News Sources, and Competitor–Colleagues,* Constable Books, London; Crouse, Timothy (1973) *The Boys on the Bus,* Random House, New York.

8. According to Goffman, a key is 'the set of conventions by which a given activity, one already meaningful in terms of some primary framework, is transformed into something patterned on this activity but seen by participants to be something quite else. . . . A rough musical analogy is intended' (Goffman, *Frame Analysis,* pp. 43, 44).

9. Rosenblum, Barbara (forthcoming) *Photographers and Their Photographs,* Holmes & Meier, New York.

10. The incident involved a national civil rights story. The network hired a local cameraman as part of its crew. The scolding was exacerbated by the fact that he had a poor reputation. 'If the network could produce better footage using him as a camera man, why couldn't we have done better?'

11. Readers are also assumed to be interested in specific persons found at localities ('people in the news'), at specific organizations (the president and the first lady), and associated with specific topics (as are movie stars and television personalities).

12. Cf. Fishman, 'Manufacturing the news'.

13. Television stations now base their ideas of what readers want to know on specially gathered survey data. These include tests of stories and of newscasters' potential popularity with viewers. Frequently, when a station hires a new anchorperson or incorporates a new feature, such as consumer news, special consulting firms test market the proposed innovation through video tapes shown, for instance, in shopping malls.

14. Until the early 1960s, *The New York Times* culture reporters 'belonged' to the city desk and the science reporters to the national desk.

38

News departments and broadcasting organizations – the institutionalization of objectivity

Peter Golding and Philip Elliott

From Golding, P. and Elliott, P. (1979) *Making the News*, Longman, London, pp. 72–6, 78–81.

Thus in all the organizations news finds itself defined as a major strut in the structure, equivalent in a formal sense to all other programmes, and embracing an output category wider than the distinction between radio and television, though naturally implementing the distinction to a greater or lesser extent internally.

The relationship between news departments and other programme departments is an important one, because it is both a cause and a result of the extent to which news broadcasters define themselves and their jobs in professional terms; that is as journalists or as broadcasters. The relationship meets its first problem in the confrontation over resources and facilities, both in the inter-departmental share-out of budgets and in the day-to-day struggle over shared facilities.

Where resources are minimal this problem can be acute. In Nigeria the film crews were invariably over-stretched by competing demands from news and programmes, and only a few were allocated exclusively to a news department. It was a common complaint that cameramen had been poached by a programmes producer or had their services unduly monopolized by other television departments. Studio facilities were also a subject of contention. No separate news studio was available at NBC TV, while the radio studios were in constant demand for rehearsal and programme preparation. Film editing and processing, viewing rooms, the use of graphic artists all have to be fought for competitively with the inevitable consolidation of a 'news versus the rest' view of inter-departmental relations.

This view is exacerbated by the rather different use made of facilities by journalists in broadcasting. Journalists like to stress the unpredictability of their material, the need for them 'to be prepared'. But if they are to be manned and equipped as though every day would bring a Kennedy assassination many expensive resources would be idle for long periods. Reluctant to concede the essential regularity of their work journalists are thus permanently asking for more than the organization is willing to devote to news broadcasting, in a way that can only seem avaricious and senseless to non-journalists. To the journalists such a judgement is the result of total ignorance of journalism and the nature of news production.

All the organizations had been or were going through discussions as to which kinds of facilities could be commandeered by news departments, and which of necessity should be shared. In Nigeria film crews and transport were the main stumbling block. Comments were often bitter: 'The cameras lean to programmes, we just don't get maximum cooperation. There's no news studio for television, there's only one car in the whole department' (Editor, WNBC).

In RTE (Ireland) a film team of reporter, cameraman, sound man and lighting man could not operate easily, being controlled from different departments. The lack of technical staff attached permanently to the newsroom was seen as the result of limited resources, and efforts were being made to attach more sound men to the newsroom. There was widespread concern that cameramen should not be organizational footballs, that being a news cameraman was a specialized skill requiring permanent association with the newsroom. Presentation staff present a similar difficulty. In Nigeria they were under the control of programmes divisions. Newsmen resented their lack of cooperation and frequent scorn for the prose produced with such care by the newsroom.

The overall budgetary allocation to news departments is summarized in Table 38.1. As a proportion of station budget in most cases, this figure seems low when compared to the proportion of broadcasting hours prepared by news departments. On the other hand news costs more per hour than the average production, though of course less than original drama and variety productions. It is possible to present figures in a variety of ways supporting or disproving the news 'cause'. The important point is that the cause exists, and represents a grievance contributing much to the sense of journalistic isolation from other broadcasting functions.

Lack of resources is very much a matter of relative deprivation. One junior journalist at WNBS expressed himself happy with transport facilities: 'yes, that's OK here, they have their own van'. Nigerian journalists looked to newspapers or, if at WNBS or RTK, to NBC for comparison. At RTE and at SR (Sweden) the reference point was the BBC or ITN in England. Whereas in Nigeria the most common cause of complaint concerned general office facilities – lack of and unpredictable efficiency of telephones, shortage of typewriters, tape recorders, even notepads – in RTE greatest discontent was

Table 38.1. News costs relative to programme costs*

		News costs per hr as ratio of all programme costs per hour	News department budget as % total station budget
SR		1.4	4.2
RTE	TV	1.6	5.5 (combined)
	Radio	1 2	
NBC	TV	2.6	8.2
	Radio	1.1	4.4

*Calculated from annual reports and other documentation current at time of observation studies.

directed at the unavailability of videotape recording at crucial times. Inadequate provincial coverage in Ireland would, it was felt, be improved by the acquisition of portable video recorders and the development of local injection points and link networks, possibly with a proliferation of small unattended studios. In Sweden disputes over the availability of video recording facilities for news and sport were very similar to the disputes over cameras in Nigeria.

Deferring for a moment the complex developments in SR, we can expand on the place of news in the organization. First, news occupies a central place in scheduling, it has an assured claim to air-time and usually a fixed time-slot. Programmers may resent the impact of this immovable fulcrum upon which their material has to be articulated. At RTE the experimental shifting of news to 10 p.m. posed a threat to producers of subsequent programmes, wary that their audience would be extinguished by the natural conclusion to an evenings viewing provided by a news bulletin ending at 10.20. For the newsroom a later bulletin left more time for preparation and greater elbow room to handle late developments in foreign and provincial news.

Second, because of its divisional status, news has a closeness to organizational centres of power. Yet within news departments there was considerable scepticism as to the importance given to news within the organization. In Nigeria 46% and in Ireland 41% of journalists felt not enough importance was given to the department. Particularly galling was what was seen as undue criticism and lack of recognition despite a difficult job well done, amplified in Nigeria by common complaints about relatively poor pay and conditions. On the other hand, news was seen as the shop window of the organization. It was at once the most sensitive and vulnerable of the outputs, and one of the most popular. 'RTE attaches sufficient importance to the newsroom. It's aware that we are one of the big local draws . . . but as an organization it has a low opinion of news' (Sub-editor, RTE). This common evaluation, that news was treated with more concern than the department that produced it, was repeated elsewhere. In the face of organizational opposition status is asserted on the only grounds left, the incontrovertible importance of the ultimate product, whether justified by audience size, political or social significance, or intrinsic merit.

Third, journalists and other programmers would use different criteria in different ways to evaluate competence. This brings the news department into conflict with engineering. The journalists were seen as technological innocents; 'those people in the newsroom who just do not understand and apparently do not wish to understand the technical and engineering aspects of broadcasting – they do not understand the nature of the medium they are using', as the situation was described by a senior RTE engineering man. The most common complaint was that the journalists had not learnt to wean themselves from newspaper styles and techniques. A senior executive in RTE described these problems: 'The people in news . . . haven't integrated themselves in RTE as a television organization with a result that they are not able to utilize facilities such as sound, cameras, etc. with anything like the expertise that the programme makers will utilize. . . . ' On the other hand the journalists felt that technical provision took little account of specifically journalistic needs:

There's been a terrible mistake in allowing new telecine facilities; telecine is unsuitable for news because you need a long warm-up . . . The management's at fault – it doesn't know anything about telecines. It's a system which suits non-news departments. The new processing plant takes an hour for colour – we use Agfa – everybody else (i.e. BBC, ITN) uses Kodachrome. Kodachrome is ideal for news . . . Because news people didn't have anything to say RTE instituted a colour film processing which suits all other departments save news (Sub-editor, RTE).

This is just one aspect of the dual identity enjoyed, or endured by broadcasting journalists. Loyal to a creed and belief system developed in another industry their occupational distinctiveness raises acute organizational problems. Administrators were often inclined to view the complaints of news staff as evidence of their limited understanding of broadcasting practices. 'News is about five to six years behind the rest of the organization . . . we still have too much of the traditional newspaper, too much of rosters, and looking to procedures, actual structures and procedures of people who feel insecure at a lot of the moves on and start to hang on for dear life . . .' (Senior Executive, RTE).

In Nigeria scorn for the technical naivety of news staff was often soured to bitterness by the evident rapid promotion of young, inexperienced staff in the newsroom caused by the rapid turnover and loss of senior men to more lucrative fields. Yet the newsmen merely felt even more vulnerable because of this, aware of their lack of political weight in organizational infighting. A cut in news bulletin lengths at WNBC was assumed to result from pressure by the commercial department to carry more advertising, raising an inevitable 'why are we always the ones to get cut?' riposte.

In many ways the most important organizational split is that between news and current affairs, representing as it does an attempt to turn a concept of news into institutional form. [. . .]

Current affairs programming at RTE has been a constant source of organizational strife. The separate divisions for news and for current affairs were the end product of a series of metamorphoses. Before 1967 television current affairs was jointly controlled by the Controller of Television Programmes and the News Division. In 1967 television current affairs became the responsibility solely of the Programmes Division. The main television current affairs effort was a twice weekly programme *7 Days*. Controversial and ambitious, its producers felt themselves to be testing the boundaries of licensed independence in broadcasting. In their own view, and to some observers they were creative young Turks pricking the hides of an overbearing administration and an anxious government. The News Division was itself experimenting with news commentary programmes at this time, and one explanation of the ensuing organizational explosion was the view of many in the hierarchy of the News Division that they were too constrained, that 'News got the scoops. Programmes Division got the comment' (Dowling and Doolan, 1969, p. 115).

After a series of rumours, accusations of interference and harassment, the Director-General, in early 1968, moved *7 Days* to the jurisdiction of the Head of News. Interpretations of this move vary: empire-building by the Head of News; an attempt to politically neuter the programme; naive mismanagement by the Controller of Programmes; a sensible rationalization of unnecessarily duplicated efforts. Whatever the reality, it was widely interpreted as intended to bring an outspoken programme into the stifling ambit of the impartiality requirements attached to news programmes. This view is supported by the Director-General's remark in a newsletter circulated to staff at the time, that he 'had frequent concern about 7 *Days* programmes which at times tended to lack impartiality' (Dowling and Doolan, 1969, p. 131). The Director-General, due to retire soon after, left the station fairly quickly.

The programme 7 *Days* returned to public attention in 1969 when it transmitted a programme on illegal money-lending in Dublin. Concern over the conclusions drawn and the methods used by the programme led to the setting up of a Judicial Tribunal of Inquiry by the Prime Minister. The Tribunal report was unflattering; the programme had used unreliable sources, not checked its facts and most wounding of all, the journalists had failed to make every effort to ensure that the facts were true and accurate. In sum, as a deputy in the Dail debates put it, 'the main lesson to be learned from the inquiry is that newsmen should always be objective' (Dail, 4 March, 1971). The programme staff had been weighed in the balance and found wanting, and the punishment was to have their noses rubbed in their own professional creed. The organizational contortions continued. In 1973 a new Current Affairs group was set up to co-ordinate all current affairs work in radio and television, including 7 *Days*, and the weekly radio news comment programme, *This Week*. The Broadcasting Review Committee Report welcomed this move of current affairs 'out of news'. The news department was less happy to see its ambitions to develop more adventurous and expansive journalistic skills frustrated, though the loss of 7 *Days* was less regretted, it having always preserved a high degree of autonomy and reserve from the rest of the News Division. The department, and particularly the Head of News, were most sad to lose *This Week*, a favoured and much admired child of the department.

This paradox, that the more news appropriates the provision of explanation and background the less like news it becomes, runs through the attitudes of journalists in all the departments we studied. For the traditional journalists in RTE the over-elaborated versions of news required by news executives were simply evidence of the effete, intellectual approach developed by those with no instinct for news, no hard news sense. This divergence of philosophy is important, and will be looked at more closely in the next chapter.

The constant confrontation of a desire to expand the horizons of news production with the constraints of traditional news values and imposed definitions of impartiality have taken place with acute organizational consequences in both SR and RTE. In Nigeria organizational differentiation has not yet evolved to the same degree, though it is ubiquitously assumed to be inevitable and desirable. Current affairs are usually produced as an appendage of news, often by the same staff. The programmes take two forms, either as compilations of news items on a particular theme – the local area, foreign news, a state visit – or as discussion programmes in the European style of current affairs programmes.

At NBC a Current Affairs Unit within the News Division was developed in 1970 to produce all current affairs output on radio. Previously handled by a section modelled on BBC Talks, with its connotations of ponderous lectures on worthy topics, the unit represented the demand by graduate news staff to do more than process agency and government releases. The work of the unit was nonetheless closely articulated around news – *Newsreel*, covering news events throughout the country; *Newstalk*, providing five-minute backgrounds to items in the news; and news magazines, providing mostly foreign news stories in miscellanies or as subjects for discussions.

In television current affairs were handled largely by a Public Affairs section within the Programmes Division. This section handled sports, a schools debating programme, discussion programmes, interview programmes and a whole range of material variably labelled elsewhere as features, public affairs or just non-fiction. Within the news department was a special events section, rarely more than one overworked, but dedicated individual, left with the task of putting together news commentary programmes. These were very largely news miscellanies or interviews and were heavily based on other news department work. There was little in the work of either Special Events or Public Affairs that forced the issue of distinguishing current affairs and news, and the greatest problems were described as 'money and red tape'. Through lack of time and resources current affairs did not stray far from the confines of news, though panel discussions were a popular format for this kind of programming. But the subject matter was defined by news output. Caution abounds in the face of governmental concern.

This was even more true at WNBC. Current Affairs here was entirely separate from news, but organizational differentiation was purely notional. In practice the current affairs unit, which also produced sports programmes, worked physically and creatively within the news department. Its output was again based on news, comprising miscellanies and interviews. Caution was well to the fore and all programmes had to be pre-recorded to facilitate clearance, if required, by the Military Governor's office. Part of the unit's output was accounted for by the transmission of old *World in Action* tapes acquired from the British commercial television company, Granada.

The Northern station, BCNN, with its more developed tradition of 'critical' journalism had introduced a current affairs unit of growing distinctiveness. However, much of the impetus was lost when the Head of the Unit, a graduate with an academic background and a reputation for sharp administrative acumen, left in 1973. He had deliberately developed the unit as an aggressive alternative to news, asserting that 'in current affairs we don't have to be bound by news objectivity'. Stories of refusals to bow to government demands abounded in the department, and the unit as a whole had obvious high morale and confidence. Most of the staff in the department were graduates, in marked distinction to those in the news department.

Reference

Dowling, J. and Doolan, L. (1969) *Sit Down and Be Counted*, Wellington, Dublin.

39

How content is produced

Muriel G. Cantor

From Cantor, M. G. (1980) *Prime-time Television*, Sage, Beverly Hills, CA, pp. 84–91

On-the-line producers

The working producer of filmed dramatic television has a key role and relative power in the selection of content once a show is bought by a network or a syndication company. Producers are in charge of hiring the cast (except possibly the stars), the directors, and the writers. They serve as coordinators between the networks for which the show is produced and/or the programme suppliers. The producer also has the final responsibility for cutting and editing the filmed product. This combination of tasks and associated power is common in the role of television producer, but is not necessarily associated with the title 'producer' in other media. The producer has many of the tasks that in the motion picture industry (especially in European productions) are assigned to the film director. When a feature film director for the theatre films is hired to do a picture, he is given a story to develop and, along with the film editor, cuts the picture. In television drama (miniseries, regular series, and even movies made for television which are often pilots for series) story development is a major function of the producer. Most on-the-line producers are hyphenates, that is, writer-producers or possibly director-producers. It is often said by people associated with the television and movie industries that the feature film is a director's medium while television is a producer's medium. Three of the major creative parts of television dramatic production – story, casting, and editing – are under the producer's control. Although casting is a joint effort among the director, casting director, and producer, the producer has final authority. The directors shoot the picture and, on the set, they are in control. However, since they are hired by the producer, they turn to the producer when problems arise on the set (Cantor, 1971).

In addition, because the producer's major responsibility is story development, he or she holds a position of power over the script writers. The producer hires the writers to do one or more scripts (if it is a series) and often works with the writers for all kinds of dramatic production, directing the tone and outcome of the script. Many freelance writers aspire to be on-the-line producers because of the relative power and autonomy vested in that role.

Because the producer is a salaried employee working for a programme supplier, he or she does not have complete control and is caught in the middle between those above in the networks and production companies and those to be supervised in the production operation. As a representative of management, the producer must fulfil the goals of the organization. Thus, if the ratings of a show are low, the show will be cancelled. Network profits depend on the ratings. No matter how creative or artistic a show may be from a critical perspective, the final determination of whether a show stays on the air is made by the networks. Thus, a producer must deliver a saleable product. A producer of a successful series may be able to generate a large amount of power and possibly can communicate both social and political values which are seemingly incongruent with those held by network executives and programme suppliers. Most of the time this is unlikely. Ideally, the producer has responsibility for the creative aspects of the show, but this is always delegated authority. Even if the producer owns, creates, and produces the show, the network retains the right to final approval of scripts, casts, and other creative and administrative matters. Should a producer fight too often with the network over creative decisions, the producer is replaced. Although the producer is the most powerful of the production team, except for the star actors, his or her power is not absolute. As noted earlier, the pool of writers and others, such as assistant directors, who are qualified to work in the capacity of producer far exceeds the demand. The number of teleplays in production at any one time never exceeds 100 and is often less. That figure includes soap operas, prime-time series, movies made for television, animated cartoons, and miniseries. Producers, along with their partners in the creative process, face sporadic employment. A number of examples could be cited where the series was in production for several years with a number of different on-the-line producers. In some cases the producer became disenchanted with the work, but often the network or programme supplier replaced one person with another who would be more compliant. Examples are *Star Trek*, *Mannix*, and *Bonanza*. Thus, the success of the series does not ensure the job of the on-the-line producer.

Actors – creative power and autonomy

The star actors of a successful series are by far the most powerful of the creative people working in television. When an actor stars in a series and that series is a success, the actor becomes the person to whom everyone else, including the writers, directors, and producers, must cater. The series depends on the actor to remain on the air, and therefore the actor's wishes are considered in all aspects of the production process. However, the above is only true for a successful series and not for drama that is unsuccessful, and this power is not transferable to the next series to which a star might become attached. In contrast to the stars, supporting actors – even those who are regulars in a series – are often the least powerful of all the creative personnel. If an actor becomes troublesome, his or her part can be written out of the series. Often when supporting actors become as popular as the star, a new series is developed for them. This is known as the spin-off. A successful series, especially those done on tape and in particular the situation comedies, often develop a following and high ratings because of their stars.

Many of these shows either are named after the star or have a name which is associated with the actor in the starring role. Examples are *The Mary Tyler Moore Show*, *The Bob Newhart Show*, *Rhoda*, *Lou Grant*, (both spin-offs from *The Mary Tyler Moore Show*), and *Marcus Welby, M.D.* None of these shows could have remained on the air without the stars appearing as the leading characters. Because of the large profit associated with a successful series, these actors have been able to generate power as long as the ratings remain high.

Actors (and other artists) have generally been perceived apart from others who earn their living from wages, salaries, commissions, and sales. Historically, it might be legitimate to separate the purveyors of culture from those who deal in producing the material artefacts and substance of a society. However, because of the way much work is organized, this is no longer a legitimate separation (if there ever really was one). The growth of mass media industries also contributed to eliminating this separation. Because many artists and intellectuals work in bureaucratic settings and are dependent upon complex technology, they have problems associated with control and autonomy that other workers do not have. Actors have an additional problem: not only do they work in a bureaucratic setting doing essentially craft work, but actors are directly espousing values and political positions which may or may not be compatible with their own ideological viewpoints. Actors are unable to select the parts they play unless they are stars. Movie stars sometimes are able to produce their own movies and then select the part. There are examples of television stars who are very powerful for a number of years because the series in which they appear have been successes. However, when these same stars try other roles, they often fail or have trouble finding a suitable series and may join the unemployed. Examples are Richard Chamberlain, who was Dr Kildare, Vince Edwards, who was Ben Casey, and even Mary Tyler Moore, who appeared in several successful series and then failed at her attempt to do a variety show. Mary Tyler Moore, with her husband Grant Tinker, owns a production company. Her star status and entree through her own production facilities did not ensure success. The ratings were poor and her variety show in 1978–9 did not last the season.

Those actors who are not stars are dependent on others who write the parts, produce the shows, and, more importantly, finance and distribute the production. Once an actor receives a part, it is likely that someone else will determine how the role is to be interpreted as well. More than any other occupation which is publicized as glamorous and creative, acting in the United States provides little freedom or autonomy for those who appear on the screen. Because actors are interpreters rather than manufacturers of symbols, they are dependent upon the enterprises that produce the shows.

Actors also have a serious problem in finding employment. As noted earlier, all of the creative people in television have employment problems, but for no other group is the problem as severe as it is for the actors. The actor 'labour force' is small compared with other groups. The U.S. Census reported only 23,430 actors in 1970 (NEA, 1976). Most screen and television actors belong to the Screen Actors' Guild, which has 39,000 members (18,000 in Los Angeles). The discrepancy in figures is due to differences in defining an actor (see Cantor and Peters, 1979). Because the Guild has many members who work in other media or other occupations, the figure is clearly inflated. Moreover, the Guild reports that only 15 percent of its members work at any one time. There are only about 2000 acting jobs available in Hollywood for about 18,000 people, if one takes the Guild figures seriously.

One might ask why the Guild does not limit membership on some criteria. Every actor and union official to whom Anne Peters and I have spoken has been firm about defining an actor. All agree that any actor should have a chance to compete for a part in a production regardless of background or present status. The producer, director, and casting director are the people with the right to decide who gets hired. The only obligation the Screen Actors' Guild has is to provide good working conditions once a member is on the job. When a non-member is hired for a part, then by the rules of the Guild he can join the union.

An obvious structural feature which contributes to the oversupply of actors is that television work is casual and similar to seasonal work in other industries. Jobs tend to be of an *ad hoc* and short-term nature, and there is little continuity of employment. Only stars and regular supporting casts of an ongoing television series have work that lasts more than a few weeks. Theatre movies, movies made for television, and other productions such as TV commercials provide work of short duration.

As noted throughout this section, the differences between the stars and non-stars are outstanding. It is beyond the scope of this book to discuss why certain actors become stars and others do not, but the star system, because it exists, is a powerful force in and of itself. All actors have the possibility of becoming stars, and with that status comes great financial and reputational success. Acting is one of the few occupations, along with professional sports and other related artistic endeavours, which provide a vehicle for the attainment of personal success and fame. There is the opportunity for a few to begin with virtually no capital or credentials and become eminently successful as actors. It is this feature of the occupation which probably explains the tenacity of some actors in the face of deprivation and compromise. However, this feature of the occupation also contributes to why the supply of actors remains large while the demand remains low. And that is not the only reason – acting is an attractive occupation and actors love their work. Every actor interviewed would not only like to work regularly if possible (as is to be expected) but also recognize that working under the present conditions would not guarantee them artistic freedom and certainly not political freedom in the marketplace.

Writers

Writers, like actors, are usually freelance; that is, a show uses various writers to write each episode. The unemployment problem for writers is similar to that of actors. However, the Writers' Guild has not encouraged a large membership of the unemployed. Rather, that Guild has two classes of membership based on earnings through writing. Thus, the Guild acts similarly to other craft and white-collar unions. However, neither the Writers' Guild nor the Screen Actors' Guild helps its members secure employment. Actors and writers are on their own to find work in an industry where work is scarce and where hiring often depends on characteristics, such as beauty and personality for actors and personal connections with important industry people for writers, other than talent, training, or skills.

The relationship of the writers to the producers has been discussed in detail (Cantor, 1971, pp. 92–105). I found in my interviewing of writers that they are closest to the stereotype of the lone artist of any of the creative people in Hollywood. Most writers say that they would like to write drama or other fiction which is more highbrow or socially significant than the material they must write for television.

Joan Moore describes the full-time television writer as having little or no control over any aspect of the writing, except the invention of dialogue and incident. 'Their work is rewritten as a matter of routine. It may be changed without their consent by a story editor, producer, director, or actor' (Moore, n.d., p. 92). My work in Hollywood and New York bears out Moore's contention. Producers have to worry about changes from the network, programme suppliers, and advertisers, but freelance writers have to be concerned about everyone in the production process continually changing scripts. The writer is powerless to control any changes and can only fight about credits which translate into money because of residual payments. The producer and writer are most closely related in function and possibly background. The producer is dependent on the writer for scripts, and the writer is dependent on the producer for assignments. Producers can write scripts because most are by profession writers, but there is not time during a season for them to write all 22 or more scripts that may be needed. Therefore, they assign others, usually writers whose work is familiar to them, to write stories that often are developed together. Few if any unsolicited scripts received by the production company are ever considered seriously. The mutual dependency of the writer and producer results in some conflicts. These conflicts may occur over screen credits, because, according to the contract between the Writers' Guild and the Motion Picture and Television Producers' Association, whoever receives screen credit as the writer receives residuals or royalties if and when the episode is shown as a re-run or as part of a syndicated series. Producers are salaried employees and, while they receive large salaries, they do not receive residuals. Writers freelance and receive payment for their scripts plus residuals when they get screen credit. Because the script is bought outright by the programme supplier or producer, changes can be made without consulting the writer. All writers know they are at the mercy of the producer when it comes to control over the script. The producer defends his right to change scripts because it is his job to maintain quality control over the production. Quality control does not necessarily refer only to artistic aspects of the film, but also includes making the scripts in line with the general concept. This is particularly important for a series. The series needs a chief writer responsible for continuing the storyline. If a producer changes or rewrites a script so that a certain percentage is changed, he may wish to receive screen credit so that he can receive the residuals. Most producers are writer-producers, and as writers they are members of the Writers' Guild. But to receive credit they must 'prove' through arbitration that they indeed wrote enough of the script to add their names to the credits. The Writers' Guild decides whether the changes warrant the change of credits. Sometimes a producer will try to supplant the writer's name with his own in order to claim all of the residuals.

Freelance writers are used primarily for the adventure, western, and crime shows. In reality, there is no such occupation as television writer. Although there are few writers who write only for television, most write plays, novels, short stories, and, if fortunate, theatre films. Very little information exists on writers' work. However, being unemployed as a writer is common, and work for the freelance writer is more precarious now than it was in 1968 and before. This is related to the few movies and television films that use freelance writers as compared with 1968. Presently, because the comedy series are so popular with the production companies, writers are salaried employees as they were in the heyday of Hollywood. For shows such as *Mork and Mindy*, *The Mary Tyler Moore Show*, and others, a team of writers is hired for the series. This, of course, limits the power of the producer but does not generate much more freedom for the writer. In such situations the 'committee' becomes powerful. The writers are assured of their screen credits, but their power is limited in the creative process by the whole production.

If the history of Hollywood were written from the perspective of the occupational roles and structures, one would find that there has never been a clear definition of any of the occupations involved with making a movie. For example, actors direct and write films and often produce them as well. Joan Moore (n.d.) makes the point that besides the difficulty of assigning an occupational role to the various people involved in production, work changes as technology and organization of Hollywood production changes. She goes on to say that one person in a year's work may create a script in which he or she has complete artistic control and one in which the script is rewritten by others and totally reshaped by directors, actors, producers, and editors. The writer and his role partners are subject to control both from the networks and other distributors as well as those attached to the actual production.

Although space here is limited and the complexities of trying to be a creative writer for television cannot be discussed in the detail the topic deserves, the occupational roles provide the ideal example of how bureaucratic organization affects creative work. Those writers who work as freelancers are no more free from the controls than those who are salaried directly by a production company.

Directors

Of the four occupational roles discussed here, that of director is the least important. Compared with his counterpart in theatre film, the television director is weak and powerless. In television production, he or she rarely stays with the production through the editing process. Directors are hired either on a freelance basis or are salaried regular employees, directing the shows on a weekly basis. When the director is hired for an episode, the time limitations often do not allow him the luxury of his contractual right of the first cut (editing). Thus, the freelance director becomes merely a technician, carrying out the mandates of the on-the-line producers. Only those directors who are hired for a season (again, this is likely in the case of situation comedies) share some authority with the on-the-line producer and the stars to determine content.

References

Cantor, M. G. (1971) *The Hollywood TV Producer: His Work and His Audience*, Basic Books, New York.

Cantor, M. G and Peters, A. K. (1979) The employment and unemployment of screen actors in the United States. Presented at the *First International Conference on Economics and the Arts*, Edinburgh, Scotland, August 11 (proceedings to be published by Abt Associates, Cambridge, MA).

Moore, J. (1961) Occupational anomie and irresponsibility. *Social Problems*, Vol. 8, No. 2, pp. 293–9.

Moore, J. (n.d.) The Hollywood writer (unpublished manuscript).

NEA (1976) Employment and unemployment of artists, 1970–75. National Endowment for the Arts, Washington, DC.

40

Journalists at war (introduction)

David E. Morrison and Howard Tumber

From Morrison, D. E. and Tumber, H. (1988) *Journalists at War: The Dynamics of News Reporting During the Falklands Conflict*, Sage, London, pp. viii–xiv.

It is strange to find journalists, whose business is to enquire into the occupations and lives of others, so frequently making the comment that it is impossible to understand their occupation unless one has oneself been a journalist. Yet journalism as a practice, and journalists as an occupational group, perhaps more than any other, have been the subject of intensive enquiry; in American schools of journalism, the findings of such studies form part of journalists' own professional training and education.

Reading the academic literature one cannot help but feel sympathy with the journalists' claim that the 'outsider' has failed to get inside the trade: it is all too formalistic, too sterile, too serious; and it is not surprising, therefore, that working journalists fail to recognize the world they are supposed to inhabit. To begin with, there are not many laughs in the academic literature, but anyone who has spent time with journalists knows how amusing they often are. Journalists are individuals whose work and working conditions involve the unpredictable, and their attempts at control and management of events and people are, especially as told by themselves, often hilarious. Journalists, as could be expected from the nature of their trade, are good story-tellers, which, generally, social scientists are not. What we have done therefore is to let the journalists tell their own story. (In doing so we hope to have corrected the outsider's failure to deliver the inside workings of a journalist's world.)

The setting is, of course, the conflict between Britain and Argentina over the Falkland Islands; but the main purpose of the study is not war reportage as such, or that war in particular, but to understand journalists through the unique facility offered by events in the South Atlantic. The advantage of using the conflict as the stage upon which the story is set is that it offers near-perfect vision, a kind of bell-jar condition, for observing journalists going about being journalists.

It has another advantage. The stage was such that the actors themselves were forced to confront the role they were playing, reflect on habits, practices and procedures that in other more normal circumstances would be taken for granted. Not only, therefore, did the Falklands Conflict offer a clear view to the outsider of journalistic procedures, it also opened the eyes of the journalists themselves, turning them into reflective witnesses of their occupation.

While the principal method of the research was the ethnographic one of having the journalists recount their experiences and comment on their approach and practices, the stories the journalists told have at times been used in the same way that an anthropologist might use stories and myths of some primitive tribe to explain the culture out of which the stories have emerged. The accuracy of some stories is not always, therefore, an essential condition of their usefulness, especially those in which journalists referred to the behaviour of their colleagues. A readiness to scorn the performance of others appeared to us, leaving aside the genuine dislike that some journalists developed towards their colleagues, to function as a technique by which to highlight their own abilities without having to name them: a silent boasting by omission. So common was this characteristic that it appeared to be an occupational one, the roots of which no doubt rest in the tendency towards insecurity that afflicts journalists in general; one which is perhaps not too surprising in an occupation that combines scholarship with showmanship, promoting the writer through the by-line to the status of a personality but denying him outright editorial control of his product. Yet by understanding this tendency towards insecurity it becomes that much easier to understand the type of behaviour engaged in by the journalists which upset and shocked the military: the internecine bickering; the hostility towards those who clogged up the signal system with over-long despatches or those who filed for foreign newspapers; the complaints that the military were unfairly dispensing favours to some journalists; the collective agreement by one group to block another group getting ashore quickly and thus robbing it of equal reporting opportunities. Compared to their own disciplined men, the military saw the journalists as childishly irresponsible, referring to them as the 'fourth form'.

Thus while we have allowed the journalists to tell their own story, we have not allowed the story to go unstructured. What we have attempted is to develop the coverage of the Falklands hostilities as a general treatise on journalism: other journalists in less dramatic situations which might not so easily be observed, would show similar patterns of behaviour. Furthermore, the behaviour exhibited by the journalists in our case study of the coverage of the Falklands would be recognizable to other journalists who have never covered a foreign story let alone a war. Although the possibility of death and the sheer physical hardship was new to some of them who were, to quote one of the journalists, 'office and bar-room trained', the manner of gathering the news was not. The situation presented new twists and turns to basic patterns of reporting: being bombed may have been new, but being lied to was not.

Too often studies of news concentrate either on the formal editorial control of content or on the informal control whereby the journalist is socialized into the news values and procedures of his organization. What is missing is any notion of the 'journalist as person'. That is, he is first and foremost regarded as a performer of a specific role with certain attributes rather than an individual with his own biography of sensibilities; for example, following the fall of Port Stanley, Ian Bruce of the *Glasgow Herald* was talking by phone to his editor, who complained that Bruce's stories sounded very bitter, to which Bruce replied: 'That's because I am fucking bitter'.

A soldier Bruce had known well and with whom he had shared a drink on many occasions failed to make it to Stanley having been badly wounded, possibly crippled, at the very close of the war. Bruce was upset, it affected him, and in doing so moulded the mood of his copy.

Of course it would be sociological madness to deny the vital importance of structural factors influencing the manner in which journalists report; the journalist does not, after all, write for himself, but for an organization. Nevertheless, insufficient attention has been paid to how the journalist as an individual exercises his own judgement in negotiating his role, and more than that, the critical politicizing of research in the area of mass communications has meant that the journalist as news gatherer has been pushed out of sight. He no longer fits, or rather researchers cannot find a place for him, in the grand indictment of the news as the reproduction of dominant ideology. If nothing else, a study such as this which examines journalists at work under the difficult conditions of the Falklands Conflict is a reminder that there is something called journalism as opposed to 'information oppression'.

This is not to deny the value and contribution to mass communications research of the 'critical' tradition, but there is a need alongside this for a more humanistically inclined individual perspective. One needs to know how those at the cutting surface of news collection operate before making statements drawn from general understanding of social processes. Content analysis can help, but even then its major benefit is in determining values; it cannot go beyond its own methodology to explain how the picture was arrived at. The values say something in that they do not appear by chance; indeed they represent the workings of social relationships which go beyond even the news industry itself and into social formation. Yet to understand the creation of news, as distinct from social relationships as demonstrated by the news, it is essential to get to grips with people as operatives within a system rather than operators of a system. The latter too easily leads to notions of conspiracy on the one hand and on the other to give social structures a life of their own.

We see our focus on journalists themselves as a method of bringing home the complexities and difficulties involved in any interpretation of happenings. It may be convenient to say that journalists got this or that wrong without defining what 'wrong' could mean; does it mean a wrong perspective; does it mean a wrong understanding in some historical sense of social movement and distribution of power within society; does it mean wrong in the sense of factually wrong?

All we can expect from journalists is a reasonable amount of accuracy and a rounded presentation of the facts. Unfortunately, however, facts are provisional upon wider understandings than that which is observed; but a factual account can be taken to be what a community accepts as reasonably accurate, given the limitations and difficulties of observing events. A correspondent for *Pravda* may have been capable of filing a factually accurate account for the *Morning Star*, but not for readers of the *Daily Star*. Facts, as we said, are provisional, but we will see how the Task Force journalists working within community-structured definitions of what is factual struggled to decide what constituted a fact and what counted as an accurate factual account.

Illustrating how the journalists operated gives a sense of reality to proceedings rather than some imagined account of what the journalists ought to have been doing and how they should have viewed events according to, let's say, some creed of abhorrence of war. Was, for example, the firing on British troops after the Argentinians surrendered at Goose Green to be taken as fact, and were the reports of the bayoneting of surrendered Argentinian soldiers by the British to be accepted as fact and, if so, given the contextual meaning of war, where death in all its forms loses the meaning that it has in civilian life, reported as fact?

These were difficult questions and not all the journalists arrived at the same conclusions, but the point is that one cannot treat journalists, any more than any observer, as if they are simply pairs of eyes. They must be seen as active, thinking human beings who make judgements, but at the same time it would be wrong to take the journalist's account of what he was doing as the account of what was going on: what he thought he was doing and what he was actually doing, if the same, would presume perfect knowledge of events. Consequently, the accounts the journalists gave us (and given their lengthy reproduction in the book they are open to inspection and interpretation by the reader) have been set within our own occupational understanding, as sociologists, of social behaviour and social organization.

The journalists, then, have not been regarded as passive observers of something called facts, but as active witnesses of happenings which called for judgements on their part. The judgements journalists make, however, take place within professional codes and set standards of accuracy which allow them to evaluate the level of interpretation present in their reports. The fact that we can see those codes and standards tested to the limits in the Falklands is one of the benefits of the study, but the holding of codes and professional standards of accuracy is no guarantee against systematic distortion since journalists may operate within an occupational ideology that prejudices them in ways they are barely aware of. That is, their accounts are not the same accounts that members of the public would give had they been present. Distortion might take place, in other words, not because of a. lack of shared agreement about facts, but because of practices of collecting facts peculiar to journalism. But again, an advantage of the situation in the Falklands was that for most of the journalists, faced by events that threatened their own lives and the deaths of soldiers they had become fond of, the basis for their own activities was opened for self-inspection to an unusual degree. Tony Snow of the *Sun* may not have slept with the light on after writing 'Up yours, Galtieri' on a Sidewinder Missile, but he could not escape reflecting, as our interview shows, on the nature of popular journalism and his procedures as a reporter. What he could not do in his copy, which included the Sidewinder episode, was to explain the basis of his judgement, and it is that basis which requires examination: it cannot be read backwards from a content analysis of his story.

Although the individual is not the object of sociological study it does not mean there is no room in sociological explanation for biographical placement, especially when the subject of investigation (the news) is constructed in the first instance by individual investment of meaning. The observer must be observed. Non-participant observation is a well-accepted technique for examining the workings of journalism; most typically conducted in the formal setting of the newsroom where the observer is attempting to distinguish patterns of behaviour or judgements made in deciding what is newsworthy. Occasionally the observer will accompany the journalists on assignment. Whether those observed behave differently under the outsider's eye is open to question. In the busy confines of the newsroom, probably not. The news must be produced and routines cannot be altered to massage the image for the watchful eye of the observer. The situation of the assignment is somewhat different. One sometimes has the feeling that the behaviour is promoted for the benefit of the observer, indeed that one is even being 'taken for a ride'. It is not surprising, there is something slightly ludicrous about all observation situations where significance is looked for in every act.

Most observational work, however, whether in the formal setting of the newsroom or the more fluid assignment situation, do not allow much insight into the personalities of those who are being observed. It is a pity, but to be expected from a trade that tends to pride itself on remaining removed from those it studies. There are some notable exceptions, and within sociology different approaches and different definitions of what constitutes correct procedure are necessary. Yet, mass communication research has been especially guided by the attempt at general description: it is the audience as the statistical average of responses, or the journalist as a 'role incumbent', or the news as the filtered expression of social arrangements, or within the tradition of political economy, the organization as a factor of production. The fact that at times, for example, within gratification studies or laboratory experiments, the numbers of people studied are small, does not mean they feature as individuals. They become statistical expressions of states of arousal or the incorporators of information.

The overall purpose is to understand journalism, or at least to gain greater insight into news-gathering than has hitherto been provided by abstract description or the attempt at formalizing procedure. Hopefully, the lengthy treatment of the journalists' accounts of what went on in the Falklands, and their differing perceptions of events will allow the reader to establish the journalists as distinct individuals and by so doing frame the activities with a measure of some understanding of the people involved. Thus Max Hastings becomes, not only the reporter from the *Evening Standard* or the *Express*, but someone with his own individualistic approach and even foibles. But, equally, Ian Bruce, from the *Glasgow Herald*, is seen not as a man just filled with hatred for Hastings, but as someone tired of the trials of obtaining the news in a situation that worked against all efforts without, as he held, the help of Mr Hastings.

What we arrive at by this method is not only an understanding of the individual journalists, but an understanding of the context within which the individuals operated and how they acted in gathering the news. However, while we lay claim for greater focus on journalists as individuals in understanding the production of news, it must be recognized that they are only one part of news production. The whole world is not open to inspection through the individual, only parts, and even those parts can resist full understanding without wider placement in the world from which the individuals have been drawn.

Thus, while the major part of our book deals almost exclusively with the Task Force journalists, three chapters examine the handling of the news in London, including the political controversy that resulted from the manner in which the Ministry of Defence released the news and the political attacks made on the media for the way in which the war was reported. This part of the story takes us directly into wider issues and into questions about the role of information in liberal democratic societies.

It is at this point that the study comes to questions, not of individual behaviour, but of power and power arrangements, the role of ideology and the value structure of society. In other words, it is one thing to give a detailed account and advance understanding of journalists as practitioners, but it is quite another to understand how the product of those practices surfaces as meaning, and even more so, how the meanings of events presented for popular consumption are digested. [. . .]

To have the press we deserve is an old adage, but it pays no attention to the press the public might want or at least it pays no attention to the type of news and reporting the public might want. The answers come at the end, but first, the journalists, then the politics, then the public.

41

The national culture

Paddy Scannell and David Cardiff

From Scannell, P. and Cardiff, D. (1991) *A Social History of British Broadcasting*, Basil Blackwell, Oxford, pp. 277–80, 286–9.

A nation, as David Chaney points out, is an abstract collectivity. It is too big to be grasped by individuals. A sense of belonging, the 'we-feeling' of the community, has to be continually engendered by opportunities for identification as the nation is being manufactured.[1] Radio and, later, television were potent means of manufacturing that 'we-feeling'. They made the nation real and tangible through a whole range of images and symbols, events and ceremonies relayed to audiences direct and live. In the course of the 1920s and 1930s BBC engineers arranged thousands upon thousands of outside broadcasts from a wide variety of sources for the growing listening public.[2] They included religious services and sacred music from churches; opera and plays from the theatres and entertainment from variety halls; dance music from cafes and concert music from the concert halls; public speeches by public persons from all sorts of public places; and ceremonies and events which ranged from royal occasions to the song of the nightingale. Added to all these was the coverage of sporting events – football, rugby, cricket, horse racing, tennis and boxing.

In presenting this material the broadcasters did not intervene to restructure it. Most programmes observed real time, the length of the broadcast corresponding to the duration of the event. Radio sought to minimize its own presence as witness, claiming simply to extend the distribution of the event beyond its particular context to the whole listening community. Their appeal, which was very great to an audience unlike today's which takes such things for granted, was that they admitted listeners to public events, to their live presence, in a way no previous technology had been able to do. A letter to *Radio Times* in 1928 poignantly expressed their effect:

> Many of your readers must be office workers. They must know what sort of a life is that of a clerk in a provincial city – a tram-ride to the office, lunch in a tea-shop or saloon bar, a tram-ride home. You daren't spend much on amusements – the pictures and that – because you've got your holidays to think of. We have no trade unions and we don't grumble, but it's not an easy life. Please don't think I'm complaining. I'm only writing to say how much wireless means to me and thousands of the same sort. It is a real magic carpet. Before it was a fortnight at Rhyl, and that was all the travelling I did that wasn't on a tram. Now I hear the Boat Race and the Derby, and the opening of the Menai Bridge. There are football matches some Saturdays, and talks by famous men and women who have travelled and can tell us about places.[3]

Such broadcasts unobtrusively stitched together the private and the public spheres in a whole new range of contexts. At the same time the events themselves, previously discrete, now entered into new relations with each other, woven together as idioms of a common national life. Nothing so well illustrates the noiseless manner in which the BBC became perhaps *the* central agent of the national culture as its calendrical role; the cyclical reproduction, year in year out, of an orderly and regular progression of festivities, rituals and celebrations – major and minor, civil and sacred – that marked the unfolding of the broadcast year. The calendar is based on natural temporal cycles – the lunar month or solar year – and is a means of regulating in the long term the manifold purposes of religious and civil life. It not only coordinates social life, but gives it a renewable content, anticipatory pleasures, a horizon of expectations. It is one means whereby 'the temporality of social life is expressed in the meshing of present with past that tradition promotes, in which the cyclical character of social life is predominant'.[4]

The cornerstone of the broadcast calendar was the religious year: the weekly observances of the Sabbath through church services and a programme schedule markedly more austere than on other days; the great landmarks of Easter, Pentecost and Christmas; the feast days of the patron saints of England, Scotland and Wales which occasioned special programmes from the appropriate 'region', though what to do with St Patrick's Day was an annually recurring headache for the programme-makers in Belfast. Bank holidays were celebrated in festive mood while the solemn days of national remembrance were marked by religious services and special feature programmes. Sport of course developed its own calendar very quickly. The winter season had its weekly observances of football, rugby and steeple-chasing, climaxing in the Boat Race, the Grand National and the Cup Final. Summer brought in cricket and flat racing, the test matches, Derby Day, Royal Ascot and Wimbledon.

Threaded through the year was a tapestry of civic, cultural, royal and state occasions: Trooping the Colour, the Ceremony of the Keys, the Lord Mayor's Banquet, the Chairing of the Bard, the Dunmow Flitch, the Shakespeare memorial celebrations at Stratford and much, much more. From the late twenties onwards programme-makers kept a watchful eye on impending anniversaries as occasions for a potential talk or feature. The 2000th anniversary of Virgil's death produced a talk on Virgil in English Poetry, while some of the more radical elements conspired to remember republican causes May Day, the Fall of the Bastille or the hundredth anniversary of the first great Chartist march.

The broadcast year fell naturally into two divisions: the indoor months of autumn and winter and the outdoor months of spring and summer. One of the first things the radio manufacturers discovered was the seasonal nature of the sale of radio sets which increased sharply as winter came on. Hence the annual trade exhibition, Radiolympia, was held in the autumn as heralding the start of the 'wireless season'. By the late 1920s output was being planned on a quarterly basis, and the autumn quarter was always carefully arranged to woo the fireside listeners with a varied menu of new plays, concerts and variety programmes. The fireside months were generally better stocked with 'serious' listening matter, but from Whitsun onwards the lighter elements in the programmes were expected to have an increasingly wide appeal. At the same time the broadcasters claimed to have redressed the balance between the seasons of the year, making it possible now to hear good music and plays throughout the summer months when the theatres and concert halls were closed.[5] Thus the programme planners tried to find broadly appropriate material to suit the climate of the year and the mood and leisure activities of the audience. The high point of these activities were the annual arrangements for Christmas Day.

From the very beginning Christmas was always the most important date in the broadcast year. It was the supreme family festival, an invocation of the spirit of Dickens, a celebration of 'home, hearth and happiness'.[6] It was no coincidence that Reith had worked hard for years to persuade the King to speak, from his home and as head of his family, to the nation and empire of families listening in their homes on this particular day. The royal broadcast (the first was in 1932) quickly became part of the ritual of the British Christmas, and is a classic illustration of that process whereby tradition is invented. It set a crowning seal on the role of broadcasting in binding the nation together, giving it a particular form and content: the family audience, the royal family, the nation as family.

Though not all these ceremonies and events recurred annually their combined effect was to create an underlying stable temporal framework for broadcasting, working through the weeks and months of the year. Programme output took on a patterned regularity that grew stronger in the National Programme during the 1930s. This was, and continues to be, an incremental process of production and reproduction in which a seemingly diverse range of material – Wimbledon, a Bank Holiday seaside special feature, a commemorative church service, a royal ceremony – becomes sedimented in annual output as the normative expression of an accessible public life. The nation as a knowable community became available to all members with access to broadcasting.

[. . .]

But when the broadcasters themselves began to put together special feature programmes for anniversaries and special days in the BBC calendar they found themselves in difficulties. The art of live commentary took time to develop. The more elaborate attempts to combine narrative with music and actuality material could give rise to uneasy transitions between the symbolic and the real. But the problems went deeper than style. How should such abstract entities as empire or nation be represented? If the broadcasters drew on older cultural traditions, on history or folk music and poetry, the material might bypass large sections of their audience. If they dealt with the contemporary and actual it might give rise to controversy. There were fissures within the imaginary unity of empire and nation: there was India, there was Ireland. To reference such divisions would defeat the purpose of the programmes. Perhaps the idealized and the actual could be combined if the perfect typification could be found; a location that embodied the essence of Britishness, a New Zealand farmer who might serve as a model for colonial virtue and honest loyalty. Producers explored a range of possibilities, but none provided an obvious way out of their difficulties.

The problems were most evident in the special feature programmes made for Christmas, New Year, Empire Day and the national saints' days. A notable feature of their development was a change in style from the symbolic, rhetorical and impersonal to the actual, vernacular and personal. The pervasive unitary metonym that stood in for the social whole was again the image of the family. In the Empire Day programme 1935 a mother was heard explaining to her daughter, ' "The British Empire, Mary, is made up of one big family." "You mean a family like ours, Mummy?" asks Mary. "Yes, darling", Mummy replies, "but very much larger" '.[7]

The royal broadcasts on Christmas Day were preceded by an elaborate feature programme which aimed to link nation and empire in a common celebration of the family festival. For the first one, described as a 'poetic juggling in time and space in terms of broadcasting', the British announcer was transmuted into an 'aerial postman' who surveyed the globe from a great height and intoned his greetings to each dominion and colony to the sound of a striking clock.[8] This pitch of poetic elevation was not sustained when the postman set foot on land with his 'Hullo Brisbane' or 'Are you awake Vancouver?' and handed over to a local announcer who might mingle expressions of loyalty to the crown with accounts of butter and cheese production or descriptions of a new hydro-electric plant.[9] While critics welcomed the programme as a technical triumph it was evident that a more intimate style would be needed if a sense of the national and imperial community as family was to be evoked.

In successive Christmas features such as *Absent Friends* in 1933 and *The Great Family* in 1935, poetic narration and the chain of empire greetings played a diminishing part.[10] Instead, listeners were offered slices of life, outside broadcasts from a lighthouse and a coal mine, church services, children's parties and family gatherings, talks from individuals representing different parts of the United Kingdom. But here the issue of what was acceptable as representative posed severe problems. Within the BBC the most successful contributor of this type was reckoned to be 'the grand old shepherd of Ilmington' who introduced the King's talk in 1934. But a critic of the 1933 programme pointedly preferred characterful episodes from a Welsh family, Rhondda miners and Highland Scots to the less distinctive Glasgow and Lancashire Christmas parties which he found 'noisy and tedious'.[11] And it was, characteristically, in Northern Ireland that the gravest exception was taken to the way in which that part of the United Kingdom was presented to the rest of Great Britain.

Belfast's contribution to *Absent Friends* lasted less than four minutes. It was intended to show how 'a distinctively Ulster household might be spending part of Christmas'. In the fortnight that followed the broadcast a long and often highly critical debate about it took place in the letter columns of the Belfast Unionist press. Over 70 letters were published, and the following extracts give something of their tone:

> 1. The feelings of thousands of Ulster people must have been outraged when listening to this 'ballyhoo' performance, coming as it did in the midst of an otherwise impressive Christmas message. One listened first to the carefully chosen words of the London announcer and to Mr Howard Marshall, delivered in their delightfully cultured voices, then to the nice, simple messages from hospital children, lighthousemen, miners, crofters, etc., in their natural dialects,

musical and unexaggerated in every case. But what a shock, when Ulster was called, to hear what was obviously considered an amusing example of Ulster dialect, but what in reality was mere parody. What must the world think of Ulster when that is the only form of Christmas message we could send on the ether?

2. It was not Ulster dialect at all, it was an imitation of the dialect of the Free State.

3. We are cut off from the rest of Ireland by the Border. We have not anything to do with it, and we never will have. Erin is Ireland. Ireland is on the other side of the Border: yet we hear the voice of Ulster proclaiming in song 'Come back to Erin'. Ye Gods! Think of it. Who arranged this programme which was of worldwide significance to our province? Who selected 'Father O'Flynn' as a typical Ulster song? Many people have thought for a long time that there is too much of the Irish pipe, the Irish jig, and the Irish atmosphere in the BBC programmes from Belfast.[12]

In an implacably divided community it was an impossible task to find acceptable symbols and images to invoke a shared sense of a common way of life. In London, as Rex Cathcart points out, there had been a tendency to regard the BBC in Northern Ireland as the BBC in Ireland. But in the 1930s the Belfast station became, under its Regional Director, George Marshall, increasingly Unionist in outlook. When North Region proposed to relay a feature in 1937 called *The Irish*, Marshall objected to the title itself as 'highly undesirable, linking under one name two strongly antipathetic states with completely different political outlooks. There is no such thing today as an Irishman. One is either a citizen of the Irish Free State or a citizen of the United Kingdom of Great Britain and Northern Ireland. Irishmen as such ceased to exist after the partition'.[13]

In such circumstances the special programmes for St Patrick's Day became an annual ordeal by fire for programme-makers in the BBC's Northern Ireland office. *Turf Smoke*, Belfast's effort for 1933, was relayed to the rest of Britain and parts of the empire. It was meant to recall for Irish exiles far from home 'those things in Ireland which have a universal appeal'. There was a prologue spoken by a number of voices and an epilogue which referred particularly to Belfast. In between there was music, poetry and songs. All the voices were anonymous. The letter columns of the Belfast newspapers registered Ulster opinion. Exception was taken to 'Father O'Flynn' and to uneducated English accents trying to assume a genuine Irish brogue. But there was praise for the clever dialogue – 'one could almost see the hills and the valleys and the little thatched cottages through the mist, and hear the sea-gulls screaming on the shores'. The tone of many of the critical letters was more in sorrow than anger, and registered a feeling that the BBC staff in Northern Ireland, being mostly English or Scottish, could not be expected to understand Ireland or the Irish.[14] By 1937 the search for exemplars of Irishness for St Patrick's Day drove the desperate producer of the programme up the Sperrin mountains in a blizzard to bring back to the studio a shepherd, a gamekeeper, an embroidress and a country fiddler.[15]

The production files for all the anniversary programmes reveal the problems producers experienced in trying to square myth with reality. Empire

Day was a constant source of embarrassment to producers who were aware that its traditional celebration involved aggressive and ultra-patriotic sentiments which might offend supporters of internationalism and the league of Nations. Yet attempts to devote the programme to current imperial themes such as constitutional change in India were abandoned for fear of controversy.[16] When the New Year's Eve feature in 1932 struck a controversial note, for once, it gave rise to a diplomatic tiff with the Polish Embassy and the banishment, it was rumoured, of its producer to northern parts. Even the Christmas features were not entirely free of politics. In 1935 it was found that there were too many difficulties in including a representative of the unemployed in *The Great Family*. This programme was criticized within the BBC as too formal and pompous. Significantly the objections came from producers in North Region where more direct and down-to-earth styles of documentary and more populist styles of presentation were being developed.[17] By the late thirties the Christmas Day features were sometimes dropped and the highlight of the day – at least as far as the popular press was concerned – was the radio stars' Christmas Party. The folksiness of the earlier Christmas features was lampooned in a stage review, *Nine Sharp* by Herbert Farjeon, which had Captain Snaggers of the North Sea Bloater Fishing Fleet quoting poetry and a BBC commentator bidding him farewell with 'Goodbye and good bloating'.[18]

In routine, day-to-day output the issues of national identity and culture posed problems which, on the one hand, arose from divisions within the supposed unity of British life and culture and, on the other, from the impact of foreign cultures and their perceived threat to traditional national values. Talks might try to preserve a harmonious vision of the British and Britishness only to have the tranquillity of their account exploded by one of the participants. The Americanization of British culture was widely debated outside the BBC, with particular reference to variety programmes and dance music. And the Music Department found itself caught in the double bind of defending a vision of musical culture without national boundaries while trying, at the same time to promote British musical interests at home and abroad.

Notes

1. Chaney, David (1986) A symbolic mirror of ourselves: civic ritual in mass society. In Collins, R. *et al.* (eds) *Media, Culture and Society. A Critical Reader*, Sage Publications, London, p. 249.
2. An article on outside broadcasts (OB) in *Radio Times*, 8 January, 1932 (p. 56), claimed that the 10,000th OB had been notched up on 24 November, 1931.
3. *Radio Times*, 20 January 1928.
4. Giddens, Anthony (1979) *Central Problems in Social Theory*, Macmillan, London, p. 201.
5. *Radio Times*, 11 May 1934.
6. Ibid., 20 December 1924.
7. Empire Day 1935. BBC WAC, Scripts. Quoted in 'An examination of the BBC Empire Service, its establishment and function, 1932–1939', Delaney, Monica, BA Media Studies Dissertation, Polytechnic of Central London, 1979, p. 21.
8. *Radio Times*, 21 December 1934, p. 974.
9. *All The World Over*, 1932. BBC WAC, Scripts.

10. Scripts for both programmes in BBC WAC.
11. Review in *Manchester Guardian*, 27 Decembe, 1933.
12. Cathcart, Rex (1984) *The Most Contrary Region. The BBC in Northern Ireland, 1924–1984*, The Blackstaff Press, Belfast, pp. 65–6.
13. Ibid., pp. 5–6.
14. Ibid., pp. 63–4,
15. Programme Director (Northern Ireland) to AC(P), 18 March 1937. BBC WAC, R34/239.
16. Rose-Troup to DT, 20 April 1932, King-Bull to Gielgud, 22 February 1930. BBC WAC, R51/134. L. Fielden to C. Cliffe, undated, 1937. R47, Empire Day, 1937.
17. BBC WAC, R19/874.
18. Quoted in Short, Ernest (1946) *Fifty Years of Vaudeville*, Eyre & Spottiswoode, London, p. 169.

Section 7

Cultural hegemony

42

Approaches to cultural hegemony within cultural studies

Chris Newbold

The cultural studies perspective as it developed in the 1960s and 1970s began to focus attention away from the more mainstream mass communication debates on media effects and audience attitude/behaviour change, towards an emphasis on the wider cultural environment. To the psychological and sociological frames that had hitherto dominated media research, cultural studies brought the benefits of a radicalized literary studies tradition, with North American (e.g. Radway, 1984), European (e.g. Barthes, 1972; and Eco, 1977) and British (e.g. Hoggart, 1958; Williams, 1958; and Hall, 1971) variants.

Also referred to as the cultural effects theory, this approach assumed that the media as part of the culture industries did have important effects; but these were not short term and immediate, or at least they were not *merely* so, but were the contribution of media to popular consciousness through the language, symbolic and cultural codes in which the media framed the world, not as neutral organizations working to serve the public good in some kind of independent 'fourth estate' or 'watchdog' role, but as institutions embedded in existing patterns of social relations and, in common with all powerful institutions within a given social system, serving to reproduce the social relations in which their own power is invested. Media work in this model is essentially ideological work, but to understand the media it is also necessary to understand their place with reference to more extensive social and cultural codes from which they draw and to which they contribute. There is considerable debate in this tradition as to the extent to which the ideological work of media is directly determined by the interests of social élites, by underlying economic forces, or whether they can function autonomously, with spaces for resistance and subversion that arise from oppositions within the system, for example between the interests of specific professional groups such as broadcasters and broader interests of the social class from which they are recruited, or between different factions of the social élite in their struggles for power. Although Marxism is a powerful influence in early manifestations of this approach, there is evidence of considerable intellectual innovation here, particularly with respect to analysis of media texts, much of which is pursued in relation to subordinate groups, including the working class, women, youth groups and ethnic communities.

Much of the work of the Frankfurt school only became available in English in the early 1960s, when it proved influential to young Marxist and neo-

Marxist radicals. Emphasizing the totalistic commercialization of culture in mass society, the Frankfurt approach offered an attractive and above all critical base for the analysis of mass media in radical opposition to the anodyne and conservative models of media effects which had prevailed hitherto. Through Marcuse (1964), furthermore, a bridge was offered between Marx and Freud, and a place found for the role of sexuality within processes of social oppression. The focus on culture raised important questions about the adequacy of Marx's own discussions of culture, and the relationship between economic 'base' and 'cultural superstructure'. A variety of positions emerged concerning the relative autonomy of culture from the economic base (see, in particular, the work of Althusser), but a theory of cultural hegemony acquired particular influence.

The notion of ideology as hegemonic derives principally from the work of the Italian Marxist Antonio Gramsci (1971), who likens it to the trench warfare of the First World War, with each side gaining and losing ground in a continual, shifting contest over time. Here ideology is not simply dominant, it is hegemonic, which is to say that the concept allows for the dimension of struggle and opposition, of confrontation between differing cultures, where hegemony has to be negotiated and won. Cultural studies, as developed in its widely influential British form, conceived of society made up of a number of competing cultures. The central question was the degree to which mass media output reflects and communicates a dominant version of culture as though it were the only culture, through which the structure and leading ideas of a world that has been organized to serve one or a range of competing élites is made to appear as part of a 'natural' order of things, beyond rational questioning, and thus completely de-legitimizing or even obliterating other possible versions or, rather, other possible visions of the world as it might be. It is through the shifting nature of power and political élites that ideological consensus evolves and is maintained.

The common ground of the articles included in this section is their concern to explain how such processes of cultural domination through the media should be conceptualized and understood. The first extract, often acknowledged as a starting point in cultural studies, is taken from Raymond Williams' *The Long Revolution*. In his chapter on 'The analysis of culture' Williams defines three related meanings of culture, of which one prefigures the position of Stuart Hall who in his introduction to the first *Working Papers in Cultural Studies*, wrote that 'culture is the way social life is experienced and handled, the meanings and values which inform human action, which are embodied in and mediate social relations, political life, etc.' (Hall, 1971, p. 6). For Hall as for Williams and Hoggart (1958) the media should be studied not as 'effecting culture', but as an indicator of social values and meanings, a text through which cultural meanings are revealed and evaluated.

There is a great deal of emphasis on the symbolic codes of textual expression, drawing from the traditions of linguistics, semiotics, sociolinguistics and literary structuralism. Within such work there is a tension between, on the one hand, the structuralist proposition that the 'meanings' of texts, including cultures-as-texts, can be revealed by accessing fundamental oppositions and their other underlying structural characteristics, and on the other hand, the view that the meanings of texts have to be understood by reference not to fundamental regularities of structure but to the ways in which texts are generated within specific social and cultural situations and among particular historically-located human beings. Paradoxically, these social contexts are themselves often investigated along structuralist lines with reference to key sociological parameters of social class, etc., whereas more recent studies, through ethnographic method, attempt to establish meanings directly from the evidence of the parties to communication.

Hall considers the various legacies which nurture culturalist and structuralist paradigms in cultural studies. He explores the all pervading nature of culture in society as expressive of ideologies. Bennett develops this to discuss the relationship between cultural studies, with its concern for subordinate and subordinated cultures, and the structuralist ingestion of the text, through the adoption of the Gramscian approach to hegemony. In doing so he illustrates the benefit to both camps of the 'reading through popular forms' that so characterizes the cultural studies approach. Inevitably both articles point the way to the 'struggle over meaning' and the polysemic nature of the message, a direction or 'turn' in cultural studies that is taken up in Section 10.

The second extract by Hall sees the emergence of the concern with ideology as critical to development of the field of mass communication study. From the standpoint of the early 1980s he reflects a paradigm shift in media studies from a largely pluralistic model to one in which media institutions, working ideologically through a wide variety of textual devices in construction and composition are understood to 'manufacture consent'.

Carey takes up this relationship between mass communication research and cultural studies, and discusses the essential difference between the behavioural science model of mass communication and the human experience approach of cultural studies His position is not dissimilar to that of Williams, for whom cultures are 'structures of feeling', which communicate and are in every sense lived. This position rejects the 'false consciousness' approach to the culture of subordinated classes which is common to Marxism, wherein working class culture is defined in terms of the extent of its self-delusion. Carey emphasizes the work of anthropologist Clifford Geertz, suggesting that for a cultural science of communication the understanding and interpretation of the meaning structure of symbols applied to contemporary culture is the key task.

Carey implicitly examines the terms of reference for mass communication, finding that it is constituted in such a way that it misses much of the wider style and focus of investigation common to a study of culture, thus isolating itself from the very emphasis on ordinary and everyday life experience which, as we have seen, Williams, Hall, and Geertz make the centre of their projects. It is this populist strand in cultural studies that lies at the heart of the eloquent criticism mounted by McGuigan in the final extract. Dwelling on the writings of Williams and Hall, and on the period in which the cultural hegemony approach dominated critical debate, McGuigan is particularly quizzical of the relationship between the culture of intellectuals and that of other people, which he sees as 'inherently paradoxical' (McGuigan, 1992, p. 5). Hall and Williams are the best examples of this since their work emerges from an engagement with left/Marxist issues during the period of the rise of Reagan and Thatcher.

This chapter charts the decline of the hegemony paradigm and looks towards a resurrection of or at least a reconciliation with the base/superstructure model, in coming to terms with the culture industries rather than just the content of their products, and together with the economic dynamics of cultural globalism.

As much as cultural hegemony proved a rallying point for those concerned with relationships between cultures and those concerned with ideology in text, it also generated sufficient points of new theoretical departure to fragment the initial ideas of writers such as Williams and Hall. The following sections of the reader stand to some extent in testament to this. Feminism, and moving image analysis emerge and pursue their own discourses apart from such classic texts as Hall's (1980) treatise on *Encoding/decoding*, or the structuralist and psychoanalytic traditions of cultural studies. In particular, any examination of ideology and ideological effects has now to be problematized in the light of the emphasis on audience decoding and ethnography often attributed to David Morley (1980) at the CCCS, but also drawing on a range of works such as those of Ang, Radway, Hobson, Brundson and others, which are cited in the references to Section 10.

References and further reading

Althusser, L. (1971) Ideology and ideological state apparatuses. In *Lenin and Philosophy and Other Essays*, New Left Books, London.

Barthes, R. (1972) *Mythologies*, Jonathan Cape, London.

During, S. (ed.) *The Cultural Studies Reader*, Routledge

Eco, U. (1977) *A Theory of Semiotics*, Macmillan, London.

Gramsci, A. (1971) *Selections from the Prison Notebooks* (edited and translated by Hoare, Q, and Nowell-Smith, G.), Lawrence and Wishart.

Hall, S, (1971) Introduction. In *Working Papers in Cultural Studies*, CCCS, University of Birmingham, Spring.

Hall, S. (1980) Encoding/decoding. In Hall *et al. Culture, Media, Language*, Hutchinson.

Harris, D. (1992) *From Class Struggle to the Politics of Pleasure: The Effects of Gramscianism on Cultural Studies*, Routledge.

Hoggart, R. (1958) *The Uses of Literacy*, Penguin.

Marcuse, H. (1964) *One-dimensional Man*, Sphere Books, London.

McGuigan, J. (1992) *Cultural Populism*, Routledge.

Morley, D. (1980) *The Nationwide Audience: Structure and Decoding*, British Film Institute.

Turner, G. (1990) *British Cultural Studies: An Introduction*, Unwin Hyman. Boston.

Williams, R. (1958) *The Long Revolution*, Chatto and Windus, London.

43

The analysis of culture

Raymond Williams

From Williams, R. (1965) *The Long Revolution*, Penguin, Harmondsworth, pp. 57–70.

There are three general categories in the definition of culture. There is, first, the 'ideal', in which culture is a state or process of human perfection, in terms of certain absolute or universal values. The analysis of culture, if such a definition is accepted, is essentially the discovery and description in lives and works, of those values which can be seen to compose a timeless order, or to have permanent reference to the universal human condition. Then, second, there is the 'documentary', in which culture is the body of intellectual and imaginative work, in which, in a detailed way, human thought and experience are variously recorded. The analysis of culture, from such a definition, is the activity of criticism, by which the nature of the thought and experience, the details of the language, form and convention in which these are active, are described and valued. Such criticism can range from a process very similar to the 'ideal' analysis, the discovery of 'the best that has been thought and written in the world', through a process which, while interested in tradition, takes as its primary emphasis the particular work being studied (its clarification and valuation being the principal end in view) to a kind of historical criticism which, after analysis of particular works, seeks to relate them to the particular traditions and societies in which they appeared. Finally, third, there is the 'social' definition of culture, in which culture is a description of a particular way of life, which expresses certain meanings and values not only in art and learning but also in institutions and ordinary behaviour. The analysis of culture, from such a definition, is the clarification of the meanings and values implicit and explicit in a particular way of life, a particular culture. Such analysis will include the historical criticism already referred to, in which intellectual and imaginative works are analysed in relation to particular traditions and societies, but will also include analysis of elements in the way of life that to followers of the other definitions are not 'culture' at all: the organization of production, the structure of the family, the structure of institutions which express or govern social relationships, the characteristic forms through which members of the society communicate. Again, such analysis ranges from an 'ideal' emphasis, the discovery of certain absolute or universal, or at least higher and lower, meanings and values, through the 'documentary' emphasis, in which clarification of a particular way of life is the main end in view, to an emphasis which, from studying particular meanings and values, seeks not so much to compare these, as a way of establishing a scale, but by studying their modes of change to discover certain general 'laws' or 'trends', by which social and cultural development as a whole can be better understood.

[. . .]

The variations; meaning; and reference, the use of culture as a term, must be seen, I am arguing, not simply as a disadvantage, which prevents any kind of neat and exclusive definition, but as a genuine complexity corresponding to real elements in experience. There is a significant reference in each of the three main kinds of definition, and, if this is so, it is the relations between them that should claim our attention. It seems to me that any adequate theory of culture must include the three areas of fact to which the definitions point, and conversely that any particular definition, within any of the categories, which would exclude reference to the others, is inadequate. Thus an 'ideal' definition which attempts to abstract the process it describes from its detailed embodiment and shaping by particular societies – regarding man's ideal development as something separate from and even opposed to his 'animal nature' or the satisfaction of material needs – seems to me unacceptable. A 'documentary' definition which sees value only in the written and painted records, and marks this area off from the rest of man's life in society, is equally unacceptable. Again, a 'social' definition, which treats either the general process or the body of art and learning as a mere by-product, a passive reflection of the real interests of the society, seems to me equally wrong. However difficult it may be in practice, we have to try to see the process as a whole, and to relate our particular studies, if not explicitly at least by ultimate reference, to the actual and complex organization.

[. . .]

If we study real relations, in any actual analysis, we reach the point where we see that we are studying a general organization in a particular example, and in this general organization there is no element that we can abstract and separate from the rest. It was certainly an error to suppose that values or art-works could be adequately studied without reference to the particular society within which they were expressed, but it is equally an error to suppose that the social explanation is determining, or that the values and works are mere by-products. We have got into the habit, since we realized how deeply works or values could be determined by the whole situation in which they are expressed, of asking about these relationships in a standard form: 'what is the relation of this art to this society?' But 'society', in this question, is a specious whole. If the art is part of the society, there is no solid whole, outside it, to which by the form of our question, we concede priority. The art is there, as an activity, with the production, the trading, the politics, the raising of families. To study the relations adequately we must study them actively, seeing all the activities as particular and contemporary forms of human energy. If we take any one of these activities we can see how many of the others are reflected in it, in various ways according to the nature of the whole organization. It seems likely, also, that the very fact that we can distinguish any particular activity, as serving certain specific ends, suggests that without this activity the whole of the human organization at that place and time could not have been realized. Thus art, while clearly related to the other activities, can be seen as expressing certain elements in the organization which, within that organization's terms, could only have

been expressed in this way. It is then not a question of relating the art to the society, but of studying all the activities and their inter-relations, without any concession of priority to any one of them we may choose to abstract. If we find, as often, that a particular activity came radically to change the whole organization, we can still not say that it is to this activity that all the others must be related; we can only study the varying ways in which, within the changing organization, the particular activities and their inter-relations were affected. Further, since the particular activities will be serving varying and sometimes conflicting ends, the sort of change we must look for will rarely be of a simple kind: elements of persistence, adjustment, unconscious assimilation, active resistance, alternative effort, will all normally be present, in particular activities and in the whole organization.
[. . .]
    I would define the theory of culture as the study of relationships between elements in a whole way of life. The analysis of culture is the attempt to discover the nature of the organization which is the complex of these relationships. Analysis of particular works or institutions is, in this context, analysis of their essential kind of organization, the relationships which works or institutions embody as parts of the organization as a whole. A key word, in such analysis, is pattern: it is with the discovery of patterns of a characteristic kind that any useful cultural analysis begins, and it is with the relationships between these patterns, which sometimes reveal unexpected identities and correspondences in hitherto separately considered activities, sometimes again reveal discontinuities of an unexpected kind, that general cultural analysis is concerned.
[. . .]
    We can go some way in restoring the outlines of a particular organization of life; we can even recover what Fromm calls the 'social character' or Benedict the 'pattern of culture'. The social character – a valued system of behaviour and attitudes – is taught formally and informally; it is both an ideal and a mode. The 'pattern of culture' is a selection and configuration of interests and activities, and a particular valuation of them, producing a distinct organization, a 'way of life'. Yet even these, as we recover them, are usually abstract. Possibly, however, we can gain the sense of a further common element, which is neither the character nor the pattern, but as it were the actual experience through which these were lived. This is potentially of very great importance, and I think the fact is that we are most conscious of such contact in the arts of a period. It can happen that when we have measured these against the external characteristics of the period, and then allowed for individual variations there is still some important common element that we cannot easily place. I think we can best understand this if we think of any similar analysis of a way of life that we ourselves share. For we find here a particular sense of life, a particular community of experience hardly needing expression, through which the characteristics of our way of life that an external analyst could describe are in some way passed, giving them a particular and characteristic colour. We are usually most aware of this when we notice the contrasts between generations, who never talk quite 'the same language', or when we read an account of our lives by someone from outside the community, or watch the small differences in style, of speech or behaviour,

in someone who has learned our ways yet was not bred in them. Almost any formal description would be too crude to express this nevertheless quite distinct sense of a particular and native style. [. . .]

The term I would suggest to describe it is *structure of feeling*: it is as firm and definite as 'structure' suggests, yet it operates in the most delicate and least tangible parts of our activity. In one sense, this structure of feeling is the culture of a period: it is the particular living result of all the elements in the general organization. And it is in this respect that the arts of a period, taking these to include characteristic approaches and tones in argument, are of major importance. For here, anywhere, this characteristic is likely to be expressed; often not consciously, but by the fact that here, in the only examples we have of recorded communication that outlives its bearers, the actual living sense, the deep community that makes the communication possible, is naturally drawn upon. I do not mean that the structure of feeling, any more than the social character, is possessed in the same way by the many individuals in the community. But I think it is a very deep and very wide possession, in all actual communities, precisely because it is on that communication depends. And what is particularly interesting is that it does not seem to be in any formal sense, learned. [. . .]

Once the carriers of such a structure die, the nearest we can get to this vital element is in the documentary culture, from poems to buildings and dress-fashions, and it is this relation that gives significance to the definition of culture in documentary terms. This in no way means that the documents are autonomous. It is simply that, as previously argued, the significance of an activity must be sought in terms of the whole organization, which is more than the sum of its separable parts. What we are looking for, always, is the actual life that the whole organization is there to express. [. . .]

We need to distinguish three levels of culture, even in its most general definition. There is the lived culture of a particular time and place, only fully accessible to those living in that time and place. There is the recorded culture, of every kind, from art to the most everyday facts: the culture of a period. There is also, as the factor connecting lived culture and period cultures, the culture of the selective tradition.

When it is no longer being lived, but in a narrower way survives in its records, the culture of a period can be very carefully studied, until we feel that we have reasonably clear ideas of its cultural work, its social character, its general patterns of activity and value, and in part of its structure of feeling. Yet the survival is governed, not only by the period itself, but by new periods, which gradually compose a tradition. Even most specialists in a period know only a part of even its records. One can say with confidence, for example, that nobody really knows the nineteenth-century novel; nobody has read, or could have read, all its examples, over the whole range from printed volumes to penny serials. The real specialist may know some hundreds; the ordinary specialist some what less; educated readers a decreasing number: though all will have clear ideas on the subject. A selective process, of a quite drastic kind, is at once evident, and this is true of every field of activity. Equally, of course, no nineteenth-century reader would have read all the novels; no individual in the society would have known more than a selection of its facts. But everyone living in the period would have had something which, I have argued, no later individual can wholly recover: that sense of the life within which the novels were written, and which we now approach through our selection. Theoretically, a period is recorded; in practice, this record is absorbed into a selective tradition; and both are different from the culture as lived.

It is very important to try to understand the operation of a selective tradition. To some extent, the selection begins within the period itself; from the whole body of activities, certain things are selected for value and emphasis. In general this selection will reflect the organization of the period as a whole, though this does not mean that the values and emphases will later be confirmed. We see this clearly enough in the case of past periods, but we never really believe it about our own. [. . .] The selective tradition thus creates, at one level, a general human culture; at another level, the historical record of a particular society; at a third level, most difficult to accept and assess, a rejection of considerable areas of what was once a living culture.

Within a given society, selection will be governed by many kinds of special interest, including class interests. Just as the actual social situation will largely govern contemporary selection, so the development of the society, the process of historical change, will largely determine the selective tradition. The traditional culture of a society will always tend to correspond to its *contemporary* system of interests and values, for it is not an absolute body of work but a continual selection and interpretation. In theory, and to a limited extent in practice, those institutions which are formally concerned with keeping the tradition alive (in particular the institutions of education and scholarship) are committed to the tradition as a whole, and not to some selection from it according to contemporary interests. The importance of this commitment is very great, because we see again and again, in the workings of a selective tradition, reversals and re-discoveries, returns to work apparently abandoned as dead, and clearly this is only possible if there are institutions whose business it is to keep large areas of past culture, if not alive, at least available. It is natural and inevitable that the selective tradition should follow the lines of growth of a society, but because such growth is complex and continuous, the relevance of past work, in any future situation, is unforeseeable. [. . .]

In a society as a whole, and in all its particular activities, the cultural tradition can be seen as a continual selection and re-selection of ancestors. Particular lines will be drawn, often for as long as a century, and then suddenly with some new stage in growth these will be cancelled or weakened, and new lines drawn. In the analysis of contemporary culture, the existing state of the selective tradition is of vital importance, for it is often true that some change in this tradition – establishing new lines with the past, breaking or re-drawing existing lines – is a radical kind of *contemporary* change. We tend to underestimate the extent to which the cultural tradition is not only a selection but also an interpretation. We see most past work through our own experience, without even making the effort to see it in something like its original terms. What analysis can do is not so much to reverse this, returning a work to its period, as to make the interpretation conscious, by showing historical alternatives; to relate the interpretation to the particular contemporary values on which it rests; and, by exploring the real patterns of the work, confront us with the real nature of the choices we are making. We shall find, in some cases, that we are keeping the work alive because it is a genuine contribution to cultural growth. We shall find, in other cases, that we are using the work in a particular way for our own reasons, and it is better to know this than to surrender to the mysticism of the 'great valuer, time'. To put on to time, the abstraction, the responsibility for our own active choices is to suppress a central part of our experience. The more actively all cultural work can be related, either to the whole organization within which it was expressed, or to the contemporary organization within which it is used, the more clearly shall we see its true values. Thus 'documentary' analysis will lead out to 'social' analysis, whether in a lived culture, a past period, or in the selective tradition which is itself a social organization. And the discovery of permanent contributions will lead to the same kind of general analysis, if we accept the process at this level, not as human perfection (a movement towards determined values), but as part of man's general evolution, to which many individuals and groups contribute. Every element that we analyse will be in this sense active: that is it will be seen in certain real relations, at many different levels. In describing these relations, the real cultural process will emerge.

44

Cultural studies: two paradigms

Stuart Hall

From Scannell, P. (ed.) (1980) *Media, Culture and Society*, Academic Press, London, Vol. 2, No. 1, pp. 59–72.

Two rather different ways of conceptualizing 'culture' can be drawn out of the many suggestive formulations in Raymond Williams' *Long Revolution*. The first relates 'culture' to the sum of the available descriptions through which societies make sense of and reflect their common experiences. The conception of 'culture' is itself democratized and socialized. It no longer consists of the sum of the 'best that has been thought and said', regarded as the summits of an achieved civilization – that ideal of perfection to which, in earlier usage, all aspired. Even 'art' – assigned in the earlier framework a privileged position, as touchstone of the highest values of civilization – is now redefined as only one, special, form of a general social process: the giving and taking of meanings, and the slow development of 'common' meanings – a common culture: 'culture', in this special sense, 'is ordinary'. [. . .]
  If this first emphasis takes up and re-works the connotation of the term 'culture' with the domain of 'ideas', the second emphasis is more deliberately anthropological, and emphasizes that aspect of 'culture' which refers to social *practices*. It is from this second emphasis that the somewhat simplified definition – 'culture is a whole way of life' – has been rather too neatly abstracted. Williams did relate this aspect of the concept to the more 'documentary' – that is, descriptive, even ethnographic – usage of the term. But the earlier definition seems to me the more central one, into which 'way of life' is integrated. The important point in the argument rests on the active and indissoluble relationships between elements or social practices normally separated out. It is in *this* context that the 'theory of culture' is defined as 'the study of relationships between elements in a whole way of life'. 'Culture' is not *a* practice; nor is it simply the descriptive sum of the 'mores and folkways' of societies – as it tended to become in certain kinds of anthropology. It is threaded through *all* social practices, and is the sum of their inter-relationship. The question of what, then, is studied, and how, resolves itself. [. . .] The purpose of the analysis is to grasp how the interactions between all these practices and patterns are lived and experienced as a whole, in any particular period. This is its 'structure of feeling'.
  It is easier to see what Williams was getting at, and why he was pushed along this path, if we understand what were the problems he addressed, and what pitfalls he was trying to avoid. This is particularly necessary because *The Long Revolution* (like many of Williams' work) carries on a submerged,

almost 'silent' dialogue with alternative-positions, which are not always as clearly identified as one would wish. There is a clear engagement with the 'idealist' and 'civilizing' definitions of culture – both the equation of 'culture' with *ideas*, in the idealist tradition; and the assimilation of culture to an *ideal*, prevalent in the élitist terms of the 'cultural debate'. But there is also a more extended engagement with certain kinds of Marxism, against which Williams' definitions are consciously pitched. He is arguing against the literal operations of the base/superstructure metaphor, which in classical Marxism ascribed the domain of ideas and of meanings to the 'superstructures', themselves conceived as merely reflective of and determined in some simple fashion by 'the base'; without a social effectivity of their own. That is to say, his argument is constructed against a vulgar materialism and an economic determinism. He offers, instead, a radical interactionism: in effect, the interaction of all practices in and with one another, skirting the problem of determinacy. The distinctions between practices is overcome by seeing them all as variant forms of *praxis* – of a general human activity and energy. The underlying patterns which distinguish the complex of practices in any specific society at any specific time are the characteristic 'forms of its organization' which underlie them all, and which can therefore be traced in each.

There have been several, radical revisions of this early position: and each has contributed much to the redefinition of what Cultural Studies is and should be. We have acknowledged already the exemplary nature of Williams' project, in constantly rethinking and revising older arguments – in going on thinking. Nevertheless, one is struck by a marked line of continuity through these seminal revisions. One such moment is the occasion of his recognition of Lucien Goldmann's work, and through him, of the array of Marxist thinkers who had given particular attention to superstructural forms and whose work began, for the first time, to appear in English translation in the mid-1960s. [. . .] 'I came to believe that I had to give up, or at least to leave aside, what I knew as the Marxist tradition: to attempt to develop a theory of social totality; to see the study of culture as the study of relations between elements in a whole way of life; to find ways of studying structure . . . which could stay in touch with and illuminate particular art works and forms, but also forms and relations of more general social life; to replace the formula of base and superstructure with the more active idea of a field of mutually if also unevenly determining forces' (*NLR* 67, May–June 1971). And here is the positive – the point where the convergence is marked between Williams' 'structure of feeling' and Goldmann's 'genetic structuralism': 'I found in my own work that I had to develop the idea of a structure of feeling . . . But then I found Goldmann beginning . . . from a concept of structure which contained, in itself, a relation between social and literary facts. This relation, he insisted, was not a matter of content, but of mental structures: 'categories which simultaneously organize the empirical consciousness of a particular social group, and the imaginative world created by the writer'. By definition, these structures are not individually but collectively created'. The stress there on the interactivity of practices and on the underlying totalities, and the homologies between them, is characteristic and significant. 'A correspondence of content between a writer and his world is less significant than this correspondence of organization, of structure'.

A second such 'moment' is the point where Williams really takes on board E. P. Thompson's critique of *The Long Revolution* (cf. the review in *NLR* 9 and 10) – that no 'whole way of life' is without its dimension of struggle and confrontation between opposed ways of life – and attempts to rethink the key issues of determination and domination via Gramsci's concept of 'hegemony'. This essay ('Base and superstructure', *NLR* 82, 1973) is a seminal one, especially in its elaboration of dominant, residual and emergent cultural practices, and its return to the problematic of determinacy as 'limits and pressures'. Nonetheless, the earlier emphases recur, with force: 'we cannot separate literature and art from other kinds of social practice, in such a way as to make them subject to quite special and distinct laws'. And, 'no mode of production, and therefore no dominant society or order of society, – and therefore no dominant culture, in reality exhausts human practice, human energy, human intention'. And this note is carried forward – indeed, it is radically accented – in Williams' most sustained and succinct recent statement of his position: the masterly condensations of *Marxism And Literature*. Against the structuralist emphasis on the specificity and 'autonomy' of practices, and their analytic separation of societies into their discrete instances, Williams' stress is on 'constitutive activity' in general, on 'sensuous human activity, as practice', from Marx's first 'thesis' on Feuerbach; on different practices conceived as a 'whole indissoluble practice'; on totality. 'Thus, contrary to one development in Marxism, it is not 'the base' and 'the superstructure' that need to be studied, but specific and indissoluble real processes, within which the decisive relationship, from a Marxist point of view, is that expressed by the complex idea of "determination" ' (*M & L*, pp. 30–31, 82).

At one level, Williams' and Thompson's work can only be said to converge around the terms of the same problematic through the operation of a violent and schematically dichotomous theorization. The organizing terrain of Thompson's work – classes as relations, popular struggle, and historical forms of consciousness, class cultures in their historical particularity – is foreign to the more reflective and 'generalizing' mode in which Williams typically works. And the dialogue between them begins with a very sharp encounter. The review of *The Long Revolution*, which Thompson undertook, took Williams sharply to task for the evolutionary way in which culture as a 'whole way of life' had been conceptualized; for his tendency to absorb conflicts between class cultures into the terms of an extended 'conversation'; for his impersonal tone – above the contending classes, as it were; and for the imperializing sweep of his concept of 'culture' (which, heterogeneously, swept everything into its orbit because it was the study of the inter-relationships between the forms of energy and organization underlying *all* practices. But wasn't this – Thompson asked – where History came in?). Progressively, we can see how Williams has persistently rethought the terms of his original paradigm to take these criticisms into account – though this is accomplished (as it so frequently is in Williams) obliquely: via a particular appropriation of Gramsci, rather than in a more direct modification.

[. . .]

Here, then, despite the many significant differences, is the outline of one significant line of thinking in cultural studies – some would say, *the* dominant paradigm. It stands opposed to the residual and merely-reflective role assigned to 'the cultural'. In its different ways, it conceptualizes culture as interwoven with all social practices; and those practices, in turn, as a common form of human activity: sensuous human praxis, the activity through which men and women make history. It is opposed to the base-superstructure way of formulating the relationship between ideal and material forces, especially where the 'base' is defined as the determination by 'the economic' in any simple sense. It prefers the wider formulation – the dialectic between social being and social consciousness: neither separable into its distinct poles (in some alternative formulations, the dialectic between 'culture' and 'non-culture'). It defines 'culture' as *both* the meanings and values which arise amongst distinctive social groups and classes, on the basis of their given historical conditions and relationships, through which they 'handle' and respond to the conditions of existence; *and* as the lived traditions and practices through which those 'understandings' are expressed and in which they are embodied. Williams brings together these two aspects – definitions and ways of life – around the concept of 'culture' itself. Thompson brings the two elements – consciousness and conditions – around the concept of 'experience'. Both positions entail certain difficult fluctuations around these key terms. Williams so totally absorbs 'definitions of experience' into our 'ways of living', and both into an indissoluble real material practice-in-general, as to obviate any distinction between 'culture' and 'not-culture'. Thompson sometimes uses 'experience' in the more usual sense of consciousness, as the collective ways in which men 'handle, transmit or distort' their given conditions, the raw materials of life; sometimes as the domain of the 'lived', the mid-term *between* 'conditions' and 'culture'; and sometimes as the objective conditions themselves – against which particular modes of consciousness are counterposed. But, whatever the terms, both positions tend to read structures of relations in terms of how they are 'lived' and 'experienced'. Williams' 'structure of feeling' – with its deliberate condensation of apparently incompatible elements – is characteristic. But the same is true of Thompson, despite his far fuller historical grasp of the 'given-ness' or structuredness of the relations and conditions into which men and women necessarily and involuntarily enter, and his clearer attention to the determinacy of productive and exploitative relations under capitalism. This is a consequence of giving culture-consciousness and experience so pivotal a place in the analysis. The *experiential pull* in this paradigm, and the emphasis on the creative and on historical agency, constitutes the two key elements in the *humanism* of the position outlined. Each, consequently accords 'experience' an authenticating position in any cultural analysis. It is, ultimately, where and how people experience their conditions of life, define them and respond to them which, for Thompson, defines why every mode of production is also a culture, and every struggle between classes is always also a struggle between cultural modalities; and which, for Williams, is what a 'cultural analysis', in the final instance, should deliver. In 'experience', all the different practices intersect; within 'culture' the different practices interact – even if on an uneven and mutually determining basis. This sense of cultural totality – of the whole historical process – over-rides any effort to keep the instances and elements distinct. Their real interconnection, under given historical conditions, must be matched by a totalizing movement 'in thought', in the analysis. It establishes for both the strongest protocols against any form of analytic abstraction which distinguishes practices, or which sets out to test the 'actual historical movement' in all its intertwined complexity and particularity by any more sustained logical or analytical operation. These positions, especially in their more concrete historical rendering (*The Making*, *The Country And The City*) are the very opposite of a Hegelian search for underlying essences. Yet, in their tendency to reduce practices to *praxis* and to find common and homologous 'forms' underlying the most apparently differentiated areas, their movement is 'essentializing'. They have a particular way of understanding the totality – though it is with a small 't', concrete and historically determinate, uneven in its correspondences. They understand it 'expressively'. And since they constantly inflect the more traditional analysis towards the experiential level, or read the other structures and relations downwards from the vantage point of how they are 'lived', they are properly (even if not adequately or fully) characterized as 'culturalist' in their emphasis: even when all the caveats and qualifications against a too rapid 'dichotomous theorizing' have been entered. [. . .]

The 'culturalist' strand in cultural studies was interrupted by the arrival on the intellectual scene of the 'structuralisms'. These, possibly more varied than the 'culturalisms', nevertheless shared certain positions and orientations in common which makes their designation under a single title not altogether misleading. It has been remarked that whereas the 'culturalist' paradigm can be defined without requiring a conceptual reference to the term 'ideology' (the *word*, of course, does appear: but it is not a key concept), the 'structuralist' interventions have been largely articulated around the concept of 'ideology': in keeping with its more impeccably Marxist lineage, 'culture' does not figure so prominently. Whilst this may be true of the Marxist structuralists, it is at best less than half the truth about the structuralist enterprise as such. But it is now a common error to condense the latter exclusively around the impact of Althusser and all that has followed in the wake of his interventions – where 'ideology' has played a seminal, but modulated rôle: and to omit the significance of Lévi-Strauss. Yet, in strict historical terms, it was Lévi-Strauss, and the early semiotics, which made the first break. And though the Marxist structuralisms have superseded the latter, they owed, and continue to owe, an immense theoretical debt (often fended off or down-graded into footnotes, in the search for a retrospective orthodoxy) to his work. It was Lévi-Strauss' structuralism which, in its appropriation of the linguistic paradigm, after Saussure, offered the promise to the 'human sciences of culture' of a paradigm capable of rendering them scientific and rigorous in a thoroughly new way. And when, in Althusser's work, the more classical Marxist themes were recovered, it remained the case that Marx was 'read' – and reconstituted – through the terms of the linguistic paradigm. In *Reading Capital*, for example, the case is made that the mode of production – to coin a phrase – could best be understood as if 'structured like a language' (through the selective combination of invariant elements). The a-historical and synchronic stress, against the historical emphases of 'culturalism', derived from a similar source. So did a pre-occupation with 'the social, *sui generis*' – used not adjectivally but substantively: a usage Lévi-Strauss derived, not from Marx, but from Durkheim. [. . .] Structuralism shared with culturalism a radical break with the terms of the base/superstructure metaphor, as derived from the simpler parts of the *German Ideology*. And, though 'It is to this theory of the superstructures, scarcely touched on by Marx' to which Lévi-Strauss aspired to contribute, his contribution was such as to break in a radical way with its whole terms of reference, as finally and irrevocably as the 'culturalists' did. Here – and we must include Althusser in this characterization – culturalists and structuralists alike ascribed to the domains hitherto defined as 'superstructural' a specificity and effectivity, a constitutive primacy, which pushed them beyond the terms of reference of 'base' and 'superstructure'. Lévi-Strauss and Althusser, too, were anti-reductionist and anti-economist in their very cast of thought, and critically attacked that transitive causality which, for so long, had passed itself off as 'classical Marxism'.

Lévi-Strauss worked consistently with the term 'culture'. He regarded 'ideologies' as of much lesser importance: mere 'secondary rationalizations'. Like Williams and Goldmann, he worked, not at the level of correspondences between the content of a practice, but at the level of their forms and structures. But the manner in which these were conceptualized were altogether at variance with either the 'culturalism' of Williams or Goldmann's 'genetic structuralism'. This divergence can be identified in three distinct ways. First, he conceptualized 'culture' as the categories and frameworks in thought and language through which different societies classified out their conditions of existence – above all (since Lévi-Strauss was an anthropologist), the relations between the human and the natural worlds. Second, he thought of the manner and practice through which these categories and mental frameworks were produced and transformed, largely on an analogy with the ways in which language itself – the principal medium of 'culture' – operated. He identified what was specific to them and their operation as the 'production of meaning': they were, above all, *signifying* practices. Third, after some early flirtations with Durkheim and Mauss' social categories of thought, he largely gave up the question of the relation between signifying and non-signifying practices – between 'culture' and 'not-culture', to use other terms – for the sake of concentrating on the *internal* relations within signifying practices by means of which the categories of meaning were produced. This left the question of determinacy, of totality, largely in abeyance. The causal logic of determinacy was abandoned in favour of a structuralist causality – a logic of arrangement, of internal relations, of articulation of parts within a structure. Each of these aspects is also positively present in Althusser's work and that of the Marxist structuralists, even when the terms of reference had been regrounded in Marx's 'immense theoretical revolution'. In one of Althusser's seminal formulations about ideology – defined as the themes, concepts and representations through which men and women 'live', in an imaginary relation, their relation to their real conditions of existence – we can see the skeleton outline of Lévi-Strauss' 'conceptual schemes between praxis and practices'. 'Ideologies' are here being conceptualized, not as the contents and surface forms of ideas, but as the unconscious categories through which conditions are represented and lived. [. . .]

The great strength of the structuralisms is their stress on 'determinate conditions'. They remind us that, unless the dialectic really can be held, in any particular analysis, between both halves of the proposition – that 'men make history . . . on the basis of conditions which are not of their making' – the result will inevitably be a naive humanism, with its necessary consequence: a voluntarist and populist political practice. The fact that 'men' can become conscious of their conditions, organize to struggle against them and in fact transform them – without which no active politics can even be conceived, let alone practised – must not be allowed to override the awareness of the fact that, in capitalist relations, men and women are placed and positioned in relations which constitute them as agents. [. . .]

This connects with a second strength: the recognition by structuralism not only of the necessity of abstraction as the instrument of thought through which 'real relations' are appropriated, but also of the presence, in Marx's work, of a continuous and complex movement *between different levels of abstraction*. It is, of course, the case – as 'culturalism' argues – that, in historical reality, practices do not appear neatly distinguished out into their respective instances. However, to think about or to analyse the complexity of the real, the act of practice of thinking is required; and this necessitates the use of the power of abstraction and analysis, the formation of concepts with which to cut into the complexity of the real, in order precisely to reveal and bring to light relationships and structures which cannot be visible to the naive, naked eye, and which can neither present nor authenticate themselves: 'In the analysis of economic forms, neither microscopes nor chemical reagents are of assistance. The power of abstraction must replace both'. [. . .]

Structuralism has another strength, in its conception of 'the whole'. There is a sense in which, though culturalism constantly insists on the radical particularity of its practices, its mode of conceptualizing the 'totality' has something of the complex simplicity of an expressive totality behind it. Its complexity is constituted by the fluidity with which practices move into and out of one another: but this complexity is reducible, conceptually, to the 'simplicity' of praxis – human activity, as such – in which the same contradictions constantly appear, homologously reflected in each. Structuralism goes too far in erecting the machine of a 'structure', with its self-generating propensies (a 'Spinozean eternity', whose function is only the sum of its effects: a truly structural*ist* deviation), equipped with its distinctive instances. Yet it represents an advance over culturalism in the conception it has of the necessary *complexity* of the unity of a structure (over-determination being a more successful way of thinking this complexity than the combinatory invariance of structuralist causality). Moreover, it has the conceptual ability to think of a unity which is constructed through the differences between, rather than the homology of, practices. [. . .]

The third strength which structuralism exhibits lies in its decentring of 'experience' and its seminal work in elaborating the neglected category of 'ideology'. It is difficult to conceive of a cultural studies thought within a Marxist paradigm which is innocent of the category of 'ideology'. Of course, culturalism constantly makes reference to this concept: but it does not in fact lie at the centre of its conceptual universe. The authenticating power and reference of 'experience' imposes a barrier between culturalism and a proper conception of 'ideology'. Yet, without it, the effectivity of 'culture' for the reproduction of a particular mode of production cannot be grasped. It is true that there is a marked tendency in the more recent structuralist conceptualisations of 'ideology' to give it a functionalist reading – as the necessary cement of the social formation. From this position, it is indeed impossible – as culturalism would correctly argue – to conceive either of ideologies which are not, by definition, 'dominant': or of the concept of struggle (the latter's appearance in Althusser's famous ISA's article being – to coin yet another phrase – largely 'gestural'). Nevertheless work is already being done which suggests ways in which the field of ideology may be adequately conceptualized as a terrain of struggle (through the work of Gramsci, and more recently, of Laclau), and these have structuralist rather than culturalist bearings.

Culturalism's strengths can almost be derived from the weaknesses of the structuralist position already noted, and from the latter's strategic absences and silences. It has insisted, correctly, on the affirmative moment of the development of conscious struggle and organization as a necessary element in the analysis of history, ideology and consciousness: against its persistent down-grading in the structuralist paradigm. Here, again, it is largely Gramsci who has provided us with a set of more refined terms through which to link the largely 'unconscious' and given cultural categories of 'common sense' with the formation of more active and organic ideologies, which have the capacity to intervene in the ground of common sense and popular traditions and, through such interventions, to organize masses of men and women. In this sense, culturalism *properly* restores the dialectic between the unconsciousness of cultural categories and the moment of conscious organization: even if, in its characteristic movement, it has tended to match structuralism's over-emphasis on 'conditions' with an altogether too-inclusive emphasis on 'consciousness'. It therefore not only recovers – as the necessary moment of any analysis – the process by means of which classes-in-themselves, defined primarily by the way in which economic relations position 'men' as agents – become active historical and political forces – for-themselves: it also – against its own anti-theoretical good sense – *requires* that, when properly developed, each moment must be understood in terms of the level of abstraction at which the analysis is operating. Again, Gramsci has begun to point a way through this false polarization in his discussion of 'the passage between the structure and the sphere of the complex superstructures', and its distinct forms and moments. We have concentrated in this argument largely on a characterization of what seem to us to be the two seminal paradigms at work in cultural studies. Of course, they are by no means the only active ones. New developments and lines of thinking are by no means adequately netted with reference to them. Nevertheless, these paradigms can, in a sense, be deployed to measure what appear to us to be the radical weaknesses or inadequacies of those which offer themselves as alternative rallying-points. Here, briefly, we identify three.

The first is that which follows on from Lévi-Strauss, early semiotics and the terms of the linguistic paradigm, and the centring on 'signifying practices', moving by way of psychoanalytic concepts and Lacan to a radical recentring of virtually the whole terrain of cultural studies around the terms 'discourse' and 'the subject'. [. . .]

A second development is the attempt to return to the terms of a more classical 'political economy' of culture. This position argues that the concentration on the cultural and ideological aspects has been wildly overdone. It would restore the older terms of 'base/superstructure', finding, in the last-instance determination of the cultural–ideological by the economic, that hierarchy of determinations which both alternatives appear to lack. This position insists that the economic processes and structures of cultural production are more significant than their cultural–ideological aspect: and that these are quite adequately caught in the more classical terminology of profit, exploitation, surplus-value and the analysis of culture as commodity. It retains a notion of ideology as 'false consciousness'. [. . .]

The third position is closely related to the structuralist enterprise, but has followed the path of 'difference' through into a radical heterogeneity. Foucault's work currently enjoying another of those uncritical periods of discipleship through which British intellectuals reproduce today their dependency on yesterday's French ideas – has had an exceedingly positive effect: above all because – in suspending the nearly insoluble problems of determination Foucault has made possible a welcome return to the concrete analysis of particular ideological and discursive formations, and the sites of their elaboration. Foucault and Gramsci between them account for much of the most productive work on *concrete analysis* now being undertaken in the field: thereby reinforcing and – paradoxically – supporting the sense of the concrete historical instance which has always been one of culturalism's principal strengths.

I have said enough to indicate that, in my view, the line in cultural studies which – has attempted to *think forwards* from the best elements in the structuralist and culturalist enterprises, by way of some of the concepts elaborated in Gramsci's work, comes closest to meeting the requirements of the field of study. And the reason for that should by now also be obvious. Though neither structuralism nor culturalism will do, as self-sufficient paradigms of study, they have a centrality to the field which all the other contenders lack because, between them (in their divergences as well as their convergences) they address what must be the *core problem* of cultural studies. They constantly return us to the terrain marked out by those strongly coupled but not mutually exclusive concepts culture/ideology. They pose, together, the problems consequent on trying to think *both* the specificity of different practices and the forms of the articulated unity they constitute. They make a constant, if flawed, return to the base/superstructure metaphor. They are correct in insisting that this question – which resumes all the problems of a non-reductive determinacy – is the heart of the matter: and that, on the solution of this problem will turn the capacity of cultural studies to supersede the endless oscillations between idealism and reductionism. They confront – even if in radically opposed ways – the dialectic between conditions and consciousness. At another level, they pose the question of the relation between the logic of thinking and the 'logic' of historical process. They continue to hold out the promise of a properly materialist theory of culture. In their sustained and mutually reinforcing antagonisms they hold out no promise of an easy synthesis. But, between them, they define where, if at all, is the space, and what are the limits, within which such a synthesis might be constituted. In cultural studies, theirs are the 'names of the game'.

45

Popular culture and 'the turn to Gramsci'

Tony Bennett

From Bennett, T., Mercer, C. and Woollacott, J. (eds) (1986) *Popular Culture and Social Relations*, Open University Press, Milton Keynes, pp. xi–xix.

Why study popular culture? It's tempting to answer: why not? To do so, however, would merely be to lend hostage to fortune, for many reasons have been advanced as to why popular culture should not, or at least need not, be studied – on the grounds that it is too slight and ephemeral to be worthy of any sustained inquiry, for example – and, for the greater part of this century, such arguments have largely carried the day. Moreover, even where they have not prevailed, the grounds upon which the study of popular culture has been justified have been mainly negative: to expose its morally corrupting influences and aesthetic poverty, for example, or, in Marxist approaches, to reveal its role as a purveyor of dominant ideology. In the context of such assumptions, to study popular culture has also meant to adopt a position against and opposed to it, to view it as in need of replacement by a culture of another kind, usually 'high culture' – the view not only of reformist critics, such as F. R. Leavis, but, oddly enough, equally influential in Marxist circles too, especially in the work of Theodor Adorno, Herbert Marcuse and the other members of the Frankfurt school.

It is one of the quirks of history that these arguments, which once nowhere had quite so much sedimented cultural weight as in Britain, have been overturned perhaps more decisively in Britain than anywhere else over the course of the last 20 to 30 years. The study of cinema, popular music, sport, youth sub-cultures and of much else besides has now developed to the point where these are well established fields of inquiry, with considerably developed bodies of theory and highly elaborated methodologies, in which debate is no longer stalked by the ghost of Leavis – or by the gloomy prognostications of the Frankfurt school, for that matter. Equally important, significant advances have been made in theorizing the sphere of popular culture as a whole. The term had previously been used quite loosely to refer to a miscellaneous collection of cultural forms and practices having little in common beyond the fact of their exclusion from the accepted canon of 'high culture'. In more recent debates, by contrast, the many and diverse practices which are typically grouped under the heading of popular culture are more usually regarded as being systematically interconnected by virtue of the parts they play in relation to broader social and political processes, particularly those bearing on the production of consent to the prevailing social order in both its patriarchal and capitalist dimensions. These theoretical developments finally, have been accompanied by a sureness of political purpose as the study of popular culture has been defined as a site of positive political engagement by both socialists and feminists in their concern to identify both those aspects of popular culture which serve to secure consent to existing social arrangements as well as those which, in embodying alternative values, supply a source of opposition to those arrangements.

[. . .]

Debates in the area during the 1970s were often deadlocked around the polar opposites of structuralism and culturalism represented, respectively, as the 'imported' and 'home-grown' varieties of cultural studies.[1] In the perspective of structuralism, popular culture was often regarded as an 'ideological machine' which dictated the thoughts of the people just as rigidly and with the same law-like regularity as, in Saussure's conspectus – which provided the originating paradigm for structuralism – the system of *langue* dictated the events of *parole*. Focusing particularly on the analysis of textual forms, structuralist analysis was concerned to reveal the ways in which textual structures might be said to organize reading or spectating practices, often with scant regard to the conditions regulating either the production or the reception of those textual forms.[2] Culturalism, by contrast, was often uncritically romantic in its celebration of popular culture as expressing the authentic interests and values of subordinate social groups and classes. This conception, moreover, resulted in an essentialist view of culture: that is, as the embodiment of specific class or gender essences. In the logic of this approach, as Roszika Parker and Griselda Pollock put it, many feminists were led to look for an authentically female culture as if this could 'exist isolated like some deep frozen essence in the freezer of male culture',[3] just as many socialists rummaged through popular culture in search of the authentic voice of the working class, as if this could exist in some pure form, preserved and nurtured in a recess immune to the socially preponderant forms of cultural production in a capitalist society.[4]

These theoretical divergences were accentuated by their association with different disciplinary perspectives, structuralism being most strongly present in the study of cinema, television and popular writings while culturalism tended to predominate within history and sociology, particularly in studies concerned with working class 'lived cultures' or 'ways of life'. Given this division of the field – a division that was sometimes provocatively and needlessly deepened, particularly by E. P. Thompson's *The Poverty of Theory*[5] – there seemed little alternative but to pay one's money and take one's choice. Worse, it seemed as though, depending on one's area of interest, one was constrained to be either a structuralist or a culturalist – the former if one studied cinema, television or popular writing, and the latter if one's interests were in sport, say, or youth sub-cultures. It was almost as if the cultural sphere were divided into two hermetically separate regions, each exhibiting a different logic. While this was unsatisfactory, it was equally clear that the two traditions could not be forced into a shot-gun marriage either. The only way out of this impasse, therefore, seemed to be to shift the debate on to a new terrain which would displace the structuralist–culturalist opposition, a project which inclined many working in the field at the time to draw increasingly on the writings of Antonio Gramsci, particularly those on the subject of hegemony.[6]

[. . .]

Put in the most general terms, the critical spirit of Gramsci's work totally shunning the intolerable condescension of the mass culture critic while simultaneously avoiding any tendency toward a celebratory populism, both avoids and disqualifies the bipolar alternatives of structuralism and culturalism. However, this is less a question of style or of Gramsci's mode of address – although these are important considerations in Gramsci's writing – than one of theory. In Gramsci's conspectus, popular culture is viewed neither as the site of the people's cultural deformation nor as that of their cultural self-affirmation or, in any simple Thompsonian sense, of their own self-making; rather, it is viewed as a force field of relations shaped, precisely, by these contradictory pressures and tendencies – a perspective which enables a significant reformulation of both the theoretical and the political issues at stake in the study of popular culture .

Politically speaking, both the structuralist and culturalist paradigms subscribe to a rather similar conception of the structure and organization of the cultural and ideological spheres viewed in relation to the antagonistic economic and political relationships between social classes. Although importantly different in other respects, both paradigms regard the sphere of cultural and ideological practices as being governed by a dominant ideology, essentially and monolithically bourgeois in its characteristics, which, albeit with varying degrees of success, is imposed from without, as an alien force, on the subordinate classes. Viewed from this perspective the main differences between the two perspectives are largely nominal or ones of orientation. In structuralism, 'popular culture', 'mass culture' and 'dominant ideology' are usually equated through a series of sliding definitions. In consequence, the chief political task assigned to the study of popular culture is that of reading through popular cultural forms and practices to reveal the obfuscating mechanisms of the dominant ideology at work within them, thus arming the reader against the occurrence of similar mechanisms in related practices. In culturalism, by contrast, popular culture, in being equated with the 'autochthonous' culture of subordinate classes, is explicitly distinguished from and opposed to dominant ideology in the form of mass culture. Where this conception prevails, analysis is dominated by a positive political hermeneutic: that of, having found the people's authentic voice, interpreting its meaning and amplifying its cultural volume. To be sure, the consequences of these contrasting orientations are by no means negligible. In spite of these, however, the two approaches share a conception of the cultural and ideological field as being divided between two opposing cultural and ideological camps – bourgeois and working class – locked in a zero-sum game in which one side gains only at the expense of the other and in which the ultimate objective is the liquidation of one by the other so that the victor might then stand in the place of the vanquished.

For Gramsci too, of course, cultural and ideological practices are to be understood and assessed in terms of their functioning within the antagonistic relations between the bourgeoisie and the working class as the two fundamental classes of capitalist society. Indeed, Gramsci's insistence that these antagonistic class relations form the ultimately determining horizon within which cultural and ideological analysis must be located constitutes the outer limit to the programme of theoretical revision he inaugurated in relation to classical Marxist theories of ideology.[7] Where Gramsci departed from the earlier Marxist tradition was in arguing that the cultural and ideological relations between ruling and subordinate classes in capitalist societies consist less in the *domination* of the latter by the former than in the struggle for *hegemony* – that is, for moral, cultural, intellectual and, thereby, political leadership over the whole of society – between the ruling class and, as the principal subordinate class, the working class.

This substitution of the concept of hegemony for that of domination is not, as some commentators have suggested, merely terminological; it brings in tow an entirely different conception of the means by which cultural and ideological struggles are conducted.[8] Whereas, according to the dominant ideology thesis, bourgeois culture and ideology seek to take the place of working class culture and ideology and thus to become directly operative in framing working class experience, Gramsci argues that the bourgeoisie can become a hegemonic, leading class only to the degree that bourgeois ideology is able to accommodate, to find some space for, opposing class cultures and values. A bourgeois hegemony is secured not via the obliteration of working class culture, but via its *articulation to* bourgeois culture and ideology so that, in being associated with and expressed in the forms of the latter, its political affiliations are altered in the process.

As a consequence of its accommodating elements of opposing class cultures, 'bourgeois culture' ceases to be purely or entirely bourgeois. It becomes, instead, a mobile combination of cultural and ideological elements derived from different class locations which are, but only provisionally and for the duration of a specific historical conjuncture, affiliated to bourgeois values, interests and objectives. By the same token, of course, the members of subordinate classes never encounter or are oppressed by a dominant ideology in some pure or class essentialist form; bourgeois ideology is encountered only in the compromised forms it must take in order to provide some accommodation for opposing class values. As Robert Gray remarks, if the Gramscian concept of hegemony refers to the processes through which the ruling class seeks to negotiate opposing class cultures onto a cultural and ideological terrain which wins for it a position of leadership, it is also true that what is thereby consented to is a negotiated version of ruling class culture and ideology:

> Class hegemony is a dynamic and shifting relationship of social subordination, which operates in two directions. Certain aspects of the behaviour and consciousness of the subordinate classes may reproduce a version of the values of the ruling class. But in the process value systems are modified, through their necessary adaptation to diverse conditions of existence; the subordinate classes thus follow a 'negotiated version' of ruling-class values. On the other hand, structures of ideological hegemony transform and incorporate dissident values, so as effectively to prevent the working through of their full implications.[9]

Although an over-rapid and somewhat abstract summary of a complex body of theory, the main points, perhaps, clear enough: that the spheres of culture and ideology cannot be conceived as being divided into two hermetically separate and entirely opposing class cultures and ideologies. The effect of this is to disqualify the bipolar options of the structuralist and culturalist perspectives on popular culture, viewed as either the carrier of an undiluted bourgeois ideology or as the site of the people's authentic culture and potential self-awakening, as unmitigated villain or unsullied hero. To the contrary, to the degree that it is implicated in the struggle for hegemony – and, for Gramsci, the part played by the most taken-for-granted, sedimented cultural aspects of everyday life are crucially implicated in the processes whereby hegemony is fought for, won, lost, resisted – the field of popular culture is structured by the attempt of the ruling class to win hegemony and by the forms of opposition to this endeavour. As such, it consists not simply of an imposed mass culture that is coincident with dominant ideology, nor simply of spontaneously oppositional cultures, but is rather an area of negotiation between the two within which – in different particular types of popular culture – dominant, subordinate and oppositional cultural and ideological values and elements are 'mixed' in different permutations.

In sum, then, the 'turn to Gramsci' has been influential in both disputing the assumption that cultural forms can be assigned an essential class-belongingness and contesting a simply 'bourgeois versus working class' conception of the organization of the cultural and ideological relationships. These reorientations have resulted in two decisive shifts of political emphasis within the study of popular culture. First, they have produced a perspective, within Marxism, from which it is possible to analyse popular culture without adopting a position that is either opposed to it or uncritically for it. The forms of political assessment of cultural practices which the theory of hegemony calls for are much more conjunctural and pliable than that. A cultural practice does not carry its politics with it, as if written upon its brow forever and a day; rather, its political functioning depends on the network of social and ideological relations in which it is inscribed as a consequence of the ways in which, in a particular conjuncture, it is articulated to other practices. In brief, in suggesting that the political and ideological articulations of cultural practices are *movable* – that a practice which is articulated to bourgeois values today may be disconnected from those values and connected to socialist ones tomorrow – the theory of hegemony opens up the field of popular culture as one of enormous political possibilities.

Equally important, the Gramscian critique of class essentialist conceptions of culture and ideology and the associated principles of class reductionism enables due account to be taken of the relative separation of different regions of cultural struggle (class, race, gender) as well as of the complex and changing ways in which these may be overlapped on to one another in different historical circumstances. Apart from being an important advance on classical Marxism, this has also served as an important check on the Foucauldian tendency to view power and the struggle against it as equally diffuse and unrelated. Most important, though, it has offered a framework within which the relations between the cultural politics of socialist movements and those of, say, feminist or national liberation struggles can be productively debated without their respective specifications threatening either to engulf or be engulfed by the others.

This is not to suggest that Gramsci's writings contain the seeds of an answer to all problems in the field of popular culture analysis. There are specific and detailed technical and theoretical problems peculiar to television and film analysis, popular music, the study of lived cultures and the field of popular writings which no amount of general theorizing might resolve. Likewise, questions concerning the relations between culture and class, culture and gender and culture and nation remained vexed and complex, requiring separate and detailed attention if progress is to be made. The value of the Gramscian theory of hegemony is that of providing an integrating framework within which both sets of issues might be addressed and worked through in relation to each other. By the same token, of course, it is liable to the criticism that it is too accommodating and expansive a framework, over-totalizing in its analytical claims and ambit. The charge has certainly been made often enough, and it seems one likely to be pressed with increased vigour, particularly in the area of cultural studies.

Notes

1. While the term 'structuralism' has a more general currency, the concept of culturalism and the structuralism/culturalism polarity are mainly attributable to the collective work of the Centre for Contemporary Cultural Studies at the University of Birmingham. For the classic statement of this position, see Hall, S. (1980) Cultural studies: two paradigms. *Media, Culture and Society*, Vol. 2, No. 1, shortened version in Bennett, T. *et al.* (eds) (1981) *Culture, Ideology and Social Process*, Batsford, London.
2. The heyday of structuralism, in this respect, is probably best represented by Umberto Eco's *The Role of the Reader*, Hutchinson, London, 1981 (first published in Italian in 1979). In addition to providing rigorous structuralist analyses of the ideological encoding of a range of popular texts (Superman, the James Bond novels, etc.), Eco's approach to the processes of reading is one in which such processes are conceived as entirely regulated by textual structure. For critical discussions of this aspect of Eco's work, see Chapter 6 of de Laurentis, T. (1984) *Alice doesn't: Feminism, Semiotics, Cinema*, Macmillan, London; and Chapter 3 of Bennett, T. and Woollacott, J. (eds) (1986) *Bond and Beyond: The Political Career of a Popular Hero*, Macmillan, London.
3. Parker, R. and Pollock, G. (1982) *Old Mistresses: Women, Art and Ideology*, Pantheon Books, New York, p. 136.
4. The most pronounced recent example of this approach is David Harker's *One for the Money: Politics and Popular Song*, Hutchinson, London, 1980.
5. Thompson, E. P. (1978) *The Poverty of Theory and Other Essays*, Merlin Press, London.
6. See, especially, Gramsci, A. (1971) *Selections from the Prison Notebooks*, Lawrence and Wishart, London. The more recent translation and publication of Gramsci's writings on culture and politics seems likely to strengthen the Gramscian influence on contemporary cultural theory: see Gramsci, A. (1985) *Selections from Cultural Writings*, Lawrence and Wishart, London.
7. There have however, been a number of attempts recently to go beyond these 'outer limits' although whether the resulting formulations are meaningfully described as Marxist is debatable. See, for example, Laclau, E. (1983) Transformations of advanced industrial societies and the theory of the subject. In Hanninen, S. and Paldan, L. (eds) *Rethinking Ideology: A Marxist Debate*, International General/ IMMAC, New York.
8. The failure to appreciate this is one of the most conspicuous shortcomings of Abercrombie, N., Hill, S. and Turner, B. S. (1980) *The Dominant Ideology Thesis*, George Allen and Unwin, London.
9. Gray, R. (1976) *The Labour Aristocracy in Victorian Edinburgh*, Clarendon Press, Oxford, p. 6.

46

The rediscovery of 'ideology': return of the repressed in media studies

Stuart Hall

From Gurevitch, M. *et al.* (eds) (1982) *Culture, Society and the Media*,
Methuen, London, pp. 56–90.

Mass communications research has had, to put it mildly, a somewhat chequered
career. Since its inception as a specialist area of scientific inquiry and research
– roughly, the early decades of the twentieth century – we can identify at
least three distinct phases. The most dramatic break is that which occurred
between the second and third phases. This marks off the massive period of
research conducted within the sociological approaches of 'mainstream'
American behavioural science, beginning in the 1940s and commanding the
field through into the 1950s and 1960s, from the period of its decline and the
emergence of an alternative, 'critical' paradigm. Two basic points about this
break should be made at this stage in the argument. First, though the
differences between the 'mainstream' and the 'critical' approaches might appear,
at first sight, to be principally methodological and procedural, this appearance
is, in our view, a false one. Profound differences in theoretical perspective and
in political calculation differentiate the one from the other. These differences
first appear in relation to media analysis. But, behind this immediate object of
attention, there lie broader differences in terms of how societies or social
formations in general are to be analysed. Second, the simplest way to characterize
the shift from 'mainstream' to 'critical' perspectives is in terms of the movement
from, essentially, a behavioural to an ideological perspective.
[. . .]

The critical paradigm

It is around the rediscovery of the ideological dimension that the critical
paradigm in media studies turned. Two aspects were involved: each is dealt
with separately below. How does the ideological process work and what
are its mechanisms? How is 'the ideological' to be conceived in relation to
other practices within a social formation? The debate developed on both
these fronts, simultaneously. The first, which concerned the production and
transformation of ideological discourses, was powerfully shaped by
theories concerning the symbolic and linguistic character of ideological
discourses – the notion that the elaboration of ideology found in language
(broadly conceived) its proper and privileged sphere of articulation. The
second, which concerned how to conceptualize the ideological instance

within a social formation, also became the site of an extensive theoretical and empirical development.
[. . .]

Cultural inventories

I shall first examine how ideologies work. Here we can begin with the influence of the Sapir–Whorf hypothesis in linguistic anthropology. The Sapir–Whorf hypothesis suggested that each culture had a different way of classifying the world. These schemes would be reflected, it argues, in the linguistic and semantic structures of different societies. Lévi-Strauss worked on a similar idea. [. . .] Lévi-Strauss was following Saussure's (1960) call for the development of a general 'science of signs' – semiology: the study for the 'life of signs at the heart of social life' (Lévi-Strauss, 1967, p. 16). Potentially it was argued, the approach could be applied to all societies and a great variety of cultural systems. The name most prominently associated with this broadening of the 'science of signs' was that of Roland Barthes, whose work on modern myths, *Mythologies*, is a *locus classicus* for the study of the intersection of myth, language and ideology. [. . .]

In the structuralist approach, the issue turned on the question of signification. This implies that things and events in the real world do not contain or propose their own, integral, single and intrinsic meaning, which is then merely transferred through language. Meaning is a social product-ion, a practice. The world has to be *made to mean*. Language and symbolization is the means by which meaning is produced. [. . .] Because meaning was not given but produced, it followed that different kinds of meaning could be ascribed to the same events. Thus, in order for one mean-ing to be regularly produced, it had to win a kind of credibility, legitimacy or taken-for-grantedness for itself. That involved marginalizing, down-grading or de-legitimating alternative constructions. Indeed, there were certain kinds of explanation which, given the power of and credibility acquired by the preferred range of meanings were literally unthinkable or unsayable (see Hall *et al.*, 1977). Two questions followed from this. First, how did a dominant discourse warrant itself as the account, and sustain a limit, ban or proscription over alternative or competing definitions? Second, how did the institutions which were responsible for describing and explaining the events of the world – in modern societies, the mass media, *par excellence* – succeed in maintaining a preferred or delimited range of meanings in the dominant systems of communication? How was this active work of privileging or giving preference practically accomplished?

This directed attention to those many aspects of actual media practice which had previously been analysed in a purely technical way. Conventional approaches to media content had assumed that questions of selection and exclusion, the editing of accounts together, the building of an account into a 'story', the use of particular narrative types of exposition, the way the verbal and visual discourses of, say, television were articulated together to make a certain kind of sense, were all merely technical issues. They abutted on the question of the social effects of the media only in so far as bad editing or complex modes of narration might lead to incomprehension on the viewer's part, and thus prevent the pre-existing meaning of an event, or the intention of the broadcaster to communicate clearly, from passing in an uninterrupted or transparent way to the receiver. But, from the viewpoint of signification, these were all elements or elementary forms of a social practice. They were the means whereby particular accounts were constructed. Signification was a social practice because, within media institutions, a particular form of social organization had evolved which enabled the producers (broadcasters) to employ the means of meaning production at their disposal (the technical equipment) through a certain practical use of them (the combination of the elements of signification identified above) in order to produce a product (a specific meaning) (see Hall, 1975). The specificity of media institutions therefore lay precisely in the way a *social practice* was organized so as to produce a *symbolic product*. To construct *this* rather than *that* account required the specific choice of certain means (selection) and their articulation together through the practice of meaning production (combination). Structural linguists like Saussure and Jacobson had, earlier, identified selection and combination as two of the essential mechanisms of the general production of meaning or sense. Some critical researchers then assumed that the description offered above – producers, combining together in specific ways, using determinate means, to work up raw materials into a product – justified their describing signification as exactly similar to any other media labour process. Certain insights were indeed to be gained from that approach. However, signification differed from other modern labour processes precisely because the product which the social practice produced was a discursive object. What differentiated it, then, as a practice was precisely the articulation together of social and symbolic elements – if the distinction will be allowed here for the purposes of the argument. Motor cars, of course, have, in addition to their exchange and use values, a symbolic value in our culture. But, in the process of meaning construction, the exchange and use values depend on the symbolic value which the message contains. The symbolic character of the practice is the dominant element although not the only one. Critical theorists who argued that a message could be analysed as just another kind of commodity missed this crucial distinction (Garham, 1979; Golding and Murdock, 1979).

The politics of signification

As we have suggested, the more one accepts that how people act will depend in part on how the situations in which they act are defined, and the less one can assume either a natural meaning to everything or a universal consensus on what things mean – then, the more important, socially and politically, becomes the process by means of which certain events get recurrently signified in particular ways. This is especially the case where events in the world are problematic (that is, where they are unexpected); where they break the frame of our previous expectations about the world; where powerful social interests are involved; or where there are starkly opposing or conflicting interests at play. The power involved here is an ideological power; the power to signify events in a particular way.
[. . .]

Central to the question of how a particular range of privileged meanings was sustained was the question of classification and framing. Lévi-Strauss, drawing on models of transformational linguistics, suggested that signification depended, not on the intrinsic meaning of particular isolated terms, but on the organized set of inter-related elements within a discourse. Within the colour spectrum, for example, the range of colours would be subdivided in different ways in each culture. Eskimos have several words for the thing which we call 'snow'. Latin has one word, *mus*, for the animal which in English is distinguished by two terms, 'rat' and 'mouse'. Italian distinguishes between *legno* and *bosco* where English only speaks of a 'wood'. But where Italian has both *bosco* and *foresta*, German only has the single term, *wald*. [The examples are from Eco's essay, 'Social life as a sign system' (1973).] These are distinctions, not of nature but of culture. What matters, from the viewpoint of signification, is not the integral meaning of any single colour-term – mauve, for example – but the system of differences between all the colours in a particular classificatory system; and where, in a particular language, the point of difference between one colour and another is positioned. It was through this play of difference that a language system secured an equivalence between its internal system (signifiers) and the systems of reference (signifieds) which it employed. Language constituted meaning by punctuating the continuum of nature into a cultural system; such equivalences or correspondences would therefore be differently marked. Thus there was no natural coincidence between a word and its referent: everything depended on the conventions of linguistic use, and on the way language intervened in nature in order to make sense of it. [. . .]

What signified, in fact, was the positionality of particular terms within a set. Each positioning marked a pertinent difference in the classificatory scheme involved. To this Lévi-Strauss added a more structuralist point: that it is not the particular utterance of speakers which provides the object of analysis, but the classificatory system which underlies those utterances and from which they are produced, as a series of variant transformations. Thus, by moving from the surface narrative of particular myths to the generative system or structure out of which they were produced, one could show how apparently different myths (at the surface level) belonged in fact to the same family or constellation of myths (at the deep-structure level). If the underlying set is a limited set of elements which can be variously combined, then the surface variants can, in their particular sense, be infinitely varied, and spontaneously produced. [. . .]

This move from the content to structure or from manifest meaning to the level of code is an absolutely characteristic one in the critical approach. [. . .]

The 'class struggle in language'

[. . .]
Because meaning no longer depended on 'how things were' but on how things were signified, it followed, as we have said, that the same event could be signified in different ways. Since signification was a practice, and 'practice' was defined as 'any process of transformation of a determinate raw material into a determinate product, a transformation effected by a determinate

human labour, using determinate means (of "production")' (Althusser, 1969, p. 166), it also followed that signification involved a determinate form of labour, a specific 'work': the work of meaning production, in this case. Meaning was, therefore, not determined, say, by the structure of reality itself, but conditional on the work of signification being successfully conducted through a social practice. It followed, also, that this work need not necessarily be successfully effected: because it was a 'determinate' form of labour it was subject to contingent conditions. The work of signification was a social accomplishment – to use ethnomethodological terminology for a moment. Its outcome did not flow in a strictly predictable or necessary manner from a given reality. In this, the emergent theory diverged significantly, both from the reflexive or referential theories of language embodied in positivist theory, and from the reflexive kind of theory also implicit in the classical Marxist theory of language and the superstructures.

Three important lines of development followed from this break with early theories of language. Firstly, one had to explain how it was possible for language to have this multiple referentiality to the real world. Here, the polysemic nature of language – the fact that the same set of signifiers could be variously accented in those meanings – proved of immense value.

Second, meaning, once it is problematized, must be the result, not of a functional reproduction of the world in language, but of a social struggle – a struggle for mastery in discourse – over which kind of social accenting is to prevail and to win credibility. This reintroduced both the notion of 'differently oriented social interests' and a conception of the sign as 'an arena of struggle' into the consideration of language and of signifying 'work'. Althusser, who transposed some of this kind of thinking into his general theory of ideology, tended to present the process as too uni-accentual, too functionally adapted to the reproduction of the dominant ideology (Althusser, 1971). Indeed, it was difficult, from the base-line of this theory, to discern how anything but the 'dominant ideology' could ever be reproduced in discourse. The work of Vološinov and Gramsci offered a significant correction to this functionalism by reintroducing into the domain of ideology and language the notion of a 'struggle over meaning' (which Vološinov substantiated theoretically with his argument about the multi-accentuality of the sign). What Vološinov argued was that the mastery of the struggle over meaning in discourse had, as its most pertinent effect or result, the imparting of a 'supraclass, eternal character to the ideological sign, to extinguish or drive inward the struggle between social value judgements which occurs in it, to make the sign uni-accentual' (1973, p. 23). [. . .]

The third point then, concerned the mechanisms within signs and language, which made the 'struggle' possible. Sometimes, the class struggle in language occurred between two different terms: the struggle, for example, to replace the term 'immigrant' with the term 'black'. But often the struggle took the form of a different accenting of the *same* term: e.g. the process by means of which the derogatory colour 'black' became the enhanced value 'Black' (as in 'Black is Beautiful'). In the latter case, the struggle was not over the term itself but over its connotative meaning. Barthes, in his essay on 'Myth', argued that the associative field of meanings of a single term – its connotative field of reference – was, *par excellence*, the domain through which ideology invaded the language system. It did so by exploiting the associative, the variable, connotative, 'social value' of language. For some time, this point was misunderstood as arguing that the denotative or relatively fixed meanings of a discourse were not open to multiple accentuation, but constituted a 'natural' language system; and only the connotative levels of discourse were open to different ideological inflexion. But this was simply a misunderstanding. Denotative meanings, of course, are not uncoded; they, too, entail systems of classification and recognition in much the same way as connotative meanings do; they are not natural but 'motivated' signs. The distinction between denotation and connotation was an analytic, not a substantive one (see Camargo, 1980; Hall, 1980). It suggested, only, that the connotative levels of language, being more open-ended and associative, were peculiarly vulnerable to contrary or contradictory ideological inflexions.

Hegemony and articulation

The real sting in the tail did not reside there, but in a largely unnoticed extension of Vološinov's argument. For if the social struggle in language could be conducted over the same sign, it followed that signs (and, by a further extension, whole chains of signifiers, whole discourses) could not be assigned, in a determinate way, permanently to any one side in the struggle. Of course, a native language is not equally distributed amongst all native speakers regardless of class, socio-economic position, gender, education and culture: nor is competence to perform in language randomly distributed. Linguistic performance and competence is socially distributed, not only by class but also by gender. Key institutions – in this respect, the family education couple – play a highly significant role in the social distribution of cultural 'capital', in which language played a pivotal role, as educational theorists like Bernstein and social theorists like Bourdieu have demonstrated. But, even where access for everyone to the same language system could be guaranteed, this did not suspend what Vološinov called the 'class struggle in language'. Of course, the same term, e.g. 'black', belonged in both the vocabularies of the oppressed and the oppressors. What was being struggled over was not the 'class belonging-ness' of the term, but the inflexion it could be given, its connotative field of reference. In the discourse of the Black movement, the denigratory connotation 'black = the despised race' could be inverted into its opposite: 'black = beautiful'. There was thus a 'class struggle in language'; but not one in which whole discourses could be unproblematically assigned to whole social classes or social groups.

This was an important step. But one could infer, immediately, two things from this. First, since ideology could be realized by the semantic accenting of the same linguistic sign, it followed that, though ideology and language intimately linked, they could not be one and the same thing. [. . .]

Second, though discourse could become an arena of social struggle, and all discourses entailed certain definite premises about the world, this was not the same thing as ascribing ideologies to classes in a fixed, necessary or determinate way. Ideological terms and elements do not necessarily 'belong' in this definite way to classes: and they do not necessarily and inevitably flow from class position. What mattered was the way in which different social interests or forces might conduct an ideological struggle to disarticulate a signifier from one, preferred or dominant meaning-system, and rearticulate it within another, different chain of connotations. This might be accomplished, formally, by different means. The switch from 'black = despised' to 'black = beautiful' is accomplished by inversion. The shift from 'pig = animal with dirty habits' to 'pig = brutal policeman' in the language of the radical movements of the 1960s to 'pig = male-chauvinist pig' in the language of feminism, is a metonymic mechanism – sliding the negative meaning along a chain of connotative signifiers. This theory of the 'no necessary class belongingness' of ideological elements and the possibilities of ideological struggle to articulate/disarticulate meaning, was an insight drawn mainly from Gramsci's work, but considerably developed in more recent writings by theorists like Laclau (1977).

[. . .]

Ideology in the social formation

This may be a convenient point in the argument to turn, briefly, to the second strand: concerning the way ideology was conceived in relation to other practices in a social formation. Complex social formations had to be analysed in terms of the economic, political and ideological institutions and practices through which they were elaborated. Each of these elements had to be accorded a specific weight in determining the outcomes of particular conjunctures. The question of ideology could not be extrapolated from some other level – the economic, for example – as some versions of classical Marxism proposed. But nor could the question of value-consensus be assumed, or treated as a dependent process merely reflecting in practice that consensus already achieved at the level of ideas, as pluralism supposed. Economic, political and ideological conditions had to be identified and analysed before any single event could be explained. Further, the presupposition that the reflection of economic reality at the level of ideas could be replaced by a straightforward 'class determination', also proved to be a false and misleading trail. It did not sufficiently recognize the relative autonomy of ideological processes, or the real effects of ideology on other practices. It treated classes as 'historical givens' – their ideological 'unity' already given by their position in the economic structure – whereas, in the new perspective, classes had to be understood only as the complex result of the successful prosecution of different forms of social struggle at all the levels of social practice, including the ideological. This gave to the struggle around and over the media – the dominant means of social signification in modern societies – a specificity and a centrality which, in previous theories, they had altogether lacked. It raised them to a central, relatively independent, position in any analysis of the question of the 'politics of signification'.

[. . .]

The weakness of the earlier Marxist positions lay precisely in their inability to explain the role of the 'free consent' of the governed to the leadership of the governing classes under capitalism. The great value of pluralist theory was precisely that it included this element of consent – though it gave to it a highly idealist and power-free gloss or interpretation. But, especially in formally democratic class societies, of which the U.S. and Britain are archetypal cases, what had to be explained was exactly the *combination* of the maintained rule of powerful classes *with* the active or inactive consent of the powerless majority. The ruling-class/ruling-ideas formula did not go far enough in explaining what was clearly the most stabilizing element in such societies – consent. 'Consensus theory' however, gave an unproblematic reading to this element – recognizing the aspect of consent, but having to repress the complementary notions of power and dominance. But hegemony attempted to provide the outlines, at least, of an explanation of how power functioned in such societies which held both ends of the chain at once. The question of 'leadership' then, became, not merely a minor qualification to the theory of ideology, but the principal point of difference between a more and a less adequate explanatory framework. The critical point for us is that, in any theory which seeks to explain both the monopoly of power and the diffusion of consent, the question of the place and role of ideology becomes absolutely pivotal. It turned out, then, that the consensus question, in pluralist theory, was not so much wrong as incorrectly or inadequately posed. As is often the case in theoretical matters, a whole configuration of ideas can be revealed by taking an inadequate premise and showing the unexamined conditions on which it rested. The 'break' therefore, occurred precisely at the point where theorists asked, 'but who produces the consensus?' 'In what interests does it function?' 'On what conditions does it depend?' Here, the media and other signifying institutions came back into the question – no longer as the institutions which merely reflected and sustained the consensus, but as the institutions which helped to produce consensus and which manufactured consent.

This approach could also be used to demonstrate how media institutions could be articulated to the production and reproduction of the dominant ideologies, while at the same time being 'free' of direct compulsion, and 'independent' of any direct attempt by the powerful to nobble them. Such institutions powerfully secure consent precisely because their claim to be independent of the direct play of political or economic interests, or of the state, is not wholly fictitious. The claim is ideological, not because it is false but because it does not adequately grasp all the conditions which make freedom and impartiality possible. It is ideological because it offers a partial explanation as if it were a comprehensive and adequate one – it takes the part for the whole (fetishism). Nevertheless, its legitimacy depends on that part of the truth, which it mistakes for the whole, being real in fact, and not merely a polite fiction.

This insight was the basis for all of that work which tried to demonstrate how it could be true that media institutions were both, in fact, free of direct compulsion and constraint, and yet freely articulated themselves systematically around definitions of the situation which favoured the hegemony of the powerful. The complexities of this demonstration cannot be entered into here and a single argument, relating to consensus, will have to stand. We might put it this way. Formally, the legitimacy of the continued leadership and authority of the dominant classes in capitalist society derives from their accountability to the opinions of the popular majority – the 'sovereign will of the people'. In the formal mechanisms of election and the universal franchise they are required to submit themselves at regular intervals to the will or consensus of the majority. One of the means by which the powerful can continue to rule with consent and legitimacy is, therefore, if the interests of a particular class or power bloc can be aligned with or made equivalent to the general interests of the majority. Once this system of equivalences has been achieved, the interests of the minority and the will of the majority can be 'squared' because they can both be represented as coinciding in the consensus, on which all sides agree. The consensus is the medium, the regulator, by means of which this necessary alignment (or equalization) between power and consent is accomplished. But if the consensus of the majority can be so shaped that it squares with the will of the powerful, then particular (class) interests can be represented as identical with the consensus will of the people. This, however, requires the shaping, the education and tutoring of consent: it also involves all those processes of representation which we outlined earlier.

Now consider the media – the means of representation. To be impartial and independent in their daily operations, they cannot be seen to take directives from the powerful, or consciously to be bending their accounts of the world to square with dominant definitions. But they must be sensitive to, and can only survive legitimately by operating within, the general boundaries or framework of 'what everyone agrees' to: the consensus. But, in orienting themselves in 'the consensus' and, at the same time, attempting to shape up the consensus, operating on it in a formative fashion, the media become part and parcel of that dialectical process of the 'production of consent' – shaping the consensus while reflecting it – which orientates them within the field of force of the dominant social interests represented within the state.

Notice that we have said 'the state', not particular political parties or economic interests. The media, in dealing with contentious public or political issues, would be rightly held to be partisan if they systematically adopted the point of view of a particular political party or of a particular section of capitalist interests. It is only in so far as (a) these parties or interests have acquired legitimate ascendancy in the state, and (b) that ascendancy has been legitimately secured through the formal exercise of the 'will of the majority' that their strategies can be represented as coincident with the 'national interest' – and therefore form the legitimate basis or framework which the media can assume. The 'impartiality' of the media thus requires the mediation of the state – that set of processes through which particular interests become generalized, and, having secured the consent of 'the nation', carry the stamp of legitimacy. In this way a particular interest is represented as 'the general interest' and 'the general interest as 'ruling'. This is an important point, since some critics have read the argument that the operations of the media depend on the mediation of the state in too literal a way – as if it were merely a matter of whether the institution is state-controlled or not. But it should be clear that the connections which make the operations of the media in political matters legitimate and 'impartial' are not institutional matters, but a wider question of the role of the State in the mediation of social conflicts It is at this level that the media can be said (with plausibility – though the terms continue to be confusing) to be 'ideological state apparatuses'. (Althusser, however, whose phrase this is, did not take the argument far enough, leaving him open to the charge of illegitimately assimilating all ideological institutions into the state, and of giving this identification a functionalist gloss.)

This connection is a systemic one: that is, it operates at the level where systems and structures coincide and overlap. It does not function, as we have tried to show, at the level of the conscious intentions and biases of the broadcasters. When in phrasing a question, in the era of monetarism, a broadcasting interviewer simply takes it for granted that rising wage demands are the sole cause of inflation, he is both 'freely formulating a question' on behalf of the public and establishing a logic which is compatible with the dominant interests in society. And this would be the case regardless of whether or not the particular broadcaster was a lifelong supporter of some left-wing Trotskyist sect. This is a simple instance; but its point is to reinforce the argument that, in the critical paradigm, ideology is a function of the discourse and of the logic of social processes, rather than an intention of the agent. The broadcaster's consciousness of what he is doing – how he explains to himself his practice, how he accounts for the connection between his 'free' actions and the systematic inferential inclination of what he produces – is indeed, an interesting and important question. But it does not substantially affect the theoretical issue. The ideology has 'worked' in such a case because the discourse has spoken itself through him/her. Unwittingly, unconsciously, the broadcaster has served as a support for the reproduction of a dominant ideological discursive field.

The critical paradigm is by no means fully developed; nor is it in all respects theoretically secure. Extensive empirical work is required to demonstrate the adequacy of its explanatory terms, and to refine, elaborate and develop its infant insights. What cannot be doubted is the profound theoretical revolution which it has already accomplished. It has set the analysis of the media and media studies on the foundations of a quite new problematic. It has encouraged a fresh start in media studies when the traditional framework of analysis had manifestly broken down and when the hard-nosed empirical positivism of the halcyon days of 'media research' had all but ground to a stuttering halt. This is its value and importance. And at the centre of this paradigm shift was the rediscovery of ideology and the social and political significance of language and the politics of sign and discourse: the re-discovery of ideology, it would be more appropriate to say – the return of the repressed.

References

Althusser, L. (1969) *For Marx*, Allen Lane, London.

Althusser, L. (1971) Ideology and ideological state apparatuses. In *Lenin and Philosophy and Other Essays*, New Left Books, London.

Barthes, R. (1972) *Mythologies*, Jonathan Cape, London

Camargo, M. (1980) Ideological dimension of media messages. In Hall, S. *et al.* (eds) *Culture, Media, Language*, Hutchinson, London.

Eco, U. (1973) Social life as a sign system. In Robey, D. (ed.) *Structuralism: An Introduction*, Clarendon Press, Oxford.

Garnham, N. (1979) Contribution to a political economy of mass communication. *Media, Culture and Society*, Vol. 1, No. 2, April.

Golding, P. and Murdock, G. (1979) Ideology and mass communication: the question of determination. in Barrett, M., Corrigan, P., Kuhn, A. and Wolff, J. (eds) *Ideology and Cultural Reproduction*, Lawrence & Wishart, London.

Hall, S. (1975) Encoding and decoding in the television discourse. *Education and Culture*, Council of Europe, Strasbourg, Vol. 6.

Hall, S. (1980) Encoding and decoding (revised extract). In Hall, S. *et al.* (eds) *Culture, Media, Language*, Hutchinson, London.

Hall, S., Connell, I. and Curti, L. (1977) The 'unity' of current affairs television. *Cultural Studies*, Vol. 9.

Laclau, E. (1977) *Politics and Ideology in Marxist Theory*, New Left Books, London.

Lévi-Strauss, C. (1967) *The Scope of Anthropology*, Jonathan Cape, London.

Saussure, F. de (1960) *Course in General Linguistics*, P. Owen, London.

Vološinov, V. N. (1973) *Marxism and the Philosophy of Language*, Seminar Press, New York.

47

Mass communication and cultural studies

James W. Carey

From Carey, J. W. (1989) *Communication as Culture: Essays on Media and Society*, Unwin-Hyman, London, pp. 40–68.

In the early 1970s I heard the late Raymond Williams, then a distinguished fellow of Jesus College, Cambridge, remark at a London meeting that 'the study of communications was deeply and disastrously deformed by being confidently named the study of "mass-communication" '. Stuart Hall, then director of the Centre for the Study of Contemporary Culture at the University of Birmingham, responded that at his centre they had considered a number of labels, including 'communications', to describe their work. In his opinion the wisest decision they had made was to tie the Birmingham Centre to contemporary culture rather than to communications or mass communications. Awash as we are in programmes of 'communications' and 'mass communications' what tell, were Williams and Hall trying to teach us?

Williams argued that it was now time (over a decade ago) to bury the term 'mass communications' as a label for departments, research programmes, and conferences. The term was disastrous, he thought, for three reasons. First, it limits studies to a few specialized areas such as broadcasting and film and what is miscalled 'popular literature' when there is 'the whole common area of discourse in speech and writing that always needs to be considered'. Second, the term 'mass' has become lodged in our language in its weakest sense – the mass audience – and stands in the way of analysis of 'specific modern communication situations and of most specific modern communications conventions and forms'. Third, because the audience was conceived as a mass, the only question worth asking was how, and then whether, film, television, or books influenced or corrupted people. Consequently, it was always much easier to get funding for these kinds of impact studies than any other kind of research.

It is easy to glide by Williams' distinctive emphasis. He was suggesting that studies of mass communications create unacceptable limitations on study and a certain blindness as well. The blindness is that the term generally overlooks the fact that communication is first of all a set of practices, conventions, and forms, and in studying 'mass situations' these phenomena are assumed to exist but never are investigated. Second, the term limits and isolates study by excluding attention to the forms, conventions, and practices of speech and writing as well as to the mass media and therefore necessarily distorts understanding. This distinctive emphasis, which derives in part from European Marxism, should not blind us to the fact that it is shared by American pragmatism as well.

Stuart Hall's objection to the word 'communication' is somewhat more opaque, though I think he had a similar intention. Hall believes that the word 'communication' narrows study and isolates it substantively and methodologically. Substantively, it narrows the scope of study to products explicitly produced by and delivered over the mass media. The study of communications is therefore generally isolated from the study of literature and art, on the one hand, and from the expressive and ritual forms of everyday life – religion, conversation, sport – on the other. The word 'culture', which in its anthropological sense directs us toward the study of an entire way of life, is replaced by the word 'communication', which directs us to the study of one isolated segment of existence. Methodologically, the word 'communication' isolates us from an entire body of critical, interpretive, and comparative methodology that has been at the heart of anthropology and the study of literature as well as modern Marxism.

We can, of course, easily dismiss this as a misunderstanding and claim that our emphasis on communications and mass communications has not divorced us from the study of speech, writing, and other contemporary products. Too much is being read into the organization of departments and journals. Or, we might argue that limitations have been placed on the range and scope of research, but only to achieve a subject matter amenable to treatment with scientific methods and scientific theories. But these dismissals jump too easily to the lips, and it would be well to suspend judgement until a more generous understanding can be gained of what is distinctive in the Williams–Hall arguments.

One way of catching these distinctive emphases is to suggest that intellectual work on culture and communications derives from different intellectual puzzles and is grounded in two different metaphors of communications. The generalization is too large, of course, and plenty of vividly particular exceptions can be found, but I express preponderant tendencies of thought related to different social conditions. As I suggested earlier, American studies are grounded in a transmission or transportation view of communication. We see communication basically as a process of transmitting messages at a distance for the purpose of control. The archetypal case of communication, then, is persuasion; attitude change; behaviour modification; socialization through the transmission of information, influence, or conditioning or, alternatively, as a case of individual choice over what to read or view. I call this a transmission or transportation view because its central defining terms have much in common with the use of 'communication' in the nineteenth century as another term for 'transportation'. It also is related strongly to the nineteenth-century desire to use communication and transportation to extend influence, control, and power over wider distances and greater populations.

By contrast, a ritual view conceives communication as a process through which a shared culture is created, modified, and transformed. The archetypal case of communication is ritual and mythology for those who come at the problem from anthropology; art and literature for those who come at the problem from literary criticism and history. A ritual view of communication is directed not toward the extension of messages in space but the maintenance of society in time (even if some find this maintenance characterized by domination and therefore illegitimate); not the act of imparting information or influence but the creation, representation, and celebration of shared even if illusory beliefs. If a transmission view of communication centres on the extension of messages across geography for purposes of control, a ritual view centres on the sacred ceremony that draws persons together in fellowship and commonality.

Now the differences between these views can be seen as mere transpositions of one another. However, they have quite distinct consequences, substantively and methodologically. They obviously derive from differing problematics; that is, the basic questions of one tradition do not connect with the basic questions of the other.

What is the relationship between culture and society – or, more generally, between expressive forms, particularly art, and social order? For American scholars in general this problem is not even seen as a problem. It is simply a matter of individual choice or one form of determination or another. There is art, of course, and there is society; but to chart the relationship between them is, for a student in communication, to rehearse the obvious and unnecessary. However, in much European work one of the principal (though not exclusive) tasks of scholarship is to work through the relationship of expressive form to social order.

The British sociologist Tom Burns put this nicely somewhere when he observed that the task of art is to make sense out of life. The task of social science is to make sense out of the senses we make out of life. By such reasoning the social scientist stands toward his material – cultural forms such as religion, ideology, journalism, everyday speech – as the literary critic stands toward the novel, play, or poem. He has to figure out what it means, what interpretations it presents of life, and how it relates to the senses of life historically found among a people.

Note what Burns simply takes for granted. There is, on the one hand, life, existence, experience, and behaviour and, on the other hand, attempts to find the meaning and significance in this experience and behaviour. Culture according to this reading is the meaning and significance particular people discover in their experience through art, religion, and so forth. To study culture is to seek order within these forms, to bring out in starker relief their claims and meanings, and to state systematically the relations between the multiple forms directed to the same end: to render experience comprehensible and charged with affect. But what is called the study of culture also can be called the study of communications, for what we are studying in this context are the ways in which experience is worked into understanding and then disseminated and celebrated (the distinctions, as in dialogue, are not sharp).

Communication studies in the United States have exhibited until recently quite a different intention. They have found most problematic in communication the conditions under which persuasion or social control occurs. Now to reduce the rich variety of American studies to this problematic is, I will admit, a simplification, yet it does capture a significant part of the truth. American studies of communication, mass and interpersonal, have aimed at stating the precise psychological and sociological conditions under which attitudes are changed, formed, or reinforced and behaviour stabilized or redirected. Alternatively, the task is to discover those natural and abstract functions that hold the social order together. Specific forms of culture – art, ritual, journalism – enter the analysis only indirectly, if at all; they enter only insofar as they contribute to such sociological conditions or constitute such psychological forces. They enter, albeit indirectly, in discussions of psychological states, rational or irrational motives and persuasive tactics, differing styles of family organization, sharp distinctions rendered between reality and fantasy-oriented communication, or the role of the mass media in maintaining social integration. But expressive forms are exhausted as intellectual objects suitable for attention by students of communication once relevance to matters of states and rates have been demonstrated. The relation of these forms to social order, the historical transformation of these forms, their entrance into a subjective world of meaning and significance, the interrelations among them, and their role in creating a general culture – a way of life and a pattern of significance – never is entertained seriously.

This difference of substance and intent is related also to a difference in strategy in dealing with a persistent methodological dilemma of the social sciences and, especially, of different meanings of that critical word *empirical*.

[. . .]

Mass communication research began as an attempt to explain communication effects by deriving them from some causally antecedent aspect of the communication process. Inspired by both behaviouristic psychology and information theory, this explanatory apparatus gave rise to a power model of communication wherein the emphasis was placed on the action of the environment, however conceived, upon a relatively passive receiver. This model was made both possible and necessary by a scientific programme that insisted on reducing cultural phenomena to antecedent causes. Some of these causes were explicitly conceptualized as psychological variables – source credibility, appeal of the message – whereas others were rooted in the structural situation of the receiver – class, status, religion, income (Hovland, Janis, and Kelley, 1953; Lazarsfeld, Berelson, and Gaudet, 1948).

An advantage of this model of antecedent causality was that it rooted cultural phenomena in the solid ground of social structure or the conditioning history of individuals. However, it had the disadvantage of yielding ambiguous predictions of behaviour. At best, modest correlations of antecedent and resultant variables were achieved, and even modest success was often purchased by carefully screening test populations (Katz and Lazarsfeld, 1955) to heighten the likelihood of significant result.

The history of mass communication research parallels that of other areas of the social sciences that deal with cultural forms. Whether it be deviance (Matza, 1964), art (Geertz, 1973), or religion (Berger, 1967), the attempt is first made to predict the presence of a creed, ideology, deviant pattern, or behaviour change on the basis of antecedent exposure and stimulation or on the basis of a social-structural variable – race, class, income, and so on. The results are usually meagre, and the conclusion comes down to 'some do, some don't'. On the basis of conditioning or class or any other of these families of antecedent variables, one concludes that some hold to the creed, some do not; some vote one way, some another; some join fascist movements, some remain apathetic. Unfortunately, one is unable to predict the doers from the underlying model, for only a minuscule amount of variation in the data – significant correlations, but usually less than 0.5 – can be explained by even complex sets of variables. An anti-essentialism is forced on us by the data rather than by the philosophy, as David Morley's (1980, 1986) contemporary studies of audiences have shown. The entire imagery of culture as a power – the opiate of the people, the hypodermic needle, the product of the environment – denies the functioning of autonomous minds and reduces subjects to trivial machines. The rich history of cultural symbolism, the complex, meaningful transactions of, for example, religion end up no more than shadowy derivatives of stimuli and structures.

The functional model arises in response to the empirical difficulties encountered in models of antecedent causality. Moreover, it engenders a shift in imagery and attention: from a view of communication as a power to one of communication as a form of anxiety release and from an interest in the source to an interest in the audience. But most important, it involves a shift in the explanatory apparatus. For in functional analysis the primary emphasis is not on determining the antecedents or origins of behaviour but on determining the import or consequences of behaviour for the maintenance of systems of thought, activity, or social groups. One explains social phenomena not merely etiologically but teleologically: the way they act as mechanisms to maintain or restore equilibrium within a system.

Functional analysis turns, then, from causes to consequences, which are viewed as a contribution to maintaining (or disrupting) the individual personality or more complex systems of social life. Whether the subject is ideology, religion, or mythology, the effect is the same. Religion, no longer characterized as a product of historical conditioning, is now shown to maintain social solidarity: the 'we're all in this together' theory. Ideology, now no longer merely caused by class interest, is shown to provide catharsis by fixating and dispelling anxiety on scapegoats – the 'Even paranoids have enemies' theory. Mass communication, rather than causing certain attitudes or behaviours, provides, by diverting audiences from their troubles, feedback into the maintenance of normalized social roles: the 'Everything we do is useful' theory.

Functionalism starts, then, from the potential malintegration of systems – social, personality, cognitive. It explains phenomena by attaching them not to causal antecedents but to future states, which they erode or more often maintain. At the level of society functional mechanisms deal with strain – surveying hostile environments; at the level of personality with anxiety, or, in the psychological equivalent to sociological functionalism, with disequilibrium. One is left with the equivocal notion that mass communication may upset or confirm social consensus, survey the environment or deceive an audience, promote solidarity or enhance animosity, relieve or exacerbate social tensions, correlate a response to crisis or fragment a community. Anecdotal evidence can be introduced to support all of these contentions, but there is no way of specifying when and under what circumstances mass communication does any or all of these things.

Although a uses and gratifications analysis on occasion comes close to motives that lie behind the consumption of mass communications, in attempting to discriminate the consequences of the behaviour the analysis becomes ambiguous. A pattern of behaviour shaped by a certain set of motivations turns out by a plausible coincidence to serve remotely related ends. A person sits down to watch a television programme because he wants to be entertained and by some mysterious process ends up dispelling his tensions, restoring his morale, or establishing solidarity with a larger community. These consequences are related to the motivations for the action in an extremely vague, unspecific, and unconvincing way. This problem, again, haunts all functional analysis. As Geertz (1973) has summarized the dilemma,

> a group of primitives sets out, in all honesty, to pray for rain and ends up by strengthening its social solidarity; a ward politician sets out to get by or remain near the trough and ends by mediating between unassimilated immigrant groups and an impersonal governmental bureaucracy; an ideologist sets out to air his grievances and finds himself contributing, through the diversionary powers of his illusions, to the continued viability of the very system that grieves him (p. 206).

Latent functions or false consciousness are devices by which the gap is closed between the intentions and consequences of conduct. This trick was inherited from Malinowski (1962) and his arguments concerning the nature of the primitive mind. In Malinowski's scheme, human action that on its face was patently irrational, superstitious, and magical was linked by a hidden indirection to meanings inherently rational and commonsensical: the primitive mentality disclosed a utilitarian mind. This form of thought left us with but two alternatives in treating behaviour; it was either intrinsically primitive and hence irrational and superstitious, or it was susceptible to transformation into utilitarian forms of thought by indication of its intrinsic sensibleness: the unconscious side of thought contributed to the stability of the personality or the ordering of society.

Either strategy has the effect of dissolving the content of the experience – the particular ritual, prayer, movie, or news story – into something pre- or protological without ever inspecting the experience itself as some ordered system of meaningful symbols. The difficulty is, of course, the virtual absence in mass communication research of anything more than a rudimentary conception of symbolic processes. There is much talk about escape, finding symbolic outlets, or solidarity being created, but how these miracles are accomplished is never made clear. In such analyses one never finds serious attention being paid to the content of experience. For example, studies of entertainment claim that fantasy is not completely 'irrational' because it eases tension, promotes solidarity and promotes learning – claims that seem ridiculous to anyone who has witnessed a community divided over the content of movies or personally disturbed by a recurrent film image. What one rarely finds is any analysis of the voice in which films speak. There is an emphasis on everything except what movies are concretely all about.

The link between the causes of mass communication behaviour and its effects seems adventitious because the connecting element is a latent function and no attention is paid to the autonomous process of symbolic formation. Functional analysis, like causal analysis, goes directly from the source to the effect without ever seriously examining mass communication as a system of interacting symbols and interlocked meanings that somehow must be linked to the motivations and emotions for which they provide a symbolic outlet. Content analyses are done, but they are referred for elucidation not to other themes or to any sort of a semantic theory but either backward to the needs they mirror or forward to the social system they maintain.

Despite that, I wish neither to gainsay – or to belabour the traditions of work on mass communication. They are indispensable starting points for everyone. I merely wish to suggest that they do not exhaust the tasks of trained intelligence. There is a third way of looking at the goals of intellectual work in communications. Cultural studies does not, however, escape Mannheim's Paradox; it embraces it in ways I hope to show. In doing so it runs the risk of falling into a vicious relativism, though Geertz himself does not see that as a problem. Cultural studies also has far more modest objectives than other traditions. It does not seek to explain human behaviour in terms of the laws that govern it or to dissolve it into the structures that underlie it; rather, it seeks to understand it. Cultural studies does not attempt to predict human behaviour; rather, it attempts to diagnose human meanings. It is, more positively, an attempt to bypass the rather abstracted empiricism of behavioural studies and the ethereal apparatus of formal theories and to descend deeper into the empirical world. The goals of communications conceived as a cultural science are therefore more modest but also more human, at least in the sense of attempting to be truer to human nature and experience as it ordinarily is encountered.

[. . .]

A cultural science of communication views human behaviour – or, more accurately, human action – as a text. Our task is to construct a 'reading' of the text. The text itself is a sequence of symbols – speech, writing, gesture – that contain interpretations. Our task, like that of a literary critic, is to interpret the interpretations. [. . .]

To speak of human action through the metaphor of a text is no longer unusual, though it is still troubling. The metaphor emphasizes that the task of the cultural scientist is closer to that of a literary critic or a scriptural scholar, though it is not the same, than it is to a behavioural scientist. 'Texts' are not always printed on pages or chiselled in stone – though sometimes they are. Usually we deal with texts of public utterance or shaped behaviour. But we are faced, as is the literary critic, with figuring out what the text says, of constructing a reading of it. Doing communication research (or cultural studies or, in Geertz's term, ethnography) 'is like trying to read (in the sense of 'construct a reading of') a manuscript – foreign, faded, full of ellipses, incoherencies, suspicious emendations, and tendentious commentaries but written not in conventionalized graphs of sound but in transient examples of shaped behaviour' (p. 10).

[. . .]

Why do we wish to construct a reading? The answer to this question shows both the modesty and importance of communication as a study of culture. The objective of cultural studies is not so much to answer our questions as, Geertz puts it, 'to make available to us answers that others guarding other sheep in other valleys have given and thus to include them in the consultable

record of what man has said' (p. 30). This is a modest goal: to understand
the meanings that others have placed on experience, to build up a veridical
record of what has been said at other times, in other places, and in other
ways; to enlarge the human conversation by comprehending what others
are saying. Though modest, the inability to engage in this conversation is
the imperative failure of the modern social sciences. Not understanding their
subjects – that unfortunate word – they do not converse with them so much
as impose meanings on them. Social scientists have political theories and
subjects have political ideologies; the behaviour of social scientists is free
and rationally informed, whereas their subjects are conditioned and ruled
by habit and superstition – not good intellectual soil for a working democracy.

Geertz is suggesting that the great need of the social sciences and one
that cultural studies is able uniquely to perform is the creation of a theory
of fictions. Fiction is used here in its original sense – fictio – a 'making', a
construction. The achievement of the human mind and its extension in
culture (though it is as much an abject necessity as an achievement) is the
creation of a wide variety of cultural forms through which reality can be
created. Science, with its claim to be the only cultural achievement that was
a veridical map of reality, held us back as much as it advanced our
understanding of how this miracle was accomplished. [. . .]

To pull off an effective theory of popular culture requires a conception of
persons, not as psychological or sociological but as cultural. Such a model
would assume that culture is best understood not by tracing it to psychological and sociological conditions or, indeed, to exclusively political or economic
conditions, but as a manifestation of a basic cultural disposition to cast up
experience in symbolic form. These forms, however implausible to the
investigator, are at once aesthetically right and conceptually veridical. They
supply meaningful identities along with an apprehended world.

If human activity is not passive or fully dependent on external
stimulation, then a corollary is that activity is not merely an emanation of
some substratum of biological needs or socially induced dispositions. Instead,
human activity, by the very nature of the human nervous system (Geertz,
1973, p. 68), is cultural, involving the construction of a symbolic container
that shapes and expresses whatever human nature, needs, or dispositions
exist. [. . .]

When the idea of culture enters communications research, it emerges as
the environment of an organism or a system to be maintained or a power
over the subject. Whatever the truth of these views – and there is truth in all
of them – culture must first be seen as a set of practices, a mode of human
activity, a process whereby reality is created, maintained, and transformed,
however much it may subsequently become reified into a force independent
of human action (Berger and Luckmann, 1966). This activity allows the human
nervous system to function by producing and maintaining a meaningful cosmos
at once both aesthetically gratifying and intellectually plausible. It is precisely
such a theory of culture – or, if you prefer, a theory of meaning, semantics, or
semiotics – that is necessary if culture is to be removed from the status of a
power or an environment.
[. . .]

It is unfortunate that to mention cultural studies to most communications researchers resurrects the image of the arguments concerning mass and popular culture that littered the field a few decades ago. That was part of the disaster Raymond Williams referred to in comments mentioned earlier. Yet many who worked in popular culture were on the right track. The question they both raised and obscured was a simple but profound one: What is the significance of living in the world of meanings conveyed by popular art? What is the relationship between the meanings found in popular art and in forms such as science, religion, and ordinary speech? How, in modern times, is experience cast up, interpreted, and concealed into knowledge and understanding?

The remarkable work of Clifford Geertz – remarkable substantively and methodologically, though the latter has not been explored in this essay – and of many others working in phenomenology, hermeneutics, and literary criticism has served to clarify the objectives of a cultural science of communications and has defined the dimensions of an interpretive science of society. The task now for students of communications or mass communication or contemporary culture is to turn these advances in the science of culture toward the characteristic products of contemporary life: news stories, bureaucratic language, love songs, political rhetoric, daytime serials, scientific reports, television drama, talk shows, and the wider world of contemporary leisure, ritual, and information. To square the circle, those were some of the conventions, forms and practices Raymond Williams felt had slipped by us when we confidently named our field the study of mass communications.

References

Berger, Peter L. (1967) *The Sacred Canopy*, Doubleday, Garden City, NY.

Berger, Peter and Luckmann, Thomas (1966) *The Social Construction of Reality*, Doubleday, Garden City, NY.

Geertz, Clifford (1973) *The Interpretation of Cultures*, Basic Books, New York.

Hovland, Carl, Janis, I. and Kelley, H. (1953) *Communication and Persuasion*, Yale University Press, New Haven.

Katz, Elihu and Lazarsfield, Paul (1955) *Personal Influence*, Free Press. New York.

Lazarsfeld, Paul, Berelson, B. and Gaudet, H. (1948) *The People's Choice*, Columbia University Press, New York.

Malinowski, Bronislaw (1962) *Sex, Culture and Myth*, Harcourt, Brace and World, New York.

Matza, David (1964) *Delinquency and Drift*, John Wiley, New York.

Morley, David (1980) *The 'Nationwide' Audience: Structure and Decoding*, British Film Institute, London.

Morley, David (1986) *Family Television: Cultural Power and Domestic Leisure*, Comedia Publishing Group, London.

48

Populism and ordinary culture

Jim McGuigan

From McGuigan, J. (1992) *Cultural Populism*, Routledge, London, pp. 13–44.

Populist sentiment

I want to argue that at the heart of British cultural studies – and also impinging upon the cognate fields of communication and media studies – there is populist sentiment, but hardly any 'sentimentality'[1] is discernible: present-day students of popular culture are too street-wise for that. Although the cultural studies approach considered here is not wholly encompassed by populism, a non-populist cultural studies is very nearly a contradiction in terms: it is an academic game which might do better calling itself something else.

To use the noun 'sentiment' is risky because it instantly invokes the adjective 'sentimental', as it does in *The Oxford English Dictionary*:

> **Sentiment** . . . n. **1.** a mental attitude produced by one's feeling about something; a verbal expression of this; an opinion. **2.** emotion as opposed to reason; sentimentality.

The next entry is '**Sentimental** . . . romantic or nostalgic feeling . . . showing or affected by emotion rather than reason'. In his invaluable *Keywords* Raymond Williams notes that such a delimitation of meaning is traceable back to late Romanticism, enunciated by Robert Southey during his conservative old age: 'the sentimental classes, persons of ardent or morbid sensibility' (quoted by Williams, 1983a, p. 283). In Williams' judgement 'this confusion permanently damaged *sentimental*'. Using the term 'sentiment' enables me to avoid using Williams' concept 'structure of feeling' to characterize "populism" as Ken Hirschkop does, a little too loosely in my view, to characterize Williams' own complex populism (Hirschkop, 1989). To suggest that a theory or a field of intellectual enquiry is grounded in certain sentiments is hardly in itself contentious except in the most rigorously positivistic discourses of social and cultural science. That cultural studies has values and that practitioners are passionate about what they do should not alarm anyone: it would be much more alarming if cultural studies lacked such qualities.

[. . .]

How are we to make sense of the meaning of this slippery phenomenon, populism, which I am suggesting lie at the heart of cultural studies? As Ernesto Laclau (1977) has observed, it is 'a concept both elusive and recurrent' (p. 143). 'Elusive', difficult to define; 'recurrent', a label readily

applied by political commentators and also, increasingly, by cultural critics.
[. . .]

For him, populism is not inherent in the movement, nor in the ideology, but in the articulation of 'non-class contradictions' into political discourses originating in class contradictions. In Laclau's subsequent theorizing, with Chantal Mouffe, 'class' looms much less large, if at all, as a fundamental and generative grounding (Laclau and Mouffe, 1985). That does not, however, substantially affect this explication. Two points are crucial here. First, 'the people' do not exist in any finite sense: they are an articulation of political discourse. Political discourse interpellates a subject, a subjectivity and a subjecthood (Althusser, 1970, 1984). This is, in a sense, a 'culturalist' argument: politics as the production of identity. The Weberian Donald MacRae (1969) said virtually as much, in rather different terms, in remarking that populism is 'about personality' (p. 160). Second, according to Laclau, politics is, furthermore, about 'the "people"/power bloc contradiction' (1977, p. 166) . It never presents itself as an unmediated struggle between classes. The problem of populism, then, is both dissolved *and* expanded to subsume the whole terrain of politics. Whoever gets to speak on behalf of 'the people' against the current construction of 'the power bloc' is winning the game, albeit only for the time being, according to the radical democratic theorization – see O'Shea (1984), on Thatcherite rhetoric from this perspective. That politics is thus culturally implicated in 'the interpellation of subjects', is what enabled Stuart Hall to say:

> Popular culture is one of the sites where this struggle for and against a culture of the powerful is engaged: it is also the stake to be won or lost in that struggle. It is the arena of consent and resistance. It is partly where hegemony arises, and where it is secured (1981, p. 239).

Hall did, however, wish to quibble with Laclau's formulation because he thought it depended too much on the Latin American experience of subordinate classes being articulated against the dominant classes through populist discourse. It neglected their articulation to the dominant classes in other contexts: for instance, Thatcherism in Britain. Thus, Hall wished to qualify the political range of 'populism' and contrast it with 'popular-democratic', which, by definition for him, is not available to the political Right (1988, p. 140). Such a view could, none the less, reasonably be considered a populism of the democratic Left, still appreciating Hall's vital distinction between something like genuine democracy and what inadequately passes for it in the British parliamentary system. There is a danger in Hall's position of reducing culture entirely to politics and, more seriously, of collapsing politics into cultural politics *tout court*.
[. . .]

In his 'base–superstructure' article (1973) Williams argued that Antonio Gramsci's conception of hegemony is superior to the dominant ideology thesis of the base–superstructure model, since it facilitates an understanding of the complex interplay of cultural forces within a social totality. When ideology is conceptualized as only the distorted 'reflection' of power relations and contradictions in 'the base' its livedness is thereby denied. That which is lived cannot be entirely illusory: it is represented in common sense, the practical reasoning of everyday life and, because hegemonic leadership is never all-pervasive, the nexus of culture and ideology is one of perpetual negotiation between contending forces. To explore the complexity of hegemony, Williams categorized cultural practice in terms of *dominant*, *residual* and *emergent* formations, with both residual and emergent subdivided into *alternative* and *oppositional*.

During the 1980s, Williams noted that hegemonic dominance was becoming progressively trans-national, motivated by the globalization of capitalism and the terror of a renewed Cold War, stated most sharply in his last great work of cultural and political analysis, *Towards 2000* (1983b).[2] Cultural power, *en route* to the millennium, was not only represented by the cardinal principle of possessive individualism: in addition, Williams identified what he called 'Plan X' – a nihilistic politics of 'strategic advantage' on a global scale (1983b, p. 244), of which Thatcherism was a local manifestation. However, Williams was no pessimist: he also discerned 'resources of hope' rising from below, subordinate cultural forces that can be clarified with reference to his model of hegemony. The dominant culture never commands the field entirely: it must struggle continually with residual and emergent cultures. Residual culture, by definition, derives from the past, usually rooted, under predominantly secular and urban conditions, in religious and rural practices, presenting resistance and challenge to the current hegemonic system: a major example would be the rise of Islamic fundamentalism. Williams himself, however, was more interested in emergent and oppositional formations, carrying potential for a new, previously unimaginable, social order. Because emergent culture is different from anything that went before, it is tempting to mistake apparent novelty, so characteristic of capitalist cycles of renewal, for forms and practices that really do make a difference. It is more reliable, perhaps, to study emergent cultures historically. From this perspective, the working-class and women's movements are justifiably seen as historical forms of emergence, signifying collective and liberating possibilities, the oppositional power of which has frequently been neutralized by incorporation into dominant hegemonic arrangements whilst also, however, winning genuine concessions.

Williams made a vital distinction between alternative and oppositional practices. Alternative culture seeks a place to coexist within the existing hegemony, whereas oppositional culture aims to replace it. For instance, there is a world of difference between a minority 'back-to-nature' cult and the ecology movement's global reach. In his later work, Williams managed to combine an enduring commitment to class politics, put into such disarray and discredit by the recomposition of capitalist hegemony, with hope in the 'new social movements', especially 'peace, ecology and feminism'. He was also sensitive to the dialectic of alternative and oppositional in more narrowly defined practices of cultural production, in film, television and so on, and the risks associated with, on the one hand, self-excluding purity and, on the other, compromised incorporation. The central problem, for Williams, turned on the articulation of popular movements and emerging forms of cultural production into a counter-hegemony, totalizing opposition to 'Plan X'. Separated and divided, they are inherently vulnerable to neutralizing and marginalizing mechanisms, institutionally, societally and globally.

Williams' comparatively later ideas speak directly to our present condition. However, it is also important to appreciate the continuity in Williams' thought from the time when he announced, polemically, that 'culture is ordinary'. Williams' populism persistently brought into the foreground the question of democracy, placing him on the incorruptible side of Hall's binary opposition between popular-democratic and merely populist politics. Writing in 1959 he said:

> Nothing has done more to sour the democratic idea, among its natural supporters, and to drive them back into angry self-exile, than the plain, overwhelming cultural issues: the apparent division of our culture into, on the one hand, a remote and self-gracious sophistication, on the other hand, a doped mass (reprinted in 1989a, p. 17).

Williams not only strove to democratize cultural theory, he intervened politically by making very specific policy suggestions. The first two policies proposed in 'Culture is ordinary' were tame indeed: comprehensive education and increased expenditure on arts and adult education. The third proposal, however, would seem, according to 1990s conventional wisdom, even more dangerously radical and unrealistic than it did at the end of the 1950s: finding ways of replacing advertising revenue for newspapers with public funds. [. . .]

If I have positioned Williams like a Colossus at the entrance to cultural studies it is not because he said it all but because his vision of a 'common culture' founded in participatory democracy remained on the agenda, at least sentimentally, through the various theoretical twists and turns over the following years, which at times virtually displaced it. By the late 1980s, Williams looked back with horror at some of those twists and turns because, in his opinion, they had led cultural studies away from its popular educational project. From the 1970s onwards, cultural studies was carried along on successive waves of what Williams considered to be idealist theorizing, mainly derived from Saussurian linguistics, resulting in specialized academicism and loss of historical imagination. Williams claimed that such 'theory' was élitist even when applied to the study of popular culture. Whether this claim was just or not, his meaning is clear when one thinks of the title of a book on popular culture edited by Colin MacCabe, a notable proponent of what Williams dubbed 'the new conformism', a legacy of heady 1970s theoreticism: *High Theory/Low Culture* (1986).[3] Williams' argument that cultural studies is peculiarly obliged to account for the formation of its own project was well put and a chastening reminder: 'the real problem of the project as a whole, which is that people's questions are not answered by the existing distribution of the educational curriculum, can be forgotten' (1989b, p. 159). Speaking at the 1986 conference of the Association for Cultural Studies, Williams urged upon his audience the paramount task of contesting the new educational utilitarianism, 'work experience' and so forth, 'a definition of industrial training which would have sounded crude in the 1860s' (1989b, p. 160).

Although he does not name him, Williams' criticisms were also aimed unmistakably at his old New Left comrade Stuart Hall, who did more than anyone to establish cultural studies as a nearly respectable subject during his directorship of the Birmingham University postgraduate Centre for

Contemporary Cultural Studies in the 1970s. Wllliams questioned Hall's dating of the inception of cultural studies from the publication of certain texts: Richard Hoggart's *The Uses of Literacy* (1957), Edward Thompson's *The Making or the English Working Class* (1963), Williams' own *Culture and Society* (1958) and *The Long Revolution* (1961), 'the original "curriculum" of the field' (Hall 1980b, p. 16). Such a text-based history, according to Williams, obscured the practices that went into making those books and the educational context in which they were made: adult education, a curriculum negotiated with working-class students from the late 1940s and throughout the 1950s. These were students who had questions to ask that could not be answered by the established disciplines of literature and history, thus, calling forth an explora-tory approach, in effect an interdisciplinary cultural studies approach. Drawing on that memory, Williams criticized the Open University's Popular Culture course of the 1980s for producing a non-negotiated curriculum in which students were positioned as passive consumers of a newly reified branch of academic knowledge as though the subject matter had little to do with their own lives.

[. . .]

Before considering Hall's maps I want to suggest that there are, broadly, three levels at which the development of cultural studies can be addres-sed. First, in terms of the movement of ideas within the field, the succession, incommensurability and interaction between different paradigms and problematic. This is the most conventional means of accounting for an academic project. Second, cultural studies may be considered in terms of its formation, as Williams insisted it should. This involves addressing institutional and historical contexts of emergence and transformation. Third, one can explore its politics of representation, the mechanisms of inclusion and exclusion which regulate agency within the field: basically, who gets to define the issues and with what purposes. My purpose in opening up the problem of accounting for cultural studies here is to draw attention to its populist impulses. This is to be clarified by Hall's maps. In effect, Hall has addressed all three levels, with a stress, however, on the first and second.

In his 'Two paradigms' essay (1980a), Stuart Hall very nearly abstracts cultural studies from its institutional and historical contexts: talking of cultural studies as though it were more than the work of the Birmingham Centre while, none the less, being mainly grounded in the ideational movements of that Centre. [. . .]

Culturalism and structuralism are not the only paradigm identified by Hall in his 'Two paradigms' essay. In addition to these 'names of the game', he offers his own synthesis and goes on to mention three other contenders, each of which he treats with scepticism. Two of these contenders are 'post-structuralist': the reintroduction of the subject, a decentred not a humanist subject, in Lacanian psychoanalysis, which evacuates the analysis of social formation for the analysis of subjectivity; Foucauldian discursive formation analysis, which traces the specificities of power/ knowledge operations but at the expense of analysing the articulation of determinate instances in a social formation; that is, it departs from the effort to theorize a non-reductive alternative to the base–superstructure model of orthodox Marxism, a project which characterized both culturalism and structuralism in their different ways. The final paradigm mentioned by Hall is the political economy of culture, which he rejects because it does not resolve Marxism's problem of economic reductionism, his own special demon.

Read in isolation, Hall's 'Two paradigms' essay would give the impression that cultural studies was perhaps a philosophical sub-discipline. And a reader unfamiliar with this theoretical terrain may not be much enlightened by the foregoing and very condensed summary of Hall's influential survey. Complicating matters even further, it is now out of date, preceding as it does the extraordinary efflorescence of post-structuralist and post-modernist theorizing in the 1980s. But if you read Hall's other mapping piece, 'Cultural studies and the Centre' (1980b), it all makes much more practical sense because the theoretical acrobatics are there situated within a particular research institute, the Birmingham Centre for Contemporary Cultural Studies itself. The second essay presents a much messier picture, identifying other important strands of thought (for instance, interpretative sociology and Sartrean existentialism), false starts, dead ends, the difference between actually doing concrete research and theorizing it, in a collective endeavour, sometimes harmoniously, sometimes antagonistically, built around workshops rather than academic individualism. Also, as well as registering the dizzying 'impact of the structuralisms', Hall registers the 'impact of the feminisms' that is, a political rather than principally intellectual movement, in the 1970s. This leads us back to considering the relationship between cultural studies, institution and history and, in particular, the political radicalism of the post-1968 research student generation before the Thatcherite backlash was to transform the rules of the game so dramatically in the 1980s.

It also connects up with the main point I want to make here concerning the representational politics of cultural studies. This can be introduced by a quotation from *Women Take Issue*, produced by the Centre's Women's Studies Group:

> When we decided to do this book we thought we were deciding to produce the eleventh issue of *Working Papers in Cultural Studies*. Ten issues, with only four articles concerning women – it seemed about time. Women's continued 'invisibility' in the journal, and within much of the intellectual work done within CCCS (although things are changing), is the result of a complex of factors, which although in this particular combination are specific to our own relatively privileged situation are not unique to it (CCCS Women's Studies Group 1978, p. 7).

The authors proceed to tell a familiar story of women's silence in a male-dominated discourse, the problem of whether to adopt a separatist stance or try to de-masculinize the whole process from top to bottom.[4] They also remark, 'Women's studies, like black studies, as a subject or discipline, has political not academic roots' (p. 9). Several years later, another graduate of the Centre, Paul Gilroy, had this to say in *There Ain't No Black in the Union Jack*:

> This book has a second more parochial aim [in addition to tracing the history of British racism] related to its origins in the field of cultural studies. It seeks to provide, more implicitly than explicitly, a corrective to the more ethnocentric dimensions of that discipline. . . . The marginalization of 'race' and racism has persisted even where cultural studies have identified themselves with socialist and feminist aspirations (1987, p. 12)[5].

These criticisms, made from female and black experiences within cultural studies, and specifically from within the Birmingham Centre, are not by any means peculiar to cultural studies. Similar criticisms have been made and acted upon in the wider society, most markedly in public-sector institutions. Cultural studies, then, like any other socially responsible intellectual practice, is affected by broad-based issues around discrimination and representation. But, and much more to the point, it is these issues, especially in their subjective and discursive aspects, that are integral to cultural studies, not only for the political sympathies of agents in the field but in deciding upon what to study and how to study it: this constitutes a democratic imperative, stimulated by 'underdog' sentiments. Although similar sentiments operate in the adjacent fields of media and communication studies, sociology and contemporary literary theory, it is in cultural studies where they have been most intensely felt and pronounced. However much we trace and map the movement of ideas in cultural studies, its institutionalization in research centres, proliferating under graduate and post-graduate degree courses, its presence in further and secondary education, the journals, associations and conferences where debates are conducted and fresh directions explored, the field of study is not intelligible without recognition of its populist impulses, and what I aim to show are some of their attendant dilemmas. Analytical objects are not only the product of academic theories. The energizing sentiments may be populist but that does not mean, however, that cultural studies could in any way be reduced to a simplistic, atheoretical populism, merely telling it from the point of view of one socially subordinate constituency or another. The theories and methods are sophisticated and various, with a will to eclecticism, the sense of which is captured in Richard Johnson's (1986) 'realist hypothesis', seeking to reconcile probably irreconcilable epistemological positions: 'What if the existing theories, their methods and their results actually correspond to different sides of the same process?' (p. 283).

'Between the grand old cause and the brand new times'

Contemporary cultural studies developed rapidly at Birmingham in the 1970s. Newly imbibed theories and proliferating socio-cultural differences spawned lines of enquiry and issues to engage, giving an impressive dynamism to the nascent field of study. The core problematic of ideological reproduction through popular culture was continually modified in response to a steady flow of mainly French ideas concerning language, power and subjectivity. And, empirical research projects were triggered off by a succession of constituencies to represent: class, generational, gender/sexual and ethnic/racial. During that most fecund period of the Birmingham Centre, specificity was linked to complexity in a totalizing framework. This was later to be called into question, usually from elsewhere, by the modish deconstructionist currents of the 1980s, frequently claiming that totalization, making holistic connections between ostensibly discrete phenomena, is somehow inherently *totalitarian*.

In the mid-1970s, however, theoretical effort was devoted to producing a revised model of the social whole against 'expressive' and 'essentialist' conceptions of totality. Stuart Hall, drawing on both Louis Althusser and Antonio Gramsci, stressed that project in his mapping essays. Society was conceived of as inherently complex: the various 'instances' of the 'super-structure' irreducible to a single 'basic' contradiction, that of the forces and relations of production. Ideological formations were separated out rigorously and their articulation to the state and (possibly) the mode of production traced rather than presumed. The approach was interactive: specific social and signifying practices related dialectically through a complex totality, with the economic only determinate in 'the last instance', if at all.

'Articulation' is probably Stuart Hall's most important conceptual addendum to Gramscian thought, inspired originally by Ernesto Laclau (1977). Hall explained his usage of the term in an interview with Lawrence Grossberg, the leading North American interpreter of British cultural studies, in 1986:

> I always use the word 'articulation', though I don't know whether the meaning I attribute to it is perfectly understood. In England, the term has a nice double meaning because 'articulate' means to utter, to !speak forth, to be articulate. It carries that sense of language-ing, of expressing, etc. But we also speak of an 'articulated' lorry (truck): a lorry where the front (cab) and back (trailer) can, but need not necessarily, be connected to one another. . . . So the so-called 'unity' of a discourse is really the articulation of different, distinct elements which can be rearticulated in different ways because they have no necessary 'belongingness' (Grossberg and Hall, 1986, p. 53).

One might observe, facetiously no doubt, that a 'back (trailer)' without a 'front (cab)' to pull it along would be stationary. Although Hall was elaborating on discourse/subjectivity in the interview with Grossberg, 'articulation' also illuminates how contemporary cultural studies theorized the relation of 'the cultural' to 'the economic', which is where it parts company with the political economy of culture. Political economists, in this field, generally insist on some necessary articulation between economic dynamics and cultural processes, whether systemically (capital accumulation and social reproduction) or institutionally (advertising, media ownership and control), though not automatically submitting the latter simply to a function of the former in either case (Garnham 1979; Golding and Murdock 1979; Jhally 1989), nor denying the importance of subjectivity, as cultural autonomists usually claim they do. Hall (1983) has conceded some ground to political economy, remarking that perhaps it is wiser to see the economic as determinate in 'the first instance' rather than in 'the last instance' (Murdock 1989a). Yet, 'the lonely hour' has scarcely ever arrived for contemporary cultural studies, early or late. Hall's concession did not substantially affect the predominantly interpretative style of research associated with Birmingham, which scrupulously avoided economic reduc-tionism by normally steering clear of economic determinations.

Contemporary cultural studies increasingly autonomized itself as a distinct 'school of thought' with a growing reputation at home and abroad. Having summarily dismissed the political economy of culture (Hall 1980a), the Centre aimed to out-distance the pioneering work of Raymond Williams as well. For instance, Hall (1980c) criticized Williams' emphasis on 'the indissoluble elements of a continuous social-material process' by arguing that '[a]nalysis must deconstruct the "lived wholeness" in order to think its determinate conditions' (p. 101).[6] This methodological protocol, in epistemological and practical terms, is not contentious. No analysis could grasp the whole of life in one totalizing movement. And, the breaking down and parcelling out of analytical tasks within a shared problematic, which happened at the Birmingham Centre, is fundamental to the intellectual division of labour in anything but the most individualized and imperious research. However, the pursuit of one question, or what is typically a cluster of questions, is likely to result in criticisms of partiality, of leaving something out, of neglecting important determinations, of not taking *absolutely everything* into account. For example, 'Why did Thatcherism become so popular?' is one such question open to the critique of partiality. It is, of course, the question which made Stuart Hall so famous in the 1980s.

Hall wanted to account for how Thatcherism, as an ideology, had won the battle for hearts and minds in the 1970s and then why it sustained hegemonic leadership through the following decade [. . .]

In concentrating on some of Stuart Hall's political writings here, my aim has been to indicate the connection between contemporary cultural studies and left-democratic populism rather than to interrogate the full subtleties of his theoretical position. Hall is not, by any means, the sole representative of this intellectual mix: he was, however, the most eloquent and credible exponent of cultural populism during the 1980s.

Towards the end of the 1980s, and before the fall of Margaret Thatcher herself, the state/ideology problematic circulating around Thatcherism began to be displaced in the pages of *Marxism Today* and also, somewhat hesitantly, in cultural studies by a very different problematic, one addressing longer-run and global forces, the key terms of which are 'culture' and 'economics':

> The 'New Times' argument is that the world has changed, not just incrementally but qualitatively, that Britain and other advanced capitalist societies are increasingly characterised by diversity, differentiation and fragmentation, rather than homogeneity, standardisation and the economies and organisations of scale which characterised modern mass society. This is the essence of the so-called transition from 'Fordism', which defined the experience of modernity in the first two-thirds of the 20th century to 'post-Fordism'. In economic terms, the central feature of the transition is the rise of 'flexible specialisation' in place of the old assembly-line world of mass production. It is this, above all, which is orchestrating and driving on the evolution of this new world. However, this must not be seen as exclusively an economic development, in the narrow sense. Just as Fordism represented, not simply a form of economic organisation but a whole culture – what Gramsci in 'Americanism and Fordism' called a new epoch of civilisation within advanced capitalism – so post-Fordism is also shorthand for a much wider and deeper social and cultural development (Hall and Jacques, 1989, pp. 11–12).

Crucially, this declaration of 'New Times' called for a further shift of attention away from the capitalist mode of production to its modes of reproduction and consumption, thus bringing to the foreground 'the cultural' to an even greater extent than before. According to the thesis, as discussed by Hall in his 'Brave new world' essay in the October 1988 edition of *Marxism Today* (reprinted with revisions as 'The meaning of new times' in Hall and Jacques, 1989), the cultural phenomena associated with 'post-modernism' ('difference', 'subjectivity', 'identity') and the economic phenomena associated with 'post-Fordism' (information technology, robotics, disorganization and reorganization of systems of production/consumption) have some sort of relation to each other, the implication being that economic causation had returned to the agenda. This is an interesting turnabout if one remembers that it was Hall who consigned the political economy of culture perspective to the dustbin of base–superstructure Marxism when he surveyed the contending paradigms of cultural studies several years ago. The New Times thesis did not, however, constitute a reversion to economic reductionism, but it did open up a space for dialogue between two hitherto counterposed positions. In my view, the separation of contemporary cultural studies from the political economy of culture has been one of the most disabling features of the field of study. The core problematic was virtually premised on a terror of economic reductionism. In consequence, the economic aspects of media institutions and the broader economic dynamics of consumer culture were rarely investigated, simply bracketed off, thereby severely undermining the explanatory and, in effect, critical capacities of cultural studies. Some believe that the New Times thesis retains those weaknesses: 'New Times was born in the throes of political pragmatism under the sign of cultural theory bereft of economic reasoning' (Sivanandan 1990, p. 4). Commenting on the *Manifesto for New Times Times*, Judith Williamson (1989) expressed a similar view, suggesting that 'New Times' displays the same excessively ideological reading of culture and politics as the earlier Thatcherism thesis, and is peculiarly complicit with the *populist* delusions fostered by the political Right since the 1970s. Nicholas Costello and his co-authors (1989) have challenged the economic analysis battened on to the New Times thesis and the inferences that are drawn from it for working-class politics and culture. It undercuts arguments for socialism and, at best, brings into the foreground 'identity' and 'new social movement' politics (Rutherford, 1990). The curious thing, however, is that the New Times thesis actually brought economic reasoning back into the cultural debate, switching from a state/ideology problematic, in the analysis of Thatcherism and authoritarian populism, to a culture/economic problematic, as Thatcherism went into decline and appeared less momentous in retrospect. The post-Fordism thesis of the regulation school of economists was seized upon for some rough-and-ready economic equivalent to the manifest cultural changes associated with post-modernity.

Recently, Angela McRobbie (1991) has tried to make sense of the paradigm crisis in contemporary cultural studies. The old Althusserian/Gramscian synthesis of the Birmingham Centre no longer holds sway. Searching questions concerning modernity/post-modernity have superseded it. McRobbie identifies two particular strands in this respect: the radical critique of post-modernism and the New Times cultural politics of consumerism and playful identity. She attacks both unreservedly. According to her, the work of Fredric Jameson (1991) and David Harvey (1989), whom she regards as entirely hostile critics of post-modernism, merely reruns a discredited economic reductionism. And, even worse, New Times writers have lost all sense of the determinate relations between production and consumption, for instance, treating shopping as unproblematically pleasurable. That consumption is part of the material and unequal drudgery of social reproduction is missed by this 'cultural populism' (p. 14), a term used entirely pejoratively by McRobbie. She recommends a return to neo-Gramscian hegemony theory, which once mapped out the field, a kind of middle-ground position between the extremities of economic reductionism and insouciant hedonism. There are two main faults in McRobbie's argument: a slippage and a misrepresentation. The first is to do with her own position, which I believe is itself rooted in cultural populism – not in my vocabulary a term of abuse. Her critique of an undialectical consumptionist perspective is incisive. Like Sinbad, however, McRobbie wants to lure the genie back into the bottle but, unlike Sinbad, she can't do it. There is no retreat into some primordial haven in a rapidly changing world. This relates to the second fault in McRobbie's argument, her misrepresentation of the work of such writers as Jameson and Harvey, who do indeed re-articulate economics and culture but not in the crudely reductionist, or 'reflectonist', manner which she suggests.

Notes

1. Michael Schudson (1987) has also discussed populist 'sentiment' in communication and cultural studies but much more perjoratively than I do here.
2. Williams' posthumously published *The Politics of Modernism* (1989b) is an incomplete collection of disparate pieces and, for this reason, cannot be considered his last major study of culture and politics, which therefore, remains *Towards 2000* from 1983.
3. Raymond Williams' characteristically oblique criticisms of structuralist and post-structuralist theoreticism were no doubt unfair and too sweeping, but he was not particularly inclined to sectarian squabbling. In fact, he displayed impressive solidarity with Colin MacCabe himself when he was denied tenureship at Cambridge in the early 1980s (see Williams, 1981).
4. For an up-to-date discussion of the relations between feminism and cultural studies, see Sarah Franklin *et al.* (1991).
5. On the question of race , the most important publication emanating from Birmingham was *The Empire Strikes Back* (CCCS, 1982) , with which Gilroy was heavily involved.
6. Hall's argument concerning the separation of analytical elements was closely modelled on Karl Marx's (1973) methodological introduction to the *Grundisse* (Hall, 1974). His work, during the 1970s, was very much influenced by Louis Althusser (1966 and 1968). However, Hall's mature theoretical positions are most adequately described as neo-Gramscian. His best-known work draws on Antonio Gramsci's *Prison Notebooks* (Hoare and Nowell-Smith) in a novel and fertile manner.

References

Althusser, L. (1970 – original French publication) Ideology and ideological state apparatuses. In *Essays on Ideology* (1984), New Left Books/Verso, London.
Angus, I. and Jhally, S. (eds) (1989) *Cultural Politics in Contemporary America*, Routledge, London.
Barrett, M., Corrigan, P., Kuhn, A. and Wolff, J. (eds) (1979) *Ideology and Cultural Production*, Croom Helm, London.
CCCS Women's Studies Group (1978) *Women Take Issue*, Hutchinson, London.
Costello, N., Michie, J. and Milne, S. (1989) *Beyond the Casino Economy*, Verso, London.
Franklin, S., Lury, C. and Stacey, J. (1991) Feminism and cultural studies – pasts, present, futures. *Media, Culture and Society*, Sage, London, Vol. 13, No. 2, April.

Garnham, N. (1979) Contribution to a political economy of mass communication. *Media, Culture and Society*, Academic Press, London; reprinted in Garnham (1990), Vol. 1, No. 2, April.

Garnham, N. (1990) *Capitalism and Communication – Global Culture and the Economics of Information*, Sage, London.

Gilroy, P. (1987) *There Ain't No Black in the Union Jack*, Hutchinson, London.

Golding, P. and Murdock, G.(1979) Ideology and the mass media – the question of determination. In Barrett, M. *et al.*

Grossberg, L. and Hall, S. (1986) On postmodernism and articulation – an interview with Stuart Hall. *Journal of Communication Enquiry*, Iowa Centre for Communication Study, Vol. 10, No. 2, summer.

Hall, S. (1980a) Cultural studies – two paradigms. *Media, Culture and Society*, Vol. 2, No. 2; reprinted in Collins, R. *et al.* (1986).

Hall, S. (1980b) Cultural studies and the centre – some problematics and problems. In Hall, S. *et al.* (1980).

Hall, S. (1980c) The Williams interviews. *Screen Education*, Vol. 34; reprinted in Eagleton, T. (1989).

Hall, S. (1981) Notes on deconstructing 'the popular'. In Samuel, R. (1981).

Hall, S. (1983) The problem of ideology – Marxism without guarantees. In Matthews, B. (ed.) *Marx 100 Years On*, Lawrence & Wishart, London.

Hall, S (1988) *The Hard Road to Renewal*, Verso, London.

Hall, S. and Jacques, M. (eds) (1989) *New Times*, Lawrence & Wishart, London.

Hall, S., Hobson, D., Lowe, A. and Willis, P. (eds) (1980) *Culture, Media, Language*, Hutchinson, London.

Harvey, D. (1989) *The Condition of Postmodernity*, Basil Blackwell, Oxford.

Hirschkop, K. (1989) A complex populism – the political thought of Raymond Williams. *News from Nowhere no. 6, Raymond Williams – Third Generation*, Oxford English Ltd.

Hoggart, R. (1957) *The Uses of Literacy*, Chatto and Windus, London.

Jameson, F. (1991) *Postmodernism or, The Cultural Logic of Late Capitalism*, Verso, London.

Jhally, S. (1989) The political economy of culture. In Angus, I. and Jhally, S.

Johnson, R. (1986) The story so far – and further transformations? In Punter, D. (ed.) *Introduction to Contemporary Cultural Studies*, Longman, London.

Laclau, E. (1977) *Politics and Ideology in Marxist Theory*, New Left Books/Verso, London.

Laclau, E. and Mouffe, C. (1985) *Hegemony and Socialist Strategy*, New Left Books/Verso, London.

MacCabe, C. (ed.) (1986) *High Theory/Low Culture*, Manchester University Press, Manchester.

MacRae, D. (1969) Populism as an ideology. In Ionescu, G. and Gellner, E.

McRobbie, A. (1991) New times in cultural studies. *New Formations*, Routledge, London, Vol. 13, Spring.

Murdock, G. (1989) Cultural studies at the crossroads. *Australian Journal of Communication*, Vol. 16.

O'Shea, A. (1984) Trusting the people – how does Thatcherism work? In *Formations of Nation and People*, Routledge, London.

Rutherford, J. (ed.) (1990) *Identity – Community, Culture, Difference*, Lawrence & Wishart, London.

Sivanandan, A. (1990) All that melts into air is solid – the hokum of new times. In *Race and Class*, Vol. 31, No. 3, Institute of Race Relations, London.

Thompson, E. P. (1963) *The Making of the English Working Class*, Gollancz, London.

Williams, R. (1958) *Culture and Society*, Chatto and Windus, London.

Williams, R. (1961) *The Long Revolution*, Chatto and Windus, London.

Williams, R. (1973) Base and superstructure in Marxist cultural theory. *New Left Review* 82; reprinted in Williams, R. (1980).

Williams, R. (1980) *Problems in Materialism and Culture*, New Left Books/Verso, London.

Williams, R. (1983a) *Keywords*, London: Fontana, London.
Williams, R. (1983b) *Towards 2000*, Chatto and Windus, London.
Williams, R. (1989a) *Resources of Hope*, Verso, London.
Williams, R. (1989b) *The Politics of Modernism*, Verso London.
Williamson, J. (1989) Even new times change. *New Statesman and Society*, 7 July.

Section 8

Feminism

49

Feminist studies of the media

Chris Newbold

The selection of articles presented in this section is designed to illustrate the breadth of approaches to the media available from feminist perspectives. The questions raised by feminist writers relate not only to the key issue of representation, which has always been a central concern of the study of media texts, but also to wider examination of the place of women in the media industries, to women as audiences, and women's ideas and under-standings of their own situation in relationship to the media. Feminist writers in general have all in some way tackled the question of women's relationship to the public and the private domains. By problematizing this, feminism undermines these natural tensions. This section aims to illustrate this core tenet of feminist work as it is applied to the media.

Amongst the articles here represented several sub-questions begin to emerge, not least of which is the argument that there is not simply one feminism or woman's movement, but many. The extract from Press for instance, directs our attention to women and class relations. Other women's movements might be sub-divided by race (see Hooks, 1990), or by the north/south divide (Enloe, 1990). Questions raised by this section might also revolve around women's relationship to technology (see *Media, Culture and Society*, 1992), or to the issue of whether increased numbers of women in the media industries might alter the image presented of women (see UNESCO, 1987).

Feminist studies, more than any other approach discussed in this reader – more so even than that of political economy and cultural hegemony – is rooted in political action and strategies for change, whether challenging sexism in everyday life, the use of sexist language, or levels of representation of women in decision making. Even over the short period represented by the articles in this volume much has changed in terms of gender roles and social justice; feminist writing and scholarship, in the media field and elsewhere, has had much to do with this.

Section 8 is concerned mainly with feminist scholarship and the media, but much of this work draws from across the broad raft of feminist academic and polemic writing. The women's movement itself considers several works of the 1960s to have provided a lead in the development of its cause, and a structure to its thought. Foremost amongst the works that were particularly influential on American and western European women were Betty Friedan's (1963) *The Feminine Mystique* and in the 1970s Germaine Greer's (1971) *The Female Eunuch*, in both of which there is substantial discussion of the media.

A specifically-focused concern with women and the media emerged in the early to mid 1970s, although there are previous works which deal with this theme (see reference to Herzog's 1946 research into women as radio soap opera listeners). A major stimulus to research came in 1979 with the publication of *Mass Media: The Image, Role, and Social Conditions of Women*, from an international survey conducted for UNESCO whose recommendations included the striking conclusion that 'our knowledge about the inter-relationship between women and mass media is far exceeded, both quantitatively and qualitatively, by what remains unexplored' (Ceulemans and Fauconnier, 1979, p. 67). The articles in this section may be seen as a continuing endeavour to redress that balance.

The article by Steeves illustrates how the terrain of feminist studies has burgeoned since the UNESCO report was published. She examines the area by dividing the research into several spheres of interest: liberal feminism, radical feminism, Marxist and socialist feminism. Steeves is able constructively to relate these areas to traditions in media research. Liberal feminism she associates with mainstream American research which looks for piecemeal remedies that do not challenge the fundamental structure of society, whilst radical feminism, which considers that society is constructed as a patriarchy, she associates with the structuralist text-oriented model. The most fruitful of the three approaches is seen to be socialist feminism which she believes offers a broader based intellectual framework with which to operate. Much can be made of the use of typologies such as these, and more recently Van Zoonen (1994) develops a useful discussion on both her own and that of others.

The extract here is concerned with Steeves' analysis of the liberal approach (other paradigms are well represented in this section). This critique of the liberal tradition is of interest in relationship with Sections 1 and 2 in the reader, where the development of the field tends to be viewed from a largely male perspective.

The extract from Brown represents a discussion from the perspective of radical feminism, and focuses on the influence of British cultural studies, and particularly structuralism and post-structuralism. In particular she examines the importance of psychoanalysis as a theoretical and one might say pivotal conceptual leap: foregrounding sexual and gender difference, feminist criticism becomes a central force in media enquiry. Foregrounding the active female audience is also important in Brown's work, where polysemy leaves room for the female viewer to construct meaning from a television text while taking account of its contradictions.

An older tradition of feminist analysis is to be found in the article extract from Tuchman; here women are very much the objects rather than active subjects. In a very real sense, the 'symbolic annihilation' of women involved not so much the portrayal of women as objects, but rather the complete absence of women altogether. Using content analysis and social statistics she established the dominance of male representation on television, comparing it with the role of women, particularly working women, in society. The main thrust of the argument revolves around socialization, Tuchman indicates that through stereotypes and taken-for-granted 'ideal' images, the media fail to provide women with positive role models. The work of Gerbner is used here to particular effect, in that through symbolic representation in the media the female audience sees the kind of positions for women that society seems to approve and value. In the symbolic world, Tuchman concludes, women appear, if they appear at all, situated in the home, divorced from the economic productivity of the labour force (although later arguments in this field turn on the exclusion from economic indicators of the importance of domestic work to the social economy).

Mattelart also addresses the relationship of women, women's work and the culture industries in her discussion of sex role discrimination in capitalism and the 'invisibility of women's work'. In this extract Mattelart takes up the role of the culture industries in integrating women who do household work into everyday life via the genre of women's broadcasts, or daytime programming. This she does by looking at two case studies of such programming in Latin America and Japan; in particular she is interested in the relative influence of fictional and informational material available to women. Mattelart recognizes that a thorough examination of the relative impact of these media would require extensive audience research within the areas of sociology, anthropology, psychoanalysis and semiotics. Andrea Press takes up this challenge in her work to connect cultural studies to empirical communication studies. The focus of her work is on how women respond to and whether they resist the patriarchal elements of mass culture. She considers how they do this according to a hegemonic process based on class, and class definitions of realism, she also indicates that television content itself upholds an 'hegemony of middle class realism' for working class women. Press is emphasizing that what is important is not simply the reading of gendered television, but the class context in which such readings take place.

Of the many critical turns in, and expansions of, feminist research into the media, this emphasis on ethnography and women's own decoding of media products has proved to be one of the most fruitful. Following the debates on representation, and considerations of the gendered content of the consciousness industries, the work of Brown, Press, and Ang (1985, Section 10) represented in this reader, illustrates how the emphasis on the 'reading' of popular texts has attempted to empower women as viewers to 'resist' or gain 'pleasure' from their experience of the media.

This notion of pleasure and the 'female gaze' has emerged out of the enquiries and the questions raised about the female spectator. In particular the essays contained in Gamman and Marshment's (1988) *The Female Gaze* take to task the psychoanalytic approach to moving image content that sees the woman as object of the male gaze, a process which serves to replicate domination and power relations in society. The work of Mulvey (1975) in particular here has come under criticism, in that she sees visual pleasure as structured by patriarchal order, thus placing women outside popular culture. The female gaze draws on the polysemic attributes of texts and according to its proponents permits alternatives in the dominant discourse.

These issues are taken up in the final extract by Kuhn who seeks not only to examine the mode of address but also the structure of dominant cinema. This she does by examining the institutional framework of dominant cinema, considering the possibilities of feminist film, although admittedly at the fringes of the industry. The second prong of this examination is the 'classic realist text' which dominates film production and practice. In looking at the film *Mildred Pierce* she illustrates her argument that women in film narratives are no longer seen in relation to 'real life', but become 'a structure governing the organization of story and plot'. This according to Kuhn is a reflection of the position of women in society and the industry, as texts do not operate independently of the social structure in which they are constructed and received.

As this section has illustrated, feminist studies are perhaps one of the most dynamic and diverse areas of research in media and mass communications at present, drawing as they do on many areas and traditions of scholarship, and infused as they are with a radical purpose of great ambition. No less significant is the influence of feminist thought on analysis of gender and studies of masculinity.

References and further reading

Ceulemans, M. and Fauconnier, G. (1979) *Mass Media: The Image, Role, and Social Conditions of Women*, UNESCO.

Creedon, P. (ed.) (1989) *Women in Mass Communication*, Sage.

Dines, G. and Humez, J. M. (1995) *Gender, Race and Class in Media: A Text Reader*, Sage.

Enloe, C. (1990) *Bananas, Beaches, Bases*, University of California Press.

Franklin, S., Lury, C. and Stacey, J. (1991) Feminism and cultural studies, pasts, presents, futures. *Media, Culture and Society*, Vol. 13, No. 2, April.

Friedan, B. (1963) *The Feminine Mystique*, Penguin Books.

Gamman, L. and Marshment, M. (1988) *The Female Game: Women as Viewers of Popular Culture*, The Women's Press.

Greer, G. (1971) *The Female Eunuch*, Paladin.

Hooks, B. (1990) *Yearning: Race, Gender and Cultural Politics*, South End Press, Boston.

Jansen, S. C. (1989) Gender and the information society: a socially structured silence. *Journal of Communication*, Vol. 39, No. 3.

Media, Culture and Society (1992) *Gender and Technology, Media, Culture and Society*, Vol. 14, No. 1, January.

Mulvey, L. (1975) Visual pleasures and narrative cinema. *Screen*, Vol. 6, No. 3, Autumn,

Pribram E. D. (ed.) (1988) *Female Spectators: Looking at Film and Television*, Verso.

UNESCO (1987) *Women and Media Decision-making: the Invisible Barriers*, UNESCO, Paris.

Van Zoonen, L. (1994) *Feminist Media Studies*, Sage.

50

Feminist theories and media studies

H. Leslie Steeves

From Eason, D. L. and Davis, D. K. (eds) (1987) *Critical Studies in Mass Communication*, Vol. 4, No. 2, Speech Communication Association, Annadale VA, pp. 100–6.

Liberal feminism

Liberal feminism has had the most influence on feminism in America (e.g. Elshtain, 1981; Jaggar, 1983). Jaggar (1983) describes liberal feminism as an application of the principles of liberal political philosophy (as expounded by Locke, Kant, Mill, Rawls, and others) to political and economic inequities experienced by women. She links the 300-year history of liberal philosophy with the history of capitalism and capitalist demands for the protection of individual autonomy and equality of opportunity.

Liberal theory assumes that rational mental development is the highest human ideal and that the state should act to assure equal opportunities for all in pursuing this goal and associated ones. Most liberal feminists therefore focus their efforts on creating and changing laws to promote women's opportunities for intellectual growth and professional success. Early liberals worked for women's suffrage and property ownership. Contemporary liberals fight for issues such as equal pay and employment.

Liberal feminism does not address the psychological origins of gender differences. Many liberal feminists believe the inequity is simply a matter of irrational prejudice that can be solved through rational argument. Many others, however, borrow ideas from socialization theory and research. Social psychologists identify childhood cognitive factors and role training as the sources of gendered behaviour. Cognitive theorists, such as Kohlberg (1966) assume that once children realize their own genders are constant, they maintain cognitive consistency by imitating behaviour of those of the same sex. In contrast, social learning theorists (Bandura, 1977; Mischel, 1966, 1970) emphasize the importance of rewards and reinforcements in children's modelling behaviour. They agree that sex-role learning does occur through the modelling of behaviour but claim it is motivated by complex cognitive processes that can be explained best by the child's reinforcement history. Both perspectives stress the importance of modelling and reinforcement (by parents, teachers, media, etc.) in the acquisition of sex-role behaviours but via somewhat different cognitive processes. Liberal feminists influenced by these perspectives maintain that rational argument and legal struggle are effective in both increasing opportunities for women and in providing role models for adult women and for girls.

Liberal feminists' belief that equal opportunity is possible within existing capitalist socio-economic systems leads to an acceptance of traditional social science research methods that treat every unit studied (subject, household, etc.) as though it were equal. Unlike radical feminists, who argue that these methods are male biased, liberals maintain that they have not yet been utilized effectively to further feminist goals (Jayaratne, 1983).

In the United States, liberal feminist approaches are common in literary and speech, as well as in media, studies. Liberal feminist scholarship, however, has developed differently in each discipline. In literary studies, liberal scholarship consists primarily of qualitative content analyses. In liberal feminist speech and media studies, scholarship consists primarily of quantitative content analyses. Famous female journalists, media processors, and media effects also are studied. Many recent liberal feminist media studies have aimed overtly to test a communication theory. This focus on communication theory may account partially for American media scholars' slower progress (compared to literary scholars) in incorporating more complex feminist theories into their work.[1]

Content analysis

In literary studies, liberal feminist assumptions are primarily manifest, though unexplicated, in the so-called 'images of women' studies, an early form of feminist criticism. According to Ruthven (1984, p. 70), images of women studies were emphasized '. . . partly because academic feminism was conceived of initially as some sort of sociology in which literary texts could be used as evidence and picked over to see what kind of role models for women they supplied'. Both Ruthven (1984) and Eagleton (1986) cite Register's liberal argument (1975) that literary works should provide role models for women that are consistent with the women's movement and that feminist criticism should evaluate texts on this basis. Eagleton (p. 2) notes that this emphasis was not challenged by important texts of the 1960s and 1970s (e.g. Ellmann, 1968; Moers, 1976; Showalter, 1977; Spacks, 1975), which focused on the works of 'white, middle-class, heterosexual (or presented as heterosexual) women, living in England and America during the nineteenth and twentieth centuries'. The 1960s and 1970s stimulated many studies, and courses, on topics related to sex-role representations in literature, including studies of contemporary novels focusing on individual women's successful liberation, such as Marilyn French's *The Women's Room* (1977). These qualitative analyses, however, have been criticized for repeating the same observations and for failing to consider factors other than gender (Newton, 1981; Robinson, 1978). Separatist, semiotic, and Marxist-influenced analyses of women's writing have become more predominant than image studies in recent years.

In media studies, content analyses of the presence or absence, stereotyping, and devaluation of women are abundant in American journals. Butler and Paisley (1980), Tuchman and her colleagues (1978), and Courtney and Whipple (1980) provide examples.[2] While these studies suffer from an underdeveloped theoretical framework, they clearly stress the liberal ideal of increasing women's public visibility and criticize traditional stereotypes. They do not elaborate theoretically on what is meant by a stereotype but simply classify character traits that are assumed to reinforce over-generalizations in the minds of individual audience members.[3] For example, Lichter, Lichter, and Rothman (1986) analyse the themes and characters on prime time network television over 31 seasons, from 1955 through 1986. They find (p. 17) that, in general:

> Female characters are less in evidence than males and, in many ways, are portrayed as the weaker sex. They are less likely to be mature adults, are less well educated, and hold lower status jobs. Their activities tend to represent the private realm of home, personal relations, and sexuality, while men represent the public realm of work, social relations, and sexuality.

Their analysis over time indicates little numerical change in these portrayals. They do, however, note a number of 'progressive flourishes' in the past 10 years. Most significantly, they count 54 instances where themes explicitly addressed women's rights, and in all such instances since 1965, the episode upheld sexual equality. They applaud such episodes and present two examples, both clearly indicative of their liberal understanding of feminism. These are an *Eight is Enough* episode where the male family members attempt, but fail, to exclude the females from a camping trip, and a *Maude* episode where Maude directs a bicentennial celebration and has to fight for the theme of famous women in history. They conclude (p. 19) that, 'What television says about women in general is often quite different from what it shows about particular women'. As will become clear later, this televised treatment is a blatant metaphor for women's situation under capitalism, where the conditions for women in general are often quite different than for particular categories of women.

A particularly striking example of a liberal feminist approach to content analysis is Suzanne Pingree and her colleagues' creation of a multi-level 'consciousness scale' (1976), which Smith (1982) praises for allowing the researcher to move beyond simple nominal classifications. The scale examines five hierarchical levels for the portrayal of women. These levels, from lowest to highest, suggest: (1) a two-dimensional mindless decoration; (2) 'in her place' in a traditional female role; (3) 'in two places', both traditional and non-traditional with a clear priority given to the former; (4) equal to a man in a non-traditional setting; and (5) as an individual outside stereotypes. Although Pingree *et al.* do not make their liberal perspective explicit, it is evident in their hierarchy.

Most American content analyses based implicitly on liberal feminism do not specify the mass communication theory that grounds the research. Many, however, work on agenda setting or cultivation effects. Agenda setting research assumes that media can set the agenda for issue salience (McCombs and Shaw, 1972; McLeod, Becker, and Byrnes, 1974). Feminist examples are Epstein's edited series of reports and essays on relationships between the marginality of women's issues in news and the agenda setting function of the press (1978) and Lazier-Smith's study of the coverage of the 19th Amendment and the proposed Equal Rights Amendment (1984).

The notion of cultivation is similar to agenda setting except that audience perceptions of social reality, as opposed to perceptions of news issue salience, are assumed to be altered by media emphases (Gerbner and Gross, 1976; Gerbner, Gross, Morgan, and Signorielli, 1980). Many content analyses of soap operas appear to assume cultivation effects. For example, Fine (1981) compares soap opera portrayals to what is known about the real world. She reports that conversations between females on soap operas are defined almost always by personal issues while conversations between males are defined professionally. The most intimate conversations are between males and females. This research exposes a negative liberal stereotype of a home-bound, romantically oriented woman, a stereotype contradicted by employment statistics and one that, the researchers assume, contributes to misleading audience perceptions.[4]

[. . .]

Effects studies

Comparatively little research from a liberal perspective has examined effects of media imagery on audiences. Most of the existing studies have sought consequences from an agenda setting, cultivation, or uses and gratifications perspective. In addition, some studies utilize socialization theory and research. Although a feminist perspective, liberal or otherwise, is not readily apparent in this research, the measures used and the assumptions made often indicate considerable consistency with liberal feminism.

Agenda setting, cultivation, and uses and gratifications. Agenda setting research has failed to compare the relationship between space or time devoted to women's issues in the media and their actual salience for audience members (Tuchman, 1978, p. 5). Some research from a cultivation perspective, however, has compared media content to audience perceptions of social reality. For example, Gross and Jeffries-Fox (1978) report that heavy television viewing correlates with lowered educational aspirations and sexist attitudes in children. Their attitude measures indicate the liberal feminist assumption that decreased sexism entails increased perceptions of women as professionally ambitious and successful. In another cultivation study, Buerkel-Rothfuss with Mayes (1981) find that exposure to soap operas correlates with the belief by viewers that men and women have affairs, get divorced, have illegitimate children, and undergo serious operations and that women are housewives, have abortions, and do no work at all. While the authors do not discuss the consequences of these distorted perceptions, except as support for the cultivation effect, the findings appear (as in Fine's 1981 study) to show a negative stereotyped perception of women from a liberal feminist perspective. Cantor and Pingree (1983, p. 145) suggest that studies of soap operas should address explicitly how soap operas affect feminist consciousness. Based on the possibility of cultivation (and socialization) effects, they further suggest that soap opera producers could make a greater effort to deal with feminist issues such as the Equal Rights Amendment and present a less conservative view of sex roles.

Other than these agenda setting and cultivation studies, little American research has examined media use by adult women. I have been able to locate only one study on the effects of feminist attitudes on media use. Lull, Mulac, and Rosen (1983) found that both men and women who held liberal feminist attitudes spent less time with television than did non-feminists and preferred alternative types of television and radio programmes consistent with their feminism. These findings are consistent with the study Andreasen and I conducted (1983) on employed women's magazine use. We found that assertive women (i.e. those who had taken action to change a discriminatory job situation) read less traditional magazines than did unassertive women.

A few additional studies on women's use of media have utilized a uses and gratifications perspective, which assumes that individuals consciously seek certain gratifications from mass media (Blumler and Katz, 1974). These studies seldom specify a feminist perspective but appear most consistent with liberal feminism in assuming that individuals may deliberately turn to the media for particular gratifications. Almost all of these studies on women have addressed soap opera viewing and listening (e.g. Compesi, 1980; Herzog, 1944; Miyazaki, 1981). In fact, perhaps the first uses and gratifications study of any type was on housewives' uses of radio soap opera (Herzog, 1944).

Allen (1985) and Cantor and Pingree (1983) provide reviews of the literature on soap operas, including uses and gratifications studies. Numerous uses and gratifications citations also are included in several studies in the Summer 1985 issue of the *Journal of Broadcasting and Electronic Media*. Cantor and Pingree's summary (1983) provides evidence that women use soap operas for emotional release via identification with other people's problems, escape into better or easier ways of life, companionship and relief from loneliness, practical information for everyday problems, and enjoyment and relaxation. Several studies reported additional analyses of the types of people that seek particular types of gratifications. In addition, recent uses and gratifications research has indicated that viewing motivations can be divided into two major types: ritualistic uses that reflect habitual and diversionary behaviour and instrumental uses that reflect more goal-directed behaviour (e.g. Rubin, 1985). Carveth and Alexander (1985) link cultivation theory with uses and gratifications in soap opera viewing, reporting that the cultivation effect is stronger among ritualistic than instrumental viewers.

Socialization studies. Most feminist studies utilizing socialization theory have examined media effects on children, and most of these have focused on television.[5] Researchers generally test whether children's exposure is related to their perceptions of stereotypic gendered behaviour (e.g. Atkin and Miller, 1975; Beuf, 1974; Freuh and McGhee, 1975; Miller and Reeves, 1976; Pingree, 1978), whether exposure, particularly to characters of the same gender, is related to actual stereotypic or non-traditional behaviour (e.g. Fischer and Torney, 1976; McArthur and Eisen, 1976), and whether children prefer to attend to media characters of their own gender (e.g. Sprafkin and Liebert, 1978). These studies show that positive relationships exist between exposure to sex-stereotyped media content and stereotypic perceptions, attitudes, and behaviours, and some studies imply media can be used to teach children non-sexist attitudes and behaviours (e.g. McArthur and Lisen, 1976; Pingree, 1978; Williams, LaRose, and Frost, 1981). In most cases, however, relationships are not strong and become weaker when variables such as IQ, age, and sex are controlled (Butler and Paisley, 1980). For example, Pingree (1978) found that third graders of both sexes and eighth grade girls who saw commercials with women in non-traditional roles were less likely to give sexist responses to attitudinal items than children who saw stereotyped commercials. The treatment, however, had no effect on eighth grade boys. In addition, Pingree and Hawkins (1980, pp. 295–8) note interesting peculiarities in some results. For example, Atkin and Miller (1975) found that children who saw a commercial with a female judge thought women could become professionals; commercials with female computer programmers and television technicians, however, failed to produce similar results. A study by Drabman, Hammer, and Jarvie (1976) showed that research can be confounded by most children's already well-formed stereotypes. Children were shown videotaped visits to Dr Mary and Nurse David and then asked simply to recall the names of the doctor and nurse. Only a tiny fraction of first and third graders gave a woman's name for the doctor and a man's name for the nurse. These types of weaknesses also are highlighted in Durkin's study of children's (aged 4 to 9) interpretations of highly stereotyped television excerpts (1984). Interviews with the children indicated that even at a very early age they bring considerable knowledge of gendered behaviour to the viewing situation and use this knowledge to interpret and embellish what they see.

Such results indicate that liberal feminist and socialization theory alone cannot account for gendered behaviour and the ideology of women's secondary status in society. In fact, these perspectives do little more than note its occurrence. There has been an increasing tendency in feminist media scholarship, as well as in literary and film studies, to explore areas of theory that include factors on broader social levels, that is, beyond the level of the individual and his or her immediate relationships.

Notes

1. Tuchman (1979, p. 528) similarly suggests that mainstream feminist media research 'has been crippled by dependence upon the academic study of mass communication'. Of course, another obvious consideration is that women's participation in mass communication study only has increased significantly within the past decade or so. In contrast, women have a long and significant history of participation in literary production and criticism.
2. Selected examples of content analyses in the mass communication literature that implicitly reflect liberal feminist assumptions include studies of *television advertising* by Courtney and Whipple (1974), Dominick and Rauch (1972), Maracek and his colleagues (1978), O'Donnell and O'Donnell (1978), and Thoveron (1986); studies of *television programming* by Fine (1981), Lichter, Lichter, and Rothman (1986), McNeil (1975), Segger, Hafen, and Hannonen-Gladden (1981), Tedesco (1974), Thoveron (1986), and Turow (1974); studies of *magazine advertisements* by Courtney and Lockeretz (1971), Pingree and her colleagues (1976), Sexton and Haberman (1974), and Wagner and Banos (1973); studies of *magazine stories* by Loughlin (1983), and Newkirk (1977); and studies of the *newspaper* (advertisements, photos, cartoons, or stories) by Blackwood (1983), Miller (1975, 1976), Guenin (1975), Potter (1985), and Streicher (1974). See also Butler and Paisley (1980), Courtney and Whipple (1980), and Tuchman *et al.* (1978) for numerous additional examples. In speech studies, there has been much quantitative research demonstrating men's

greater visibility and superiority in language content and use. See Thorne *et al.* (1983) for examples.
3. See Perkins (1979) and Seiter (1986) for further discussion on the concept of stereotype. Perkins suggests ways stereotypes function to legitimize and sustain various ideologies of oppression. Seiter points out that social psychologists have generally defined stereotypes cognitively, and that the methods such a definition promotes mask economic, historical, and political questions.
4. See Cassata and Skill (1983) for several examples of soap opera content analyses that assume cultivation effects. See also Allen (1985) for an excellent review and critique of empiricist content analyses of soap operas.
5. Some content analyses utilize social learning and cognitive developmental theorists in research rationales and discussions. Examples are Busby (1974), Franzwa (1974), Smith and Matre (1975), and Weitzman, Eifler, Hokada, and Ross (1972). For a full discussion and review of research on sex-role stereotyping with regard to children and television in both content analyses and effects studies, see Williams, LaRose, and Frost (1981). In addition to socialization studies involving children, some experimental research from a social psychological perspective has examined effects of pornography on male perceptions of, and aggression against, women. See Malamuth and Donnerstein (1984) for a review of the literature.

References

Allen, R. C. (1985) *Speaking of Soap Operas*, University of North Carolina Press, Chapel Hill.

Andreasen, M. and Steeves, H. L. (1983) Employed women's assertiveness and openness as shown in magazine use. *Journalism Quarterly*, Vol. 60, pp. 449–57.

Atkin, C. and Miller, M. M. (1975, April) The effects of TV advertising on children: Experimental evidence. Paper presented to the *Annual Convention of the International Communication Association*, Chicago.

Badura, A. (1977) *Social Learning Theory*, Prentice-Hall, Englewood Cliffs, NJ.

Beuf, A. (1974) Doctor lawyer, household drudge. *Journal of Communication*, Vol. 24, No. 2, pp. 142–45.

Blumler, J. and Katz, E. (eds) (1974) *The Uses of Mass Communications*, Sage, Beverly Hills.

Buerkel-Rothfuss, N. L., with Mayes, S. (1981). Soap opera viewing: The cultivation effect. *Journal of Communication*, Vol. 31, No. 3, pp. 108–15.

Butler, M. and Paisley, W. (1980) *Women and the Mass Media*, Human Sciences Press, New York.

Cantor, M. and Pingree, S. (1983) *The Soap Opera*, Sage, Beverly Hills.

Carveth, R. and Alexander, A. (1985) Soap opera viewing motivations and the cultivation process. *Journal of Broadcasting & Electronic Media*, Vol. 29, No. 3, pp. 259–73.

Compesi, R. (1980) Gratification of daytime TV serial viewers. *Journalism Quarterly*, Vol. 57, pp. 155–8.

Courtney, A. and Whipple, T. (1980) *Sex Stereotyping in Advertising: An Annotated Bibliography*, Marketing Science, Cambridge, MA.

Drabman, R., Hammer, D. and Jarvie, G. (1976) Children's perceptions of media – portrayed sex roles across ages. University of Mississippi Medical Center, Department of Psychiatry and Human Behavior, Jackson.

Durkin, K. (1984) Children's accounts of sex-role stereotypes in television. *Communication research*, Vol. 11, No. 3, pp. 341–62.

Eagleton, M. (ed.) (1986) *Feminist Literary Theory: A Reader*, Basil Blackwell, New York.

Ellmann, M. (1968) *Thinking About Women*, Harcourt, Brace, & World, New York.

Elshtain, J. B. (1981) *Public Man, Private Woman: Women in Social and Political Thought*, Princeton University Press, Princeton, NJ.

Epstein, L. K. (ed.) (1978) *Women and the News*, Hastings, New York.

Fine, M. G. (1981) Soap opera conversations: the talk that binds. *Journal of Communication*, Vol. 31, No. 3, pp. 91–107.

Fischer, P. and Torney, J. (1976) Influence of children's stories on dependency: a sextyped behavior. *Developmental Psychology*, Vol. 12, pp. 489–90.

French, M. (1977) *The Women's Room*, Summit Books, New York.

Freuh, T. and McGhee, P. (1975) Traditional sex-role development and amount of time spent watching television. *Development Psychology*, Vol. 11, pp. 109.

Gerbner, G. and Gross, L. (1976) The scary world of TV. *Psychology Today*, Vol. 9, pp. 41–5.

Gerbner, G., Gross, L., Morgan, M. and Signorielli, N. (1980) The 'mainstreaming' of America: Violence profile No. 11. *Journal of Communication*, Vol. 30, No. 3, pp. 19–29.

Gross, L. and Jeffries-Fox, S. (1978) What do you want to be when you grow up, little girl? In Tuchman, G., Daniels, A. K. and Benét, J. (eds) *Heart and Home: Images of Women in the Mass Media*, Oxford University Press, New York, pp. 240–65.

Herzog, H. (1944) What do we really know about daytime serial listeners? In Lazarsfeld, P. F. and Stanton, F. (eds) *Radio Research, 1942–1943*, Duell, Sloan & Pearce, New York, pp. 3–33.

Jaggar, A. M. (1983) *Feminist Politics and Human Nature*, The Harvester Press, Sussex.

Jayaratne, T. E. (1983) The value of quantitative methodology for feminist research. In Bowles, G. and Klein, R. D. (eds) *Theories of Women's Studies*, Routledge & Kegan Paul, London, pp. 140–61.

Kohlberg, L. (1966). A cognitive developmental analysis of sex-role concepts and attitudes. In Maccoby, E. (ed.) *The Development of Sex Differences*, Stanford University Press, Stanford, CA, pp. 821–83.

Laxier-Smith, L. (1984, August) Coverage or cover-up: A comparison of newspaper coverage of the 19th Amendment and the Equal Rights Amendment. Paper presented to the *Annual Convention of the Association for Education in Journalism and Mass Communication*, Gainesville, FL.

Lichter, R. S., Lichter, L. S. and Rotheman, S. (1986). From Lucy to Lacey: TV's dream girls. *Public Opinion*, Vol. 9, No. 3, pp. 16–19.

Lull, J., Mulac, A. and Rosen, S. L. (1983) Feminism as a predictor of mass media use. *Sex Roles*, Vol. 9, No. 2, pp. 165–77.

McArthur, L. and Eisen, S. (1976) Achievements of male and female storybook characters as determinants of achievement behavior by boys and girls. *Journal of Personality and Social Psychology*, Vol. 33, pp. 467–73.

McCombs, M. E. and Shaw, D. L. (1972) The agenda-setting function of the media. *Public Opinion Quarterly*, Vol. 36, pp. 176–87.

McLeod, J. M., Becker, L. B. and Byrnes, J. E. (1974). Another look at the agenda-setting function of the press. *Communication Research*, Vol. 1, No. 2, pp. 131–65.

Miller, M. and Reeves, D. B. (1976) Children's occupational sex-role stereotypes: the linkage between television content and perception. *Journal of Broadcasting*, Vol. 20, pp. 35–50.

Mischel, W. (1966) A social-learning view of sex differences in behavior. In Maccoby, E. (ed.) *The Development of Sex Differences*, pp. 56–81. Stanford University Press, Stanford, CA.

Mischel, W. (1970) Sex typing and socialization. In Mussen, P. (ed.) *Carmichael's Manual of Child Psychology*, 3rd edn, John Wiley, New York, pp. 3–72.

Miyazaki, T. (1981) Housewives and daytime serials in Japan: a uses and gratifications perspective. *Communications Research*, Vol. 8, No. 3, pp. 323–41.

Moers, E. (1976) *Literary Women: The Great Writers*, Doubleday, Garden City, NY.

Newton, J. (1981) *Women, Power, and Subversion: Social Strategies in British Fiction,* 1778–1860. University of Georgia Press, Athens, GA.

Pingree, S. (1978) The effects of non-sexist television commercials and perceptions of reality on children's attitudes about women. *Psychology of Women Quarterly,* Vol. 2, pp. 262–277.

Pingree, S. and Hawkins, R. (1980) Children and media. In Butler, M. and Paisley, W. (eds) *Women and the Mass Media, Human Sciences Press,* New York, pp. 279–99.

Pingree, S., Hawkins, R., Butler, M. and Paisley, W. (1976) A scale for sexism. *Journal of Communication,* Vol. 26, Vol. 4, pp. 193–200.

Register, C. (1975) American feminist literary criticism: a bibliographical introduction. In Donovan, J. (ed.) *Feminist Literary Criticism,* University of Kentucky Press, Lexington, pp. 1–28.

Robinson, L. (1978) *Sex, Class, and Culture,* Indiana University Press, Bloomington.

Rubin, A. (1985) Uses of daytime television soap operas by college students. *Journal of Broadcasting & Electronic Media,* Vol. 29, No. 3, pp. 241–258.

Ruthven, K. K. (1984) *Feminist Literary Studies: An Introduction,* Cambridge University Press, Cambridge, MA.

Showalter, E. (1977) *A Literature of Their Own: British Women Novelists from Brontë to Lessing,* Princeton University Press, Princeton, NJ.

Smith, M. Yodelis (1982) Research retrospective: feminism and the media. *Communication Research,* Vol. 9, No. 1, pp. 145–60.

Spacks, P. M. (1975) *The Female Imagination,* Alfred A. Knopf, New York.

Sprafkin, J. and Liebert, R. M. (1978) Sex-typing and children's preferences. In Tuchman, G., Daniels, A. K. and Benét, J. (eds) *Hearth and Home: Images of Women in the Mass Media,* Oxford University Press, New York, pp. 228–39.

Tuchman, G. (1978). The symbolic annihilation of women by the mass media. In Tuchman, G., Daniels, A. K. and Benét, J. (eds). (1978). *Hearth & Home: Images of Women in the Mass Media,* Oxford University Press, New York, pp. 3-38.

Tuchman, G., Daniels, A. K., and Benét, J. (eds) (1978) *Hearth & Home: Images of Women in the Mass Media,* Oxford University Press, New York.

Williams, F., LaRose, R. and Frost, F. (1981) *Children, Television, and Sex-role Stereotyping,* Praeger, New York.

51

Feminist cultural television criticism – culture, theory and practice

Mary Ellen Brown

From Brown, M. E. (ed.) (1990) *Television and Women's Culture: The Politics of the Popular*, Sage, London, pp. 11–17.

The evolution of the feminist television criticism was encouraged by the women's movement in general and mediated by several strands of critical thought. Primary in its evolution are two ideas, one is the use of theory and the other is the close, fresh and specific examination of television programmes and audiences.

The theory, which can be loosely labelled post-structuralist, makes clear but limited use of structuralist thinking while recognizing its social construction. The works of Sigmund Freud, Jacques Lacan, and Claude Lévi-Strauss apply here. In discerning what meaning is and how meaning is made, the theories of Ferdinand de Saussure, Umberto Eco, and Roland Barthes provide the semiotic underpinnings. Its Marxist social and philosophical position evolves out of the work of Louis Althusser in France, Raymond Williams and Stuart Hall in England and Antonio Gramsci in Italy. Feminist theoretical underpinnings are harder to pinpoint.

The French feminist thinkers, Hélène Cixous, Julia Kristeva, Catherine Clément, Luce Irigaray, Michèle Montrelay and Monique Wittig, mostly gathered around the publishing house *des femmes*, are an influence because the French feminists have been willing to conceptualize a level of writing, *écriture féminine*, which speaks directly and uniquely to women. The British feminist film theorists, centred around *Screen* and *Screen Education*, the journals which brought to English-speaking cultures the French Marxist political film critique of *Cahiers du Cinéma*, began the serious feminist critique of Hollywood cinema – critics and theorists like Claire Johnston, Laura Mulvey, Annette Kuhn and Pam Cook. This critique, psychoanalytic in bent, is carried on in America by the *Camera Obscura* collective. The feminist psychoanalytic film critique remains a major, if not the major, strand of film theory in the United States. Theorists like Kaja Silverman and Teresa de Lauretis have attempted to combine psychoanalysis and semiotics in recent works. It is, however, to the women in the British culturalist critique of popular culture that the criticism presented here is most indebted.

Feminist culturalist television criticism

In this section I shall attempt to delineate how the streams of theoretical and critical work which I have mentioned have come together to form what

I am calling feminist culturalist television criticism. A similar and often overlapping theoretical approach has been called resistance theory.

Resistance theory comprises a body of work which addresses the issue of how ordinary people and subcultural groups can resist hegemonic, or dominant pressures, and consequently obtain pleasure from what the political, social and/or cultural system offers, despite that system's contradictory position in their lives. Recently, studies of audiences' conversations about television have been labelled 'reading reception theory' or 'reception and response criticism'. Reception and response criticism uses a combination of interviews, participant observation and conversation analyses to determine how audiences respond to various textual practices on television.

While the British cultural studies movement redefined working class culture, feminist writers/ethnographers working at the Birmingham Centre for Contemporary and Cultural Studies (CCCS) stood their ground for an investigation as well as a redefinition of the invisible 'other' in working-class culture – its girls and women. Out of their collective work evolved publications such as *Women Take Issue* and the work of authors like Charlotte Brunsdon, Marion Jordan, Dorothy Hobson, Christine Ceraghty and Angela McRobbie.[1] These authors re-examined our common sense assumptions about media using both ethnographic methodology and theoretical perspectives which assume that audiences have a great deal of control over their reading practices.

Concurrent with these events, some American feminists had begun to use content analysis to describe women's presence on television. The first assumption behind content analysis is that broadcast television has a moral obligation to serve (and therefore to represent) all of a country's citizens. The political argument here assumes that equality can, as a practical matter, be achieved within patriarchal capitalism. The major problem with such an approach is that content analysis is only descriptive and fails to critique the discursive construction of women within representational systems like television. A second assumption behind content analysis is psycho-logical/ideological; and has to do with modelling behaviour. The notion is that people's perceptions of themselves hinge on seeing other people, like themselves, acting out particular roles. Content analysis takes for granted that women's 'real lives' are a given unproblematic and naturalized concept – an idea that most feminist culturalists would question.

While early feminist television studies in the United States centred on content analysis and film criticism centred on psychoanalysis, feminist literary and art criticism concentrated on restructuring the canon of the great writers and artists. This restructuring involved the re-writing of art and literary history to include the women, and the re-evaluating of what is classified as 'great art' or 'great literature'. Patchwork quilts and diaries, for example, have had their status elevated in the process. Attention has also been paid to the role of institutions like the gallery system and the academic system, as well as to the social context in which girls and women are culturally subordinated, to show how the meaning of the term 'high art' has been constructed to exclude women's work.

The British cultural studies movement, on the other hand, has seen it as essential to accept a redefined meaning of the term 'culture' as all that we do, say and believe, that is the practice of everyday living – a definition which has virtually eliminated the high/low distinction in terms of the analysis of cultural practices and artefacts. Cultural studies, of which feminist culturalist television criticism is a part, replace aesthetic criteria based on a notion of culture as the 'best' that has been thought and created in the world as defined by T. S. Eliot and Matthew Arnold, for instance. Instead, cultural studies offer an analysis of how ideology is produced and functions within television products and practices and how audiences use and interact with television in their lives. It involves textual, contextual, theoretical and anthropological analysis. Its aim is understanding and empowerment.

[. . .]

Like ideology itself, the grass-roots women's movement eluded the simple classifications that capitalist and patriarchal press analysis was prone to make. Thus the expression 'the personal is political', which has several levels of meaning, in this case functioned to identify an ideological stance which bound women together in positions for which current social myths about women had no set position, i.e. loyalty to other women could replace jealousy over men or aggressiveness in women could exist alongside tenderness. These women developed the idea of a woman's culture based on theory and practice which cut across existing constructions of the feminine. A major concern within the academic, critical and research aspects of the women's movement has to do with a preference for theory rather than for practice since practice is considered the essence of a political movement. I would argue that the development of theory is a type of practice and that in feminist television criticism one can apply feminist theories to the process of deconstructing ideology, an aspect of the 1970s women's movement that has been essential to its politics since the beginning.

Feminist practice and television criticism

What then are the terms of feminist practice within current television criticism? Since language is the medium in which feminist television criticism operates, the evolution and meanings of the terms 'female' and 'male', their various derivatives and the ways in which they are used, are of primary importance. The terms 'feminine' and 'masculine' are used to define social constructions of woman and man as opposed to biological, essential, and/or natural, inherited properties of men and women. This is not to ignore completely biological differences between women and men, but to see the influence of biological differences and indeed sexuality itself, as constructed over time through discourse. Discourse is here used in the Foucauldian sense, as a network of possible ways of speaking or being spoken, being, belonging, empowering, and consequently socially and physically enforcing normalcy. In other words, the ways that people can live, their social practices, are 'constructed' by the way these practices can be spoken about or conceptualized in language.

Another way of looking at language in this context is semiotically, as a system of codes and signs, non-linguistic as well as linguistic, which construct meaning. A sign is anything that stands for something else. Signs also acquire meaning from the things that they fail to stand for, that is the other possible meanings available to us the audience (or subject), and from their position in social myths that we already understand. Television's languages and texts are seen as polysemic sites for potential ideological meaning generation. Television texts are not, however, isolated in their generation of meanings. They gain meaning by interacting with other media and cultural forms and, in addition, audiences composed of differing social and cultural groups can use television texts for their own purposes and in different ways from each other.

As feminist practice, these approaches – the re-evaluation of language, discourse and signifiers and the consideration of audiences not as masses but as unique, shifting, and respected groups – coincide with other similar feminist notions which relate to research practices.

The first of these is that past histories and research approaches have been constructed according to ideological, social, and political needs based on power relationships. Thus, research methodologies are structured by the power relationships of the people who construct them. Feminist researchers, theorists and critics favour research methods which empower the subjects, which are often non-quantitative and which avoid hierarchies.

Secondly, the idea of looking at audiences as unique and specific allows for the fact that women and men and sub-groups of both may see things differently because of their position in society. They may construct meanings in terms of class, gender, race or any number of variables, and texts may be constructed to these positions. Such research also tries to place the researcher *with* the audiences, not above and/or apart from them. Like consciousness-raising, it respects each person's personal experience while recognizing her or his construction ideologically in society and language.

The audience/spectator and feminist criticism

It is clear then that the conceptualization of 'the audience' is crucial to our reading of televisual texts. The pivotal feminist inquiry into the nature of the audience or spectator in film criticism is Laura Mulvey's 'Visual pleasure and narrative cinema'.[2] Her article argues that the spectator, controlled by the economy of the gaze and involved with the psychoanalytical concepts of voyeurism, scopophillia and fetishism, is constructed as masculine. This conceptualization presents a problem for feminist critics as long as the text is considered to have the power to construct its reader as masculine. Mulvey's insights into the construction of certain narrative forms, with their cause and effect relationships and ultimate resolution as masculine, generated an interest in looking at the form of a work as possibly gender-related and thus shaped, at least in part, by its intended audience.

Once film criticism had begun to use psychoanalysis as a theoretical tool, the idea of difference (particularly sexual difference) became important. Feminist critics then began to use the psycho-analytic theories of Freud and Lacan to analyse the patriarchial cultural and psychoanalytical implications of Hollywood narrative ideology. Their analysis was textual in that its emphasis was on the power of the text to create its subject.

Like the British culturalists they relied at least partially on the re-interpretation of cultural Marxism by Althusser, along with the use of Lacan's theory that the unconscious is structured like a language. Psychoanalysis was coupled with Althusser's notions of 'hailing' and 'interpolation', implying that particular audience positions (or subject positions) are created through the audience's acknowledgement of a place created for them by a text. This implied a theory of subjectivity in which the text was theorized as being more or less all powerful. Since much of the work using the type of psychoanalytic theory briefly described here was published in the British film journal, *Screen*, it is often referred to as *Screen* theory.

Broadcast television, although it incorporates traditional narrative form (usually referred to as classical Hollywood realism or sometimes simply as realism), is essentially segmented. Audiences incorporate it into their lives differently from the way audiences incorporate film, or for that matter, radio or reading. Audiences *use* it much more freely than many other media forms. Television's segmented, serial and series forms are different from classical Hollywood narratives. What this difference is and how it works are important to feminist culturalist television criticism. Therefore this type of criticism incorporates both the semiotic analysis of textual form and content and the context and uses made of television by its audiences in the practice of viewing and in the incorporation of television into other cultural practices, like gossip networks.

Notes

1. Women's Studies Group (eds) (1978) *Women Take Issue*, Hutchinson, London.
2. Mulvey, L. (1975) Visual pleasure and narrative cinema. *Screen*, Vol. 16, No. 3, Autumn, pp. 6–18.

52

The symbolic annihilation of women by the mass media

Gaye Tuchman

From Tuchman, G., Kaplan Daniels, A. and Benét, J. (eds) (1978) *Hearth and Home: Images of Women in the Mass Media*, Oxford University Press, New York, pp. 3–17.

In 1920, 24 percent of the nation's adult women worked for pay outside the home and most of them were unmarried. Fifty years later, in 1976, over half of all American women between the ages of 18 and 64 were in the labour force, most of them married. [. . .] In the face of such change, the portrayal of sex roles in the mass media is a topic of great social, political, and economic importance.

[. . .]

If the stereotyped portrayal of sex roles is out-of-date, the media may be preparing youngsters – girls, in particular – for a world that no longer exists.

Suppose for a moment that children's television primarily presents adult women as housewives, non-participants in the paid labour force. Also, suppose that girls in the television audience 'model' their behaviour and expectations on that of 'television women.' Such a supposition is quite plausible for

> what psychologists call 'modeling' occurs simply by watching others, without any direct reinforcement for learning and without any overt practice. The child imitates the model without being induced or compelled to do so. That learning can occur in the absence of direct reinforcement is a radical departure from earlier theories that regarded reward or punishment as indispensable to learning. There now is considerable evidence that children do learn by watching and listening to others even in the absence of reinforcement and overt practice. . . . (Lesser, quoted in Cantor, 1975, p. 5).

And psychologists note that 'opportunities for modeling have been vastly increased by television' (Lesser, quoted in Cantor, 1975, p. 5), It is then equally plausible that girls exposed to 'television women' may hope to be homemakers when they are adults, but not workers outside the home. [. . .]

Two related ideas are central to our discussion. These are *the reflection hypothesis* and *symbolic annihilation*. According to the reflection hypothesis, the mass media reflect dominant societal values. In the case of television (see Tuchman, 1974, 1976), the corporate character of the commercial variety causes programme planners and station managers to design programmes for appeal to the largest audiences. To attract these audiences (whose time and attention are sold to commercial sponsors), the television industry offers programmes consonant with American values. The pursuit of this aim is solidified by the fact that so many members of the television industry take those very values for granted: dominant American ideas and ideals serve as resources for programme development, even when the planners are unaware of them, much as we all take for granted the air we breathe. These ideas and ideals are incorporated as *symbolic representation of America society, not as literal portrayals*. Take the typical television family of the 1950s: mother, father, and two children living in an upper middle-class, single residence suburban home. Such families and homes were not the most commonly found units in the 1950s, but they were the American ideal. Following George Gerbner (1972, p. 44), we may say that 'representation in the fictional world', such as the 1950s ideal family symbolizes or 'signifies social existence'; that is, representation in the mass media announces to audience members that this kind of family (or social characteristic) is valued and approved.

Conversely, we may say that either condemnation, trivialization, or 'absence means symbolic annihilation' (Gerbner, p. 44). Consider the symbolic representation of women in the mass media. Relatively few women are portrayed there, although women are 51 percent of the population and are well over 40 percent of the labour force. Those working women who are portrayed are condemned. Others are trivialized: they are symbolized as child-like adornments who need to be protected or they are dismissed to the protective confines of the home. In sum, they are subject to *symbolic annihilation*.

The mass media deal in symbols and their symbolic representations may not be up-to-date. A time lag may be operating, for non-material conditions, which shape symbols, change more slowly than do material conditions. This notion of a time lag (or a 'culture lag,' as sociologists term it) may be incorporated into the reflection hypothesis. As values change, we would expect the images of society presented by the media to change.

The reflection hypothesis also includes the notion that media planners try to build audiences, and the audiences desired by planners may vary from medium to medium. For instance, television programmers may seek an audience of men and women, without distinguishing between women in the labour force and housewives. But the executives at women's magazines may want to attract women in the labour force in order to garner advertisements designed for those women. Accordingly, we might expect the symbolic annihilation of women by television to be more devastating that of *some* women's magazines.

[...]

From children's shows to commercials to prime-time adventures and situation comedies, television proclaims that women don't count for much. They are under-represented in television's fictional life – they are 'symbolically annihilated'. From 1954, the date of the earliest systematic analysis of television's content through 1975, researchers have found that males dominated the television screen. With the exception of soap operas where men make up a 'mere majority' of the fictional population, television has shown and continues to show two men for every woman. In 1952, 68 percent of the characters in prime-time drama were male. In 1973, 74 percent of those characters were male. In 1973, Women were concentrated in comedies where men make up 'only' 60 percent of the fictional world. Children's cartoons include even fewer women of female characters than adult's prime-time programmes do.

That message is reinforced by the treatment of those women who do appear on the television screen. When television shows reveal someone's occupation, the worker is most likely to be male.

Those few working women included in television plots are symbolically denigrated by being portrayed as incompetent of inferior to male workers. Soap operas provide even more powerful evidence or the portrayal of women as incompetents and inferiors. Although Turow (1974) finds that soap operas present the most favourable image of female workers, there to they are subservient to competent men. Women do not appear in the same professions as men: men are doctors, women, nurses; men are lawyers, women secretaries; men work in corporations, women tend boutiques.

The portrayal of incompetence extends from denigration through victimization and trivialization. When television women are involved in violence, unlike males, they are more likely to be victims than aggressors (Gerbner, 1972). Equally important, the pattern of women's involvement with television violence reveals approval of married women and condemnation of single and working women. As Gerbner (1972) demonstrates, single women are more likely to be victims of violence than married women, and working women are more likely to be villains than housewives. Conversely, married women who do not work for money outside the home are most likely to escape television's mayhem and to be treated sympathetically. More generally, television most approves those women who are presented in a sexual context or within a romantic or family role (Gerbner, 1972; cf. Liebert *et al.*, 1973). Two out of three television-women are married, were married, or are engaged to be married. By way of contrast, most television men are single and have always been single. Also, men are seen outside the home and women within it, but even here, one finds trivialization of women's role within the home.

[. . .]

Although a higher proportion of adult women appear on children's programming in public television than is true of commercial television, Cantor (Isber and Cantor, 1975) finds 'both commercial and public television disseminate the same message about women although the two types of television differ in their structure and purpose'. Her conclusion indicates that commercialism is not solely responsible for television's symbolic annihilation of women and its portrayal of stereotyped sex roles. Rather, television captures societal ideas even when programming is partially divorced from the profit motive.[1]

Male domination has not been measured as directly for television commercials, the other kind of televised image that may be used to test the reflection hypothesis. Since so many of the advertised products are directed toward women, one could not expect to find women neglected by commercials. Given the sex roles commercials play upon, it would be bad business to show two women discussing the relative merits of power lawn mowers or two men chatting about waxy build-up on a kitchen floor.

However, two indirect measures of male dominance are possible: (1) the number of commercials in which only men or only women appear; and (2) the use of males and females in voice overs. (A 'voice-over' is an unseen person speaking about a product while an image is shown on the television screen; an unseen person proclaims 'two out of three doctors recommend' or 'on sale now at your local . . .'.)

On the first indirect measure, all-male or all-female commercials, the findings are unanimous. Schuetz and Sprafkin (in this volume), Silverstein and Silverstein (1974) and Bardwick and Schumann (1967), find a ratio of almost three all-male ads to each all-female ad. The second indirect measure, the use of voice-overs in commercials, presents more compelling evidence for the acceptance of the reflection hypothesis. Echoing the findings of others, Dominick and Rauch (1972) report that of 946 ads with voice-overs, 'only six percent used a female voice; a male voice was heard on 87 percent.' The remainder use one male and one female voice.

The commercials themselves strongly encourage sex-role stereotypes. Although research findings are not strictly comparable to those on television programmes because of the dissimilar 'plots,' the portrayals of women are even more limited than those presented on television dramas and comedies. Linda Busby (1975) summarized the findings of four major studies of television ads. In one study,

- 37.5 percent of the ads showed women as men's domestic adjuncts
- 33.9 percent showed women as dependent on men
- 24.3 percent showed women as submissive
- 16.7 percent showed women as sex objects
- 17.1 percent showed women as unintelligent
- 42.6 percent showed women as household functionaries.

Busby's summary of Dominick and Rauch's work reveals a similar concentration of women as homemakers rather than as active members of the labour force:

- Women were seven times more likely to appear in ads for personal hygiene products than not to appear [in those ads]
- 75 percent of all ads using females were for products found in the kitchen or in the bathroom
- 38 percent of all females in the television ads were shown inside the home, compared to 14 percent of the males
- Men were significantly more likely to be shown outdoors or in business settings than were women
- Twice as many women were shown with children [than] were men
- 56 percent of the women in the ads were judged to be [only] housewives
- 43 percent different occupations were coded for men, 18 percent for women.

In sum, then, analyses of television commercials support the reflection hypothesis. In voice-overs and one-sex (all male or all female) ads, commercials neglect or rigidly stereotype women. In their portrayal of women, the ads banish females to the role of housewife, mother, homemaker, and sex object, limiting the roles women may play in society.

What can the pre-school girl, the school girl, the adolescent female and the woman learn about a woman's role by watching television? The answer is simple. Women are not important in American society, except *perhaps* within the home. And even, within the home, men know best, as the dominance of male advice on soap operas and the use of male voice-overs for female products, suggests. To be a woman is to have a limited life divorced from the economic productivity of the labour force.

Note

1. Sponsors do play a role in public broadcasting. As underwriters of programmes, they may refuse to fund controversial materials. Some critics claim the Corporation for Public Broadcasting has avoided controversial topics to maintain corporate grants, and has designed dramatic series to appeal to corporations and foundations. According to informants at WNET, corporate underwriters object when the station delays airing their programmes to squeeze in public appeals for contributions to the station.

References

Bardwick, Judith and Schumann, Suzanne (1967) Portrait of American men and women in TV commercials. *Psychology*, Vol. 4, No. 4, pp. 18–23.

Busby, Linda J. (1975) Sex-role research on the mass media. *Journal of Communication*, Vol. 25, No. 4, pp. 107–31.

Cantor, Muriel G. (1975) Children's television: sex-role portrayals and employment discrimination. In Mielke K. *et al.* (eds) *The Federal Role in Funding Children's Television Programming*, United States Office of Education, USOE OEC–074–8674, Vol. 2.

Dominick, Joseph and Rauch, Gail (1972) The image of women in network TV commercials. *Journal of Broadcasting*, Vol. 16, No. 3, pp. 259–65.

Gerbner, George (1972) Violence in television drama: Trends and symbolic functions. In Comstock, G. A. and Rubinstein, E. A. (eds) *Media Content and Control*, Television and Social Behavior, U.S. Government Printing Office, Washington, DC, Vol. 1, pp. 28–187.

Isber, Caroline and Cantor, Muriel (1975) *Report of the Task Force on Women in Public Broadcasting*, Corporation for Public Broadcasting, Washington.

Liebert, R. M., Neale, J. M. and Davidson, E. S. (1973) *The Early Window: Effects of Television on Children and Youth*, Pergamon Press, New York.

Silverstein, Arthur Jay and Silverstein, Rebecca (1974) The portrayal of women in television advertising. *FCC Bar Journal*, Vol. 1, pp. 71–98.

Tuchman, Gaye (1974) *The TV Establishment: Programming for Power and Profit*, Prentice-Hall, Englewood Cliffs, NJ.

Tuchman, Gaye (1976) Media values. *Society*, November/December, pp. 51–4.

Turow, Joseph (1974) Advising and ordering: daytime, prime time. *Journal of Communication*, Vol. 24, No. 2, pp. 138–41.

53

Women and the cultural industries

Michèle Mattelart (translated by K. Reader)

From McBarnet, A. (ed.) (1982) *Media, Culture and Society*, Academic Press, London, Vol. 4, No. 2. pp. 135–50.

It is in the everyday time of domestic life that the fundamental discrimination of sex rôles is expressed, the separation between public and private, production and reproduction. The sphere of public interests and production is assigned to man, that of private life and reproduction to woman. The hierarchy of values finds expression through the positive value attached to masculine time (defined by action, change and history) and the negative value attached to feminine time which, for all its potential richness, is implicitly discriminated against in our society, interiorized and lived through as the time of banal everyday life, repetition and monotony.

Invisible work

For a few years now, the international feminist movement, with the aid of analytical work by specialists in social science (male and female), has been vigorously denouncing the negative value attached to women's household work, which becomes transparently obvious when we think that it has been regarded as self-evident that this work should be unpaid. Now, 'as a rule, once manual work is paid, it takes on economic value, so that any unpaid work (such as women's housework) becomes economically, and thus also socially and culturally, devalued (Stavenhagen, 1980).[1]

The part played by this *invisible work* in the functioning of economies has been amply demonstrated. Everywhere, in developed and developing countries alike, women form the mainstay of the *support economy* which makes it possible for all the other activities to be carried on. A woman at home performs a fundamental rôle in any economy: she restores the labour force each day. This economic activity, carried on by most layers of the female population, is of great importance; but the indicators by which the socioeconomic situation of each country is defined, and its development measured, conceal the economic value of household work.

The arrival of capitalism, which introduced the factory and institutionalized the sale of labour-power, undoubtedly represented a decisive moment in the segregation of sex rôles in the productive process, by depriving the family of its old function as a productive unit. But we should beware of a nostalgic attitude, and of the tendency to idealize the situation that traditional society gave women in productive activities. It has been shown (with reference to Africa, for example) that this often went hand in hand with forms of slavery.

Capitalism merely continued and deepened a hierarchical division of labour which had come into being well before as modes of production developed, reserving for males the most prestigious and best-rewarded work and restricting women to the lowest kind. This sex rôle discrimination is fundamental to the maintenance of the capitalist economy, and it has been shown that 'but for this vast female underpinning, the women who provide food and clothing for the proletariat in a world where the necessary facilities for a collective restoration of labour energy simply do not exist, the hours of surplus value extorted from the worker by capital would be fewer. We can even say that women's work in the home is expressed through men's work outside by the creation of surplus value' (Larguia and Dumoulin, 1975).

Gradually separated from the world of production, through the long process of consolidation of the monogamous family which brings about a close link between the system of relations within the family unit and that of private property, woman, by virtue of the kind of tasks she carries out at home and her dependence on man, is the cement of class society. This division of labour finds expression in a definition of masculine and feminine qualities transmitted, reinforced and rearticulated by the different institutions of society (the Church, schools, the media). Girls will be docile, submissive, clean, chaste, prudish; they will play quiet games and enjoy indoor activities. Conversely, boys will be sexually aggressive, prone to show off their physical strength, to develop their 'innate' sense of leadership and so forth.

The invisibility of women's work and the concealment of the productive value of their household tasks are of decisive importance in determining the image of them projected by the media and the media's relationship with them. The media have made a point of following the traditional household timetable. Radio and television programming is very revealing in this respect. It punctuates the day with moments that make women's condition 'all worth while' and helps to compensate for being shut up at home all day. It makes women's work legitimate, not as work but as a duty that forms part of their natural function.

The genre of these women's broadcasts may differ (afternoon magazines, television serials, radio serials); the values around which their themes are structured can correspond to different points in women's relation to capital, and to the more or less modern and free-thinking character of the sections of the bourgeoisie that produce them. But they still have in common the role of integrating women into their everyday life.

The exception confirms the rule – adventure consecrates routine

In this process of integration, the melodramatic serial on radio or television has traditionally played a supremely important part. Most serials take as their target the family audience. On the other hand, the melodramatic serial, which carries on in radio and television where 'lonely-hearts' columns leave off, addresses primarily the working-class female public. Because of the immense impact of this genre in Latin America and other Catholic countries, there is a tendency to think of it as a Latin genre. But we can see that it exists, with variations, on the screens and the air waves of every country in the world, at least the capitalist part of it. It is all too well known that the more a channel declares itself to be fulfilling a cultural function and/or that of a public service, the fewer serials it will broadcast; and this is even truer of melodramatic serials, which on the other hand are everywhere on commercial channels. The profile of their audience, and their very regularity, make them excellent terrain for advertisers (in one hour of these serials in Venezuela for example, there are 20 minutes of advertising).

In Latin America, undoubtedly the supreme territory for this genre (known as *Telenovela*) and more and more a major centre of diffusion, the state channels (insignificant compared with the commercial ones – they attract only 10 percent of the public on average) display a tendency to win over the large public audience of this genre by making it more 'up-market'. Major authors of contemporary Latin American literature (Salvador Garmendia in Venezuela, Gabriel Garcia Marquez in Colombia, Jorge Amado in Brazil) have been invited to contribute to this strategy of renewal, which opposes ('to the commercial model of the dominant channels the cultural alternative ('cultural television'). There is no doubt that the works that stem from this collaboration offer female audiences (and others) the chance to encounter cultural products which show a much richer and more complex approach to human experience and emotion. But can we here still speak of melodramatic serials or 'telenovelas'?

The conditions of production currently prevalent in commercial Latin American broadcasting companies encourage directors. In order to keep costs down and profits up, to adhere to rules of serialization that lead to stereotyped banalities shooting-time is minimal; the script of the following day's episode is improvised from one day to the next within the context of the time-honoured formulae of these mass-produced artefacts. The stereotyped structure of these productions annuls the possibility of openness to public reaction and criticism which this 'on-the-spot' shooting would otherwise make possible, in obvious contrast to the mode of production in other sectors of the cultural industry. The rule of commercialism, which has as its first principle to mine the same vein to exhaustion, means that these stories go on and on interminably. The Venezuelan government had to limit the number of episodes by decree.

There is no denying that the interplay in this or that country between cultural channels (even in a minority) and commercial ones can lead the latter to modify their programming, and particularly the raise their level, especially when they realize that the new 'cultural serials' attract large audiences. Even so, in the current circumstances, these serials, like the 'lonely-hearts' press, remain dominated by a principle of obscurantism, one of segregation of audiences. That is the key to the matter. This genre conforms to the principles of division of the market that govern the culture industry. In the press, to refer to socially distinct targets (from the standpoint of both purchasing power and cultural power), publishers and publicists alike speak of 'upmarket' and 'downmarket'. In the field of television the melodramatic serial indisputably belongs in the second category. As we said when talking about the duality of the female market, a duality which increasingly pervades the whole mass-cultural apparatus (one of market democratization and segregation at the same time):

These two products of modern capitalism, women's magazines on one hand and photo-novels on the other, belong to specific moments and represent different mechanisms of bourgeois domination. They are complementary. Photo-novel magazines may tend to develop more in the context of the obscurantism caused by fascism or other present-day authoritarian regimes. But they are still there amid the everyday normality of liberal democracy. Furthermore, women's magazines correspond to the enlightened dimension of the most up-to-date section of the ruling class. The two genres express the different alliances that the bourgeoisie tries to conclude with women from different strata of society. And the variations that may, depending on the historical moment, indicate the dominance of one genre over another are indissolubly linked to the type of consensus the state may be able to produce and the model of development it favours (Mattelart, 1979).

It remains true that the melodramatic serial on radio or television is the fictional genre most clearly addressed to a mass female public. These productions usually bear a woman's name as their title – *Natacha, Simplemente Maria, Rafaela* or whatever. It has been shown that this is a condition of their success. The serials whose titles included men's names had less of an impact. In Latin American countries, these productions continue to exist side-by-side with imported series (generally North American), or more up-to-date programmes fully involved with the symbolic universe of the industrialized world and reflecting the relative emancipation of women participating in professional life on an equal footing with men. But the traditional productions still enjoy more success. It is through these serials that the principal audience-battle between the different stations is fought out.

There have been enough content analyses and ideological readings of melodramatic serials and linked genres (such as photo-novels) for us to feel able to give a highly condensed summary here (cf. Mattelart, 1977, Dardigna, 1978, Butler Flora and Flora, 1978). The plot generally revolves round the ups and downs of a love affair which brings together people separated by social class (or age, or previous ties, or a combination of all three). The family context tends to be riddled in rather higgledy-piggledy fashion with social pathology and individual problems – unhappy homes, incurable diseases, illegitimate children, alcoholism, incestuous or quasi-incestuous cohabitation and so on. The variations run the whole gamut from romantic adventures to social dramas. In Latin America, the serials are very much marked by sex and violence, obsessively present (though always shrouded in implication and innuendo) in the form of blackmail or rape (at least, that is what one deduces must have happened). The unrolling of the story through all kinds of ambiguities, avowals, mistaken identities and interventions of a *deus ex machina* reveals a highly normative message whose structure is Manichean: the good and the virtuous are rewarded. Love sanctioned by the legitimate union of marriage is better than passion, which is always punished by fate. The female characters ennoble the values of purity and virginity for girls, who often become heroic martyrs to men who in fact get away with abusing their masculine authority and class-power; but, after putting her through great suffering and temptation, they confirm the happiness of the girl from a modest background by offering her a ring and married life. The sacrifice, courage, and self-denial of wives and mothers are other attitudes reinforced by these messages, crowned as they are by the return of the husband, the renewed gratitude of the son, or the simple satisfaction that comes from doing one's duty.

Monotony also has its exceptions. The serial makes possible a symbolic revenge on the triviality of everyday life, whose monotonous repetitiveness is countered by the day-by-day episodes of the heroine's exceptional adventure. Household work, experienced as unproductive and of low socio-economic standing, is countered by programmes which give value to the realm of private life and a female world dominated by 'love' and 'emotion'.

We can notice that from the 'content' point of view a tendency to increase the realism of these discourses brings them closer to the real situations of working people. These new serials, at any rate in Venezuela, show an increasing concern to stick to real life. Let us look at one such example, and observe the unchanged manner in which it smooths over points of conflict. The serial 'Dona Juana' explicitly refers to a problem that affects all social strata, but principally the working people, and implacably brings out the sexist character of society – that of irresponsible paternity, of illegitimate children brought up by their mothers alone, not recognized by the father who abandons the mother after making her pregnant. 'Dona Juana' portrays these woman, and their brave struggle against male hostility and recklessness. but this woman, or humble background, does not learn to define herself as an independent individual, even through her struggle shows the strength and energy she can display as head of the family. The *dénouement* still follows a conservative and conventional pattern: thanks to an almost miraculous stroke of luck, the father finds his daughter and recognizes her. He thereby satisfies simultaneously the mother's dream and that of her daughter – that the child can bear its father's name and thus escape the stigma of illegitimacy.

It is no secret that the ideological function of these narrative discourses resides primarily in the fact that they are given as representations of reality, and therefore cleave to certain features of the reality of social and class conflict, which they implicitly explain (through the mechanisms of the story) from a certain point of view, itself likewise linked to the objective reality of class struggle. The serial's twin task – of representing reality and explaining it – defines its rôle of reproducing the conditions of production of the social formation, predisposing women to accept the 'natural' explanation of their domination.

The balance between fiction and information

Various studies have clearly brought out the split that can exist within one television channel between *informative* programmes intended for women and *fictional* ones (drama series, serials, etc.). This split can even be seen as distinguishing the informative programmes intended for women, and hence conveying a particular image of them, from the rest of the programmes, which convey another.

Let us first of all look at '*The influence of audio-visual media upon the social and cultural behaviour of women in Japan*' (Nuita, 1980). The author shows how, immediately after the end of World War II, the Japanese state broadcasting authority (NHK) helped women to free themselves from their virtual confinement within the family; this was achieved through the programme 'Woman's Hour' and even more by group listening to radio, especially to educational programmes. These programmes were entirely in accord with the policy of modernization in Japan, started by the occupying forces and taking the form for women of a policy of emancipation. The programme was then reinforced by another series – *NHK Female Classes* – which dealt with a variety of themes, from problems of family consumption to political, economic and social questions, first on radio, then on television. Around these broadcasts – and this initiative is emblematic of the break that had been made with traditional conceptions of women in the media – were set up women's study groups to fight the tendency to isolation and domestic imprisonment which could have been perpetuated, or even made worse, by solitary listening to broadcasts. Thus, the whole enterprise of civic education for women was served by these NHK programmes, which came to a stop in 1969, partly because Japan's rapid economic development between 1965 and 1969 meant that more and more women took outside jobs, which made it difficult to organize daytime group meetings. It is interesting to note that, by starting to bring women together, the media had in a way played a role analogous to work, until economic expansion brought paid work back onto the agenda. Nowadays, there are a certain number of strictly educational programmes which still serve as a focus for female study groups. But we have to interpret this use of the media to promote the development of society in the light of the overall characteristics of media programming in Japan, and particularly of the dominant image of woman transmitted by the media. Nuita says that both drama serials and television plays purvey a stereotyped image of woman. These occupy an enormous amount of programme-time, so that traditional social norms are reinforced. 'Traditionally the Japanese woman has been brought up to fulfil her role as daughter, wife, and mother'; hence, the characters of the 'tender mother' or the 'good little wife' are dominant. There are a few television plays that show pioneering or resistant female characters, but as a rule 'these plays present woman as always willing to conform to the dominant attitude, and go to reinforce traditional female ways of thinking'.

This duality can also be observed in some magazines, especially those which are reluctant to adopt a squarely modernist approach and would rather remain within the confines of a part-traditional, part-modern attitude.[2] The editorials may evince some kind of 'progressive' intention, conforming to a mildly liberal image of woman in their treatment of permissive morality. But, in the same issue, the fiction (a novel serialized over several numbers) will portray woman in the most conventional light imaginable: passive, dependent, prone to a sugary-sweet view of life.

This leads us to deepen our analysis to the media as they operate in liberal democracies. Their political function is to reproduce the co-existence of different social classes and groups. Thus they constitute a place where social tensions are reduced; everybody has a part to play. But at the same time society has to reassert its cohesiveness by reproducing the legitimacy of public opinion (defined as that of an 'average citizen').[3] This 'average citizen' – in fact an abstract entity in the service of social inertic – becomes the basic norm to mediate change and ensure the continuance of tradition. It is in the interests of this basic norm that the balance between information and fiction is established.

This is what the author of the Japanese study says in her remarks on dramatic and other kinds of fiction: 'Overall, society demands that women correspond to the type of the good wife and good mother. This is why the main characteristic of the female characters in family plays is not a sense of independence, but conformity with existing social standards.' Information programmes, on the other hand, meet the demands of other groups, which the media are under an obligation to satisfy if they are to fulfil their task of communication and satisfy divergent interests while mediating their contradictions.

But there is more than one element to take into account. To the crucial question 'What is the relationship between information and fiction?', we have offered two kinds of answer, that given by the Japanese broadcasting system and that given by certain magazines. We could find similar examples in other developing and developed countries. As the terrain on which social negotiation takes place, the media make possible – indeed necessary – the co-existence of may varied points of view. The diversity of genres within television and radio, like that of sections within a magazine, expresses (in however trite a way) this necessity, which relates to a rather more complex aspect of the media's answer to the problem of 'diversity'. We should here point out a fundamental difference which stems from the different places the media occupy in the social formation. Some are under a statutory obligation to favour variety and diversity, others to go further and respect *pluralism*. This distinction is an important one, for it determines the different kinds of answers different media give to a single problem, and thus highlights their specific institutional functions.

A magazine, especially a women's magazine, addresses a fairly consistent and equally defined public. The magazines that interest us – those which circulate in accordance with market laws (i.e. not those produced by government organizations or political groups) – are usually controlled by a press group, answerable only to itself and its public. Its task is to take its public through the different stages of a development whose success is gauged by the volume of sales. Within a press group which aims at the female market, a division of labour generally occurs: some magazines cater for the demand of one sector of the population, others for a different kind. (The same holds good for the daily press.) So the same group, as we have already seen, will publish photo-novel magazines and modern, not to say *avant-garde*, ones – a distinction known as 'down-market' *versus* 'up-market' both turning out equally professional products. This division of labour, we have suggested, can also arise within one particular magazine. This division and variety bring into play a complex but logical array of elements governed by commercial as much as ideological factors. The ideology professed by a magazine is invariably the result of its commercial situation (except – cf. Mattelart, 1976 – in a period of crisis).

On the other hand, a medium such as television, especially when it is · controlled by criteria of public service, has to give air-time to identifiable public groups whose opinions and ideologies are different, or even incompatible – the very groups that mark the pluralism of a liberal society. The definition of a public service enjoins upon it, in different ways depending on the situation, a rôle of information and social leadership, and of development of democratic life. It has to favour the development of citizens' abilities so that they may be better aware of their rights and better placed to defend them. It also has to show all the major currents of opinion and act as the platform on which society can express itself. *But* it cannot turn itself into an *avant-garde* medium. Its task of ensuring the maintenance of the social order implies a rigorous codification of its pluralism, so that it can cultivate a certain conservatism in the service of the *status quo*. The natural interplay between the informative broadcasts which boost women's role and image and the bulk of the fictional ones thus appears as a basic mechanism of this conservatism. The limits of pluralism have been judiciously assessed:

> Pluralism admits several ideologies, opinions and moralities. From this liberality it derives a system, banishing dogmatism and opposing repressive systematis- ation. Quite right too. Yet liberal pluralism itself is systematic and dogmatic in its own way. The number of accepted opinions is few; the liberal accepts several moral codes, but demands some kind of morality. He accepts several religions, but demands some kind of religious sentiment. Old or new, liberalism tends to institutionalize accepted opinions, acceptable moralities or ideologies. . . . This leads to a tendency to hallow establishment opinions and values (Lefebvre, 1970).[4]

[. . .]

Of the two areas of information and fiction, which has the greater pubic impact, from the nebulous point of view of its 'effects', i.e. the attitudes, ambitions and models it transmits? To answer this, we should need an extensive study of audiences, in an interdisciplinary perspective combining the approaches of sociology, anthropology, psychoanalysis and semiology. This may be highly controversial. We should begin by pointing out that it has long been recognized by cultural critics that mass-culture brings together a variety of different areas: the 'real' and the 'imaginary' [in their Lacanian sense—trans.], the effect of fictional conventions upon the field of information the sensationalist tendency of that field and so forth. The boundary between reality and fiction becomes progressively vaguer. [. . .]

We are inclined on balance to think that fiction has a greater impact upon the majority of people than informative programmes. A life-style is more easily transmitted fictionally than non-fictionally. Fictional programmes – serials, series, family comedies – are the places where the feelings and ideas of the 'silent majority' are confirmed, where accepted wisdom on the hierarchy of rôles and values is reiterated and repermuted in such a way as to reinforce the beliefs and practices of the greatest number. They are also the place where disruptive elements are digested, and non-conformist ideas absorbed. This zone of mass-culture is the privileged space where authority does not need to speak politically in order to act politically.

Fiction and information do not refer to the same things. However affected by fictional values they may be, information programmes still refer to *reality*. Fictional programmes refer to the other text, the already-said, the already-written. Reality manifests tension, effort, history, and an openness to the future, the developing, the unknown. The already-said reiterates the past, renews the sense of security which in spite of everything it gives.

Notes

1. A great many women and women's groups have studied this problem (viz. Baxandall *et al.*, 1976; *IDS Bulletin*, 1979; Dalla Costa, 1972).
2. This happens with a number of French magazines, some of which have lost out through too sudden a change of direction. *Bonne Soirée'* decided after 1968 to react against its traditional format by including rather more 'contemporary material', and proceeded to lose 300,000 readers in six months. These women's magazines are read primarily in the provinces.
3. Pierre Bourdieu has shown that 'public opinion' is in fact a mystification (Bourdieu, 1979).
4. It is worth pointing out that commercial stations, less under the thumb of public interest and morality, can show themselves more tolerant than state channels. This is suggested by the Japanese author when she says that (several private programmes at one time were criticized for depicting adultery or other non-legitimate types of sexual relation).

References

Butler Flora, C. and Flora, J. L. (1978) The footnovela as a tool for class and cultural domination, *Latin American Perspectives*, Issue 16, Vol. V, No. 1.

Dardigna, A. M. (1978) *La Presse Féminine, Fonction Idéologique*, Maspero, Paris.

Larguia, I. and Dumoulin, J. (1975) Towards a science of women's liberation. *Latin America and Empire Report*, North American Congress on Latin America, No. 6, New York.

Lefebvre, H. (1970) *Le Manifeste Différentialiste*, Gallimard, Paris.

Mattelart, M. (1976) Chile: the feminine version of the Coup d'etat. In Nash, J. and Safa, H. (eds) *Sex and Class in Latin America*, Praeger, New York.

Mattelart, M. (1977) *La Cultura de la opresiòn Femenina*, Editorial Era, Mexico.

Mattelart, M. (1979) Notes on modernity: a way of reading women's magazines. In Mattelart, A. and Siegelaub, S. (eds) *Communication and Class Struggle, an Anthology*, International General, New York.

Nuita, Y. (1980) L'influence des Medias Audiovisuels sur le Comportement Socioculturel des Femmes au Japon. In *L'influence des Medias Audiovisuels sur le Comportement Socioculturel des Femmes. 2 Exemples: le Japon et le Canada*, Dossier Documentaire, No. 17, Section Développement culturel, UNESCO, Paris.

Stavenhagen, R. (1980) La femme invisible. *Courrier de l'UNESCO*, July.

54

Class and gender in the hegemonic process: class differences in women's perceptions of television realism and identification with television characters

Andrea Press

From Sparks, C. (ed.) (1989) *Media Culture and Society*, Sage, London, Vol. 11, No. 2. pp. 229–51.

In this paper I compare the ways in which American working-class women receive television entertainment programming differently than do middle-class women. Specifically, I compare the type of identification with television characters made by each group, and differences between the way in which members of each group judge television content to be 'realistic'. I demonstrate that while many of our society's hegemonic values are present in television programming, they reach women of different social classes in class-specific ways. Working-class women are more likely to notice the middle-class material world which television depicts, and to judge this world to be representative of the real world. Middle-class women, in contrast, are more likely to identify personally with television characters and their problems, particularly those related to the family and situated in a family context.

As scholars theorizing the relationship between gender and class might predict, I conclude that the hegemonic process operates quite differently for working-class as opposed to middle-class women. While working-class women are much more susceptible to the class-specific features of the liberal, middle-class ideology characterizing the television entertainment medium, middle-class women are more responsive to its gender-specific features. As working-class women are lulled into accepting that their *wishes* regarding material reality constitute that reality itself, middle-class women are similarly encouraged by television's portrayal of the family to accept the interpersonal and familial ideals and goals which television presents, and to evaluate both their *own* lives *and* the behaviour of television characters in light of these overall hegemonic views.

Theoretical framework: cultural studies and the emergent feminist tradition

The cultural tradition as it has developed in the fields of both communication and sociology has been aimed specifically at questions of social values, and the role of the mass media in creating, supporting and interacting with social values. I am interested specifically in what the cultural approach has to offer to feminist theory, and to empirical feminist research in communication. It is in this tradition that I locate my own work.

Both the communication and sociology fields have always focused at least some critical attention on issues of social and cultural values, raising questions such as these:

1. Where – in what social texts or artifacts – in what specific teachings – are our social values inscribed?

2. How do we as a society use these texts as tools and means with which to socialize new generations into our cultural value systems?

3. What dissonance occurs among competing values? How is this expressed in our society? Does our society and our culture provide us with any *basis* upon which to evaluate the merits of these competing points of view? Through what mechanism are these evaluative criteria communicated? (Here I refer specifically to the terms of the Habermas–Gadamer debate.)

4. Finally, the question raised specifically by the Marxist intellectual roots shared by members of the critical school, do our values simply uphold and reinforce an inherently oppressive class and gender social structure? Or again, do they make it possible for members of our society to engage in critical and constructive dialogue concerning these issues, and debating means of their possible resolution?

Feminist scholars, both sociologists and especially the inter-disciplinary group of feminist scholars involved in communication studies, have carried this dialogue and its critique of our cultural consciousness even further. While now fairly well established in the broader communication studies field, primarily by those working in the humanities, feminist communication study and research in *the social sciences* has been slower to develop. While feminist *theory* in the communication field has 'taken off', so to speak, and is considered by many to be one of its most exciting and generative areas of theoretical growth, empirical research inspired by these ideas has been somewhat slower to issue forth. Part of the reason for this, of course, may lie in the abstract nature of much of the feminist theorizing which has occurred. The relationship between feminist ideas and feminist research, when these ideas are as abstract as those of the deconstructionist and post-modern feminist theorists and those working with psycho-analytic concepts, is admittedly often perplexing. Another reason for the slower growth of feminist research *vis-à-vis* theory may be the greater need for research funding in the social sciences, and the lack of a tradition of funding feminist research.

Empirical research informed by a feminist theoretical approach has a great deal to offer to culturally focused communication studies. Many areas of study – women's cultural experience, their reception of cultural messages and products, cultural images of gender, and the potential existence of separate and *gendered* cultural spheres – have only begun to be examined through feminist research.

The questions occupying this work carry the critical project of cultural communication sociology one step further, bringing the traditional concerns of this group to bear alongside issues arising specifically from the consideration of gender. Questions central to this body of work include the following; some are shared with feminist theory generally, others specific to those interested in studying the issue of culture in particular:

1. Can we call Western society – and most other known societies as well, feminists argue – *patriarchal* (meaning that gender domination occurs in an intrinsic, characteristic cultural element within the value systems of these societies)? Where – again, in what social texts or artifacts, in which teachings – and patriarchal values inscribed? (This question is shared by feminist theorists working in most disciplines.)

2. How do patriarchal traditions provide the basis for their own critical appropriation by those interested in resisting and subverting patriarchal values? Where can we look for sources, inscriptions, and evidence of this resistance? How can women be both the products of patriarchal society, and its critics as well?

3. Finally, does it make sense to speak of a 'women's culture' existing at some level as a viable subculture of resistance (or accommodation) within complex societies? What other divisions – e.g. social class, race, ethnicity may be relevant to locating and documenting specific women's cultures as they exist and have existed in Western societies?

I see my work as situated within this emergent tradition of empirical feminist research, both regarding the theoretical frame work which inspired it, and the methodology I used. I attempt to address resistance (or the lack of it) to elements of mass culture by examining responses to television narrative and characters among women of different classes in the U.S.

Case study I: *I Love Lucy* and women's identification with comic characters

First, I look at a case study comparing working-class and middle-class women's identification with the central character in one of the most-watched entertainment shows on television, the *I Love Lucy* show. The *I Love Lucy* show is one of the most successful television shows of all time. Lucy (Lucille Ball), the star of the show, is television's prototypical comic woman. Zany, dingy, wild, but ultimately feisty and strong-willed, the character of Lucy serves as a complex image for women of our time. Predating the era of women's liberation from the post-war era home, Lucy is a traditional wife and mother constantly plotting and scheming to get into her husband's business, the professional entertainment world. The power of her image, however, resonates beyond its surface qualities, and she was one of the most talked-about figures in my interviews.

There are marked differences between what working-class and middle-class women notice about the image of Lucy. While the show was popular with respondents of both classes, it was more popular with the middle-class women to whom I spoke, who gave me many more, and more impassioned, comments about it. Most significantly, it was popular in different ways with women of each class. Members of both classes thought Lucy a funny character, but for middle-class women she had more of a positive identity, often as a comedienne in distinction from her comic persona. They also noticed the liberatory or feminist aspects of the Lucy character more often than did working-class informants, identifying her as a strong, independent role model for women. [. . .]

'*I Love Lucy* was a very funny show. Everybody enjoyed it. But [and this in a disparaging tone] I couldn't really follow it as real life in any way'. And I wish to stress here that the issue of whether the show was true-to-life was brought up by my informants themselves; it was not an issue which I introduced into the interview situation. It was their own criteria, used to evaluate their likes and dislikes of television programming and characters. These findings led me to suspect that women of different classes may respond differently, specifically to comic female figures. Lucy is almost a feminist figure for middle-class women; whereas these feminist qualities which strike middle-class women so strongly are repudiated by working-class women viewers.

Possible interpretations of these results, and judgements of their significance for the broader issue I investigate, are several. On a method-ological note it is possible that working-class women hesitated to tell me that they identified with a character whom they perceived to be so silly. They may have been embarrassed, more so than were middle-class women, to admit to a professional sociologist that they could associate themselves with a character who it seemed to them was not taken entirely seriously. I believe that this is, in part, a reason for some of the responses I received. It was certainly true that working-class women were more easily embarrassed and more hesitant in my presence than were my middle-class informants.

More was at issue on the Lucy questions, however, in my view. Judging from the working-class responses I received overall, my feeling is that while the embarrassment factor may have been operating for some of my respondents, interfering with the very possibility of their admitting an identification with any comic character, it was certainly not the cause of most of the responses I received. I claim this because many informants did not appear embarrassed to discuss their feelings about television shows with me, even feelings about shows they considered to be silly, comic or stupid. This was especially evident in most responses I received to questions about *I Love Lucy*, which provoked much spontaneous enthusiasm among middle-class and working-class informants alike. For the enthusiastic, relaxed working-class women who discussed the Lucy character, factors other than embarrassment or hesitancy seemed to be clearly operating in their lack of identification with her.

For working-class women, I maintain that it is comedy's lack of realism when literally interpreted which accounts for the paucity of their identification with comic television characters. More so than do women of the middle class, working-class women believe that television is, or should be, a mirror of the world, or at least should reflect the world they would like to see. This conviction has a strong impact on the way in which they perceive and interpret television characters and shows, and on the occurrence and manner of their identification with television females. Morley (1986) also found that working-class women dislike slapstick comedy, particularly in a domestic setting. They were disturbed, he claimed, by portrayals of the disruption of domestic order, an order which they work long and hard to maintain. Certainly, the working-class women with whom

I spoke seemed quite disturbed by Lucy's challenge to the orderly domestic life which might have prevailed in the absence of her comic shenanigans. Ultimately, I assert, the realistic aura which television assumes for working-class women gives it more power, and power of a different sort, over their lives than it exerts over the lives of middle-class women.

Middle-class women, on the other hand, pick up more directly on the family dynamics, and Lucy's position within them, which are portrayed on the *I Love Lucy* show. They more freely incorporate her comic qualities into their admiration of the Lucy character for her ongoing struggle to free herself from the confines of an essentially oppressive marriage.[1] Paradoxically, in this instance television operates almost counter-hegemonically for middle-class women, offering them a feisty female image whose rebellion is directed specifically against her traditional role in the nuclear family.

Case study II: The *Cosby Show* and women's perceptions of realism

Moving to my second case study, I investigate more deeply working-class perceptions of realism on television in the context of comparing working-class and middle-class women's reactions to the *Cosby Show*. The *Cosby Show* features a decidedly upper-middle-class family. Bill Cosby, who plays the father, is Dr Heathcliff Huxtable, a medical doctor. His wife Clair (Phylicia Ayers-Allen) is a lawyer. They are black. They live in an extremely nice home and have five children, one of whom they are sending to college. Certainly the Huxtable family is not representative of black families overall. In fact, with two highly paid professional parents, they are not even representative of white families overall.

[. . .]

Given that the percentage of dual professional black families is exceedingly small, I find that the vigour with which one woman argues that the *Cosby Show* is realistic to be quite a tribute to the ability of television images to establish, for some, an alternative vision of the real world. Even if this woman had known one successful, middle-class black family, surely there is enough evidence in the world around her to confirm the high incidence of poverty and unemployment among blacks; in fact, this woman lived in a city area which bordered an extremely poor, largely black section of town. There should have been ample evidence in her experience to support the position alternative to the one she argued.

This woman's attitude attests to the real triumph of that aspect of the hegemonic ideology which states that those who work hard will succeed. It is as though she believes it would be racist to admit that some blacks, or that blacks as a group, have not succeeded, that to believe this would be tantamount to labelling blacks to be lazy and incompetent individuals. Otherwise, how to explain their failure? Her statement indicates the possibility that shows like *Cosby* could have an extremely conservative effect on perceptions of the true position and needs of minority group members in our society. If shows like *Cosby* are perceived as an advance for minorities, as capable of correcting racist misconceptions that blacks are poor, they undoubtedly strengthen an individualistic interpretation of poverty's causes, and its remedies. Paradoxically, then, the increasing appearance of minority images on popular

television, packaged as they are within the terms of the white middle-class hegemony, may progressively discourage accurate perceptions of minority groups, poverty and prejudice in our society.
[. . .]

Again, middle-class women, while noticing the lack of realism on the show, become involved in the familial relationships which are portrayed and identify with persons and situations despite a perception and judgement of unreality, in line with their greater fundamental similarity to what is, after all, a middle-class family. In their comments, middle-class women more easily move back and forth between their own experience and descriptions of the television characters and situations which directly inspire particular memories and what often adds up to an overall feeling of personal relatedness, which is not quite present in more working-class women's remarks. In general, however, none of the female characters on *Cosby* inspired the same strong degree of identification which the character of Lucy did for middle-class women. Perhaps too little of the show's conflict and action revolves around them for these characters to command the level of adulation and response which is accorded to Lucy.

Case study III: Working-class women respond to *Alice* and *Who's the Boss*

Finally, I compare working-class women's perceptions of realism in *Alice*, one of the few shows to feature specifically working-class characters in a working-class setting, with their response to the white middle-class show *Who's the Boss*. *Alice* concerns the daily adventures of a widow with a small son who works as a waitress at Mel's Diner. Situations revolve primarily around workplace experiences of Alice (Linda Lavin), her fellow waitresses Flo (Polly Holliday) and Vera (Beth Howland), and their boss Mel (Vic Tayback), who makes a mean bowl of chilli ('Mel's Famous Chilli'). Flo was later replaced by Belle (Diane Ladd) and then Jolene (Celia Weston) when she left the series in 1980 to star in her own spin-off series, *Flo*.

Several working-class women with whom I spoke remarked on the unreality, in their view, of the situations, characters, and particularly the boss–worker relationships portrayed in *Alice*. Their perceptions of this unreality seemed to interfere significantly with their pleasure in watching the show.
[. . .]

The distinction made here between the viewer's expectations of a character who she perceives to be 'strong' or dramatic (Alice) as opposed to a character whom she perceives to be comic (Flo) are interesting in light of my discussion of working-class women's response to television's comic women in the discussion of *I Love Lucy*, above. Remember too that this woman specifically mentions her affection for, and enjoyment of, the character Flo, that she stopped watching the show when Flo left it. As in the case of judgements working-class women made of the Lucy character (was Flo strong also? If she was, why should she remain working in Mel's Diner? was Alice the only strong figure in the diner? why was Flo a more realistic character than Alice?).
[. . .]

What is reality? Escapism for working-class women

One problem working-class women may experience in attempting to identify with the working-class images which do appear on television may involve the fact that many working-class images on television are comic images. Working-class women do not readily identify with comic images[2] in part because they perceive them to be unrealistic. For example, several told me that they enjoyed the show *Laverne and Shirley*, which pictures the adventures of two young working-class women, but they phrased their comments in terms of noticing and praising the show's humour rather than in their ability to identify with, or relate to, the main characters. Another woman remembers herself laughing hysterically when watching *The Honeymooners*, a show about a working-class couple. This woman had been a battered wife for many years, but had never related her experiences to the many arguments or threats of violence depicted between husband and wife in that show. Again, here it may be that comedy interfered with the identification process. Or that working-class women avoid identifying with images which somewhat too realistically evoke real-life pain.

One working-class woman stated her desires from television for me quite clearly. She had just described in great detail a soap opera to which she was addicted, criticizing many of the characters and situations for their lack of realism. However, when asked if she would prefer more realistic characters or situations on television – poor women, for example, or women who worked for a living – she denied it. While she liked television to be fairly realistic, she did not wish to see too problematic a reality:

> It takes the fantasy away. When it's something that's totally unreal you expect it to stay that way. Who wants to see welfare mothers or working women who go home to a bunch of screaming kids? You don't want to see that on TV.

She goes on to illustrate her point in the context of describing the show *Kate and Allie*, and her reaction to it. Kate (Susan Saint James) and Allie (Jane Curtin) were two divorced women, old friends, who decided to move in together with their children to form a household following their divorces. Allie, the old-fashioned one, kept house for Kate, the glamorous career woman. The show is interesting in that it plays the roles of the two women – traditional and modern – off each other. Plots revolve around various problems one or both of the two women experience in the course of their lives. It has been widely praised among television critics for its realism, and for the sensitivity with which the relationship between the two women in particular is portrayed.

My informant describes the show in these unflattering terms:

> Well, it was these two women with their problems. I don't know what it was like 'cause I just didn't like it too much. I just watched it because it was supposed to be so good.

She ends up, not surprisingly, criticizing the show for its lack of (of all things) realism:

> Well, I guess the repartee, and the way they discuss and handle them [their problems] seems still unreal. I mean, life is really slow. It's not always an incident or entertaining, funny issue. Real life is just – can be quite a drudge. You know, the same old problems. You have to make your challenges.

On the one hand, we are told that the drudge of real life is an unfitting subject for television – 'it takes the fantasy away'. On the other, *Kate and Allie*, a show about problems, is unreal, failing to capture the dull drudgery of real life. This woman, at least, seems caught between the desire for more realistic television and a desire for fantasy or escape.

Another woman expresses a similar sentiment, arguing that television shows depicting children on drugs and in other sorts of trouble hit too close to home – are a little too realistic – and that people she knows certainly don't want to see this, to be reminded of the potential problems they or their children might face. She too is a working-class woman who maintained throughout her interview a strong preference for realistic television,

> They think that the children want to see children who are screwed up – because that's what they are – and children who are promiscuous, children who are alcoholics, children who are on drugs. Maybe the children want to see it; I don't think that the old people want to see it. First of all they are happy that their children weren't on it.

She goes on to describe her particular fears regarding her children's exposure to the drug scene in college. As demonstrated above in other contexts, when television images hit too closely to home, or touch topics actually troubling a woman at a given moment in time, she is likely to judge these images to be unrealistic. The situation in which television presents her with idealized images that have less actual relationship to her real life, but more easily conform to her fantasies and dreams, is more likely to meet with both her general approval and, from working class women, specific praise for its 'realism'.

Conclusion

In this work I have used an open-ended, unstructured interviewing technique in order to investigate differences between the way in which working-class and middle-class women understand, identify with, and use television narrative and characters. Results yielded interesting differences between the classes of women I have studied. Working-class women and middle-class women have different expectations of television. The former criticize television for its lack of realism, and evaluate shows at least in part on their success in mimicking real-life people and events. The more 'realistic' working-class women find a show and its characters to be, the more likely it is that they have enjoyed it sufficiently to watch it fairly regularly. Their evaluations of realism, however, seem to reflect their wishes about reality – reality, particularly material reality, as they would like it to be – rather than some more objective assessment of television's truly realistic character. There is a tension between the working-class search for realism in television, and working-class women's desire to use television for escapist purposes, which is also pervasive.

Overall, I found that the less solidly, soberly middle class or upper class are female characters on television, the less likely are working-class women to identify with them. In fact, the few television women showing any signs of dissatisfaction with their societal status, Lucy for example, or the few solidly working-class television women characters, are often loudly denounced by working-class informants for their lack of realism, even though, as in the

Lucy example discussed above, these same characters can serve as feminist, critical figures for middle-class viewers. Middle-class characters, however, whom the television critic might judge to be just as unrealistic as are television's working-class characters, were much more often accepted as realistic by working-class informants. One might say that working-class women define realism, in effect, to mean what they *wish* real life to be, rather than what they experience their own lives to be.

Because the vast majority of television characters are middle-class or upper-class, my study indicates that television seems to support what I call an 'hegemony of middle-class realism' for working-class women, and as such may operate in part to blind working-class women to the realities of their own situation in society. When their experience is addressed directly, as the few working-class images on television begin to do, working-class women are moved to articulate their difference from, and reality apart from, these images. However, because this happens so rarely, American television entertainment in its present form encourages the denial of this experience, or its submergence under an ultimately unrealistic belief in television's idyllic picture of middle-class life.

For middle-class women, however, already living the middle-class material life depicted in the vast majority of television products, television's hegemonic importance rests more in the form of the family, and of women's role within it, which it portrays in the context of middle-class life. With some exceptions, television portrays women, even professional women, who put family duties and responsibilities before those of their jobs or careers, and who seem unconflicted about this choice. However, when television women do express dissatisfaction with their role in the family, as is striking in the case of the *I Love Lucy* show, television can operate counter-hegemonically for female middle class viewers. Many label Lucy to be a strong and determined woman fighting for autonomy in an oppressive marriage. Like Morley (1986), who found that working-class women dislike comic disruptions of domestic order, I too found that working-class women were prevented by the *I Love Lucy* show's comic context from discerning and identifying with the liberated woman which middle-class women found so inspiring.

In sum, there are important differences regarding the way in which television is perceived, experienced, and used between class-differentiated groups of women in the contemporary United States. These differences may relate to broader class differences which may exist. Questions concerning the possibility that social classes and genders in our society occupy different cultures, speak different languages, and are oriented to the world in fundamentally different ways, have all been raised in other contexts in the social scientific study of classes and cultures in contemporary societies.[3] The possibility that differences between groups of women can be traced to class-specific characteristics poses a fundamental challenge to feminists who have argued that women themselves in our society constitute a specific culture (Hacker, 1951) or class (Hartmann and Bridges, 1979). Considerations of class in particular (along with race and ethnicity) have raised serious questions regarding some of the foundations of much of the feminist theory concerning women's status as a social group, ideas which have been central to both academic and political feminists movements in our time.

This study raises the possibility that the categories of class and gender are crucially important for the study of media audiences. In my work I argue that television is a complex medium which bolsters the patriarchal hegemony in class-specific and gender specific ways. Television entertainment can be seen to foster a two-edged hegemony of beliefs and practices, which serve our society's dominant class and gender interests. Much more work on audience reception of television remains to be done before the full contribution of these ideas, both to media theory and to broader questions of feminist theory, can be assessed. I hope that this preliminary work will be useful for future researchers and theorists in both of these fields.

Notes

This paper was first presented at the 1988 International Television Studies Conference. The data presented are culled from a larger study involving interviews with approximately 20 working-class and 20 middle-class women. See Press, *Women Watching Television* (University of Pennsylvania Press, Philadelphia, forthcoming), for a fuller explanation of the methodology of that study.
1. See Press (1987), especially Chapter 2, for a fuller discussion and analysis of the plotlines characteristic of the *I Love Lucy* show. As I demonstrate there, much of the show is characterized by Lucy's struggle against her dominating husband.
2. See my discussion of the difficulty working-class women have in identifying with comic images in my dissertation (Press, 1987), particularly in Chapter 3 which is entitled 'Women's identification with television narrative and characters'.
3. On questions of class culture, see Hyman (1953) and Lewis (1959 and 1966). Regarding differences between working-class and middle-class languages, see Bernstein (1958 and 1966). Schatzman and Strauss (1955), in a dated yet relevant piece, raise the issue of class-specific orientations to thought.

References

Bernstein, Basil (1958) Some sociological determinants of perception. *British Journal of Sociology*, Vol. IX, No. 2, pp. 159–74.
Bernstein, Basil (1966) Elaborated and restricted codes: their social origins and some consequences. In Smith, A. G. (ed.) *Common Culture*, Holt, Rinehart and Winston, New York (first published 1964).
Hacker, Helen (1951) Women as a minority group. *Social Forces*, Vol. 30, pp. 60–9.
Hartman, Heidi and Bridges, Amy (1979) The unhappy marriage of Marxism and feminism: towards a more progressive union. *Capital and Class*, Summer.
Hyman, Herbert (1953) The value systems of different classes. In Bendix, R. and Lipset, S. M. (eds) *Class Status and Power*, Free Press, Glencoe, IL, pp. 426–42.
Lewis, Oscar (1959) *Five Families: Mexican Case Studies in the Culture of Poverty*, Basic Books, New York.
Lewis, Oscar (1966) *La Vida: A Puerto Rican Family in the Culture of Poverty – San Juan and New York*, Random House, New York.
Morley, David (1986) *Family Television*, Comedia, London.
Press, Andrea (1987) Deconstructing the audience: class differences in women's identification with television narrative and characters. Ph.D. thesis, Sociology Department, University of California at Berkeley.
Schatzman, Leonard and Strauss, Anselm (1955) Social class and modes of communication. *American Journal of Sociology*, Vol. LX, No. 4, pp. 329–38.

55

The pleasure machine

Annette Kuhn

From Kuhn, A. (1993) *Women's Pictures: Feminism and Cinema*, Verso, London, pp. 21–43.

In this chapter, I will examine the dominant cinema from two points of view: first in terms of its nature as an economic and social institution, and then in relation to its textual features. Dominant cinema may be defined both as the industrial frameworks surrounding the production, distribution, and exhibition of films for world-wide mass markets, and also as the distinctive characteristics of the films themselves – what they look like and the kinds of readings the construct. Hollywood is usually considered to be the limiting case, the ideal-type, of dominant cinema, although of course the institutions and forms characteristic of dominant cinema are by no means confined to the Hollywood film industry.
[. . .]
　Although the apparatus of dominant cinema acquires its historically specific character from the relationships between its economic and ideological conditions of existence, I will examine these two categories separately, as 'institutions' and 'texts' respectively. It cannot be emphasized too strongly, however, that in concrete situations institutions and texts do not operate in isolation from one another, but are inter-related in any and every specific form taken by dominant cinema. Nevertheless, the conceptual distinction is quite useful for the purpose of dealing with the relationship of feminism and cinema, because it permits a consideration of feminist film practices which focus, implicitly or explicitly, on one rather than the other, as well as practices aimed at transcending and distinction between them.

Institutions

[. . .]
It seems clear, first of all, that film – considered as a complex commodity having certain relationships with structures of production, distribution and exhibition – has become, as a vehicle of representations, relatively marginalized. Audiences in film theatres continue to decline alongside the growth of functional alternatives to this form of cinema – network television producing TV movies, home video and subscriber cable television broadcasting films round the clock. This particular formation of the institutions of dominant cinema, which is frequently regarded as symptomatic of a state of crisis in the film industry, has a number of implications with regard to feminism. Firstly, the rise of small film production

companies on the fringes of institutions of dominant cinema has opened up a space within the purview of dominant cinema for films which may be read as 'feminist': such a space did not exist during the period of ascendancy of the studio system. These films operate broadly within the institutional and textual parameters of dominant cinema, while at the same time appearing to offer alternative representations of women. The situation also has implications for the position of women and feminists working within the industry and for the degree of control which they are able to exert over their own work.

Claudia Weill's film *Girlfriends* (1977) is a significant case in point, in that it highlights some of the contradictions within dominant cinema. The film began as a low-budget ($10,000) independent short, financed by a series of grants, loans and private donations. It then grew, over a production period of several years, into a full-length narrative feature. When it attracted attention at a number of film festivals, Warner Brothers acquired worldwide distribution rights to the film, and it was widely exhibited and favourably received. Weill, whose directorial experience had come from work on documentaries for American public television, was then contracted by Warners to make three more feature films. *Girlfriends* is interesting because, although it was widely read as a feminist film, it constructs a kind of feminism which is in some degree assimilable by the structures of dominant cinema. First, it can be situated within the recent-revived genre of 'women's pictures', and secondly, the fact that it is a feature narrative permits it to be slotted relatively easily into existing structures of distribution and exhibition, while its approach to cinematic narrative is compatible with the textual characteristics of dominant cinema. At the same time, however, the film's conditions of production marginalize it in relation to dominant structures. The history of *Girlfriends* may be understood as marking a crisis over representation, of women and of feminism in particular, within the film industry.

A further set of potential consequences in relation to feminism of changes in the institutional structures of dominant cinema revolves around transformations in the conditions of reception of films. The fact that films can now be viewed not only in the public or semi-public setting of the film theatre, but also in the privacy of the spectator's home, has a variety of consequences. One is that, to the extent that film viewing takes place in private, it is no longer susceptible to the forms of censorship to which public representations may be subject. This immediately raises the question of texts as they intersect with institutions: various institutions for the control and censorship of cinematic representations have, precisely because their domain is 'the public', sought to circumscribe what is representable in cinema. To the extent that institutions of film censorship concern themselves with the nature and the audience of films considered to be 'pornographic', for example, cinematic representations of women are at stake. A change in relations of exchange and reception of films whereby they are increasingly consumed in private may thus open up a space for transformations in certain representations of women. This in turn may operate retroactively on the textual characteristics of certain types of films to generate, for example, changes in the nature of pornographic representations.

Finally, the increasingly privatized conditions of film reception, taken together with changes in relations of production, distribution and exhibition in dominant cinema, suggest that the social characteristics of cinema audiences are themselves likely to be transformed. While, with relatively few exceptions, films are decreasingly being produced for mass general audiences, low-budget independent films are able to address themselves to small audiences with specialized or sectional interests. This has implications for the reading and reception of film texts. The point to be emphasized here is that among these fragmented or specialized cinema audiences are audiences for films of feminist interest. Indeed, certain recent examples of Hollywood (or, like *Girlfriends*, quasi-Hollywood) films may be read as addressing themselves exactly to such audiences. All this may take place largely within dominant cinema, but might none the less be considered in some respects as a challenge to its institutional boundaries.

Texts

There are some core constituents of the dominant cinematic text which pervade all forms of dominant cinema, and indeed – such is their power as ideological constructs – also spill over into a variety of institutionally 'non-dominant' film practices. The textual model for dominant cinema is the 'classic realist text', in relation to film sometimes called the classic Hollywood text, classic cinema, or classic Hollywood cinema. I take all these terms to refer to a type of film text organized around both a certain kind of narrative structure, and a specific discourse or set of signifiers, which become the vehicle of the narrative, the means by which the story is told. It should be emphasized that this set of textual operations is not confined to films made in Hollywood. However, Hollywood films, and in particular the products of the studio system of the 1930s and 1940s, may again be regarded as ideal-typical. I shall examine in turn narrative structure and narrative discourse, at this stage simply signalling a number of points which are of relevance to the question of cinema and feminism.
[. . .]
  Structural analysis can be applied to various forms of narrative expression, and the method provides a useful point of entry to the narratives of individual films. For example, a breakdown of the plot of *Mildred Pierce* (Curtiz, Warner Brothers, 1945) can be instrumental in untangling the somewhat complex inter-relationship between story and plot in this film. The film's story follows, more or less, the story in the novel by James Cain on which the film is based. It concerns the rise to wealth of an 'independent' woman who parts from her husband, opens up a successful restaurant business, and has an affair with a millionaire playboy. The woman, Mildred Pierce, has two daughters, with one of whom she has an almost incestuously close relationship that ends in the downfall of both of them. The film's plot reverses the story order by setting up as its narrative disruption the central element in the heroine's downfall – the murder of her lover. The task of the plot of the film, as against that of the novel, is to solve the murder. The story is told in three flashbacks which relate events leading up to the murder: it is this which makes for the complexity of the film's plot–story relationship. A breakdown or segmentation of the plot of *Mildred Pierce* based

on the film's articulation of narrative time is given in Figure 55.1. The first segment sets up the villainy – a murder – which it is one of the tasks of the narrative to explain and solve. The plot may be regarded as a series of retardation devices which function to delay the solution until the penultimate segment, when the 'truth' is revealed by the detective and the murder solved. The second segment constructs a further enigma, this time in the form of a lack centring on Mildred's relationship with her husband: the lack is liquidated in the final segment, when the two are reunited. These resolutions constitute a final equilibrium and permit narrative closure at the levels of both plot and story. The complex relationship of plot and story in this film turns on its peculiar manipulation of temporal order, such that the end of the story becomes the beginning of the plot, which then moves in and out of various levels of narrative time. This is effected by the film's juxtaposition of flashbacks from different narrative view points (Mildred's and the detective's) with sequences in the film's narrative present. A breakdown of narrative structure along these lines may clear the way for further textual analysis, as is demonstrated by feminist readings of *Mildred Pierce* itself (Cook, 1978; Nelson, 1977).

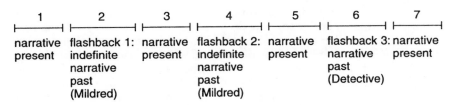

1. The murder. Mildred is found on the beach and taken to police station.
2. Mildred tells detective events in her past.
3. Detective interrupts.
4. Mildred proceeds with her story.
5. Mildred's daughter is brought into police station.
6. The 'truth' is revealed by the detective and the murder solved.
7. Mildred leaves police station with her former husband.

Figure 55.1. *Mildred Pierce*: a segmentation of the plot.

Another procedure for a structural analysis of narratives involves isolating the basic units, or moves, of the story – the 'functions' of the narrative. In the relatively simple case of the fairy tale, Propp deals with only one type of function, which he defines largely in terms of narrative action. Since narrative function is regarded as 'an act of a character defined from the point of view of its significance for the course of the action' (Propp, 1968, p. 21), characters in fairy tales are seen simply as vehicles for narrative action, or agents. Analyses of narrative forms have elaborated on Propp's model by putting forward other kinds of function. Barthes, for example, has added three groups of functions to Propp's in order to account for data relating, for example, to the spatial location of the narrative and to characters in the story (Barthes, 1977).

The notion of character is in fact crucial to any consideration of the classic realist text, cinematic or otherwise. While the classic realist text may mobilize elements of story and plot and produce enigmas and resolutions in the ways I have described, it derives its specificity from its articulation of character as a narrative function. In the classic realist text, action typically pivots on central characters who are rendered in psychological depth and tend to become objects of identification for readers. These characters are fictional persons whose fate is tied up with the progress of the narrative, indeed on whom may be centred the very disruption that sets the narrative in motion. For example, the second sequence of *Mildred Pierce* shows the heroine in a series of close-ups and medium close-ups: this immediately signals the centrality of the Mildred character to the film's narrative. Because a sequence showing a murder has immediately preceded these shots of Mildred, the villainy becomes linked with the figure of the heroine, and her fate tied up with the solution of the crime. In classic Hollywood cinema, character and action are typically intertwined in this way. To the extent that, as in *Mildred Pierce*, the central character is female, we may consider how 'woman' as a structure or narrative function operates within the textual organization of certain types of film. Is it possible, for example, to isolate recurrent or typical narrative functions or interactions of character and narrative action in dominant cinema, and if so, how do these relate specifically to 'woman'?

There are a number of possible approaches to this question. The one which perhaps presents itself most immediately, and which was in fact adopted early on in feminist critical work on dominant cinema, actually departs from the premises of structural analysis in being inductive rather than deductive (in induction, general conclusions are drawn from particular cases). An inductive approach ideally demands a thoroughgoing empirical critical method, which is exemplified to some extent by Molly Haskell's historical/critical survey *From Reference to Rape* (Haskell, 1975). Haskell deals largely with changes over time in the images and roles of female figures in Hollywood films, from the vamp of the 1920s to the victim of male violence of the 1960s and 1970s. She then relates these stereotypes to female 'star' images in each of the periods in question. Her method is basically a descriptive survey of a large number of films, with some general inductive conclusions. In Haskell's analysis, cinematic representations of women tend to be perceived in terms of roles, stereotypes or images, a perspective which is often accompanied by the assumption that there is some direct or reflective relationship between these representations and the social formation of which they are part. A structural approach to narrative, on the other hand, starts out with a rather hermetic view of the film text, focusing in the first instance on its internal structures. It is deductive in the sense that it advances a general model of underlying narrative structures and suggests ways in which particular narratives may be read as expressing or articulating their ground rules. These rules are both logically prior to the innumerable narratives existing in the world and also not open to immediate observation. It is clear, then, that a structural approach to the study of narratives does not necessarily demand an empirical methodology, at least in a positive sense. It may be considered sufficient, for example, to examine a single narrative in terms of its expression of underlying structures, for the structures themselves are seen as manifest only in their operation in actual narratives.

The point at issue here is that any structural approach to the analysis of 'woman' in narratives is faced with a model of woman that departs from the one characteristic of inductive approaches to film narratives. No longer is 'woman' regarded as a concrete gendered human being who happens to exist on the cinema screen rather than in 'real' life: 'she' becomes, on the contrary, a structure governing the organization of story and plot in a narrative or group of narratives. The ways in which a 'woman-structure' activates narratives must clearly be related in some way to the wider question of the position of women in the society which produces the narrative, but in a structural model a simple relationship of reflection cannot be assumed. The question of how the woman-structure informs cinematic narratives may be re-phrased, then, within the terms of structural analysis, by asking whether there are any recurrent structures of enigma-resolution, of movement of plot from disrupted beginning equilibrium to resolution, associated with woman as a narrative function. Such a question calls for inductive and empirical study of films as well as for analysis of individual narratives on the deductive model.

A project which opens up this area of study has been undertaken by Mary Beth Haralovich, who has analysed ten randomly-sampled Warner Brothers films of the 1930s and 1940s. Within the terms of an explanatory model which takes in the narrative structures of the films, the roles of their women characters, and the place of the films within their immediate institutional and broader historical contexts, Haralovich has concluded that narrative closure is always dependent on the resolution of enigmas centring on heterosexual courtship:

> If a woman is in a non-normative role in economic control and production, she will cede that control to a man by the end of the film. Romantic love seems to be the normative role which most strongly influences her decision (Haralovich, 1979, p. 13).

Not only, then, is woman recuperated into the male/female bond by the closures of these films (Dalton, 1972), but the courtship process itself constitutes a structuring element of their entire narratives.

There seems, therefore, to be a tendency on the part of the classic Hollywood narrative to recuperate woman. Moreover, it is often woman – as structure, character, or both – who constitutes the motivator of the narrative, the 'trouble' that sets the plot in motion. In *Mildred Pierce*, for example, the narrative's reconstruction of Mildred's life is a prior condition of the detective's access to the truth of the matter, and thus to the solution of the murder. In this way, the film's resolution depends on the resolution of the particular 'woman-question' set up by its narrative: woman may thus have to be returned to her place so that order is restored to the world. In classic Hollywood cinema, this recuperation manifests itself thematically in a limited number of ways: a woman character may be restored to the family by falling in love, by 'getting her man', by getting married, or otherwise accepting a 'normative' female role. If not, she may be directly punished for her narrative and social transgression by exclusion, outlawing or even death. In *Mildred Pierce*, both forms of resolution of the woman-question are at work. Mildred is restored to the family in the film's final sequence by being reunited with her former husband. Her daughter, on the other hand, is punished for transgressing the law: not only by having committed the crime of murder, but also through the unbridled and quasi-incestuous sexuality (she sleeps with her mother's lover) which is the unspoken narrative motivation for the actual act of murder.

Fortunately for feminists, things are not always so clear cut in dominant cinema. Perhaps the only thing that can be concluded with any degree of certainty is that, structurally and thematically, the classic Hollywood narrative attempts to recuperate woman to a 'proper place'. This attempt may not always be completely successful, though, particularly in cases where the narrative sets up questions that cannot be contained by any form of closure. Such excess of narrative disruption over resolution has been seen as signalling Hollywood's intermittent failure to contain woman within the confines of the classic narrative structure. An interesting case of persistent narrative excess in Hollywood cinema is exemplified by the film noir genre of the 1940s. In films noirs, whose narratives are typically structured around crime and its investigation by a detective figure, it is very common for a woman character to be set up as an additional mystery demanding solution, a mystery independent of the crime enigma (Kaplan, 1978). In many film noirs, in fact, the focus of the story may shift between the solution of crimes and the solution of the woman-question. However, if only because of the way in which enigmas are constituted in film noirs, there is a tendency to narrative excess in-built in the genre. This excess often centres precisely on the inability of the narrative to cope fully with the woman-question. As a genre, film noir is, historically speaking, very much a part of dominant cinema and yet at the same time it contains the potential, within its own characteristic narrative structure, to subvert the textual organization of dominant cinema. This internal contradiction is a point at which are directed a number of feminist readings of films. These readings are aimed exactly at exposing some of the ideological operations and contradictions embedded in the textual practices of dominant cinema.

So far, I have been considering the textual characteristics of dominant cinema in relation exclusively to narrative structures. Much of what I have said could therefore be applied not only to cinema but to all narrative forms of expression. My discussion has not yet touched on cinematic discourse – the ways in which stories are told through film as opposed, say, to the novel. Is it possible to identify modes of discourse intrinsic to dominant cinema? It is commonly accepted that across all its forms of expression, the classic realist text is marked by a denial of its own operation in the signification process, in that the discourse seems to be nothing more than the vehicle of telling the story (MacCabe, 1974). The point here is that all narrative discourse does produce meaning in and by itself, and does therefore constitute a form of address to its recipients, but one of the defining features of the classic realist text is that its recipients are not normally aware that this is taking place.

In any consideration of the textual characteristics of dominant cinema, then, an important question must be: how do signifiers in cinema produce meanings, and how does this work specifically in relation to narrative meanings? To answer these questions, it is necessary to penetrate the surface transparency of classic narrative discourse. Signifiers in film texts may or may not be specific to cinema: cinema mobilizes some vehicles of meaning production, or codes – written and spoken language, for instance – which also operate in other narrative forms of expression, as well as some – such as editing – that operate exclusively, or virtually so, in cinema. All films create meanings through the articulation of their signifiers, and each narrative film creates its own meanings through a particular configuration of signifiers, some of which are cinematically specific (Heath, 1973; Metz, 1974). According to this argument, classic Hollywood cinema produces narrative as it produces meanings – that is, it produces narrative meanings. Not only, then, is meaning conterminous with narrative meaning in this form of cinema, meaning also presents itself as transparent, as 'already there' in the story, rather than as the outcome of active processes of signification. In dominant cinema, it might be said, signifiers work unobtrusively in the service of the narrative. How does this operate in actual films? In dealing with this question, I will consider four sets of codes: the photographic image, *mise en scène*, mobile framing, and editing. I will argue firstly that the operations of these codes in dominant cinema are historically specific and contingent, and secondly that they construct modes of address which draw spectators into film narratives by making the reading of film texts seem effortless.

Cinema uses the technologies of cinematography as a basis for its own practices of meaning production. As such, while it draws on some of the codes of still photography, the cinematographic image also possesses codes of its own. Moreover, further codes are associated with narrative discourse in cinema. Among the signifying features of the cinematographic image is framing: long shots, medium shots and close-ups, for example, generate their own meanings. A cut-in close-up, for instance, can emphasize detail which may be read as having some significance within the narrative. Close-ups very commonly also operate in relation to characterization: close-ups of players' faces became increasingly common in Hollywood films of the 1920s and after as a means of conveying the emotions of characters. To the extent that close-ups are most commonly of central characters in film narratives, they may function to constitute that psychological realism of character which is a mark of the classic narrative.

Mise en scène is a term employed in theatre to designate the contents of the stage and their arrangement. In cinema, however, the reference is rather to the content of the film frame, including the arrangement of the profilmic event, of everything, that is, which is in front of the camera – settings, costumes and props. *Mise en scène* also refers more broadly to what the spectator actually sees on the screen – the composition of the image and the nature of movement within the frame. As an element of *mise en scène*, composition of the cinematic image, for example, may produce narrative meanings relating to the spatial location of the story. Movement within the frame, particularly the movements of players, can also have narrative functions in relation to characterization. In any one film, *mise en scène* will work in conjunction with other codes to produce narrative meanings. In a scene from Howard Hawks' film noir, *The Big Sleep* (Warner Brothers, 1946), for example, the signifying effects of within-frame movements of the hero, Philip Marlowe, around the house of the film's first murder victim, Arthur Geiger, in the course of the detective's search for clues, combine with the effects of camera movement and editing to establish the series of disruptions and enigmas which structure the narrative of the first part of the film (Kuhn, 1981). Mobile framing – the effect of zooming and of camera movements of different kinds (Bordwell and Thompson, 1979, p. 121) – can also produce narrative meaning in a variety of ways. For instance, in zoom-in, like a cut-in close-up, can emphasize detail which may then be read in context as bearing particular significance within the narrative. Camera movement may operate simply to move the plot along, as in the case of the series of pans and tracking shots which orchestrate Marlowe's movements around Geiger's house in his search for clues to Geiger's murder.

Finally, the question of the forms of editing developed and privileged in classic Hollywood cinema is of the utmost importance to any consideration of the textual operations of dominant cinema and their construction of narrative meaning. The term editing refers basically to the practice of splicing together pieces of film. Nevertheless, editing may be performed according to various principles. Dominant cinema, however, has institutionalized a highly specific set of rules for film editing, and the mobilization of these rules has important consequences for cinematic signification. Continuity editing, as this set of conventions is called, was not firmly established in Hollywood itself until the early 1920s, but it is the culmination of a series of experiments with the cinematic rendering of narratives which began in the earliest years of cinema. The rules of continuity editing are written up in manuals of film technique and are invariably represented to learning film makers as the only possible approach to editing. The explicit objective of the continuity system is to construct – by ensuring that cuts are as unobtrusive to the spectator as possible – the appearance of a seamless and coherent narrative space and time. The effect of this is to make cinematic discourse – the process of meaning production – invisible. Each of the rules of continuity editing functions to this end (Bordwell and Thompson, 1979, p. 163; Reisz and Millar, 1973). In narrative cinema, an apparently coherent fictional world is produced which carries with it the 'impression of reality'. Spectators are thus drawn effortlessly into a narrative which seems to unfold before them as a series of already-constituted meanings. At the same time, the invisible ellipses of space and time brought about by continuity editing move the story along, keeping the plot on track towards its resolution.

The question of the woman-structure in the textual organization of classic narrative cinema may now be raised in relation to he specific question of cinematic signification. What, then, is the relationship between 'woman' and narrative discourse in dominant cinema? This begs two further questions: in what sense may 'woman' be regarded as a signifier in cinema? And what kind of relationship of reading might a notion of 'woman' as signifier suggest? Much of the discussion in the present chapter concerning the textual characteristics of dominant cinema may, because of its emphasis on the internal features of film texts, seem overly formalistic. However, despite the fact that analytical work on film texts may be justified to the degree that it sheds light on the ideological operation of dominant cinema, it is important to remember that texts do not function independently of their institutional conditions of existence. Texts are part of the cinematic apparatus, and the cinematic apparatus is also constituted by the contexts within which the film texts are received. What a discussion of cinematic codes and narrative structures in dominant cinema suggests is that the point at which cinematic discourse departs from non-cinematic discourse rests precisely in its address, in the ways it speaks to and is received by spectators. Cinematic address operates visually and through time: the pictures we see are moving pictures.

References

Barthes, Roland (1977) Introduction to the structural analysis of narratives. In *Image-Music-Text*, Fontana, London.

Bordwell, David and Thompson, Kristin (1979) *Film Art: An Introduction*, Addison-Wesley, Reading, MA.

Cook, Pam (1978) Duplicity in *Mildred Pierce*. In Kaplan, E. Ann (ed.) pp. 68–82.

Dalton, Elizabeth (1972) Women at work: Warners in the thirties. *Velvet Light Trap*, No. 6, pp. 15–20.

Haralovich, Mary Beth (1979) Woman's proper place: defining gender roles in film and history. Unpublished paper for an independent study with Professor Jeanne Allen, University of Wisconsin-Madison.

Haskell, Molly (1975) *From Reverence to Rape: the Treatment of Women in the Movies*, New English Library, London.

Heath, Stephen (1973) The work of Christian Metz. *Screen*, Vol. 14, No. 3, pp. 5–29.

Kaplan, E. Ann (ed.) (1978) *Women in Film Noir*, British Film Institute, London.

Kuhn, Annette (1981) *The Big Sleep*: a disturbance in the sphere of sexuality. *Wide Angle*, Vol. 4, No. 3, pp. 4–11.

MacCabe, Colin (1974) Realism and the cinema: notes on some Brechtian theses. *Screen*, Vol. 15, No. 2, pp. 7–27.

Metz, Christian (1974) *Language and Cinema*, Mouton, The Hague.

Nelson, Joyce (1977) *Mildred Pierce* reconsidered. *Film Reader*, No. 2, pp. 65–70.

Propp, Vladimir (1968) *Morphology of the Folktale*, University of Texas Press, Austin.

Reisz, Karel and Millar, Gavin (1973) *The Technique of Film Editing*, Hastings House, New York.

Section 9

Moving image

56

Analysing the moving image

Chris Newbold

The extracts in this section are concerned with the two most pervasive areas of moving image theory. If it can be said that all moving image output can be understood and classified by genre, then equally it can be said that all are structured by narratives. For this reason genre and narrative study are an expanding area of mass communication, media and cultural studies. But like all terms derived from literary criticism their description and usage are much argued and debated over. This section aims to clarify and illustrate the major areas of engagement.

Moving image is here used to describe all products of the film, television and video industries. It is not intended to preclude the analysis of the still image nor indeed the written word; however, the phrase 'moving image' encourages us to focus on those media which, arguably, represent the richest cocktail of symbolic forms of communication and which can call upon the widest range of human senses, but especially those of sight and hearing.

Both areas of study have a long history, emerging from literary criticism and developing from analysis of the nineteenth century novel. But genre exists in all art forms to some extent. It emerged in film theory as a major force with articles published by people such as Warshow (1948, 1954) and from a growing dissatisfaction with the Auteur theory in film analysis. This theory tended to privilege the director as sole artistic creator of meaning for the audience through the text, whereas genre critics argue that meaning is essentially 'inter-textual' and relies on audience experience and knowledge of previous genre products. Genre critics recognize that films are watched within the context of other films, and of other media products such as novels, radio programmes and even advertising. The word itself is taken to mean type or kind, and is used in moving image analysis as a means of understanding the set of principles by which we associate one film, television or video product with others of its like, that is, how moving image products relate to each other, and what they have in common. Thus we talk of thrillers, Westerns, horror, soap operas, news and even music videos. Ultimately genre study is not about realism – moving image genre products are not an imitation of real life, but, rather, their reference points are to other moving image and indeed non-moving image products, and understanding them is about understanding the relationships between texts.

Genre study itself is based largely on description and classification, and is to a considerable extent dependent on a sophisticated application of researchers' own reading. Thus the genre debates discussed in this section illustrate the various attempts to classify and establish genres. Although much of the discussion in this section is textually based, it is also important to take into account the tripartite relationship that exists between industry, audience and genre. Genre or 'formula' products are largely generated by the industry as and when there is perceived to be a demand for them from the audience, Thomas Schatz (1981) develops this argument with particular reference to Hollywood cinema. This approach represents one of the three main strands of genre study namely, the *ritual* approach which is concerned with genre as an exchange between industry and audience. The other two approaches are the *ideological* or structural approach, concerned with the way genre products reflect and reproduce the myths, meanings and values of society, and the *aesthetic* approach dealing with the creativity and artistic values inherent in genre products.

Although in this section the extracts tend to discuss genre and narrative in moving image as separate components or features of texts, it will become apparent that there are many connections between the two, for instance, narrative structures are of key importance in understanding genre and generic patterns.

The first extract by Will Wright illustrates this use of narrative and genre analysis but also draws on other critical methods to create a structural study of the Western. Much of the literature on moving image genre, especially film genre tends to consist of studies of American 'Western' films. This reflects the enduring influence and potential for universality of that particular genre. For examples of this and also of the influence of sociological and structuralist thought in Western genre analysis see Cawelti (1984) and Kitses (1969).

Wright discusses Lévi-Strauss' notion of myth and in particular the operation of binary oppositions to understand the way in which the Western is structured to symbolically represent the American value or belief system. Combined with this is an application of Vladimir Propp's analysis of the structure of folk tales to Western films and their myths. In line with Lévi-Strauss, myths here are taken to be the means by which society organizes itself and symbolically comes to terms with faults or problems that arise, thus maintaining its value consensus. Narrative structures and binary oppositions have their place in this, hence the victory of good over evil, civilization over wilderness and the law over lawlessness.

The extract from Solomon takes issue with this style of approach, foregrounding instead qualitative distinctions and artistic achievement. Genre study for Solomon should be seen in terms of the traditional aesthetic values that are applied to other works of art. He is particularly critical of formula studies and cultural approaches, in particular their preoccupation with categories and their insistence on the sociological significance of the repetition in films of certain formulas. Genre analysis for Solomon is about the way in which categories illuminate particular films.

Neale in the third extract updates his classic (1980) text and considers the development of approaches to genre throughout the 1980s. Specifically he talks about the role of the spectator, bringing in the audience dimension of the tripartite system mentioned earlier. Here notions of expectations and pleasure figure highly in genre analysis. This is the direction of much recent work in the area, particularly on women's genre preferences and viewing.

Indeed, this extract shows how vibrant the area of genre study still is, feeding as it does into cultural studies, feminist studies and audience research.

Genre, as discussed in the above extracts, directs our expectations of how narratives might work given particular sets of information enshrined in images, icons and *mise-en-scène*. The connection between narrative study and genre study is inevitably interwoven through the formal analysis of the text and with the audiences' understanding of it. Narrative can be seen as the devices and strategies, the conventions and sequencing of events with characterization, which constitutes a story, be it fictional or factual. It is undoubtedly the case that story telling is a basic human need, the world comes to us in the form of stories, and language itself is narrativized, that is sentence construction syntactics has much in common with the narrative structure of stories.

It is this commonality of narrative in human experience that drew Propp to examine the folk tale origins of stories and to establish the similarities in the structures of stories from one culture to another. The extract from Propp focuses on his method and the identification of functions as the basic units of narratives which are organized into the sequential development of plot. Propp argues that there is an underlying plot structure to the one hundred Russian folk tales which he analyses, regardless of their overt subject matter. As we saw in the extract from Wright, Propp's work on deep narrative structure and plot paradigms has been developed in much structuralist work.

The extract from Chatman takes Propp's analysis as a starting point and considers it in terms of the complexity of modern narratives. Undoubtedly, modern narrative theory in moving image analysis has been dominated by the classic realist text or the Hollywood narrative structure, that is, one where the logical sequence of events dominates and subordinates all actions, time and space to narrative cause and effect and the resolution of enigmas posed during the film. Chatman grounds this style of narrative and its analysis in literary theory, and considers narrative as a semiotic structure with a substance and a form, but as a form of communication it must also have a sender and a receiver. Bordwell is also interested in the spectator and the process of narrative comprehension; this he pursues by connecting two particular attributes of narrative, one the *fabula*, is the construct of the narrative or story we create in our minds, the other, the *syuzhet* composes the pattern of events or plot. The *syuzhet* is crucial in that its style of presentation will affect audience construction of the *fabula*; if too much information is provided then the fabula will be confused, or if to little it will be difficult to construct.

The consideration of narrative in these two extracts and the majority of narrative theory is one that largely derives from the understanding of narrative as a chain of events in a cause and effect relationship, based on the resolution of a central narrative. This owes much to the work of Lévi-Strauss (1967), Barthes (1974, 1977) and particularly Todorov (1975) who is concerned with movement in the text from a state of equilibrium, through disruption to action and then to a new equilibrium. It is this structure common to literary narratives and films that Feuer in the last extract, considers to be inappropriate when examining the more open ended textual operation of television, especially in episodic series and the genres of situation comedy and soap opera.

References and further reading

Barthes, R. (1974) *S/Z*, Jonathan Cape.

Barthes, R. (1977) *Image-Music-Text*, Fontana.

Berger, A. A. (1992) *Popular Culture Genres: Theories and Texts*, Sage.

Bordwell, D. and Thompson, K. (1993) Narrative as a formal system. In *Film Art: An Introduction*, 4th edn, McGraw-Hill, Chapter 3.

Cawelti, J. G. (1984) *The Six-gun Mystique*, Bowling Green State University Popular Press.

Cook, P. (1985) *The Cinema Book*, British Film Institute, London.

Fisk, J. (1987) Narrative. In *Television Culture*, Methuen.

Grant, B. K. (ed.) (1986) *Film Genre Reader*, University of Texas Press.

Kitses, J. (1969) *Horizons West*, Thames and Hudson.

Kozloff, S. (1992) Narrative theory and television. In Allen, R. C. (ed.) *Channels of Discourse, Reassembled*, 2nd edn, Routledge.

Lévi-Strauss, C. (1967) *The Structural Study of Myth*, Routledge & Kegan Paul.

Neale, S. (1980) *Genre* British Film Institute, London.

Schatz, T. (1981) *Hollywood Genre Formulas, Filmmaking and the Studio System*, Random House, New York.

Todorov, T. (1975) *The Fantastic*, Cornell University Press.

Turner, G. (1993) *Film as Social Practice*, 2nd edn, Routledge.

Warshow, R. (1948) The gangster as tragic hero. In *Partisan Review*, February.

Warshow, R. (1954) Movie chronicle: the westerner. In *Partisan Review*, March–April.

57

Myth and meaning

Will Wright

From Wright, W. (1975) *Six Guns and Society: A Structural Study of the Western*, University of California Press, Berkeley, CA, pp. 185–94.

Lévi-Strauss argues that tribal myths are cognitive rather than emotional attempts to classify and understand the world; and Kenneth Burke takes a similar approach to works of literature in modern societies. In this study, I have argued that the Western is a myth of contemporary American society. As such, it contains a conceptual analysis of society that provides a model of social action. This is an unusual argument for two reasons. First, most anthropologists – including Lévi-Strauss – as well as most literary critics have tacitly agreed that primitive societies have myths whereas modern societies have history and literature. Myth is viewed either as a non-historical (i.e. primitive) form of history and philosophy (Lévi-Strauss and Malinowski), or as a patterning of archetypes (gods, origins, revolutions) that writers appropriate and manipulate to create great works of literature (Northrop Frye and Leslie Fiedler). In either case, the agreement is that modern societies do not have myths in the sense of popular stories that serve to locate and interpret social experience. They may have folktales and legends, but they have history and science to explain origins and nature and literature to express the archetypes of the collective unconscious. They don't need myths. On the other hand, I have assumed that modern America does have myths in the sense of popular stories and that the Western is one. Its function is similar to that of myths in other societies.

While Lévi-Strauss, Burke, and others have stressed the conceptual dimension of myths and literature, their function as a paradigm or model of social action has been more or less unnoticed. In most analyses, the primary interest has been in the social symbolism of the myth rather than in the movement of the story, the conflicts and resolutions of the plot. The narrative aspect of myth has been taken for granted as a necessary framework for the expression of the symbolism, not particularly interesting in itself; like the stadium for a football game, it is useful for the game but does not need to be included in the commentary. By stressing the narrative structure of the Western, I have tried to show that it is through the narrative action that the conceptual symbolism of the Western, or any myth, is understood and applied by its hearers (or viewers). Thus, the analogy should be to the rules, not the stadium, of the football game; for the narrative structure constitutes the myth just as the rules constitute the game. There can be different rules (or symbols), but without the rules there is no game. And this is the second reason why my argument is unusual.

The narrative structure is determined by the requirements of the narrative sequence – a beginning and ending description of one situation with a middle statement that explains a change in that situation. It is through the logic of this sequence that a narrative 'makes sense', tells a story rather than giving a list of events. More specifically, the narrative sequence provides the rules by which characters are created and the conflicts are resolved in a story. When the story is a myth and the characters represent social types or principles in a structure of oppositions, then the narrative structure offers a model of social action by presenting identifiable social types and showing how they interact. The receivers of the myth learn how to act by recognizing their own situation in it and observing how it is resolved.

If they are to recognize their own situation, the narrative structure must reflect the social relationships necessitated by the basic institutions within which they live. As the institutions change because of technology, war, migration, or depression, so the narrative structure of the myth must change. The social types symbolized by the oppositional structure will generally remain the same, since they are fundamental to the society's understanding of itself; but the conceptual relationships between those types will change as the real relationships between people change with the institutions of the society. Thus, it is in the narrative structure that the relationship between a myth and its society is most apparent, and it is because they have generally ignored the narrative dimension that most commentators on myths have interpreted them as revealing universal archetypes, biological traumas, or mental structures rather than as conceptual models of social action for everyday life.

[. . .]

The Western has presented a series of models of relevant social action in the context of economic institutions. All myths fulfil this function for their societies, and therefore the Western, though located in a modern industrial society, is as much a myth as the tribal myths of the anthropologists. Lévi-Strauss (and others) would disagree with this, on the general argument that tribal myths provide a society with a unique, synthetic pattern of thought through which the society explains its relationship to history and to nature. On the other hand modern societies are seen to have an analytic mode of thought which we express in history and science, and therefore in the same sense as tribal societies. It is true that both tribal myths and our myths, including the Western, are about the past, we have history to explain the past, whereas tribal societies do not. For them life is cyclical; the past, except for the mythical past, is like the present, a recurring cycle of seasons and rituals. For us, the past is history; it is necessarily different from the present.

But for this very reason, history is not enough: it can explain the present in terms of the past, but it cannot provide an indication of how to act in the present based on the past, since by definition the past is categorically different from the present. Myths however can use the setting of the past to create and resolve the conflicts of the present. Myths use the past to tell us how to act in the present. In tribal societies, since the mythical past is the only past worth knowing, myths can stand for history. In our society they cannot, but they can fulfil a major function, which is to present a model of social action based upon a mythical interpretation of the past.

One consequence of this mythical use of the past as a model for the present is that the setting of the past becomes relevant to the present in an unusual way. The elements of this setting may no longer be practically useful or important, but through the myth they become conceptually important and take on meanings that have little if any relation to actual meanings associated with the setting as it was experienced in the past. In more concrete terms, some aspects of the American West in the late nineteenth century have become quite significant in modern America, but for reasons that are clearly different from the reasons for their actual significance in the historical West. One obvious case is clothes. Western attire is perennially popular and makes periodic forays into the 'mod' look for both men and women.

[. . .]

Why does the wilderness mean so much in the context of modern American society? [. . .] While other societies reaffirm themselves through religious rituals and traditional observances, we seem to accomplish this, at least in part, through a return to faith in the land of the West.

In fact, it seems this land has become our tradition – a tradition based not on the West itself but on the myth of the West. The meanings of this tradition are to be found in the Western, particularly in the Western film, where the land's natural beauty is photographed with magnificent significance by such masters as John Ford, Anthony Mann, and John Sturges. In these films, the wilderness/civilization opposition establishes associations with the land that we can then experience in our own contact with it. As we have seen, the land is the hero's source of strength, both physical and moral; he is an independent and autonomous individual *because* he is part of the land. The strength that makes him unique and necessary to society and the beauty that makes him desirable to the girl are human counterparts to the strength and beauty of the wilderness. Moreover, the weakness of society and the villainy of the villains stem from their ignorance of the wilderness and their identification with the trappings of civilization. Thus, the man who accepts the wilderness, believes in it, and communes with it is stronger than civilization and capable of making it into something worthwhile. All the characters outside of society, good and bad, are identified with the land. Here is where freedom, independence, and strength lie as opposed to the cowardice, stupidity, greed, and conformity of society. Respect, friendship, and love are available to people who associate with the land, who may work in or for society (*Rio Bravo, The Professionals, True Grit, The War Wagon*) but whose under standing and comfort derive from the wilderness.

In the mythical context, it is clear how the land that embodies such meanings can become a fount of social values. Individuality, respect, acceptance, strength, freedom, and goodness are all associated with and therefore derived from the mountains and deserts, lakes and streams of the West. The Western myth has taken the historical setting and shaped it into a model of the present, which states in concrete images the conceptual conflicts of modern America and resolves them through types of action. The Western land, particularly the visual images of its landscape, is an integral part of the understanding and resolution of these conflicts; if the myth is to succeed as a myth, the land must take on these meanings. To the extent that the myth succeeds in making the past like the present, it also makes the present *like* the myth of the past. If the myth of the past is to provide a model for action in the present, then relevant aspects of the present must take on the meanings of that myth. In our association of historical landscape with mythical meanings, we are remarkably similar to primitive societies. [. . .]

One more problem remains to be discussed. Why myths? What properties do myths possess that make them capable of fulfilling the conceptual functions I have described – signifying social differences necessitated by institutional contradictions and establishing possibilities of reconciliation based upon models of interaction? I have tried to show the relation between myths and society by arguing that myths reconcile deep social conflicts through models of action; myths do this through their binary structure of images and their narrative structure of action. But I have not shown why myths satisfy these conceptual needs. This is essentially a psychological question – what is the relation between myths and the mind? – whereas my interest has been primarily social. This question is the central concern of Lévi-Strauss, who feels that anthropology, properly done, is a branch of psychology and that myths in particular are especially revealing of the properties of the human mind. His answer to the question is that myths reproduce and manifest the structure of the mind; therefore, they have meaning to the mind through their formal structure alone, a meaning which logically precedes any socially determined meanings this structure might contain. Myths can reconcile, or at least make understandable, the conceptual contradictions in a society because these concepts are embodied in a structure that communicates directly with the mind. Lévi-Strauss concludes his argument that each myth is a matrix of meanings in which both meanings and matrix refer to other meanings and matrices as follows:

> And if it is now asked to what final meanings these mutually significative meanings are referring – since in the last resort and in their totality they must refer to something – the only reply to emerge from this study is that myths signify the mind that evolves them by making use of the world of which it is itself a part. Thus, there is simultaneous production of myths themselves, by the mind that generates them and, by the myths, of an image of the world which is already inherent in the structure of the mind (Lévi-Strauss, 1969, p. 341).

If the 'structure of the mind' means biological structure, as it sometimes seems to, then the argument is a definition, since Lévi-Strauss produces no independent evidence of biological structure. On the other hand, if it means the structure of symbolic consciousness, then I am in agreement with the analysis, except that it no longer explains the unique role of myth since this structure would be shared by all forms of symbolic communication – language, literature, conversation, and so forth.

I would like to suggest another interpretation of the special place of myth in the process of human consciousness, which is at least as plausible as the 'structure of the mind' notion of Lévi-Strauss. My interpretation stresses the one aspect of myths that is most responsible for their popularity, which Lévi-Strauss chooses to ignore systematically – their nature as stories or narratives. Rather than asking 'why myths?', let us ask 'why stories?'. Stories appear in every human society: this is a universal social fact that is well known yet does not arouse the speculative interest and respect accorded such solid and dignified universals as the incest taboo and kinship structures. Stories are entertaining, and this generally suffices as an explanation of the form. The particular content of a story may be sociologically significant, but the form itself is rarely, if ever, considered problematic. Stories (myths) relieve boredom, permit escape, relate custom and history, enrich experience, reinforce values, relieve psychological conflict, produce social cohesion, create social conflicts (Leach), strengthen status demands, teach children violence; but all these alleged functions of stories are performed by their content. What is it about the form itself that gives stories this remarkable ability to accomplish such varied tasks? What is the relation between narrative and consciousness?

I cannot answer this question, but I can suggest a direction in which an answer might lie. Narratives explain change; they have a beginning, middle, and end. A narrative is a temporal account of a sequence of events related by similarity of topic and by a relationship of explanation, or causality. These properties make possible the analysis of narrative structure that we have utilized in our theory of myth and in our study of the Western. There is also another very important aspect of narrative which we have not sufficiently considered. In a story, everything is important, all the actions and events are meaningful with respect to the unifying topic. To one degree or another all stories reconstruct events based upon the actual, possible, or desirable experiences of life. Yet all stories share a basic difference from life: every event experienced in a narrative is relevant to the success or failure of its actors, whereas many, if not most, of the events experienced by an individual in life are not at all relevant to his success or failure. Events in life must be *interpreted* as significant, events in narratives are *inherently* significant. In a story, if someone is late for an appointment, either something *has* happened or *will* happen as a result, or it gives an insight into the character important for an understanding of the conclusion – that is, either the event has been caused by something, will cause something, or provides the basis for another event to cause some thing. *Every* event is a beginning, middle, or end of a narrative sequence that explains a significant change.

[. . .]

Thus, the narrative form is maximumly meaningful. It provides a far greater context of understanding than is possible in life itself. Yet it reproduces the order and experiences of life, at least in terms of motivations and communication. As humans – the users of symbols – we seek to find meaning in our ordinary experience. We must constantly choose, consciously or unconsciously, which of our experiences to consider significant and which insignificant, which to invest with emotional force and which to ignore. One way, perhaps the only way, to make this choice is to determine whether or not the experience can be connected with another significant experience as either its beginning, its cause, or its result. By locating an experience in a narrative sequence with other experiences, experiences are given meaning. The form stories take can be seen as a paradigm for making sense of life. Not only do stories demonstrate that experience can make sense, they also demonstrate *how* it makes sense, by showing that one important event causes another and by ignoring the unimportant events. Narrative *form* – the thing that makes a story a story and not a list of events – is also the form which human consciousness imposes on real experience to give it meaning. If I lose my job, it is because of the boss's perfidy, not my incompetence. Thus, the narrative sequence – I have a job, the boss is unfair, I lose the job – gives meaning to the experience and allows me to incorporate it into a larger sequence – I am happily married, I lose my job, my wife leaves me – and so on. Thus, narratives resonate, with human consciousness: one naturally by selecting events to fit the form, and one less naturally by forcing the form to fit all experience.

In life meaning is problematic, in narrative it is not. Narrative form – the fact that in a story all events have meaning and all events are explained – interacts with the content of a narrative – its characters and events – to create a structure that communicates conceptual meaning to the individuals who hear the story. The structure of narrative communicates ideas about social action; the form of narrative establishes the possibility of meaning – it is a primer for making sense of experience. This is probably why stories, even bad ones, are usually entertaining: the meaningful organization of events is in itself psychologically satisfying as well as instructive. This is probably also why all societies tell stories: they not only aid in the understanding of social action but reflect and reinforce the formal process of consciousness itself.

What then is the relation between myths and consciousness? Myths are narratives, but they are a special case. Perhaps the most characteristic feature of myths, as opposed to other stories, is that their images are structured into binary oppositions. Lévi-Strauss argues that this reflects the structure of the mind, while I have argued that these oppositions create the symbolic difference necessary for simplicity of understanding together with the maximum resources for conceptual abstraction. The binary structure enables the images of myths to signify general and complex concepts (nature/culture, good/bad) and make them socially available. Myths also present images that are immediately recognizable, concrete objects and events that already have cultural meaning. Myths are easily understood, conceptually deep, and socially relevant; they reflect and reveal basic concerns and directions of their society. They may also model the fundamental approaches to the meaning and ordering of experience available to human consciousness.

If the form of myth as narrative is a model for making sense of experience, then the content of particular myths embodies and makes possible this model. Structurally, myths present a conceptual model of felt social–psychological differences and of actions capable of bridging these differences, while formally myths present a structural model of meaning itself. The conceptual definition of social reality given in a myth is incorporated into, and understood with the structural definition of consciousness by which we comprehend reality. The social meanings of myth may become identified with the fundamental organization of understanding by which the mind knows itself and its world. For this reason, it is apparent that if we are fully to understand and explain specific human actions, we must be able to relate those actions to the social narratives or myths of the society to which the actor belongs. It is at least partly through these myths that he makes sense of his world, and thus the meaning of his actions – both to himself and his society – can only be grasped through a knowledge of the structure and meaning of myth.

Reference

Lévi-Strauss, Claude (1969) *The Raw and the Cooked*, Harper and Row, New York.

58

Defining genre/genre and popular culture

Stanley J. Solomon

From Solomon, S. J. (1976) *Beyond Formula: American Film Genres,*
Harcourt Brace Jovanovich, New York, pp. 1–9.

My intentions differ sharply from those apparent in most contemporary studies
of film genre. The prevailing attitude of even the most knowledgeable critics
and theorists suggests only casual recognition of the value of genre analysis.
I want to promote the thesis that genre study incorporates critical evaluation
– that such study need not rely, as it now seems to do, on the more faddish
critical tendencies of sociology and of cultural archaeology, which often consists
merely of sifting and digging among the gravestones of Monogram Pictures.

Popular as genre critiques have become in recent years, the subject still
lacks the kind of intellectual grounding in theory that would qualify the
genre approach as a plausible category of film criticism. The current level
of genre comprehension can be seen from a recent study of film theories:

> It is precisely for this reason that *genre* notions are so potentially interesting.
> But more for the exploration of the psychological and sociological interplay
> between filmmaker, film, and audience. . . . Until we have a clear, if speculative,
> notion of the connotations of a *genre* class, it is difficult to see how the critic,
> already besieged by imponderables, could usefully use the term, certainly not
> as a special term at the root of his analysis.[1]

Such attitudes toward genre are common and reflect only a limited approach.
Yet the deficiencies of such an approach may denigrate the entire subject,
since the kind of criticism that cannot establish qualitative distinctions is
of little use in any attempt to understand artistic achievement.

The theory I advocate starts with the view that the truly typical elements
of a genre, both visual and dramatic, are not necessarily the most obvious
props and devices shared by bad films and television parodies. Secondly
– and basic to the apprehension of qualitative variations within the genre
– whatever these typical elements may be, they are not trite, repetitive
patterns stored in film studio libraries or file cabinets, but artistic insights
stored in the minds of such filmmakers as Alfred Hitchcock and John Ford.

From these premises evolves my belief that *the most generic works* – the
most 'typical' works – of a significant genre are, artistically and intellectually,
the best works of that genre. The best films never do what certain critics
always assert they must do in order to succeed – that is, genre classics never
'go beyond the limitations of the genre', but in fact incorporate the generic
elements to the fullest degree. Since these elements often include
premises basic to a film's artistic strengths, it appears to me that genre study
not only permits but suggests analytical approaches to the evaluation of

individual works. Ultimately, genre study contributes to our understanding of major films, to our perception of how artists shape their creative materials.

Defining genre

The problem of defining film genre does not seem very great until one reads the critics. Then what appears to be a genre to one writer becomes a sub-genre to another, and what to one is merely a technique or a style becomes to another an identifiable manner of grouping films. In practice, the term *genre* has an almost unlimited number of valid connotations.

The identification of groups of films is not at all a matter of preconceived logical categories, but of common practice. I reject some of the common practices only on the grounds that they seem unusable to me. For example, there are books published on 'the thriller' and 'suspense in the cinema', categories that, from my point of view, are so vague as to include films the public could more easily recognize as belonging to a number of genres more perceptible than those two – for techniques or styles by themselves can tell us little of the content or effect of most films. Similarly, I cannot get a critical handle on a generic immensity now much esteemed, the *film noir*, a classification that includes most of the sombre melodramas of the 1940s, mainly on the basis of mood or lighting, though I discuss several of these films under crime or detective genres. Nor do I consider comedy as a genre. Comedy is a mode of presentation, one of three possibilities (along with tragedy and tragicomedy).

For a different reason, I also reject some of the currently popular types of categories that I have elsewhere called 'conceptual genres'.[2] By locating a theme or an ideological topic that recurs in a group of films – for example, 'politics in film' or 'sex in the cinema' – some critics and historians are able to construct genres for the study of certain attributes that seem to me less cinematic than sociological. With the virtually unlimited possibilities that confront a critic willing to write on such a popular theme of the day as 'images of women in the cinema', a random selection of twenty films would produce generalizations hardly likely to be closely matched by any equivalent selection. When ideology dominates the critical endeavour, the sense of cinema is ignored – or made less important than it is when studied as a perceivable *art form*, of ultimate importance in and for itself.

The genres discussed here – for the most part the usual ones the public recognizes as genres – are all based on perceptual patterns that filmmakers intend to be observable from film to film, though all of these do not occur in all instances of the genre. (If some element does seem to occur in every memorable film made in a particular genre, then very likely we are confronting an essential aspect of the genre's meaning.) Broadly put, a genre film is one in which the narrative pattern, or crucial aspects of that pattern, is visually recognizable as having been used similarly in other films.

Generic cores

Although definitions of particular genres are too often confined to the assembling of characteristics, it seems to me that the defining aspect of a genre is a certain mythic structure, formed on a core of narrative meaning found in those works that are readily discernible as related and belonging to a group. The core can be composed of different sorts of elements. For example, if genre A evolves from the main character's occupation while genre B develops from the visual environment, it might seem that the qualities central to A may be so different from those central to B that A and B are not comparable genres. But in fact, genres can be formulated on different bases and still be widely recognized by critics and general audiences as comparable, though distinct, groupings. Genre A, for instance, might be established on the basis of the hero's being a private investigator, while genre B is premised on the action taking place in the West. The source of each is important for the study of the particular genre, but what ever the source, the results are similar: identifiable narrative patterns develop from a core of ideas that in turn stem from the concept 'private investigator' or 'Western locale'.

Neither of these two generic cores would necessarily suggest any particular meaning to us were we questioned about them apart from the American cinema. Yet when considered in the framework of the American motion picture industry, 'private investigator' and 'Western locale' immediately begin to assume a visual dimension, culminating eventually in a list of attributes. [. . .]

It is, of course, quite possible to make a film about a private detective on vacation who falls in love with a woman, marries her, retires, and opens a successful grocery store. But obviously what we mean by the private investigator genre comprehends films about a professional engaged in the work of his profession. Indeed, it is extraordinarily clear that the real-life profession has little to do with the genre's meaning – real-life private investigators do not track down murderers, but take pictures of spouses in compromising situations and provide personal security services. And when a film at last is made entirely from the reality of a private investigator's routine, then a new genre will have been created. In the meantime, the immediate narrative core of this genre remains one in which a highly skilled professional detective is hired to do something, discovers some crime in the course of his investigation, and solves it. This is the basic material. The implications of that material seem strongly to suggest an underlying mythic structure that reappears in all the memorable works of the genre.

Narrative patterns and iconography

A good deal of the popular sense of a film genre relates to its recurring elements, including dialogue patterns (for instance, the ironic repartee of the private eye), rather than to its underlying structure. These characteristic images are sometimes referred to as the *iconography* of the genre, but those who employ the term do not always seem to realize that iconography means the images or visual symbols *that represent something else*. That something else is the deeper reality that justifies genre art. Those genre enthusiasts who refuse to go beyond the literal surfaces they enjoy so much – the contorted faces of monsters coming alive in laboratories, the shootouts between sheriff and badman, the private detective mocking the police – reveal an infinite patience for small variations, but they surely seem out of touch with their own sensibilities. We sometimes identify very strongly with genre situations and heroes, and such films may become significant to our perception of our world. But if the unexamined life is not worth living, as Socrates said, then perhaps the unexamined genre is not worth loving.

I deliberately avoid systematically surveying the iconography of any genre, the repeated visual characteristics and motifs that serve to identify, in the public mind, both the best and the worst films of a genre. Furthermore, I am uncertain about too many aspects of what other writers sometimes bring forth as the typical evidence of a genre – all the way from the decor of costume drama to the dialogue of a Western. If my generalization is true that the most typical genre film is likely to be the best genre film – not for its surface properties, but for its artistic statement – then probably there are not enough 'best' films or close-to-best films in any genre to justify a survey of iconography that would hold true of the lesser, but numerically greater, films in the same genre. For example, in a memorable sequence from Francis Ford Coppola's *The Godfather* (1972), the displeasure of a crime family don with a defiant movie producer, who is unwilling to give a part to one of the don's friends, leads to a rather gruesome scene in which the movie producer wakes up one morning to find the severed head of his horse in bed with him. Now this particular method of persuasion had never, to my knowledge, been seen in a film before, so it cannot be claimed as a bit of conventional scenic design in the gangster film. Yet without taking anything away from its horror and originality (and artfulness, because it shows at once the crudeness, violence, and omnipotence of the mob), the sequence belongs crucially to the conventions of the gangster genre. In the genre's heyday, the 1930s, the mob that wished to make its power apparent would 'bump off' someone or break up a rival distillery or night-club. But the element of psychological warfare – gaining a point by proving to a holdout that the gang can reach him and destroy him – is entirely common elsewhere in the genre. The image of the horse's head becomes an icon of the genre.

I am open to the argument that every convention, no matter how seemingly minor, helps us to comprehend the nature of a genre. But I believe that at this point in the study of cinematic genre, less attention has been paid to understanding the major narrative patterns than to the elements of iconographic design. For instance, it seems to me at least theoretically possible to make a successful Western without a pistol (that is, an icon), but not to make a good private eye film without the detective coming across as highly moralistic and honest (that is, a pattern of meaning). Failure to understand the pattern (as distinct from the iconography) of any genre – for example, to underestimate the integrity of the private eye – leads to a lot of poor genre films, by filmmakers who think they are being original when in fact they have simply failed to grasp the materials at hand. Much of would-be genre parody is merely self-parody by those who have never understood the nature of the genre they think so suitable for ridicule.

Genre and originality

There remains one more element essential to a definition of genre, and that is the matter of originality. The final criticism offered by those who do not respect genre art is that there is implicit in all genre works, except for the earliest examples, a lack of originality. Genre, as partially defined in the preceding discussion, has much to do with the familiar. But there is a difference between the reproduction of familiar patterns and outright repetition – the trademark of lesser films, whether they belong to a recognizable genre or borrow from many. Everything depends on how genre filmmakers, who we assume are skilful to begin with, handle basic story structures, conventional environmental factors, and the conception of major characters. If they want merely to repeat the surface elements that have recently proven successful – to vary them with, for example, some new styles of murder, but to retain the essential thrills that brought audiences to the theatre the last time – then such filmmakers are exploiting the blatant imagery of the genre, but, contrary to creating genre art, they are merely reproducing genre formula. To achieve genre art, filmmakers must be committed to exploring new facets of the familiar setting, elaborating on their insights into the mythic structures of the genre. For above everything else, genre is a convenient arrangement of significant human actions that can be returned to, over and over again, to provide new understanding of basic human motivations or needs. Genres may originally be derived unconsciously, by accident. But the patterns are repeated on purpose because other filmmakers see, in those first films of a genre, latent possibilities for the reinterpretation of human conduct in archetypal situations.

Genre and popular culture

A too-easy association is often made between film studies based on genre and film studies based on popular culture. Popular culture studies describe, categorize, and analyse in regard to the sociological and psychological phenomena apparent in films. In contrast, genre criticism is concerned with the traditional values of art as they happen to appear in a group of related works. For the purposes of popular culture, any well-worked-over genre that is still current is worthy of study. But to dismiss popular culture as a serious scholarly pursuit because, for its purposes, *Love Story* is sometimes just as important as *The Birth of a Nation*, is to neglect the aspect of it that is indeed analogous to genre study: the search for underlying patterns that can relate a particular cultural or artistic experience to some universal truth about human nature or the society we live in.

I believe that the widespread insistence on regarding generic patterns as either artistically indiscriminate or as detracting from the artistic value of individual films is based on a simple failure to discern what those patterns really are. To assert that the worst examples of the Western film are the most typical – the most generic – works of the genre is to confuse genre with formula. Formula, indeed, it can be argued, is the essence of almost all the longer studies that purport to analyse and classify genres. And it is in the large area of formula that genre study and popular culture analysis may overlap, the latter expounding a view that the frequent reappearance of a formula in itself denotes sociological significance. Yet no one wants to defend the value of a particular film just because it purposely exploits a current formula. Such films usually convey no aesthetic quality, since the general formula itself attracts all the attention. In contrast, genre study probes beneath surface details for whatever dimensions of meaning adhere to the patterns manifest in the individual example. Whereas exponents of popular culture seek to reveal a category, students of genre explore the ways in which the category illuminates particular films.

Until the relatively recent growth toward respectability of popular culture studies, few critics had written on the theory of genre without conveying a sense of suppressed laughter, or at least condescending amusement, at what the masses found entertaining. Among the first to write with perception about the subject as it pertains to film was Robert Warshow. He treated genre as an important manifestation of a psychological aspect of mass culture that deserved analysis because of what it revealed about all of us. In this sense, he functioned as a precursor to all popular culture studies that aspire to serious analysis in our day. Warshow's approach was to make a generalization about society and to link it to a popular film genre's narrative pattern, thereby making a lucid connection between a general cultural idea or condition and its manifestation in popular art.

There is, however, one negative aspect of Warshow's methodology – although of course he cannot be blamed for instituting it – and it is the process of generalization, which is probably indigenous to genre criticism. It makes sense to generalize when one's subject matter is a group of films that have reproduced a certain formula, even though individual works within the group show marked differences. The problem with later critiques of genre – all of them more detailed than Warshow's two famous essays on gangster and Western films – is that often the generalizations have counted for everything and the comparisons have verged on the absurd – true in a *general* sense, but preposterous in regard to *many specific genre films*. Yet generalizations about genre are essential or else there can be no analysis of a category in the first place. The problem is really one of defining a basis for such generalizations, and here again the issue seems to me a matter of separating the popular-culture approach from the aesthetic analysis of narrative art. The critical endeavour that strives for an all-inclusive approach to a massive body of popular works is dealing virtually by definition with popular culture, regardless of the author's specific intent. And at this level of criticism, certain formularizations, as they apply to the innumerable works of passing interest – films of the day – if they have any validity at all may help us to deal with chaotic data as we receive it from contemporary trends in our culture. This kind of approach helps us to classify, and therefore comprehend, the ordinary and the mediocre – works that defy extended aesthetic analysis because they are intended to be meaningful primarily or entirely on the level of popular entertainment. I do believe that popular entertainment must be studied and its impact understood, but I am more interested in the admittedly narrower question of how genres within a certain form of popular entertainment – motion pictures – affect the artistry of certain films that are to my way of thinking far better than ordinary. Genre in the cinema, as elsewhere, surely provides refuge for much mediocrity, but it also provides us with much art, and it is this aspect of genre that concerns me.

Notes

1. Tudor, Andrew (1974) *Theories of Film*, Viking, New York, pp. 139–42.
2. Solomon, Stanley J. (1974) Film study and genre courses. *College Composition and Communication*, Vol. XXV, October, pp. 277–83.

59

Questions of genre

Steve Neale

From Caughie, J. (ed.) (1990) *Screen*, Oxford University Press, Vol. 31, No. 1, pp. 45–66.

This article will discuss some of the issues concepts and concerns arising from work on genre in the cinema published over the last decade or so. It seeks to highlight a number of questions and problems which may pinpoint some possible directions for future research. I will be particularly concerned with the constitution of generic corpuses: with the extent to which they are constituted by public expectations as well as by films, and with the rôle of theoretical terms, on the one hand, and industrial and institutional terms, on the other, in the study of genres. The concept of verisimilitude is central to an understanding of genre, as is the question of the social and cultural functions that genres perform. These, too, will be discussed. Stress will be laid throughout on the changing, and hence, historical nature, not just of individual genres, but of generic regimes as well.
[. . .]

Expectations and verisimilitude

There are several general, conceptual points to make at the outset. The first is that genres are not simply bodies of work or groups of films, however classified, labelled and defined. Genres do not consist only of films: they consist also, and equally, of specific systems of expectation and hypothesis which spectators bring with them to the cinema, and which interact with films themselves during the course of the viewing process. These systems provide spectators with means of recognition and understanding. They help render films, and the elements within them intelligible and therefore explicable. They offer a way of working out the significance of what is happening on the screen: a way of working out why particular events and actions are taking place, why the characters are dressed the way they are, why they look, speak and behave the way they do, and so on. Thus, if, for instance, a character in a film for no reason (or no otherwise explicable reason) bursts into song, the spectator is likely to hypothesize that the film is a musical, a particular kind of film in which otherwise unmotivated singing is likely to occur. These systems also offer grounds for further anticipation. If a film is a musical, more singing is likely to occur, and the plot is likely to follow some directions rather than others.

Inasmuch as this is the case, these systems of expectation and hypothesis involve a knowledge of – indeed they partly embody – various regimes of verisimilitude, various systems of plausibility, motivation, justification, and belief. Verisimilitude means 'probable' or 'likely'.[1] It entails notions of propriety, of what is appropriate and *therefore* probable (or probable and therefore appropriate).

Regimes of verisimilitude vary from genre to genre. (Bursting into song is appropriate, therefore probable – therefore intelligible, therefore believable – in a musical. Less so in a thriller or a war film.) As such these regimes entail rules, norms and laws. (Singing in a musical is not just a probability, it is a necessity. It is not just likely to occur, it is bound to.) As Tzetan Todorov, in particular has insisted, there are two broad types of verisimilitude applicable to representations: generic verisimilitude on the one hand, and, on the other, a broader social or cultural verisimilitude. Neither equates in any direct sense to 'reality' or 'truth'.

[. . .]

There are several points worth stressing here. The first is the extent to which, as the example of singing in the musical serves to illustrate, generic regimes of verisimilitude can ignore, side-step, or transgress these broad social and cultural regimes.

The second is the extent to which this 'transgression' of cultural verisimilitude is characteristic of Hollywood genres. This has implications for conventional notions of 'realism'. There is, of course, always a balance in any individual genre between purely generic and broadly cultural regimes of verisimilitude. Certain genres appeal more directly and consistently to cultural verisimilitude. Gangster films, war films and police procedural thrillers, certainly, often mark that appeal by drawing on and quoting 'authentic' (and authenticating) discourses, artefacts and texts: maps, newspaper headlines, memoirs, archival documents, and so on. But other genres, such as science fiction, Gothic horror, or slapstick comedy, make much less appeal to this kind of authenticity, and this is certainly one of the reasons why they tend to be despised, or at least 'misunderstood', by the critics in the 'quality' press. For these critics, operating under an ideology of realism, adherence to cultural verisimilitude is a necessary condition of 'serious' film, television of literature. As Todorov goes on to argue, realism as an ideology can be partly defined by its refusal to recognize the reality of its own generic status, or to acknowledge its own adherence to a type of generic verisimilitude.

A third point to be made is that recent uses of the concept of verisimilitude in writing on genre tend to blur the distinction between generic and cultural verisimilitude, and tend therefore to vitiate the usefulness of the term.

The fourth point is that, at least in the case of Hollywood, generic regimes of verisimilitude are almost as 'public', as widely known, as 'public opinion' itself. It is not simply in films or in genres that the boundaries between the cultural and generic are blurred: the two regimes merge also in public discourse, generic knowledge becoming a form of cultural knowledge, a component of 'public opinion'.

Fifth, and finally, it is often the generically verisimilitudinous ingredients of a film, the ingredients, that is, which are often least compatible with regimes of cultural verisimilitude – singing and dancing in the musical, the appearance of the monster in the horror film – that constitute its pleasure, and that thus attract audiences to the film in the first place. They too, therefore, tend to be 'public', known, at least to some extent, in advance.

These last two remarks lead on to the next set of points, which concern the rôle and importance of specific institutional discourses, especially those of the press and the film industry itself, in the formation of generic expectations, in the production and circulation of generic descriptions and terms, and therefore, in the constitution of any generic corpus.

Genre and institutional discourse

As John Ellis has pointed out, central to the practices of the film industry is the construction of a 'narrative image' for each individual film:

> An idea of the film is widely circulated and promoted, an idea which can be called the 'narrative image' of the film, the cinema's anticipatory reply to the question, 'What is the film like?'[2]

The discourses of film industry publicity and marketing play a key rôle in the construction of such narrative images; but important, too, are other institutionalized public discourses, especially those of the press and television, and the 'unofficial', 'word of mouth' discourses of everyday life.

Genre is, of course, an important ingredient in any film's narrative image. The indication of relevant generic characteristics is therefore one of the most important functions that advertisements, stills, reviews and posters perform. Reviews nearly always contain terms indicative of a film's generic status, while posters usually offer verbal generic (and hyperbolic) description – 'The Greatest War Picture Ever Made' – and as anchorage for the generic iconography in pictorial form.

These various verbal and pictorial descriptions form what Gregory Lukow and Steven Ricci have called the cinema's 'inter-textual relay'.[3] This relay performs an additional, generic function: not only does it define and circulate narrative images for individual films, beginning the immediate narrative process of expectation and anticipation, it also helps to define and circulate, in combination with the films themselves, what one might call 'generic images', providing sets of labels, terms and expectations which will come to characterize the genre as a whole.

This is a key point. It is one of the reasons why I agree with Lukow and Ricci on the need to take account of all the component texts in the industry's inter-textual relay when it comes to studying not only films, but genre and genres. [. . .]

Clearly, generic expectations and knowledge do not emanate solely from the film industry and its ancillary institutions; and clearly, individual spectators may have their own expectations, classifications, labels and terms. But these individualized, idiosyncratic classifications play little part, if any, in the public formation and circulation of genres and generic images. In the public sphere, the institutional discourses are of central importance. Testimony to the existence of genres, and evidence of their properties, is to be found primarily there.

A distinction needs to be made, then, between those studies of genres conceived as institutionalized classes of texts and systems of expectation, and studies which use critically or theoretically constructed terms as the basis for discussing classes of films. (Studies of *film noir* are obvious examples of the latter.) A distinction also needs to be made between institutionally recognized sub-genres, cycles and categories ('operetta' and 'the singing Western') and theoretically or scholarly based classifications ('The Fairy Tale Musical', 'The Show Musical', and 'The Folk Musical'). This is not to argue that theoretically based studies and classifications are somehow illegitimate. (Far from it. These examples all illustrate how productive they can be.) It is, however, to insist on the pertinence of Todorov's distinction for an understanding of what it is that is being studied.

[. . .]

Genre as process

It may at first sight seem as though repetition and sameness are the primary hallmarks of genres: as though, therefore, genres are above all inherently static. But as Hans Robert Jauss and Ralph Cohen (and I myself) have argued, genres are, nevertheless, best understood as *processes*.[4] These processes may, for sure, be dominated by repetition, but they are also marked fundamentally by difference, variation and change.

The process-like nature of genres manifests itself as an interaction between three levels: the level of expectation, the level of the generic corpus, and the level of the 'rules' or 'norms' that govern both. Each new genre film constitutes an addition to an existing generic corpus and involves a selection from the repertoire of generic elements available at any one point in time. Some elements are included; others are excluded. Indeed some are mutually exclusive: at most points in its history, the horror film has had to characterize its monster *either* supernaturally – as in *Dracula* (1930) – or psychologically – as in *Psycho* (1960). In addition, each new genre film tends to extend this repertoire, either by adding a new element or by transgressing one of the old ones. Thus, for instance, *Halloween* (1979) transgressed the division between psychological and supernatural monsters, giving its monster the attributes of both. In this way the elements and conventions of a genre are always *in* play rather than being, simply, *re*-played;[5] and any generic corpus is always being expanded.

Memories of the films within a corpus constitute one of the bases of generic expectation. So, too, does the stock of generic images produced by advertisements, posters and the like. As both corpus and image expand and change with the appearance of new films, new advertising campaigns, new reviews, so also what Jauss has termed the 'horizon of expectation' appropriate to each genre expands and changes as well.

This is one reason why it is so difficult to list exhaustively the characteristic components of individual genres, or to define them in anything other than the most banal or tautological terms: a Western is a film set on the American Western frontier; a war film is a film that represents the waging of war; a detective film is a film about the investigation of criminals and crime, and so on.

Exclusive definitions, list of *exclusive* characteristics, are particularly hard to produce. At what point do Westerns become musicals like *Oklahoma!* (1955) or *Paint Your Wagon* (1969) or *Seven Brides for Seven Brothers* (1954)? At what point do Singing Westerns become musicals? At what point do comedies with songs (like *A Night at the Opera* (1935)) become musical comedies? And so on.

These examples all, of course, do more than indicate the process-like nature of individual genres. They also indicate the extent to which individual genres not only form part of a generic regime, but also themselves change, develop and vary by borrowing from, and overlapping with, one another. Hybrids are by no means the rarity in Hollywood many books and articles on genre in the cinema would have us believe. This is one reason why, as Marc Vernet has pointed out, 'a guide to film screenings will often offer to the spectator rubrics like: Western, detective film, horror film, and comedy; but also: dramatic comedy, psychological drama, or even erotic detective film'.[6] Indeed, in its classical era, as Bordwell, Staiger and Thompson have shown, nearly all Hollywood's films were hybrids insofar as they always tended to combine one type of generic plot, a romance plot, with others.[7] Moreover, it is at least arguable that many of the most apparently 'pure' and stable genres, both inside and outside the cinema, initially evolved by combining elements from previously discrete and separate genres either within or across specific generic regimes. [. . .]

Hence the importance of *historicizing* generic definitions and the parameters both of any single generic corpus, and of any specific generic regime. For it is not that more elaborated definitions are impossible to provide, just that they are always historically relative, and therefore historically specific. It is not that the process-like nature of genres renders generalization invalid. Genre films, genres and generic regimes are always marked by boundaries and by frameworks: boundaries and frameworks which always have limits. Thus even hybrids are recognized as hybrids – combinations of specific and distinct generic components – not as genres in their own right.

Genre history: three approaches

There currently seem to exist three major ways in which genre history has been conceived. The first is what Jauss has called 'the evolutionary schema of growth, flowering and decay'.[8] This schema is open to several objections: it is teleological; it is (for all its organic metaphors) highly mechanistic; and it treats genres in isolation from any generic regime.

Similar objections apply to a second model of evolutionary development used by Thomas Schatz, in which genres progress towards self-conscious formalism. [. . .]

The third historical model is the one provided by the Russian formalists.[9] It has the virtue of embedding the history of individual genres within the history, not just of generic formations, but of wider cultural formations as well. It is perhaps best known for Tynyanov's concept of 'the dominant' (with its correlative concept of genre history as the displacement of one dominant genre by another),[10] and by Shklovsky's idea that such displacements occur according to a principle known as 'the canonization of the junior branch': 'When the "canonized" art forms reach an impasse, the way is paved for the infiltration of the elements of non-canonized art, which by this time have managed to evolve new artistic devices'.[11]

[. . .]

There is clearly a great deal here that is both attractive and useful. As a theory or model, it takes account of the historicity, not only of genres, but of specific generic regimes; it takes account of their process-like nature; and, in its insistence on the importance of an interplay between canonized and non-canonized forms of representation, and between canonized and non-canonized genres, it takes account both of the transience of generic hierarchies, and of the role of hybridization in the formation and dissolution of individual genres.

In sketching the application of this model to the American cinema, one could argue, for instance, that the cinema itself arose in, and as, the conjunction of a variety of art forms – canonized and otherwise – from photography, through pictorial entertainments and spectacles like the diorama, the zoëtrope and the magic lantern show, to magic itself, and to the vaudeville routine. Its earliest generic regime, in America as elsewhere, was dominated by the genres associated with these forms: the moving snapshot or 'view', re-enacted and reconstructed news, trick films, and slapstick and gag-based comedy. Subsequent to this, there is a shift to a predominance of fiction, in particular of melodrama (whether in its thrilling, mysterious, domestic or spectacular guise) on the one hand, and of comedy on the other. With accompanying subdivisions, and with the addition of genres like the musical, this 'dominant' came to be stabilized in the era of oligopoly and studio control. Later, in a period of crisis and re-adjustment, 'adult' drama and 'epic' values – marked by, and derived principally from, the epic itself, and spreading from there to the Western, the war film, the musical and even with films like *The Great Race* (1965) and *It's a Mad, Mad, Mad, Mad World* (1963), to slapstick comedy – gained a position of dominance, though by now beginning to jockey for position with 'exploitation' genres, and the 'juvenilization' of Hollywood's output. Finally, more recently, the process of juvenilization has continued, with the emergence of the 'teenpic', and the predominance of sci-fi and horror. Meanwhile, in exemplary illustration of Shlovsky's thesis, some of these genres, in combination with serial-derived individual films like *Raiders of the Lost Ark* (1981) and *Romancing the Stone* (1984), have been promoted from the 'junior branches' of Hollywood's output to achieve hegemony within the realms of the family blockbuster.

What is particularly valuable about the formalists' model is that it neither prescribes the conditions for generic outmodedness, nor specifies any single mechanism by which non-canonized forms, devices or genres might find a place within generic regimes or assume a position of dominance within them. It allows for a variety of factors and reasons. This is especially important in the case of the cinema, where, for example, the initial predominance of actuality genres is as much a consequence of technological factors as it is of their popularity or 'canonization' elsewhere in the contemporary culture, and where, on the other hand, the promotion and predominance of 'juvenile' genres is as much a consequence of market research and the targeting of audiences,[12] and, in some cases, of new special-effects techniques, as it is of any new-found aesthetic vitality.[13]

What, meanwhile, is particularly striking about this historical sketch is the extent to which many genres either originated in forms and institutions of entertainment other than the cinema, or were (and are) circulated additionally by them. Melodrama, for example, originated on the stage. It fed from there, in a process of increasing and mutual interaction, firstly into written fiction then into the cinema. All the while, in all three fields, it generated sub-divisions like the crime story, the mystery, the adventure story and the romance, as well as domestic drama. Comedy came from vaudeville, the circus, burlesque and the newspaper cartoon strip, as well as from the 'legitimate' stage, and, later, from radio and television. The musical came from Broadway (and its songs from Tin Pan Alley). Cheap hardback and paperback books, meanwhile, together with both 'slick' and 'pulp' magazines, comic books, comic strips and mass-produced fiction of all kinds, helped in some cases to originate, and in all cases to circulate, genres like the Western, the detective story and the thriller, horror, science-fiction, war and romance. This generic fiction often appeared in series or serial format with precise generic titles and names: *Adventure Library* (1897), *The Detective Library* (1917), *Western Story Magazine* (1919), *Thrill Book* (1919), *Love Story Magazine* (1921), *Love Story Library* (1926), *War Stories* (1922), *Gangster Stories, The Magazine of Fantasy and Science-Fiction* (1942), *Bestseller Mysteries* (1942), *The Vault of Horror* (1950), and so on.[14]

It is worth, at this point, signalling the need for a great deal more as a corollary, on the particular contributions of individual institutions and forms.[15] More research is needed, too, on the aesthetically specific transformations and adaptations each genre undergoes in each institution and form.[16]

Finally, I should like to move on to discuss a set of questions to do with the aesthetic characteristics of mass-produced genres, their institutional functions within the cinema, and their putative social, cultural and ideological significance.

The first point to make here is, again, an historical one. It concerns the provenance, and status, of the term 'genre' itself, its applicability to the cinema, and its role in characterizing not only the cinema, but mass-produced art and entertainment in general. It is a point which, once more, has usefully been focused by Williams:[17]

> Perhaps the biggest problem with genre theory or genre criticism in the field of cinema is the word *genre*. Borrowed, as a critical tool, from literary studies . . . the applicability of 'genre' as a concept in film studies raises some fairly tough questions. Sample genres are held to be Westerns, Science Fiction Films, more recently Disaster Films, and so on. What do these loose groupings of works – that seem to come and go, for the most part, in ten- and twenty-year cycles – have to do with familiar literary genres such as tragedy, comedy, romance, or (to mix up the pot a bit) the epistolary novel or the prose poem?

He continues,

> For the phrase 'genre films', referring to a general category, we can frequently, though not always, substitute 'film narrative.' Perhaps *that* is the real genre. Certainly there is much more difference between *Prelude to Dog Star*

Man and *Stars Wars* than there is between the latter and *Body Heat*. It's mainly a question of terminology, of course, but I wonder if we ought to consider the principal genres as being narrative film, experimental/avant-garde film, and documentary. Surely these are the categories in film studies that have among themselves the sorts of significant differences that one can find between, say, epic and lyric poetry. If we reserve this level for the term *genre*, then film genres will by definition have the kind of staying power seen in literary genres. What we presently call film genres would then be *sub-genres*.[18]

In many ways, it seems to me, Williams is right about this. However, apart from the fact that, as he himself says, it is 'probably too late' to change things, there is an important qualification to be made.

As Ralph Cohen has pointed out, the term 'genre' is a nineteenth century term.[19] Thus, although the concept is clearly much older, the term itself emerges precisely at the time that popular, mass-produced generic fiction is making its first appearance (its genres, incidentally, just as susceptible to Williams' strictures). At the same time, also, there began to emerge a distinct shift in the value placed on generic literature by 'High Culture' artists and critics. As Terry Threadgold has explained, prior to the advent of Romanticism 'it was *literature* that was generic'.

> The rest, the 'popular culture' of political pamphlets, ballads, romances, chapbooks, was not only *not* literature, but also *not* generic; it escaped the law of genre, suffering a kind of rhetorical exclusion by inclusion in the classical distinction between high, middle, and low styles. It was seen as a kind of anarchic, free area, unconstrained by the rules of polite society and decorum, by *genre* in fact.[20]

With the emergence of new technologies, new capital, mass production, new means of distribution (notably the railway), with the formation of a relatively large, literate (or semi-literate) population (with the formation, therefore, of a market), and with the commodification of all forms of leisure and entertainment, the equation is reversed. Now it is 'popular culture', mass culture, that is generic, ruled as it is by market pressures to differentiate to a limited degree in order to cater to various sectors of consumers, and to repeat commercially successful patterns, ingredients and formulas. By contrast, 'true literature' is marked by self-expression, creative autonomy, and originality, and hence by a freedom from all constrictions and constraints, including those of genre.

It is at this point absolutely crucial to disentangle a number of assumptions and conflations, for it is at this point that a great deal of 'genre theory' (indeed 'popular cultural theory' in general) tends to go astray. Firstly, of course, it has to be recognized that no 'artist', in whatever sphere of aesthetic production, at whatever period in history, in whatever form of society, has ever been free either of aesthetic conventions and rules, or of specific institutional constraints (whether he or she has reacted against them or not). Secondly, as Geoffrey Nowell-Smith has recently re-emphasized, *all* cultural and artistic production in Western societies is now, and has been for some time, subject to capitalist conditions of production, distribution and exchange, hence to commodification.[21] (This means, among other things, both that High Cultural art that still draws upon 'traditional', pre-capitalist genres like lyric poetry, and High Cultural art that eschews both 'traditional' and modern, 'popular' genres is still itself 'generic' insofar as it is thereby still engaged in catering for a sector of the market, still involved in a form of product differentiation.)[22] The third point is that it is indeed, therefore, the case that mass-produced, popular genres have to be understood within an economic context, as conditioned by specific economic imperatives and by specific economic contradictions – in particular, of course, those that operate within specific institutions and industries. That is why it is important to stress the financial advantages to the film industry of an aesthetic regime based on regulated difference, contained variety, pre-sold expectations, and the re-use of resources in labour and materials. It is also why it is important to stress the peculiar nature of films as *aesthetic* commodities, commodities demanding at least a degree of novelty and difference from one to another, and why it is necessary to explore the analogies and the distinctions between cycles and genres in the cinema, on the one hand, and models and lines in the field of non-artistic commodity production, on the other.

Failure to recognize these points results in approaches to genre which are inadequate and simplistic. It is worth specifying two such approaches here. The first is what Altman has called the 'ritual' approach, and Thomas Schatz (along with Will Wright and John Cawelti, a pioneer of this particular approach) once again serves as an example.[23] Here is Williams' summary:

> The repetitive nature of genre production and consumption produces active but indirect audience participation; successful genres are 'stories the audience has isolated through its collective response'. Hence genre filmmaking can be examined as 'a form of collective cultural expression' (pp. 12–13).[24]

Quite apart from the doubtful assumption that consumer decision-making can be considered a form of 'cultural expression', and quite apart from the tendency of such an approach to conflate the multiplicity of reasons for consumer 'choices' and a multiplicity of readings of these 'choices', the 'ritual' theory of genres is open to question on other grounds. Principal among these is that it ignores the role of institutional determinations and decisions, by-passing the industry and the sphere of production in an equation between market availability, consumer choice, consumer preference, and broader social and cultural values and beliefs. This is an equation open to challenge on its own grounds. During the studio era, for instance, Westerns were regularly produced in large numbers, despite the fact that, as Garth Jowett has shown, such market research as was conducted at this time indicated that the genre was popular only with young adolescent boys and sectors of America's rural population, and that it was *actively disliked* more than it was liked by the viewing population as a whole.[25]

Second, objections can also be made to what Altman calls, the 'ideological approach' to genre, an approach which recognizes the capitalist nature of the film industry, and the status of its films as commodities, but which treats genres simply as vehicles for 'capitalist' (or 'the dominant') 'ideology'.[26] This approach is open to the charges of reductivism, economism, and cultural pessimism.[27] It tends to presume, in the final analysis, that representations reflect their social and economic conditions of existence, that institutions and social formations necessarily secure their own reproduction, and, in Colin MacCabe's words, that 'the meanings of texts . . . are always finally anchored in a class struggle which is not to be understood in cultural terms'.[28] As both MacCabe and Geoffrey Nowell-Smith have each, in their different ways, insisted, 'stressing the capitalist character of modern cultural production is in itself neither optimistic nor pessimistic.'[29] The ideological significance of any text – or any genre – is always to be sought in a context-specific analysis. It cannot simply be deduced from the nature of the institution responsible for its production and circulation, nor can it ever be known in advance.

Both these theories for all their differences, suffer from the fact that they pay little attention to aesthetics – for them form is always, and only, a wrapping for the cultural or ideological content in which they are almost exclusively interested. Insofar as they do discuss form, they tend to stress the repetitive, 'stereotypical' aspects of genres, setting aside the differences within and between them in order to provide themselves with a stable corpus, and in order to substantiate their underlying premise: that the reasons for the popularity and longevity of genres are relatively uniform, as are, aside from a few Lévi-Straussian antinomies, the genres themselves, the meanings they convey, and the culture (or ideology) that underpins them. While it may be the case that repetition is important, it is also the case, as we have seen, that variation and difference are crucial. Equally, while it may be the case that Hollywood genres are in most instances best considered as sub-genres of 'narrative film', and while these sub-genres may not be marked by the kinds of apparent discursive peculiarities that tend to differentiate the narrative film from documentary or the structuralist avant garde, there is still a great deal of scope for the investigation of specific discursive characteristics. Aside from my own attempt, in *Genre*, to explore the ways in which different genres exploit in different ways the features and characteristics of the narrative film (an attempt somewhat marred by an over-schematic approach, by a lack of attention to hybridization, and, above all, by a lack of attention to history), the basis for an approach can perhaps be found in the Russian formalist idea that genres can each involve a 'dominant' (or dominating) aesthetic device (or ideological element).[30]

On this basis, particular genres can be characterized, not as the only genres in which given elements, devices and features occur, but as the ones in which they are dominant, in which they play an overall, organizing role.

Approaches to individual genres – and to individual genre films – that draw centrally on the notion of a generic dominant are few and far between. However, it could be argued, for example, that the epic is marked by the dominance of spectacle; that the thriller and the detective genre, especially as discussed by Dennis Porter and Kristin Thompson , are dominated by the devices of suspense, narrative digression, and hermeneutic delay;[31] and that, as the Russian formalists themselves have argued, melodrama involves the subordination of all other elements 'to one overriding aesthetic goal: the calling forth of "pure", "vivid" emotions'.[32] In doing so, however, emphasis again must be placed on the fact that dominant elements are not necessarily exclusive elements, elements that occur only in the genre concerned. Clearly, spectacle, digression, suspense and the generation of passion and emotion are properties common to all Hollywood films.

By way of conclusion, I would like to stress the need for further research, further concrete and specific analyses, and for much more attention to be paid to genres hitherto neglected in genre studies, like the adventure film: for example, the war film and the epic. In stressing this, I can do no better than to quote, for the last time, from Williams. In his own summation, he calls for a 'return to film history', for 'genre studies with real historical integrity':

> This would mean (1) starting with a genre's 'pre-history', its roots in other media; (2) studying all films, regardless of perceived quality; and (3) going beyond film content to study advertising, the star system, studio policy, and so on in relation to the production of films.[33]

I would merely add that the scope of this investigation needs to be extended beyond individual genres to encompass specific generic regimes both inside, and outside, the cinema.

Notes

1. For discussions of verisimilitude and genre see Ben Brewster (1987) 'Film' in Cohn-Sherbok, Dan and Irwin, Michael (eds), *Exploring Reality*, Allen & Unwin, London, esp. pp. 147–9; Genette, Gerard (1969) *Vraisemblance et motivation*, in *Figures*, Seuil, Paris, Vol. 3; and Todorov, Tzvetan (1977) 'The typology of detective fiction' and 'An introduction to verisimilitude' in *The Poetics of Prose*; Cornell University Press, Ithaca, and (1981) *Introduction to Poetics*, The Harvester Press, Brighton, esp. pp. 118–19.
2. Ellis, John (1981) *Visible Fictions: Cinema. Television: Video*, Routledge, London, p. 30.
3. Lukow, Gregory and Ricci, Steve (1984) The 'audience' goes 'public': intertextuality, genre, and the responsibilities of film literacy. *On Film*, No. 12, Spring, p. 29.
4. Cohen, Ralph (1986) History and genre. *New Literary History*, Vol. 17, No. 2, Winter, p. 205–6; Jauss, Hans Robert (1982) *Towards an Aesthetic of Reception*, The Harvester Press, Brighton, p. 80, Neale, *Genre*, British Film Institute, London, p. 19.
5. I owe this phrase to an unpublished lecture on genre by Elizabeth Cowie.
6. Vernet, Marc (1978) Genre. *Film Reader*, Vol. 3, February, p. 13.
7. Bordwell, David, Staiger, Janet and Thompson, Kristin (1985) *The Classical Hollywood Cinema: Film Style and Mode of Production to 1960*, Routledge, London, pp. 16–17.
8. Jauss, op. cit. (see Note 4), p. 88.
9. See, in particular, Eikenbaum, Boris 'The theory of the formal method' and Tynyanov, Jury 'On literary evolution', both in (1978) Matejka, Ladislav and Pomorska, Krystyna (eds) *Readings in Russian Poetics: Formalist and Structuralist Views* Michigan Slavic Publications, Ann Arbor, MI; and Viktor Shklovsky's views as summarized both in these works and in Erlich, Victor (1981) *Russian Formalism: History-Doctrine*, Yale University Press, New Haven, pp. 259–60.
10. Tynyanov, op. cit. (see Note 9), pp. 72–3.
11. Quoted in Erlich, op. cit. (see Note 9), p. 260.
12. On exploitation, juvenilization and the emergence of the teenpic, see Docherty, Thomas (1988) *Teenagers and Teenpics: the Juvenilization of American Movies in the 1950s*, Unwin Hyman, Boston.
13. On the role of special effects see Neale, Steve (1981) Hollywood strikes back – special effects in recent American cinema. *Screen*, Vol. 21, No. 3, pp. 101–5.

14. Dates for series titles indicate initial year of publication. On mass produced fiction, series and genres, see, among others, Bold, Christine (1987) *Selling the Wild West: Popular Western Fiction, 1860–1960*, Indiana University Press, Bloomington; Tony Goodstone (ed.) (1970) *The Pulps: Fifty Years of American Pop Culture*, Chelsea House, New York; Goulart, Ron (1986) *Great History of Comic Books*, Contemporary Books, Chicago; Peterson, Theodore (1956) *Magazines in the Twentieth Century*, University of Illinois Press, Urbana; Radway, Janice A. (1984) *Reading the Romance: Women, Patriarchy and Popular Literature*, University of North Carolina Press, Chapel Hill; Reynolds, Quentin (1955) *The Fiction Factory, or, From Pulp Row to Quality Street*, Random House, New York; Schick, Frank L. (1958) *The Paperbound Book in America*, R. R. Bowker, New York; and Schreuders, Piet (1981) *The Book of Paperbacks: A Visual History of the Paperback*, Virgin Books, London.

15. The only books dealing with a number of genres across a variety of institutions and forms, remain, so far as I am aware, Cawelti, John G. (1976) *Adventure, Mystery, and Romance*, University of Chicago Press, Chicago; and Toll, Robert C. (1982) *The Entertainment Machine: American Show Business in the Twentieth Century*, Oxford University Press, Oxford. Research is also needed on the institutional connections between the cinema, the theatre, radio, television and popular music which in part enable cross-media generic circulation. For a summary and bibliography of some of the work to date, see Pryluck, Calvin (1986) Industrialization of entertainment in the United States. In Austin Bruce A. (ed) *Current Research in Film Audiences Economics and Law*, Ablex, New Jersey.

16. The kind of studies I have in mind are best instanced, to date, by Altman's book on the Musical, especially his emphasis on edited alternation in constructing a 'dual focus' narrative, and his concepts of the 'Audio' and 'Video' dissolve. Altman, Rick (1989) *The American Film Musical*, Indiana University Press, Bloomington and British Film Institute, London, esp. pp. 16–17 and 59–89; John Meuller's book (1986) *Astaire Dancing: The Musical Films*, Hamish Hamilton, London, especially the section on 'Astaire's use of the camera', pp. 26–34; and Christine Saxton's (1988) *Illusions of Grandeur: The Representation of Space in the American Western*, UMI Dissertation Information Service, University Microfilms, Ann Arbor, MI.

17. Williams, Alan (1984) Is a radical genre review possible? *Quarterly Review of Film Studies*, Vol. 9, No. 2, p. 121.

18. Williams, op. cit. (see Note 17), pp. 121–2.

19. Cohen, op. cit. (see Note 4), p. 203.

20. Threadgold, Terry (1989) Talking about genre: ideologies and incompatible discourses. *Cultural Studies*, Vol. 3, No. 1, January, pp. 121–2.

21. Nowell-Smith Geoffrey (1987) Popular culture. *New Formations*, No. 2, Summer.

22. For a discussion of this in relation to the cinema, see Neale, Steve (1981) Art cinema as Institution. *Screen*, Vol. 22, No. 1.

23. Cawelti, op. cit. (see Note 15), Schatz, Thomas (1981) *Hollywood Genres: Formulas, Filmmaking and the Studio System*, Random House, New York. Wright, Will (1975) *Sixguns and Society: A Structural Study of the Western*, University of California Press, Berkeley.

24. Williams, op. cit. (see Note 17), p. 123.

25. Jowett, Garth S. (1985) Giving them what they want: movie audience research before 1950. In Austin, Bruce A. (ed.) *Current Research in Film: Audience, Economics and Law*, Ablex, Norwood, New Jersey, Vol. 1.

26. Altman, op. cit. (See Note 16), p. 94.

27. Possibly the worst example I have come across is Judith Hess Wright's article (1986) 'Genre films and the status quo'. In Grant, Barry Keith (ed.) *Film Genre Reader*, University of Texas Press, Austin.

28. MacCabe, Colin (1986) 'Introduction' to MacCabe (ed.) (1986) *High Theory/ Low Culture: Analysing Popular Television and Film*, Manchester University Press, Manchester, p. 4.
29. Nowell-Smith, op. cit. see Note 19, p. 88.
30. See Tynyanov, op. cit. (see Note 9).
31. Dennis Porter (1981) *The Pursuit of Crime: Art and Ideology in Detective Fiction*, Yale University Press, New Haven. Thompson, Kristin (1988) *Breaking the Glass Armor: Neoformalist Film Analysis*, Princeton University Press, Princeton, esp. pp. 49–86.
32. Gerould, Daniel (1978) Russian formalist theories of melodrama. *Journal of American Culture*, Vol. 1, No. 1, Spring, p. 154.
33. Williams, op. cit. (see Note 17), p. 124.

60

Morphology of the folktale

Vladimir Propp

From Propp, V. (1968) *Morphology of the Folktale* (translated by Scott, L.), University of Texas Press, Austin, TX, pp. 19–24.

Let us first of all attempt to formulate our task. As already stated in the foreword, this work is dedicated to the study of *fairy* tales. The existence of fairy tales as a special class is assumed as an essential working hypothesis. By 'fairy tales' are meant at present those tales classified by Aarne under numbers 300 to 749. This definition is artificial, but the occasion will subsequently arise to give a more precise determination on the basis of resultant conclusions. We are undertaking a comparison of the themes of these tales. For the sake of comparison we shall separate the component parts of fairy tales by special methods; and then, we shall make a comparison of tales according to their components. The result will be a morphology (i.e. a description of the tale according to its component parts and the relationship of these components to each other and to the whole). What methods can achieve an accurate description of the tale? Let us compare the following events:

1. A tsar gives an eagle to a hero. The eagle carries the hero away to another kingdom.[1]
2. An old man gives Súčenko a horse. The horse carries Súčenko away to another kingdom.
3. A sorcerer gives Iván a little boat. The boat takes Iván to another kingdom.
4. A princess gives Iván a ring. Young men appearing from out of the ring carry Iván away into another kingdom, and so forth.[2]

Both constants and variables are present in the preceding instances. The names of the dramatis personae change (as well as the attributes of each), but neither their actions nor functions change. From this we can draw the inference that a tale often attributes identical actions to various personages. This makes possible the study of the tale *according to the functions of its dramatis personae*.

We shall have to determine to what extent these functions actually represent recurrent constants of the tale. The formulation of all other questions will depend upon the solution of this primary question: how many functions are known to the tale?

Investigation will reveal that the recurrence of functions is astounding. Thus Bába Jagá, Morózko, the bear, the forest spirit, and the mare's head test and reward the stepdaughter. Going further, it is possible to establish that characters of a tale, however varied they may be, often perform the same actions. The actual means of the realization of functions can vary, and as such, it is a variable. Morózko behaves differently than Bába Jagá. But the function, as such, is a constant. The question of *what* a tale's dramatis personae do is an important one for the study of the tale, but the questions of *who* does it and *how* it is done already fall within the province of accessory study. The functions of characters are those components which could replace Veselóvskij's 'motifs', or Bédier's 'elements'. We are aware of the fact that the repetition of functions by various characters was long ago observed in myths and beliefs by historians of religion, but it was not observed by historians of the tale (cf. Wundt and Negelein[3]). Just as the characteristics and functions of deities are transferred from one to another, and, finally, are even carried over to Christian saints, the functions of certain tale personages are likewise transferred to other personages. Running ahead, one may say that the number of functions is extremely small, whereas the number of personages is extremely large. This explains the two-fold quality of a tale: its amazing multiformity, picturesqueness, and colour, and on the other hand, its no less striking uniformity, its repetition.

Thus the functions of the dramatis personae are basic components of the tale, and we must first of all extract them. In order to extract the functions we must define them. Definition must proceed from two points of view. First of all, definition should in no case depend on the personage who carries out the function. Definition of a function will most often be given in the form of a noun expressing an action (interdiction, interrogation, flight, etc.). Secondly, an action cannot be defined apart from its place in the course of narration. The meaning which a given function has in the course of action must be considered. For example, if Iván marries a tsar's daughter, this is something entirely different than the marriage of a father to a widow with two daughters. A second example: if, in one instance, a hero receives money from his father in the form of 100 rubles and subsequently buys a wise cat with this money, whereas in a second case, the hero is rewarded with a sum of money for an accomplished act of bravery (at which point the tale ends), we have before us two morphologically different elements – in spite of the identical action (the transference of money) in both cases. Thus, identical acts can have different meanings, and vice versa. *Function is understood as an act of a character, defined from the point of view of its significance for the course of the action.*

The observations cited may be briefly formulated in the following manner:

1. Functions of characters serve as stable, constant elements in a tale, independent of how and by whom they are fulfilled. They constitute the fundamental components of a tale.
2. The number of functions known to the fairy tale is limited.

If functions are delineated, a second question arises: in what classification and in what sequence are these functions encountered?

A word, first, about sequence. The opinion exists that this sequence is accidental. Veselóvskij writes, 'The selection and *order* of tasks and encounters (examples of motifs) already presupposes a certain freedom'. Šklóvskij stated this idea in even sharper terms: 'It is quite impossible to understand why, in the act of adoption, the *accidental* sequence [Šklóvskij's italics] of motifs must be retained. In the testimony of witnesses, it is precisely the sequence of events which is distorted most of all'. This reference to the evidence of witnesses is unconvincing. If witnesses distort the sequence of events, their narration is meaningless. The sequence of events has its own laws. The short story too has similar laws, as do organic formations. Theft cannot take place before the door is forced. Insofar as the tale is concerned, it has its own entirely particular and specific laws. The sequence of elements, as we shall see later on, is strictly *uniform*. Freedom within this sequence is restricted by very narrow limits which can be exactly formulated. We thus obtain the third basic thesis of this work, subject to further development and verification:

3. The sequence of functions is always identical.

As for groupings, it is necessary to say first of all that by no means do all tales give evidence of all functions. But this in no way changes the law of sequence. The absence of certain functions does not change the order of the rest. For the present we shall deal with groupings in the proper sense of the word. The presentation of the question itself evokes the following assumption: if functions are singled out, then it will be possible to trace those tales which present identical functions. Tales with identical functions can be considered as belonging to one type. On this foundation, an index of types can then be created, based not upon theme features, which are somewhat vague and diffuse, but upon exact structural features. Indeed, this will be possible. If we further compare structural types among themselves, we are led to the following completely unexpected phenomenon: functions cannot be distributed around mutually exclusive axes. For the time being, it can be interpreted in the following manner: if we designate with the letter A a function encountered everywhere in first position, and similarly designate with the letter B the function which (if it is at all present) *always follows A*, then all functions known to the tale will arrange themselves within a single tale, and none will fall out of order, nor will any one exclude or contradict any other. This is, of course, a completely unexpected result. Naturally, we would have expected that where there is a function A, there cannot be certain functions belonging to other tales. Supposedly we would obtain several axes, but only a single axis is obtained for all fairy tales. They are of the same type, while the combinations spoken of previously are subtypes. At first glance, this conclusion may appear absurd or perhaps even wild, yet it can be verified in a most exact manner. Such a typological unity represents a very complex problem on which it will be necessary to dwell further. This phenomenon will raise a whole series of questions.

In this manner, we arrive at the fourth basic thesis of our work

4. All fairy tales are of one type in regard to their structure.

Here it should be recalled that the study of the tale must be carried on strictly deductively, i.e., proceeding from the material at hand to the consequences (and in effect it is so carried on in this work). But the *presentation* may have a reversed order, since it is easier to follow the development if the general bases are known to the reader beforehand.

Before starting the elaboration, however, it is necessary to decide what material can serve as the subject of this study. First glance would seem to indicate that it is necessary to cover all extant material. In fact, this is not so. Since we are studying tales according to the functions of their dramatis personae, the accumulation of material can be suspended as soon as it becomes apparent that the new tales considered present no new functions. Of course, the investigator must look through an enormous amount of reference material. But there is no need to inject the entire body of this material into the study. We have found that 100 tales constitute more than enough material. Having discovered that no new functions can be found, the morphologist can put a stop to his work, and further study will follow different directions (the formation of indices, the complete systemization, historical study). But just because material can be limited in quantity, that does not mean that it can be selected at one's own discretion. It should be dictated from without .

If repetition is great, then one may take a limited amount of material. If repetition is small, this is impossible. The repetition of fundamental components exceeds all expectations. Consequently, it is theoretically possible to limit oneself to a small body of material. We are not interested in the quantity of material, but in the quality of its analysis.

Notes

1. *'Car'daet udal'cu orla. Orel unosit udal'ca v inoe carstvo'* (p. 28). Actually, in the tale referred to (old number 104a = new number 171), the hero's future bride, Poljuša, tells her father the tsar that they have a *ptica-kolpalica* (technically a spoonbill, although here it may have meant a white stork), which can carry them to the bright world. For a tale in which the hero flies away on an eagle, see 71a (= new number 128). [L.A.W.]
2. See Afanás'ev, Nos. 171, 139, 138, 156.
3. Wundt, W., Mythus und Religion. *Völkerpsychologie*, Vol. II, Section I; Negelein, *Germanische Mythologie*. Negelein creates an exceptionally apt term, *Depossedierte Gottheiten*.

61

Story and discourse (introduction)

Seymour Chatman

From Chatman, S. (1978) *Story and Discourse: Narrative Structure in Fiction and Film*, Cornell University Press, London, pp. 15–42.

The Russian formalist tradition, especially the work of Vladimir Propp, emphasized simple narratives: folk tales,[1] myths, *romans policiers*. But modern narrative fiction entails additional complexities of structure. The rigid homogeneity of plot and simplicity of characterization found in the Russian fairy tale are obviously not typical of many modern narratives. Still, much can be learned from these investigations, particularly about the theory of plot and the necessity of separating narrative structure from any of its mere manifestations, linguistic or otherwise. Certain disadvantages must also be considered, particularly classificatory reductivism. On balance, what constitutes a viable and modern narrative theory?

To begin, let me sketch the general conception of literature and of art in terms of which the present theory is conceived.

Narrative and poetics

Formalists and structuralists argue that it is not the literary text itself that is the subject of poetics but rather – to use Roman Jakobson's phrase – its 'literariness'. The question for poetics (unlike literary criticism) is not 'What makes *Macbeth* great?' but rather 'What makes it a tragedy?' [. . .]

Like modern linguistics, literary theory might well consider a rationalist and deductive approach rather than the usual empiricist one. It should assume that definitions are to be made, not discovered, that the deduction of literary concepts is more testable and hence more persuasive than their induction. Poetics should construct 'a theory of the structure and functioning of literary discourse, a theory which presents a set [*tableau*] of possible literary objects, such that existing literary works appear as particular realized cases'.[2] Aristotle provides a precedent; the *Poetics* is nothing less than a theory of the properties of a certain type of literary discourse. Northrop Frye is outspokenly deductive in *Anatomy of Criticism*. We need not expect actual works to be pure examples of our categories. The categories plot the abstract network upon which individual works find their place. No individual work is a perfect specimen of a genre – novel or comic epic or whatever. All works are more or less mixed in generic character.

To put it another way, genres are constructs or composites of features. The novel and the drama, for example, require features like plot and character, which are not essential to the lyric poem; but all three may utilize the feature of figurative language. [. . .]

Narrative theory has no critical axe to grind. Its objective is a grid of possibilities, through the establishment of the minimal narrative constitutive features. It plots individual texts on the grid and asks whether their accommodation requires adjustments of the grid. It does not assert that authors should or should not do so-and-so. Rather, it poses a question: What can we say about the way structures like narrative organize themselves? That question raises subsidiary ones: What are the ways in which we recognize the presence or absence of a narrator? What is plot? Character? Setting? Point of view?

Elements of a narrative theory

Taking poetics as a rationalist discipline, we may ask, as does the linguist about language: what are the necessary components – and only those – of a narrative? Structuralist theory argues that each narrative has two parts: a story (*histoire*), the content or chain of events (actions, happenings), plus what may be called the existents (characters, items of setting); and a discourse (*discours*), that is, the expression, the means by which the content is communicated. In simple terms, the story is the *what* in a narrative that is depicted, discourse the *how*. Figure 61.1 illustrates this. This kind of distinction has of course been recognized since the *Poetics*. For Aristotle, the imitation of actions in the real world, *praxis*, was seen as forming an argument, *logos*, from which were selected (and possibly rearranged) the units that formed the plot, *mythos*.

The Russian formalists, too, made the distinction, but used only two terms: the 'fable' (*fabula*), or basic story stuff, the sum total of events to be related in the narrative, and, conversely, the 'plot' (sjužet), the story as actually told by linking the events together.[3] To formalists, fable is 'the set of events tied together which are communicated to us in the course of the work', or 'what has in effect happened'; plot is 'how the reader becomes aware of what happened,' that is, basically, the 'order of the appearance (of the events) in the work itself',[4] whether normal (abc). flashed-back (acb). or begun *in medias res* (bc). [. . .]

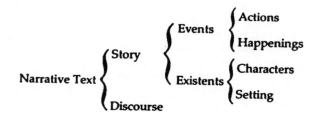

Fig. 61.1.

Is narrative a semiotic structure?

Narrative is a structure: we may go on to ask if it is independently meaningful, that is, conveys a meaning in and of itself, separately from the story it tells. Linguistics and semiotics, the general science of signs, teach us that a simple distinction between expression and content is insufficient to capture all elements of the communicative situation. Crosscutting this distinction, there is that between substance and form. Figure 61.2 is familiar to everyone who has read Ferdinand de Saussure and Louis Hjelmslev. Units of the expression plane convey meanings, that is, units of the content plane. In languages, the substance of expression is the material nature of the linguistic elements, for example, the actual sounds made by voices, or marks on paper. The substance of content (or 'meaning') is, on the other hand, 'the whole mass of thoughts and emotions common to mankind independently of the language they speak'.[5] Now each language (reflecting its culture) divides up these mental experiences in different ways. Hence the *form* of the content is 'the abstract structure of relationships which a particular language imposes ... on the same underlying substance'.[6] The vocal apparatus is capable of an immense variety of sounds, but each language selects a relatively small number through which to express its meanings.

	Expression	**Content**
Substance		
Form		

Fig. 61.2.

If narrative structure is indeed semiotic – that is, communicates meaning in its own right, over and above the paraphraseable contents of its story – it should be explicable in terms of the quadripartite array above. It should contain (1) a form and substance of expression, and (2) a form and substance of content.

What in narrative is the province of expression? Precisely the narrative discourse. Story is the content of the narrative expression, while discourse is the form of that expression. We must distinguish between the discourse and its material manifestation – in words, drawings, or whatever. The latter is clearly the *substance* of narrative expression, even where the manifestation is independently a semiotic code. But commonly codes serve other codes as substance; for instance, Barthes has shown that in the world of fashion, the codes of clothing 'enjoy the status of systems only in so far as they pass through the relay of language, which extracts their signifieds (in the forms of usages or reasons)'. He concludes that 'it is ... difficult to conceive a system of images and objects whose *signifieds* can exist independently of language'.[7] In precisely the same way, narratives are *langues* conveyed through the *paroles* of concrete verbal or other means of communication.

As for narrative content, it too has a substance and a form. The substance of events and existents is the whole universe, or, better, the set of possible objects, events, abstractions, and so on that can be 'imitated' by an author (film director, etc.). This is illustrated in Fig. 61.3.

	Expression	Content
Substance	Media insofar as they can communicate stories. (Some media are semiotic systems in their own right.)	Representations of objects & actions in real & imagined worlds that can be imitated in a narrative medium, as filtered through the codes of the author's society.
Form	Narrative discourse (the structure of narrative transmission) consisting of elements shared by narratives in any medium whatsoever.	Narrative story components: events, existents, and their connections.

Fig. 61.3.

But what does it mean practically to say that narrative is a meaningful structure in its own right? The question is not 'What does any given story mean?' but rather 'What does narrative itself (or narrativizing a text) mean?'. The *signifiés* or signifieds are exactly three – event, character, and detail of setting; the *signifiants* or signifiers are those elements in the narrative statement (whatever the medium) that can stand for one of these three, thus any kind of physical or mental action for the first, any person (or, indeed, any entity that can be personalized) for the second, and any evocation of place for the third. We are justified, I believe, in arguing that narrative structure imparts meanings, of the three kinds listed above, precisely because it can endow an otherwise meaningless ur-text with eventhood, characterhood, and settinghood, in a normal one-to-one standing-for relationship. There are animated cartoons in which a completely contentless object is endowed with characterhood, that is, takes on the meaning 'character' because it engages in a suitably anthropomorphic action (that is, a movement on the screen that is conceived as an instance of human movement). [. . .]

Substance will be discussed where it seems to facilitate an understanding of narrative form. For instance it is clear that verbal narratives express narrative contents of time summary more easily than do cinematic narratives, while the latter more easily show spatial relations. A purely gratuitous visual link may tie together two shots (the line of the roof support in Charles Foster Kane's childhood home in *Citizen Kane* 'turns into' a string wrapping a Christmas package given him by his cold-hearted guardian; the sweep of the curve of a Hollywood starlet's body on top of St. Peter's in *La Dolce Vita* 'turns into' the sweep of a saxophone braying in an outdoor night-club).

The above considerations prompt a redrawing of our first diagram to that shown in Fig. 61.4.

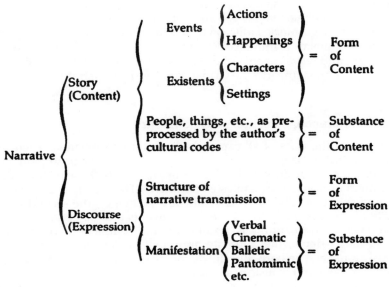

Fig. 61.4.

Manifestation and physical object

Story, discourse, and manifestation must further be distinguished from the mere physical disposition of narratives – the actual print in books, movements of actors or dancers or marionettes, lines on paper or canvas, or whatever.

This issue is resolved by phenomenological aesthetics, particularly by Roman Ingarden, who has established the fundamental difference between the 'real object' presented to us in museums, libraries, the theatre, and so on, and the 'aesthetic object'.[8] The real object is the thing in the outside world – the piece of marble, the canvas with pigment dried on it, the air waves vibrating at certain frequencies, the pile of printed pages sewn together in a binding. The aesthetic object, on the other hand, is that which comes into existence when the observer experiences the real object aesthetically. Thus it is a construction (or reconstruction) in the observer's mind. Aesthetic objects may exist in the absence of a real object. One can have an aesthetic experience through purely fictitious objects; for example, we may 'only imagine the "letters" or the corresponding sound, e.g., when we are repeating a poem from memory'. Thus the material book (or whatever) is not 'a literary work, but only a means to 'fix' the work, or rather to make it accessible to the reader'. To a certain point, the physical condition of a book (or other artefact) does not affect the nature of the aesthetic object fixed by it: *David Copperfield* remains *David Copperfield* whether it is read in an elegant library edition or a dirty, water-stained paperback version. Further, *mere* reading is not an aesthetic experience, just as merely looking at a statue is not one. They are simply preliminary to the aesthetic experience. The perceiver must at some point mentally construct the 'field' or 'world' of the aesthetic object.

The aesthetic object of a narrative is the story as articulated by the discourse, what Susanne Langer would call the 'virtual' object of the narrative. A medium – language, music, stone, paint and canvas, or whatever – actualizes the narrative, makes it into a real object, a book, a musical composition (vibrating sound waves in an auditorium or on a disc), a statue, a painting: but the reader must unearth the virtual narrative by penetrating its medial surface.

Narrative inference, selection, and coherence

If discourse is the class of all expressions of story, in whatever medium possible to it (natural language, ballet, 'programme' music, comic strips, mime, and so on), it must be an abstract class, containing only those features that are common to all actually manifested narratives. The principal features are order and selection. The first I have already spoken of; the second is the capacity of any discourse to choose which events and objects actually to state and which only to imply. For example, in the 'complete' account, never given in all its detail, the 'ultimate argument,' or *logos*, each character obviously must first be born. But the discourse need not mention his birth, may elect to take up his history at the age of ten or twenty-five or fifty or whenever suits its purpose. Thus *story* in one sense is the continuum of events presupposing the total set of all conceivable details, that is, those that can be projected by the normal laws of the physical universe. In practice, of course, it is only that continuum and that set actually inferred by a reader, and there is room for difference in interpretation.

A narrative is a communication; hence, it presupposes two parties, a sender and a receiver. Each party entails three different personages. On the sending end are the real author, the implied author, and the narrator (if any); on the receiving end, the real audience (listener, reader, viewer), the implied audience, and the narratee.

The sense modality in which narrative operates may be either visual or auditory or both. In the visual category are non-verbal narratives (painting, sculpture, ballet, pure or 'unbubbled' comic strips, mime, etc.), plus written texts. In the auditory category are bardic chants, musical narratives, radio plays, and other oral performances. But this distinction conceals an important commonality between written and oral texts. All written texts are realizable orally; they are not being performed but could be at any moment. That is, they are innately susceptible of performance.

Whether the narrative is experienced through a performance or through a text, the members of the audience must respond with an interpretation: they cannot avoid participating in the transaction. They must fill in gaps with essential or likely events, traits and objects which for various reasons have gone unmentioned. [. . .]

A sketch of narrative structure

Narrative discourse consists of a connected sequence of narrative *statements*, where 'statement' is quite independent of the particular expressive medium. It includes dance statement, linguistic statement, graphic statement, and so on. 'Narrative statement' and 'to state narratively' are used here as technical terms for any expression of a narrative element viewed independently of its manifesting substance. The term has a broad discursive sense, not a grammatical one. For example, a narrative statement may be manifested by questions or commands as well as by declarative constructions in natural language.

Narratives are communications, thus easily envisaged as the movement of arrows from left to right, from author to audience. But we must distinguish between real and implied authors and audiences: only implied authors and audiences are immanent to the work, constructs of the narrative-transaction-as-text. The real author and audience of course communicate, but only through their implied counterparts. What is communicated is *story*, the formal content element of narrative; and it is communicated by *discourse*, the formal expression element. The discourse is said to 'state' the story, and these statements are of two kinds – *process* and *stasis* – according to whether someone did something or something happened; or whether something simply existed in the story. [. . .]

'Reading' and 'reading out'

Though this chapter has treated story as an object, I do not mean to suggest that it is a hypothesized object, separate from the process by which it emerges in the consciousness of a 'reader' (using that term to include not only readers in their armchairs, but also audiences at movie houses, ballets, puppet shows, and so on). This kind of 'reading out' is qualitatively different from ordinary reading, though so familiar as to seem totally 'natural'. [. . .] From the surface or manifestation level of reading, one works through to the deeper narrative level. That is the process I call, technically, *reading out*. Reading out is thus an 'inter-level' term, while mere 'reading' is 'intra-level.' I am trying to avoid technical vocabulary wherever possible, but this seems a necessary distinct-ion, and reading out a relatively transparent term for 'decoding from surface to deep narrative structures'. Narrative translation from one medium to another is possible because roughly the same set of events and existents can be read out. I do not minimize the problems entailed in the surface reading, itself a profoundly cultural and by no means 'natural' process. Witness the reports of anthropologists that aborigines have difficulty in even seeing what are, to us, 'self-evident' video and cinematic images. But it is at the 'reading-out' level that occur the problems of the elementary literature class, where students understand the meaning of every sentence in isolation, but cannot make any sense (or any satisfying sense) out of the whole narrative text.

Notes

1. See *Morfologia Skazi* (Leningrad, 1928), translated by Laurence Scott as *The Morphology of the Folktale*, 2nd edn (Austin, 1970). A summary of Propp's analysis appears in the article 'Les Transformations des contes fantastiques', in (1966) Todorov, Tzvetan (ed.) *Théorie de la littérature*, Paris, pp. 234–62; and also Bremond, Claude(1964) Le messag narratif. *Communications*, Vol. 4, pp. 4–10.
2. Todorov, Poétique, p.103.

3. Erlich, Victor (1965) *Russian Formalism: History, Doctrine*, 2nd edn, The Hague, pp. 240–41.
4. Tomashevsky, Boris (1925) *Teorija literatury (Poehka)*, Leningrad. The relevant section, Thématique, appears in Todorov, (ed.) *Théorie de la littérature*, pp. 263–307; and in Lemon and Reis (eds) *Russian Formalist Criticism*, pp. 61–98. The quotations here translate the French text in Todorov (ed.) p. 268. The distinction between *fabula* and *sjužet* appears on p. 68 of Lemon and Reis.
5. Lyons, John (1969) *Introduction to Theoretical Linguistics*, Cambridge, p. 56.
6. Ibid., p.55.
7. Barthes, Roland (1967) *Elements of Semiology* (translated by Lavers, Annette and Smith, Colin), Boston, p. 10.
8. Roman Ingarden (1967) Aesthetic experience and aesthetic object. In Lawrence, Nathaniel and O'Conner, Daniel (eds) *Readings in Existential Phenomenology*, Englewood Cliffs, NJ, p. 304.
9. Langer, Susanne (1953) *Feeling and Form*, New York, p. 48, and *passim*. The section on narrative is on pp. 260–5.

62

Principles of narration

David Bordwell

From Bordwell, D. (1985) *Narration in the Fiction Film*, Methuen, London, pp. 49–53.

Theories of narration founder upon superficial analogies between film and other media – literature or theatre (the mimetic approach); literature, speech, or writing (the diegetic approach). The theory I propose sees narration as a formal activity, a notion comparable to Eisenstein's rhetoric of form. In keeping with a perceptual–cognitive approach to the spectator's work, this theory treats narration as a process which is not in its basic aims specific to any medium. As a dynamic process, narration deploys the materials and procedures of each medium for its ends. Thinking of narration in this way yields considerable scope for investigation while still allowing us to build in the specific possibilities of the film medium. In addition, a form-centred approach sets itself the task of explaining how narration functions in the totality of the film. Narrational patterning is a major part of the process by which we grasp films as more or less coherent wholes.

Fabula, syuzhet, and style

I have assumed a difference between the story that is represented and the actual representation of it, the form in which the perceiver actually encounters it. This crucial distinction may go back to Aristotle,[1] but it was most fully theorized by the Russian formalists, and it is indispensable to a theory of narration.

Presented with two narrative events, we look for causal or spatial or temporal links. The imaginary construct we create, progressively and retroactively, was termed by formalists the *fabula* (sometimes translated as 'story'). More specifically, the fabula embodies the action as a chronological, cause-and-effect chain of events occurring within a given duration and a spatial field. In *Rear Window*, as in most detective tales, there is an overt process of fabula construction, since the investigation of the crime involves establishing certain connections among events. Putting the fabula together requires us to construct the story of the ongoing inquiry while at the same time framing and testing hypotheses about past events. That is, the story of the investigation is a search for the concealed story of a crime. By the end of the typical detective tale, all story events can be fitted into a single pattern of time, space, and causality.

The fabula is thus a pattern which perceivers of narratives create through assumptions and inferences. It is the developing result of picking up narrative cues, applying schemata, framing and testing hypotheses. Ideally, the fabula can be embodied in a verbal synopsis, as general or as detailed as circumstances require. Yet the fabula, however imaginary, is not a whimsical or arbitrary construct. The viewer builds the fabula on the basis of prototype schemata (identifiable types of persons, actions, locales, etc.), template schemata (principally the 'canonic' story), and procedural schemata (a search for appropriate motivations and relations of causality, time, and space). To the extent that these processes are intersubjective, so is the fabula that is created. In principle, viewers of a film will agree about either what the story is or what factors obscure or render ambiguous the adequate construction of the story.

It would be an error to take the fabula, or story, as the profilmic event. A film's fabula is never materially present on the screen or soundtrack. When we see a shot of Jeff looking out his window, his action is a representation which signals us to infer a story event (Jeff looks out his window). The same piece of information might have been conveyed many other ways, many of them requiring no sight or sound of Jeff at all. The staging of the action, as Eisenstein showed, is itself a representational act. This theoretical move lets us avoid that a priori favouring of certain film techniques characteristic of mimetic theories.

'The fabula', writes Tynianov, 'can only be guessed at, but it is not a given'.[2] What is given? What sorts of phenomenally present materials and forms do we encounter? We can analyse the film as consisting of two systems and a remaining body of material, diagrammed in Fig. 62.1. The *syuzhet* (usually translated as 'plot') is the actual arrangement and presentation of the fabula in the film. It is not the text *in toto*.[3] It is a more abstract construct, the patterning of the story as a blow-by-blow recounting of the film could render it. The syuzhet is a system because it arranges components – the story events and states of affairs – according to specific principles. As Boris Tomashevsky puts it: 'The fabula is opposed to the syuzhet, which is built out of the same events, but the syuzhet respects their order in the work and the series of information processes which designate them'.[4] 'Syuzhet' names the architectonics of the film's presentation of the fabula; hence the rightward arrow in the diagram.[5] Logically, syuzhet patterning is independent of the medium; the same syuzhet patterns could be embodied in a novel, a play, or a film.

Style also constitutes a system in that it too mobilizes components – particular instantiations of film techniques – according to principles of organization. There are other uses of the term 'style' (e.g., to designate recurrent features of structure or texture in a body of films, such as 'neo-realist style'), but in this context, 'style' simply names the film's systematic

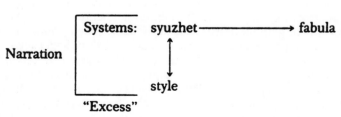

Fig. 62.1.

use of cinematic devices. Style is thus wholly ingredient to the medium. Style interacts with syuzhet in various ways; hence the two-way arrow in the diagram.

An example may illustrate how syuzhet and style differ. In *Rear Window*, the syuzhet consists of the particular pattern of events (actions, scenes, turning points, plot twists) depicting the tale of Mrs Thorwald's murder and its investigation and the tale of Lisa and Jeff's romance. The same film, however, can be described as a steady flow of applications of cinematic techniques – mise-en-scène, cinematography, editing, and sound. In one scene, Jeff and Stella are spotted by Thorwald. They step quickly back into Jeff's room (figure movement, setting); they whisper (sound) and douse the lamp (lighting); the camera tracks quickly back to a long shot (cinematography); and all of this occurs after the crucial shot of Thorwald turning to look out his window (editing).

Note that in a narrative film these two systems coexist. They can do this because syuzhet and style each treat different aspects of the phenomenal process. The syuzhet embodies the film as a 'dramaturgical' process; style embodies it as a 'technical' one. While it would often be arbitrary to separate the two systems in the process of perception, the distinction has precedent in much narrative theory.[6] Indeed, we shall discover one mode of narration that requires us to keep syuzhet and style conceptually separate. Assuming that the distinction is warranted, I want now to spell out the relations between syuzhet and fabula, and syuzhet and style.

In discussing the spectator's activity, I stressed the role of narrative schemata.[7] The theoretical concept of the syuzhet offers a way of analysing the aspects of a film that the spectator organizes into an on-going story. The latter, we can now see. comprises schematic assumptions about both the fabula and the syuzhet. The viewer's tendency to assume that characters have goals pertains to causality in the fabula; it does not imply anything about syuzhet organization. But the assumption that the spectator will encounter an exposition or an ending pertains to the organization of the syuzhet. The 'canonic story' nonetheless offers an example of how assumptions about syuzhet and fabula factors play a considerable role in narrative comprehension.

As a distinction, the fabula/syuzhet pair cuts across media. At a gross level, the same fabula could be inferred from a novel, a film, a painting, or a play. Thus one difficulty of enunciative theories – the forced analogy between linguistic categories and non-verbal phenomena – vanishes. As Meir Sternberg puts it, any narrative medium utilizes 'a largely extraverbal logic' that includes 'the twofold development of the action, as it objectively and straightforwardly progresses in the fictive world from beginning to end (within the fabula) and as it is deformed and patterned into progressing in our mind during the reading-process (within the syuzhet)'.[8] The conception of syuzhet avoids surface-phenomena distinctions (such as person, tense, meta-language) and relies upon more supple principles basic to all narrative representation. Consequently, and contrary to what some writers believe, the fabula/syuzhet distinction does not replicate the *histoire/discours* distinction held by enunciation theories.[9] The fabula is not an unmarked enunciative act; it is not a speech act at all but a set of inferences.

I asserted that the syuzhet composes story situations and events according to specifiable principles. When we perceive and comprehend a narrative text, we tend to construct certain patterns among events. We can now see how the film's syuzhet provides a basis for this activity. Three sorts of principles relate the syuzhet to the fabula.

1. *Narrative 'logic'*. In constructing a fabula, the perceiver defines some phenomena as events while constructing relations among them. These relations are primarily causal ones. An event will be assumed to be a consequence of another event, of a character trait, or of some general law. The syuzhet can facilitate this process by systematically encouraging us to make linear causal inferences. But the syuzhet can also arrange events so as to block or complicate the construction of causal relations. This happens with the false clues in *Rear Window*. Narrative logic also includes a more abstract principle of similarity and difference which I call *parallelism*. Thorwald's murder of his wife has no significant effect on most of his neighbours; one function of the courtyard vignettes is to parallel the romantic relations of Jeff and Lisa with other male/female relations. What counts as an event, a cause, an effect, a similarity, or a difference – all will be determined within the context of the individual film.

2. *Time*. Narrative time has several aspects, well analysed by Gerard Genette. The syuzhet can cue us to construct fabula events in any sequence (a matter of *order*). The syuzhet can suggest fabula events as occurring in virtually any time span (*duration*). And the syuzhet can signal fabula events as taking place any number of times (*frequency*). These aspects can all assist or block the viewer's construction of fabula time. Again, temporal representation will vary with historical convention and the context of the individual film.

3. *Space*. Fabula events must be represented as occurring in a spatial frame of reference, however vague or abstract. The syuzhet can facilitate construction of fabula space by informing us of the relevant surroundings and the positions and paths assumed by the story's agents. The confinement to Jeff's courtyard in *Rear Window* is an instance of the use of syuzhet devices to advance our construction of fabula space. But the film could also impede our comprehension by suspending, muddling, or undercutting our construction of space.

Depending on how the syuzhet presents the fabula, there will be particular spectatorial effects. Armed with the notion of different narrative principles and the concept of the syuzhet's distortion of fabula information, we can begin to account for the concrete narrational work of any film. It is obvious, for instance, that *Rear Window* depends upon withholding certain fabula information; we can now see that our schematizing and hypothesizing activities are guided by the syuzhet's cues about causality, time, and space. The basic training aspect of the film's early portions – its tendency to give visual cues, let us draw inferences, and then confirm or disconfirm them by verbal statement – arises from manipulation of causal information. To take a specific scene: while Jeff is asleep, we see a woman leave with Thorwald and wonder if she is his wife; the syuzhet has generated this suspicion that Mrs Thorwald is still alive by not showing us this woman (who is not Mrs Thorwald) entering the apartment. The syuzhet of *Rear Window* also blocks our knowledge by limiting space; we can use only narrowly restricted views of the courtyard to construct the fabula. And *Rear Window* is not exceptional in its limitations, concealments, and revelations. For theoretical purposes it may sometimes be convenient to take as an ideal baseline an instance in which the syuzhet is constructed so as to permit maximum access to the fabula. But every syuzhet uses retardation to postpone complete construction of the fabula. At the very least, the end of the story, or the means whereby we arrive there, will be withheld. Thus the syuzhet aims not to let us construct the fabula in some logically pristine state but rather to guide us to construct the fabula in a specific way, by arousing in us particular expectations at this or that point, eliciting our curiosity or suspense, and pulling surprises along the way.

In some cases, the syuzhet will include masses of material that block our construction of the fabula. Such material may encourage us to treat the syuzhet as interpreting or commenting on the fabula. In *October*, both Kerensky and General Kornilov appeal to the slogan 'For God and Country'. Suddenly we cut to a series of statues of gods from many cultures. These shots do not help us to construct the spatial, temporal, or logical connections among story events; in fabula terms they are a digression. Nonetheless, the sequence constitutes syuzhet manipulation. As a little dissertation on the very idea of God, the passage emphasizes the cultural variability of religion and suggests that an appeal to the holy often veils political opportunism. The inserted material insists in its patterned development that we motivate it transtextually, as a species of rhetorical argument. A novelist's commentary, however digressive, forms an integral part of the syuzhet, and so do Eisenstein's essayistic interpolations.

The syuzhet, then, is the dramaturgy of the fiction film, the organized set of cues prompting us to infer and assemble story information. As Figure 62.1 suggests, the film's style can interact with the syuzhet in various ways. Film technique is customarily used to perform syuzhet tasks – providing information, cueing hypotheses, and so forth. In the 'normal' film, that is, the syuzhet system controls the stylistic system – in formalist terms, the syuzhet is the 'dominant'. For example, patterns in the syuzhet's presentation of story information will be matched by stylistic patterns, as when at the close of *Rear Window* a camera movement homologous to that in the opening underlines the changes in the lives of the courtyard's inhabitants.

Still, this is not to say that the systematic employment of film techniques – that is, the film's style – is wholly a vehicle for the syuzhet. When alternative techniques exist for a given syuzhet purpose, it may make a difference which technique is chosen. For instance, the syuzhet may require that two story events be cued as occurring simultaneously. The simultaneity may be denoted by crosscutting from one event to the other, by staging the two actions in depth, by use of split-screen techniques, or by the inclusion of particular objects in the setting (such as a television set broadcasting a 'live' event).

Whatever stylistic choice is made may have different effects on the spectator's perceptual and cognitive activity. Style is thus a notable factor in its own right, even when it is 'only' supporting the syuzhet.

Film style can also take shapes not justified by the syuzhet's manipulation of story information. If in *Rear Window* Hitchcock systematically cut from Jeff's gaze to close ups of misleading or irrelevant objects which he could not see, then the stylistic procedure itself could vie for prominence with the syuzhet's task of presenting the story. True, we might take this stylistic flourish as a syuzhet manoeuvre to baffle us about causality or space; but if the device were repeated systematically across the film with no clear link to the developing syuzhet and fabula, then the more economical explanation would be that style has come forward to claim our attention independent of syuzhet/fabula relations. For analytical purposes, then, we must grant a potential disparity between the stylistic system and the syuzhet system, even if such a tendency is rare.

It is evident that both syuzhet and style invite the spectator to apply motivational rationales. At the syuzhet level, when Jeff and Stella recoil from Thorwald's look, the audience justifies this event as psychologically plausible and compositionally necessary for what follows. At the stylistic level, when Jeff scans the apartment block and the next shot is of Thorwald's windows, we assume the shot to be compositionally relevant, grant it a certain realism (Jeff's point of view), and acquiesce to a generic convention (this could be a suspenseful build-up). In the hypothetical example of patterned cutaways to irrelevant objects, we would try to motivate them compositionally, realistically, or transtextually; but if all were unequal to the task set by the style, we would have a case of 'artistic motivation', whereby the materials and forms of the medium constitute the chief object of interest.

It is time for a formal definition. In the fiction film, narration is the *process whereby the film's syuzhet and style interact in the course of cueing and channelling the spectator's construction of the fabula.* Thus it is not only when the syuzhet arranges fabula information that the film narrates. Narration also includes stylistic processes. It would of course be possible to treat narration solely as a matter of syuzhet/fabula relations, but this would leave out the ways in which the filmic texture affects the spectator's activity. We have already seen that the spectator possesses stylistic schemata as well as others, and these invariably affect the overall process of narrative representation. Moreover, by including style within narration, we can analyse stylistic departures from the syuzhet's project. In an earlier example, a cut from Jeff's gaze to irrelevant objects would be a narrational act as much as would a cut to relevant ones. Narration is the dynamic interaction between the syuzhet's transmission of story information and what Tynianov called 'the movement, the rise and fall of the stylistic masses'.[10]

Is there anything in a narrative film that is not narrational? Any image or sound can contribute to narration, but we can also attend to an element for its sheer perceptual salience. Roland Barthes has spoken of a film's 'third meaning', one lying beyond denotation and connotation: the realm in which casual lines, colours, expressions, and textures become 'fellow travellers' of the story.[11] Kristin Thompson has identified these elements as 'excess', materials which may stand out perceptually but which do not fit either narrative or stylistic patterns[12] (see Fig. 62.1). As we have seen, the spectator's categories push her or him to construct objects and denotative meaning from the outset. The canonic story in particular favours the dominance of story-world factors. From this standpoint, it is as if nothing but narration matters. But in the first shot of *Rear Window*, we can choose not to construct a story world and instead savour random colours, gestures, and sounds. These 'excessive' elements are utterly unjustified, even by aesthetic motivation. Now, this attitude is actually quite difficult to maintain over a long period, since it offers little perceptual and cognitive payoff. The *trouvailles* will never add up. Nonetheless, there may be aspects of a film that we cannot attribute to narration. In some cases, as Thompson shows with *Ivan the Terrible*, 'excess' may offer a useful way into the film's overall formal work. 'A perception of a film that includes its excess implies an awareness of the structures (including conventions) at work in the film, since excess is precisely those elements that escape unifying impulses. Such an approach to viewing films can allow us to look further into a film, renewing its ability to intrigue us by its strangeness.[13]

Notes

1. See Aristotle (1968) *Poetics* (commentary by Lucas, D. W.), Clarendon Press, Oxford, pp. 53–4, 100.
2. Tynianov, Yuri (1978) Plot and story-line in the cinema. *Russian Poetics in Translation*, Vol. 5, p. 20.
3. Since writing Chapters 1–7 of Bordwell, David, Staiger, Janet and Thompson, Kristin (1985) *The Classical Hollywood Cinema: Film Style and Mode of Production to 1960*, Columbia University Press, New York, I have reconsidered the plot/story distinction. There Chapter 2 asserted that plot (syuzhet) consists of 'the totality of formal and stylistic materials in the film', and Chapter 3 called narration that aspect of plot which transmits story information. This formulation now seems to me inadequate, both as a reading of the formalists and as an account of film form. For the reasons presented in the present chapter, I take narration to be the all-inclusive process which uses both syuzhet and style to cue spectators to construct a *fabula*, or story. This revision of theoretical terms does not seem to me to affect the analytical and descriptive claims I make in *The Classical Hollywood Cinema*, but it does offer greater theoretical precision.
4. Tomashevsky, Boris (1965) Thematics. In Lemon, Lee T. and Reis, Marion J. (eds) *Russian Formalist Criticism: Four Essays*, University of Nebraska Press, Lincoln, pp. 66–7.
5. My emphasis upon the fabula as an emergent spectatorial construct is characteristic of 'late' Russian formalist poetics; the early writings of Shklovsky in particular tend to treat the fabula as a pre-existent raw material for artistic elaboration. Nonetheless, at times we must use the language of carpentry or sculpture in describing the syuzhet's operations. For the narrative artist does in some sense work 'on' the fabula as *he may assume that the perceiver will construct it*. In the previous chapter, I claimed that the narrative film is so made as to encourage the spectator to execute story-constructing activities. These activities can in turn be presupposed by the film-maker. For the artist, presenting a story 'out of' chronological order is just that: a transformation of that arrangement which a spectator would presumably make when presented with more 'linear' cues. (Here a theoretical approach emphasizing narrative as a *structure* overlaps with that treating narration as a temporal *activity*.) The perceiver, given a narrative text, is invited to recognize a syuzhet and infer a fabula from it, whereas the artist constructs a syuzhet

according to assumptions about how the spectator could infer a fabula from it. And these assumptions will form part of the artist's material.

6. Most Russian formalist narrative theory assumes a distinction between syuzhet and style, as witnessed in the title of Viktor Shklovsky's 1919 essay, 'On the connection between devices of syuzhet construction and general stylistic devices' (1972, *Twentieth Century Studies*, Nos. 7/8, December, pp. 48–72). Although Shklovsky believed that syuzhet construction and stylistic elements often parallel each other, he presupposed them to occupy distinct domains. Boris Tomashevsky and Boris Eichenbaum also held this view. More recently, both Meir Sternberg and Seymour Chatman exclude style from the realm of the syuzhet. See Sternberg, *Expositional Modes and Temporal Ordering in Fiction* (1978, Johns Hopkins University Press, Baltimore, p. 34); and Chatman, *Story and Discourse: Narrative Structure in Fiction and Film* (1978, Cornell University Press, Ithaca, pp. 10–11, 24). Yuri Tynianov speaks of the syuzhet as 'the story's dynamics, composed of the interactions of all the linkages of material (including the story as a linkage of actions) – stylistic linkage, story linkage, etc.' (1981, On the foundations of cinema. In Eagle, Herbert (ed.) *Russian Formalist Film Theory*, University of Michigan Slavic Publications, Ann Arbor, p. 96). The passage is cryptic, but it suggests that the syuzhet includes both 'story linkage' and style, in which case Tynianov's conception would be structurally congruent with mine: what I and others call 'syuzhet,' he calls 'story linkage,' and what he calls 'syuzhet' I call narration.
7. See p. 31, above.
8. Sternberg, *Expositional Modes and Temporal Ordering in Fiction*, p. 34.
9. cf. Chatman, *Story and Discourse*, pp. 19–20; Genette, Gérard (1966) *Figures II*, Seuil, Paris, p. 66.
10. Tynianov, Yuri (1978) Plot and story-line in the cinema. *Russian Poetics in Translation*, Vol. 5, p. 20.
11. Barthes, Roland (1977) The third meaning. In Heath, Stephen (ed. and translator) *Image Music Text*, Hill and Wang, New York, p. 64
12. Thompson, Kristin (1981) *Ivan the Terrible: A Neoformalist Analysis*, Princeton University Press, Princeton, pp. 287–95.
13. Ibid., p. 302.

63

Narrative form in American network television

Jane Feuer

From MacCabe, C. (ed.) (1986) *High Theory/Low Culture: Analysing Popular Television and Film*, Manchester University Press, Manchester, pp. 102–14.

Television narrative structure

Most theories of cinematic narrative have stressed a linear, causal model derived from the work of Roland Barthes and others. That this is the dominant model for conceptualizing cinematic narrative is illustrated by a definition of 'narrative' given in a popular film introductory text as 'a chain of events in cause/effect relationship occurring in time'.[1] Following Barthes, the narrative structure of the classical Hollywood text is seen as proceeding through a chain of narrative 'enigmas' towards closure. Although much criticism has been levelled at such a totalizing theory of cinematic narrative (not the least because it describes masculine genres better than feminine genres), I believe that it is even less applicable to the operation of television. The television apparatus works against logical notions of causality and closure. According to John Ellis, television narrative operates through the segment, i.e. a relatively self-contained scene that is discontinuous with other segments. Ellis goes on to argue that 'movement from one segment to the next is a matter of succession rather than consequence'. Thus, for Ellis, all television narrative is *serial* rather than linear, in the sense that 'the series implies the form of the dilemma rather than that of resolution and closure'.[2] In this sense, neither of the two forms of television narrative that I will discuss – the episodic series and the continuing serial – correspond to the dominant model of popular cinematic narrative. However, their methods of non-correspondence differ.

Meta-psychology

The dominant model of the 'cinematic apparatus' based on the work of Metz, Baudry and others does not account very well for television. Television may be seen to possess a different 'imaginary' from cinema, to articulate a different position for its subject, and to demand ways of looking which do not correspond to mirror-identification and voyeurism as they have been described for the cinema. In another context, I have argued that so-called magazine format non-fiction television sets up an idealized quasi-nuclear

493

family whose unity is seen as an attribute of the medium itself.[3] This representational strategy has its completion in the mode of address of the apparatus – 'from our family to yours'. (These are the actual words used in the Christmas message sent to 'my family' by the local news 'team' in my market.) That is to say that the 'implied spectator' for television is not the isolated, immobilized pre-Oedipal individual described by Metz and Baudry in their meta-psychology of the cinema, but rather a post-Oedipal, fully socialized family member. Thus we need to revise a model of specularity derived from the cinema by providing for television a new destination to Metz's quest in *The Imaginary Signifier* for an analogue to the Lacanian mirror.[4] For television, we would have to dispute or at least reformulate Metz's claim that the spectator's own body is never reflected in the mirror. To be perversely literal-minded (in keeping with the spirit of much meta-psychological speculation of this ilk), the television screen *does* reflect the body of the family, if we turn the images off. This is perhaps a metaphorical way of arguing that the representational content of television proposes a reflection, however distorted, of the body of the familialized viewing subject. We are not dealing with the same degree of signification-by-absence that can be deduced from an examination of the 'basic cinematographic apparatus' if only because, as I have argued at length elsewhere, television disseminates an ideology of presence that has its basis in the presumed 'live' status of the apparatus.[5]

By extension, the unevenly developed dialectic of voyeurism and exhibitionism that Metz theorizes for the cinema does not operate with the same force for television. Far from wanting to disguise its discourse as story, television seems to want to foreground its discursive status. As Robert Stam has written regarding television news, 'if illusionistic fictions disguise their discourse as history, television news, in certain respects, wraps up its history as discourse'.[6] This calls into question a model of spectatorship based upon voyeurism. Television's foremost illusion is that it is an *interactive medium*, not that we are peering into a self-enclosed diegetic space. This generalized stance of the apparatus as a whole, due in part to the property of 'flow', tends to carry over to the more cinematic narrative modes of the episodic series and the continuing serial, if only because these 'diegetic' fictions are continually interrupted (especially on American television) by more discursive structures in the form of voice-over announcements, commercials, and promotional 'spots'. The 'diegesis' in television can never be sustained in the imaginary of the cinema either at a narrative level or at the level of modes of reception. As Raymond Williams has explained, the historically determined mode of reception for television in the West depends upon a social use of technology 'which served an at once mobile and home-centred way of living: a form of *mobile privatisation*'.[7] This is in sharp contrast to the psychoanalytical view of the historical conditions of reception for theatrical cinema which might be described as 'immobilized public consumption'. In this regard, it is important to take into account studies which demonstrate the viewer's 'talking back' to television – a process now literalized on certain cable systems by interactive cable capability, but also an implied feature of network television. The very concept 'diegesis' is unthinkable on television. One rather astonishing example of television's tendency to 'break' the cinematic diegesis (that I have observed recently) is a pattern of interrupting the ten o'clock drama with 'promos' for the eleven o'clock local news in which the news anchors, in direct address, attempt to draw parallels between the presumed diegetic fiction and a 'real' happening that will be 'covered' in the forthcoming news broadcast. For example, a 'news report' on college students' ritualistic viewing of *Dynasty* was announced during the commercial break preceding the last segment of *Dynasty* and then broadcast during the news report directly following *Dynasty*. Similarly, following a 'trauma drama' on teen suicide, the eleven o'clock news announced and subsequently presented 'expert' psychological advice on how to recognize suicidal tendencies in 'your' children. The example appears all the more bizarre if considered in terms of screen theory, when one recognizes that the identical 'expert advice' had already been given within the diegesis of the made-for-TV film in the form of a public address to a self-help group given by the mother of one of the dead children. Yet it does not appear bizarre to the viewing subject thus addressed precisely because such disregard for the diegetic is a *conventional* television practice, not an exceptional one. Television as an ideological apparatus strives to break down any barriers between the fictional diegesis, the advertising diegesis, and the diegesis of the viewing family, finding it advantageous to assume all three are one and the same.

Familialized technology

Although both the episodic series and the continuing serial are serial forms constituted by the media's economically derived need for perpetual self-reduplication, they differ in their narrative strategies. The self-replication of the episodic series depends upon a continual re-integration of the family; that of the continuing serial depends upon a continual disintegration of the family.

In almost Lévi-Straussian terms, the dominant binary opposition informing television's representational practices is that of inside the family/outside the family. Both the episodic series and the continuing serial have as their 'irresolvable' cultural contradiction the need to explain factors which in reality are 'outside' in terms of the 'inside'. For television, both the economic and the socio-political cannot be thought except in terms of 'inside the family'- an impossible dilemma, if indeed such dilemmas cannot be resolved inside the family. The social may not be equivalent to the familiar, but for ideological reasons, television's narrative representations would have it so. Here we must part company with Lévi-Strauss, in order to note that the inability to resolve the inside/outside contradiction is not a universal attribute of the human mind but rather an ideological construct derived from the social formation as a whole and buttressed by the specific role of the television apparatus as a mechanism for reproducing ideology. Thus the television 'apparatus' is historically determined.

Recent revisionist broadcast historians have emphasized the extent to which a *social* conception of broadcast technology influenced the development of that technology in the direction of Williams' 'mobile privatization'. According to these historians, the technology by no means determined its innovation as an apparatus for private consumption within the family. In its experimental period, television's initial location was in the public theatre, and it was primarily its association with radio that led to television's innovation as a home-based advertising media in America.[8] Radio itself had been instrumental in the growth of consumerism, the process of changing the American home into a unit for consumption rather than production. In this changing ideology of the home, the radio receiver played a significant role in conferring status.[9] Whereas the radio industry had initially sought in the family a market for its receiving equipment (as had the BBC in its formative years), the American radio manufacturers from their first attempts to innovate television in the 1930s already had in mind a model for selling families to advertisers. This socio-economic relationship between the apparatus and the familial viewing subject has its counterpart in television's textual strategies.

[. . .]

For the continuing serial, the very need to 'rupture' the family in order for the plot to continue can be viewed as a 'dangerous' strategy in the sense that it allows for a reading of the disintegration as a critique of the family itself. Specifically, it threatens to explode the strategy of containment common to both the series and serial by which all conflicts are expressed in terms of the family. In the sitcom, the threatening forces are re-expelled each week. The continuing serial, by contrast, maintains its 'outside' within the family structure. The outside forces which threaten the sitcom family become the inside forces which threaten the internal disintegration of the continuing serial family. In allowing the family to be perennially torn apart, there is always the danger that 'the outside' will explode upon the inside. We cannot, however, guarantee that this will lead to *politically* progressive readings of continuing serials. Rather than set up an opposition between the episodic series and the continuing serial along reactionary/radical lines, I would prefer to view them as two different responses to television's dual ideological compulsions: the need to repeat and the need to contain.

Notes

1. Bordwell, David and Thompson, Kristin (1979) *Film Art: An Introduction*, Addison-Wesley, Reading, MA.
2. Ellis, John (1982) *Visible Fictions*, Routledge and Kegan Paul, London, pp. 145–60.
3. 'The concept of live TV: ontology as ideology'. In Kaplan, E. Ann (ed.) *Regarding Television*, University Publications of America, Fredrick, MD, pp. 12–22.
4. Metz, Christian (1975) *The Imaginary Signifier*, Indiana University Press, Bloomington, pp. 1–88.
5. Kaplan, op. cit. (see Note 3).
6. 'Television news and its spectator'. In Kaplan (ed.) op. cit., p. 38 (see Note 3).
7. *Television: Technology and Cultural Form* (1975) Schocken Books, New York, p. 26.
8. Allen, Jeanne 'The social matrix of television: invention in the U.S.'. In Kaplan, op. cit. (see Note 3).
9. Boddy, Willian (1979) The rhetoric and the economic roots of the American broadcast industry. *Cine-Tracts*, Vol. 2, spring.

Section 10

New audience research

64

Approaches to 'new audience research'

Oliver Boyd-Barrett

If obliged to define a single distinguishing feature of media study over the past 15 years many scholars would focus on new approaches to audience or 'reception' analysis. Audience analysis is exceptionally important in media study because even when scholars do research issues other than audience issues, such as the industrial structure of the media or processes of production, the significance of their research is premised on the assumption that in the final analysis they can illuminate something about the nature of the influence which the media exercise through readers and audiences. Influence need not be direct, but may be reflected in the ways in which media processes interact with the political process (see Blumler and Gurevitch in this volume), or even more abstractly in the relationship between communication systems and different kinds of human society (Innis, 1972) but one can usually unpack such discourses in terms of an underlying belief in media effects, e.g. that the media intervene in the political process because politicians believe the potential for persuasion through media to be so great that political institutions and processes need to be re-organized to take media coverage into account.

Audience research is certainly not new in media study, and reaches back to its earliest days. In what ways, then, has anything new happened in the past 15+ years? The 'new audience research', in the U.K. at least, is sometimes traced back to David Morley's 1980 book, *The Nationwide Audience*. Morley's study was an application developed from Hall's 1973 hypothetical differentiation between different textual decodings. Hall's model borrowed from Parkin (1971), and distinguished among: (i) decodings which operate inside the 'dominant code' of the text (i.e. within the structure of denotative and connotative meanings which the authors of the text intend should frame understanding – the 'preferred reading'; (ii) decodings which 'negotiate' the dominant code in some way; and (iii) 'oppositional' decodings which 'retotalize the message within some alternative frame of reference'. The significance of intentionality is discussed by Morley (1992). Authors typically work within existing meaning systems and discourses, drawing from previous textual knowledge without conscious reflection, and these, more than specific intentions, will structure the 'preferred meaning' of the text which they have 'authored'. It is a feature of the post-modern critique of textual analysis that the inter-textual character of texts demotes the significance of the concept of 'authorship'.

Morley's 1980 work was an empirical investigation of different interpretations of the same two programmes by different groups. The study demonstrates that readings of the programmes 'were founded on cultural differences embedded within the structure of society – cultural clusters which guide and limit the individual's interpretations of messages' (Morley, 1992, p. 118). This can be related to the radicalization of sociolinguistics by Fairclough (1989) who sees variations of language use not simply in terms of individual choice, but in terms of the culturally-influenced choice of a given language variety in any given situation from a range or repertoire of possibilities, the extent and content of which is determined by culture and the individual's position within that culture. Both encodings and decodings, in other words, are complex culturally-derived competencies.

A distinguishing feature of Morley's work therefore, and evident in 'new audience research' as a whole, one which has become increasingly more refined and sensitive to different situations, is the importance it attributes to different readings of any given text and the relationship of such differences to cultural and social contexts. There is increasing wariness about simplistic categorizations of social context, and about simplistic categorizations of responses to texts. The original model drawn from Parkin and Hall, depended too much on political texts (Dyer, 1977). Reacting to a text is more than just a question of agreement or disagreement, but is also a matter of effect and of comprehension (both of which may be expressions of cultural rather than just individual values).

There are important questions about the factors which influence how and in what ways people come to texts in the first place (see Morley, in this section): for example, as a site for unpressurized relaxation and intensive involvement, as in the case of a man sitting down for an evening's television entertainment after a hard day's work, or pressurized and fragmented as in the case of a woman attending intermittently to television during a rota of household chores and childcare responsibilities? There is also a relationship between text and social context such that some texts have closer correspondence than others with given social and cultural contexts, as, for example in the case of the privileged place of a school textbook within a context of teacher–pupil interaction in formal education, where the formal context of use may be said to reinforce the 'inscription of readers' by the text.

The process of 'reading', in other words, is influenced by a range of factors that includes the structure of the text itself, the social context within which the text is read, the cultural affinities of readers and the ways in which cultural factors influence their reading competencies, predispositions, opportunities, and likes and dislikes. The potential complexity of these interrelationships makes it unlikely that readings can be predicted solely on the basis of the classic sociological parameters of class, education, occupation and, less classically, gender, ethnicity and age. These may be influential, but are fragmented by a myriad of other sources of difference, many of them cultural formations which do not map neatly on to these privileged categories.

If the key insight of new audience research is that different readers read texts differently, then why is it new? This is the question posed by the extract from Curran in this section. Curran argues that the 'reconceptualization' of media introduced by the 'new' audience research is identical to views of the media that emerged from 1940s and 1950s empirical research. This earlier 'effects' tradition 'prefigures revisionist arguments by documenting the multiple meanings generated by texts, the active and creative role of audiences and the ways in which different social and discourse positions encourage different reading'. Curran acknowledges some achievements of new audience research: its stronger focus on the text, better understanding of processes of interpretation, and location of these processes in a 'more adequate sociological context', but worries about its lack of quantification and the loose construction of 'decoding' (but see Morley's later discussion, above).

The original 'effects' or, rather, the 'limited effects' model of media influence, based on empirical research of the 1940s and 1950s, and summarized by Joseph Klapper's concepts of selective exposure, selective attention, selective comprehension, selective retention was a reaction to what had previously been a view of the media as extremely powerful. Likewise, the 'new audience research' is a reaction to the dominance for over two decades of 'critical', often neo-Marxist or cultural hegemony perspectives, which attributed to the media very great power – through ideological reinforcement rather than behavioural or attitudinal *change*.

Curran's charge of 'revisionism' is in line with concerns of radical political economists namely, that scholarly preoccupation with the diversity of readings has politically undesirable consequences. If texts do not determine audience readings, then producers need feel less responsible for the readings that result. If the media are not powerful, why worry about the media? If a set range of texts can generate an infinity of readings, then need producers worry about the limited repertoire of texts that they mass produce for mass audiences? Revisionism undermines the force of the radical critique of mass communication: that it serves the interests of the powerful and contributes to social reproduction of inequality.

Coming from a re-evaluation of approaches to the text, new audience research was linked with the study of language and literature. Hall and Morley had come through the Centre for Cultural Studies in Birmingham, located in a university English department. Radway's contribution in this section had its origin in American Studies and American literature. It is a reaction against formalist study of 'great works' (which unpacked the meaning of culturally prized texts in terms of their underlying structures, without reference to *actual* readers), in favour of ethnographic analysis of the readings of popular literature as a way to understand the place of such texts in the lives of ordinary Americans. Radway's ethnographic approach is a key moment, therefore, in the American wing of 'new audience research', which in the U.S. has been more closely associated with feminism than in the U.K. where, in the early work of Hall and Morley, it had mainly to do with political critique of the 'hegemonic consensus'.

Radway shares with Morley a strong concern for empirical investigation of the reading of texts. Both works celebrate ethnography. They both explore the problematics of a tradition adopted from social anthropology in which it was originally assumed that the life or experiences of the 'other' could be represented – given sufficient attention to detail, and 'faithfulness' to the data – in some kind of neutral, non-judgemental way. Both recognized that 'readings' are influenced by cultural groups to which the readers belong, and that any culture can be defined in part by its strategies for the construction, handling and interpretation of texts. In Radway's research, women talked about the reading of romances in terms of their taking time for themselves within a context of stressful family demands on their time.

Radway observes close parallels between her work and contemporaries who had also studied women's media consumption, including Dorothy Hobson, David Morley, Charlotte Brunson. (There are important connect- ions, perhaps still to be made, between study of the embedding in culture of different kinds of media text, and the study of different kinds of literacy as culturally embedded – as in the work of Shirley Brice-Heath, 1982). Radway found regularities in the meanings that her readers took from texts, and associated these with her subjects' situation and feelings as wives and mothers within patriarchal marriage. Just as Morley originally privileged social class, Radway privileges gender and she later reflects that she would like to have explored how readings also interacted with other broad sociological parameters in influencing textual interpretations. In the extract chosen for this section she explores the relationship between reading, reading strategies, social competencies and, drawing on Chodorow's psychoanalysis – pleasure. This is an additive process where the act of reading reinforces certain reading competencies (a theory of learning which is explored in the work of Salomon, 1979) and these in turn are inter-related with cultural experiences which sensitize a reader to particular genres and interpretations of genre.

Like Radway and Hobson, Ien Ang's now classic study of interpretations of the American soap opera *Dallas* is focused on women; she divides her respondents among those who profess to hate the programme, others who love it, and yet others who combine both condemnation and pleasure in a posture of irony. Her focus in this extract is on how readings of *Dallas*, and the pleasures associated with viewing it, can survive even the same viewers' subscription to an ideology of mass culture, globally widespread and linked to a discourse of cultural imperialism that is hostile to popular and especially American popular culture. In effect, viewers position themselves in relation to the programme, to the dominant ideology and to the views which they imagine that others would hold of their liking for *Dallas*. They do so in ways that allow them to maintain positive self-image, even to retain their 'critical' awareness of, or ironic detachment from, the programme (in conformity with the dominant anti-populist ideology), yet also to derive pleasure from it. The circle is not, however, squared: there is no resolution, no equally coherent set of beliefs that completely neutralizes the power of the dominant ideology, with only the tentative exception of viewers who can fall back on an oppositional 'ideology of populism', one which valorizes autonomous taste and judgement.

Morley's empiricism in *Nationwide* entailed a comparative structure, organizing viewers into discrete occupational groups. This raised questions about the validity of inferences based on relatively 'unnatural' viewing conditions, and about the status of any articulation in such a context of views which might not otherwise have been articulated (discussion about media, as Moss, 1989, argues, has at least as much to do with group dynamics as about media experiences). The methodology may be more sophisticated (but not necessarily yielding more valid data) than that of Radway (interviews with women) or of Ang (letters in response to an advertisement).

Concern for a degree of comparative rigour resurfaces in the studies of

Liebes and Katz, represented in this section. Like Ang they too focus on *Dallas*. Their interest is to explore different patterns of involvement with *Dallas* among different cultural groups. In their study they organized some 50 small groups of viewers in each case by asking an initial couple to invite two other couples who might have joined them anyway. Following the programme, an observer switched on his tape recorder and put a series of open questions to the group. The researchers applied this method to five ethnic communities, four of them in Israel, and to groups of second generation Americans in Los Angeles. The focus is on viewer involvement as represented through group talk, and in particular on how viewers 'involve' or 'distance' themselves from the story depicted on the screen. This can be related to the work of Ang, inasmuch as the 'ludic' or 'playful' ('meta-linguistic') keyings, in which the authors are particularly interested, suggest that viewers negotiate their reactions to programmes through dominant ideologies of mass (or western) culture, although Liebes and Katz are not specifically interested in ideology. They suggest that the groups which are most familiar with and whose culture is most in tune with such cultural products are more likely to 'distance' themselves from the programme, readier to analyse it in 'meta' terms, demonstrating awareness of the production and commercial contexts and discussing its content playfully rather than moralistically. Perhaps we can say that they are more competent in negotiating their 'pleasure' around problems of programme reality, and morality. The authors worry that the nihilistic lack of a moral defence makes Western audiences more rather than less susceptible than those who are more directly 'involved', to the programme's values. The 'involved' groups, by contrast, perceive themselves or their culture as more moral than that of the programme, and consider that their culture is vulnerable to its immorality while in practice they may perhaps be better 'protected' from it. There are links to be made here with Tomlinson's (1992) view of cultural imperialism as the spread of modernity, involving the simultaneous rejection of tradition and a sense of *loss* in face of its irreplaceability. A viewer from a non-modern context is participating in modernity, taking its forms of cultural expression at face value and *therefore* condemning modernity even while finding pleasure in it.

The focus of Bausinger in this section moves away from the content of television to the social meanings of television technology in domestic context. In other words to understand the significance of television we need to look at how social relations are articulated in, around and through the use of television: who has what kind of influence over which programmes that family members watch, in the presence of whom, and what kinds of talk about television take place in viewing contexts? This fruitful line of investigation, which is also touched on in Radway's analysis of romantic literature in the home, has been developed much further in more recent work, among others, of Lull (1989), Moores (1990), Moss (1989), Morley (1992) Silverstone *et al.* (1994). It is a line of investigation which lends itself yet more readily to the anthropological mode of media ethnography, as it is less about interviewing people about media experience than about observing the everyday cultural embeddedness of television in the social practices that govern the 'taking of meaning' and of pleasure from television. This is also a feature of Morley's (1986) work on television in the family, in this section, which focuses on television, gender and gender differences in attitudes to talk about television. This links back to and enriches our understanding of Ang's ideology of mass culture, adding masculine/feminine to the range of oppositions articulated by that discourse, including passivity/activity, commercial/non-commercial, national/foreign, profound/shallow, authentic/stereotypical, good popular culture/bad popular culture.

The extract from Allor, in this section, traces the study of audiences to major different traditions of media study, principally political economy, post-structuralist film theory, feminist criticism, cultural studies and post-modernism. It does not map the field in exactly the same terms employed in this volume but its map can be overlaid with the one here in most respects save for post-modernism, and in this way the article also serves an overview or revision function, probably better than one of introduction, and is a useful source of recommendations for further reading in addition to those which are supplied at the end of this chapter. The major weakness of the approach of political economy to audiences, is that while it explores the commodification of audiences, it ignores actual viewing practices. In post-modernist film theory (covered in 'moving image' here) we see that audiences are theorized as subjects positioned by textual discourse rather than empirically investigated. This had moved further, at the time of Allor's writing, to a consideration of the structural similarities between texts and the cultural conditions (still theorized rather than investigated) which determine viewing. The contribution of feminist criticism (here called feminist media theory) has been to expand the range of texts in literary criticism and to identify textual and reading practices related to the ways in which feminine roles are culturally embedded. The work of Morley and CCCS is located by Allor in cultural studies and more particularly in the investigation of ideological hegemony. Reference is made to significant contributions which have not been included here, including those of Fiske, Walkerdine, McRobbie. Generally, Allor identifies a movement away from a focus on social class and ideology to an interest in social sites of media consumption and the relationship between consumption, pleasure, fantasy and identity. Post-modernism, finally, seeks to undermine familiar oppositions of individual and social, text and audience, representation and represented, real and unreal.

References and further reading

Brice-Heath, S. (1982) What no bed-time story means. *Language in Society*, Vol. 2, No. 1, pp. 49–74.

Brundson, C. (1986) Women watching television. *MedieKulture*, Vol. 4.

Chodorow, N. (1978) *The Reproduction of Mothering: Psychoanalysis and the Sociology of Gender*, University of California Press, Berkeley.

Dyer, R. (1977) Victim: hermeneutic project. *Film Forum*, Vol. 1, No. 2.

Fairclough, N. (1989) *Language and Power*, Longman, Harlow.

Fiske, J. (1986) Television: polysemy and popularity, *Critical Studies in Mass Communication*, Vol. 3, pp. 391–408.

Hall, S. (1973) Encoding/decoding in television discourse. Reprinted in Hall *et al.* (eds) *Culture, Media, Language*, Hutchinson, London.

Hobson, D. (1982) *'Crossroads': Drama of a Soap Opera*, Methuen, London.

Lull, J. (1989) *Families Watching Television*, Sage, London.

McRobbie, A. (1984) Dance and social fantasy. In McRobbie, A. and Nava, M. (eds) *Gender and Generation*, Macmillan, London, pp. 130–61.

Moores, S. (1990) Texts, readers and contexts of reading: developments in the study of media audiences. In *Media, Culture and Society*, Vol. 12, pp. 9–29.

Morley, D. (1992) *Television, Audiences and Cultural Studies*, Routledge, London.

Moss, G. (1989), *Unpopular Fictions*, Virago, London.

Parkin, F. (1971) *Class Inequality and Political Order*, Paladin, London.

Salomon, G. (1979) *Interaction of Media, Cognition and Knowledge*, Jossey-Bass, London.

Silverstone, Hirsch, E. and Morley, D. (1992) Information and communication technologies and the moral economy of the household. In Silverstone and Hirsch (eds) *Consuming Technologies*, Routledge, London.

Tomlinson, J. (1992) *Cultural Imperialism*, Pintor, London.

Walkerdine, V. (1986) Video replay: families, films, and fantasy. In Burgin, V., Donald, J. and Kaplan, C. (eds) *Formations of Fantasy*, Methuen, London, pp. 167–99.

65

The new revisionism in mass communication research: a reappraisal

James Curran

From Blumler, J. G. *et al.* (eds) (1990) *European Journal of Communication*, Sage, London, Vol. 5, No. 2, pp. 145–51.

Revisionist assessments of audience reception

However, it is around the issues raised by the production of meaning and audience reception that revisionist writing has had most public impact. The radical tradition of mass communication research was for the most part grounded in a relatively unproblematic analysis of meaning. But a new tradition of revisionist scholarship emerged that emphasized the inconsistencies, contradictions, gaps and even internal oppositions within texts. The shift is exemplified by a comparison between the pessimistic 'state-of-the-art' collection of essays on women and the media edited by Helen Baehr (1980) and more optimistic, redemptive readings of texts by revisionists like Cook and Johnston (1988)[1] and Modleski (1982) which emphasize internal points of resistance to patriarchal values or crucial ambivalences. This shift is expressed in its most extreme form in the claim that TV is a medium that often produces relatively open and ambiguous programmes, 'producerly texts' that 'delegate[s] the production of meaning to the viewer producer' (Fiske, 1989c). A similar argument has been advanced in relation to rock videos (Larsen, 1989).

The second key shift was a reconceptualization of the audience as an active producer of meaning. This is an area of media research that has been extensively mythologized – a theme to which we shall return later. It is sufficient to note here that the assumption that audiences responded in prescribed ways to fixed, preconstituted meanings in texts, to be found in certain forms of formalist analysis, was challenged by the notion that meaning was constructed through the interaction of text and the social and discourse positions of audiences. This point was well made in a notable study of reactions to two *Nationwide* programmes by David Morley, one of the most distinguished and influential revisionist critics. He showed that divergent groups responded in very different ways to *Nationwide*, and that these differences reflected the different discourses and institutions in which they were situated. It was a particularly acute analysis, not least because of the way it illuminated the importance of different subcultural formations within the same class in generating different audience responses (Morley, 1980).

The revisionist stress on audience autonomy has encouraged a more cautious assessment of media influence. Typical of this revisionist reorientation is a case study of a 'moral panic' that not only failed but backfired by creating increased sympathy for the intended victim (Curran, 1987). Similarly, the failure of trans-European satellite TV to secure a mass audience has been explained in terms of audience autonomy rooted in linguistic and cultural differences (Collins, 1989).

Finally, the implicit conclusion that the media had only limited influence encouraged some researchers to shift their focus of interest. The political aesthetic gave way to the popular aesthetic; the focus of investigation shifted from whether media representations advanced or retarded political and cultural struggle to the question of why the mass media were popular. This encouraged 'readings' of media content that sought to infer the nature of people's pleasure in them (e.g. Drotner, 1989), and ethnographic studies of the audience that sought to probe the roots of their pleasure (e.g. Kippax, 1988).

Rediscovering the wheel?

This revisionism is often presented in assertive terms as an example of intellectual progress in which those hitherto mired in error have been confounded and enlightened. Thus, Morley (1989, pp. 16–17) recounts how 'the whole tradition of effects studies' was dominated by 'a hypodermic model of influence' until the uses and gratifications approach advanced the concept of the active audience. This was an improvement, we are told, because 'from this perspective one can no longer talk about the 'effects' of a message on a homogeneous mass audience who are expected to be affected in the same way'. However, even this improvement was 'severely limited', because it ultimately explained differential responses to the media in terms of 'individual differences of personality or psychology'. Only the new revisionism, we are informed, introduced a more satisfactory and rounded account.

This is a breath-taking, though often repeated,[2] caricature of the history of communications research that writes out a whole generation of researchers. It presents as innovation what is in reality a process of rediscovery. This mythologizing also has the effect of obscuring the multiple lines of intersection between past media research in the pluralist tradition and the new revisionism emerging out of the radical tradition. Effects research cannot be said in any meaningful sense to have been 'dominated' by the hypodermic model. On the contrary, its main thrust ever since the 1940s was to assert the independence and autonomy of media audiences and dispel the widespread notion that people are easily influenced by the media. It did this by developing many of the same insights that have been proclaimed afresh in the recent spate of 'reception' studies, albeit in a different technical language and sometimes with less subtlety.

Thus, effects researchers argued long ago that the predispositions that people bring to texts crucially influence their understanding of these texts, and that different predispositions generate different understandings. Thus, to cite one now forgotten study almost at random, Hastorf and Cantril (1954) showed a film of a particularly dirty football match between Dartmouth and Princeton to two groups of students, one from each university and asked them among other things to log the number of infractions of the rules committed by each side. The Princeton students concluded that the Dartmouth team committed more than twice as many fouls as their side, whereas the majority of the Dartmouth group concluded that both sides were about equally at fault. This prompted the authors to advance a 'transactional' perspective, in which 'it is inaccurate or misleading to say that different people have different attitudes to the same thing. For the thing is *not* the same for different people, whether the thing is a football game, a presidential candidate, communism, or spinach'. By implication, the apophthegm 'seeing is believing' should be recast as 'believing is seeing'.

This study was not unusual for this period in attributing differences of audience response to differences of shared disposition rather than, as Morley dismissively puts it, to 'individual differences of personality or psychology'. But it was also characteristic in offering a relatively simple, one-dimensional account of audience adaptation of meaning.

However, some effects researchers developed a much more complex model of audience interactions which anticipated revisionists' subsequent discovery of 'the interdiscursive processes of text-reader encounters'. An early example of this more sophisticated approach is provided by Patricia Kendall and Katherine Wolff's (1949) analysis of reactions to anti-racist cartoons. These featured Mr Biggott, an unattractive and cantankerous middle-aged man whose absurdity (highlighted by cobwebs coming out of his pin-point head) and extreme views were intended to discredit racist ideas. The study showed that 31 percent failed to recognize either that Mr Biggott was racially prejudiced or that the cartoons were intended to satirize racism, and that in general there was a considerable diversity in the way in which audience members understood the cartoons. Some resisted their propagandistic intention by resorting to various means of disidentification; they viewed Mr Biggott negatively not because of his views (which they shared) but because he was judged to be intellectually or socially inferior. A few even found in the cartoons confirmation of their prejudices, completely subverting the cartoons' intention.[3]

But perhaps the most illuminating part of this study was its explanation of why respondents negotiated the cartoons' meanings in the way that they did, based on lengthy individual interviews. One group of respondents who were secure in their racist beliefs felt no need to distance themselves from Mr Biggott's racism and remained unaware that the cartoon was attacking their opinions. Another group of prejudiced respondents had a momentary understanding of the satirical purpose of the cartoon, experienced it as punishing, did a double-take by disidentifying with Mr Biggott (in one case identifying him as a Jew) and thus succeeded in obscuring from themselves the proselytizing intention of the cartoon. The key to understanding their complex reaction was their own feelings of guilt, uncertainty or embarrassment about their racist views. A third group of young prejudiced men imposed a different frame of reference that cut across the intended framework of meaning in the cartoon. Instead of seeing the cartoons as an attack on their own views, they viewed them as a satirical attack on the older generation in which Mr Biggott symbolized the weakness, powerlessness and absurdity of flawed authority figures (with one respondent referring overtly to his father). In some of the interviews with this group, one had a glimpse of the cartoons 'working' in the sense that they encouraged a reappraisal of prejudiced views within a discourse of modernity directed against the parental generation.

That audiences perceive mass-communicated meanings differently has thus been a central finding of media effects research for nearly half a century. Another aspect of the relative autonomy of the audience, documented by Lazarsfeld, Berelson and Caudel as early as 1944, is the tendency of people to seek out media content that reinforces what they think and to avoid content that challenges their beliefs. But since the early 1950s, researchers have hotly contested the extent of selective audience exposure, and the evidence suggests that the rise of TV has reduced deliberate avoidance of media messages. However, defensive avoidance of dissonant messages persists to some degree, particularly when it is defined as inattention rather than as mere abstention.[4]

During the 1940s researchers also showed that sub-cultural formations within the audience influenced the extent to which media representations were *accepted* or not (e.g. Hyman and Sheatsley, 1947). This has become a recurrent finding of 'effects' research, as can be briefly illustrated by a clutch of studies about *All in the Family*, the successful American TV series, that featured a bigoted, chauvinist, politically reactionary but 'lovable' working class protagonist, Archie Bunker, who had regular arguments with his liberal-minded son-in-law, Mike. Racially prejudiced adolescents in Canada and the U.S. were much more inclined to think that bigoted Archie made sense and won in the end than young viewers with less prejudiced views (Vidmar and Rokeach, 1974; cf. Brigham and Giesbrecht, 1976). A comparable study in Holland revealed a more complex picture in which groups with different clusters of attitudes – whether ethnocentric, authoritarian or traditionalist – responded to the series in partially different ways (Wilhoit and de Bock, 1976). However, the most interesting study, based on responses of six- to ten-year-olds to a single programme, produced a classic summation of some of the themes of the new revisionism: 'different types of children, bringing different beliefs, attitudes, and values to the viewing of the show as a result of different socialization processes, are affected in distinctly different ways' (Meyer, 1976).

Brief reference should be made to two other strands of the 'effects' tradition, both of which are underdeveloped in 'reception' studies. The first is the stress on the dynamic processes of peer group mediation in blocking, reinforcing or modifying mass-communicated messages, following Katz and Lazarsfeld's land mark research (1955).[5] The other is the emphasis given in some studies to the selective retention of information. Levine and Murphy (1943) found that pro- and anti-communist groups tended to remember information which accorded with what they already believed, and to forget information which did not fit their world view; and that this selective forgetfulness increased over time. Subsequent research on retention has since substantially revised and refined understanding of the variables affecting selective memory.

The 'effects' tradition thus prefigures revisionist arguments by documenting the multiple meanings generated by texts, the active and creative role of audiences and the ways in which different social and discourse positions encourage different readings. In short, the research of the new revisionists is only startling and innovative from a foreshortened perspective of communications research in which the year AD begins with textual analyses of films and TV programmes in the journal *Screen*, and everything before that is shrouded in the eddying mists of time.

This said, the revisionist approach taken as a whole represents at one level an advance. It does focus more attention on the text, provides a much richer and fuller understanding of interdiscursive processes in audience reception and, above all, locates these in a more adequate sociological context. But it also represents at another level a backward step in its reluctance to quantify; its over-reliance on group discussions and consequent failure to probe adequately intra-group and individual differences;[6] and its invocation of the loose concept of 'decoding' which some researchers in the effects tradition have more usefully broken down analytically in a form that distinguishes between attention, comprehension, acceptance and retention.

This is also an appropriate point to consider parallels between revisionist, ethnographic studies of the audience and the uses and gratifications approach. It has become commonplace among revisionists to point to the shortcomings of uses and gratifications research as a preliminary to proclaiming the superiority of their own research. Thus, Ang (1985) argues that the revisionist approach is an improvement because, unlike the older tradition, it pays more attention to the mechanisms by which pleasure is aroused and it does not adopt an essentialist conception of need and gratification. There is some truth in her arguments, but the claim that the older tradition adopted an essentialist definition of need is only partly correct.

There are, in fact, considerable points of affinity between revisionist, ethnographic research and the earlier tradition that she attacks. This can be illustrated by comparing her own clever and illuminating study of Dutch reception of *Dallas* with a uses and gratifications study of radio serial listening in the U.S. conducted by Herzog (1944) some four decades earlier. Both enquiries pointed to the way in which soap opera can relativize the problems of audience members and make them more bearable or indeed pleasurable. Both also indicated the way in which soap opera provides scope for idealized but playful identification. But while Herzog paid little attention to the actual content of soap operas, she did not resort to an essentialist definition of need and gratification. Indeed, she provided in some ways a more socially situated account of women's pleasure in soap opera than Ang because she drew upon interview material rather than, as in Ang's case, letters. This enabled Herzog to illustrate what Ang calls 'the tragic structure of feeling' in terms of the particular predicaments that women found themselves in, even if she did not generalize a feminist perspective.

Quite simply, uses and gratifications research does not always resemble the way in which it is represented by those asserting the novelty of the revisionist approach. There are similarities between the two traditions. Moreover, the inferences derived from reception analysis *as a whole* have not always pointed to new directions. In some cases, they have resulted in old pluralist dishes being reheated and presented as new cuisine.

Notes

1. In fact, Cook and Johnston's admirable essay was first published in 1974 in an obscure film festival publication, and has only recently been properly distributed. It was ahead of its time.
2. Ironically, Morley (1980) offered a more complex and slightly less misleading historical account nine years earlier.
3. This last point is only brought out fully in the analysis of the same data undertaken by Cooper and Jahoda (1947).
4. For further discussion of this, see Tan (1985).
5. For a useful, brief discussion of the ways in which Katz and Lazarsfeld's two-step flow model of mediation has been complexified, see McQuail and Windahl (1981).
6. There is a certain inherent implausibility in the relatively high degree of group consensus that Morley (1980) encountered in his field work. Greater intra-group differences would probably have emerged if he had conducted individual interviews. For a recent example of research that highlights striking individual differences within groups in the processing of news, see Graber (1988).

References

Ang, Ien (1985) *Watching Dallas*, Methuen, London.

Baehr, Helen (ed.) (1980) *Women and the Media*, Pergamon Press, Oxford.

Brigham, John and Giesbrecht, Linda (1976) 'All in the family': racial attitudes. *Journal of Communication*, Vol. 26, No. 3.

Collins, Richard (1989) The language of advantage: satellite television in western Europe. *Media, Culture & Society*, Vol. 11, No. 3, pp. 351–71.

Cook, Pam and Johnston, Claire (1988) The place of woman in the cinema of Raoul Walsh. In Penley, Constance (ed.) *Feminism and Film Theory*, Routledge, London.

Curran, James (1987) The boomerang effect: the press and the battle for London, 1981–6. In Curran, James, Smith, Anthony and Wingate, Pauline (eds) *Impacts and Influences*, Methuen, London.

Drotner, Kirsten (1989) Intensities of feeling: emotion, reception and gender in popular culture. In Skovmand, Michael (ed.) *Media Fictions*. University of Åarhus Press, Åarhus.

Fiske, John (1989) Moments of television: neither the text nor the audience. In Seiter, Ellen *et al.* (eds) *Remote Control*, Routledge, London.

Hastorf, Albert and Cantril, Hadley (1954) They saw a game: a case study. *Journal of Abnormal and Social Psychology*, Vol. 49, pp. 129–34.

Herzog, Herta (1944) What do we really know about daytime serial listeners? In Lazarsfeld, Paul and Stanton, Frank (eds) *Radio Research 1942–1943*, Duell, Sloan and Pearce, New York.

Hyman, Herbert and Sheatsley, Paul (1947) Some reasons why information campaigns fail. *Public Opinion Quarterly*, Vol. 9, pp. 412–23.

Katz, Elihu and Lazarsfeld, Paul (1955) *Personal Influence*, Free Press, New York.

Kendall, Patricia and Wolff, Katherine (1949) The analysis of deviant case studies in communications research. In Lazarsfeld, Paul and Stanton, Frank (eds) *Communications Research 1949–1949*, Harper, New York.

Kippax, Susan (1988) Women as audience: the experience of unwaged women of the performing arts. *Media, Culture & Society*, Vol. 10, No. 1, pp. 5–21.

Larsen, Peter (1989) Beyond the narrative. Rock videos and modern visual fictions. In Skovmand, Michael (ed.) *Media Fictions*, Åarhus University Press, Åarhus.

Lazarsfeld, Paul, Berelson, Bernard and Gaudet, Hazel (1944) *The People's Choice*, Columbia University Press, New York.

Levine, Jerome and Murphy, Gardner (1943) The learning and forgetting of controversial material. *Journal of Abnormal and Social Psychology*, Vol. 38, pp. 507–17.
Meyer, Timothy P. (1976) The impact of 'all in the family' on children, *Journal of Broadcasting*, Winter issue.
Modleski, Tania (1982) *Loving with a Vengeance*, Archon Books, Hamden, CT.
Morley, David (1980) *The 'Nationwide' Audience*, British Film Institute, London.
Morley, David (1989) Changing paradigms in audience studies. In Seiter, Ellen *et al.* (eds) *Remote Control*, Routledge, London.
Vidmar, Neil and Rokeach, Milton (1974) Archie Bunker's bigotry: a study in selective perception and exposure. *Journal of Communication*, Vol. 24, No. 2, 240–50.
Wilhoit, G. Cleveland and de Bock, Harold (1976) 'All in the family' in Holland. *Journal of Communication*, Vol. 26, No. 3.

66

Reading *Reading the romance*

Janice A. Radway

From Radway, J. A. (1987) *Reading the Romance: Women, Patriarchy, and Popular Literature*, Verso, London, pp. 10–15.

Having identified what he takes to be the principal sociological problems with his earlier work on the 'Nationwide' audience, Morley suggests that audience research might be more successful if it turned to a genre-based theory of interpretation and interaction instead of to a simple encoding–decoding model. Such a theory, he observes, might more adequately theorlze the process of reading as a complex and inter-related series of actions which involves questions of relevance/irrelevance and comprehension/incomprehension in addition to that of ideological agreement. A theory in which genre is conceived as a set of rules for the production of meaning, operable both through writing and reading, might therefore be able to explain why certain sets of texts are especially interesting to particular groups of people (and not to others) because it would direct one's attention to the question of how and where a given set of generic rules had been created, learned, and used. This genre framework would focus attention on inter-discursive formations, that is, on questions about the kinds of cultural competencies that are learned as a consequence of certain social formations and how those are activated and perpetuated within and through multiple, related genres or discourses. Thus, just as one might want to ask what sorts of social grammars prepare working-class kids to understand Kung-fu movies and to find them interesting, so one might also want to ask what competencies prepare certain women to recognize romances as relevant to their experience and as potential routes to pleasure.

Although *Reading the Romance* does not use Morley's terms, it does work toward a kind of genre theory as he conceives it. To begin with, it attempts to understand how the Smithton women's social and material situation prepares them to find the act of reading attractive and even necessary. Secondly, through detailed questioning of the women about their own definition of romance and their criteria for distinguishing between ideal and failed versions of the genre, the study attempts to characterize the structure of the particular narrative the women have chosen to engage because they find it especially enjoyable. Finally, through its use of psychoanalytic theory, the book attempts to explain how and why such a structured story might be experienced as pleasurable by those women as a consequence of their socialization within a particular family unit. I would like to elaborate briefly on each of these moments in *Reading the Romance* in order to prepare the reader for what she or he will find in the subsequent pages and point to issues which would repay further exploration.

Most of the first half of *Reading the Romance* is devoted to a discussion of the social and material situation within which romance reading occurs Thus I initially survey the collection of social forces resulting in the mass production of romances in the 1970s and 80s, which are marketed in ways particularly appropriate to women that is through mail order and at commercial outlets largely frequented by them.[1] Although the move is analogous to Dorothy Hobson's detailed effort to explore the production of *Crossroads*, I have not gone so far as to investigate the professional ideologies informing the writing and editing of romances as she has done with the soap opera. The text does however recognize the importance of the romance-writing community even to readers because the Smithton women made it absolutely clear that they understood themselves to be reading particular and individual authors whose special marks of style they could recount in detail rather than identical factory-produced commodities. Despite the mediations of the publishing industry romance reading was seen by the women as a way of participating in a large exclusively female community. Were I conducting this study today I would want to compare the meaning and significance of the romance as it is inserted in the day-to-day existence of both writers and readers, for such a move might demonstrate the problems inherent in a simple reading off of cultural meaning or ideology from a single text.[2]

Turning from the particular processes impinging on production which create the conditions of possibility for regular romance purchases, *Reading The Romance* then attempts a parallel look at the conditions organizing women's private lives which likewise contribute to the possibility of regular romance reading. It is in this context that I distinguish analytically between the event of reading and the text encountered through the process. I found it necessary to do so, the reader will discover, because the Smithton women so insistently and articulately explained that their reading was a way of temporarily refusing the demands associated with their social role as wives and mothers. As they observed it functioned as a 'declaration of independence' as a way of securing privacy while at the same time providing companionship and conversation. In effect what Chapters two and three try to do as a result is to unpack the significance of the phrase 'escape' by taking it somewhat more literally than have most analysts of the media in order to specify the origin and character of the distance the women find it necessary to maintain between their 'ordinary' lives and their fantasies.[3] I have therefore tried to take seriously the dual implications of the word escape, that is, its reference to conditions left behind and its intentional projection of a utopian future.

It is this move I think that specifically relates *Reading the Romance* to Hobson's 'Crossroads' work, to her work on housewives, and to McRobbie's work on the culture of working-class girls. Indeed there are remarkable similarities to the way all of the women who contributed to these studies use traditionally female forms to resist their situation *as women* by enabling them to cope with the features of the situation that oppress them. Thus just as the adolescent girls studied by McRobbie manipulate the culture of femininity to 'combat the class-based and oppressive features of the school' and the housewives in Hobson's study rely on radio and TV to address their extreme loneliness, so the romance readers of Smithton use their books to erect a barrier between themselves and their families in order to declare themselves temporarily off-limits to those who would mine them for emotional support and material care. What the reader will find in Chapter three, then, is an effort to explore the myriad ways in which the simple act of taking up a book addresses the personal costs hidden within the social role of wife and mother. I try to make a case for seeing romance reading as a form of individual resistance to a situation predicated on the assumption that it is women alone who are responsible for the care and emotional nurturance of others. Romance reading buys time and privacy for women even as it addresses the corollary consequence of their situation, the physical exhaustion and emotional depletion brought about by the fact that no one within the patriarchal family is charged with *their* care. Given the Smithton women's highly specific reference to such costs, I found it impossible to ignore their equally fervent insistence that romance reading creates a feeling of hope, provides emotional sustenance and produces a fully visceral sense of well-being.

It was the effort to account for the ability of romance reading to address the women's longing for emotional replenishment that subsequently directed my attention to the cultural conditions that had prepared the women to choose romances from among all the other books available to them. Thus I found myself wondering how, given the particular 'needs' the event of reading seemed to address for the Smithton women, the romance story itself figured in this conjuncture. I began to wonder what it was about the romance heroine's experience that fostered the readers' ability to see her story as interesting and accounted for their willingness to seek their own pleasure through hers precisely at the moment when they were most directly confronting their dissatisfaction with traditionally structured heterosexual relationships. What contribution did the narration of a romance make to their experience of pleasure? Why didn't the Smithton women choose to read detective stories, westerns or best-sellers in their precious private moments?

In thus searching for a way to link a specific desire with a particularly chosen route to the fulfilment of that desire, I turned to psychoanalytic theory in general and to Nancy Chodorow's feminist revision of Freud in particular. Her work seemed relevant in this context because it insistently focused on the precise manner in which the social fact of parenting by women constitutes a female child with an ongoing need for the style of care associated originally with her primary parent, that is, with her mother. What I was trying to explain was the fact that the Smithton women apparently felt an intense need to be nurtured and cared for and that despite their universal claim to being happily married (a claim I did not doubt), that need was not being met adequately in their day-to-day existence. Romance reading, it appeared, addressed needs, desires, and wishes that a male partner could not. Chodorow's work looked useful precisely because it theorized an asymmetrical engendering process constituting women and men in profoundly mismatched ways. That work appeared additionally relevant when an investigation of the romances the Smithton women like best revealed that the heroines they most appreciated were virtually always provided with the kind of attention and care the Smithton women claimed to desire and further that the hero's ministrations were nearly always linked metaphorically with maternal concern and nurturance. Thus I found Chodorow's theories attractive because they could account for the ongoing search for the *mother* that I detected in the Smithton women's discussion of the act of romance reading and in their preferences for particular examples of the genre.

Chodorow's revisions of the psychoanalytic account of the family romance was interesting to me, in other words, because it postulated in women an ongoing, unfulfilled longing for the mother even after the Oedipal turn to the father and heterosexuality had been negotiated. Although Chodorow's principal argument was that the tripartite internal object configuration with which women are therefore endowed is addressed by a woman's subsequent turn to mothering and to her child (an argument that might be taken to imply that the constructed desire for the pre-Oedipal mother may be met through particular social arrangements), it seemed to me that what the Smithton readers were saying about romance reading indicated that in fact not even the activity of mothering could satisfy that lack or desire for the mother, at least for some women.[4] I thought this might be true because so much of what the women consciously said and unconsciously revealed through their evaluative procedures pointed to the centrality of the fact that in ideal romances the hero is constructed androgynously. Although the women were clearly taken with his spectacularly masculine phallic power, in their voluntary comments and in their revealed preferences they emphasized equally that his capacity for tenderness and attentive concern was essential as well. Chodorow's theories seemed helpful because of their capacity to explain what I thought of as the twin objects of desire underlying romance reading, that is, the desire for the nurturance represented and promised by the pre-Oedipal mother and for the power and autonomy associated with the Oedipal father. Romance reading, it seemed to me, permitted the ritual retelling of the psychic process by which traditional heterosexuality was constructed for women, but it also seemed to exist as a protest against the fundamental inability of heterosexuality to satisfy the very desires with which it engendered women.[5]

Reading the Romance turns to Chodorow's revision of psychoanalytic theory in order to explain the construction of the particular desires that seem to be met by the *act* of romance reading. However, it additionally uses that theory to explore the psychological resonance of the romantic *narrative* itself for readers so constructed and engendered, a narrative which is itself precisely about the process by which female subjectivity is brought into being within the patriarchal family. Psychoanalysis is thus used also to explain why the story hails these readers, why they believe it possible to pursue their own pleasure by serving as witness to the romantic heroine's achievement of hers. What the psychoanalytically-based interpretation reveals is the deep irony hidden in the fact that women who are experiencing the consequences of patriarchal marriage's failure to address their needs turn to a story which ritually recites the history of the process by which those needs are constituted. They do so, it appears, because the fantasy resolution of the tale ensures the heroine's achievement of the very pleasure the readers endlessly long for. In thus reading the story of a woman who is granted adult autonomy, a secure social position, and the completion produced by maternal nurturance, all in the person of the romantic hero, the Smithton women are repetitively asserting to be true what their still-unfulfilled desire demonstrates to be false, that is, that heterosexuality can create a fully coherent, fully satisfied, female subjectivity.[6]

In the end, *Reading the Romance* argues that romance reading is a profoundly conflicted activity centred upon a profoundly conflicted form. Thus the view of the romance developed here is similar to Valerie Walkerdine's account of girls' comics as a practice that channels psychic conflicts and contradictions in particular ways. It is also close to the view developed by Valerie Hey[7] as well as to that of Alison Light, who argues in her conclusion to her analysis of Daphne du Maurier's *Rebecca* that women's romance reading is 'as much a measure of their deep dissatisfaction with heterosexual options as of any desire to be fully identified with the submissive versions of femininity the texts endorse. Romance imagines peace, security and ease precisely because there is dissension, insecurity and difficulty'.[8] Light herself points to the crucial question raised by these fundamental ambiguities surrounding and infusing the act of romance reading, that is, to the crucial question of the ultimate effects the fantasy resolution has on the women who seek it out again and again. Does the romance's endless rediscovery of the virtues of a passive female sexuality merely stitch the reader ever more resolutely into the fabric of patriarchal culture? Or, alternatively, does the satisfaction a reader derives from the act of reading itself, an act she chooses, often in explicit defiance of others' opposition lead to a new sense of strength and independence? *Reading the Romance* ends without managing to resolve these questions, asserting that an adequate answer will come only with time and with careful investigation of the developmental trajectory of the lives of adult romance readers. However much I would like to resolve the issue here, once and forever, I continue to believe that such a resolution is theoretically impossible simply because the practices of reading and writing romance continue and their effects, even now, are not fully realized.

Recent critical work on the romance that focuses both on developments within the genre and within the changing profession of romance writing itself suggests that the recontainment of protest and the channelling of desire staged by the form have not been perfect enough to thwart all change. Indeed, Ann Jones has shown in an analysis of recent Mills & Boon romances that the genre has found it increasingly necessary to engage specifically with feminism.[9] She demonstrates that the contradictions within the genre have been intensified by a tendency to consolidate certain feminist agendas for women in the character of a working, independent heroine even while disparaging the women's movement itself, usually through the speeches of the hero. This 'conflict between feminism as emergent ideology and romance as a residual genre', contends Jones, produces three kinds of contradiction, including narrative discontinuity, irreconcilable settings, and inconsistency in realist dialogue.

Notes

1. I should perhaps note here that this boom was initiated in the U.S.A. by the Canadian firm of Harlequin Enterprises, which began its rise to prominence in mass market publishing by reprinting the romances of Mills & Boon in the 1950s

and 60s. The genre look off in the USA when Harlequin began to issue romance written by American women and when other firms simultaneously introduced explicit sex into the genre. The Smithton women did not confine themselves to a single kind of romance but read widely in the genre and appreciated many different variations.

2. On this point, see Grossberg's discussion in 'Critical theory and the politics of research', *Mass Communications Yearbook 6* (forthcoming, 1987).

3. The tendency to deplore the 'escapist' nature of popular fantasy seems much less pronounced in British work than in American. See, for instance, Valerie Walkerdine's sensitive discussion of the nature of fantasy escape for girls in 'Some day my prince will come: young girls and the preparation for adolescent sexuality', in (1984) McRobbie, Angela and Nava, Mica (eds) *Gender and Genderation*, Macmillan London, pp. 162–84.

4. The British reader will no doubt note that this did not lead me to reconsider Chodorow's work and its relation to object–relations theory. Walkerdine's comments in 'Some day my prince will come' (pp. 178–81) have since suggested to me that the revision romance reading caused me to propose in Chodorow's theory may be of more significance than I had thought. It may not be the case that mothering fails to work only for some (aberrant) women, but in fact that the struggle over gender identity is never resolved as she suggests, following Freud, Lacan, and Rose.

5. For a somewhat different use of Chodorow that also connects romance reading to the search for pre-Oedipal merging, see Angela Mile's fascinating unpublished article, 'Confessions of a Harlequin reader: romance and the fantasy of male mothering'.

6. Cora Kaplan has recently advanced an argument which suggests that readers do not identify only with the romantic heroine but in fact identify in multiple and wandering fashion with the seducer, the seduced, and the process of seduction itself. See 'The thorn birds: fiction, fantasy, femininity', in (1986) *Sea Changes: Feminism and Culture*, Verso, London, pp. 117–46. Although I found little evidence of this kind of multiple identification in the group I interviewed (at least at a conscious level), I have been told by many romance writers that the act of writing a romance is especially enjoyable because it gives them the opportunity to imagine themselves as the hero. It is also interesting to note that several American publishers of romances have recently permitted writers to experiment with the writing of a romance entirely from the hero's point of view. Thus it might be possible that this sort of multiple identification actually varies from reader to reader and therefore can be increased by cultural or personal changes.

7. Hey, Valerie (1983) The necessity of romance. University of Kent at Canterbury, Women's Studies Occasional Papers, No. 3.

8. Light, Alison (1984) 'Returning to Manderley' – romance fiction, female sexuality and class. *Feminist Review* 16, April, pp. 7–25.

9. Jones, Ann Rosaline (1986) Mills & Boon meets feminism. In Radford, Jean (ed.) *The Progress of Romance: The Politics of Popular Fiction*, Routledge & Kegan Paul, London, pp. 195–220.

67

Television and gender

David Morley

From Morley, D. (1986) *Family Television: Cultural Power and Domestic Leisure*, Comedia, London, pp. 146–50, 155–8.

The interviews identified the following major themes, which recur across the interviews with the different families, where I can point to a reasonable degree of consistency of response. Clearly, the one structural principle working across all the families interviewed is that of gender. These interviews raise important questions about the effects of gender in terms of:

- power and control over programme choice;
- viewing style;
- planned and unplanned viewing;
- amounts of viewing;
- television-related talk;
- use of video;
- 'solo' viewing and guilty pleasures;
- programme type preference;
- channel preference;
- national versus local news programming;
- comedy preferences.

Before going on to detail my findings under these particular headings I would first like to make some general points about the significance of the empirical differences which my research revealed between the viewing habits of the men and women in the sample. As will be seen below, the men and women offer clearly contrasting accounts of their viewing habits – in terms of their differential power to choose what they view, how much they view, their viewing styles and their choice of particular viewing material. However, I am not suggesting that these empirical differences are attributes of their essential biological characteristics as men and women. Rather, I am trying to argue that these differences are the effects of the particular social roles that these men and women occupy within the home. Moreover, as I have indicated, this sample primarily consists of lower middle-class and working-class nuclear families (all of whom are white) and I am not suggesting that the particular pattern of gender relations within the home found here (with all the consequences which that pattern has for viewing behaviour) would necessarily be replicated either in nuclear families from a different class or ethnic background, or in households of different types with the same class and ethnic backgrounds. Rather, it is always a case of how gender relations interact with, and are formed differently within, these different contexts.

However, aside from these qualifications, there is one fundamental point which needs to be made concerning the basically different positioning of men and women within the domestic sphere. It should be noted that in the earlier chapters of this book there was much emphasis on the fact that this research project was concerned with television viewing in its domestic context. The essential point here is that the dominant model of gender relations within this society (and certainly within that sub-section of it represented in my sample) is one in which the home is primarily defined for men as a site of leisure – in distinction to the 'industrial time' of their employment outside the home – while the home is primarily defined for women as a sphere of work (whether or not they also work outside the home). This simply means that in investigating television viewing in the home one is by definition investigating something which men are better placed to do wholeheartedly, and which women seem only to be able to do distractedly and guiltily, because of their continuing sense of their domestic responsibilities. Moreover, this differential positioning is given a greater significance as the home becomes increasingly defined as the 'proper' sphere of leisure, with the decline of public forms of entertainment and the growth of home-based leisure technologies such as video, etc.

These points are well illustrated in research by Ann Gray into women's viewing and the use of video in the home. Gray argues that many women do not really consider themselves as having any specific leisure time at all in the home and would feel too uncomfortably guilty to 'just' sit and watch television when there always are domestic tasks to be attended to.[1]

When considering the empirical findings summarized below, care must be taken to hold in view this structuring of the domestic environment by gender relations as the backdrop against which these particular patterns of viewing behaviour have developed. Otherwise we risk seeing this pattern as somehow the direct result of 'essential' or biological characteristics of men and women *per se*. As Charlotte Brunsdon has put it, commenting on research in this area we could

> mistakenly ... differentiate a male – fixed, controlling, uninterruptible – gaze, and a female – distracted, obscured, already busy – manner of watching television. There is some empirical truth in these characterisations, but to take this empirical truth for explanation leads to a theoretical short circuit. . . Television is a domestic medium – and indeed the male/female differentiation above is very close to the way in which cinema and television have themselves been differentiated. Cinema, the audiovisual medium of the public sphere [demands] the masculine gaze, while the domestic (feminine) medium is much less demanding, needing only an intermittent glance. This, given the empirical evidence ... offers us an image of male viewers trying to masculinise the domestic sphere. This way of watching television, however, seems not so much a masculine mode, but a mode of power. Current arrangements between men and women make it likely that it is men who will occupy this position in the home.[2]

From this perspective we can then see the empirical differences between the accounts of their viewing behaviour offered by the men and women in the sample as generated within this structure of domestic power relations.

Power and control over programme choice

Masculine power is evident in a number of the families as the ultimate determinant on occasions of conflict over viewing choices ('we discuss what we all want to watch and the biggest wins. That's me. I'm the biggest', Man, Family 4). More crudely, it is even more apparent in the case of those families who have an automatic control device. None of the women in any of the families use the automatic control regularly. A number of them complain that their husbands use the channel control device obsessively, channel flicking across programmes when their wives are trying to watch something else. Characteristically, the control device is the symbolic possession of the father (or of the son, in the father's absence) which sits 'on the arm of Daddy's chair' and is used almost exclusively by him. It is a highly visible symbol of condensed power relations (the descendant of the medieval mace perhaps?). The research done by Peter Collett and Roger Lamb in which they videotaped a number of families watching television over an extended period shows this to comic effect on at least one occasion where the husband carries the control device about the house with him as he moves from the living-room to the kitchen and then engages in a prolonged wrestling match with his wife and son simultaneously so as to prevent them from getting their hands on it.[3]

F2 Daughter: 'Dad keeps both of the automatic controls – one on each side of his chair'.

F3 Woman: 'Well, I don't get much chance, because he sits there with the automatic control beside him and that's it . . . I get annoyed because I can be watching a programme and he's flicking channels to see if a programme on the other side is finished, so he can record something. So the television's flickering all the time, while he's flicking the timer. I just say, 'For goodness' sake, leave it alone'. I don't get the chance to use the control. I don't get near it.'

F15 Woman: 'No, not really. I don't get the chance to use the automatic control. I leave that down to him. It is aggravating, because I can be watching something and all of a sudden he turns it over to get the football result.'

F9 Daughter: 'The control's always next to Dad's chair. It doesn't come away when Dad's here. It stays right there'.
F9 Woman: 'And that's what you do [her husband], isn't it? Flick, flick, flick – when they're in the middle of a sentence on the telly. He's always flicking it over'.
F9 Man: 'The remote control, oh yes, I use it all the time'.
F9 Daughter: 'Well, if you're in the middle of watching something, Dad's got a habit of flicking over the other side to see the result of the boxing'.

F8 Woman (to Son): 'You're the keeper of the control aren't you?'
F8 Son: 'Either me or Dad has it. I have it mostly.'

F16 Man: 'Oh yes, quite a bit. I think, Oh I'll just see what's on the other side.'

In most of these families, the power relations are fairly clear. The man in F8 helpfully explains their family's way of resolving conflicts over viewing preferences:

F8 Man: 'We normally tape one side and watch what I want to watch'.

Interestingly, the main exceptions to this overall pattern concern those families in which the man is unemployed while his wife is working. In these cases it is slightly more common for the man to be expected to be prepared to let other family members watch what they want to when it is broadcast, while videotaping what he would like to see, in order to watch that later at night or the following day – given that his timetable of commitments is more flexible than those of the working members of the family. Here we begin to see the way in which the position of power held by most of the men in the sample (and which their wives concede) is based not simply on the biological fact of being men but rather on a social definition of a masculinity of which employment (that is, the 'breadwinner' role) is a necessary and constituent part. When that condition is not met, the pattern of power relations within the home can change noticeably.[4]

One further point needs to be made in this connection. It has to be remembered that this research is based on people's accounts of their behaviour, not on any form of direct observation of behaviour outside of the interview context itself. It is noteworthy that a number of the men show some anxiety to demonstrate that they are 'the boss of the household' and their very anxiety around this issue perhaps betokens a sense that their domestic power is ultimately a fragile and somewhat insecure thing, rather than a fixed and permanent 'possession' which they can always guarantee to hold with confidence. Hence perhaps the symbolic importance to them on physical possession of the channel control device.

[. . .]

Television related talk

Women seem to show much less reluctance to 'admit' that they talk about television to their friends and workmates. Very few men (see below for the exceptions) admit to doing this. It is as if they feel that to admit that they watch too much television (especially with the degree of involvement that would be implied by finding it important enough to talk about) would be to put their very masculinity in question (see the section on programme type preference below). The only standard exception is where the men are willing to admit that they talk about sport on television. All this is clearly related to the theme of gender and programme choice and the 'masculinity/femininity' syllogism identified there. Some part of this is simply to do with the fact that femininity is a more expressive cultural mode than is masculinity. Thus even if women watch less, with less intent viewing styles, none the less they are inclined to talk about television *more* than men, despite the fact that the men watch more of it, more attentively.

F1 Woman: 'Actually my mum and my sister don't watch *Dynasty* and I often tell them bits about it. If my sister watches it, she likes it. And I say to her, "Did you watch it?" and she says no. But if there's something especially good on one night – you know, you might see your friends and say, "Did you see so and so last night?" I occasionally miss *Dynasty*. I said to a friend, "What happened?" and she's caught me up, but I tend to see most of the series. Marion used to keep me going, didn't she? Tell me what was happening and that'.

F2 Man: 'I might mention something on telly occasionally, but I really don't talk about it to anyone'.

F5 Woman: 'At work we constantly talk about *Dallas* and *Dynasty*. We run them down, pick out who we like and who we don't like. What we think should happen next. General chit-chat. I work with quite a few girls, so we have a good old chat . . . We do have some really interesting discussions about television [at work]. We haven't got much else in common, so we talk a lot about television'.

F6 Woman: 'I go round my mate's and she'll say, "Did you watch *Coronation Street* last night? What about so and so?" And we'll sit there discussing it. I think most women and most young girls do. We always sit down and it's "Do you think she's right last night, what she's done?" Or, "I wouldn't have done that", or "Wasn't she a cow to him? Do you reckon he'll get . . . I wonder what he's going to do?" Then we sort of fantasise between us, then when I see her the next day she'll say, 'You were right,' or "See, I told you so . . ." '.

F16 Woman: 'Mums at school will say, "Have you seen any good videos?" And when *Jewel in the Crown* was on, yes, we'd talk about that. When I'm watching the big epics, the big serials, I would talk about those'.

F8 Daughter: 'I like to watch *Brookside*, it's my favourite programme . . . 'cause down the stables everyone else watches it – it's something to chat about when we go down there . . .'.

F17 Man: 'If we do talk, it'll be about something like a news programme – something we didn't know anything about – something that's come up that's interesting'.

F18 Woman: 'I'll talk about things on telly to my friends. I do. I think it is women who talk about television more so than men. I work with an Indian girl and when *Jewel in the Crown* was on we used to talk about that, because she used to tell me what was different in India. *Gandhi* we had on video. She told me what it was like and why that was interesting. Other than that it's anything. She went to see *Passage to India* and she said it was good, but it was a bit like *Jewel in the Crown*'.

F18 Man: 'I won't talk about television at work unless there'd been something like boxing on. I wouldn't talk about *Coronation Street* or a joke on Benny Hill, so other than that, no'.

There is one exception to this general pattern – in F10. In this case it is not so much that the woman is any less willing than most of the others in the sample to talk about television but simply that her programme tastes (BBC2 drama, etc.) are at odds with those of most of the women on the estate where she lives. However, in describing her own dilemma, and the way in which this disjunction of programme tastes functions to isolate her socially, she provides a very acute account of why most of the mothers on her estate do spend so much time talking about television.

F10 Woman: 'Ninety-nine percent of the women I know stay at home to look after their kids, so the only other thing you have to talk about is your housework, or the telly – because you don't go anywhere, you don't do anything. They are talking about what the child did the night before or they are talking about the telly – simply because they don't do anything else'.

In the main, the only television material that the men will admit to talking about is sport. The only man who readily admits to talking to anyone about other types of television material is the man in F11, who is a Civil Service manager. Primarily he talks about television at work, quite self-consciously, as a managerial device, simply as a way of 'opening up' conversations with his staff, so he can find out how they're getting on, 'using it as a topic, rather than you actually wanting to discuss what was on TV', or 'as the first sort of gambit for establishing rapport . . . it's always a very good common denominator – "What did you see on the telly last night?" '.

Interestingly, beyond this conscious use of television as a conversational device in his role at work this middle-class man, exceptionally in my sample, also admits to having the kind of conversations with his men friends about fictional television programmes which, on the whole, only the women in my sample are prepared to admit to doing. Thus, this man is a keen fan of *Hill Street Blues* and will readily discuss with his friends issues such as 'Should Renko marry? Should Furillo go back on the drink?'. Even if there is a conscious tone of self-mocking irony in his account of their discussions, most of the men will not admit to having conversations of this type with the friends (especially about fictional television) at all.

The issue of the differential tendency for women and men to talk about their television viewing is of considerable interest. It could be objected that, as my research is based only on respondents' accounts of their behaviour, the findings are unreliable in so far as respondents may have misrepresented their actual behaviour – especially when the accounts offered by my respondents seem to conflict with established survey findings. Thus in principle it could be argued that the claims many of the male respondents make about only watching 'factual' television are a misrepresentation of their actual behaviour, based on their anxiety about admitting to watching fictional programmes. However, even if this were the case, it would remain a social fact of some interest that the male respondents felt this compulsion to misrepresent their actual behaviour in this particular way. Moreover, this very reluctance to talk about some of the programmes they may watch itself has important consequences. Even if it were the case that men and women in fact watched the same range of programmes (contrary to the accounts they gave me), the fact that the men are reluctant to talk about watching anything other than factual programmes or sport means that their viewing experience is profoundly different from that of the women in the sample. Given that meanings are made not simply in the moment of individual viewing, but also in the subsequent social processes of discussion and 'digestion' of material viewed, the men's much greater reluctance to talk about (part of) their viewing will mean that their consumption of television material is of a quite different kind from that of their wives.

Notes

1. See Gray, Anne (1987) Women and video. In Baehr, Helen and Dyer Gillian (eds) *Boxed In: Women On and In Television*, Routledge Kegan Paul, forthcoming, 1987.
2. Brunsdon, Charlotte (1986) *Women watching television*. Paper to Women and The Electronic Mass Media Conference, Copenhagen, 1986, unpublished.
3. Collett, P. and Lamb,R.
4. See Marsden, D. and Duff, E. (1975) *Workless: Some Unemployed Men and Their Families*, Penguin, 1975, for more on these issues.

68

Dallas and the ideology of mass culture

Ien Ang

From Ang, I. (1991) *Watching Dallas* (translated by Couling, D.),
Routledge, London, pp. 102–11.

Loving Dallas

But what about those who 'really' like *Dallas*? How do they relate to the
ideology of mass culture?

Ideologies organize not only the ideas and images people make of reality,
they also enable people to form an image of themselves and thus to occupy
a position in the world. Through ideologies people acquire an identity, they
become subjects with their own convictions, their own will, their own
preferences. So, an individual living in the ideology of mass culture may qualify
him or herself as, for example, 'a person of taste', 'a cultural expert' or 'someone
who is not seduced by the cheap tricks of the commercial culture industry'.
In addition to an image of oneself, however, an ideology also offers an image
of others. Not only does one's own identity take on form in this way, but the
ideology serves also to outline the identity of other people. As Göran Therborn
puts it, 'in one's subjection to and qualification for a particular position, one
becomes aware of the difference between oneself and others'(Therborn, 1980,
p. 27). Thus a dividing line is drawn by the ideology of mass culture between
the 'person of taste', the 'cultural expert', etc. and those who, according to
this ideology, are not such. Or to be more specific, between those who do
recognize *Dallas* as 'bad mass culture' and those who do not.

One *Dallas*-hater thus tries to distance herself from those who like *Dallas*:

> I don't understand either why so many people watch it, as there are lots of
> people who find it a serious matter if they have to miss a week. At school you
> really notice it when you turn up on Wednesday morning then it's 'Did you
> see *Dallas*, wasn't it fabulous?'. Now and then I get really annoyed, because I
> find it just a waste of time watching it. [. . .] Then you hear them saying that
> they had tears in their eyes when something happened to someone in the film,
> and I just can't understand it. At home they usually turn it on too, but then I
> always go off to bed (Letter 33).

She outlines the identity of the others, those who like *Dallas*, in a negative
way, and with a particular degree of confidence: lovers of *Dallas* are almost
declared idiots by this letter-writer! Roughly the same pattern, but in
somewhat milder terms, emerges in the following extract: 'Reading through
it [her own letter], it's a serial a normal person shouldn't watch, because
you feel someone else's sorrow and difficulties. For me that's also the reason

why so many people find the serial good' (Letter 38). The image of the others, of those who do not recognize *Dallas* as 'bad mass culture', can be summed up shortly but forcefully from the viewpoint of the ideology of mass culture: 'The aim is simply to rake in money, lots of money. And people try to do that by means of all these things – sex, beautiful people, wealth. *And you always have people who fall for it'* (Letter 35, my italics). The ideology of mass culture therefore definitely does not offer a flattering picture of those who like *Dallas*. They are presented as the opposite of 'persons of taste', 'cultural experts' or 'people who are not seduced by the cheap tricks of the commercial culture industry'. How do lovers of *Dallas* react to this? Do they know that this negative image of them exists and does it worry them at all?

In the small advertisement which the letter-writers replied to, I included the following clause: 'I like watching the TV serial *Dallas* but often get odd reactions to it'. It seems to me that the phrase 'odd reactions' is vague at the very least: from the context of the advertisement there is no way of knowing what I meant. Yet various lovers of *Dallas* go explicitly into this clause in their letters: the words 'odd reactions' seem sufficient to effect an 'Aha!' experience in some fans.

> I have the same 'problem' as you! When I let drop in front of my fellow students (political science) that I do my utmost to be able to watch *Dallas* on Tuesday evenings, they look incredulous (Letter 19).

> It always hits me too that people react 'oddly' when you say you like watching *Dallas*. I think everyone I know watches it but some of my friends get very worked up over this serial and even go on about the dangerous effects on the average TV viewer. I really don't know what I should think of this (Letter 22).

These extracts lead one to suspect that the rules and judgements of the ideology of mass culture are not unknown to *Dallas* fans. What is more, they too seem to respond to this ideology. But they tend to do so in a completely different way from those who hate *Dallas* or who love it ironically. 'Really' loving *Dallas* (without irony) would seem to involve a strained attitude toward the norms of the ideology of mass culture. And it is this strained relationship which the fans have to try to resolve.

In contrast to the haters and ironic lovers, who, as we have seen, express their attitude to the ideology of mass culture in a rather uniform and unconflicting way, the 'real' fans use very divergent strategies to come to terms with its norms. One strategy is to take over and internalize the judgements of the ideology of mass culture itself:

> I just wanted to react to your advertisement concerning *Dallas*. I myself enjoy *Dallas* and the tears roll down when something tragic happens in it (in nearly every episode, that is). In my circle too people react dismissively to it, they find it a typical commercial programme far beneath their standards. I find you can relax best with a programme like this, although you just have to keep your eye on the kind of influence such a programme can have, it is role-confirming, 'class-confirming', etc., etc. And it's useful too if you think what kind of cheap sentiment really does get to you (Letter 14).

There is a remarkable about-face in this letter. Instead of stating why she likes *Dallas* so much (which was the question I had put in my advertisement), the letter-writer confines herself to reiterating a reasoning which derives from the ideology of mass culture in answer to the 'dismissive reactions' of her milieu. She doesn't adopt an independent attitude towards this ideology but merely takes over its morals. But whom is she addressing with these morals? Herself? Me (she knows from my advertisement that I like watching *Dallas*)? All *Dallas* fans? It is as though she wants to defend the fact that she enjoys *Dallas* by showing that she is in fact aware of its 'dangers' and 'tricks'; aware, in other words, that *Dallas* is 'bad mass culture'. A similar reasoning can be read in the following letter extract:

> In fact it's a flight from reality. I myself am a realistic person and I know that reality is different. Sometimes too I really enjoy having a good old cry with them. And why not? In this way my other bottled-up emotions find an outlet (Letter 5).

In other words: watching *Dallas* is all right if you know that it is not realistic and therefore 'bad'.

But a protective strategy can also be employed by actually challenging the ideology of mass culture.

> I am replying to your advertisement as I would like to speak my mind about *Dallas*. I've noticed too that you get funny reactions when you like watching *Dallas* (and I like watching it). Many people find it worthless or without substance. But I think it does have substance. Just think of the saying: 'Money can't buy happiness', you can certainly trace that in *Dallas* (Letter 13).

But what has been said here against the ideology of mass culture remains caught within the categories of that ideology. Against the opinion 'no substance' (= 'bad') is placed the alternative opinion 'does have substance' (= 'good'); the category 'substance' (and thus the difference 'good/bad') is therefore upheld. This letter-writer 'negotiates' as it were within the discursive space created by the ideology of mass culture, she does not situate herself outside it and does not speak from an opposing ideological position.

But why do these *Dallas* lovers feel the need to defend themselves against the ideology of mass culture? They obviously feel under attack. Obviously they can't get round its norms and judgements, but must stand out against them in order to be able to like *Dallas* and not to have to disavow that pleasure. But it is never pleasant to be manoeuvred into a defensive position: it shows weakness. To have to defend oneself is nearly always coupled with a feeling of unease.

> You are right in saying that you often get these strange reactions. Such as 'So you like watching cheap mass entertainment, eh?' Yes, I watch it and I'm not ashamed of it. But I do try to defend my motivation tooth and nail (Letter 7).

'Tooth and nail'; the pent-up intensity of this expression reveals the strong desire of this letter-writer to defend herself and to justify herself, in spite of her contention that she 'is not ashamed of it'.

And another letter-writer says:

> Oh well, I'm one of those people who sit in front of the box every Tuesday for the *Dallas* programme, actually to my own amazement. . . . I must honestly confess that I do like watching the serial now. By 'confess' I mean this: at first I felt a bit guilty about the fact that I had gone mad on such a cheap serial without any morals. Now I look at it rather differently (Letter 11).

'To my own amazement', she writes, in other words 'I hadn't thought it possible'. Her feeling of guilt arises precisely because she has not escaped the power of conviction of the ideology of mass culture, from the branding of *Dallas* as a 'cheap serial without any morals'.

Finally, yet another defence mechanism against the ideology of mass culture is possible. That is, strangely enough, irony again. But in this case irony is not integrated so unproblematically in the experience of watching *Dallas* as in the case of the ironic fans we encountered earlier. On the contrary, here irony is an expression of a conflicting viewing experience. One letter-writer has put this psychological conflict clearly into words. In her account there is an uncomfortable mixture of 'really' liking *Dallas* and an ironic viewing attitude:

> Just like you I often get odd reactions when I say that at the moment *Dallas* is my favourite TV programme. [. . .] I get carried along intensely with what is happening on TV. I find most figures in the serial horrible, except Miss Ellie. The worst thing I find is how they treat one another. I also find them particularly ugly. Jock because he doesn't have an aesthetically justifiable head, Pamela because she has to seem so smart, I find that 'common'. I can't stand it that everyone (in the serial) finds her sexy when she looks like Dolly Parton with those breasts. Sue Ellen is really pathetic, she looks marvellously ravaged by all that drink. J.R. needs no explanation. He keeps my interest because I always have the feeling that one day that wooden mask is going to drop. Bobby I find just a stupid drip, I always call him 'Aqualung' (his former role in a series). They are a sad lot, so honest, stinking rich, they want to seem perfect but (fortunately for us!) none of them is perfect (even Miss Ellie has breast cancer, and that cowboy Ray, whom I've really fallen for, is always running into trouble) (Letter 23).

The distance from the *Dallas* characters is great for this letter-writer – witness the annihilating judgement that she passes so ironically on them. Nevertheless her account is imbued with a kind of intimacy which betrays a great involvement in the serial ('I get carried along intensely'. . . , 'I can't stand it'. . . , 'I am interested in him'. . . , 'whom I've really fallen for'). The detached irony on the one hand and the intimate involvement on the other appear difficult to reconcile. So it emerges from further on in her letter that irony gains the upper hand when watching *Dallas* is a social occasion:

> I notice that I use *Dallas* as a peg for thinking about what I find good and bad in my relations with others. I notice this in particular *when I'm watching with a group of people* because then we usually can't keep our mouths shut; we shout disgraceful! and bastard! and bitch! (sorry, but emotions really run high!). We also sometimes try to get an idea of how the Ewings are all doing. Sue Ellen has postnatal depression and that's why she is so against her baby. Pamela is actually very nice and suffers because of Sue Ellen's jealousy. J.R. is just a big scaredy-cat, you can see that from that uncertain little laugh of his (Letter 23, my italics).

The ironic commentaries are presented here as a *social* practice. This is confirmed by the sudden transition from the use of 'I' to 'we' in this extract. Is it perhaps true to say that the need to emphasize an ironic attitude to viewing, thereby creating a distance from *Dallas*, is aroused in this letter-writer by the social control emanating from an ideological climate in which 'really' liking the programme is almost taboo? In any case intimacy returns further on in the letter as soon as she is talking again in terms of 'I'. And the irony then disappears into the background.

> Actually they are all a bit stupid. And oversensational. Affected and genuinely American (money–appearance–relationship–maniacs–family and nation! etc.). I know all this very well. And yet. . . . The Ewings go through a lot more than I do. They seem to have a richer emotional life. Everyone knows them in *Dallas*. Sometimes they run into trouble, but they have a beautiful house and anything else they might want. I find it pleasant to watch. I do realize their ideals of beauty. I look at how their hair is done. I'm very impressed by their brilliant dialogues. Why can't I ever think what to say in a crisis? (Letter 23).

Real love and irony – both determine the way in which this letter-writer relates to *Dallas*. It is clear that they are difficult to reconcile: real love involves identification, whereas irony creates distance. This ambivalent attitude to *Dallas* seems to stem from the fact that on the one hand she accepts the correctness of the ideology of mass culture (at least in a social context), but on the other hand 'really' likes *Dallas* – which is against the rules of this ideology. The irony lies here then in the 'social surface'; it functions, in contrast to the ironizing lovers, for whom irony is interwoven with the way in which they experience pleasure in *Dallas*, as a sort of screen for 'real' love. In other words, irony is here a defence mechanism with which this letter-writer tries to fulfil the social norms set by the ideology of mass culture, while secretly she 'really' likes *Dallas*.

We can draw two conclusions from these examples. First, the fans quoted seem spontaneously, of their own free will, to take the ideology of mass culture into account: they come into contact with it and cannot apparently avoid it. Its norms and prescriptions exert pressure on them, so that they feel the necessity to defend themselves against it. Second, it emerges from their letters that they use a very wide variety of defence strategies: one tries simply to internalize the ideology of mass culture, another tries to negotiate within its discursive framework, and yet another uses surface irony. And so it would appear that there is not one obvious defence strategy *Dallas* fans can use, that there is no clear-cut ideological alternative which can be employed against the ideology of mass culture - at least no alternative that offsets the latter in power of conviction and coherence. And so the letter-writers take refuge in various discursive strategies, none of which, however, is as well worked out and systematic as the discourses of the ideology of mass culture. Fragmentary as they are, these strategies are therefore much more liable to contradictions. In short, these fans do not seem to be able to take up an effective ideological position – an identity – from which they can say in a positive way and independently of the ideology of mass culture: 'I like *Dallas* because . . .'.

But this weak position the fans are in, this lack of a positive ideological basis for legitimizing their love of *Dallas*, has tiresome consequences. Whereas those who hate the programme can present their 'opponents' as, for example, 'cultural barbarians', 'people with no taste' or 'people who let themselves be led astray by the tricks of the commercial culture industry' (thus implying that they themselves are *not*), the fans do not have such a favourable representation to hand. They are not in a position to hit back by forming in their turn an equally negative image of those who dislike *Dallas*; they can only offer resistance to the negative identities that *others* ascribe to them.

According to Therborn, such a psychologically problematic situation is characteristic for subject positions which get the worst of it ideologically. From an ideologically dominant subject position it is possible to stigmatize 'the others' as it were. For the victims of this dominant ideology, however, no such reassuring position is available: they find themselves in a position which, 'while also involving a perception and evaluation of the differences between ego and alter, tends towards resistance to the Other rather than towards forming him or her. This difference is inscribed in the asymmetry of domination'(Therborn, 1980, p. 28). This situation can have disastrous consequences for *Dallas* fans who feel pushed into a corner by the ideology of mass culture. They can easily be reduced to silence because they can literally find no words to defend themselves. The ground is cut from under them. As one of the letter-writers says: 'I personally find it terrible when I hear people saying they don't like *Dallas*' (Letter 2). As finding it 'terrible' is her only word of defence – apparently nothing else occurred to her – isn't that a form of capitulation?

Reference

Therborn, G. (1980) *The Ideology of Power and the Power of Ideology*, Verso, London, pp. 27 and 28.

69

Patterns of involvement in television fiction: a comparative analysis

Tamar Liebes and Elihu Katz

From Blumer, J. G. *et al.* (eds) (1986) *European Journal of Communication*, Vol. 1, No. 2, pp. 152–4, 166–70.

Method

Ideally, we should like to have empirical data on how people talk naturally about television: whether they refer to the medium or to specific programmes; how they decode what they see and hear; how they help each other to do so; whether and how they weave the experience of viewing into their social and political roles; whether they have categories for criticism, and if so, what these are. The only data we know come from several quasi-anthropological studies of family interaction (Bryce and Leichter, 1983; Lull, 1981); two analyses of peer group discussion of film (Custen, 1982; Laulan, 1983) focus group discussions of a news programme (Morley, 1980) and a radio marathon (Merton, 1946);[1] and two questionnaire studies attempting to clarify the critical ability and vocabulary of television audiences (Neumann, 1982; Himmelweit, 1983).

We tried to combine these methods in our own study, although what we have done does not pretend to solve the problem of truly unobtrusive observation of natural conversations concerning television. We organized some 50 small groups of viewers of *Dallas* by asking an initial couple to invite two other couples from among their friends. The group viewed an instalment of *Dallas* in a living room setting, together with others who might have joined them anyway.[2] Following the programme, our observer switched on his tape recorder and put a series of open questions to the group; in some cases recording was begun during the viewing period to catch spontaneous conversation.

First, the group was asked to retell the episode in their own words, then to describe the attributes and motivations of the three leading characters, following which we introduced a series of somewhat more specific queries such as 'How would you end the series?' 'Is the programme real?' 'Are they trying to tell us something?' 'What does the programme say about America?', etc. In short, we were interested not so much in effect, not even in gratifications, but rather in what is understood and how it is talked about.

We applied this method to five ethnic communities, four of them in Israel (Israeli Arabs, veteran Moroccan Jews, Russian Jews only recently arrived, and kibbutz members, mostly second-generation Israelis) and to groups of second-generation Americans in Los Angeles. The Israeli groups represent a naive attempt to simulate the diverse cultures that have made *Dallas* a world-wide hit, while the U.S. groups are the audience for whom the programme was presumably intended in the first place. An effort was made to make groups comparable as to age and education, but we did not have full control over the invitations, and certainly not over the correlation between ethnicity and education in the general population. We wanted to see whether the American readings differed from those of the Israelis and whether the Israelis differed among themselves. We chose *Dallas* not only because of its popularity, but because of its dependence on words, because it is so American in form and content. The puzzle of how most of the world manages to understand it all may thereby be revealed.

The generic problem of the study, then, is addressed through analysis of how viewers use the narrative to discuss their own lives. Our object is to discover the mechanisms through which the viewer interacts with the programme, becoming involved with it, and perhaps affected by it, in different ways and to different degrees.

A major indicator of involvement – or, better, a measure of the viewer's ability to distance himself from the reality of the programme – is the extent to which he or she invokes the 'meta-linguistic' rather than the 'referential' frame in responding to the programme. The 'referential' (Jakobson, 1980) connects the programme and real life, as if the viewers were relating to the characters as real people and in turn relating these real people to their own real worlds.

The 'critical' (Jakobson's 'meta-linguistic') frames discussions of the programme as a fictional construction with aesthetic rules. Referential readings are probably more emotionally involving; critical readings are more distant, dealing as they do with genres, dynamics of plot, thematics of story and so on. We shall see, however, that certain uses of the critical my betray an effort at self-protection, a refusal to admit emotional involvement.
[. . .]

Conclusions

This article originates in discussions of an episode of the American television series, *Dallas*, by small, quasi-natural groups from four ethnic communities in Israel and matched groups of second-generation Americans.

The article – part of a larger project – examines cultural differences in patterns of talk about the programme, with particular reference to the rhetorical mechanisms by means of which viewers 'involve' or 'distance' themselves from the story as depicted on the screen. Four such mechanisms are analysed: (1) *framings*, the context to which viewers' statements about the programme are assigned: 'referential' (dealing with real life) and 'critical' (dealing with the story as an artistic construction); (2) *keyings*, the register in which referential statements are made: 'realistic' or 'playful'; (3) *referents*, the real-life object to which some element of the story is connected, defined in terms of the pronouns, 'I', 'we', 'they'; and (4) *value orientations*, the extent to which a 'realistic' statement is purely interpretive or evaluational as well: 'value-free' or 'normative'. The five ethnic communities were compared in terms of each of these rhetorical mechanisms separately, and then an effort was made to discover patterned variations in 'involvement' or 'distance' by scoring the groups in terms of a single, multi-dimensional scale made up of all four mechanisms.

All this seems to add up as follows. First, most statements, in all groups, are based on perception of the programme as real. That is, there are far more referential than critical (meta-linguistic) statements, and, within the referential, far more keyings to the 'real' (serious, indicative, familiar) than to 'play' (fantasy, subjunctive, hypothetical). Moreover, most statements, in all groups, refer to people in general or general categories of people ('they') and fewer statement are in the 'I' or 'we' form. These statements are interpretive in character – observations and explanations of behaviour – without value judgements; evaluational ('normative') statements are far fewer. 'Pragmatic' may be a good name to describe this overall tendency to the 'real' and the 'value-free'.

Overall, then, one may say that discussion of *Dallas* – presuming that we have successfully simulated such discussion – accepts the programme as real and as morally unproblematic in spite of the back-stabbing and corruption which underlie the human relations that are the subject of the referential statements.

Second, the subjects of the statements are similar enough among the ethnic groups to suggest that a programme like *Dallas* may indeed set agendas for thinking and talking, not so much by imposing these subjects, but by evoking primordial concerns and perhaps even by offering opportunities for discussing them. This may be a clue to the world-wide comprehensibility of such programmes and their popularity. Ostensibly, it would seem likely that the social world of *Dallas* would be more readily recognizable in the modern Western societies, where 'immorality pays'. This, however, may be incorrect, both because Western viewers may discount the programme as unreal, and because some of the characteristics of the Ewing family may indeed be more traditional than modern.

Patterned deviations from the dominant pragmatic pattern ('real' and 'value-free') are the concern of this paper. On the one hand, we are interested in use of the 'critical' (meta-linguistic) at the expense of the 'referential' and in use of 'play' keyings at the expense of 'real' keyings. That is, we are interested in identifying those groups, and those situations, in which the viewer distances himself from the reality by using meta-linguistic frames and ludic keyings. On the other hand, we are equally interested in the move from the abstract 'they' and the 'value-free' in the direction of more intimate referents ('I' and 'we') and more evaluative, therefore more emotionally loaded, orientations.

Examining cultural differences in these terms, a third conclusion can be drawn. We find the Arabs at the one extreme that appears to maximize involvement: they talk in referential frames, with real keyings, and make moral judgements about the programme in terms of the opposing norms of their own society ('we'). At the other extreme stand the second-generation Americans who appear to have all of the mechanisms of distancing and discount at hand. They speak 'critically' of genres and production problems;

they speak playfully and pragmatically of the real-life implications of the programme for themselves ('I') and each other. The Russians differ from the native Americans and Israelis in generalizing the programme to 'they', but balance this distancing with a belief that the programme is 'real' and, consequently, dangerous.

Fourth, arraying the cultures on the multi-dimensional scale of 'involvement' or 'distancing', the ostensible conclusion must be that the more 'modern' groups are less involved in the programme, knowing the mechanisms of distancing and discount, while the more traditional groups are more 'involved'. If this is indeed so, as the data strongly suggest, the explanation is easy: the Western groups, certainly the native Americans and kibbutzniks, have been socialized in the genres of television (Hall, 1980), have good reason to question its reality, and know how to relate to it light-heartedly (Stephenson, 1967), not considering it worthy of moral outrage. (Only the Russians indicate concern for the possibility of ideological manipulation.)

Two caveats need mention here. There is the possibility that the ludic may be no less involving than the real – more distant and more serious – keyings. Once entered, play can be very absorbing, of course, and one's only protection is to remember that it is a game. Some of the ludic interactions we have analysed end in intimate revelations of the real. The other caveat is that the generalizations that follow the referent 'they' may be so all-embracing to those who speak them that the lesser involvement which we attribute to 'they' may be incorrect. If this is the case, the Russians, who specialize in interpreting the 'they' almost as participant observers, may be more enveloped than those who speak of 'I' and 'we'. Both these caveats need to be borne in mind.

Finally, presuming, nevertheless, that we have successfully arrayed the several cultures in terms of their distance from the equation of story and real, we must push harder on the central question of this article and ask whether the mechanisms of distance inoculate against the influence of the programme. The answer appears to be 'yes'. The more traditional groups, lacking the rhetorical mechanisms of defence, seem to be more vulnerable. In the absence of discounting mechanisms, the admission of the agenda of the programme to the most intimate circles – even women are gradually infiltrating the traditionally male audience, sometimes even sitting together – poses a competing paradigm which cannot but shake the system.

But again, we must propose a caveat in that the Western groups lack a *normative* defence. Along with the variety of mechanisms for cognitive discounting of television fiction, the fact is that their moral defences are down. Even in 'play', moral nihilism may have an effect. In the absence of the Arab moral shock, and the Russians' ideological suspiciousness, exposure to a steady stream of programmes, each one of which pushes the boundaries of conventional morality one step further back, may, in the last analysis, make Western audiences as vulnerable as the others.[3]

These conclusions, we repeat, are based on two sorts of assumptions which must be borne in mind: (1) that we are correct in our decisions about what is 'high' and 'low' involvement; and (2) that the more highly involved are more likely to be affected. Thus, we believe we are correct in assigning 'ludic' and 'they' keyings to low involvement and 'real' and 'we/I' keyings to high involvement, but we may be wrong.

We also may be wrong in assuming that involvement makes for vulnerability. 'Normative' rebuttals, as we have said, may make Arab viewers less vulnerable by virtue of their higher involvement. By the same token, 'ludic' viewers – if they are properly coded as less involved – may be more influenced by virtue of their lowered defences. These are the points at which mass communications research has need of a psychology of drama.

Notes

1. The focus group method is widely used in the commercial pre-testing of films, programmes and products by marketing and communications research organizations. It would be very useful to have academic access to these data.
2. Questionnaires were administered to group members following the discussion. It is quite clear from the response that the programme is typically watched in a social setting, and typically talked about afterwards. The protocols of the discussions themselves contain references to conversations about *Dallas* that took place prior to the meetings organized by us. It is safe to say that viewers of *Dallas* discuss the programme and that our constructed groups often coincide with natural groupings of viewers and discussants.
3. The creator of *Dallas*, David Jacobs, told us that escalating immorality, and proposing its acceptability, is one of the secrets of the success of the series.

References

Bryce, Jennifer W. and Leichter, Hope Jensen (1983) The family and television: forms of meditation. *Journal of Family Issues*, Vol. 4, pp. 309–28.

Custen, G. F. (1982) Film talk: viewers responses to a film as a socially situated event. Ph.D. dissertation, University of Pennsylvania.

Hall, Stuart (1980) Encoding and decoding of the television discourse. In Hall, S. *et al.* (eds) *Culture, Media, Language*, Hutchinson, London, pp. 128–38.

Himmelweit, H. (1983) The audience as critic. In Tannenbaum, Percy (ed.) *Entertaiment functions of Television*, Lawrence Erlbaum, Hillsdale, NJ.

Jakobson, Roman (1980) Linguistics and poetics. In DeGeorge, K. and DeGeorge, F. (eds) *The Structuralists From Marx to Lévi-Strauss*.

Laulan, Anne-Marie (1983) Le Role des mediateurs dans l'access a l'ouevre d'art filmique. Doctoral thesis presented to the University of Paris V. Lille, Atelier National de Reproduction des Theses, Universite de Lille III, 2 vols.

Lull, James (1981) Collective ethnographic data in studies of media audience behaviour. Paper read in International Communications Association.

Merton, Robert K. (1946) *Mass Persuasion*, Harper, New York.

Morley, Dave (1980) *The Nationwide Audience*, BFI, London.

Neuman, W. Russell (1982) Television and American culture: the mass medium and the pluralist audience. *Public Opinion Quarterly*, Vol. 46, pp. 471–87.

Stephenson, William (1967) *The Play Theory of Mass Communications*, University of Chicago Press, Chicago.

70

Media, technology and daily life

Hermann Bausinger

From Scannell, P. (ed.) (1984) *Media, Culture and Society*, Academic Press, London, Vol. 6, No. 4, pp. 344–50.

But to come back to the sphere of the media. Let us begin with some general questions regarding the relationship between the every day and the technical. This is a theme which has been completely neglected, even by the analysts of the everyday, supposedly because in the everyday (if the everyday was not labelled negatively from the start) one endeavoured to evoke the mystique of immediacy; the everyday being conceived as devoid of all technical devices. But technology has long since been integrated into the everyday. Tools themseleves are distinguished by the fact that they rapidly take on the character of artificial limbs: one hits with a hammer, and cuts with a sickle as if they were extensions of the body. (In case this is difficult for academics who are often not very good at hammering, to grasp, let me say that as far as a car driver is concerned, the inner and outer limits of his/her epidermis are displaced on to the car's body, otherwise there would be many more accidents!).

Now it could be argued that simple tools do not signify technology in a more refined sense. But is there not a level of development from which technology stands opposed to the everyday, and cannot therefore be easily integrated with it? In *Capital*, Marx makes the dividing line, the decisive, qualitative difference between cottage (or artisan) manufacturing and factory production and machinery. The development from craft to large-scale manufacturing is for Marx a significant regression: from skill to semi-skill. The all-round skill of the craftsperson gets divided, reduced, but is not quite destroyed yet. But then comes for Marx the decisive point, 'The lifelong speciality of handling the same tool now becomes the lifelong speciality of serving the same machine'. An active relationship thus becomes a passive one.

> In handicrafts and manufacture, the worker makes use of a tool; in the factory, the machine makes use of him [cf. Marx K. (1979) *Capital*, Penguin, London, Vol. 1, pp. 547–9. See especially Chapters 14 and 15].

The sharpness of the distinction between these two phases will not be discussed here, but machine technology brings a new dimension into the game. It is in effect also a qualitative leap in generally assessing the question of the integration or non-integration of technology into everyday life. From a cultural–historical point of view we do not know very much about it, but there are occasional notes relating to the subject. A prime example is the debate on the early days of the railway. According to the cultural historian Riehl, writing in 1853, the peasants had already 'constructed a circle of legends about the railway', and he gives some examples.

> There is a widespread belief amongst the peasants that the railway would after a certain period of time, disappear (this was predicted with great assurance), just as suddenly as it had arrived. Their allotted time is similar to that which the devil grants to those seeking a short cut to earthly pleasures. In the Baden region there is a legend that everytime the railway stops at one of the larger stations, one person is missing, taken by the devil as his reward; and in the Alsace in 1851 it became necessary for there to be sermons from the pulpit against railway superstitions.

Certainly only a special investigation, evaluating all the material, could establish to what degree such peasant beliefs were not merely reflexes of a conservative scepticism, *vis-à-vis* new technical means, which was well established and penetrated right into the aristocracy. The fact is that even in the literature and art of the time, the poetry of the new means of transport blends in easily with its demonology. King Ludwig I of Bavaria wrote, in his poem *The Steam Engine*:

> In the steam the old ways are now disappearing,
>   and men are at the mercy of its power
> The relentless bringer of universal sameness,
>   now destroying the people's love for its native land.
> Unstable humanity, roaming the earth, everywhere and
>   nowhere at home, as unstable as the steam.
> The racer has started off down the track;
>   the finish is out of sight.

Even around the turn of the century a painting (made popular in reproduction) of 'the broad and the narrow path' was to be found in many pious bourgeois houses, and in it the railway was associated with the broad path, a vehicle of hell, so to speak. Commentary on the picture does, however, point to the other side of the coin by allowing that the railway is 'in itself a good and useful discovery which also assists the kingdom of God'. But then the main emphasis is set without doubt: 'Altogether though it serves more to spread the kingdom of the anti-Christ, for it carries many sins in its suit, e.g. the desecration of Sunday etc.'

The same tendency to denigrate, i.e. by expressing the technical as an incomprehensible demonic threat, can be found in other areas. But this is only one side. Those who used the machines – and there is evidence for this – developed an illusion of power, of mastery, which can easily be recognized as ideological, in as much as it diverts attention away from the fact that those machines were not being mastered, but merely integrated with their immediate surroundings.

This appropriation was generally determined by a new relationship with technology: a neutralization, an embourgeoisement. The relationship with the technical has increasingly become marked by the fact that it was never reflected upon, rather, one contented oneself with the manipulation of levers and buttons – and only in the case of breakdowns were, and are, there regressions into magical modes of thought.

If one pursues the more recent transformations of technology, not in the sense of the history of technology, but in relation to the everyday, then what is most significant is a rise in the inconspicuous omnipresence of the technical. It is true that the generation of our grandparents was already served by the products of technology, but these products hardly had a technical touch; the things were not machines themselves – apart perhaps from the sewing machine. But even the sewing machine was kept going in a very traditional fashion, with the feet, so that it mainly serves today as either a nostalgic piece of furniture or as a dangerous child's toy. In the meantime not only the number of products has multiplied, but everyone owns a number of machines, and has directly to handle technical products – from the vacuum cleaner to the electric shaver, from the record player to the food mixer. But none of this seems odd, it penetrates the everyday and it is consumed and absorbed by the everyday. Today machines, technical instruments, are no longer things which give offence, no longer things which demonstrate processes – they have been ironed out, disguised with façades, technology is absorbed.

Mistrusting the new was a dominant feature up to the time of our grandparents. But today this mistrust of the new has broken down gradually, washed away by the flood of innovations. One of the consequences of this acceleration is a dehistoricized understanding of technology – paradoxically, the rapid rate of change does not allow it to be perceived in terms of comparisons. It is like a revolving wheel which, at a certain speed seems to the observer to be stationary. Progress seems no longer to develop straight towards a goal, instead it appears as something which exists, which spreads, which seems to take place more in space than in time, and which is experienced accordingly.

If it is indeed a question of the attitudes towards technology, it seems proper, once again, to relativize. The findings are by no means consistent. The functions of technology, the attitudes towards technology, can hardly be clearly distilled and defined; technology in the everyday can only ever be grasped conjuncturally. This does not only mean that the technical may be fitted in to altogether different, earlier forms of thought; it also means that the attitudes of different people are different, that with regards to different functions different attitudes come to light, and that fundamentally these attitudes can be psychically ambiguous and ambivalent.

An additional fact is that technical phenomena are by no means uniform in character. The very concept of 'the' technology is a problematical generalization even though it may derive a certain justification from the determining principles of all technical phenomena. The associations are varied – from the massive machinery of the smelting works, to the shiny new technologies of IBM and Packard; from the kitchen mixer to the nuclear power station: technology, a dubious umbrella term. This is true for the present as it is for the past.

These conjunctures, these different attitudes, also have to be taken into consideration when one focuses on a particular area of the technical, namely the media in a more narrow sense. There is an irrational mistrust of the media – in the debate about the so-called new media this certainly plays an important part, besides making for highly debatable critical arguments. But there also exists a feeling of power with regard to technology, which is mediated to young people through advertising, and which is practised by them in their skilled handling of hi-fi gear and video, but which also becomes visible in 'channel-hopping' or 'zapping': the *sindromo del telecomande* (the rapid switching over on the TV set) – a term I learned from an essay by Claus Rath. However, even here, what seems to me to be in the foreground with regard to this intercourse with the technical is the very essence of the process of the everyday: naturalization. But what does this mean and how does it manifest itself? Media research tells us little or nothing about it. At this point the analyst of the media as agencies of the everyday encounters two different types of analysis.

On the one hand empirical investigations into very limited contexts and correlations, which therefore often reify media communication, conceiving it as either the content and/or effect of episodic, self-contained units. Abraham Kaplan's critique of 'substantialism', which is on the look-out for things, instead of investigating processes, which are not easily encloseable, and hence not easily measurable, comes to mind.

On the other hand an essentialist perspective has gathered momentum; a kind of morphology, an attempt to grasp complex processes more precisely by encircling them with meanings. I admit that I lean more towards the latter. It is more important to understand something than to measure it. The obvious danger is that the playful encircling of the object becomes infatuated with its own motion, and so loses sight of it.

It is therefore important for me to relate such theorizations to empirical data, produced however by forms of empirical research in which qualitative methods predominate – participant observations, introspections, depth interviews, case studies, etc.

Let me give a harmless example: I ask how Mr Meier deals with the weekend sports coverage in the context of both his family and his everyday life. It is Saturday afternoon and Mr Meier has had two important experiences: he drove his wife to the market and couldn't find a parking space (a negative experience), and he washed the car (a positive experience as he's that type). After a late lunch he attempts to have a nap, and succeeds somehow until his eldest son leaves the house, slamming the door behind him and roaring off on his motorcycle.

Mr Meier picks up the newspaper. He has already worked his way through the political and local news, and now he reads the sports pages, looking for the previews of the day's matches. He considers going to the football ground, but he is a person with principles – his club has lost twice in a row, so punishment must be administered. He goes on reading, he dozes off again; his little daughter comes in and complains that she wants to read but it's too noisy. Mr Meier overhears on the radio the frantic commentary from some stadium. He supports his daughter against his little son, who has turned up the volume of the radio so high, but his altruism is hypocritical, for he does not really want to hear the football reports on *Samstag im Stadium* ('Saturday in the Stadium'), he wants to save his excitement until 18.05. The son gives in, turns down the volume, but a few minutes later Mr Meier hears 'Goal! goal!' In his mind he imagines what in fact is happening – Hansi Mueller on the point of knocking one in. His resolution begins to waver but he decides to persevere.

After a while his son walks into the room, beaming. 'D'you want to know the result?' he asks. His father is relieved, 'United' has won. But he is also angry, 'No!', he says, because he wants to watch the game. However, as the sports round up starts his anger increases, United's match is not going to be shown. The presenter announces that only the top games are being transmitted – as if United were a candidate for relegation! His little 10-year-old son has the advantage, he has experienced the game live, even though not in its entirety as reports are not continuous on the Saturday afternoon radio sports magazine programme. But the circumstances have given rise to a kind of competition, a series of small struggles for domination within the family in their passive participation in weekend sport.

The consequence is that, during the sports review programme the father talks more than usually, although still only a little. When it comes to Verdingen he states that the goal-keeper looks like Sepp Maier, his son disagrees. When it comes to the next match his son says, 'I support Bayern, what about you?'. He also supports Bayern. But he found Breitner weak in the cup-tie. His son didn't. In addition to this there are short asides, such as 'Great! Fantastic! Wasn't that offside? That was no dirty foul! I don't know if that was deliberate'. In between the son asks if he can buy a United tee-shirt, and in order not to be distracted the father quickly says yes. Rummenige is on the point of making a shot-on-the turn – 'This will be the goal of the month', says the father. Towards the end he has a chance to score. The commentator says 'That was a well timed (*getimete*) pass'. The son mishears and asks, 'Why does he say "a well meant (*gemeinte*) pass" ', and the father explains.

In the evening he gets involved in conversation, otherwise he would at least have watched the regional news; so he does not see the results again until after the news. In a way he wanted to go to bed early, and that is what he told his wife. But now he has a faint hope of being able to see the Mueller goal on the Second Channel sports programme. However he would have to switch channels. He tells his wife she looks tired. She is surprised that he cares, but she does go up to bed. He fetches a beer from the kitchen. Unfortunately his wife comes back to get a drink. Suddenly the penny drops. 'My God! The sports programme! That's why you sent me to bed!'. He doesn't want to get involved, and quickly goes to the toilet. In the meantime it happens. His wife shouts, 'Hey Max Schmeling is on!' He doesn't react. He can't stand Schmeling because he has something to do with Coca-Cola. He deliberately doesn't hurry. When he comes back United's game is in progress. He is just in time to see the second, rather third-rate, goal.

Late on Sunday morning he goes to the station, sees the *Welt am Sonntag* on the news-stand, and skims the headline. In *Bild* he reads: 'Chancellor has heart trouble again', and 'It was double-murder'. Contrary to habit he buys *Bild*, looks at it at home, reads that Hansi Mueller took a knock, that Maradona is even more expensive, and that a player for Cologne has had a car accident. His needs for sport and 'sport' have been satisfied.

In the afternoon a neighbour tells him that his club has lost again – which is what he thought anyway, because when there is no wind he can hear the crowd in the stadium from his balcony and there had been no shouting. He goes for a walk with his wife and their younger children; some acquaintances delay him. When he comes home his elder son is watching the sports review after having slept till midday. Meier gets angry because he has wasted the day, and even more so when his son asks, 'Have you heard, United won 2:0!' As if he was an idiot! He gives his son the *Bild*, and the son says, 'I thought you didn't read that'. Offended, the father goes to his room, while the mother sits down next to her eldest son and watches the sports review with him. It does not interest her, but it is an attempt at making contact.

One could go on like this, but I would like to make some general points:

1. To make a meaningful study of the use of the media, it is necessary to take different media into consideration, the media ensemble which everyone deals with today. The media conglomerate on the production side has long since found its counterpart on the reception side. The recipient integrates the content of different media – in the above example, radio, TV, newspapers, a list to which others can be added.

2. As a rule the media are not used completely, nor with full concentration. Meier reads parts of the sports previews, he skims through the *Bild*, he doesn't get the whole of the sports programmes. But even if he got everything, it would surely not involve his sole concentration on the content of the media. One speaks of secondary activities – I would rather use the term parergic media consumption, as it is not easy to determine what is primary and what is secondary. Both the evaluations and the relationships differ. The same man who swears because the sports programme has been delayed by ten minutes because of the Pope's visit, then spends the sports programme working on the flower stand he is making, and hardly notices the programme.

3. The media are an integral part of the way the everyday is conducted. First, on the surface, there are interactions and interferences with non-media-related forms of behaviour; the degree of attention depends on the time of day, on moods, the media message competes with other messages – for instance that one's spouse is talking about something. But this extends to deeper levels: the need for sport cannot be isolated. It is not a question of psychological motivations which can be turned on and off like a switch; but rather a structured set within a very complex household of needs. Here, too, there exists an inter-relationship and a parallel relationship. If, for instance, there is a very high proportion of females watching *Aktuelle Sportstudio* on Saturday night, then this could be related to the presentational form; it could be a certain interest in sport; it could be Harry Valerian's personal appeal, but it could also be an attempt on the part of women to save some of the togetherness of Saturday. Or when the son questions his father about the *Bild*, it is only in order to castigate him for buying it. In any case, media behaviour cannot be reduced to the correlation between content and effect, or to usage inside a clearly defined field. There are very conscious decisions, such as the decision to defer gratification (I will watch the sports programme later on and will not listen to the radio commentary beforehand) but such decisions are constantly crossed through and influenced by non-media conditions and decisions.

4. It is not a question of an isolated, individual process, but of a collective process. Even when reading a newspaper one is not truly alone, it takes place in the context of the family, friends, colleagues. The degree of interest differs amongst the members of the family. Young people are, contrary to

current opinion, not very interested in sport or sports programmes. Watching them is rather a form of post midlife-crisis participation in sport, when other, more active, forms have been left behind. Obviously there are also differences between the sexes. But even where there is a weak interest, or no interest at all, the influence of others is always possible.

5. Media communication cannot be separated from direct personal communication. Media contents are materials for conversation. Sport, for instance, is one common denominator in our highly specialized and differentiated society. How ever, we should not overestimate the expertise and the intensity of conversation. But there is an inter-relationship which plays a part in reception. We are all familiar with two-step flow theory, which, though since modified, has not actually been refuted. In addition there are problems of understanding, which are clarified in speech. Even if it has been said that television is a common activity which consists mainly of silence, direct communication has to be taken into account.

6. Some academics have taken a fancy to the idea that books do not exist, but rather that they are created in the process of reception. But as they cannot really engage in multiple processes of reception, they have discovered the implicit reader, and therefore arrive, again, at the text. This might be possible with regard to the book. With regard to media offerings the story of the synthetic average viewer surely does not work. Not only do the contents have more than one meaning with regard to their interior structure, the ambiguity is heightened by the open field in which communication takes place.

In an American experiment cameras which switched on automatically were installed in a number of people's TV sets in order to investigate the choreography of the use of television. This example is often quoted as proof of how little the arrangements of experiments bother people after a short time; for, after a very limited period, all kinds of things took place in front of the television. Amongst other things, people made love in front of the running TV set. So far so good. But what does this mean? The couples intended to make use of the information on the television, but didn't register the running wallpaper; is it therefore, in a strict sense, a question of ritualized behaviour? Or was the television a participant, a third party producing aphrodisiac effects, a kind of a technically mediated narcissism? The ambivalence is, I think, obvious.

This indicates that television or other media do not impart a slice of reality, in that they reproduce it in a slice-like and fragmented fashion, but rather that reality consists of that which has been mediated both by the media and by other things, and is constantly constructed anew. The content of television radiates out into the rest of reality, which therefore cannot be separated from it. Riha has pointed to the over-formation of sports events through electronics, to the superimposed record times, to the loudspeakers in the stadium, and also to the consumer of sports programmes who now approaches other sectors of reality with his results-table-gaze and record-eyes, which he transfers onto areas unrelated to sport. Is it not the case that we partly watch the news within the framework of 'who against whom'?

71

Relocating the site of the audience

Martin Allor

From Eason, D. L. and Davis, D. K. (eds) 1988 *Critical Studies in Mass Communication*, Speech Communication Association, Annandale VA, Vol. 5, No. 3, pp. 219–28.

In giving a brief résumé of a range of critical approaches to audience, I focus on several factors: the qualities of the audience (and the human subject) that they identify, the particular ways that they position the audience in relation to the social sphere, the model of social power they employ, and the way that they work to maintain the theoretical space of the audience as an abstracted totality. I consider, in turn, political economy, post-structuralist film theory, feminist reader-response criticism, cultural studies, and post-modernism.[1]

Political economy

The main thrust of political-economic analysis has been to shift attention away from the question of individual effects to the circulation of communications as commodities and to the question of the market structure and state/corporate power relations.[2] The question of impact on the individual has usually been inferred within Marxist models of reification and alienation. The political economy of communications, however, has over the last decade directly addressed the site of the audience in the debate inaugurated by Dallas Smythe's article, 'Communications: blindspot of western Marxism' (1977; see also Jhally, 1982; Murdock, 1978). From within the labour theory of value, this approach conceptualizes the audience as the commodity form of advertiser-supported media because it is the audience's potential attention that is sold to the advertiser. The approach frames leisure time as off-the-job work time that produces and reproduces labour power:

> The material reality under monopoly capitalism is that all non-sleeping time of most of the population is work time. This work time is devoted to the production of commodities in-general . . . and in the production and reproduction of labour power. . . . Of off the job work time, the largest single block is time of the audiences which is sold to advertisers (Smythe, 1977, p. 3).

Granting its most obvious limitation of narrowing the question of audience to advertiser-supported communication situations, this particular analysis, nevertheless, has pointed out some of the key ways that the audience, as a sedimented concept, functions within the broadcast industry (perhaps most cogently in its analysis of the 24-hour rock video channels, where the distinction between programming and advertising tends to dissolve). But, as a model of the relation of the practices of audience to social power, the approach is restricted by its functioning solely within a capital logic. It takes the broadcast industry's positioning of the audience as an adequate material description and simply reverses its meaning within the terms of Marxist labour theory. The audience function, then, becomes simply a subset of the alienation effects already critiqued within the Marxist category of commodity fetishism: television viewers are alienated from their own acts of labour in conceiving of their 'work' as leisure. Other practices of the audience, such as the reading of media texts, are subordinated to the global analysis of labour power.

The political liability of this theoretical restriction is even clearer in recent elaborations. Sut Jhally and Bill Livant (1984; 1987) extend the argument directly to the question of the production of surplus value and to the nature of watching as a productive practice. They (1984, p. 22) argue more rigorously within Marxist labour theory and attempt to offer an audience-centred account of commodity production within capitalist media by conceptualizing 'watching time' as productive labour: 'Just as workers sell labour power to capitalists so audiences sell *watching power* to media owners; and just as the use value of labour power is labour, so the use value of watching power is watching, the capacity to watch'. In this view, the social practices of television viewing, normally thought of as a form of consumption, are directly productive of value. The practices of watching either produce necessary value or surplus value: 'In programmes, audiences create *meanings for themselves* while in advertising audiences create *meaning for capital*' (Jhally and Livant, 1984, p. 36). The argument condenses corporate and representational practices with the interpretive practices of television viewers. The audience, here, functions as an abstract representation of productive labour practices that allows for the making of meaning consonant with capital formation. The argument, for example, fails to consider that *meanings for oneself* and *meanings for capital* could be constructed by viewers in both programmes and advertisements.

The political liability of this position is in its theoretical subordination of questions of consciousness and human subjectivity to the analysis of commodity relations. In attempting to link the nature of the audience to the questions and levels of abstraction of Marxist political economy, the approach ignores viewing practices and other levels of determination. The abstract totality 'audience', then, merely is made coterminous with another totality 'labour', and the critique of the conditions of audience membership is epochal: the development of the mass media represents the continued material appropriation of human activity, the expansion of the domain of capital.

Post-structuralist film theory

The materialist approach to the audience within film theory over the last decade has drawn upon different theoretical sources, particularly the decentring of the subject within structural Marxism and Lacanian psychoanalysis. Post-structuralist film theory has displaced the question of ideological effects and the nature of the individual/social relationship onto the discursive plane. Its questioning has been directly epistemological and ideological: how is it that the cinematic and televisual texts position viewers in relationships of knowledge to their conditions of existence? Providing a meta-psychological answer to this question involves a condensation of psycho-analytic accounts of primary identification processes and the practices of the audience in watching films. For example, Christian Metz (1982, p. 49) props his account of the cinematic signifier and its positioning effects on a pheno-menological privileging of the act of looking 'the spectator *identifies with himself*, with himself as a pure act of perception (as wakefulness, alertness): as the condition of possibility of the perceived and hence as a kind of transcendental subject which comes before every *there* is'.

From the ground of this psychoanalytic account of primary identification, post-structuralist film theory developed a sophisticated account of the discursive production of secondary identifications. Within this approach, the audience member becomes the spectator within the text, filling subject positions within particular discursive practices. In the moment of 'high' *Screen* theory, the textual forms of dominant media systems (e.g. the classical continuity editing system) were related to psychoanalytic accounts of the construction of ways of seeing and forms of investment (fetishism, scopophilia). In focusing on the processes of *subject formation*, film theory displaced the problem of audience activity and effects (and questions of the social formation) onto the level of discourse. The spectator was a construction of the text/in the text:

> What moves in film finally, is the spectator immobile in front of the screen. Film is the regulation of that movement, the individual as subject held in a shifting and placing of desire, energy, contradiction, in a perpetual retotalization of the imaginary (the set scene of image and subject). This is the investment of film in narrativization; and crucially for a coherent space, the unity of place and vision (Heath, 1981, p. 107).

By approaching the practices of the spectator through the generalized question of the subject and the 'suturing' operations through which film stitched viewers into passive forms of interpretation, Lacanian film theory rewrote the audience as the subject strictly within the terms of its meta-psychological problematic. The question of the social effectivity of viewing was repositioned within an analysis of the necessary precursor to sociality, subjectivity. This problematic conceptualizes social power as the reproduction of forms of interpellation and investment. But the rigour of the position's account of the inscribed relations between textual systems and their potential viewers has tended to preclude the integration of any other level of analysis.

The more recent revisions of this problematic have begun to deal with the problem of the dichotomy between the discursively constructed subject-ivity of texts and the actual practices of viewers. Their main focus, however, has been to construct more detailed accounts of particular textual systems (Kuhn, 1985) and to assume homologies between particular forms of address and socially occurring ideological structures. In an account of MTV, for example, E. Ann Kaplan (1986, p. 12) argues that 'MTV constructs a de-centered, a-historical model spectator, which coincides with the cultural formations of contemporary teenagers who appear to live in a timeless but implicitly "futurized" present'. As the position has developed, then, the central condensation of audience/spectator/ suture has continued as the central abstraction and framing problematic. The analysis of audience remains largely a discursive operation.

Feminist criticism and the reader

North American literary criticism has undergone a series of transformations over the last 20 years.[3] The literary canon has been broadened and has become less important, and the methodological hegemony of the formalism of 'new criticism' has eroded. The reasons for these shifts are complex, but among the most important has been the challenge of feminism. Within their political moment, different feminisms have intervened to disrupt the status quo within the academy. As a series of theoretical accounts of the effectivity of gender within the social formation, feminism has challenged the received problematics of all the human sciences. And, as critical practices, feminism has called into question the role of literary criticism itself.

Among the feminist revisions within literary criticism, the most significant with regard to the question of audience have been those that interrogate the relations between gender and reading. Building from the assumptions and methods of reader-response theory (Iser, 1978) and North American feminist psychology (Gilligan, 1982), reader oriented feminist criticism has introduced the 'audience function' into critical practice in two ways. First, in critiquing the textual 'maleness' of the literary canon, it has extended critical investigation to 'feminine' genres (melodrama, Gothic novels, the Harlequin romance). Second, in privileging gender as the pivot point for the questioning of the reader's role in the effectivity of literature, it has offered the possibility of grounding the universality of ideal readers at a particular site of social difference.

Feminist reader-response criticism, then, has developed a broad problematic of gendered textual practices (modes of address, represented experiences) and gendered reading practices. It relates critical readings of novels to gender ascribed interpretive schema. More significantly, the position also develops models for hermeneutic inquiry into readers' interpretations. The position employs social psychological research on gender differentiated schema (i.e. inferential structures, language styles [Crawford and Chaffin, 1986]) within a phenomenological model of reading. What emerges is a particular model of gendered engagement with 'the other'. For example, Elizabeth Flynn (1986, p. 268) utilizes a typology of reader/text relations drawn from Georges Poulet:

> The reader can resist the alien thought or subject and so remain essentially unchanged by the reading experience. In this case the reader dominates the text. Or the reader can allow the alien thought to become such a powerful presence that the self is replaced by the other and so effaced. In this case the text dominates the reader. . . . A third possibility, however, is that self and other, reader and text, interact in such a way that the reader learns from the experience without losing critical distance; reader and text interact with a degree of mutuality.

Flynn utilizes these ideal types of reader/other relations to frame an inquiry into gender differences in reading literature. Feminine readings, she suggests, rarely dominate the text but more often involve empathetic identification with characters and represented experiences or negotiate a critical distance that can only come after identification. She argues that the attributes of feminine psychology ('sensitivity to emotional nuance' and 'the ability to empathize with and yet judge' [p. 286]) are coterminous with those of accomplished literary readers. The reader, then, emerges in this account as a problematic condensation of a gendered interpretive competence, an ideal phenomenological hermeneutic critic, and life experiences within patriarchal social formations.

The strengths and liabilities of a condensed model of text/reader relationship are even clearer in work that focuses more specifically on the social consumption of women's genres. Tania Modleski's work (1982) draws on a psychoanalytic theory and sociological accounts of women's practice to provide an analysis of the pleasure of reading popular women's narratives. 'The formal properties of daytime television thus accord closely with the rhythms of women's work in the home. Individual soap operas as well as the flow of various programs and commercials tend to make repetition, interruption, and distraction pleasurable' (p. 102). Modleski finds homology among form of life, narrative structure, psychical structure, and interpretive pleasure. Reading women's narratives is simultaneously pleasure and capture within patriarchal representations. Modleski makes sense of the popular genres by reading texts and social practices as mirroring structures. While she argues against phenomenological models of response (its positive political intervention), real readers are less a presence in the analysis than a structuring absence. The reader in this account is the form of investment capable of articulating particular forms of narrative representation and gendered social practices. Reading as psychic work simultaneously produces passivity and pleasure. Power invests the site of the audience in the production of colonized fantasies.

Janice Radway's more elaborated analysis of the practice of reading romance fiction (1984) presents the same oscillation between the critic's analysis of the genre's textual features and the fans' interpretations. Radway's reading of her respondents' talk frames consumption as both escape and instruction, a symbolic response to lived contradictions:

> Romantic escape is, therefore, a temporary but literal denial of the demands that women recognize as an integral part of their roles as nurturing wives and mothers. It is also a figurative journey to a utopian state of total receptiveness where the reader, as a result of her identification with the heroine, feels herself the *object* of someone else's attention and solicitude (p. 97).

Radway, however, quickly returns to the textual questions of romance, constructing an idealization of her readers in order to ask how Harlequin romance responds to, frames, and ultimately restrains the consequences of patriarchy:

> The reader thus engages in an activity that shores up her own sense of her abilities, but she also creates a simulacrum of her limited social world within a more glamorous fiction. She therefore justifies as natural the very conditions and their emotional consequences to which her reading activity is a response (p. 214).

Radway reads her respondents within the terms of oppositions similar to Modleski's. The romance readers' talk is a manifest symptom of latent ideological work. The activity of reading is both strategic negotiation (escape and instruction) on the psychological level and ultimate incorporation at the social level.

The 'audience' that emerges in these feminist critical engagements is less one of gendered readers than gendered readings. Even in work that includes interviews with readers, the practice of criticism privileges text and context over the reader. The critic interprets from the grounds of (and in relation to) two discursive fields: literary criticism and feminist political analysis. The hermeneutic circle runs from critic to the genre to the work the genre does for the social formation and back again.

While this feminist criticism has placed real women's readings of mass produced narratives in question, it has not so far called into question the certainty of its own readings by placing them in dialogue with the readers' interpretations. The position does not fully investigate the ways in which the practice of reading women's popular narratives 'works' in relation to other practices or other planes of determination such as age, race, sexual orientation, and class. Rather, the critical act judges the ideological work the texts do for the patriarchal context and interrogates women's readings for utopian moments within the capturing discourse. The subject of these reading practices, then, is the abstract and general female psyche analysed as the construction of patriarchy. The 'gendered reading' of the audience functions as the emancipatory space between sociality and textuality.

Cultural studies

The critical approach that has most directly taken up the question of the audience has been cultural studies. At face value, the greatest strength of this media studies work has been to attempt to relate the question of audience interpretation (decoding) to several levels of determination. Seeking to directly link discursive, textual, and social processes, cultural studies recentred the question of audience and power at the site of grounded interpretive practices:

> The audience must be conceived of as composed of clusters of socially situated individual readers, whose individual readings will be framed by shared cultural formations and practices pre-existant to the individual: shared 'orientations' which will in turn be determined by factors derived from the objective position of the individual in the class structure. These objective factors must be seen as setting parameters to individual experience, although not 'determining' consciousness in a mechanistic way; people understand their situation and react to it through the level of subcultures and meaning systems (Morley, 1980, p. 15).

This subcultural approach to the audience seems to have the advantage, at first glance, of theorizing both the discursive and the social structural determinations on individual decoding. It approached social texts (Morley, 1980; 1981) within a conception of limited polysemy. The model of 'preferred readings' and structures of decodings (dominant, negotiated, and oppositional) framed a way of investigating the relationships among discursive structures, social location, and positioned interpretive practices. Upon closer examination, however, this investigation of the practice of audience members can be seen to be limited by the larger theoretical problematic within which it has been framed.

The media studies work inaugurated at the Centre for Contemporary Cultural Studies should be seen as a subset of the centre's larger questioning of the role and functions of ideology and hegemony in 'democratic' social formations. That is to say that the encoding/decoding model that framed the audience research within cultural studies placed the question of the audience firmly within the ambit of the sociological pull of the problematic of hegemony. The kinds of decodings that were investigated originally were limited in two ways. First, the studies focused on news and public affairs programs, semiotic systems most obviously engaged in the representation of the social order. Second, the subcultural groups studied fit quite mechanically into positions located at the nexus of class and educational/occupational determinations.

The levels of determination brought to bear on the site of audience within cultural studies are then somewhat less complex than they first appear. Class discursive competencies, and the practices of decoding were investigated in relation to only one axis of power: the reproduction of dominant represent-ations of the social formation.

More recent work on the audience within cultural studies has attempted to overcome the condensations contained in the decoding model by situating levels of determination. The most predominant work returns to a discursive or textual level of analysis. Ien Ang's analysis of *Dallas* fans' letters in the Netherlands (1985) pushes toward a textual analysis of television melodrama and its construction of a 'tragic structure of feeling' as an ideological form. John Fiske's discussion of television's popularity (1986) centres on a semiotic analysis of the polysemy of particular texts. And Tony Bennett (1986), in developing a model of 'reading formations', has extended the work on audience as a discursive competence.

Perhaps more interesting is recent work that has focused on specific sites as articulations of multiple determinations. David Morley's most recent work (1986) isolates the family as a social contextualization of decoding and analyses television viewing as a strategic instrumentality within family processes. Thus Morley turns from the decoding model of his earlier studies to a more situated analysis of the concrete determinations circulating in and between television practices and family processes. Similarly, Valerie Walkerdine (1986), draw-ing upon a more clinical model of psychoanalysis than *Screen* theory, traces the ways in which the practice of home video watching interpenetrates with pre-existing familial positionings. Finally, Angela McRobbie (1984) considers dance as a site of consumption/production, a move that enlarges the range of audience activity studied from a concern with 'active' electronic media reception and the decoding of meanings:

> Dance evokes fantasy because it sets in motion a dual relationship projecting both internally towards the self and externally towards the 'other'; which is to say that dance as a leisure activity connects desires for the self with those for somebody else. It articulates adolescence and girlhood with feminity and female sexuality and it does this by and through the body (p. 144).

In these most recent analyses of the audience, cultural studies has moved away from the liabilities of the class/ideological condensations of the decoding model. These studies focus on the specific locations where people 'consume' video and broaden the question of the audience to the articulations between leisure practice and identities. The articulations among class, gender, sub-cultures, reading formations, fantasy, identity, and ideology become the ground of questioning rather than the reproductive logic of decodings that necessarily make meanings for the dominant formation. Generative abstractions replace condensed abstractions.

Post-modernism

Post-modernism, the most recent development within critical discourses on the media, offers both a dizzying concatenation of sites and levels of analysis and a new direction into the question of the individual/social relationship. Post-modernist theory circulates in a wide variety of disciplines, but it has been the work of Jean Baudrillard that has led to a radical rewriting of the media/audience relationship.[4] Baudrillard's project involves the destruction of sociological models of the reproduction of the social formation. He challenges the veracity, indeed the referentiality, of socialization models that describe the relation of the individual to the social field of norms or ideology.

For Baudrillard, the social exists as a global plane of effectivity, an open system of systems entailing all action and all structures. Within this social field, the collective action of individuals is regulated neither by law nor by rationality but by information flows as stimulation (simulation). The increasing circulation of signs, media, and representational systems over the last century collapsed the real into its simulated representations. Since knowledge of one's conditions of existence depends on a closed circuit of signs about signs, no grounds remain for the individual to recognize collective identities (class, gender) around which 'authentic' action might take place.

This version of post-modernism challenges not only traditional socialization models, it refuses any notion of mediation between the individual and the social, between signification and the real. This collapse of the subject into the social and of the real (and representation) into simulacra predicates dual axes for the play of power: the media and the mass. The aggregate of individuals absorbed into the electronic media function in Baudrillard's variant of post-modernism as the locus of (and metaphor for) social action that is no longer based on meaning or identity. The audience as the mass is simultaneously the object (the end point) of simulations and the disinterested subject of the circulation (the enactment) of indifferent social action:

> Quite different is the refusal of socialization which comes from the mass [the audience]; from an innumerable, unnamable and anonymous group, whose strength comes from its very destruction and inertia. Thus, in the case of the media, traditional resistance consists of reinterpreting messages according to the group's own code and for its own ends. The masses, on the contrary, accept every thing and redirect everything *en bloc* into the spectacular, without requiring any other code, without requiring any meaning, ultimately without resistance, but making everything slide into an indeterminate sphere which is not even that of non-sense, but that of overall manipulation/fascination (Baudrillard, 1983, pp. 43–4).

This audience functions as the central pivot point for post-modernism's destruction of the subject and the social. Baudrillard locates power at the site of the disinterested viewing of the mass. In the absence of collective identity, resistance takes the form of 'hyperconformity': the mass resists in the 'fatal' strategy of the recycling of signs.

The 'mass' in post-modernism functions as a term that denies the possibility of any collective representation of individuals and as an immense theoretical condensation that allows the theorist to speak at the same time (and in the same way) of individual psychology, class action, and social codings. Baudrillard's 'mass' has been incorporated into audience analysis in two key ways. The first has been in the elaboration of the general model of the simulation of the masses in the media, particularly television. The second has been in the analysis of new cinematic or televisual forms in relation to their simulation affects on implied viewers. In developing the first tactic, Arthur Kroker (1985, p. 40) has argued:

> The audience is constituted on the basis of 'its relation to the object and its reaction to it'; the audience is nothing more than a 'serial unity' ('beings outside themselves in the passive unity of the object'); membership in the TV audience is always only on the basis of 'alterity' or 'exterior separation'; . . . 'abstract sociality' is the false sociality of a TV audience which as an empty, serial unity is experienced as a negative totality.

The television audience becomes in this account the ideal specification of the mass. Outside any social connection or personal embodiment, it becomes the perfect metaphor for a model of media power that echoes the totalizing vision of the Frankfurt School's critique. In developing the second tactic, recent film and television analysis focuses on purely textual features, such as pastiche, genre blending, and self-referentiality, as representing new forms of sociality. Texts as different as *Miami Vice* and Pepsi commercials or *Happy Days* and *Jane Fonda's Workout* are seen as foregrounding forms of identification that have more to do with simulation effects than ideology. In a manner similar to *Screen* theory, these post-modernist critiques tend to condense conceptualizations of the audience with the simulating positions that are interpreted in these texts (e.g. Morse, 1987–8; Polan, 1986).

The conception of mass in post-modernism opens up the question of the effectivity of the audience/text relationship outside of the consideration of practices of making meaning. Power in this model is centred on relations of affect rather than ideological reception. This opening, however, has been sealed off by lines of inquiry that condense the audience/mass, on the one hand, with an account of the death of the social and, on the other, with accounts of differences in contemporary discursive forms. (One of the paradoxes of post-modernism is that, while it begins with a critique of representation, its analytic practice is even more exclusively textual than that of post-structuralism.) Both of these lines of inquiry evacuate the site of audience in its specificity in favour of general theoretic accounts of sociality and textuality in the late twentieth century. In rejecting the problematic at the heart of audience research (effects as mediating), post-modernism points out absurdly, as it were, the impossibility of constructing a single analysis of audience. By pushing the concept of an abstracted totality to its logical extreme, post-modernism signals the necessity of partial reconstructions of both the individual and the social as level of abstraction in media studies.

Notes

1. This critical survey is a strategic one in the sense that it is meant to be a signpost, across theoretical problematics, to the liabilities inherent in the kind of analytic closure that arises from abstract conceptualizations of objects of inquiry. The examples discussed are not exhaustive of the range of positions in play: they are representative of a wider practice of theorizing. Moreover, none of the positions is exhaustively analysed. The positions themselves are not mutually exclusive. Feminist theory is a major presence in all of the domains discussed. There is a good deal of overlap among the models of textuality contained in film theory, cultural studies, and post-modernism. Finally, it should be clear that my purpose is not to adjudicate the truth or falsity of the various concepts at hand. Rather, in evaluating the strengths and liabilities of each conception of audience, I hope to engage with others in the process of continuing to theorize. The order of presentation of positions thus reflects my own theoretical commitments within cultural studies and the current debates over the status of post-modernism.
2. For a discussion of the general contribution of political economy to communication, see Garnham (1986).
3. It should be clear from this discussion that feminist contributions to the critical analysis of audience cut across the fields of film theory and cultural studies and are not limited to the reader-response approach. In any case, the works discussed in this section are not pure examples of reader-response criticism. They could be more properly described as feminist engagements with the practice of textually based analysis of the impacts of ideologies.
4. It is of course misleading to privilege Baudrillard's position as the major problematic within post-modernist accounts of audience functions. Because the term 'post-modernism' labels a contradictory spectrum of positions, its articulations are complicated and beyond the scope of this essay. Nevertheless, I think it is inarguable that the move away from questions of representation and decoding ideally expressed in Baudrillard's work has functioned as a kind of master code for other, more synthetic, post-modernist analyses of audience. See Grossberg (1987) for an approach that works through both cultural studies and post-modernism.

References

Ang, I. (1985) *Watching Dallas*, Methuen, London.

Baudrillard, J. (1983) *In the Shadow of the Silent Majorities. . . . Or the End of the Social.* Semiotext, New York.

Bennett, T. (1986) Texts in history: the determination of readings and their texts. In Attridge, D., Bennington, G., and Young, R. (eds) *Post-structuralism and the Question of History*, Cambridge University Press, Cambridge.

Crawford, M. and Chaffin, R. (1986) The reader's construction of meaning: cognitive research on gender and comprehension. In Flynn, E. and Schweikart, P. (eds) *Gender and Reading: Essays on Readers, Texts, and Contexts*, Johns Hopkins University Press, Baltimore, pp. 3–31.

Fiske, J. (1986) Television: polysemy and popularity. *Critical Studies in Mass Communication*, Vol. 3, PP. 391–408.

Flynn, E. (1986) Gender and reading. In Flynn, E. and Schweickart, P. (eds) *Gender and reading: Essays on readers, texts, and contexts*, Johns Hopkins University Press, Baltimore, pp. 267–88.

Gilligan, C (1982) *In a Different Voice: Psychological Theory and Women's Development.* Harvard University Press, Cambridge, MA.

Heath, S. (1981) *Questions of Cinema.* Indiana University Press, Bloomington.

Iser, W. (1978) *The Act of Reading*, Johns Hopkins University Press, Baltimore.

Jhally, S. (1982) Probing the blindspot: the audience commodity. *Canadian Journal of Political and Social Theory*, Vol. 6, No. 1–2.

Jhally, S. and Livant, B. (1984) The valorization of consciousness: extensions of the domain of capital. Unpublished manuscript.

Jhally, S. and Livant, B. (1987) Watching as working: the valorization of audience consciousness. *Journal of Communication*, Vol. 36, No. 3, pp. 124–43.

Kaplan, E. A. (1986) History, the historical spectator and gender address in music television. *Communication Inquiry*, Vol. 10, No. 1, pp. 3–14.

Kroker, A. (1985) T.V. and the triumph of culture: three theses. *Canadian Journal of Political and Social Theory*, Vol. 9, No. 3, pp. 37–47.

Kuhn, A. (1985) *The Power of the Image*, Routledge & Kegan Paul, London.

McRobbie, A. (1984) Dance and social fantasy. In McRobbie, A. and Nava, M. (eds) *Gender and Generation*, Macmillan, London, pp. 130–61.

Metz, C. (1982) *The Imaginary Signifier*, Indiana University Press, Bloomington.

Modlaki, T. (1982) *Loving with a Vengeance: Mass-produced Fantasies for Women*, Methuen, London.

Morley, D. (1980) *The 'Nationwide' Audience: Structure and Decoding*, British Film Institute, London.

Morley, D. (1981) 'The nationwide audience': a critical postscript. *Screen Education*, Vol. 39, pp. 3–14.

Morley, D. (1986). *Family Television*. Comedia, London.

Morse, M. (1987–8). Artemis aging: exercise and the female body on videocassette. *Discourse*, Vol. 10, No. 1, pp. 20–54

Murdock, G. (1978) Blindspots about Western Marxism: a reply to Dallas Smythe. *Canadian Journal of Political and Social Theory*, Vol. 2, No. 2, pp. 109–19.

Polan, D. (1986) Brief encounters: mass culture and the evacuation of sense. In Modleski, T. (ed.) *Studies in Entertainment: Critical Approaches to Mass Culture*, University of Indiana Press, Bloomington, pp. 167–87.

Radway, J. (1984) *Reading the Romance: Women, Patriarchy, and Popular Literature*, University of North Carolina Press, Chapel Hill.

Smythe, D. (1977) Communications: blindspot of western Marxism. *Canadian Journal of Political and Social Theory*, Vol. 1, No. 3, pp. 1–28.

Walkerdine, V. (1986) Video replay: families, films and fantasy. In Burgin, V., Donald, J. and Kaplan, C. (eds) *Formations of Fantasy*, Methuen, London, pp. 167–99.

Author index

Subject index